The Financial System of Canada

The Financial System of Canada

ITS GROWTH AND DEVELOPMENT

E. P. Neufeld

Macmillan of Canada

ISBN 7705-0858-8

Library of Congress Catalogue Card No. 70-178200

Design / Peter Maher

Printed in Canada for the
Macmillan Company of Canada Limited
70 Bond St., Toronto

Outline of Contents

Detail of Contents

1 Introduction

2 The Emergence of Financial Institutions

3 The Growth of Financial Intermediaries

4 The Chartered Banks

7 The Building Societies and Mortgage Loan Companies

8 Insurance Companies and Societies

9 The Trust Companies

10 Sales Finance and Consumer Loan Companies

11 Mutual Funds, Investment Trusts and Development Companies

Tables

Chart

12 Caisses Populaires and Credit Unions

13 Government Financial Intermediaries and Pension Plans

Tables

15 Interest Rates

16 Concluding Observations

Preface

The essential purpose of this book is to present a comprehensive study of the growth and development of the Canadian financial system or, broadly defined, the Canadian capital market. It traces that development from the very beginning of the emergence of financial institutions in Canada to the present, and it pays particular attention to the forces that seem to explain the changing growth experience of Canada's individual types of financial institutions—the chartered banks, savings banks, private bankers, building societies, mortgage loan companies, investment contract companies, life insurance companies, friendly societies, fire and casualty insurance companies, trust companies, sales finance companies, small loan companies, money lenders, mutual funds, investment trusts, development companies, credit unions and caisses populaires, pension funds, a wide range of government financial institutions, stockbrokers, bond dealers and the stock, bond, and money markets. It also traces long-term trends in Canadian interest rates.

By presenting this analysis both of the current character of the financial system and the way it has evolved, it is hoped that the reader will gain valuable perspective on current developments and useful insights into the likely nature of developments among financial institutions in future. Choice of language as well as the balance between descriptive and analytical material and the way that material is presented, reflect my conscious attempt to make the study useful and, hopefully, interesting both to officers of financial institutions and to researchers.

When one considers the importance to a nation of its financial system it is perhaps surprising that such a study has not previously been attempted. Historians such as Adam Shortt and R. M. Breckenridge confined their attention largely to currency and banking. They emphasized institutional description and did not analyse the economic role and growth of financial institutions. Analytical articles that began to appear after the turn of the century concerned themselves largely with monetary policy and central banking. In more recent years royal commission reports and studies—in particular the Royal Commission on Canada's Economic Prospects and the Royal Commission on Banking and Finance—have set the focus of their attention more broadly but, of necessity, have tended to concentrate on the details of current operations of financial institutions. This study differs from those in that it examines how the whole range of financial institutions has evolved over the decades, it measures their absolute and relative growth rates and attempts to explain their changing growth experience, and it also discusses recent developments in the financial system.

In order to acquire a comprehensive and integrated understanding of the growth and development of the Canadian financial system it seemed absolutely essential to have a statistical base for our analysis and for our descriptive institutional material. For this reason I have made an estimate, on an annual basis, of the size of Canadian financial intermediary assets over about the last century and these data are included in the Statistical Appendix. Those statistics are used frequently in the study, for they show clearly the changing relative size of the various types of financial intermediaries as well as the growth of financial intermediary assets in total. Where it seemed useful to do so I have also shown the growth of individual companies within a sector of the financial system, for example individual banks and life insurance companies.

There are, of course, many places where one would have wished that both description and analysis could have gone further. Technical details of institutional operations soon became voluminous and had to be sharply curtailed, while more vigorous testing of a number of hypotheses was precluded by the absence of necessary statistical data as well as by limitations of time and space. Further institutional material on the chartered banks was excluded because it is so readily available from other sources, while a chapter on the development of the currency and of monetary management was finally withdrawn for generally similar reasons. It is hoped that this study will facilitate and encourage deeper examination of many areas of the financial system.

A number of people have assisted me over the ten-year period during which I have concerned myself with this study. I cannot even list all the librarians, company officials, regulatory authorities both federal and provincial, and officers of trade associations who have provided me with information, but I am nonetheless indebted to them. Research assistants who have spent several months helping me include Carl Hall, David Nowlan, Peter Campbell and Erwin Doak. Mrs. Elizabeth Plumb assisted me greatly in gathering information, arranging for typing, and in the preparation of the index.

I am very grateful to Mr. A. H. Cameron and to the late Mr. E. M. Saunders whose research grant, made available to me through the University of Toronto, encouraged me to begin the study for it helped to defray initial costs of research and typing.

Finally my thanks go to the Canada Council for granting me a leave fellowship, to the University of Toronto for providing the environment and the sabbatical leave that made research possible and enjoyable, and to the Economics Department of Stanford University where, as a Visiting Scholar in 1970-1971, I was able to complete the study.

E. P. Neufeld
UNIVERSITY OF TORONTO
1971

1

Introduction

The Canadian financial system, as we know it today, has evolved out of at least a century and a half of economic growth, financial experimentation and legislative control. Indeed, the introduction in New France almost three centuries ago, in 1685, of the first official paper money made out of playing cards was in its day as bold a financial experiment as Canada has seen. Considerable legislation relating to currency and interest rates had appeared before the beginning of the nineteenth century, and in 1792 an attempt was made in British North America to form a bank. In 1809 the Halifax Fire Insurance Association was formed, and the Bank of Montreal in 1817. Before Confederation Canadian savings banks, life insurance companies and building societies, as well as chartered banks, had appeared in number, as had stockbrokers and rudimentary stock exchanges. Further development came swiftly. Experimentation and innovation in the capital market prior to 1900 were as significant and dramatic as those of the present century. To ignore that period would be to deny ourselves much vital material, and essential perspective for understanding the characteristics of a developing capital market.

Tracing the growth and the development of the Canadian capital market over such a long period of time is an exciting adventure. A sweep of the eye over the history of the market reveals an intriguing and unfolding pattern of financial institutions and financial relationships between institutions: new types of organizations rise to prominence, challenging the position of well-established ones; some of those well-established institutions slip into insignificance; individual companies in some cases enjoy a success, or a failure, that cannot at all be explained by the performance of the group in which they are found. Legislation plays a part in shaping that pattern: at times it defies rationalization, at other times it is only too clearly based on disarmingly naïve misconceptions, and at still other times it provides heartening evidence of the constructive role that government can play in shaping the nation's industry of finance.

But the pattern of development is, at first, somewhat bewildering. There have been, and still are, many different types of borrowers and lenders in the market, as well as types of institutions competing for the profitable privilege of shifting funds from those with funds to spare to credit-worthy borrowers in need of funds. There have also been many institutions whose principal function is to make more liquid, through organized trading, the complex variety of securities which the aforementioned process inevitably creates. The list of individual companies within given types of financial institutions over the years is almost endless; many of these companies have failed but some have made their mark on the industry. "Scandals" seem to have had a special affinity for the capital market, and over the years the market has had its share of forceful and colourful characters.

What does one make of it all? It is clear that comprehension demands rigorous selection. It is also certain that selection must be based on a conceptual framework of the functioning of a capital market which is understood at the outset. The human interest elements of the history of the market may frequently explain very little about the forces that have shaped the market we see today. The unusual experience of a single company may tell us little that is new about the type of institution or the group of companies of which that company is a member, but it cannot be assumed that it never will do so. It is essential, therefore, to provide a broad framework into which the myriad of data and developments can be fitted if our central purpose is to be served. If such a framework is constructed and not forgotten, it is possible to combine description with analysis in a way that will make each more meaningful. Our immediate task is to provide an outline of the structure and of the functioning of a free capital market, which will provide guidelines for our researches.

Role and Structure of the Financial System

Our conception of what constitutes the "capital market" or "financial system" is best understood in terms of the basic financial functions performed in any economy and the principals that perform them. Let us anticipate some of our discussion and define a capital market as being composed of institutions and individuals engaged in transferring funds from those in surplus to those in deficit and in facilitating changes in ownership of financial claims that that process inevitably creates. The first part of that definition refers to the *financial intermediation* function and to *financial intermediaries* that perform it. The second refers to the *financial brokerage* function and to the stockbrokers and investment dealers, including underwriters and jobbers, who perform it. It should also be noted that financial counselling has become an identifiable, and in some cases specialized, function of participants in the capital market and so financial counsellors may usefully be regarded as being a part of the institutional framework of the capital market. The same principals may of course perform all these functions; that is, they may at the same time be financial intermediaries and financial brokers and financial counsellors.

There are numerous examples of the way these functions were performed in early Canada. Solicitors were active in bringing individual borrowers and lenders together and arranged for the latter to take the real estate mortgage of the former. This was an example of direct financing where the solicitor acted as a broker and counsellor. When Canadian banks began to appear in the early 1800s they offered their stock and their notes and deposit liabilities in order to obtain specie as a necessary reserve for their operations, and they then made loans, the borrowers accepting as media of exchange the banks' notes and deposit liabilities. This simple transaction involved (a) the accumulation of funds; (b) the creation of "indirect securities" which were the liabilities of a financial intermediary, that is bank stocks, deposits and notes; and (c) the creation of financial instruments which were the liabilities (primary securities) of the ultimate borrower, i.e., the bills and notes of the commercial community.

The solicitor already referred to would sometimes arrange for the mortgage to be sold to a third party, and such a transaction would involve the capital market's function of facilitating the transfer of ownership of existing financial claims. Local dealers in real estate began to arrange for the sale of stocks and debentures long before stock exchanges existed.

We will now examine the basic functions of the capital market in greater detail.

FINANCIAL INTERMEDIATION

A simple diagram will help to illustrate the essential characteristics of this financial function. Terminology used is that which has become accepted in analyses of financial systems.[1]

---

1. See John G. Gurley and Edward S. Shaw, *Money in a Theory of Finance* (Washington, D.C.: Brookings Institution, 1960).

Diagram 1

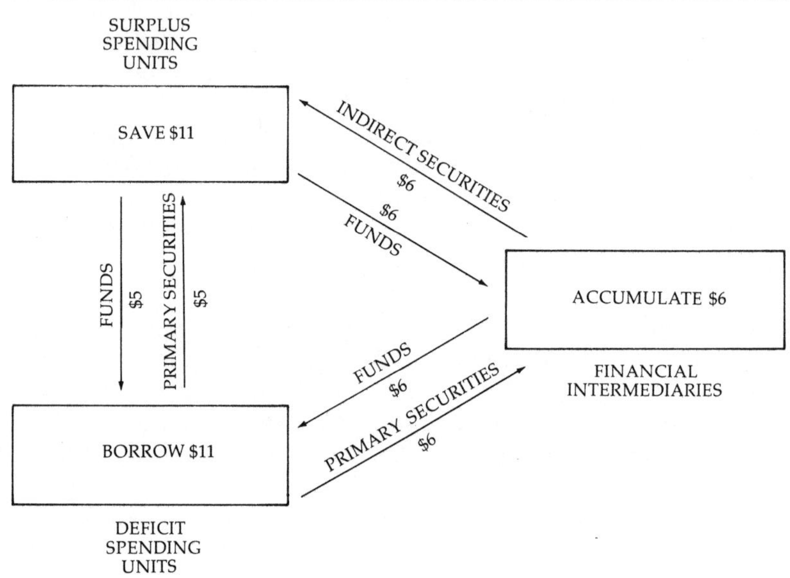

In any economy there are individual corporations, unincorporated businesses, individuals, non-profit organizations and governments (some of which may be non-residents) which in a given period have surplus funds after deducting from their current income the purchase of current output of goods and services. These may be referred to as surplus spending units or ultimate lenders. By way of example, the aggregate of their surplus funds is shown in Diagram 1 as amounting to $11 in a given period. At the same time there are other members of the aforementioned groups whose purchases of goods and services within a given period exceed their income (deficit spending units, or ultimate borrowers), and who must borrow the funds of surplus spending units by issuing "primary securities." Finally there are institutions which specialize in accumulating surplus funds by issuing their own "indirect securities" and distributing those funds by purchasing "primary securities" or even other "indirect securities." That is, their liability instruments in the form of indirect securities are their source of funds, and their assets in the form of indirect and primary securities indicate how they have used their funds. These institutions are referred to as financial intermediaries.

In this institutional environment surplus spending units can invest their funds in the primary securities of deficit spending units or in the indirect securities of financial intermediaries. Deficit spending units can sell their primary securities to surplus spending units, or to financial intermediaries. In Diagram 1 surplus spending units use their surplus of $11 to purchase $5 primary securities directly from deficit spending units, and $6 indirect securities (or liability instruments) of financial intermediaries. Financial intermediaries use the $6 of funds they receive to purchase $6 of primary securities of deficit spending units, so their assets and liabilities have increased by $6. In this way all deficits have been financed, all surplus funds have been disposed of, and financial intermediaries have distributed all the funds they have received. A total of $11 of primary securities has been issued, which is equal to the deficit of deficit spending units; but, because of financial intermediation, an additional amount of $6 indirect securities has been issued, or $17 of securities in total.

In this simple model of financial activity one principal function of the capital market is amply illustrated. This function is to transfer funds that surplus spending units have available for investment in securities, to deficit spending units. The function, however, is performed in two different ways: by the direct purchase of primary securities by surplus spending units, in which case the capital market function of financial institutions would simply be that of bringing saver and spender together, that is, it would be to act as a broker (or underwriter); and secondly by financial institutions accumulating funds through selling their own liability instruments to ultimate lenders on sufficiently attractive terms, and purchasing securities from borrowers, in which case the function of financial institutions would be to act as a financial intermediary.

In order to illustrate the relationship between the capital market and real capital formation, and to outline the basis for growth in the volume of securities and of financial intermediaries in the long-run period, it is now necessary to examine a slightly more complicated illustrative model of the capital market. Table 1:1 provides illustrative figures which, while incomplete in many respects, will assist us in our explanations. Following national accounts concepts, total net saving must equal total net real capital formation, the latter including any change in net holdings of foreign assets. Business savings arise when business retains earnings; personal savings when personal income exceeds personal expenditures on consumer goods and services; government savings when tax and similar revenues exceed current, not capital, expenditures; and non-residents supply savings when their exports exceed their imports.

Table 1:1 An Illustrative Model of Savings, Capital Expenditures, and Security Issues

	SAVINGS[1]	CAPITAL SPENDING[1]	SOURCE OF FINANCING OF CAPITAL SPENDING AND DEFICITS		PURCHASE OF SECURITIES		
			INTERNAL SAVINGS	PRIMARY SECURITIES SOLD	PRIMARY	INDIRECT	TOTAL
	(1)	(2)	(3)	(4)	(5)	(6)	(7)
Business							
– net savers	+6	+4	+3	+1	+1	+2	+3
– net dissavers	−4	+3	0	+7	0	0	0
– Total	+2	+7	+3	+8	+1	+2	+3
Individuals							
– net savers	+9	+1	+1	0	+4	+4	+8
– net dissavers	−3	0	0	+3	0	0	0
– Total	+6	+1	+1	+3	+4	+4	+8
Government							
– net savers	+3	+2	+2	0	0	+1	+1
– net dissavers	−1	+1	0	+2	0	0	0
– Total	+2	+3	+2	+2	0	+1	+1
Non-resident	+1	0	0	0	+1	0	+1
TOTAL	+11	+11	+6	+13	+6	+7	+13
Financial intermediaries	0	0	0	0	+7	0	+7
GRAND TOTAL	+11	+11	+6	+13	+13	+7	+20

[1]Assume that savings exclude depreciation funds and capital spending is net of depreciation.

Column (1) in Table 1:1 shows savings to have amounted to $11. But it also emphasizes that not all individual spending units were savers, with "gross" savings amounting to $19, and "gross" dissaving to $8. Some in each of the major categories of business, individuals and government were dissavers: in business because some companies were experiencing losses, among consumers because some individuals spent more than their current income on consumer goods and services, among governments because tax revenues of some governments were smaller than current expenditures. The existence of "dissavers" increases the volume of primary securities created. This act of dissaving could be thought of as "current account deficit spending."

Column (2) shows that there was a net accumulation of real capital by each sector, totalling $11, or the same as net savings. The question now arises, how many securities will there be created to effect the necessary transfers of savings? What is immediately obvious is that it might well be in excess of the volume of net capital formation, because of the need to finance the "dissavers" in each category. But on the other hand, if sectors use their own earnings for capital spending the volume of securities to be issued will to that extent be reduced.

Columns (3) and (4) show the extent to which sectors used internal funds and issues of primary securities to finance their capital spending *and* their "current account" deficits, while columns (5) and (6) show how spending units of each sector with funds remaining after expenditures on goods and services divided those funds between purchases of primary and indirect securities. In the business sector, for example, retained earnings of profit companies amounted to $6, capital spending to $4 with the latter financed to the extent of $3 by retained earnings, and $1 by issues of primary securities, leaving $3 which was used to purchase primary securities of $1 and indirect securities of $2. Loss companies financed a current account deficit of $4, and capital spending of $3, by the sale of $7 primary securities.

In total, capital spending amounted to $11, deficits to $8, and this $19 was financed by internal savings of $6 and issues of primary securities of $13. Since $7 indirect securities was purchased (which is also a measure of the growth of financial intermediaries in the period) total security or financial claims issues amounted to $20, much in excess of net real capital formation. We have not shown any transactions between financial intermediaries, and such transactions would increase the total of securities issued even further. It should be noted that if financial intermediaries also have retained earnings and if they issue securities to build premises and buy equipment (as they certainly do) they must to the extent of those operations be included in the business sector. Furthermore, when businesses, individuals and governments borrow funds to relend to others, as many of them do, they should to the extent of those operations be included in the financial intermediary sector.

So on what would the growth of the stock of securities depend in this exceedingly simplified model? If we were to assume that the total of capital spending and current account deficit spending were a function of total output; that gross savings were a function of total income; that internal financing, purchases of primary securities and purchases of indirect securities each were a function of gross savings, then we could say that the annual absolute increase and percentage increase in financial claims would depend on (a) the size and growth of income or output, (b) the capital-output ratio, (c) the ratio of current account deficit spending to output and (d) the individual ratios of internal financing, purchases of primary securities, and purchases of indirect securities to gross savings. The model outlined above could easily be expanded to include "layering," that is, the purchase and sale of indirect claims between financial intermediaries, broadly defined, which certainly is a further factor determining the long-term growth of the stock of securities. It could also be extended so as to include depreciation funds in savings and also to include funds raised by the sale of existing real assets.

In the short run, cyclical and other changes in prices, interest rates, and real output and income, accompanied also by changes in the desire to hold money instead of other financial claims or real assets, could of course bring about sharp changes in the growth of the stock of securities. But our emphasis is on long-term trends and our purpose is merely to illustrate the major forces at work.

This general summary of forces behind the growth of financial assets in the long run leaves a large number of specific questions unanswered. For one thing, it does not specifically distinguish between the forces inducing growth of the stock of primary securities, and those inducing growth of the stock of indirect securities. Yet this distinction for our purposes is highly significant, for it is the latter that represents the growth of financial intermediaries. Furthermore it tells us nothing of the motivation leading deficit spenders to issue securities and surplus spenders to buy them, that is, of the forces that actually cause the market to function. It is to a consideration of these and other points that we must now turn.

Primary borrowers and primary securities: The long-term growth of primary securities, it would seem from previous discussion, would depend on the growth of income, on the relative size of capital formation and current account deficits of spending units, and on the relative importance of internal financing as a source of funds. If the capital-output ratio and the current account deficit-spending-to-output ratio were both constant, and if the relative importance of internal financing remained unchanged, then we would expect that the stock of primary securities would grow at the same rate as income.

Unfortunately, the statistical data necessary to reveal what changes have occurred in Canada in all of these areas are not available. Nor is there an accurate estimate of the growth of the stock of primary securities. In the United States the ratio of a rough estimate of such securities to G.N.P. seems to have been about 2.4 in 1880, 2.9 in 1922 and 3.6 in 1929, and then it declined to 2.5 by 1949 – almost the same as the 1880 level.[2] So over the very long-term period primary securities may have grown no faster than G.N.P.

As far as the effect of capital formation on the growth of the stock of primary securities is concerned, this would depend as we have seen on the relative size of capital to output, that is, on the capital-output ratio. The larger the ratio, the higher the stock of primary securities, other things being equal. It is interesting in this regard that the capital-output ratio in the United States seems to have declined since the 1920s – which would be fully consistent with the already noted decline in the ratio of primary securities to G.N.P. over that period.[3]

One would not obviously expect that the relative size of the current account deficits of spending units would change over time, but statistical evidence could dispute this *a priori* judgment.

As for the relative importance of internal financing, there is no obvious reason why it should either increase or decrease over time, although there is some reason to believe that in a country with a relatively competitive private sector and a democratically controlled public sector it would not change significantly. Internal financing of the early family companies must have been relatively important, while the development of the limited liability industrial corporation after the 1850s undoubtedly facilitated external financing, as did the development of financial intermediaries after the early 1800s. In a

---

2. Primary securities estimated by subtracting assets of financial intermediaries from total intangible assets using data found in R. W. Goldsmith, *Financial Intermediaries in the American Economy Since 1900*, National Bureau of Economic Research (Princeton: Princeton University Press, 1958), pp. 321 and 332. Gross national product data as shown in *Historical Statistics of the United States Colonial Times to 1957*, U.S. Department of Commerce, Bureau of the Census, 1960.
3. For capital-output ratios see Simon Kuznets, *Capital in the American Economy*, National Bureau of Economic Research (Princeton: Princeton University Press, 1961), p. 199.

competitive economy the ability of corporations to *manipulate* product prices so as to provide a desired flow of savings for internal use is likely to be limited, even though the total flow of internal savings is significant; while the ability of governments to use tax proceeds instead of borrowed funds to finance long-lasting real capital assets is also probably circumscribed by public attitudes toward levels of taxation. But these conjectures merely serve to illustrate the need for statistical data that do not now exist.

Data for the United States economy do reveal some pattern of behaviour in internal financing. They show that over the period 1900-56 there was only a slight decline in the ratio of internal financing to gross capital formation.[4] The Royal Commission on Banking and Finance estimated that the ratio of major Canadian primary debt obligations outstanding (a far from complete series of primary securities) to G.N.P. was about the same in the 1920s as in the 1950s—with substantial volatility in between, owing to cyclical changes in gross national product.[5] We have found (see below p. 510) that over the three decades up to 1969 gross issues of bonds grew at about the same rate as G.N.P., and most of those bonds came from primary borrowers.

These scattered statistical data and *a priori* judgments do seem to suggest that the supply of primary securities will, in the long run, be closely related to the major economic aggregates of gross national product and gross capital formation—although much research remains to be done in this area. The growth of indirect financial claims, as we shall see, is quite another matter.

What motivates the various primary borrowers—corporations, governments and individuals—to issue primary securities? A comprehensive answer would be difficult to give. A business corporation will be induced to use internal funds because of the low administrative costs involved in raising funds in that way and because it may wish to perpetuate existing ownership arrangements; but, as already mentioned, it will be limited in doing this at some stage by its need to remain competitive in the market for its output. Expansion plans may exceed internal funds available, requiring access to external funds through the issue of primary securities. For corporations to be induced to issue such securities would usually require the expected rate of return on the funds so obtained to be in excess of their cost after allowance for risk.

The flow of primary securities issued by government will, in the

4. *Ibid.*, chap. 5.
5. See *Report of the Royal Commission on Banking and Finance* (Ottawa: Queen's Printer, 1964), p. 6.

long run, be related to the capital stock which is needed to produce the goods and services supplied by the public sector of the economy in amounts desired by the public (the latter indicated by the taxes people are prepared to pay); and it will also be related to the relative amount of internal financing (through surpluses on current operations) available to the government. Over shorter periods, for reasons of economic stabilization, for example, even some current expenditures may be financed by the issue of primary securities; while at other times the flow of primary securities may be negative as a result of tax and other similar revenues exceeding both current and capital expenditures of government.

Individuals provide the market with primary securities when they sign promissory notes and other documents showing their indebtedness arising from availing themselves of personal and instalment credit for purchasing goods and services. The use of consumer credit facilitates building up capital stock in the consumer sector (e.g., a washing machine in the basement is as much a capital good as one in a laundromat, for both provide a stream of consumer services – as do all consumer durable goods); such credit enables consumers to even out the effects on spending of interrupted income payments; and frequently, as in the case of monthly charge accounts and credit cards, it offers administrative convenience to the individual, including the cost advantages of mass accounting.

By buying consumer durable goods with credit, the consumer is sometimes able to substitute less expensive inside services for more expensive outside services, as in the case of the washing machine referred to above, or television entertainment as a substitute for going to the movies.[6] Also consumer credit may permit individuals to acquire certain expensive items that they would not acquire at all otherwise, because they may need the discipline of saving through periodic payments. This is partly because rental facilities are imperfect or, in many cases, non-existent.[7] For all these reasons consumer credit may enhance consumer satisfaction and increase economic efficiency. And this in turn provides ample economic justification for the issue of primary securities by individual consumers.

Primary lenders: Let us now consider the demand for securities. Spending units with current revenues in excess of current expendi-

---

6. See J. V. Poapst and W. R. Waters, "Rates of Return on Consumer Durables," *Journal of Finance*, December 1964.
7. For a more detailed discussion see E. P. Neufeld, "The Economic Significance of Consumer Credit," in J. S. Ziegel and R. E. Olley, eds., *Consumer Credit in Canada* (Saskatoon: University of Saskatchewan, 1966).

tures can utilize the resulting savings by holding money balances, by acquiring other financial assets (both primary and indirect), or by acquiring real assets. It is difficult to determine why people save the proportion of income they do save. It may depend partly on such things as past, present and expected income experience of the public, the relative attractiveness of return on real and financial assets, prices of goods and services, and the size of the existing stock of real and financial assets owned. Regardless of the proportion of income saved, savings as such provide a demand for securities, as well as other assets.

A saver has a broad spectrum of both primary and indirect securities to choose from in disposing of income he has saved, and in making his choice among such opportunities he is likely to be influenced by yield, risk, convenience and special services or benefits inherent in the security. It is because different investors prefer different combinations of yield, risk, convenience and other attributes that the opportunity exists for primary and indirect borrowers to innovate in the form of types of securities supplied. In other words, savers are likely to shift their savings into relatively more attractive financial assets if borrowers are able through ingenuity and imagination to create them.

But the demand for non-monetary financial assets is not based only on the current flow of savings. Such demand can change because of a shift into or out of money balances (i.e., a change in money velocity, or alternatively, in the demand for money balances), or because of a change in the supply of money, normally initiated by the monetary authorities. It could also arise from a change in the demand for real assets. Such shifts, by affecting the prices of various assets, could produce changes in income and so in savings, thereby affecting over-all demand for (and supply of) financial assets. But this is not the effect we have in mind at the moment. It is obvious that the supply of funds available for investment in securities in any given period need not be fixed. Quite apart from the actions of the monetary authorities and the effects of income changes, that supply can be expanded by offering holders of cash balances relatively more attractive primary and indirect securities in which to invest. The more attractive the securities offered, the greater will be the addition to flows of funds in the capital market from activation of idle balances.

This ability of surplus spending units to increase the flow of funds through working to lower minimum cash holdings has interesting implications for the development of a capital market. Its implications for economic policy are widely understood and need only be referred to briefly. During periods of full employment, when net real capital formation is limited to net domestic savings and net savings inflow from abroad, an increase in the velocity of money (i.e., a decrease in the demand for cash balances) will be inflationary, either directly so if the cash balances are used to purchase goods and services or indirectly so if they are used to purchase new issues of securities, or if they tend to reduce interest rates by being channelled into existing securities. During periods of unemployment the tendency would be for such velocity changes to increase spending and increase real output through the re-employment of idle resources.

But from the point of view of the development of the capital market, the most interesting aspect of the possibility for money velocity to change is that it more readily permits innovation among financial intermediaries than would otherwise be the case. A new financial intermediary which offers either a new or improved form of credit or a new and relatively more attractive form of liability instrument than those of existing intermediaries can become established and grow because it can appeal both to savers and to holders of idle cash balances. The appeal to the latter could of course be indirect in that holders of the liability instruments of existing financial intermediaries might sell them at attractive prices to holders of cash balances and use the proceeds to purchase the liability instruments of the new intermediaries.

Financial intermediaries: In our discussion of primary borrowers, we drew some very tentative and, for our purposes, not too interesting conclusions about the supply of primary securities. Then, in discussing primary lenders, we commented on the demand for both primary and indirect securities. The source of supply of those indirect securities has not yet been discussed. It arises from the operations of the financial intermediaries and it is to those institutions that we now turn.

As we explained earlier, surplus funds may be transferred directly to final users of funds, as when a corporation sells stock to individuals, or a government sells bonds to individuals, or they may first be accumulated by financial intermediaries who in turn, by purchasing the securities of final users of funds, complete the transfer. The accumulation of surplus funds, which may or may not arise from saving out of income, and the subsequent distribution of those funds (usually to final users) is the major economic function of financial intermediaries. In order to accumulate such funds, financial intermediaries issue indirect securities, so termed because the proceeds will not be used directly to purchase goods and services but rather to purchase primary and indirect securities. In other words, an increase in financial intermediation means an increase in the relative importance of indirect as compared with direct financing. (It could also mean an increase in "layering," that is in the relative amounts of financial intermediary liabilities held as assets by other financial intermediaries). What are the major forces determining the split between direct and indirect financing, and so determining the growth of financial intermediaries? That is the major question we seek to answer at this stage of our discussion.

It seems to us that there are really only two reasons why there is indirect as well as direct financing in the economy: the advantages of economies of scale, and the advantages of product differentiation. Economies of scale undoubtedly appear on both the accumulation and the distribution sides of the intermediation process. For many individual savers it would be exceedingly expensive in terms of time and effort expended, and perhaps even direct outlay of funds, to invest their savings only in primary securities and real assets. In availing themselves of the facilities of financial intermediaries, individuals are free to devote more of their time to other pursuits, which will increase living standards (i.e. consumer satisfaction), whether those other pursuits are income-generating or involve increased leisure or, more likely, do both. This, it must be understood, is because the unit real costs of financial intermediaries investing funds is likely to be much less than the unit real costs of individuals alone doing it through the purchase of primary securities directly from borrowers.

Similar cost advantages also arise from the intermediation process for the ultimate borrower. For them there undoubtedly are cost advantages in selling large blocks of securities to a few financial intermediaries rather than to many small investors. Financial intermediation, in short, is one route by which the economy achieves productivity increases in the transfer of funds from those in surplus to those in deficit. That is, it leads to more efficient resource allocation within the financial system itself. This in turn would contribute to increasing the economy's real rate of growth.

Another advantage arising out of economies of scale relates to the quality of the investment decisions (i.e., capital allocation decisions) of financial intermediaries as compared with those of individuals. The development of specialized investment departments on the part of the former should mean that better capital allocation (i.e., economically more efficient allocation) is achieved in the economy generally, and this would also increase the nation's economic growth. At the same time, to the extent that financial intermediaries become rigid and unimaginative in their investing decisions, they may misallocate capital and slow down the nation's real growth rate.

One way in which the quality of decision-making may be increased is through a certain specialization among financial institutions. This specialization can take the form of either the kind of credit supplied, that is, the kind of securities purchased by a given type of intermediary, or the kind of liability instrument offered to the saver in exchange for his surplus funds. Up to a point one would think that such specialization would reduce costs of administration and increase the return on assets; however, it is not a simple relationship and it is quite possible that innovation in matters of administration may enable particular institutions to benefit from reduced specialization.

The advantages of intermediation along lines of economies of scale probably diminish with the increase in the individual amounts saved and available for investment in securities, and with the individual amounts borrowed. Individual ultimate savers with large amounts of savings may be justified in buying primary securities directly, rather than buying indirect securities issued by financial intermediaries. Furthermore, the services of a knowledgeable broker, who can provide investment advice at an economic cost because of the volume of business *he* does, will assist them in this. Investment counselling services will reduce the size of individual savings at which it becomes sensible for individuals to purchase securities directly rather than, say, leaving their funds on deposit with financial institutions. What this means, therefore, is that simply from the viewpoint of economies of scale there is no *a priori* reason to believe that indirect financing should completely replace direct financing. This in turn means that there is competition not merely between individual financial intermediaries but also between financial intermediaries in general, and direct financing (including the important role of brokers in it) in general.

Apart from economies of scale the advantages of intermediation arise from the greater diversity of financial claims that they make possible—varying in net monetary yield, risk, associated non-monetary services, denomination, transferability, ease of acquisition and storage, and in the division of income from them between capital gains and interest. In other words, financial intermediation creates new "products." Chartered bank deposits provide some interest income (at least some of them do), and also valuable media of exchange services; life insurance contracts provide protection against the financial problems created by the death of the income-earner and also offer the conveniences of contractual savings; mutual funds enable the small investor to invest intelligently (if he chooses the right fund) in the stock market on a regular basis and thereby avail himself of a hedge against the depreciation of his financial assets through inflation and also obtain the rewards of increased yet limited risk-taking; investing in credit unions or caisses populaires may give an individual unique satisfaction in that it may make him feel that he is helping his less fortunate brother; and pension funds involve convenient contractual savings and provide a certain income security. The very nature of financial intermediary operations means that risks are being spread for the person leaving funds with them, instead of investing directly, except for the risk of mismanagement on the part of the intermediary itself, which at times, it is true, is not negligible. What all this means is that by creating new forms of financial claims, the process of financial intermediation increases the sum total of monetary and non-monetary returns that can be obtained from a given amount of savings.

The benefits to be derived from increased financial intermediation may also be understood in a general way by noting the conditions that led to the appearance of the early intermediaries. The first significant financial intermediary in Canada was the chartered bank. There can be little doubt that the woeful scarcity of a reliable medium of exchange for effecting domestic trade was the major factor enabling the banks to "sell" their demand notes to the public and thereby to make loans and discount notes.[8] However, the first really important non-bank financial intermediaries in Canada were the permanent building societies that appeared in the 1850s, or mortgage loan companies as they later were called. The prospectus of the first of these societies, The Canada Permanent Building and Savings Society, written in 1855, outlines lucidly and comprehensively the advantages of financial intermediation to borrowers and lenders:

> As it is now constituted, it is believed that a lender can invest his capital through the medium of this Institution, at least as profitably as and more satisfactorily than by a direct transaction with the borrower. He relieves himself from the trouble of having to investigate the title to the property offered in security, or the risk of its proving defective; from all concern as to the ability, or inclination of the borrower, to meet his engagements punctually; from the importunities of improvident or unfortunate debtors; from his being obliged to consent to delays and indefinite extension, with the knowledge that presuming on his forbearance, opportunities for making timely provision have been neglected; or, from the unpleasantness, anxiety and uncertainty of law suit. All these contingencies and many more are provided against, or assumed by the Society. Nor are all the advantages above to the investor. The borrower applies to the institution as a matter of right, and chooses his own time for redemp-

8. See below, pp. 72-3.

> tion, with the assurance that he is giving fair value for what he receives, and therefore in nowise compromises his independence; that, by promptly meeting the small periodical payments on his shares, which no individual mortgagee would accept, he is gradually paying off his mortgage; that he is not subject to the caprice of any individual who may sacrifice his property by enforcing payment unexpectedly; and that should he wish to sell, exchange, or redeem his property, he can at any time accomplish his purpose on certain equitable principles.

We may summarize our discussion of the advantages of indirect financing or financial intermediation in this way: it increases economic efficiency within the financial system by reducing administrative costs of transferring funds from those in surplus to those in deficit, to the financial benefit of both borrowers and lenders; it increases the satisfaction that lenders receive from a given stock of wealth, by making an increased variety of financial claims available to them; and it increases economic efficiency outside the financial system by improving the way the nation's capital is allocated, this at times through innovating in the kinds of securities it will buy, i.e., the kind of credit it will supply. As for the relative importance of indirect financing and the relative size of financial intermediaries in the economy, in the long term this will depend heavily on the extent to which the financial intermediaries are able to exploit the aforementioned potential advantages. This is why there is no *a priori* reason to believe that the growth of financial intermediaries, that is the growth of indirect financial claims, should be tied to the growth of income as, in a general and loose sort of way, we found was the case with primary securities.

It is implicit in the foregoing discussion, and exceedingly important to note for future reference, that increased financial intermediation may be closely related to successful innovation in the capital market. Such innovation may take place in the kind of credit offered by intermediaries (as shown by their asset structure) and the form and manner in which it is supplied; it may take place in the kind of liability instruments offered to savers, and it may take place in the area of administration. Such innovation may sometimes be encouraged by the growth of income of the economy, or by the growth of the stock of wealth of the economy (as when savers' "tastes" change with an increase in the stock of wealth). It may even be encouraged by structural changes in the economy if, for example, such changes involve the provision of a new type of credit. In a sense, therefore, these forces invite innovation.

We shall see in succeeding chapters that new types of financial intermediaries have appeared periodically in the Canadian capital market over the last century and a half. It is a reasonable hypothesis that specific changes of an innovatory character will explain their appearance, their development, and indirectly their decline. The preceding discussion provides a guide as to where to look for such innovations. Innovation, the absence of innovation, and the reasons for both require our close attention when we attempt to explain the growth and development of financial intermediaries in the chapters that follow.

Bank and non-bank financial intermediation: It has become customary to distinguish between bank and non-bank financial intermediaries in discussions of the development of financial intermediaries. However, in order to avoid confusion, it is prudent to outline at this stage the basis of that distinction, particularly since it is perhaps a less fundamental one than has generally been believed. When we speak of banks we mean media-of-exchange-issuing institutions. That is, in our terminology an institution is a bank to the extent that its liability instruments are in fact used as media of exchange, or "money."

In a general sense the same variables will explain the growth of all financial intermediaries. The three most important variables, apart from the growth of the economy, determining the growth of existing financial intermediaries are their cost of funds (or the yield at issue of the liability instruments they sell to accumulate funds), the costs of administration (including costs of selling their liability instruments), and the return on the credit they extend (that is the yield of the financial assets they in turn hold). When the costs of additional funds, including administrative costs, begin to equal or exceed the returns on financial assets purchased, there is no profit incentive for further expansion of assets. What volume of liability instruments a financial intermediary will be able to sell at given unit cost (say in percentage terms), excluding national income growth, will depend on how attractive the package of attributes (including interest return and embodied services, as well as others) can be made to appear to investors. What volume of credit the intermediary will be able profitably to place will depend on the loan rates and other services that the intermediary can make known to and available to borrowers. Furthermore, the intermediary's success in both borrowing and lending will depend partially on its success in minimizing administrative costs.

These generalizations apply as much to banks as to non-bank intermediaries. While at any given time the size of bank assets will depend largely on the amount of bank cash made available by the central bank, the latter itself will in the long term depend heavily on how successful the banks are in convincing investors that their deposits are a good thing to hold. More specifically, the more successful the banks are in this, the more cash the Bank of Canada will have to make available to create given credit conditions. Or expressing it in another way, if the banks can convince depositors to hold more deposits at the same rate of interest, the central bank will have to increase cash if it wishes to maintain existing interest rate levels; or if the banks, through reducing administrative costs or increasing the return on their assets, are able to offer depositors increased interest rates relative to those offered by other institutions, the central bank will have to increase bank cash if it wishes to maintain existing credit conditions. To be more precise about it, if total deposits are fixed and an increased proportion is held in the form of idle savings deposits, the reduced amount available for transaction purposes (i.e., the reduction in demand deposits available) will induce business to sell financial assets in order to restore their demand deposits. Such sales will raise interest rates. If the central bank does not wish to see credit conditions change, it will have to permit bank cash and bank deposits to expand. In both cases bank assets would rise relative to those of other financial institutions even though the banks were subjected to central bank cash control. Nor, in the long run, would this conclusion be altered if the central bank did not supply the extra cash, for eventually this would result in a lower price level being established with the banks still experiencing an increase in their assets relative to those of other financial intermediaries. So the long-term growth of the chartered banks can be discussed within the same conceptual framework as that of non-bank financial intermediaries.

What about the short term, for example the cyclical growth of bank and non-bank financial intermediaries? Again we must point out that there are important similarities between the two groups. For one thing, both may engage in multiple credit expansion. The non-bank intermediaries may do so by taking action that has the effect of increasing the velocity of circulation of money, and the banks may do so in the same way, as well as by increasing deposits absolutely as a result of having received new cash from the central bank or operating to a lower cash-to-deposit ratio. Let us explain this further.

Consider a period of economic recovery. Improved profit and sales expectations will increase the demand for credit, and will increase the rate that borrowers are prepared to pay for credit. This the financial intermediaries will see as an increase in the rate of return they can receive on new credit extended, i.e., on new financial assets acquired. They will therefore be in a position to increase the rate of interest on the liability instruments they issue, thereby inducing individuals to part with bank savings deposits, and so increasing the velocity of circulation of the supply of money. The banks too may expand credit through velocity increases by selling securities to holders of savings deposits and by increasing loans.

Either process could be inflationary if it continued to expand the supply of credit (i.e., the demand for primary securities) after an inflationary level of effective demand had been created. The more closely the rate of return (in monetary and non-monetary terms) on bank deposits moves with the rate of return on the liability instruments of non-bank financial intermediaries, the more closely would the cyclical growth of non-bank financial intermediary assets approximate the cyclical growth of bank assets; and the more closely both types of rates move with the rate of return on primary securities, the smaller would be the cyclical volatility of national income, primary securities, and financial intermediary assets. In the absence of interest rate restrictions, and assuming the banks are willing to compete actively for deposits, there is no *a priori* reason to believe that monetary restrictions would slow down the cyclical growth of banks more than that of non-bank financial intermediaries.

The only significant difference between banks and non-bank financial intermediaries is that banks offer the public a liability instrument that is extensively accepted as and used as a medium of exchange, with changes in ownership effected through the clearing system, while non-bank financial intermediaries offer the public liability instruments that are not so used, but that have other attractive characteristics. This difference, nonetheless, is important. Banks, because they issue readily accepted media of exchange, by definition would be able (in the absence of cash control) to increase their holdings of financial assets (both primary and indirect) as long as the public retained confidence in bank deposits as acceptable media of exchange. In other words, the banks could bid for primary and indirect securities, thereby inducing a shift into bank deposits, and since this would lower the whole structure of interest rates, including the rate on bank savings deposits, the process could continue until secondary repercussions began to have their effect. This is why it is meaningful to regard the banks as being able to engage in multiple expansion and contraction not just of credit, as can other institutions under certain circumstances, but also of the supply of money which other intermediaries cannot do.

Secondary repercussions would end the process. That is, price increases would begin to emerge as reduced interest rates increased the demand for credit and real output, and as expectations of further price increases would begin to lead individuals to believe that the real value of bank deposits (and other fixed income securities) would fall significantly or simply that the banks would be unable to redeem their deposits with legal tender on demand. In other words, a run on the banks would end it.

What all this means really is that because of the medium of exchange characteristics of bank deposits, it is necessary for the government to influence their short-term growth if it wishes to achieve certain price and interest rate objectives. One way of exercising such influence is to control banks, but there are other ways as well. However, we will defer further discussion until we discuss the chartered banks in chapter 4, except for one final point.

Earlier we noted that the non-bank intermediaries as well as the banks were able to expand credit by increasing money velocity (i.e., by reducing the demand for idle cash balances). Now we have noted that official authorities must control bank asset growth so as to control the growth of the supply of money. Does it follow that they should also control non-bank asset growth so as to control the velocity of money? This is an empirical question. We have already noted that complete flexibility in the structure of interest rates might mean that cyclical growth of non-bank assets would be no greater than cyclical growth of bank assets. If empirical investigation were to find that interest rate changes were insufficient to preclude non-bank institutions from expanding the supply of credit to the point of facilitating an effective demand of inflationary proportions, then control over them for stabilization purpose would be justified. Empirical evidence to date does not suggest that such control is necessary in Canada.

The structure and growth of financial intermediation: While we leave to chapters 2 and 3 the task of analysing in detail the growth and development of financial intermediation in Canada, it may help to impart a certain air of reality to the preceding discussion to present a small part of it at this point. We have already noted that while the growth of primary securities may well be confined in a general way to the growth of national income and output, this need not at all be the case with indirect securities, that is, with financial claims issued essentially for the purpose of acquiring other financial claims – hence the possibility that financial intermediaries may grow faster than gross national product. Chart 1:1 shows the ratio of total financial intermediary assets to gross national product for both Canada and the United States. (The statistics, of course, exclude the cases of individuals and non-financial institutions and corporations issuing debt to

Chart 1:1 — Assets of Financial Intermediaries as a Proportion of Gross National Product 1880-1968

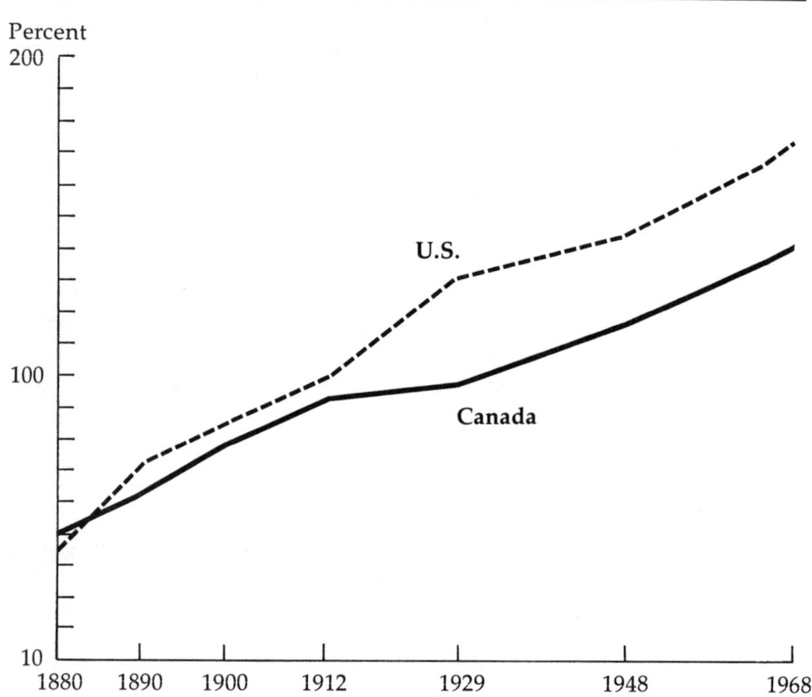

SOURCE: See Statistical Appendix.

purchase financial assets.) There is no doubt, as can readily be seen from the chart, that the long-term trend in both countries has been for total financial intermediary assets to grow faster than gross national product although, as we shall discuss later, Canada experienced a curious pause in that development from several years before the First World War until the mid 1920s.

In 1870 Canadian financial intermediary assets compiled amounted to about one-third of G.N.P., while by the end of the 1920s they were about equal to G.N.P. The high ratios of the depression of the 1930s and their subsequent decline should be ignored because they resulted from highly volatile G.N.P. figures. But an upward trend has again existed in Canada since the early 1950s with the ratio standing at 1.41 in 1968.

Table 1:2 Major Groupings of Canadian Financial Intermediary Assets as a Proportion of Gross National Product 1870-1970 (selected years)

	TOTAL F.I. ASSETS	PRIVATE F.I. ASSETS	CHARTERED BANK CANADIAN ASSETS	PRIVATE NON-BANK F.I. ASSETS	PUBLIC F.I. ASSETS
	%	%	%	%	%
1870	31	28	22	6	3
1880	50	45	28	17	5
1890	62	55	31	24	7
1900	79	71	41	29	8
1910	80	73	47	25	7
1920	75	67	46	21	8
1926	88	79	44	35	9
1930	100	92	46	46	8
1935	146	130	62	67	16
1940	120	103	49	54	17
1945	119	95	55	41	24
1950	115	91	48	43	24
1955	110	88	42	46	22
1960	119	93	38	56	26
1963	130	102	39	63	27
1965	134	106	39	67	28
1966	129	100	37	63	30
1967	136	105	39	66	31
1968	141	108	41	67	33
1969	n.a.	n.a.	40	66	n.a.
1970	n.a.	n.a.	40	n.a.	n.a.

SOURCE: See Statistical Appendix.

Table 1.2 shows Canadian data disaggregated into two major groupings of private and public financial intermediaries, with the private grouping divided again into chartered banks and non-bank intermediaries. Private financial intermediary assets rose faster than G.N.P. until the 1930s, and did so again after 1950. Of this group the chartered banks grew faster than G.N.P. only until about 1910; with the exception of the somewhat artificial period of the 1930s and the Second World War, their Canadian assets grew less than G.N.P. after that although the decline may have "bottomed out" after 1966. The ratio for the banks was 41% in 1900, 41% in 1968 and 40% in 1970.

The private non-bank ratio was 29% in 1900 and 67% in 1968, with a period of relative decline from the mid thirties until the end of the Second World War followed by a fairly steady increase in the ratio from about 1950. Government financial intermediaries grew faster than G.N.P. from about 1870 to 1900, but then ceased doing so for the next thirty years. However, after 1930 they increased more quickly than G.N.P. and by 1968 the ratio was 33% as compared with 8% in 1930.

So while there has been a long-term increase in the degree of financial intermediation, this increase has by no means been shared equally by the major groupings. Later we shall see that the experience of individual types of intermediaries has varied much more over the years than even the major groups discussed above.

THE FINANCIAL BROKERAGE FUNCTION — BROKERS, JOBBERS, UNDERWRITERS

In the preceding pages we have concerned ourselves essentially with the financial intermediation function of the financial system, and we used Diagram 1 to describe it. That same diagram can be used to explain the second major function of the capital market. It will be seen from the diagram that the transfer of funds has resulted in the creation of both primary and indirect securities. Original purchasers will not all wish to hold their securities until they mature — an obvious point made even more obvious in the case of perpetual bonds and stocks. Once financial claims have been created it is necessary to facilitate a change in their ownership. So some financial institutions are engaged in, and institutional arrangements are directed toward facilitating changes in ownership of financial claims. In the case of bank deposits it is the banks through their payments and clearing system that facilitate the transfer; for stocks it is largely stockbrokers acting through the stock exchanges; for fixed interest securities it is the investment dealers acting through the "over-the-telephone" money and bond markets, and also specialized mortgage brokers; and for foreign currencies it is the foreign exchange brokers and dealers.

The institutions that facilitate a change in ownership of financial claims are essentially financial brokers. However, those among them that act as principals — the bond and money market dealers and jobbers, underwriters, and foreign exchange dealers — that is, those that hold an inventory of financial claims (financed largely with borrowed money) in order to facilitate their brokerage operations, are, strictly speaking, a cross between brokers and financial intermediaries. Those that act entirely as agents are "pure" brokers. The same individual or institution may, of course, act as a "pure" broker in some transactions and as a jobber and underwriter in others.

The economic function of the "pure" broker is to facilitate the transfer of securities from one holder to another, and thereby reduce price variations arising from market imperfections, and in this he is assisted by brokers organizing themselves into stock exchanges. His commission is payment for those services, and its size, together with volume of business, must be such that he receives a competitive return on his capital while paying competitive rates for hired services, including his own.

The return required by jobbers and underwriters can be viewed the same way, but their functions are slightly different. The jobber, by taking a position in securities that are being traded, reduces short-term price fluctuations in that way and thereby improves the functioning of the market, an improvement based on his superior knowledge of market values. The underwriter, by agreeing to take up a new issue if he is unable to distribute it before delivery date, also reduces price fluctuations based on market imperfections – assuming his judgment of the inherent value of the issue is subsequently proven to be correct. An underwriter who depends on pre-issue orders before assuming an underwriting liability is really a broker. It can be seen that brokers, jobbers and underwriters all facilitate the distribution of primary and indirect securities by providing a focal point for buyers and sellers of securities, and that thereby the liquidity of securities is increased, price fluctuations in short-term trading activity are reduced, the smooth flow of funds into securities with the highest rate of return (given the risk) is enhanced, and the spread between buying and selling prices is minimized.

FINANCIAL COUNSELLING

The efficient functioning of the capital market can be enhanced by the communication of specialized knowledge of security values from the active participants in the market to those whose interest is more distant. This advice can be given by almost any one of the active participants in the market referred to above, but with the growth of the market there begin to be opportunities for individuals and companies specializing only in that kind of activity. Such advice can flow to those with surplus funds to invest, to financial intermediaries with accumulated funds to invest, to borrowers faced with the prospect of having to sell security issues, and even to brokers, jobbers, and underwriters who may lack specialized knowledge of either some areas of the market, or of the factors which influence the behaviour of the market. Presumably, as long as the fee charged by the counsellor is smaller than the monetary advantages to his clients for having received his advice, his existence will be economically justified.

SUMMARY

In the abstract, the functioning of the capital market, as a market in financial claims, involves an attempt on the part of savers with surplus funds to maximize the return in yield and services on the primary and indirect securities they purchase (within complicated constraints of tastes or preferences). It involves a tendency for financial intermediaries to maximize profits by minimizing the cost of funds accumulated through the issue of indirect securities and the costs of administration, maximizing the return on the primary and indirect securities purchased with those funds and expanding assets and liabilities until marginal costs and marginal returns are equal. It involves final users of funds minimizing the cost of funds obtained through the issue of primary securities, and expanding the issue of such securities until rewards from acquiring additional funds (which will differ materially in character as between business, government and individuals) are equal to the cost of additional new funds. It involves the effort of brokers, jobbers and underwriters to provide a focal point for buyers and sellers of securities, thereby facilitating the placement of new issues of primary and indirect securities, and the transfer of existing securities from one holder to another, which in turn will reduce price fluctuations and encourage the movement of surplus funds into the highest-yielding securities after due allowance for risk.

This is the outline of the structure and operation of the market that we will wish to keep in mind when tracing the development of the capital market. It provides a framework both for describing the capital market and its development, and for appraising the deficiencies of the functioning of the capital market.

It does not allow, however, for the impact of government, apart from government as a controller of the medium of exchange and government as a borrower and lender of funds. And yet government has exercised an influence on the functioning of the institutions in the capital market over the whole of the period of this study, beginning with the early bank charters. It is therefore necessary to provide an outline which will indicate the general character of government intervention in the operation of financial institutions.

The Basis for Government Regulation

REASONS FOR REGULATION

In the hypothetical business world that economists refer to technically as a "perfectly competitive economy" there would not be much justification on economic grounds for government intervention in the capital market. The capital market would help achieve maximum efficiency through competition, assisted by the existence of perfect knowledge, in the sense of achieving efficiency in resource allocation both in the rest of the economy, and within its own operations. Through competition funds would go to most productive borrowers and measurement of productivity would take into account both private and social costs of production. Through competition there would be an "optimum" division of internal and external financing and, within the latter, between direct and indirect financing. Through competition financial intermediaries and financial brokerage institutions would be of "optimum" size and would be operating at minimum cost and "normal" profits. Types of securities issued would perfectly reflect the portfolio preferences of savers and, given those preferences, they would constitute a mix of claims that would minimize borrowing costs of individual borrowers. Finally, the prices of outstanding financial claims would reflect only inherent differences between claims. On economic grounds the role of government in the capital market would possibly be confined to controlling the supply of media of exchange so as to achieve a certain desired price level objective.

The *actual* existence of government intervention in the capital market may for purposes of clarification be viewed as arising for four broad and interrelated reasons: first, as the economy experiences instability in its price, employment and economic growth behaviour, governments have used their control over financial variables such as money supply to reduce such instability; second, the capital market in reality is not perfectly efficient and government intervention may have as its objective the removal of market rigidities that have led to inefficiency in resource allocation, or the neutralization of the undesirable effects of such rigidities by, for example, providing incentives for funds to flow in certain directions; third, quite apart from the beneficial effects its actions may have on resource allocation, the government may feel that it must provide a certain degree of protection to savers and borrowers, to buyers and sellers of securities; fourth, the government may wish to achieve a host of non-economic objectives other than those automatically achieved by either a perfectly efficient or a less than perfectly efficient capital market.

Each of these reasons for government intervention must be examined closely in order to indicate more clearly their implications for government intervention in the financial system.

Government actions that affect the capital market and are designed to achieve the first objective essentially would include attempts to influence the rate of spending on current output of goods and services by changing the flow of income and the stock of liquid assets through controlling the supply of money, influencing the cost and availability of credit by techniques that supplement control over the supply of money, changing the level and structure of taxation and of borrowing and spending (including changes in tariffs, depreciation allowances, debt structure, subsidies and similar items).

The first objective also involves attempts on the part of government to exert a stabilizing influence on market prices of foreign exchange and of securities. With respect to the exchange rate, absolute stabilization exists when the government maintains a fixed rate of exchange, but at other times stabilization involves influencing the extent to which free-market forces in the foreign exchange market are permitted to determine the rate of exchange. From time to time official authorities also attempt to influence other financial markets, as when they influence stock purchases on margin and intervene in the government securities markets. Sometimes such attempts at stabilization may be explained by government debt management objectives, but at other times by the government's view that the market may from time to time generate price fluctuations that may compromise the smooth and efficient functioning of the financial system.

As for the second reason for government intervention, there are in fact several groups of reasons why inefficiency may emerge in the way the capital market operates and allocates the nation's resources.

(a) The optimum size of some capital market operations may constitute a monopoly or near monopoly, and this may require the kind of regulation that one normally associates with natural monopolies, or it may require the emergence of public ownership. The best examples would be control of the supply of money which to a large extent is vested in the Bank of Canada, and the arguments for a national pension plan which have led to the Canada Pension Plan and the Quebec Pension Plan.

(b) Ignorance on the part of issuers, buyers, sellers, brokers and underwriters of financial claims and also on the part of investment advisers may lead to an economically inefficient allocation of funds, which also of course involves unfair treatment of innocent parties, and such ignorance may pave the way for fraud. Ignorance itself may arise because of the inadequate disclosure of information that is being or could be generated, in which case the remedy may be disclosure requirements. It may arise because of inadequate compilation of information that is disclosed, in which case the answer may be regulations relating to the form in which information is disclosed, or the establishment of independent information services. It may arise because of misrepresentation of information, in which case disclosure provisions may have to be supplemented by penalties for misrepresentation or fraud. It may arise because some information is inherently so complex that the normal investors or borrowers may not be able to understand it, at least not in the time available to them for attempting to do so (which identifies the need for investment advisers and for ensuring that their operations in fact serve to improve decision-making in the capital market). It may arise because of careless consideration of even easily understood and readily available information, which may imply the need for public education in financial matters and for rules designed to protect individuals against themselves, as for example regulations giving individuals a period for reconsideration prior to signed contracts becoming legally binding. It may arise because some information is difficult to document and to present – such as gross errors of judgment on the part of new or deteriorating management – in which case a certain amount of official surveillance and control reporting to official authorities may be needed. It may arise because some important information cannot be available to everyone at the same time, thereby giving certain groups unjustified advantages, which may necessitate regulations such as those relating to "insider" trading, to the timing of release of information (e.g., quarterly statements or releases relating to special developments), or to "arm's length" transactions. Finally, ignorance may arise because some significant information just cannot be made available, as for example the chances of a mine being found, in which case information relating to the *absence* of information (that is, relating to the degree of "riskiness"), may be needed.

(c) Economic inefficiency in the allocation of funds may also arise because the cost of funds to borrowers and the return on funds to savers may not reflect fully both private *and* social economic costs and returns. That is, there may be "external" costs and returns that the capital market ignores when it accumulates and allocates funds, for it is normally concerned only with costs and returns that appear on the income statements of borrowers. A simple example would be when a company increases its net return by failing to adopt anti-pollution devices, thereby increasing the costs of public anti-pollution policies. Various techniques, such as special taxes and regulation of industrial activities (with penalties), may be used to overcome the problem, and while these may essentially be unrelated to the capital market and therefore outside the bounds of our discussion, they could improve the allocation of funds.

(d) Government intervention in the allocation of capital might also be justified in cases where it could convincingly be argued that its appraisal of future returns on projects being considered is better than that of the private sector. In most instances it is difficult to see why this should be the case. However, one, possibly hypothetical, case may be noted. Where future returns on projects are partially contingent on appropriate supporting government policy, and where government is more confident that such support will be forthcoming than is business, and assuming that government is justified in its greater confidence, then it may be that government appraisal of future returns will be superior to that of the private sector. A system of subsidies for borrowers or the operation of government financial intermediaries might then be utilized to improve capital allocation. Or, it is sometimes argued that local governments in some cases are better informed of local investment opportunities than are the members of the capital market who make allocation decisions in cities far away.

We have already noted that, quite apart from their undesirable impacts on resource allocation, imperfections in the functioning of the capital market may impair the financial position of unsuspecting buyers and sellers of securities and other financial claims. Thirdly, therefore, intervention may be required to provide protection simply on the grounds of fairness and decency. All the various disclosure provisions referred to earlier will of course serve to provide such protection, as well as to improve the economic efficiency of the capital market. But there may need to be others, particularly as they relate to the functioning of financial intermediaries. Historically, statutory prescriptions and official surveillance relating to permitted lending, investing and borrowing activities of financial intermediaries have been introduced essentially so as to reduce the "riskiness" of their operations and thereby give protection to individuals dealing with them. The use of deposit insurance is another, and more recent, example of government providing protection. Some would argue that maximum consumer loan rates would be another, as would provisions relating to the right to renegotiate contracts after a certain period of time as under the Interest Rate Act, or to restricting the rights of repossession of items purchased under conditional sale agreements. Quite obviously, the need to provide minimum protection is going to be of continuing concern to regulatory authorities.

As for the fourth reason, there is no need to discuss here why government may decide that for social or political reasons it should intervene in the financial system. Recently, limitation of foreign ownership has been a prime example of such intervention. Also the government may feel that more funds should be directed toward certain sectors even though economically more productive uses of those funds are available. A direct or indirect subsidy on the cost of funds would therefore be involved. Such an objective could be achieved by altering the rules governing the operations of existing financial intermediaries (i.e., requiring them to hold securities they would not otherwise hold) or giving appropriate instructions to government-sponsored financial intermediaries. The threats that the achievement of these non-economic objectives pose for economic efficiency should of course be recognized.

Several general observations must be made with respect to these various objectives and the government's attempts to achieve them. Government may have in mind more than one objective when using a particular technique to influence the market, as for example when it stabilizes markets so as to preclude chaotic markets from interfering with economic growth. Also, government attempts to achieve one of those objectives might well interfere with some of the other objectives of government intervention, as when action taken to stabilize economic activity or to protect the position of borrowers and lenders prevents capital from flowing to its most productive uses. Furthermore, some techniques for achieving given objectives may conflict less with the other objectives than other techniques for achieving the same objectives: for example, techniques designed to remove rigidities from the capital market and improve capital allocation in that way are likely to be more in harmony with the efficient functioning of the capital market than are attempts to offset the effects of rigidities by imposing additional regulations on financial intermediaries or introducing new government-sponsored financial intermediaries; and aggregate monetary and fiscal techniques designed to influence aggregate spending may distort the functioning of the capital market less than selective controls designed to influence selected sectors of the economy. Government intervention may also at times explain the growth behaviour of different types of financial institutions and must therefore be considered in any explanation of the growth and the decline of financial institutions.

TYPES OF REGULATION

In Canada regulation of capital market activity is divided first of all between "self-regulation" and "government regulation." The former refers to the rules of operation of the stock exchanges, the Investment Dealers' Association of Canada, the Broker-Dealers' Association of Ontario, and to a lesser extent the various associations of financial intermediaries—e.g., the Canadian Bankers' Association, the Canadian Life Insurance Association, the Trust Companies' Association of Canada, the Federated Council of Sales Finance Companies, Canadian Consumer Loan Association, the Canadian Mutual Funds Association and the Association of Canadian Investment Companies. We will not discuss the matter of "self-regulation" here, except merely to note that its existence has for decades been officially recognized and that the amount of government regulation required will in part be determined by the success or failure of self-regulation.

It is the nature of government regulation and control of the financial system that primarily concerns us here. Classified into type of activity, such regulation relates essentially to (a) the issue and management of currency, or more generally "money"; (b) the issue of new securities and the sale and purchase of securities; and (c) the control of the detailed operations of financial intermediaries.

Classified by approach of the regulation, government on the one hand can attempt to remove obstacles that prevent the market from functioning efficiently and on the other hand can attempt to offset the undesirable economic effects of such obstacles by redirecting the flow of funds. Points (a) to (c) that follow would fall essentially in the former category and point (d) in the latter. The various approaches are: (a) disclosure—at least an element of which is found in almost every federal and provincial statute concerned with the capital market, particularly important examples of which are prospectus requirements; (b) stipulating prohibited activity for purposes of providing protection and generally establishing standards of conduct—as found in the Criminal Code and in provincial securities and anti-fraud regulations; (c) stipulating required procedures and permitted or approved activity, and objective operational requirements—as for example outlined in legislation relating to selling securities, to the borrowing and lending activities of financial intermediaries, and to the various financial intermediaries' reserve requirements; (d) direct government influence on the flow of funds—as in the case of the many government-guaranteed loan schemes, and industrial development agencies including the operation of government-owned financial intermediaries.

Finally, classified by the mechanics of control we can identify (a) regular reports to official authorities that reveal whether objective statutory requirements are being met; (b) on-going surveillance of authorities and the exercise of discretionary power by them with respect to current operations and standards of conduct—an approach that may involve, not objective statutory criteria of operations, but only subjective judgments of official authorities; (c) the submission of operating material (e.g. prospectuses) to official authorities for approval; (d) for purposes of directly affecting the allocation of capital, the use of grants to borrowers, guaranteed loans, favourable tax treatments, and the establishment of government financial intermediaries including a variety of lending agencies.

It should be noted that the various approaches to regulation may to some extent be substitutes for each other for the purpose of achieving desired objectives. Economic efficiency in a particular instance, for example, might be served by disclosure regulations, and the more effective such regulations are, the less reliance need be placed on rules relating to standards of conduct and to what constitutes "permitted" activity. Or, the more detailed the enquiries of official authorities are as to current operations, and the more willing they are to exercise discretionary judgments in particular cases, the less reliance would need be placed on the establishment of objective statutory requirements and on regular reporting relating to such requirements. Or, the use of devices such as deposit insurance may reduce the minimum required degree of official surveillance and control of intermediary operations.

Presumably, therefore, a rational government would seek to achieve an "optimum" structure of government regulation, this being one that would best achieve the efficiency and protection objectives being sought with the least cost in the form of real resources used for regulation. Such a structure of regulation would involve achieving an appropriate balance between the three approaches of (a) disclosure, (b) specification of prohibited activities with penalties for infraction and (c) specification of required procedures, permitted activity and minimum operational requirements, and regular reporting relating thereto.

We can now move from this somewhat abstract view of the structure and functioning of the financial system, and of government regulation, to an examination of the actual development of the Canadian capital market.

2

The Emergence of Financial Institutions

There is a danger that, in tracing the development of particular types of financial institutions, perspective on the growth of the capital market in general will not be acquired. Past concentration on the development of the chartered banking system seems to have had this result. Yet detailed investigation of the growth of each type of financial institution is desirable. To reconcile these conflicting objectives we intend in this chapter to outline in a general way the establishment of financial institutions in Canada, while leaving statistical analysis and the details of the growth and development of institutions to later chapters. We shall, however, draw on the conclusions of subsequent chapters whenever this assists us in our immediate task of describing the growth and the development of the capital market in general.

Period Up to Confederation

Innovation in the capital market in the sense of the establishment of new financial intermediaries is not a new phenomenon. Most of the major types of intermediaries presently in existence were established prior to the turn of the century and, as we shall see, the growth rate of financial intermediaries was probably greater before the turn of the century than after, while the increase in the relative importance of non-bank financial intermediaries in this century compared with the period prior to 1900 has perhaps been rather less than is commonly assumed.

Table 2:1 outlines the date of appearance of various types of Canadian financial intermediaries.

Table 2:1 Canadian Financial Intermediaries: Date of Appearance

	YEAR
Fire and casualty insurance companies	1809
Chartered banks[1]	1817
Savings banks	1819
Terminating building societies	1844
Life insurance companies[2]	1847
Permanent building societies or mortgage loan companies	1855
Government Note Issue	1866
Federal Government Savings Bank[3]	1867
Federal Government Post Office Savings Bank	1867
Government insurance and pension account[4]	1870
Trusteed pension plans[5]	1874
Trust companies	1882
Caisses populaires and credit unions	1900
Closed-end investment trusts[6]	1901
Federal government annuities	1908
Finance companies	1916
Provincial agricultural loan schemes[7]	1917
Government housing loans[8]	1918
Provincial government savings offices	1920
Consumer loan companies	1928
Farm Credit Corporation (formerly Canadian Farm Loan Board)	1929
Mutual funds	1932
Bank of Canada	1935
Registered small loan companies and money lenders	1939
Investment contract companies	1940
Industrial Development Bank	1944
Provincial industrial loan schemes[9]	1944
Government export insurance[10]	1944
Development companies	1953
National pension plans	1965
Deposit insurance	1967

[1]The first charter was actually granted in 1820. The Bank of Montreal operated without a charter from 1817 to 1822.
[2]The first Canadian life insurance company—The Canada Life Assurance Co.—began operations in 1847. British and U.S. companies had agents in Canada from the 1830s onward.
[3]Had been trustee savings banks operated by Nova Scotia and New Brunswick prior to Confederation.
[4]The federal government introduced its civil servants' pension plan that year.
[5]In 1874 the Grand Trunk Railway introduced a contributory pension plan for its cler-

Prior to Confederation innovation among financial intermediaries took the form of the establishment of chartered banks as the predominant suppliers of medium of exchange and short-term credit; the establishment of trustee savings banks (an experiment that ended in failure), and the permanent emergence of the Quebec savings banks; the establishment of fire insurance companies and, ultimately much more important for the capital market, the establishment of the first Canadian life insurance company and the appearance of British and American life insurance underwriting agents in Canada; and the emergence of terminating building societies and their evolution to permanent societies, along with the appearance of joint-stock loan companies operating under royal charter (the land companies are not here included as capital market institutions even though they sometimes assumed credit granting functions). An examination of these financial intermediaries reveals not only that they had appeared prior to Confederation but also that some of them had already undergone significant changes by 1867.

While the natural inclination of the local community to protect itself against the financial hazards of fire had led to the appearance of British fire insurance agents in 1804 and to the formation of the Nova Scotia Fire Association (later the Halifax Fire Insurance Association) in 1809, it was the formation of Canadian banks beginning with the Bank of Montreal in 1817 that marked the appearance of the first significant financial intermediary in Canada.

There can be no doubt that the overwhelming economic impetus to the formation of the first Canadian banks was the shortage of medium of exchange. This shortage had been chronic and it had extended over many years. The colonies of British North America had not had their own coinage. Nor had New France before the Conquest, apart from a few insignificant issues. A hodge-podge of foreign coins was heavily depended upon for hand-to-hand cur-

---

ical and indoor staff which may have been the first pension plan in private industry.

[6]Year of appearance of the oldest surviving investment trust. Other short-lived corporations that might be classed as investment trusts had appeared earlier from time to time.

[7]This is when they began in a serious way. There were small loan programs before that date, however.

[8]The federal government made funds available to the provinces for financing residential construction at the municipal level.

[9]This is only an approximation of the commencement of serious lending by provinces to industry—it being the date of the appearance of the Nova Scotia Industrial Loan Fund. Other provincial loan schemes soon followed. However, isolated instances of such lending activity occurred long before 1944.

[10]Formation of the federal Export Credits Insurance Corporation, now Export Development Corporation.

rency, and the Pillar Dollar of Spain, the "piece of eight," was the predominant large coin. Experimentation with playing-card money in New France over a period of sixty-five years had been quite successful during time of peace, and it suggested that paper money could be a substitute for scarce metallic media of exchange; but overissue through financing war expenditures discredited it and the British forbade the issue of paper money in the colonies except under conditions of war. This attitude was not hospitable to the formation of financial institutions issuing paper currency.

It is true that further minor experimentation with paper money occurred prior to the formation of the chartered banks. John McGill, appointed Commissary of Stores in Upper Canada in 1792, and soon Agent of Government Purchases, was given permission to pay for his supplies with transferable certificates suitable for hand-to-hand circulation—although they were not endowed with legal tender properties. In 1761 Nova Scotia began to issue treasury notes to finance its expenditure; after 1773 it was possible to make these payable to bearer; and in 1813 they were made non-interest-bearing. Prince Edward Island issued its first treasury notes in 1790 and these were clearly designed to alleviate the scarcity of money in circulation.[1]

But these experiments did not begin to overcome the shortage of reliable media of exchange and a persistent flow of merchants' I.O.U.s (or "bons" in French Canada) joined the foreign coinage in hand-to-hand circulation. Just how unsatisfactory the currency was is illustrated by a writer to the *Acadian Recorder* of October 21, 1820, who noted that after buying 6 pence worth of squash with a 20 shilling provincial note (of which 3 pence was a discount on the note itself) he received in exchange 5 shillings in the note of George Leggett, 5 shillings in the note of Wm. Lawson, 1 shilling in the team boat note of H. H. Cogswell, 1 shilling 3 pence in the note of Adam Esson and a similar note of John A. Barry, three 7½ pence notes of Wm. Smith, 7½ pence in silver, and 3 shillings 6 pence in copper.[2]

The opportunities for the formation of note-issuing banks (that is, banks for the issue of even-denomination readily accepted paper currency) were early realized by local prominent merchants—merchants who had actively been pursuing the merchant banking business of financing international and domestic trade. In 1792 three of these (Phyn, Ellice & Inglis; Todd, McGill & Co.; and Forsyth, Richardson & Co.) issued a circular, reprinted in the *Official Gazette,*

1. See Victor Ross, *The History of the Canadian Bank of Commerce* (Toronto: Oxford University Press, 1920), vol. 1, p. 424.
2. Quoted in H. A. Innis and A. R. M. Lower, *Select Documents in Canadian Economic History 1783-1885* (Toronto: University of Toronto Press, 1933).

proposing the establishment of a note-issuing bank. The close relationship between the early establishment of Canadian banks and the shortage of medium of exchange is nowhere better illustrated than in that circular, which read:

> The undersigned, having experienced great inconvenience in Canada from the deficiency of specie or some other medium to represent the increasing circulation of the Country, as well as from the variety of the money now current, and knowing the frequent loss and general difficulty attending receipts and payments, have formed the resolution of establishing a Bank at Montreal, under the name of the "Canadian Banking Company".
>
> The business proposed by the Company, and usually done by similar establishments, is: To receive deposits in cash. To issue notes in exchange for such deposits. To discount Bills and notes of hand. To facilitate business by keeping cash accounts with those who choose to employ the medium of the Bank in their receipts and payments ...[3]

The attempt was unsuccessful, as was a further attempt in 1808. Then came the war of 1812-14. The Parliament of Lower Canada in July 1812 passed an act to finance the new expenditures of the army. Specie was scarce, so that sales of bills on London would have depressed the rate of exchange. Shipment of specie from London was risky and in any case England had earlier suspended payment. So it was decided that the Governor, as Commander of the Army, should be authorized to issue "Army Bills" of small denominations intended for local circulation but redeemable in government bills of exchange on London. Denominations of $1.00, $2.00, $3.00, $4.00, $5.00, $10.00, $12.00, $16.00, $20.00, $25.00, $50.00, $100.00 and $400.00 were issued at one time or another. The first issue was limited to £250,000, but this was raised in several stages to £1,500,000. The amount outstanding at the end of the war was £1,249,000. Bills of denominations of $25.00 or over bore interest and, at the option of the issuers, were redeemable in cash or bills on London, while the smaller bills did not bear interest and were redeemable only in cash.[4] Significantly, smaller notes could be exchanged for interest-bearing larger notes, so that shifts between them provided for a flexible currency and an investment security at the same time. The bills were seen essentially as a means for overcoming fiscal difficulties, and this was confirmed

---

3. Quoted in James Stevenson, "The Currency of Canada after the Capitulation," *Transaction of the Literary and Historical Society of Quebec*, Sessions of 1876-7, pp. 105-34, and reprinted in E. P. Neufeld, ed., *Money and Banking in Canada*, Carleton Library no. 17 (Toronto: McClelland and Stewart, 1964), pp. 28-9.
4. Ross, *op. cit.*, pp. 8-9.

by their hasty redemption after war emergencies disappeared. But while they were outstanding they constituted a highly satisfactory medium of exchange and clearly established the benefits of a paper currency which merely required specie, or its rough equivalent in the form of bills of exchange, as a reserve and which was not subject to disappearance through external drain as was circulating specie coinage. This successful experimentation with Army Bills reduced public suspicion toward paper money and eased the way for the establishment of note-issuing chartered banks—particularly when the redemption of the Bills once more subjected the economy to all the inconveniences of a short supply of medium of exchange.

Even so, the first bank, the "Montreal Bank," when it began operations in 1817 had not been granted a charter and operated, probably illegally, as a limited-liability company under private articles of association. The first "chartered" bank was the Bank of New Brunswick, which received its charter in March 1820. In the following year chartered banking was finally established with the granting of charters to the Bank of Montreal, Quebec Bank, Bank of Canada, and Bank of Upper Canada. Those early charters reflected both the major restrictions on banking operations and the approach to control of the banks by government that was to prevail and evolve over the whole history of the chartered banks. The charter of the Bank of Montreal, given royal assent on July 22, 1822, provided for a ten-year charter. It prohibited the bank from owning real estate beyond that required for the "... convenient conduct and management of the business of the said Bank"; it prohibited the bank from lending on mortgages, hypothèque, or land, or other fixed property, although the bank could take mortgages as additional security on a loan already made; it required the bank to present an annual report, with specified information, to shareholders; and it forbade the bank from taking "...any interest exceeding the lawful interest of six per centum per Annum, as fixed by the laws of this Province." The general prohibition against mortgage lending, except for some government-guaranteed mortgages, was not removed until 1967 but the banks enjoyed great freedom in most other types of lending and investing. Government control over the years was to take the form, not of detailed investment prescriptions, but of general and increasing supervision based on a progressively more detailed system of reporting and inspection.

While the Canadian chartered banks soon dominated the commercial banking field after their first appearance in the 1820s, and for many years dominated also the capital market in general, this success did not come without experimentation with other forms of banking. It was not until 1837 that legislation in Upper and Lower Canada prohibited the issue of notes by private banks, and up to that time (and in other parts of British North America even after that) there were many attempts at establishing private note-issuing banks under deed of settlement. Banks of this type which were in operation at the time of the 1837 legislation (the Farmers' Banking Company, the Bank of the People, the Niagara Suspension Bank, and the Agricultural Bank) soon disappeared. There were also banks operating under royal charter. The Bank of British North America, also at first a joint-stock bank, was formed in Great Britain, began operations in Canada in 1836, received local authorization to sue and be sued in the name of the resident officer, obtained a royal charter in 1840 and was absorbed by the Bank of Montreal in 1918. The Bank of British Columbia began operations in 1862 under royal charter and was absorbed by the Canadian Bank of Commerce in 1900.

During part of the period 1837-9 the chartered banks, because of political unrest, were permitted to suspend specie payment, and this prompted a number of spurious banks to circulate notes. These banks, of which at least sixteen have been listed, had no charters and were merely groups of individuals operating mainly out of Buffalo. They circulated notes in British North America and even more so in the United States and whatever offices they established in Canada quickly disappeared when notes were offered for redemption. With resumption of specie payment these "banks" disappeared.

Another type of commercial bank which appeared was the "free" bank introduced by banking legislation of the Province of Canada in 1850. This legislation permitted the function of banking to be extended to individuals and corporations, a function denied them since the legislation of 1837. Only unit banks could be established under the legislation, capital of the not inconsiderable amount of $25,000 was required, and notes for circulation could only be obtained after the deposit of an equal amount of provincial securities with the Receiver General—a requirement which in effect ensured that the banks could not be very profitable but would provide a demand for the securities of a hard-pressed provincial government. The system did not work and soon was inoperative. Six banks operated under the legislation: the Bank of British North America, which did so partly to obtain the privilege of issuing notes of less than $4, a privilege denied it by its royal charter; the Zimmerman Bank established in 1855, which became the Clifton Bank in 1858 and had its charter repealed in 1863; the Bank of the Niagara District (at St. Catharines), which soon applied for and obtained a charter but then encountered difficulties and was absorbed by the Imperial Bank of Canada in 1875; the Molson's Bank (Montreal), which also soon obtained a charter, and operated successfully as a chartered bank until 1925 when it was absorbed by the Bank of Montreal; the Provincial Bank (Stanstead); and the Bank of the County of Elgin (St. Thomas), which operated only from 1856 to 1862.

This was the end of experimentation with different forms of note-issuing commercial banks, and it had come before Confederation. The local bankers who took deposits, made loans, and frequently rose to prominence in Ontario and the North West from then until the First World War constituted the only important innovation in commercial banking over those years – apart from the demand deposits which some of the loan companies experimented with and the banking business of the two Quebec savings banks. After the Second World War caisses populaires, credit unions, and trust companies began actively to solicit chequing deposits, which must be viewed as innovations in commercial banking in that they involve offering liability instruments that serve as media of exchange.

Experimentation with savings banks in Canada began in 1819 with the formation of a savings bank in Montreal and the introduction of legislation to encourage their establishment by New Brunswick in 1825. Similar legislation was also introduced by the other colonies, all of which followed closely the trustee savings bank legislation of the United Kingdom. These banks, of which a number were established, were intended specifically to provide savings facilities to the "... lower orders of society ..." to whom commercial banks did not cater, and to thereby encourage thrift among them. Management was honorary, and the rate of interest allowed on savings usually was generous; in some cases funds could only be invested in government securities, while in others wide freedom for choosing investments existed. The banks, for various reasons, were not a success. They failed to shed the characteristics of the original trustee savings banks – the aura of charity, the voluntary and somewhat casual management, and the concentration on the "industrious poor" as a source of funds – and so could not evolve into profit-motivated, commercially viable institutions. The Act of 1855 of the Province of Canada ensured their end, not in that it required new savings banks to be formed along other than trustee lines, but rather because it imposed impossible capital requirements on them and not on the new upstarts, the building societies. The two Quebec savings banks had by then been established. They were the only trustee savings banks to successfully overcome early disabilities and evolve into successful intermediaries, and one of them is still in operation as a savings bank. This successful transition had to a substantial degree occurred by Confederation, although periods of financial difficulties for them still lay ahead. It was not until 1871 that legislation of the new Dominion required all existing savings banks to obtain charters if they wished to continue in business, and to meet a capital requirement of $200,000, as well as to satisfy other provisions. Over the years details of the legislation changed, but no more savings banks appeared, and existing legislation does not even specifically provide for the formation of additional savings banks.

The institutions that began to challenge the savings banks as collectors of the funds of small savers were the terminating building societies. These, like the savings banks, were modelled on institutions operating in the United Kingdom, and the legislation which governed their operations was also at first greatly influenced by legislation of the United Kingdom. The Port Sarnia Syndicate, formed in 1844, was the first of them to appear, but they sprang up all over Upper Canada after the passing in 1846 of the Upper Canada Building Society Act. Their decisive advantages over the savings banks (and over the chartered banks) were that they catered to the very strong demand for real estate credit and they introduced the innovation of the contractual savings agreement in the form of instalment payments for shares.

However, they, like the savings banks, suffered from inefficient management, and also from the fact that the individual societies in theory were to terminate when total funds paid in and profits on loans were equal to the full value of the shares contracted for. Many abuses crept into their operations as well, and the institutions were well on the way to oblivion when further innovation saved some of them and permitted new ones to be formed on more successful lines. In 1855 the first step toward permanent societies was taken when one society introduced the practice of enrolling new members, and so a new cycle of share payments, every month, and of confining payment of profits to investors. The next step was taken when, in 1859, legislation permitted societies to capitalize paid-up shares and confirmed that they could take deposits as some had already been doing. Finally, in 1874 they were given authority to issue debentures, which soon placed them in the preferred and enviable position, among Canadian financial intermediaries, of being able to tap the United Kingdom capital market for funds. By Confederation the transition from terminating societies to permanent societies was virtually complete in some cases, although terminating shares did not completely disappear for many years. Certainly the concept of permanent building societies, soon to be called loan and savings societies or companies, and then mortgage loan companies, was firmly established and widely understood by Confederation.

It must also be mentioned that in addition to the appearance of building societies designed to cater to the demand for funds secured on real estate mortgages, there appeared also the Trust and Loan Company of Upper Canada with the same objective. It, however, was a limited liability company incorporated in 1843, which received a royal charter in 1845, but it was not really successfully launched till 1851. Later a few other mortgage loan companies with royal charters appeared but the companies that arose from permanent building society legislation were in terms of numbers and size of total assets the most important form of mortgage loan company in Canada.

Contractual savings agreements were also introduced in the pre-Confederation period by the life insurance companies. These companies, however, were also in a position to offer a liability instrument that was distinctly different from others that existed at the time – one that permitted individuals to insure themselves against the financial hazards of death. This unique characteristic of the product they could offer to savers and the contractual payments arrangement implicit in it were undoubtedly the major reasons why life insurance companies grew steadily in relative importance for three-quarters of a century.

British (and American) companies had agents in British North America in the 1830s, but the first Canadian life insurance company to be formed was the Canada Life Assurance Company, which began operations in 1847 in Hamilton. The non-Canadian companies appear to have been exporters of capital in that period and were important to the development of the Canadian capital market before Confederation primarily in that they familiarized Canadians with life insurance and they provided the Canadian company with the principles and the practice of establishing a life insurance business. It was not until 1871 that additional Canadian life insurance companies became active, so that at the time of Confederation the industry as a supplier of funds to borrowers was not important.

The result of all these developments was that by 1867 there were 33 chartered banks with about 123 branches in Canada, and assets which accounted for about 78% of the assets of all the financial intermediaries we have listed. There were about 28 building societies, many of which had begun to be permanent societies, and their assets accounted for about 9% of the assets of all recorded financial intermediaries. There were about 6 savings banks with 3% of all assets. The assets of one Canadian life insurance company amounted to about 1% of the total of all financial intermediaries listed; but in addition there were 13 British and 9 U.S. companies writing insurance in Canada whose assets in Canada are not known, but were not large, probably amounting to no more than 1% of total financial intermediary assets. There were 30 fire insurance companies (in 1869), 11 Canadian, 13 British, and 6 American, and their assets in Canada accounted for about 3% of the assets of all financial intermediaries in that year. The Government Note Issue appeared in 1866 and amounted to about 4% of the assets of all financial intermediaries in 1867, and the Federal Government Savings Bank and Post Office Savings Bank assets were about 3% of total financial intermediary assets. In dollar terms the total assets of financial intermediaries listed amounted to just over $100 million, which was roughly just under one-third the size of Gross National Product.

Specialized houses with brokerage functions were also beginning to appear, although typically the broker up to Confederation and a few years thereafter dabbled in a number of things: bonds and stocks were bought and sold on commission; real estate transactions were common, as was sale of life, fire and marine insurance; mortgage loans were arranged, foreign exchange business was solicited, deposits were taken and advances were made by some of them. The most important credit instrument for their business was the stock of the chartered banks, although a few utility, industrial and mining stocks were also occasionally available, and the debentures of the larger cities and of the various Ontario municipalities had appeared and provided an opportunity for brokerage business. Toronto brokers organized themselves into an exchange in 1852, while Montreal brokers began to meet regularly in 1832 and formed a Board of Stock and Produce Brokers in 1842. Reproduced below are the stock quotations of the two exchanges for April 8, 1857, as they appeared in the press. Bank stocks were the most important stock traded, and it is interesting that the credit instrument of a financial intermediary provided a substantial impetus to the formation of another financial institution – the stockbroker. (After Confederation loan companies also provided an important supply of instruments to the broker, and it was not until toward the end of the nineteenth century that industrial corporations began to do so in volume). The 1857 report for the Toronto exchange lists six banks, two gas utilities, three fire insurance companies, one railroad, and Province of Canada, Municipal Loan Fund, and Municipal (County and Town) debentures, a total of 15. The Montreal stock market report lists 20, including six banks, five mining stocks (surprisingly enough), three railroads, two utilities, and debentures of the Province of Canada, Municipal Loan Fund, one railroad, and the exchange itself. In 1865 the Toronto exchange press report still listed only 18 issues.[5] But neither exchange was publicly incorporated prior to Confederation.

5. See Bank of Nova Scotia, *Monthly Review*, September 1960.

MONTREAL STOCK MARKET—PREPARED BY THE BOARD OF BROKERS.

BOARD ROOM EXCHANGE, MONTREAL, March 28th, 1857.

DESCRIPTION.	Shares.	Paid Up.	Dividend Last Six Months.	Buyers.	Sellers.
	£ s. d.				
Bank of Montreal	50 0 0	whole.	4 per cent.	17 prem.	17 prem.
Bank of Montreal, New Stock	50 0 0	40 per cent.	4 per cent.	$15\frac{3}{4}$ prem.	16 prem.
Bank of British North America	50 0 0 stg.	whole.	3 per cent.	40 prem.	43 prem.
Commercial Bank of Canada	25 0 0	whole.	4 per cent	$12\frac{1}{4}$ prem.	$12\frac{1}{4}$ prem.
City Bank	20 0 0	whole.	4 per cent.	10 prem.	11 prem.
City Bank, New Stock	20 0 0	10 per cent.	......	10 prem.	11 prem.
Bank of Upper Canada	12 10 0	whole.	4 per cent.	3 prem.	3 prem.
People's Bank	12 10 0	do	4 per cent.	1 prem.	1 prem.
Montreal Mining Company's Consols	5 0 0	3 13 9	None.	10s. 0d.	10s 0d.
Quebec and Lake Superior Mining Company	2 0 0	1 0 6	.....	None.	None.
Lake Huron Silver and Copper Mining Company	1 5 0	0 3 9	.....	2s. 6d.	None.
Canada Mining Company	1 5 0	0 4 6	....	0s. 6d.	None.
Huron Copper Bay Mining Company	1 0 0	0 1 3	....	0s. 6d.	0s. 9d.
Champlain and St. Lawrence Railroad Company	50 0 0	whole.	None.	None.	$82\frac{1}{2}$ dis.
Grand Trunk Railroad Company	25 0 0	whole.	6 per cent. per annum.	$53\frac{1}{2}$ dis.	$53\frac{1}{2}$ dis.
Great Western of Canada	25 0 0	whole.	4 per cent., 6 mos.	None.	None
Montreal Telegraph Company	10 0 0	whole.	5 per cent., 6 mos.	$14\frac{1}{2}$ prem.	15 prem.
Montreal City Gas Company	10 0 0	whole.	3 per cent., 6 mos.	$5\frac{1}{4}$ dis.	par.
Government Debentures, 20 years	...	...	6 per cent. per annum.	2 prem.	$2\frac{1}{2}$ prem.
Con. M. L. F. Debentures	...	...	6 per cent. per annum.	$5\frac{1}{2}$ dis.	5 dis.
Champlain and St. Lawrence Railroad Bonds	....	...	7 per cent. per annum.	40 dis.	30 dis.
Montreal Exchange	100 0 0	whole.	7 per cent. per annum.	None.	10 dis.

STOCKS.

BANK OF MONTREAL.—(DO. NEW STOCK.)—Heavy at 17 prem. for "old" and 16 prem. for "new" stock.

BANK OF BRITISH NORTH AMERICA.—Quotations nominal. None in market.

COMMERCIAL BANK MIDLAND DISTRICT.—Has slightly advanced, 12½ per cent prem. having been paid.

CITY BANK.—Heavy at the quotations—say buyers at 10, sellers 11 prem

BANK OF UPPER CANADA.—Transactions at 3 per c. pr.

PEOPLE'S BANK.—Very little in market, "new" stock being asked for at 1½ prem.

MONTREAL MINING COMPANY CONSOLS.—Inactive at 10s per share.

CHAMPLAIN AND ST. LAWRENCE RAILROAD.—Nothing whatever doing either in Stock or Bonds.

GRAND TRUNK RAILROAD.—Has slightly advanced. Sales took place during the week at 55 dis., but it has since been taken at 53½ dis.

GREAT WESTERN OF CANADA.—None in market.

MONTREAL TELEGRAPH COMPANY STOCK.—Sales at 14½ to 15 per cent prem.

MONTREAL CITY GAS COMPANY.—Without change in the nominal rate, but nothing doing.

GOVERNMENT DEBENTURES.—Sales to some extent at 2½ per cent prem., but this price is not to-day procurable.

CONSOLIDATED MUNICIPAL LOAN FUND DEBENTURES.—Buyers at 5½ per cent dis. Holders demanding 5 dis.

IN OTHER STOCKS.—Nothing to report.

EXCHANGE.—Bank, 60 days, on London, procurable at 9½ prem. Private 8½ to 9 prem. Bank, on demand New York, ¼ to ½ prem.; Private, par to ¼ dis.

SOURCE: *The Canadian Merchants' Magazine and Commercial Review*, Volume 1, April-September 1857 (Toronto: Wm. Weir & Co., 1857)

TORONTO STOCK MARKET.

(CORRECTED BY F. P. STOW.)

Toronto, 8th April, 1857.

DESCRIPTION.	SHARES. £ s. d.	PAID UP.	DIVIDEND LAST SIX MONTHS.	RATE.
Bank of Upper Canada	12 10 0		4 per cent.	No transaction.
Bank of Montreal	50 0 0		4 per cent.	16 per cent premium.
Commercial Bank	25 0 0		4 per cent.	12 per cent. premium.
Bank of British North America	50 0 0 Sterling.		3 per cent.	None offering.
Gore Bank	10 0 0 Curren'y	All.	4 p. c. & 10 bonus.	1 @ 2 per cent premium.
City Bank, Montreal	20 0 0		4 per cent.	11 per cent. premium.
Toronto Gas Company	12 0 0		5 per cent.	2 per cent. premium.
Hamilton Gas Company	10 0 0		5 per cent.	Par.
Western Assurance Company		15 per cent.	None.	Nominal.
British America do	12 10 0	45 per cent.	None.	Nominal.
Provincial do	20 0 0	20 per cent.	None.	Nominal.
Great Western R. R.	{ 25 0 0 Curren'y 20 10 0 Sterling. }	All.	4 per cent.	5 per cent. premium.
Government Debentures	...	...	{ 6 per cent. inter't per annum.	Par.
Municipal Loan do	...	...	do.	5 @ 6 per cent discount.
County & Town do	...	...	do.	1 @ 3 dis. per annum.

SOURCE: *The Canadian Merchants' Magazine and Commercial Review,* Volume 1, April-September 1857 (Toronto: Wm. Weir & Co., 1857)

While some of the aforementioned brokers dealt in exchange, the important principals in the foreign exchange business, from the first appearance of chartered banks to the present, have been the chartered banks which had inherited it from the merchants of Montreal.

After Confederation

From the year 1870 it has been possible to compile statistics of the assets of almost all the financial intermediaries in Canada, although the uneven quality of the figures requires that they be used with care. However, before examining the changing relative size of the various types of intermediaries, it is perhaps useful first to note the timing and the circumstances surrounding the appearance of additional financial intermediaries in Canada.

The terms of Confederation required the federal government to assume the liabilities of the savings banks operated by Nova Scotia and New Brunswick, and these the federal government operated for many years through the Department of Finance; the new Dominion government also established the Post Office Savings Bank in 1867. The former were gradually merged with the latter and disappeared as separate entities in 1929. But from 1867 to 1887 they experienced remarkable growth, with their deposits in the latter year amounting to 39% of the deposit liabilities of the chartered banks. Thereafter they declined steadily in importance until they were insignificant in size. In 1968 the Post Office Savings Bank was abolished.

While statistics of their assets are not available, it should be mentioned that in Ontario and to a smaller extent in the Northwest Territories, from Confederation to the turn of the century, there appeared a number of private bankers who took deposits, made loans, and fulfilled most other functions associated with commercial banking, apart from issuing notes (which of course they were forbidden to do). In 1890, 189 of such private bankers were listed, a year when there were only 426 chartered bank branches in Canada, so in terms of numbers they were not insignificant. These private bankers could become established primarily because the chartered banks had not yet fully established their system of branches. It is significant, for example, that many of them operated in centres where no chartered bank branch existed and that when the density (branches to population) of the branch system finally attained the level that has become relatively fixed, the private bankers disappeared.[6]

6. See below, pp. 171-3.

The federal government's pension plan for civil servants was introduced in 1870, but the beginning of private trusteed pension plans is more uncertain, even though their growth to significant size did not occur until after the 1930s. However, it may be that the first such plan was the contributory pension plan established by the Grand Trunk Railway for its clerical and indoor staff in 1874.

It was in 1872 that the first trust company, the Toronto General Trusts Company, was incorporated but that company did not really begin operations until 1882. Several more companies appeared in the later 1880s but marked interest in forming such companies developed in the 1890s.

The trust companies enjoyed the singular advantage of being able to act in a fiduciary capacity—the only incorporated institution so privileged. This, alone, set them apart from other financial institutions. However, that function is not really one of financial intermediation. Originally, as we shall see (chapter 9), the federal and provincial governments attempted to prohibit trust companies from taking deposits and issuing debentures, thereby hoping to keep them out of the "banking" and "mortgage loan company" business. However, since the trust companies were permitted to take funds "in trust" either in the form of deposits or guaranteed investment certificates, the practical (if not the strictly legal) obstacles to their engaging in deposit banking and in "debenture" financing were in effect soon overcome. So the trust companies could become established because they offered unique non-intermediary type services and because that activity could be supplemented by their encroaching on the activity of the chartered banks and mortgage loan companies.

The caisses populaires first appeared in 1900, and they were really in the tradition of the early trustee savings banks in their emphasis on encouraging thrift among the low-income groups. Later some of them (particularly the credit unions of English-speaking Canada) emphasized their function of making loans at reasonable cost to members as well as providing savings facilities. The caisses populaires and credit unions did not really experience significant growth until after the Second World War.

In 1901 appeared what is certainly the oldest surviving closed-end investment trust, the Debenture and Securities Corporation of Canada. It was incorporated by special act of the Parliament of Canada. Other such companies soon followed but it was not until the later 1920s that they appeared in large numbers. Not until 1932 did the first mutual fund, Canadian Investment Fund, Ltd., appear, and while several other mutual funds appeared before the Second World War, it was not until the postwar period that their numbers increased greatly.

Instalment finance companies made their appearance in 1916 when Continental Guaranty Corporation Canada (now Commercial Credit Corporation Ltd.) was formed, followed in 1919 by a branch office in Toronto of General Motors Acceptance Corporation of New York, and in 1920 by Traders Finance Corporation Limited, a Manitoba-based company. Other Canadian companies and United States branches and subsidiary companies appeared in the 1920s but again it was not until after the Second World War that their greatest growth was experienced. The establishment of these companies is explained primarily by the demand for a new type of credit that arose from the successful introduction of the automobile as popular transportation. As other durable consumer goods appeared, the same companies provided the necessary credit, but they also diversified their activities into other lending areas.

The first of what are now called personal or consumer loan companies – excluding the small individual money lenders that seem always to have been present – appeared in 1928 as the Central Finance Corporation (changed in 1937 to Household Finance Corporation). Then in 1939 federal legislation prompted the successful emergence of the *registered* money lenders. Their appeal was largely to one particular type of borrower – the small borrower who did not have collateral adequate for obtaining funds from chartered banks and who required a loan for a reason other than that of purchasing a durable good. These intermediaries were permitted to charge adequate interest rates, yet were subjected to rate limitations so as to protect the frequently inexperienced borrower.

In the period after the Second World War there have appeared a number of private companies that specialize in lending medium- and long-term capital, and also, significantly, in providing management assistance and advice to new, or small and medium-sized existing, companies. It is their emphasis on assisting the formation and development of new or relatively new companies that distinguishes them for the other financial intermediaries such as the closed-end investment trusts. These "industrial and commercial development corporations" are perhaps the only "new" type of private financial intermediary that has appeared after the Second World War, although many of the older ones have undergone substantial change.

We have already noted the formation of the Federal Government Savings Bank after Confederation. Its insurance and pension account first appeared in 1870, and in 1908 it established its Annuity Fund. In 1917 the Canadian provinces first began seriously to establish facilities for extending loans to farmers, but these efforts were superseded by the operations of the federal government's Canadian Farm Loan

Board (now Farm Credit Corporation) in 1929. Government participation in house financing began in 1918 when the federal government made $25 million available to the provinces, under the War Measures Act for re-lending to municipalities for housing purposes, while the Dominion Housing Act of 1935 gave the federal government a continuing role in residential financing, a role implemented after 1945 by Central Mortgage and Housing Corporation.

It was in the 1920s that a large number of pension and superannuation plans for provincial civil servants and teachers began to appear, and these have subsequently become relatively important.

The Manitoba government opened a savings office in 1920, but it ceased operating in 1932. The Ontario Government Savings Bank began operations in 1922 and the Alberta Treasury branches in 1939, and both are still in operation. The nation's central bank, the Bank of Canada, replaced the Dominion Note Issue in 1935, and the Industrial Development Bank, a subsidiary of the Bank of Canada, appeared in 1944. Since the Second World War most of the provinces have established an assortment of facilities for extending loans to farmers, fishermen, industry, municipalities and public service institutions.

As to the appearance since Confederation of new forms of brokers and dealers, the most significant event was the emergence in the decade before the turn of the century of specialized bond dealers. Stockbrokers had of course been present for many years, even prior to Confederation. The Montreal Stock Exchange was publicly incorporated in 1874, and the Toronto Stock Exchange followed in 1878. Two mining exchanges were formed in Toronto in the 1890s which in a few years became the Standard Stock and Mining Exchange and which in turn merged with the Toronto Stock Exchange in 1934. The Winnipeg Stock Exchange was established in 1903, the Vancouver Stock Exchange in 1907, and the Calgary Stock Exchange in 1914, while in 1926 the Montreal Curb Market was organized and it changed its name to the Canadian Stock Exchange in 1953. By the First World War the Toronto Stock Exchange list had increased to over 200 stocks and the Montreal list to 182 issues. This reflected not only the rapid growth of organized exchange business but also the early beginning of the emergence of the Toronto Exchange as the dominant exchange in Canada.

But the specialized bond dealer (with or without a stock brokerage adjunct) did not emerge until just before the turn of the century. However, in the decade after 1900 bond dealers appeared in remarkably large numbers—well before the impetus given to such development by the financing of the Dominion government during the First

World War. Specialized investment counsellors seem not to have emerged successfully until after the Second World War.

Changes in the Relative Size of Financial Intermediaries

While the history of each of the major financial intermediaries will be discussed in subsequent chapters, it is perhaps worthwhile noting briefly at this stage the major changes that have occurred in their relative size. Table 2:2 outlines this information for the years 1870, 1900, 1930 and 1968. Even though we discuss the quality and sources of our statistical data in an appendix, it is prudent to comment briefly on those data at this point. The basic concept used was assets arising out of business in Canada, not total assets where foreign operations were involved. The financial intermediaries not included, either because of the absence of adequate data or because our concept of what constitutes a financial intermediary ruled them out, are the following: the local private banks which were numerous in the nineteenth century; provincial life insurance companies and some provincial fraternal benefit societies; the estates, trusts and agency funds of trust companies; provincial fire and casualty insurance companies, apart from Ontario companies; brokers and dealers; and the book credit of merchants. While some of these should ideally have been included, their omission does not alter the long-term trends described below and we estimate that more than 95% of the assets of organized financial intermediaries are included over the whole of the period. Our emphasis is on long-term trends and generally speaking the data should not be used to make year-to-year comparisons of developments in the assets of financial intermediaries. By compiling annual statistics of the assets of almost all of the financial intermediaries, we believe that long-term developments have been accurately revealed, much more so than would have been the case if data for a few years only had been compiled.

Perhaps the most conspicuous change indicated by Table 2:2 is the long-term relative decline of the chartered banks. In 1870 their assets amounted to 73% of total financial intermediary assets while in 1968 the corresponding ratio was 29%. In the period up to 1900 it was the growth of the mortgage loan companies, the life insurance companies, and the Post Office and Government Savings Banks that accounted for the relative decline of the chartered banks. From 1900 to 1930 the banks' relative size declined moderately (although it

Table 2:2 Relative Size of Canadian Assets of Canadian Financial Intermediaries 1870-1968 (selected years)

	1870	1900	1930	1968
	PER CENT OF TOTAL			
I Chartered banks – total	72.6	52.6	45.9	28.9
II Private non-bank – total	18.9	37.2	46.1	47.7
Quebec savings banks	3.7	2.5	1.4	.6
Life insurance companies	2.4	13.1	26.0	13.6
Fraternal benefit societies	–	1.0	1.8	.5
Fire and casualty insurance	3.2	3.3	3.8	2.5
Building societies and mortgage loan companies	9.6	16.2	5.0	3.0
Trust companies	–	1.2	4.4	5.0
Consumer loan and finance companies	–	–	.7	4.9
Mutual funds	–	–	–	3.4
Closed-end funds	–	–	2.9	.9
Credit unions and caisses populaires	–	–	.2	4.2
Pension funds	–	–	–	8.9
Development companies	–	–	–	.1
III Public – total	8.4	10.2	8.0	23.4
(a) Federal – total	8.4	10.2	5.9	19.2
Dominion Note Issue and Bank of Canada	5.2	3.4	3.0	4.6
Post Office and Government Savings banks	3.2	6.7	.4	–
Annuity insurance and pension account	–	–	1.4	8.4
Industrial Development Bank	–	–	–	.4
Farm Credit Corporation	–	–	.1	1.1
Veterans Land Act	–	–	.9	.4
Central Mortgage and Housing Corporation	–	–	–	3.9
Export Credits Insurance Corporation	–	–	–	.4
Canada Deposit Insurance Corporation	–	–	–	–
(b) Provincial – total	–	–	2.1	4.2
Canada Pension Plan	–	–	–	2.1
Caisse de dépôt	–	–	–	.7
Savings banks	–	–	.7	.3
Annuity insurance and pension accounts	–	–	.1	.4
Agricultural loan schemes	–	–	1.0	.5
Industrial loan schemes	–	–	–	.2
Miscellaneous	–	–	.4	–

SOURCE: See Statistical Appendix.

varied substantially within that period as we shall see in chapter 4), but it was a period in which the mortgage loan companies declined from 16% of total assets in 1900 to 5% in 1930, and the federal Post Office and Government Savings Banks to less than 1% from 6% in 1900, while the life insurance companies experienced great growth—their portion of assets amounting to 26% of the total in 1930 as compared with 13% in 1900. Trust companies and closed-end trusts became conspicuous in the market in that period, the assets of the former amounting to 4% of total intermediary assets, and the latter to 3% in 1930.

From 1930 to 1968 the chartered banks' share of total assets declined from 46% to 29% (although in fact the ratio increased from about 1933 to 1945). Over that same period the relative size of life insurance company assets declined from 26% in 1930 to 14% in 1968, and declines in relative size also occurred among mortgage loan companies and fire and casualty insurance companies. Trust companies did slightly better than hold their own, while the credit unions, finance companies, and trusteed pension funds all rose to new prominence. Private non-bank financial intermediaries as a group accounted for 46% of total assets in 1930 and 48% in 1968.

Government financial intermediaries amounted to 8% of total financial intermediary assets in 1930 (about the same as in 1870), of which 2% were provincial and 6% were federal; by 1968 the total had increased to 23%, 19% federal and 4% provincial—a most significant development. Pension plans and house financing were especially conspicuous in that increase, but a number of government loan schemes appeared as well.

It is apparent from Table 2:2 that by 1968 the assets of financial intermediaries were divided much more evenly between the various types of financial intermediaries than at any other time in the nation's history.

We shall now examine the growth and changing relative size of our major groupings of financial intermediaries, and of individual types of intermediaries, in some detail.

3

The Growth of Financial Intermediaries

We have already noted that there is no *a priori* reason why the growth of financial intermediary assets might not exceed the growth of the economy. The existence of unexploited cost advantages in increased indirect financing, and even in increased "layering" among financial intermediaries, as well as the appearance of new cost advantages in intermediation as the economy increases in size and changes in structure, could cause such a development. Such growth could also be caused by the appearance of new indirect claims which savers, up to a point, might consider superior to existing primary securities. It seems plausible that in an economy with an advanced capital market the latter might be a stronger force than the former. It might also be that the rate of development of a capital market over time is indicated by the rate of change of the stock of financial intermediary assets, as compared with the flow of output, and that the "maturity" of a capital market is indicated by the ratio of financial intermediary assets to output (or financial intermediary assets to total real and financial assets).

While we are unable in this study to test that hypothesis by international comparisons through "cross-section" analysis, it is one that is worthwhile keeping in mind when examining Canadian time series data.

Growth of Financial Intermediaries in Relation to G.N.P.

Let us for a moment recall the ratio of financial intermediary assets to gross national product discussed in chapter 1. The figures of Table 1:2 are shown graphically in Chart 3:1. What is immediately apparent from that chart is that the period from 1870 to 1900 or even 1910 was one of remarkable development of financial intermediation, since total financial intermediary assets grew much faster than did G.N.P. over those years. From 1900 to the early 1920s total financial intermediary assets grew at about the same rate as G.N.P.; from the early 1920s to 1930 they again grew faster; then from 1930 to 1940 the ratios were distorted by the low G.N.P. levels, and from 1940 to 1950 by war finance and its aftermath; but from 1950 total financial intermediary assets again grew at a substantially faster rate than G.N.P.

From 1870 to 1968 G.N.P. in current dollars rose at an annual rate of 5.3%, while our figure for total financial intermediary assets in current dollars rose by 6.9% per annum. In the most recent period of increase in the ratio of financial intermediary assets to G.N.P., that is, 1950 to 1968, G.N.P. rose at an average annual rate (in current dollars) of 8.0%, and total financial intermediary assets at about 9.2%, while from 1926 to 1968 the G.N.P. growth figure was 6.5%, and the financial intermediary asset growth figure was 7.6%. It seems that the per annum rate of increase in the stock of financial intermediary assets in current dollars is about 1% to 1½% greater than G.N.P. over long periods of time.[1]

The chartered banks' "Canadian" assets grew faster than G.N.P. until 1910, but after that made no further permanent progress, even declining on balance until 1960. Private non-bank intermediaries grew much faster than G.N.P. until 1900, but the end of the rapid development of mortgage loan companies resulted in a decline in the ratio until about 1920. It rose throughout the 1920s, and following the disruptions caused by the depression and the Second World War, again began to rise—a pattern quite different from that of the chartered banks. Public financial intermediaries, because of the growth of the Post Office and Government Savings Banks, rose faster than G.N.P. until 1900; they rose at about the same rate until 1930, but have increased much faster than G.N.P. thereafter. If Bank of Canada assets are excluded from 1935 onward, it becomes clear that the post-Second World War growth of public intermediaries in relation to G.N.P. is explained by the growth of public intermediaries other than the Bank of Canada, primarily government pension and superannuation plans, Central Mortgage and Housing Corporation,

1. It is to be remembered that G.N.P. figures prior to 1926 are not entirely comparable to those from 1926 to the present, and are not as reliable as the later figures. For a discussion of this see M. C. Urquhart and K. A. H. Buckley, eds., *Historical Statistics of Canada* (Toronto: Macmillan Company of Canada, 1965), p. 129.

Chart 3:1 — Major Groupings of Canadian Financial Intermediaries as a Proportion of G.N.P. 1870-1968 (selected years)

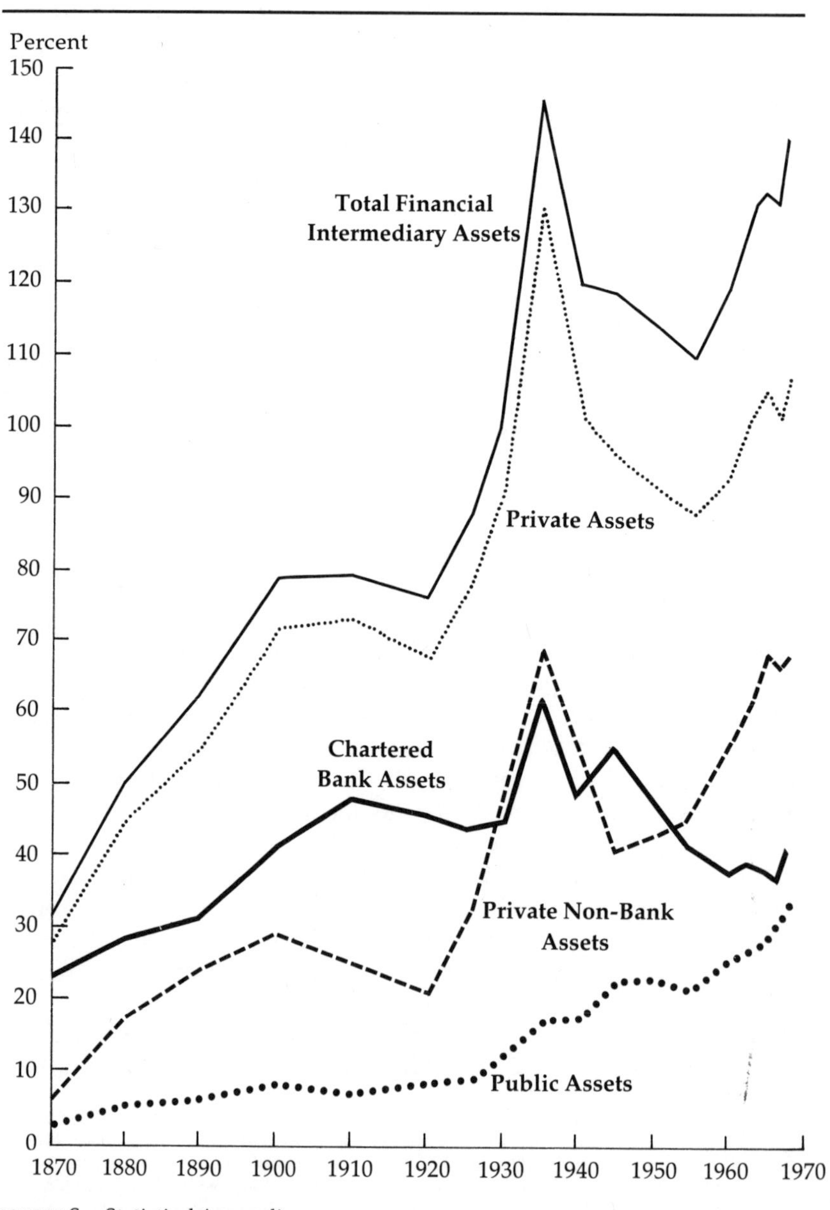

SOURCE: See Statistical Appendix.

Industrial Development Bank, provincial industrial loan schemes, Farm Credit Corporation, and Export Credits Insurance Corporation (now Export Development Corporation).

Annual Growth Rate of Financial Intermediaries

Let us now examine specifically the annual growth rate of Canadian financial intermediaries in current dollars, constant dollars and constant dollars per capita. Chart 3:2 shows Canadian data in the aforementioned form and Table 3:1 shows the growth rates implied by the slopes of the curves in Chart 3:2. A glance at Chart 3:2 immediately reveals an interesting pattern in the growth of Canadian financial intermediaries: an historically high growth rate in constant dollars and constant dollars per capita up to 1910, then a decade or more of almost zero real growth (because of rising prices) and finally a period of relatively steady growth.

A clearer impression of these growth rates can be obtained by examining Table 3:1. It shows that financial intermediary assets in constant dollar terms rose by 6.1% per annum from 1870 to 1910, well above the 5.4% rate for the period 1926-68, and also well above the long-term (1870-1968) average of 5.2%. Similarly, in terms of constant dollar per capita figures, the growth rate was 4.4% from 1870 to 1910, as compared with 3.4% from 1926 to 1968 and 3.4% from 1870 to 1968. Once more we see that the period prior to the First World War was one of historically rapid development of financial intermediation.

Over the period from 1910 to the early 1920s financial intermediary assets per capita in constant dollars did not rise at all, and the growth rate from 1910 to 1926 was only .7%, compared with the 1870 to 1968 average of 3.4% and the 4.4% of the 1870 to 1910 period.[2]

The period from 1926 to 1968 was one in which financial intermediary development was about in line with the long-term (1870 to 1968) trend. Table 3:1, for example, shows that the annual growth rate of financial intermediary assets, using constant dollar per capita figures, rose by 3.4% from 1926 to 1968, and by 3.9% from 1950 to 1968, and that the 1870-1968 average was 3.4%.

---

2. This pattern is very similar to that of real G.N.P. per capita, which also rose at an historically low rate from 1910 to 1930: see O. J. Firestone, *Canada's Economic Development 1867-1953*, Income & Wealth Series VII (London: Bowen & Bowen, 1958), Table II, p. 68.

Chart 3:2 – Assets of Canadian Financial Intermediaries 1870-1968

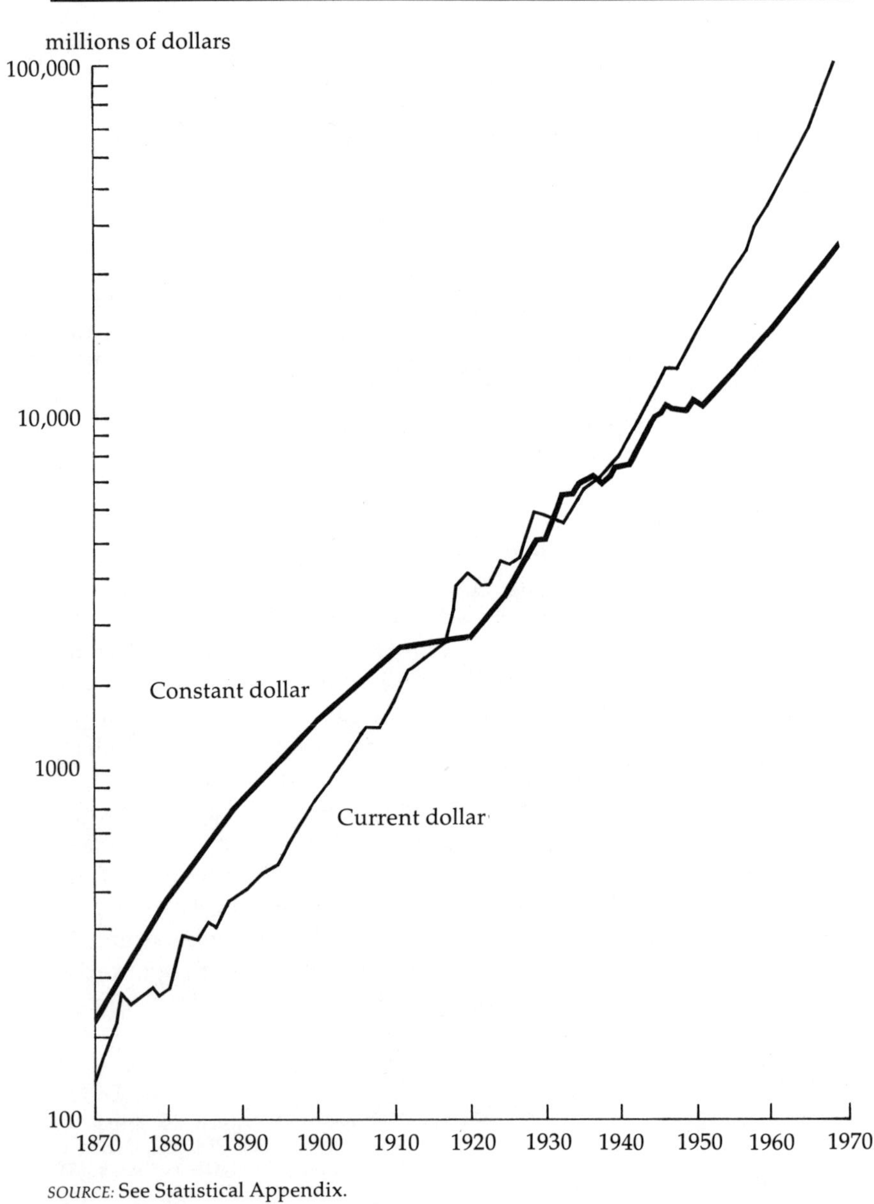

SOURCE: See Statistical Appendix.

Table 3:1 Average Annual Growth Rates of Canadian Financial Intermediaries 1870-1968 (selected periods)

	1870-1910 %	1910-1926 %	1926-1968 %	1950-1968 %	1870-1968 %
Current dollar assets	6.5	6.0	7.6	9.2	6.9
Constant (1935-1939) dollar assets	6.1	2.7	5.4	6.3	5.2
Constant dollar per capita assets	4.4	.7	3.4	3.9	3.4

SOURCE: See Statistical Appendix.

Canada – United States Comparisons

Table 3:2 shows Canadian constant dollar per capita financial intermediary assets, and G.N.P., as a proportion of the same U.S. figures. It also shows the "degree" of financial intermediation in the two countries in the figure of the ratio of financial intermediary assets to G.N.P. While the quality of much of those data is such that conclusions drawn must be exceedingly tentative, it seems worthwhile to refer to several interesting points. If the average degree of financial intermediation for the years 1880, 1890, 1900, 1912 for Canada is taken as a proportion of the U.S. degree of financial intermediation, it works out at 96% – that is, Canadian intermediation was almost as far advanced as that in the United States; while the average for the years 1929, 1948, 1968 placed it at 78% – signifying a lag in the development of financial intermediation in Canada relative to the United States. Similarly, for the years 1880, 1890, 1900, 1912 the average ratio of constant dollar per capita financial intermediary assets in Canada to those in the United States was 74%, a figure that declined to 59% in the years 1929, 1948, 1968. The ratio of constant dollar per capita G.N.P. in Canada to the same figure in the United States for the earlier period was 85% and for the latter period it was 72%. In other words, our financial intermediary asset data support the G.N.P. data to the effect that Canada experienced a slow-down in economic growth relative to the United States some time after the turn of the century, which continued on until the 1920s (possibly

Table 3:2 Financial Intermediation 1880-1968 Canadian and United States Experience Compared

	1880	1890	1900	1912	1929	1948	1965	1968
Canadian figure as a percentage of the U.S. figure								
G.N.P. constant (1929) dollars per capita	77	80	91	90[1]	72	65	79	80
Financial intermediary assets constant (1929) dollars per capita	85	70	78	62	53	58	65	65
Financial intermediary assets as a proportion of G.N.P.								
Canada	50	62	79	92[1]	95	115	134	140
United States	45	71	85	98	130	144	167	172

SOURCE: United States G.N.P. statistics based on data in S. Kuznets, *Capital in the American Economy*, National Bureau of Economic Research, Princeton University Press, 1961, pp. 561, 563, and U.S. Department of Commerce, *Historical Statistics of the United States Colonial Times to 1957*, 1960, p. 139, and current issue of *Survey of Current Business;* financial intermediary asset data were kindly supplied to me by Professor Raymond W. Goldsmith, and also from his volume *Financial Intermediaries in the American Economy Since 1900*, National Bureau of Economic Research, 1958, and *Financial Institutions*, Random House, New York, 1968. Current data from Federal Reserve System, *Federal Reserve Bulletin*. Canadian G.N.P. data from sources outlined for Chart 1:1; financial intermediary data from the Statistical Appendix to this volume; and implicit price index data partly from O.J. Firestone, *Canada's Economic Development 1867-1953*, p. 66, and from Dominion Bureau of Statistics, *National Accounts Income and Expenditure*.

[1]Canadian G.N.P. data very roughly estimated by the author.

from 1906 to 1924). From then onward constant dollar per capita G.N.P., constant dollar per capita financial intermediary assets, and the ratio of financial intermediary assets to G.N.P. all seem to have risen more quickly in Canada than in the United States but not nearly quickly enough to recover the ground lost in the years after the turn of the century.

What the causes were for both the slow real economic growth and the halt in the growth of financial intermediaries in relation to G.N.P. over the two decades preceding the mid 1920s we cannot examine here. But our financial intermediary data suggest that those interested in explaining present per capita output differences between

Canada and the United States should begin with an examination of that period of slow real and financial development.[3]

Is it possible that if the real income gap were to disappear so would the "degree of financial intermediation gap"? Is the latter a function of the former? Or is it possible that the process of financial intermediation in Canada has independently developed more slowly than in the United States and has impeded growth? Again we cannot pursue these questions here, but the rather crucial role of financial intermediaries in allocating financial, and therefore real, resources makes it at least plausible that the line of causation may have run in both directions.

Relative Size of Canadian Financial Intermediaries

Preceding discussion left us with the clear impression that the period 1870 to, say, 1910 was one of rapid financial intermediary growth and development; the period roughly from 1910 to 1926 was one of slow growth and development; and the period 1926 to the present was one in which intermediary growth was normal in relation to our long-term (1870-1968) trend. It remains now to determine the experience of individual groups and types of financial intermediaries within that aggregate pattern. Table 3:3 shows that the historically high growth rate of total financial intermediary assets from 1870 to 1910 was in fact the combined result of historically high growth rates for all three of our major groupings—chartered banks, private non-banks and public financial intermediaries. Similarly, the historically low growth rate of financial intermediary assets in the 1910-26 period was accounted for by historically low growth rates for all three groups—but particularly so for the banks.

The historically "normal" growth rate of the 1926-68 period saw the banks continue to grow below their long-term average rate; the private non-bank group first grew below their long-term normal rate and then in the 1950-68 period grew well above their long-term average rate; and the public intermediaries grew at a rate well above their long-term average.

Perhaps the simplest way to show how the different types of financial intermediaries explain the growth experience of financial inter-

---

3. See the analysis in J. H. Dales, *The Protective Tariff in Canada's Development* (Toronto: University of Toronto Press, 1966).

Table 3:3 Average Annual Growth Rate of Chartered Banks, and of Private Non-Bank and Public Financial Intermediaries (constant (1935-39) dollar data) 1870-1968

	1870-1910	1910-1926	1926-1968	1950-1968	1870-1968
	%	%	%	%	%
1. Chartered banks	5.6	1.5	4.0	4.1	4.3
2. Private non-bank	7.5	4.1	5.9	7.8	6.2
3. Public	6.2	3.9	7.5	7.0	6.3
4. TOTAL:	6.1	2.7	5.4	6.3	5.2

SOURCE: See Statistical Appendix.

mediaries in the aggregate is to examine the change in relative size of each over the periods of growth we have already identified. Table 3:4 has been compiled for this purpose. It may be noted that in 1870 the chartered banks accounted for 72.6% of total financial intermediary assets, while in 1910 they accounted for 59.6%. This decline of 13.0 percentage points was accounted for entirely by the increase of 13.0 percentage points of the private non-bank group, and within that group it was the life insurance companies in particular, but also the fraternal benefit societies, trust companies and mortgage loan companies, that saw increases in their relative size.

In the period of slow over-all financial intermediary growth, that is, from 1910 to 1926, it was the chartered banks, Quebec savings banks and mortgage loan companies that declined relatively in size, while the life insurance companies continued to expand very rapidly, and the other private financial intermediaries did so marginally.

In 1926 chartered bank Canadian assets accounted for 49.9% of total financial intermediary assets, but by 1968 this had declined to 28.9%, a total decline of 21.0 percentage points. Private non-bank financial intermediaries only accounted for 7.8 percentage points of that decline (with increases in relative size occurring among the trusteed pension funds, investment companies, instalment finance and consumer loan companies, credit unions and caisses populaires, trust companies, and declines among the life and fire and casualty insurance companies, fraternal benefit societies, mortgage loan companies, and Quebec savings banks). Public intermediaries increased their share by 13.2 percentage points. This general pattern also held for the 1950-68 period, except that by that time the mortgage loan companies had ended their long-term relative decline.

Table 3:4 Ratio of Assets of Specific Financial Intermediaries to Total Canadian Financial Intermediary Assets 1870-1968 (selected years)

	PER CENT OF TOTAL FINANCIAL INTERMEDIARY ASSETS					CHANGE IN PER CENT OF TOTAL FINANCIAL INTERMEDIARY ASSETS				
	1870	1910	1926	1950	1968	1870-1910	1910-1926	1926-1968	1950-1968	1870-1968
Private—Total	91.5	91.5	89.8	79.2	76.6	0	−1.7	−13.2	− 2.6	−14.9
1. Ch. Bks.	72.6	59.6	49.9	41.9	28.9	−13.0	−9.7	−21.0	−13.0	−43.7
2. Q.S.B.	3.7	2.1	1.7	1.0	.6	− 1.6	− .4	− 1.1	− .4	− 3.1
3. Life Ins.	2.4	11.9	21.6	19.4	13.6	+ 9.5	+9.7	− 8.0	− 5.8	+11.2
4. Frat. Soc.	—	1.8	2.1	.9	.5	+ 1.8	+ .3	− 1.6	− .4	+ .5
5. Fire & Cas.	3.2	3.3	3.6	2.7	2.5	+ .1	+ .3	− 1.1	− .2	− .7
6. Mtge. Loan	9.6	10.9	6.4	1.9	3.0	+ 1.3	−4.5	− 3.4	+ 1.1	− 6.6
7. Trust	—	1.9	2.6	2.1	5.0	+ 1.9	+ .7	+ 2.4	+ 2.9	+ 5.0
8. Cons. Loan	—	—	.5	2.3	4.9	—	+ .5	+ 4.4	+ 2.6	+ 4.9
(a) Con. L.	—	—	—	.6	1.6	—	—	+ 1.6	+ 1.0	+ 1.6
(b) Fin.	—	—	.5	1.7	3.4	—	+ .5	+ 2.9	+ 1.7	+ 3.4
9. Inv. Cos.	—	—	1.3	1.0	4.3	—	+1.3	+ 3.0	+ 3.3	+ 4.3
(a) Mut.	—	—	—	.3	3.4	—	—	+ 3.4	+ 3.1	+ 3.4
(b) Non-Res.	—	—	—	—	.1	—	—	+ .1	+ .1	+ .1
(c) Closed	—	—	1.1	.4	.4	—	+1.1	− .7	—	+ .4
(d) Holding	—	—	.2	.3	.4	—	+ .2	+ .2	+ .1	+ .4
10. CP & CU—lcs.	—	—	.2	1.5	3.7	—	+ .2	+ 3.5	+ 2.2	+ 3.7
11. CP & CU—cens.	—	—	—	.2	.5	—	—	+ .5	+ .3	+ .5
12. Pension	—	—	—	4.2	8.9	—	—	+ 8.9	+ 4.7	+ 8.9
13. Dev. & other	—	—	—	—	.1	—	—	+ .1	+ .1	+ .1
Public—Total	8.4	8.5	10.2	20.8	23.4	+ .1	+ 1.7	+ 13.2	+ 2.6	+15.0
14. Dom. Notes	5.2	5.1	4.6	—	—	− .1	− .5	− 4.6	—	− 5.2
15. B. of C.	—	—	—	11.4	4.6	—	—	+ 4.6	− 6.8	+ 4.6
16. P.O.	3.2	3.2	.7	.2	—	—	−2.5	− .7	− .2	− 3.2
17. Fed. Ann.	—	.1	.9	4.8	8.4	+ .1	+ .8	+ 7.5	+ 3.6	+ 8.4
18. I.D.B.	—	—	—	.2	.4	—	—	+ .4	+ .2	+ .4
19. F.C.C.	—	—	—	.1	1.1	—	—	+ 1.1	+ 1.0	+ 1.1
20. V.L.A.	—	—	1.8	.9	.4	—	+1.8	− 1.4	− .5	+ .4
21. C.M.H.C.	—	—	—	1.9	3.9	—	—	+ 3.9	+ 2.0	+ 3.9
22. E.C.I.C.	—	—	—	—	.4	—	—	+ .4	+ .4	+ .4
23. C.D.I.C.	—	—	—	—	—	—	—	—	—	—
24. C.P.P.	—	—	—	—	2.1	—	—	+ 2.1	+ 2.1	+ 2.1
25. C. de dépôt	—	—	—	—	.7	—	—	+ .7	+ .7	+ .7
26. Pr. Sav.	—	—	.7	.6	.3	—	+ .7	− .4	− .3	+ .3
27. Pr. Ann.	—	—	.1	.2	.4	—	+ .1	+ .3	+ .2	+ .4
28. Pr. Ag. Lo.	—	—	.8	.4	.5	—	+ .8	− .3	+ .1	+ .5
29. Pr. Ind. Lo.	—	—	—	—	.2	—	—	+ .2	+ .2	+ .2
30. Pr. Misc.	—	—	.5	.1	—	—	+ .5	− .5	− .1	—

SOURCE: See Statistical Appendix, which also gives unabbreviated headings.

Over the period 1870 to 1968 the chartered banks' "Canadian" assets declined by 43.7 percentage points to a 1968 level of 28.9%. Of this, the private non-bank group accounted for 28.8 percentage points with substantial gains being made by the life insurance companies (11.2 percentage points), trusteed pension funds (8.9), sales finance and consumer loan companies (4.9), trust companies (5.0), credit unions and caisses populaires (3.7) and investment companies (4.3). Public financial intermediaries increased their relative size by 15.0 percentage points, which was largely accounted for by the federal Annuity, Insurance and Pension Account (8.4 percentage points), Central Mortgage and Housing Corporation (3.9), Canada and Quebec pension plans (2.8), Farm Credit Corporation (1.1), provincial agricultural loans (.5), Industrial Development Bank (.4), Veterans Land Act loans (.4), Export Credits Insurance Corporation (.4), provincial superannuation and pension accounts (.4), provincial savings banks (.3) and provincial industrial loan programs (.2). The federal Post Office Savings Bank declined by 3.2 percentage points, and the Dominion Note Issue and Bank of Canada combined declined by .6 percentage points.

Relative Decline of the Chartered Banks

Perhaps the most obvious development revealed in the preceding section was the long-term relative decline of the chartered banks. While we will be examining the experience of the chartered banks in detail in chapter 4, it is useful at this stage to look somewhat more closely at the banks' relative decline than we have done up to this point.

Chart 3:3 outlines the relative size of our major groups of financial intermediaries for the period 1870 to 1968, based on annual data. It is immediately obvious from that chart that the relative decline of the chartered banks has not been uninterrupted over the years. They declined fairly rapidly from 1870 (the first year shown) to 1896, but then they grew sharply in relative size until 1906. (One could also regard that period of increase as extending from 1896 to 1919, for war finance caused a peak in the banks' relative size in the latter year, but on balance the period 1896 to 1906 appears more suitable.) The banks therefore may be thought of as declining in relative size from 1906 to about 1934; then, largely because of war finance, increasing up to the year 1945, followed by a final period of decline from 1945 to 1966, with a slight improvement in 1967 and 1968. If one were to ignore the

Chart 3:3 — Ratio of Assets of Major Groupings of Canadian Financial Intermediaries to Total Financial Intermediary Assets 1870-1968

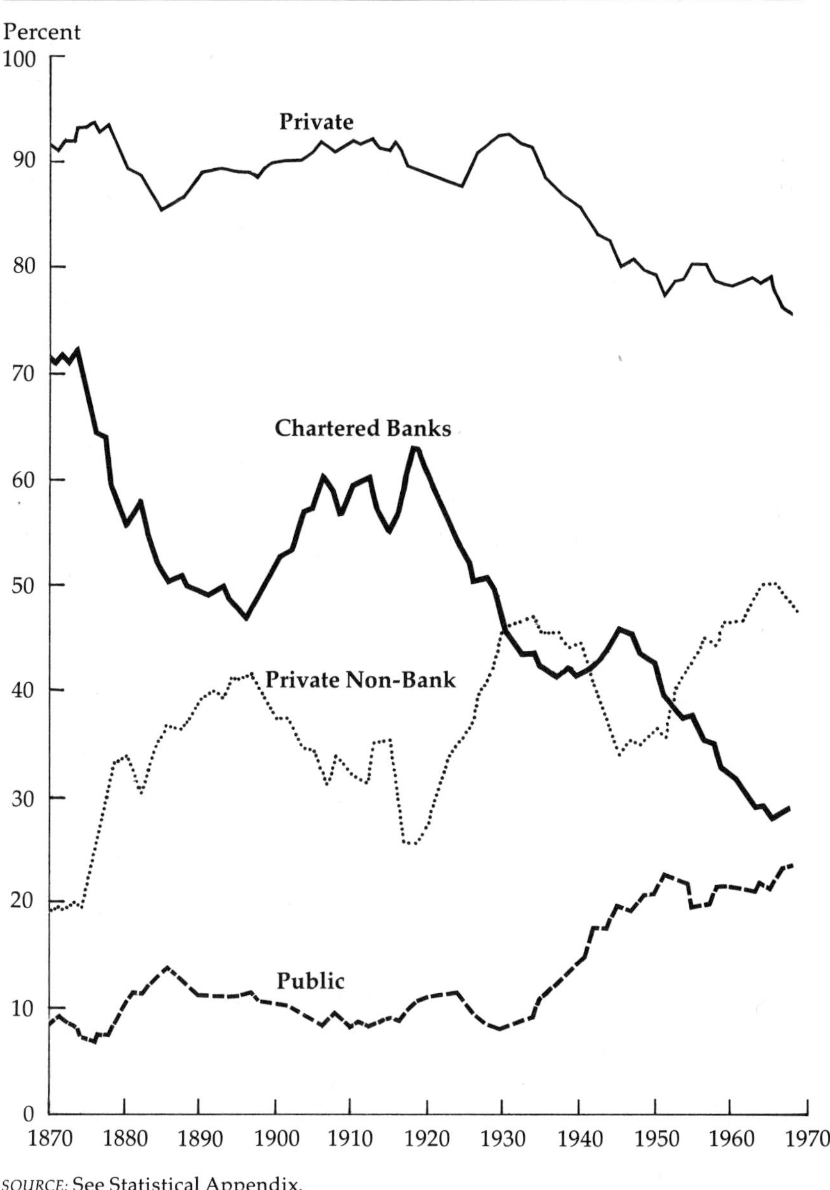

SOURCE: See Statistical Appendix.

effects of First and Second World War finance, the period of relative decline would have extended from 1906 to 1966, with the only important peacetime reverse of the decline from Confederation onward coming in the period 1896 to 1906.

From the Statistical Appendix it is possible to determine clearly which financial intermediaries increased and decreased in relative size over the previously outlined long swings in the relative size of the chartered banks. From 1870 to 1896 chartered bank "Canadian" assets declined from 72.6% of total financial intermediary assets to 47.7%, a decline of 24.9 percentage points, which was much greater than the decline from 1906 to 1934, or even from 1945 to 1968. Remarkable expansion of the mortgage loan companies, life insurance companies, and Post Office and Government Savings Banks may be thought of as being responsible for it, particularly since the chartered banks' growth rate over that period was historically very high; and therefore we will in later chapters pay particular attention to the reasons for the growth of those three intermediaries prior to the turn of the century.

From 1896 to 1906 the relative size of chartered bank assets rose by 12.7 percentage points, and it was the relative decline of the mortgage loan companies (which was to continue steadily until the early 1950s) and of the Post Office and Government Savings Banks, as well as the temporary slowdown in the expansion of life insurance companies and an acceleration in the growth rate of the banks themselves, that explained the change. These are also developments on which we will focus some attention in discussing the experience of those intermediaries in succeeding chapters.

The period of long-term decline in the relative size of the chartered banks, from 1906 to 1934, over which bank Canadian assets declined by 17.9 percentage points, was one in which the life insurance companies made tremendous gains—rising by 18.7 percentage points. It was also a period in which trust companies increased in relative size to a level not again exceeded until the 1960s. Both closed-end investment companies and mutual funds made their appearance in this period.

From 1934 to 1945 the banks increased in relative size, but only by 3.6 percentage points, and this was largely because war finance caused them to have a relatively high growth rate. Private non-bank intermediaries lost 13.9 percentage points and public intermediaries gained 10.3. Almost all private non-bank financial intermediaries declined in relative size—notably the life insurance companies which began their long period of relative decline. The intermediary that showed the greatest increase in relative size was the Bank of Canada.

The period after the Second World War for the most part saw a continuation of the long-term decline in the relative size of the chartered banks. Their loss of 17.2 percentage points from 1945 to 1968 was gained to the extent of 13.7 percentage points by private non-bank intermediaries and 3.5 percentage points by public intermediaries. Among private intermediaries trusteed pension funds gained the most (6.1); next came mutual funds (3.3), finance companies (3.0) although they levelled off before the end of the period, caisses populaires and credit unions (3.2) and trust companies (3.0). The Federal Annuity, Insurance and Pension Account increased substantially (5.2), as did Central Mortgage and Housing Gorporation (3.7) and the Canada and Quebec pension plans (2.8). Smaller gains were made by many of the others. The life insurance companies continued their relative decline, falling by 6.8 percentage points, and the relative size of the Bank of Canada declined sharply, by 9.8 percentage points.

Growth of Financial Intermediaries since 1950

It may be of interest to examine briefly the growth experience of the various financial institutions over recent years. Table 3:5 shows the percentage growth of their assets over the periods 1950-68, 1960-8, 1965-8 and, for some of them, 1968-9 and 1969-70. While we need not describe the developments shown in that table, since they are plain enough, several points may be noted. From 1950 to 1968 financial intermediary assets grew by 387%, with private intermediary assets rising by 371% (banks by 235% and non-bank intermediaries by 525%) and public assets by 448%. Among the private intermediaries the growth of mutual funds was the greatest; then came consumer loan companies, caisses populaires and credit unions, trust companies, trusteed pension funds and sales finance companies. Data for the 1965-8 period show all those groups, except the sales finance companies, still experiencing the highest growth rates, and also show an interesting improvement in the growth of the chartered banks. Pension funds largely explain the high growth of public intermediary assets.

Table 3:5 Percentage Increase in Canadian Financial Intermediary Assets 1950-1970 (selected periods)

	1950-1968 %	1960-1968 %	1965-1968 %	1968-1969 %	1969-1970 %	ASSETS $MNS 1968
Private—total	+ 371	+118	+ 32	12	n.a.	7691
I. Chartered banks Can. assets	+ 235	+104	+ 37	+ 7	+ 8	28939
II. Non-bank financial intermediaries—total	+ 525	+128	+ 30	8	n.a.	47852
Quebec savings banks	+ 180	+ 84	+ 33	− 5	+ 5	571
Life insurance assets in Canada	+ 242	+ 71	+ 20	+ 5	n.a.	13667
Fraternal benefit societies	+ 171	+ 63	+ 15	− 1	n.a.	506
Fire and casualty insurance companies	+ 357	+ 81	+ 29	+10	+12	2516
Mortgage loan companies	+ 669	+215	+ 23	+11	+15	2977
Trust companies	+1029	+281	+ 45	+16	+14	4980
Consumer loan companies	+1411	+176	+ 44	+ 9	n.a.	1556
Sales finance companies	+ 824	+ 92	+ 7	17	n.a.	3371
Mutual funds	+5702	+263	+ 70	− 5	−12	3423
Closed-end funds	+ 411	+120	+ 33	+ 4	−10	455
Holding companies	+ 675	+138	+ 12	− 9	−13	434
Caisses populaires and credit unions	+1136	+188	+ 48	+ 9	+12	4278
Trusteed pension funds	+ 925	+150	+ 37	+11	n.a.	8972
Other	—	—	—	+ 3	—	145
Public—total	+ 448	+141	+ 52	n.a.	n.a.	23519
I. Federal—total	+ 380	+111	+ 34	n.a.	n.a.	19282
Bank of Canada	+ 97	+ 52	+ 17	n.a.	+11	4636
Other	+ 777	+141	+ 41	n.a.	n.a.	14646
II. Provincial—total	+1458	+567	+289	n.a.	n.a.	4237
TOTAL	+ 387	+123	+ 37	n.a.	n.a.	100310

SOURCE: See Statistical Appendix.

Summary and Conclusions

Of the numerous developments discussed, the following seem to us to be the most important from the point of view of the evolving character of financial intermediation in Canada. Some of these points also serve as a guide to analysing the experiences of individual financial intermediaries in later chapters.

(1) The growth of the stock of financial intermediary assets has typically exceeded the growth of the gross national product, using current dollar data, with the average annual growth rate of the former being 1% to 1½% greater than the latter. Assuming that the stock of primary securities has increased at about the same rate as G.N.P., it is the continuing advantages of increased financial intermediation as such that have accounted for the aforementioned growth rate differential. This, in turn, might have happened because existing advantages were never fully exploited. Or, if we assume continuing equilibrium between direct and indirect financing, it could have happened because of economies of scale of intermediation as the economy increased in size. Or it could simply have occurred because of innovation by financial intermediaries in financial claims made available to savers or accepted from borrowers, as well as because of new or improved administrative processes that reduced the cost of intermediation and increased the return on assets through more efficient allocation of funds.

(2) The period 1870-1910 was one in which financial intermediary assets grew at an historically high rate, with the constant dollar per capita asset figure rising at 4.4% per annum, as compared with the long-term average of 3.4% and the 1950-68 average of 3.9%. It was also a period in which financial intermediary assets grew much more quickly than did gross national product. On the whole the period is an exceedingly important one in the history of the evolution of the Canadian capital market.

The most significant developments among financial intermediaries within that period were: (a) the spectacular growth of the mortgage loan companies and the beginning of their relative decline; (b) the emergence of life insurance companies as important financial intermediaries; (c) the rapid growth and earlier stages of relative decline of the federal government's Post Office and Government Savings Banks; and (d) the relative decline of the chartered banks until 1896 followed by a decade of relative increase – the only peacetime decade of the past century in which the banks were able to increase in relative size.

(3) After the turn of the century there were about two decades of slow development (we have shown it as 1910-26, for statistical reasons). Canadian financial intermediary assets grew very

slowly, in relation both to long-term trends and to U.S. intermediary growth at that time, and this was accompanied by slow G.N.P. growth.

The latter undoubtedly helps to explain the former, but probably not entirely so, since the financial intermediary assets to G.N.P. ratio ceased rising for part of that period. The unusually slow growth rate of the chartered banks (their 1918 "Canadian" assets in current dollars were actually higher than their 1926 assets), the continuing decline of the mortgage loan companies, and the unspectacular growth of other intermediaries except the life insurance companies, are particularly to be noted.

(4) From 1926 to the present, financial intermediary growth was equal to its long-term average performance. The chartered banks continued to decline in relative size and grew no faster than gross national product. The life insurance companies began their period of relative decline. The finance companies increased greatly in relative size, and then levelled off. Government financial intermediaries rose to new prominence, particularly in the pension fund area. Total financial intermediary assets were more evenly distributed among the various financial intermediaries than at any other time.

(5) Since 1950 the high rate of growth of mutual funds, consumer loan companies, caisses populaires and credit unions, trust companies, trusteed pension funds, government operated pension funds, and for a period, sales finance companies stand out noticeably; as does the slow growth rate of the banks, Quebec savings banks, life insurance companies, fraternal benefit societies, and Bank of Canada.

4
The Chartered Banks

In Canada the emergence of successful specialized financial institutions begins essentially with the establishment of banks. Granting of articles of association to the "Montreal Bank" in June 1817 was a significant event in the history of the capital market, for it gave Canada its first successful bank of "issue, discount and deposit."

As a result of the work primarily of Adam Shortt and also of R. M. Breckenridge, much is known about the subsequent history of the Canadian banking system. We will review here only those aspects of that history that are required to place the development of the banking system in historical perspective and those that are essential for explaining its growth as a major type of financial intermediary.[1]

The Period Prior to Confederation

Before the appearance of banks, the functions of banks had been assumed by merchants. This is the way one historian has described the arrangements in Upper and Lower Canada at the end of the eighteenth century:

> ...there was little occasion for banking services throughout the rural districts of Lower Canada while in Upper Canada the leading merchants in the rising towns performed practically all the func-

1. Some of the material in this chapter appeared in E. P. Neufeld, "The Relative Growth of Commercial Banks," in C. R. Whittlesey and J. S. G. Wilson, *Essays in Money and Banking in Honour of R. S. Sayers* (London: Oxford University Press, 1967).

> tions of a bank except the issue of notes, although some of them provided an irregular issue of Bons.
>
> In Western Canada particularly the larger merchants were both exporters and importers of practically every variety of goods required in the settlements. Nearly all exchanges were made through them; credits were extended by them and orders for goods and money drawn upon them. They also conducted the external exchanges, procuring from their Montreal agents such foreign bills as might be required. The larger importers in Montreal discharged all the ordinary functions of a banker for their regular customers, the merchants of the upper province. They received deposits of money and bills, made payments to order and advanced loans or credits, to be met later by produce bills or cash.[2]

It is obvious from the foregoing that any bank that wished to become established would be successful only if it were able to supplant the "merchant banker." To do so it would have to enjoy advantages denied the merchant. The vitally important advantage which the new chartered banks were to enjoy was the superior form of bank notes or medium of exchange which they were able to offer the public.

Economic Basis of the New Banks

Throughout the history of the chartered banks the one unique characteristic which has ensured for them a significant place in the capital market has been the general acceptance by the public of their liability instruments (first mainly notes, then notes and deposits, now entirely deposits) as media of exchange and the near-monopoly position of those instruments in providing for the nation's medium of exchange requirements. It was above all the unsatisfactory state of the country's currency which led to the establishment of the first banks in the early 1800s. And in the 1960s fully 90% of the banks' liabilities were in the form of chequing deposits or deposits which could without cost or delay be changed into chequing deposits or Bank of Canada notes. Furthermore, in the 1960s, and in spite of the chequing privileges offered by credit unions and trust and loan companies, the banks continued to supply the major portion of the medium of exchange instruments, even though they had over the years lost the privilege of issuing bank notes which in the beginning of their history had been so important to them.

---

2. A. Shortt and A. G. Doughty, eds., *Canada and its Provinces*, vol. 4 (Toronto: Glasgow Brook and Co., 1914-17), p. 605.

The need for dependable and simplified currency at the time the banks first appeared is graphically indicated by contemporary comments on the state of the currency to which historians frequently refer, comments which usually illustrate the tendency for specie or "hard money" to disappear from circulation because of its being used to finance an insatiable demand for imports, and the complex and cumbersome nature of the substitutes which then were used in their place. One observer in Upper Canada notes that "... from the King's Receiver General to the Sergeant Major of the Rangers, from the first Commercial houses to the person who retails drams, *Everybody makes money*. As to security that is now not thought of. In a payment the other day of twenty five pounds I received the bills of twelve different persons; to realize this by a draft on Montreal would require an application to as many different people, some at Detroit, some of York, some the Lord knows where."[3] And we have already noted the hodge-podge of change received by one individual writing in the *Acadian Recorder* of October 21, 1820.

Not only was the state of the currency unsatisfactory but in Upper and Lower Canada it threatened to deteriorate. This was because after the War of 1812 the British government immediately began to redeem the Army Bills which it had issued to finance the purchase of supplies and payment of troops, and which had proved to be a welcome addition to the medium of exchange of the nation as well as a successful and encouraging experiment with paper currency. At one time or another during the war these Army Bills had appeared in various denominations. The small bills did not bear interest and were payable in cash on demand. In terms of Halifax currency there were £800,000 of interest-bearing and £449,000 of non-interest-bearing bills outstanding at the end of the war. This entirely satisfactory experience with paper money had proved so beneficial, and its prompt redemption so effective in reducing the suspicion toward paper money, that it must have been of direct help in the banks' becoming established through the issue of their own bank notes.[4] Adam Shortt, in his critical review of Breckenridge's pioneering work *The Canadian Banking System*, remarks that "... the pressing difficulty of this time, and the one to which all the bank petitions referred, was the scarcity of a circulating medium of any kind after the withdrawal of the Army Bills."

A financial institution that could so manage its affairs as to provide

3. Quoted in H. A. Innis and A. R. M. Lower, *Select Documents in Canadian Economic History 1783-1885* (Toronto: University of Toronto Press, 1933), pp. 369 and 433.

4. See Victor Ross, *A History of the Canadian Bank of Commerce* (Toronto: Oxford University Press, 1920), vol. 1, pp. 8-10.

a reliable currency in the form of its notes and deposits was obviously one which, in the above illustrated environment, could secure for itself an important and permanent source of funds for relending and investing. That the early attempts at forming banks arose primarily from a recognition of the potential demand for a reliable currency is indicated by the wording of the articles of agreement and charters under which they operated. This is well illustrated by the announcement in the official gazette of October 18, 1792, of the formation of the Canada Banking Company, which we have already noted.[5]

It is worthwhile asking how the banks might be expected to improve the state of the currency and alleviate the scarcity of specie. Improvement lay essentially in the substitution of the bank notes of relatively few banks, issued in even denominations, for the great variety of coins, government bills and merchants' notes which were being used. The extent of the improvement would depend on the extent to which such substitution occurred. The fact that the Canadian currency remained in a state of disarray for many years after the formation of the banks is a reflection of a number of factors: the long time it took for the aforementioned substitution to take place; the delay by government in improving the coin currency of the country; and the suspicion occasionally cast on bank notes themselves as a result of bank failures, which were by no means few in number.

As to alleviating the shortage of specie, the direct contribution of the banks was likely to be small. To the extent that bank notes were substitutes for circulating specie, some of the specie could be freed for financing imports. The amount freed would be the difference between specie no longer needed for circulation and the amount that the banks would wish to hold as a reserve against their note liabilities. Their indirect contribution, however, was likely to be greater than this. By establishing efficient machinery for the transfer of foreign capital into the country, the supply of specie would likely be enhanced. But most important of all, perhaps, it would be expected that the effect on the currency of a loss of specie through a balance of payments deficit would be less severe with banks than without them. This is because banks would be inclined to take such measures as restricting their discount business to protect their reserve of specie (that is, their reserve backing notes and deposit liabilities), and in that way induce greater stability in the supply of medium of

5. Excerpt from James Stevenson, "The Currency of Canada after the Capitulation," *Transaction of the Literary and Historical Society of Quebec*, Sessions of 1876-7, and reprinted in E. P. Neufeld, ed., *Money and Banking in Canada*, Carleton Library no. 17 (Toronto: McClelland and Stewart, 1964), pp. 28-9.

exchange; whereas without banks specie would simply disappear from circulation in payment for imports until a severe shortage of medium of exchange had developed.

While the obvious need for a reliable currency undoubtedly served to make the new bank notes welcome, the banks in this were also assisted by governmental experiences with paper money. As noted above, the Army Bills issued for several years as a result of problems of financing the War of 1812-14 proved popular and, since they were redeemed, left the public with a favourable impression concerning paper money. In Nova Scotia, too, government paper money had proved useful and reliable. So attempts at forming banks finally were successful.

The First Banks

As early as 1792 two Montreal merchants and a London house established a private banking association, called the Canada Banking Company, which issued some notes. However, it did not long survive.[6] Attempts on the part of some citizens of Quebec City to be incorporated as a bank of issue in 1807 were unsuccessful and further attempts in 1808 by Quebec and Montreal merchants to be incorporated as the "Bank of Canada" were declined by the legislature.[7] The attempt in 1810 of Kingston merchants to incorporate the Bank of Upper Canada was also frustrated. After the War of 1812-14 Montreal merchants once more sought a bank charter, but after several defeats they decided to proceed with their plan under articles of association (regarded as a distinctly inferior arrangement) and it is in this way that the "Montreal Bank," or the Bank of Montreal, came into existence in June 1817. Another private partnership, known as the Quebec Bank, was formed in July 1818 by citizens of Quebec City and a third one by Montreal interests in August 1818 in the name of the Bank of Canada. All three were finally granted charters in 1822. A Bank of Upper Canada operated as a private institution in Kingston from 1818 to 1821, ending in failure, and a more permanent bank of the same name began operations under charter in York in 1821.[8]

The first public bank to operate under charter in British North

6. See Ross, *op. cit.*, pp. 7-8. This section of the volume was written by Adam Shortt.

7. See R. M. Breckenridge, *The Canadian Banking System 1817-1890* (Toronto: 1894), p. 19, and E. P. Neufeld, *op. cit.*, pp. 30-40.

8. R. Craig McIvor, *Canadian Monetary, Banking and Fiscal Development* (Toronto: Macmillan Company of Canada, 1958), pp. 31 and 32.

America was the Bank of New Brunswick, which received its charter in 1820. Attempts to establish an incorporated bank in Nova Scotia appeared as early as 1801 and recurred in 1819, 1822 and 1825.[9] Because these attempts failed, the merchants of Halifax in 1825 formed the Halifax Banking Company, a private association which soon became a powerful financial institution in that port city. Indeed, it was the monopoly position of that bank which was primarily responsible for steps being taken to form the Bank of Nova Scotia, which received its charter in March 1832.[10]

The first bank in Prince Edward Island, the Bank of Prince Edward Island, was not established until 1856, and failed in 1881; the Union Bank of Newfoundland appeared in 1854 and failed in 1894; the Bank of British Columbia was incorporated in 1862 and disappeared in a merger in 1900.

From these early beginnings in each of the British North American colonies there soon developed repeated, sometimes frantic attempts to establish banks. We have already seen[11] that prior to Confederation four main types of commercial banks of issue had appeared: banks chartered by the colonial legislature, banks operating under royal charter, private or "joint-stock" banks without corporate power to sue, and "free" banks operating under the Free Banking Act of 1850. From 1837 to 1839, during the period of suspension of specie payment of the chartered banks, there were also some spurious "Canadian banks," operating mainly out of Buffalo, which circulated notes in the British North American colonies and in the United States. In addition there were local private bankers who carried on all aspects of banking except the issue of notes and who became particularly prominent in Ontario after Confederation.[12] However, it was the chartered bank that always dominated banking in Canada.

The establishment of each chartered bank is a story in itself, but an adequate impression, for our purposes, of the attempts to establish chartered banks can be obtained from Table 4:1. That table shows the number of active banks present each year from 1820, when the first public chartered bank appeared, to 1970, as well as the number of new active banks that appeared each year, the numbers of new banks that appeared but did not use their charters, and the number of banks that failed or had their charters repealed. The large increases in the number of active chartered banks occurred in several distinct

---

9. Betty Hearn, "Letter to the Editor," *The Canadian Banker*, vol. 69, no. 2 (Summer 1962), pp. 86-90.
10. *The Bank of Nova Scotia*, 1832-1932, privately published in 1932, p. 22.
11. See above, pp. 39-41.
12. See Chapter 6.

Table 4:1 Number of Canadian Chartered Banks 1820-1971

DATE	NO. ACTIVE AT BEGINNING OF YEAR	NEW BANKS, ACTIVE	NEW BANKS, CHARTERS NOT USED	FAILURES (OR CHARTER REPEALED)	MERGERS	NO. ACTIVE AT END OF YEAR
1820	0	1	0	0	0	1
21	1	1	0	0	0	2
22	2	3	0	0	0	5
23	5	0	0	0	0	5
24	5	0	0	0	0	5
25	5	1	0	0	0	6
26	6	0	0	0	0	6
27	6	0	0	0	0	6
28	6	0	0	0	0	6
29	6	0	0	0	0	6
1830	6	0	0	0	0	6
31	6	1	0	1	0	6
32	6	1	0	0	0	7
33	7	1	0	0	0	8
34	8	3	0	0	0	11
35	11	3	0	0	0	14
36	14	7	0	0	0	21
37	21	1	0	3	0	19
38	19	1	0	1	1	18
39	18	0	0	0	1	17
1840	17	0	0	1	0	16
41	16	0	2	0	0	16
42	16	0	0	1	0	15
43	15	1	0	0	0	16
44	16	0	0	0	0	16
45	16	0	0	0	0	16
46	16	0	0	0	0	16
47	16	0	2	0	0	16
48	16	0	1	0	0	16
49	16	0	0	1	0	15
1850	15	0	0	0	0	15
51	15	0	0	0	0	15
52	15	0	0	0	0	15
53	15	0	0	0	0	15
54	15	1	0	0	0	16
55	16	7	1	0	0	23
56	23	3	2	0	0	26
57	26	3	1	0	0	29

Table 4:1 (continued)

DATE	NO. ACTIVE AT BEGINNING OF YEAR	NEW BANKS, ACTIVE	NEW BANKS, CHARTERS NOT USED	FAILURES (OR CHARTER REPEALED)	MERGERS	NO. ACTIVE AT END OF YEAR
1858	29	1	1	0	0	30
59	30	3	1	3	0	30
1860	30	1	0	0	0	31
61	31	2	0	0	0	33
62	33	1	0	3	0	31
63	31	0	1	2*	0	29
64	29	3	1	0	0	32
65	32	3	8	1	0	34
66	34	1	0	2	0	33
67	33	2	0	0	0	35
68	35	0	1	1	1	33
69	33	2	0	0	0	35
1870	35	0	0	0	1	34
71	34	3	2	0	0	37
72	37	8	2	0	0	45
73	45	6	3	1	0	50
74	50	1	1	0	0	51
75	51	0	1	0	1	50
76	50	1	1	0	2	49
77	49	0	0	1	0	48
78	48	0	0	0	0	48
79	48	0	0	4	0	44
1880	44	0	0	0	0	44
81	44	0	0	1	0	43
82	43	1	3	0	0	44
83	44	2	1	1	1	44
84	44	2	2	0	0	46
85	46	0	0	0	0	46
86	46	0	0	0	0	46
87	46	0	0	5	0	41
88	41	0	0	0	0	41
89	41	0	0	0	0	41
1890	41	0	1	0	0	41
91	41	0	0	0	0	41
92	41	0	0	0	0	41
93	41	0	0	1	0	40
94	40	0	0	2**	0	38
95	38	0	0	1	0	37
96	37	0	0	0	0	37

DATE	NO. ACTIVE AT BEGINNING OF YEAR	NEW BANKS, ACTIVE	NEW BANKS, CHARTERS NOT USED	FAILURES (OR CHARTER REPEALED)	MERGERS	NO. ACTIVE AT END OF YEAR
1897	37	0	0	0	0	37
98	37	0	1	0	0	37
99	37	0	0	1	0	36
1900	36	0	1	0	1	35
01	35	1	0	0	1	35
02	35	2	1	0	1	36
03	36	3	5	0	2	37
04	37	1	0	0	0	38
05	38	1	1	1	1	37
06	37	0	1	1	1	35
07	35	0	0	0	1	34
08	34	1	2	3	1	31
09	31	0	0	0	1	30
1910	30	1	0	2	1	28
11	28	1	0	0	1	28
12	28	0	1	0	2	26
13	26	0	0	0	2	24
14	24	0	1	1	1	22
15	22	0	1	0	0	22
16	22	0	0	0	0	22
17	22	0	0	0	1	21
18	21	0	0	0	2	19
19	19	0	0	0	1	18
1920	18	0	1	0	0	18
21	18	0	0	0	0	18
22	18	0	0	0	1	17
23	17	0	1	1	1	15
24	15	0	0	0	2	13
25	13	0	0	0	2	11
26	11	0	0	0	0	11
27	11	0	0	0	0	11
28	11	0	1	0	1	10
29	10	1	0	0	0	11
1930	11	0	0	0	0	11
31	11	0	0	0	1	10
32	10	0	0	0	0	10
33	10	0	0	0	0	10
34	10	0	0	0	0	10
35	10	0	0	0	0	10

Table 4:1 (continued)

DATE	NO. ACTIVE AT BEGINNING OF YEAR	NEW BANKS, ACTIVE	NEW BANKS, CHARTERS NOT USED	FAILURES (OR CHARTER REPEALED)	MERGERS	NO. ACTIVE AT END OF YEAR
1936	10	0	0	0	0	10
37	10	0	0	0	0	10
38	10	0	0	0	0	10
39	10	0	0	0	0	10
1940	10	0	0	0	0	10
41	10	0	0	0	0	10
42	10	0	0	0	0	10
43	10	0	0	0	0	10
44	10	0	0	0	0	10
45	10	0	0	0	0	10
46	10	0	0	0	0	10
47	10	0	0	0	0	10
48	10	0	0	0	0	10
49	10	0	0	0	0	10
1950	10	0	0	0	0	10
51	10	0	0	0	0	10
52	10	0	0	0	0	10
53	10	1	0	0	0	11
54	11	0	0	0	0	11
55	11	0	0	0	1	10
56	10	0	0	0	1	9
57	9	0	0	0	0	9
58	9	0	0	0	0	9
59	9	0	0	0	0	9
1960	9	0	0	0	0	9
61	9	0	0	0	1	8
62	8	0	0	0	0	8
63	8	0	0	0	0	8
64	8	0	0	0	0	8
65	8	0	0	0	0	8
66	8	0	0	0	0	8
67	8	0	1	0	0	8
68	8	1	0	0	0	9
69	9	1	0	0	0	10
1970	10	0	0	0	1	9
71	9	0	0	0	0	9

SOURCE: Compiled from data received from the Inspector General of Banks, Ottawa.

*Charters repealed
**Both Newfoundland

periods: from 1831 to 1836, when they increased from 6 to 21; from 1854 to 1858, a period of intense speculative economic activity, when they increased from 16 to 30; and from 1870 to 1874, when they increased from 34 to the record number of 51. After that, failures and mergers exceeded new formations and by 1961 only 8 banks remained in active operation, although shortly thereafter several new charters were applied for and in 1970 there were 9 chartered banks.

From 1820 to 1970 the record relating to chartered banks can be summarized in this way:

Number of banks chartered	157
Number of charters not used	60
Number of active banks	97
Number of active banks that failed or were wound up	45
Number of active banks whose charters were repealed	2
Number of banks that merged with other banks	41
Number of active banks, 1971	9

The large number of failures is rather surprising in view of the Canadian banking system's reputation for solvency. From 1820 to Confederation there were 19 failures; after Confederation there were 28 failures. While the record of terminating building societies prior to Confederation, as well as of savings banks prior to Confederation, is worse than that of the chartered banks, it appears that as a group the chartered banks have a record for solvency after Confederation that is more tarnished than that of any other financial intermediary examined.

Government Influence and Chartered Bank Growth

We have seen that the early banks appeared essentially because of the existence of a strong demand for the unique services they were able to supply through introducing the paper bank note. However, a further prerequisite for the development and growth of the chartered banking system was the development of principles and procedures for bank operations that would enable the banks to remain solvent and profitable while providing their unique services to the public. This, in turn, involved two parallel influences—the external influence of government and the internal influence in the form of the evolution of banking policies and procedures. Both contributed to the success of the banks. However, both were also potential hazards to the development of the banks, the first because of the possibility that supervision and control would be overly restrictive and the second because policies and procedures might become unnecessarily rigid. These generalizations are worth keeping in mind when examining the historical experience of the banks.

What then was the government's influence in engendering confidence in the new bank notes and deposits? From the first bank charters, the issue of notes was limited to some portion of capital, and notes had to be redeemed in specie on demand. The Imperial Government Select Committee of the Privy Council for Trade in 1830 adopted regulations for colonial bank charters that were to influence Canadian bank charters. These included provisions that prohibited banks from becoming merchants, that prohibited a bank from holding its own shares or making advances against them, that limited the amount of a loan made to directors or officers of a bank, and that required a new bank to have half its capital paid in before it could commence operations. Required capital for chartered banks was relatively high. Double shareholder liability was first introduced in the charter of the Central Bank of New Brunswick in 1834, and partly so in the charter of the Bank of Nova Scotia in 1832, being eventually extended to all banks. It was not modified until the 1934 revision, when it was reduced in proportion to the reduction in chartered bank note circulation introduced in the same revision. Finally in 1950, by which time all chartered bank notes had to be withdrawn, double liability vanished completely.

Government supervision has also depended on the banks' making reports on their operations. At first, yearly and half-yearly statements of assets and liabilities were usually submitted to the government, and from the early 1850s monthly reports were required of the banks in the Province of Canada, and of all banks after Confederation. The reports became increasingly more detailed over the years following Confederation.

While we are interested for the moment primarily in the pre-Confederation period of banking development, it is convenient at this stage also to refer to certain developments after Confederation. Many detailed amendments to the Bank Act after Confederation could be viewed as being directed toward improving the banks' chances of remaining solvent, and so to increasing public confidence in them. But the major changes from this viewpoint were the following: (a) limitation of dividends paid until a certain reserve had been accumulated, as outlined in the 1870 Bank Act, and amended later; (b) definite recognition of the note holder as a preferred creditor (1880 revision); (c) establishment of a "Bank Note Circulation Redemption Fund," with contributions by each bank of an amount equal to 5% of its note issue, and the provision that notes of failed banks would be paid off with interest at 6% (1890 revision); (f) recognition of the Canadian Bankers' Association as the agent for, among other things, supervising the appointment of curator for failed banks (1900 revision); (g) arrangements for a shareholders' audit (1913 revision); and (h) appointment of an Inspector General of Banks following the Home Bank failure of 1923. The Finance Act of 1913 gave the banks access to a source of emergency cash in the form of advances of Dominion notes from the Government of Canada, and lender-of-last-resort facilities for the banks were introduced by the Bank of Canada when it replaced the Finance Act and began operations in 1935.

All these post-Confederation developments, as well as the numerous bank failures arising not just from incompetence but also from fraud and contravention of Bank Act provisions, which we note below, suggest that the pre-Confederation trend toward government inspection was necessary for the development of the banking system but that it still had very far to go.

Over the years the feeling seems to have grown that no government could permit a chartered bank to fail in a way that would lead to loss of funds by depositors and holders of chartered bank notes. Formally, however, the government has never endorsed this view, and it is likely that in the future, as in the past, such loss would be avoided by timely mergers acquiesced in by Ministers of Finance. We will refer to the merger question again.

There remains the question of whether bank legislation inhibited the development of banks in any way in the pre-Confederation period. Prior to 1870 the principal restriction on the operations of the banks was the requirement, embodied in the first charters, that the chartered banks had to redeem their notes in specie on demand. In the Province of Canada payment could also, after the Provincial Notes Act of 1866, be made in provincial notes. No cash ratio was imposed and indeed none appeared until 1934. Apart from the redemption requirement, early legislation also imposed limits on the size of a bank's note issue in relation to its capital and required government approval for any increase in the authorized capital of a bank.

The first charters of the banks of Upper and Lower Canada (1821) and that of the Bank of Nova Scotia (1832) required that the total indebtedness or liabilities of a bank, *excluding liabilities arising from the deposit of specie*, but including notes, should not exceed three times the paid-up capital, while the limit in the charter of the Bank of New Brunswick (1820) was twice the paid-up capital. In addition the charter of the first bank of Upper Canada forbade the issue of notes under five shillings (one dollar). In 1830 the charter of the Bank of

Montreal first introduced the limit on the amount of bank notes under five shillings to one-fifth the paid-up capital. In the 1841 revision of the charter this was changed to notes of less than one pound or four dollars.

The 1841 revision of the charters of three banks in Lower Canada and later the charters of other banks in the United Provinces were based on the final report (1841) of the Select Committee on Banking and Currency, which in turn was to a large extent based on an 1840 despatch from the imperial government. Changes included the restriction of all debts *excluding liabilities arising from the deposit of specie and government paper* to three times the paid-up capital; the limitation of a bank's note circulation to the amount of its paid-up capital; a tax of 1% on a bank's note circulation; and, as mentioned above, the restriction of notes of under one pound or four dollars to one-fifth the paid-up capital. Theoretically, this enabled an infinite expansion of bank assets taking the form of government securities with funds from capital stock and deposits, but its limited importance in practice is indicated by a measure first introduced in 1854 (and cancelled in 1871) requiring the banks to hold 10% of their paid-up capital in government securities.

While in its discussion stage the Provincial Notes Act of 1866 threatened to end the issue of chartered bank notes, in the form in which it was passed it merely gave the banks an incentive to surrender that privilege – an offer taken up only by the Bank of Montreal, and this for only several years. The same act introduced what later became the Dominion Note Issue and in effect first permitted the banks to hold government notes as cash.

This essentially was how matters stood until the innovations introduced in the Bank Acts of 1870 and 1871. Expansion of bank notes depended on the demand for credit, on the demand of the public for bank notes in preference to other media of exchange, on the ability of the chartered banks to obtain and retain a supply of specie which would permit them to honour the redemption obligation at all times, on their obtaining permission to increase their capital stock, and on public demand for bank stock. The latter two influences seem not to have impeded the banks significantly, as can be seen in Table 4:2 below. It shows that until 1864 the banks in the Canadas for the most part maintained a ratio of paid-up capital to total liabilities of almost 50% and only after that did the long-term decline in that ratio, which for so long was a feature of Canadian banking, begin to assert itself. This ratio was necessary not for fulfilling statutory requirements but rather in order to provide sufficient protection against risks inherent in banking at that time.

Table 4:2 Selected Chartered Bank Liabilities as Per Cent of Total Liabilities 1832-1875

Date	Capital Stock Paid Up: Canadas %	New Brunswick %	Bank of Nova Scotia %	All Chartered Banks	Note Circulation: Canadas %	New Brunswick %	Bank of Nova Scotia %	All Chartered Banks	Deposits: Canadas %	New Brunswick %	Bank of Nova Scotia %	All Chartered Banks	Other: Canadas %	New Brunswick %	Bank of Nova Scotia %	All Chartered Banks
1832-4	41[1]	38	58[2]		31[1]	52	19		24[1]	9	22		4[1]	1	1	
1841	50	58	40		20	28	28		19	10	22		11		10	
1851	44	49	48		25	29	20		26	16	29		5	6	3	
1856	40		31		33		31		24		35		3		3	
1857	49		32		25		34		23		29		3		5	
1858	48				24		28		24				4			
1859	48				22		28		27				3			
1860	46				23		25		29				2			
1861	45	43	35		23	32	28		32	16	30			9	7	
1862	47				17		26		35				1			
1863	45				17		28		37				1			
1864	47				13		31		38				2			
1865	42				16		27		41				1			
1866	42				14		24		39				5			
1867	42	37	29	42	11	25	26	12	42	26	40	41	5	12	5	5
1868	38				12		20		48				2			
1869	36				12		19		50				2			
1870	32				17		18		49				2			
1871	32				19		20		47				2			
1872					19		26									
1873							22									
1874	34				15		17		45				6			
1875	41		28		14		15		43		28		2			

SOURCE: Based on statistics in R. M. Breckenridge, *The Canadian Banking System 1817-1890*, pp. 41, 166; C. A. Curtis, *Statistical Contributions to Canadian Economic History*, The Macmillan Co. of Canada, 1931; *History of the Bank of Nova Scotia, 1832-1900*.

[1] Lower Canada only, as at January, 1834.
[2] As at February 1833, which was the Bank's first Annual Report.

While there is evidence that the banks found ways to delay meeting the redemption obligation, there was only one period, 1837 to 1839, when the banks in general suspended specie payment. As to the restraints imposed by the need to obtain a charter, by the capital and note requirements, and by the demand for bank stocks, these appear not to have been serious. From 1820 to 1867, 78 charters were issued, and 56 banks commenced business, a not inconsiderable number. There was frequently some delay in granting increased authorized capital and occasionally some disappointment at the speed with which new stock was taken up by investors, but nevertheless over the period 1841 to 1867 the paid-up capital of banks in the United Province of Canada increased twelve-fold, notes in circulation increased nine-fold, and the average annual rate of expansion of chartered bank notes and deposit liabilities, as well as assets, was about 12% per annum.[13] Also the following figures show that in 1837 the note circulation of the banks was less than the paid-up capital even though the legislation restricting the note issue to the paid-up capital was not introduced until 1841.

1837	*Paid-up capital*	*Notes in circulation*	*Specie*
Bank of Montreal	£250,000	£180,692	£68,811
City Bank	200,000	104,576	15,934
Bank of Upper Canada	200,000	168,906	37,850
Commercial Bank	196,597	116,092	23,102
Gore Bank	80,381	34,246	17,932

The banks themselves favoured surrendering their right to issue smaller denomination notes in 1871, so this type of issue appears not to have been important to them and even troublesome during periods of economic unrest.

One of the principal reasons why legislative restraints on bank liabilities did not inhibit the growth of the chartered banks was that they did not restrict the growth of bank deposit liabilities at a time when that source of funds was beginning to become increasingly important. Table 4:2 outlines the ratios of paid-up capital, notes in circulation and deposit liabilities to total liabilities for the banks of Upper and Lower Canada, New Brunswick, and the Bank of Nova Scotia. The ratios, for various reasons, are somewhat volatile and the statistics used suffer from many limitations, but several generalizations can safely be made. Until 1861 note circulation accounted for

13. See Breckenridge, *op. cit.*, p. 50, for original statistics.

about 25% of the banks' liabilities in the Canadas, but in the succeeding decade they declined to about 15% (remaining, however, above 10% until 1900). In the Maritimes the ratio was slightly higher and did not decline decisively until 1868. Until 1858 deposits in the Canadas were about as large as notes in circulation, but thereafter always exceeded notes outstanding. This is also approximately true for the Bank of Nova Scotia, whose deposits exceeded its notes every year after 1856. This almost parallel movement of deposits and notes until the later 1850s is interesting. It suggests that, until about that time, deposits served primarily as a repository of specie and notes for the public, whereas after that they served increasingly as a medium of exchange through the development of the practice of drawing cheques against accounts for settling indebtedness, particularly since the savings deposit business had not yet been developed. It was therefore in the late 1850s that the deposit began to develop into a substitute for the bank note.[14] Prior to that time the note issue was of particular importance to the banks. Interference with the banks' near monopoly in the issue of notes would have been a more serious threat to their business before the late 1850s than after, for it was through the note issue that the banks could satisfy the demand for a satisfactory medium of exchange. And government notes did not really appear until 1866.

Nor was the significance of the note issue in the early years of banking in Canada diminished by the fact that 75% of the liabilities of the banks were made up of items other than notes—principally paid-up capital and deposits. In those years paid-up capital was a relatively expensive source of funds, for to be competitive banks were expected to pay dividends of about 8%,[15] while usury laws fixed the loan rate, with penalties for infractions, at 6% until 1858 and 7% until 1866 (although evasion of those laws by the banks may have occurred to some extent). Paid-up capital provided the banks with a source of specie, and, in effect, with a reserve to meet contingencies such as bad debts and defalcations. Indeed, after 1841 the note issue of banks in the Canadas was limited to the size of the paid-up capital so that expansion in the former required expansion of the latter. But it was the note issue and deposits that provided them with inexpensive funds. And, as already suggested, without being able to offer a

---

14. Nor is this generalization negated by other reasons for the relative decline in the size of the banks' notes during those years. The Government Note Issue was not introduced until 1866, and in 1870 the aggregate of the Dominion and chartered bank notes outstanding amounted to only one-half of the deposits of the chartered banks.

15. See Breckenridge, *op. cit.*

medium of exchange in the form of notes the early banks would to a great extent have been denied deposits as a source of funds – until deposits themselves became a medium of exchange. It is because of this that the development of a note issue in which the public had confidence and the freedom to expand it were so important to the establishment of commercial banking institutions in Canada.

Legislative restrictions on bank lending appear not to have impeded the growth of the chartered banks any more than did restrictions on the banks' sources of funds. Until 1858 most lenders in the Province of Canada were subject to the 6% interest ceiling of the usury laws, and from 1858 to 1866 this was raised from 6% to 7% for the banks and abolished entirely for others.[16] After 1866, and until 1934, the banks too could charge what they wished, but could not use legal processes to recover interest in excess of 7%. These were not restrictions that placed the banks in any significantly inferior position.

From the first charters of the banks, there existed a prohibition against mortgage lending by the banks. But it was a period when chartered bank funds were truly short term and when formalized mortgage lending processes and institutions were not yet well developed. The rule of thumb of confining lending to short-term, self-liquidating loans was probably necessary to ensure survival of the banks in the first fifty years of their existence. All "responsible" bankers favoured it, as they continued to do until after the Second World War – that is, long after the banks had become savings banks and long after the techniques of mortgage lending had been exceedingly well developed by others.

In general the period prior to Confederation was one in which the ease of obtaining bank charters and increased bank capital permitted the chartered banking system to grow at an historically high rate. Public acceptance of the bank note as a substitute for existing media of exchange was the dominant force behind that growth. The emergence of the chequing demand deposit in that period provided the basis for continued growth, while the beginning of the decline in the relative importance of bank stock as a source of funds did so as well.

At the time of Confederation the banks dominated the financial scene. They accounted for three-quarters of financial intermediary assets; they handled the foreign exchange business; and their stock was by far the most important security traded on the embryonic stock exchanges. But the banking system was far from being fully developed. While there were about 35 banks in operation, the ratio of

16. For a full discussion of government control of interest rates see below, chapter 15.

branches to population was only about one to 29,000,[17] as compared with one to about 3500 that became "normal" many years later. Nor did the banking system enjoy unqualified public confidence, for good reasons. In 1866 there were two insolvencies; in 1865 there was one, and eight charters granted were not even used; in 1863 two charters were repealed; and in 1862 as well as in 1859 there were three insolvencies. Both internal bank management and external bank supervision had not yet been effectively developed. This was to happen in the second half-century of the banks' existence.

The Growth of the Chartered Banks after Confederation

After Confederation the banks entered a fifty-year period of continued remarkable growth. Table 4:3 shows that it averaged consistently above the 1870-1970 average of 4.2% in constant dollars, and Chart 4:1 shows that this occurred even though there were short-term interruptions to that growth. This high growth rate in real terms ended around 1910, although in current dollar terms it continued until about 1920 largely because of First World War financing. While annual constant dollar data are not available for the earlier years it would appear that this period of slow growth in real terms ended in about 1926. In current dollars chartered bank assets were actually lower in 1934 than in 1919.[18] Certainly this prolonged period of slow chartered bank growth, whether we see it as having extended from 1919 to 1934 (with interruptions) using current dollars, or from 1910 to 1926 using constant dollars, is one of the most unusual episodes in the history of the chartered banks, and we will seek an explanation for it. After that period of slow growth ended, the banks entered a period in which their growth in real terms approximated that of their average long-term (1870-1970) experience.

We have already noted the long-swings that occurred in the relative size of the chartered banks. Chart 4:1 shows this aspect of the chartered banks from two points of view. It shows that the ratio of chartered bank assets to total private financial intermediary assets has had very much the same trend as the ratio of their assets to total financial intermediary assets. In other words, the latter is not explained essentially by the appearance of public financial intermediaries.

It should also be noted that the relative decline in the size of the

17. See Table 4:7 below.
18. See Chart 4:1.

Table 4:3 Growth Rate of Chartered Bank Assets 1870-1970

	TOTAL RECORDED ASSETS GROWTH RATE PER ANNUM (CURRENT DOLLARS) %	TOTAL "CANADIAN" ASSETS GROWTH RATE PER ANNUM (CURRENT DOLLARS) %	TOTAL "CANADIAN" ASSETS GROWTH RATE PER ANNUM (CONSTANT DOLLARS) %
1870-1880	5.6	4.5	4.7
1880-1890	3.1	4.4	4.5
1890-1900	6.8	5.9	6.3
1900-1910	9.4	9.3	7.0
1910-1920	9.5	9.1	1.4
1920-1930	.3	.4	3.0
1930-1940	1.7	2.3	3.0
1940-1950	9.7	10.1	4.6
1950-1960	6.0	5.1	1.9
1960-1965	8.9	8.1	6.0
1965-1970	12.5	9.7	5.5
1870-1970	6.2	6.0	4.2

SOURCE: See Statistical Appendix.

Canadian banking system is not a unique phenomenon. Table 4:4 shows the ratio of commercial bank assets to total financial intermediary assets for both Canada and the United States for selected years over approximately a century. Most strikingly illustrated is the similarity between the two banking systems with respect to both their relative size and their relative decline. In 1880, for example, Canadian chartered bank assets amounted to 55% of total Canadian financial intermediary assets, while U.S. commercial bank assets amounted to 59% of total U.S. financial intermediary assets. Eighty-eight years later, the two systems were still much the same in terms of their relative size, both having undergone about the same relative decline. Thus, in 1968, after both banking systems had been subjected to a great variety of, and not always identical, external influences (economic and political or legal), the Canadian system accounted for 29% of total financial intermediary assets and the United States commercial banking system for 32% of such assets.

A further point indicated by Table 4:4 is that the decline in the relative size of the U.S. banking system, as of the Canadian, was not an

Chart 4:1 – Growth and Relative Size of Chartered Bank Assets 1870-1970

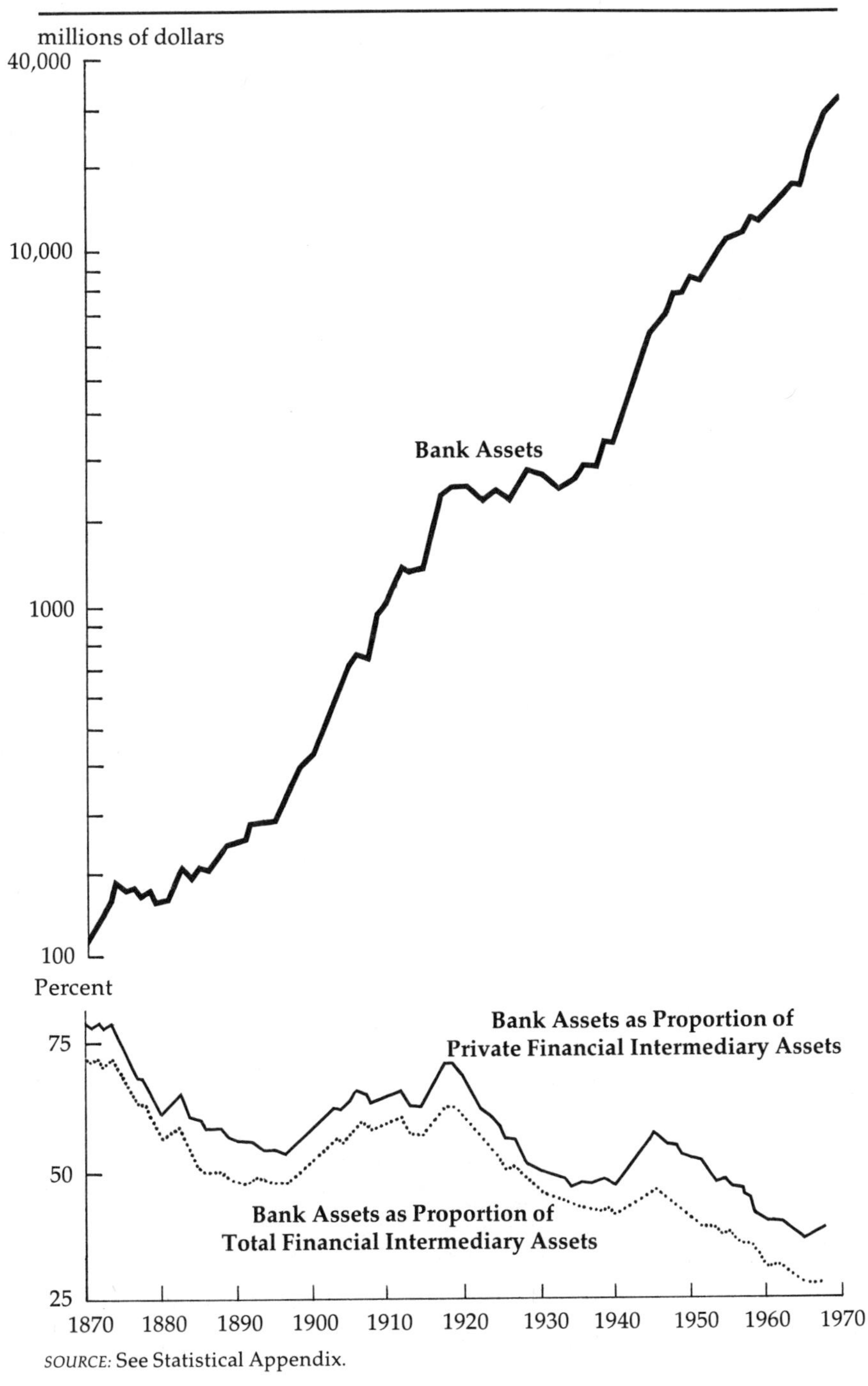

SOURCE: See Statistical Appendix.

Table 4:4 Assets of Commercial Banks in Canada and the United States as a Proportion of Total Financial Intermediary Assets 1860-1968 (selected years)

	CANADA %	UNITED STATES %
1860	n.a.	65
1870	73	n.a.
1880	55	59
1890	50	58
1900	53	63
1912	60	64
1929	49	50
1939	42	40
1948	44	41
1960	32	33
1965	29	32
1968	29	32

SOURCES: Statistics relating to U.S. financial intermediary assets were made available to me by Professor Raymond W. Goldsmith, for which I am most grateful. See also Raymond W. Goldsmith, *Financial Institutions*, Random House, New York, 1968, p. 158. Canadian data were compiled by the author from a variety of sources. See Statistical Appendix.

uninterrupted process. There was a period that began before the First World War when both systems increased in relative size. Both systems declined again until the 1930s – the U.S. system more than the Canadian, almost certainly because of the complete absence of bankruptcies among Canadian banks in the 1930s. Then both systems increased in relative size, beginning in the late 1930s and continuing on into the years of the Second World War. Finally both systems entered into their most recent period of relative decline at the end of the Second World War.

There is also the question of whether the growth of the banks should be compared with that of the group of intermediaries that are often regarded as being their competitors. The difficulty here is whether they should be grouped according to the similarity of their assets (i.e., competition in the lending market) or according to the similarity of their liabilities (i.e., competition in accumulation of funds). Furthermore, to the extent that institutions operate with flexibility and so minimize the development of segmented markets, there is little justification for dividing financial intermediaries into subgroups for purposes of comparison. However, for what it is worth we have compared the relative growth of the chartered banks with the

Table 4:5 Change in Relative Size of Assets of Canadian Financial Intermediaries 1870-1968

	PERCENTAGE POINT CHANGE 1870-1968
I Chartered banks	−44
II Near competitors of the banks	
Quebec savings banks	− 3
Mortgage loan companies	− 7
Trust companies	+ 5
Credit unions and caisses populaires	+ 4
Consumer loan and sales finance companies	+ 5
Dominion Note Issue and Bank of Canada	—
Post Office and Government Savings Banks	− 3
Provincial savings banks	—
TOTAL	+ 1
III Distant competitors of the banks	
Life insurance companies	+11
Fraternal benefit societies	—
Fire and casualty insurance companies	− 1
Investment companies	+ 4
Trusteed pension funds	+ 9
Federal Annuity, Insurance and Pension Account	+ 8
Industrial Development Bank	—
Farm Credit Corporation and Veterans Land Act	+ 2
Central Mortgage and Housing Corporation	+ 4
Canada Pension Plan	+ 2
Other government intermediaries	+ 3
TOTAL	+42

SOURCE: See Statistical Appendix.

growth of those that may be regarded, in a general sort of way, as their "near competitors" and their "distant competitors." The results are shown in Table 4:5.

They show that whereas the banks' relative size declined by 44 percentage points from 1870 to 1968, this loss for the most part was gained not by their near competitors, which group only increased by

1 percentage point, but rather by the distant competitors who gained 42 percentage points.

To complete this survey of the record of bank asset growth we may recall our previous comparison of that growth with the growth of G.N.P. The statistics of Chart 3:1 above suggest that until 1910 chartered bank assets grew much more quickly than G.N.P.; then they levelled off at roughly 45% of G.N.P., with the ratio, however, rising much above that in the 1930s because of a depressed G.N.P. and in the 1940s because of war finance; and in the 1960s the ratio became stabilized at around 39% of G.N.P. So since 1910 chartered bank assets have not grown faster than G.N.P., and the level at which they seem to have become stabilized in the 1960s was roughly 6 or 7 percentage points of G.N.P. lower than the level at which they were stabilized in the period 1910-30.

Forces behind Chartered Bank Growth

We must now consider a number of different developments that will enable us finally to form a view concerning the forces that lay behind the banks' absolute and relative growth experience.

A word about the nature of the potential forces behind their growth is in order, particularly since there seems to have been some confusion over the matter. We explained in the first chapter that apart from the global economic forces, such as national income and output, which are likely to affect the growth of all financial intermediaries, the growth of individual financial intermediaries, including the chartered banks over long periods of time, will depend on their success in innovation with respect to (a) the type of liability instruments they can offer to surplus spenders; (b) the type of credit instruments they are prepared to take from deficit spenders; and (c) the administration of the intermediation process. Lack of success in innovation may arise from inadequate imagination and initiative and from legislative or other official constraints; but on the other hand changes introduced by government as well as the exercise of imagination and initiative may prompt innovation.

But how can this view be reconciled with the view that chartered bank asset growth will depend on the size of the cash base of the banking system and on the cash-to-liability ratio (i.e. cash ratio) that the banks choose to observe or are officially required to observe? The point really is that this is a theory of short-term bank asset growth, while the one outlined above is a theory of long-term bank asset growth.

Let us examine this more closely. From the point of view of financial intermediation, commercial banks fulfil the same general function as other financial intermediaries—they transfer funds from surplus spenders to deficit spenders. As such they are in a position to exploit economies of scale advantages over direct financing. If they were thought to suffer from externally imposed disadvantages in this activity, it would have to be because of legal constraints on such things as branch banking. Also, if they were thought to suffer from external disadvantages in the provision of new financial claims to the public or new forms of credit to borrowers, it would have to be because of legal restrictions on their borrowing and lending activities.

But what is the significance for the growth of the commercial banks of their liability instrument – the bank deposit – being accepted generally as a medium of exchange? To the extent that commercial bank deposits provide the major part of the nation's medium of exchange, the banks are able to finance the purchase of revenue-earning assets by issuing deposits sufficient to satisfy the transaction's demand for money. If the banks issued only media of exchange instruments, if they retained their share of the total "market" for media of exchange, and if the ratio of media of exchange to output did not change over time, then satisfying the demand for media of exchange would of course permit the banks to grow at the same rate as gross national product. Further, because they issue financial claims that are readily accepted as media of exchange, they must endure external controls that limit the long-term growth of such media of exchange to – in the above instance – the rate of growth of G.N.P. If the objective of the external controllers is price stability, the relevant rate would be growth of real G.N.P. The question that needs to be answered is whether the banks' long-term growth rate suffers because monetary controls must be imposed on them.

The answer seems to be "no," for controls on the rate of growth of media of exchange do not imply controls on the rate of growth of financial claims other than media of exchange. To be specific, if banks increased the attractiveness of their deposits as an asset to hold through, say, appropriate interest rate, insurance, and non-monetary service incentives, it would be necessary for the central banking authorities to increase cash reserves at an increased rate—assuming they retained their original price-level objectives. So monetary controls by themselves do not appear to inhibit the long-term growth of commercial banks. The introduction of competing forms of media of exchange would of course do so.

If the above analysis is correct, then it should also be the case that a sudden expansion of bank cash, without any change in the character (i.e. relative attractiveness) of bank deposits will not lead to a permanent increase in the size of commercial banks relative to other financial intermediaries. One would expect a sudden expansion of bank cash to be followed by an equally sudden expansion of bank loans, investments and deposits as banks individually seek to maximize profits (each knowing it has no control over market interest rates), and by a decline in interest rates of all kinds, including bank loan and savings deposit rates. The public's holdings of bank deposits for non-transactions purposes will now be excessive. They will tend to restore equilibrium (which may take some time) through purchases of current output and real and financial assets, with possible further (although temporary) declines in interest rates and increases in prices and money incomes thus accelerating the growth of non-bank financial intermediaries. As long as bank deposits continue to retain public confidence as media of exchange this process will not drain cash from the banks (apart from the *normal* increase in note circulation) and so will not reverse the earlier expansion in bank assets. When the process is complete there is no obvious reason to believe that the ratio of bank to non-bank financing will have changed. This ratio will remain constant for three principal reasons: because there seems to be no reason why the structure of interest rates, and specifically the position of bank deposit and loan rates within that structure, would have changed; because we assume that the public has retained confidence in bank deposits as media of exchange; and because we assume there has been no other change in the character of bank deposits.

The experience of the Canadian banking system in the periods influenced by First and Second World War financing support these conclusions concerning the long-term impact on the relative size of the banks of a large expansion of cash reserves. In both periods the relative size of the banking system increased noticeably during wartime monetary expansion, and in both instances this relative increase proved to be transitory, as the banks soon resumed their long-term decline in relative size (see Chart 4:1).

One additional point must be noted. If the banks permanently operate at a lower cash ratio this will improve their competitive position to the extent that it will increase the proportion of their assets in earning asset form, and so will increase their real rate of return per unit of asset; as we have seen, it will not permanently do so merely because it has permitted multiple expansion of bank assets and liabilities. This point does not fundamentally distinguish banks from any other financial intermediaries, for an improved distribution of assets on their part would improve their competitive position as well.

We may now proceed to examine the various influences that may help us explain the growth experience of the banks, including the following: increased concentration in the industry; increased density of branches; improvement in bank operations; legislative restrictions; the nature of chartered bank assets; the structure of their liabilities; the appearance of competitors; and foreign banking operations.

CHARTERED BANK CONCENTRATION

The extent and timing of the move toward bank concentration is readily apparent from Table 4:1 above. At the end of 1867 there were 35 active banks. An historical peak of 51 active banks existed at the end of 1874. Then the long period of decline in the number of banks began. By 1910 there were only 30 banks and when the number finally declined to 11 in 1925 the process in effect was complete. It is not surprising that almost as many individual banks disappeared in the fifteen years after 1910 as in the thirty-five years before, when it is recalled that the former period was one of historically slow growth for the system and the latter one of historically high growth. The financial loss involved in the insolvencies in the period after Confederation was largely confined to shareholders, for note-holders of suspended banks were in almost all cases paid off at 100%, and in many cases depositors also recovered all their funds.[19]

One reason why the banking system was able to become more concentrated, and presumably thereby to obtain the advantages of economies of scale of operation, was that no legislation prohibited mergers and indeed may have encouraged them. Until 1900 bank mergers required special acts of Parliament which were not easy to obtain; of the twenty-one banks that disappeared from the beginning of 1875 to the beginning of 1900, only four disappeared in mergers. The remainder simply failed. From the Bank Act revision of 1900 onward mergers merely required approval of the Governor-in-Council on the recommendation of the Treasury Board. This paved the way for mergers, and of the thirty-six banks that disappeared from 1900 to 1926, no less than twenty-seven disappeared in mergers.

Also it is possible that the Bank Act revision of 1890, which raised the minimum paid-up capital for a new bank from $100,000 to $250,000 and required that that capital had to be raised, and the permit to begin operations received within one year of the charter being granted, may have deterred new banks from entering the industry.

---

19. See A. J. Glazebrook, "Finance and Banking: Economic Development of Canada, 1867-1921," *Cambridge History of the British Empire* (Cambridge: At the University Press, 1930), vol. 6, p. 640.

The merger movement did not go unnoticed. Fearful that harmful concentration might result from it, the government introduced a provision into the 1913 Bank Act that merger agreements could not be entered into until the Minister of Finance had given his consent in writing. The merger movement nonetheless went forward, and this in spite of strong political controversy over it.[20] Time and again the Minister of Finance had to explain that mergers had been permitted because they would strengthen the banking system. In many cases this was not simply because of economies of scale of operation, but also because one or other of the banks involved was experiencing difficulties. The number of banks that failed is not a complete indication of the number of banks that were mismanaged, or that faced oblivion for other reasons. The dilemma of a Minister of Finance in deciding whether he should permit mergers and face increased concentration, or should prohibit them and see confidence in the banking system shaken through a possible bank failure, has been present for many decades.[21] So far he has always chosen the first alternative, thereby confirming that in practice there has been no effective anti-merger influence from government. Studies of economies of scale in Canadian banking upon which a rational merger policy might be constructed seem not to have been made.

Be that as it may, there is no evidence that legislation in any way impeded the trend toward fewer banks, particularly after 1900, so that the banks were able to acquiesce to forces that greatly increased their individual average relative size. Whether this process went up to or beyond the point of individual optimum size is not possible to say.

What the relative size of the individual banks has become is indicated in Table 4:6, which, however, is based on their total assets, both Canadian and foreign. One important change from earlier years is that no one bank dominates the industry the way the Bank of Montreal did at the time of Confederation. The quite remarkable increase in the relative size of the Royal Bank of Canada from about 1900 to 1930, as well as the increase in the size of the Canadian Bank of Commerce over those same years and through its merging with the Impe-

---

20. For an interesting, although preliminary, discussion of the economic forces involved in the merger movement see David E. Bond, *The Merger Movement in Canadian Banking*, 1890-1920, *Some Preliminary Findings*, unpublished paper presented at the Annual Meeting of the Canadian Economics Association, June 1969.

21. See B. H. Beckhart, *The Banking System in Canada*, and particularly pp. 325-46, or sections reprinted in E. P. Neufeld, *op. cit.*, pp. 196-205.

Table 4:6 Relative Size of Individual Chartered Banks 1870-1970 (selected years)

DEC. 31ST	1870 %	1880 %	1890 %	1900 %	1910 %	1920 %	1930 %	1940 %	1950 %	1960 %	1969 %	1970 %
Bank of Montreal	28.3	22.4	18.4	19.0	18.1	18.1	25.6	26.4	23.6	20.7	19.7	19.5
Royal Bank of Canada	—	1.5	2.2	3.6	7.5	18.7	27.2	25.3	26.2	25.1	25.0	25.1
Canadian Bank of Commerce[1]	8.2	12.2	8.9	10.7	12.4	15.2	19.7	19.4	18.7	18.3 }	22.2	22.7
Imperial Bank of Canada[1]	—	2.5	3.9	4.4	4.9	4.3	4.2	5.0	5.7	6.0 }		
Bank of Nova Scotia	n.a.	2.2	3.4	4.5	4.4	7.8	8.4	8.8	8.9	11.8	13.9	13.6
Bank of Toronto[2]	4.8	3.5	4.7	4.0	4.0	3.2	3.9	4.5	5.2 }	10.8	12.1	12.0
Dominion Bank[2]	—	3.1	4.8	4.8	5.1	4.6	4.5	4.1	4.9 }			
Banque Provinciale du Canada	2.6	.9	1.1	.6	.8	1.4	1.6	1.5	1.8	2.2	2.1	2.2
Banque Canadienne Nationale	—	.7	1.1	2.0	1.9	2.4	4.6	4.3	4.7	4.6	4.1	4.3
Other—	56.1	51.0	51.4	46.4	40.9	24.3	(.2)	(.6)	(.4)	(.5)	(.8)	(.6)
—Number in "other" category	(15)	(27)	(29)	(27)	(19)	(9)	(2)	(1)	(1)	(1)	(3)	(2)
TOTAL—%	100	100	100	100	100	100	100	100	100	100	100	100
—$mns	111	193	260	502	1230	3057	3144	3731	9496	16917	42578	47307
Two largest—%	36.5	34.6	27.3	29.7	30.5	36.8	52.8	50.7	49.8	45.8	47.2	47.8
Five largest—%	—	43.7	40.7	43.4	48.0	64.4	85.5	83.4	83.1	86.7	92.9	92.9

SOURCE: Monthly Returns of the Chartered Banks, *Canada Gazette*, Queen's Printer, Ottawa, and C.A. Curtis, "Statistics of Banking," *Statistical Contributions to Canadian Economic History*, Vol. I, The Macmillan Company of Canada Ltd., 1931.

[1]Canadian Imperial Bank of Commerce after 1960.
[2]Toronto-Dominion Bank after 1955.

rial Bank of Canada in the 1960s, left them both larger in terms of assets than the Bank of Montreal. The Bank of Nova Scotia has also increased in relative size over the years, as have the other banks shown in Table 4:6, albeit to a lesser extent. The gain in relative size of the aforementioned banks came from the disappearence of the large number of small banks and from the decline in the relative size of the Bank of Montreal. In 1880 the five largest banks accounted for 44% of bank assets, and in 1970, 93%. So there has been both a substantial increase in concentration of assets among the few largest banks and a much more even distribution among those banks. In the last decade or two the three largest banks have not gained in relative size; indeed they have declined on balance, whereas the Bank of Nova Scotia and the Toronto-Dominion Bank have increased, as has La Banque Provinciale du Canada.

Foreign ownership of Canadian banks is small and was steadily becoming smaller even before the ownership restrictions of the 1967 Bank Act were introduced. While data are not available, it would seem that some years ago individual United Kingdom investors held a substantial proportion of Canadian bank stock. In 1958 Canadian residents owned 79.0%, other Commonwealth residents 15.9% and United States residents 4.2%, while in 1966 the equivalent figures were 89.1%, 7.3% and 3.0%. The trend has continued, for in 1969 Canadian residents owned 93.1%, other Commonwealth residents owned 4.1% and United States residents owned 2.2%.[22]

The sale by a Netherlands bank in 1963 of its Mercantile Bank of Canada to the First National City Bank of New York alarmed the federal government, and was one reason why it introduced ownership restrictions. Another reason seems to have been the possibility, in 1964, that the government of British Columbia might become a major shareholder in the Bank of British Columbia, thereby compromising the British North America Act provision that gives the federal authority exclusive jurisdiction over banking. In any case there had been emerging a general consensus in the country that foreign ownership of financial institutions should be restricted, and such a policy had gradually been emerging from the time that the federal government in 1957 permitted the mutualization of life insurance companies as a way of preventing the transfer of life company ownership into the hands of foreign investors.

The 1967 Bank Act prohibits ownership of the voting shares of a

---

22. See Canadian Bankers' Association, *Factbook—Chartered Banks of Canada* 1970, Toronto.

bank by a government, limits ownership by an individual shareholder and his associates, whether resident or non-resident, to 10% (except that residents are permitted to hold more than 10% of the shares of a new bank), and limits total non-resident ownership of a bank to 25%. The government also established that any bank with more than 25% non-resident ownership, which in effect meant the Mercantile Bank, could not increase its total liabilities in excess of twenty times its authorized capital, and an increase in authorized capital requires the approval of the Governor-in-Council. In January 1970 the First National City Bank of New York announced that it would sell shares of the Mercantile Bank to the Canadian public and reduce its holdings in it to 25%. This move paves the way for future expansion of the only Canadian bank with a significant element of foreign ownership.

DENSITY OF THE BRANCH SYSTEM

While the number of banks diminished, the number of branches increased greatly as can be seen from Table 4:7. In 1868 there were 123 branches or one branch for every 28.9 thousand of the population. This was far from an adequate banking service and prompted the appearance of a large number of private local banks and the establishment of the government's Post Office Savings Bank. Until about 1910, when there were 3.0 thousand people for every branch, branches appeared in much greater number than can be explained by increases in population. It was a period, in other words, when the banks filled the backlog of demand for banking services. In view of the remarkably stable number of branches per population since 1940 – about one for every 3½ thousand people – the period 1910 to 1940 was undoubtedly one of over-expansion followed by inevitable contraction in the branch system, for at one point in that period there was one branch for fewer than two thousand people. At the same time, in 1968 there were also 2,144 registered small-loan company and money-lender branches and 531 trust company branches, while in the 1920s there were only a small number; it is possible therefore that after the 1930s the banks permitted the number of their branches to fall below the "optimum" level, the others coming in in part to fill a gap that was thereby created. Nevertheless, there were other factors that were possibly even more important, such as the failure of the banks for many years to enter the consumer credit business, to develop more savings instruments and to improve their hours of business.

The explosive increase in the number of branches from 1890 to

Table 4:7 Density of Chartered Bank Branches in Canada 1868-1970 (selected years)

	TOTAL	PEOPLE PER BRANCH (in thousands)
1868	123	28.9
1879	295	14.4
1890	426	11.3
1900	708	7.6
1910	2,367	3.0
1920	4,676	1.9
1930	4,083	2.5
1940	3,311	3.4
1950	3,679	3.7
1960	5,051	3.5
1965	5,724	3.5
1968	5,953	3.5
1969	6,038	3.5
1970	6,199	3.5

SOURCE: *Canada Year Book*, Queen's Printer, Ottawa, Annual and Canadian Bankers' Association, *Factbook—Chartered Banks of Canada*, Annual.

1920 (426 to 4,676) was accompanied by the virtual disappearance of the local private banker and a substantial decline in the relative size of the Post Office Savings Bank. There is little doubt that the former caused the latter two developments.[23] Absence of legal restrictions on the formation of branches made this branch development possible. It was a development that, apart from growth through population increases, was largely complete by 1910. Ironically the over-density of branches after that came at a time when the banks had entered into a period of historically slow growth.

IMPROVEMENT IN BANK OPERATIONS

The chartered banks, while enjoying remarkable freedom in pursuing their business, had nonetheless to develop rules of operations or to have rules of operations imposed on them to avoid pitfalls ending in insolvency and in losses to note-holders and depositors. An impression of the nature of these pitfalls can be gained by the following contemporary comments on various individual bank failures.

23. See below, pp. 173-5.

...The trial and conviction of a bank cashier for making fraudulent returns to the Government is so strange an occurrence amongst us as to deserve something more than a passing notice. . . . Mr. Cotte, though an able man, was not a banker. . . . After a time therefore he made just such mistakes as an inexperienced person would fall into. Many of the loans made by the bank degenerated into "lock ups", and, as time went on the amount of such lock ups became so serious that the available resources of the bank were heavily diminished....[24]

...In two years no less than $1,200,000 was written off on account of the Detroit and Milwaukee Railway bonds. . . . The gold speculations of the Merchants' in New York... had latterly proved unprofitable....There were besides other losses in New York, making the whole loss there $198,000. Then there were losses at several of the agencies in Canada. . . . It is confessed that there had been, at the head office, inadequate supervision of the transactions of the agencies, mistaken motives of economy having prevented the employment of an adequate staff for this purpose.[25]

...The directors are culpable in permitting one of their number, who, although clever, is a bold and self-willed man, to have all the money desired by the firm of which he was a ruling spirit to lock up in ships.[26]

...The losses of the Consolidated Bank have not been in the ordinary course of business. . . . It is the recklessness with which enormous sums have been squandered in loans to men of little or no capital, to irresponsible schemes and desperate speculation, which has aroused those feelings of resentment. . . .[27]

...We beg to announce that on the 28th ult. this Bank suspended specie payments, owing to complications and unauthorized advances made by our late Cashier, who has for the present left the country. . . .[28]

...Thomas Craig, the manager, who owes the bank something like $226,000, has absconded, or at least he is not to be found. To the moment of his departure, he continued in charge. . . . It now comes out that the bank has never even inspected since he was placed in charge. . . . The Bank's money was contrary to law, loaned on or invested in its own stock. . . .[29]

...The advances made by the bank to several of its customers were unwise and excessive. In one case, where the advances exceeded, we are told, half a million, the margin is mainly in real estate, the value of which is problematical. . . .[30]

---

24. *Monetary Times*, Nov. 3, 1876, p. 504, regarding Jacques Cartier Bank.
25. *Monetary Times*, July 6, 1877, regarding the Merchants' Bank.
26. *Monetary Times*, Oct. 18, 1878, p. 504, regarding the Merchants' Bank of P.E.I.
27. *Monetary Times*, Sept. 26, 1879, p. 384.
28. Circular issued by the Board of Directors, Bank of Prince Edward Island, Dec. 31, 1881. See *Monetary Times*, Dec. 16, 1881, p. 731.
29. *Monetary Times*, Dec. 7, 1883, p. 629, regarding the Exchange Bank of Canada.
30. *Monetary Times*, July 19, 1895, p. 78, regarding La Banque du Peuple.

> ... It appears that this firm owed the bank the altogether disproportionate sum of $490,000....[31]
>
> ... It is understood that under "Other Securities" was placed $778,000 which had no existence. Stock transactions were carried on with a New York Broker's firm, which lost $485,000.
>
> At various times the Ontario Bank purchased $220,000 of its own shares in the name of the officers' guarantee fund, in order to protect the price in the open market. With speculative losses of $170,000 in Minneapolis and St. Louis Railway Stock, these four items amount to a loss of $1,653,000....[32]

Evidence relating to the many other bank failures, or even to the circumstances of some bank mergers, is of the same character. An examination of that evidence leads us to conclude that loss of confidence in banks almost always resulted from their having made imprudent loans and investments or from suffering defalcations, and almost never from external forces over which the banks had no control. It was hardly ever a case of having made good long-term loans which could not be realized when depositors and note-holders for extraneous reasons demanded legal tender; but rather it was usually a case of having made imprudent loans (sometimes of a short-term, other times of a long-term, nature) which subsequently led to loss of confidence. This is why the general prohibition against mortgage security was no guarantee of bank solvency and why it would probably have been better, at least in later years, to have permitted the banks to become experienced in taking such security. In many cases, also, loans made to individual borrowers were too large in relation to a particular bank's total resources or reserves, and not infrequently bank directors were involved in such loans. The fault lay with internal operations.

The major improvements in the operations of the banks that appear to have been required were the training of professional bankers for all the agencies and branches as well as head offices of the banks; the development of adequate internal accounting and auditing procedures; the establishment of the system of branches; the successful application of accounting, audit and inspection procedures to such a system; and the development of general principles for appraisal of risks, which could be applied to an ever-increasing number of individual credits. In addition the increased size of individual banks, through mergers as well as ordinary growth, increased the size of individual loans that could safely be made and undoubt-

---

31. *Monetary Times*, March 10, 1905, pp. 1205-6.
32. *Monetary Times*, Oct. 20, 1906, p. 575.

edly reduced unit costs of operations. It is difficult to determine by what period all these improvements had successfully been made, although it appears that the period from Confederation to the First World War saw many of them become generally adopted. After that, consolidation and refinement seem to have predominated.

All these developments, leading to fewer and fewer bank failures, engendered increasing public confidence in the bank note and the bank deposit as media of exchange and as a way for holding savings in liquid form. The failure of the Home Bank in 1923 was the last failure.

LEGISLATIVE RESTRICTIONS ON THE BANKS

Perhaps the most discussed legal restriction on the banks' operations was the interest rate ceiling on loans. We have already noted that by an act of 1866 banks in the Province of Canada no longer faced any penalties for charging more than the 7% ceiling rate that had been established in 1858 following many decades of a 6% ceiling.[33] This provision was introduced into legislation of the new Dominion and applied to all banks in Canada in 1867, which had the effect in Nova Scotia and New Brunswick of raising the ceiling from 6% to 7% and apparently of removing their penalties for "usury." It also indicated that the banks could not use legal processes to recover interest in excess of 7%, but in practice this was hardly a significant restriction. A Privy Council decision of 1913 established that if a borrower voluntarily paid more than 7%, he could not recover it and this in turn meant that the banks were able to charge any rate they wished as long as interest was deducted when the loan was granted. This is how matters stood until 1934, when penalties for charging in excess of 7% were re-introduced, having been absent since 1866. In 1944 the rate was lowered to 6%. However, from 1934 to about 1955 or 1956 it could hardly be said that the ceiling was a restriction, for several reasons. First of all, interest rates in general were so low that for most loans the ceiling was of no consequence. Second, beginning in 1936 the Canadian Bank of Commerce (now the Canadian Imperial Bank of Commerce) entered the personal instalment loan field and by deducting interest when the loan was made, by requiring instalments to be paid into a savings account on which half-yearly payments of bank interest on minimum quarterly balances were permitted, and by making certain service charges, the bank was able to raise its annual average percentage yield on personal loans to just

33. See below, pp. 542-50, for a full discussion of the interest rate ceiling.

over 10%.[34] To an outside observer it is apparent that this personal loan scheme was welcomed by members of Parliament, even though political exigencies appear to have prevented successive governments from explicitly confirming its legality. In 1958 the other banks began to enter the field, having received the legal authority to take chattel mortgage security in 1954.

When all the preceding points are considered it is apparent that in no meaningful sense of the word were the chartered banks placed at a competitive disadvantage because of the interest rate ceiling until the later part of 1955. It may be recalled that in early 1955, less than a year after the chartered banks had entered the National Housing Act mortgage lending field, they bid the rate on such mortgages *down* to 5%, hardly evidence that the ceiling was harmful to them.

What about the impact of other legislative restrictions on the operations of the banks? The cash ratio is frequently mentioned. The matter of a fixed cash ratio arose first in 1870 when the bank charters were up for renewal, and Sir Francis Hincks, Minister of Finance, favoured its introduction. The bankers opposed it and George Hague has explained why: "...They took the unassailable ground that a reserve that must be kept is no reserve at all. A reserve that cannot be used is obviously an absurdity; just as the reserve of an army would be if a general were forbidden to bring it into action."[35]The bankers were right, for the arguments in support of fixed reserves were not at that time related to their contribution to increasing the effectiveness of monetary controls, which was in any case a largely irrelevant factor until 1914, when the requirement that bank and Dominion notes had to be redeemed on demand with specie was suspended. In 1934 a 5% cash ratio was introduced, although the banks in practice held about 10%, and in 1954 it was changed to 8%. Then in the 1967 Bank Act a 12% ratio was stipulated for demand deposits and a 4% ratio for savings deposits which, taking into account the way the banks' deposits are divided between those two types, resulted in an average cash ratio of about 6½%. So, until 1954, in no sense could it be said that legislation with respect to the cash reserve ratio placed the banks at a competitive disadvantage. Since the effect of the 1954 legislation was to increase the proportion of assets that the banks in fact held in earning asset form, it is difficult to see how the legislation, at least

34. See W. C. Hood, *Financing of Economic Activity in Canada* (Ottawa: Queen's Printer, 1958), p. 398, and Canada, House of Commons, Standing Committee on Banking and Commerce, *Minutes of Proceedings and Evidence*, Thursday, April 8, 1954, Appendix "C".

35. "Bank Reserves," *Journal of the Canadian Bankers' Association*, vol. 1, 1893-4, and reprinted in E. P. Neufeld, *op. cit.*, pp. 192-5.

in the first instance, was disadvantageous to the banks. Whether or not it began sometime after 1954 to be disadvantageous is not at all clear, but it almost certainly was not after 1967.

Before the days of central banking and managed money the purpose of a cash reserve was to ensure that the banks would be in a position to honour their obligation to redeem on demand with legal tender (specie or Dominion notes) their note and deposit liabilities, and the level of reserves held for this purpose would depend on the volatility of seasonal and cyclical forces as well as less periodic developments that engendered financial crises from time to time. But when the Finance Act of 1913 began to give the banks an official source of cash throughout the year, and particularly when the Bank of Canada began in 1935 to manage cash so as to offset seasonal swings and also to act as a lender of last resort to the banking system, the original purpose of the cash reserves virtually disappeared. Since the Bank of Canada provided a flexible supply of cash there was no longer any pressing need for the actual cash held by the banks to vary as it used to do, and so the fixed cash ratio as such probably imposed no net new restriction on the banks. The only important question that remains is whether, having in mind the kind of assistance supplied by the Bank of Canada, the cash ratio is higher than the banks would want it on average to be if no legal ratio at all were required. Whenever it is higher than they would want it to be, it should be lowered. Finally, it is difficult to see how the arrangement that the banks receive no interest on cash deposits with the Bank of Canada imposes a restriction that would not exist if the Bank of Canada were not present. The banks would almost certainly have to maintain reserves on which they would receive no interest, and it is conceivable that the amounts they would maintain would be even larger than the amounts they would wish to maintain with the Bank of Canada present. It is significant that from 1934 to 1954, when the banks were required to hold only 5% of their note and deposit liabilities in the form of non-interest-earning bank cash, they in fact held about 10% in that form. So again we feel that the only significant issue is whether the reserves are larger than the banks would want them to be, and we conclude that until at least 1954 they obviously were not. All this is not to prejudge the issue as to whether monetary policy would be as effective without a minimum cash reserve ratio as with one, something which we cannot discuss here.

From May 1956 until the 1967 Bank Act the chartered banks, through a voluntary agreement with the Bank of Canada, maintained a minimum reserve of liquid assets (cash, day-to-day loans and treasury bills) equal to 7% of their Canadian deposit liabilities in addition to the cash ratio of 8%. There is no doubt that this imposes a rigidity on bank operations, and we would argue that it does not contribute significantly to making monetary policy effective. But that it impaired the banks' competitive position in any significant way is doubtful, since the banks could readjust their liquid assets not covered by the arrangement in a way that would, to some extent at least, offset the effect of the ratio. Under the 1967 Bank Act the banks, if and when required by the Bank of Canada, were obliged to maintain a secondary reserve ratio and the 1967 Bank of Canada Act stipulated that the Bank could require a reserve ratio of from 6% to 12% with monthly changes limited to 1%.

The new Dominion bank legislation of 1870 and 1871 imposed no new specific controls on bank liabilities at all. The note circulation was limited only by the already familiar requirement that it not exceed a bank's paid-up capital (and capital could now be increased by a mere vote of shareholders, government approval no longer being required) and of course the banks had to pay specie or Dominion notes on demand. The Provincial Notes Act of 1866 in effect became the Dominion Notes Act in 1870, thereby permanently breaking the chartered banks' monopoly of the note issue. How important were these various provisions? Prior to 1900 the chartered banks' peak seasonal note circulation (this being for the month of October) was well below 80% of paid-up capital, so the provision limiting note circulation to paid-up capital was not a restrictive one. A few years later, however, it threatened to become restrictive. Because of this the banks from 1908 onward were permitted by government to increase their seasonal note circulation in excess of paid-up capital up to 15% of capital and rest fund. In this way the banks were spared the need to raise expensive equity capital to meet the demand for notes.

The problem had arisen not from any great increase in the seasonal note circulation but rather from the cyclical expansion in economic activity that began after 1895; and also from the reluctance of the banks to increase their paid-up capital in the amounts required to meet the demand for notes. The result was that the chartered banks were easily able to retain their share of the "market" for bank notes even with the existence of Dominion notes. For example, from the early 1870s until the early 1930s chartered bank notes accounted for over 80% of bank notes held by the public. Virtually until the formation of the Bank of Canada in 1934, governmental influences on the chartered bank note issue did not impede the growth of the chartered banks.

We have already seen that until 1934 the chartered banks were not required to maintain any cash ratio against notes or deposits. Nor were they ever required to maintain any deposit-to-capital ratio. Consequently, no legal impediments existed for the secular decline in the ratio of deposits to equity (that is, paid-up capital and rest). In 1883, for example, that ratio was 178% whereas by 1900 it had risen to 348% and by 1914 to 510%. The banks made no attempt to cultivate liability instruments other than bank notes, deposits, and for a number of years deposit certificates (they began to issue short-term notes in the early 1960s) even though they were not prohibited by the Bank Act from doing so.

Legal restraints on bank assets, that is on bank lending, did not significantly restrict the banks' operations for most of the period of their existence. This was because the bankers themselves, until well after the Second World War, argued strongly against their participation in mortgage lending, and because the decennial revision of the Bank Act permitted the banks to enter new fields of short-term lending as they emerged. And they have always enjoyed great freedom in their security purchases.

The banks began operations essentially by discounting commercial notes or bills of exchange. By a special act of 1859 they were authorized to make loans against the security of bills of lading and warehouse receipts covering certain commodities; this was the beginning of what later became the famous section 88 of the Bank Act. Legislation relating to this type of lending was extended on numerous occasions over the years, as need arose.[36]

In 1879 a special act of Parliament, passed prior to an election and following public criticism of stock speculation, prohibited a bank from making loans against any bank's stock. In itself this restriction probably has never been important to the banks; but it still exists, and for this reason the environment surrounding its introduction might with interest be recalled. A report in the *Monetary Times* of January 31, 1879, outlines it graphically:

> ... Amongst the important changes introduced in the present [i.e. 1871] Act, was that of allowing Banks to lend upon the stock of other Banks.... It could never have been dreamed that in such an apparently innocent clause, such tremendous powers of mischief lay concealed. Under the present Banking Act, considerable facilities were given for the incorporation of new institutions, and as Banking at that time, and for some years afterwards, partook of the general inflation which then characterized all departments of business, a general movement for the increase in capital, and for the

36. See A. B. Jamieson, *Chartered Banking in Canada* (Toronto: Ryerson Press, 1955), pp. 3-168.

> establishment of new banks set in.... Considerable amounts of capital subscribed could only be paid up by borrowing, and by pledging the stock so subscribed for....
>
> ...After 1874, a gradual wave of depression set in....One consequence of this has been that it has been found impossible to take up the masses of loans on bank stock, and they have accordingly been kept floating about, now in one form, and now in another, held by this broker and that, advanced upon, changing hands from this bank to that bank, month after month, and year after year, until at present there is somewhere about four millions of bank capital (at par value) in this state of suspension. It is upon this amount of floating capital that the prodigious mania of speculation has been built up, which is one of the greatest evils of the time. Operators know that this immense field lies open to them, in which to form their combinations and carry out their plans either for a rise or fall. Bank stocks, therefore, have been for years buffeted about, and tossed up and down at the mercy of speculators....[37]

So it was a combination of a rash of new bank formations and the expansion of existing ones based on bank loans, embarrassment to borrowers caused by a depression, questionable speculative behaviour, and a certain revulsion against stock speculation as such (and bank stocks were the main item being traded in the stock exchange), as well as the political implications of all this, that led to the prohibition. It is difficult to imagine that present circumstances continue to justify the prohibition.

While, as mentioned earlier, lending provisions under the "pledge" sections of the Bank Act continued to be adjusted almost every time the Bank Act was revised, it was not until 1936 that the banks entered into other new types of lending. In that year the chartered banks began making home improvement loans, with a 15% government guarantee against loss of the aggregate of loans authorized by and made under the Home Improvement Loans Guarantee Act of 1937. Also in 1936, as we have seen, the Canadian Bank of Commerce began a personal instalment loan business under which the effective rate of interest was almost double the 6% ceiling; other banks did not enter the field until 1958. The principle of a government guarantee against loss up to a certain amount of the aggregate loans made was adopted in 1944 for short-term and intermediate-term loans made to farmers under the new Farm Improvement Loans Act. This act also broke new ground in that it permitted the banks to take land mortgage security against F.I.L.A. loans. Similar guarantee principles and collateral provisions were adopted in the Veterans Business and Professional Loans Act of 1946, and the Small Business Loans Act of 1960.

---

37. *Monetary Times*, Jan. 31, 1879, p. 949.

In 1954 the chartered banks took a further step toward mortgage lending when they began to make government-guaranteed residential mortgage loans under the National Housing Act, and when they were permitted to take chattel mortgages as security for bank loans — a step further into the personal loan business. But the major change in mortgage lending provisions of the Bank Act did not occur until 1967 when the new Bank Act enabled the banks for the first time to make conventional unguaranteed mortgage loans. There is no doubt that this is the most significant change in bank lending power that has occurred for decades. It is interesting that, like the many changes in section 88, it occurred within a few years of the banks' expressing a desire for such a change.

It seems clear that the banks did not, over the years, labour under harmfully restrictive legislation with respect to their borrowing and lending activities. Changes in lending regulations came soon after they were desired while provisions relating to bank liabilities did not restrict the banks' operations — with the exception of the requirement that the banks until 1913 had to pay off their notes in specie on demand, had to maintain a minimum cash reserve ratio after 1934, and were gradually deprived of the note issue after that year. Growth of the banks, apart from the force of competition from other intermediaries and general economic conditions, depended heavily on the ingenuity exercised by the banks themselves.

What then may we conclude about the impact of legislative restrictions on the banks? First, not until at least 1955 did the legal interest rate ceiling or legal cash ratio requirements place the banks at a competitive disadvantage. Second, the banks obtained new lending powers almost as soon as they wanted them, because of the decennial revision of the Bank Act; and not until 1962 did they themselves publicly argue in favour of being permitted to make conventional mortgage loans. Third, the banks have enjoyed almost complete legislative freedom in the type of liability instruments they can issue. So the greater part at least of the relative decline in the size of the chartered banks cannot be explained by restrictive legislation. Nor can the changing growth rates of the banks over time be explained by it. We must turn to other factors explaining the growth experiences of the banks.

THE NATURE OF CHARTERED BANK ASSETS

We have noted that the only restriction on bank lending and purchases of securities that persisted over the years was the ban on mortgage loans and on loans secured with bank shares. Furthermore, we noted that in the case of the former it was not until 1962 that the banks expressed a desire to have the ban (by that time, the partial ban) on mortgage lending removed. What this means, then, is that the structure of bank assets over the years is a reflection not of legislative restriction but of bankers' preferences.

Consistent long-term series of the structure of bank assets are not easy to compile, because of changes in items reported by the banks. But Table 4:8 provides a broad outline of the major changes, even though the series shown there are not ideal for our purpose and are not entirely consistent over the whole of the period. A number of observations about the structure of bank assets may be made.

(1) There appears to have been no significant long-term trend in the proportion of non-interest-earning assets held by the banks, at least not until 1955. Column 1 of Table 4:8 shows that the ratio of Canadian cash items to total assets for the periods shown (using year-end figures) moved between 6.6% and 8.8% from 1873 to 1910, and between 7.2% and 8.9% from 1926 to 1955. Over the period from 1911 to 1925 it was somewhat higher, which is interesting in that it was also a period of slow growth for the banks; and after the establishment of the legal 8% cash-to-deposit ratio in 1954, the Canadian cash-items-to-total-assets ratio declined to historically low levels. From 1900 onward more meaningful figures for foreign cash items are available, and if these are added to the Canadian cash items and a ratio to total assets taken (see col. 3, Table 4:8) the results again confirm an absence of any long-term trend. Indeed, this ratio stood at 10.3% in the 1901-05 period and at 11.0% in the 1961-5 period, with 11% at the end of 1966 as well. The increase after 1966 reflected a new influence—chartered bank activity in the emerging Euro-dollar market. The decline in the ratio of Canadian cash items after 1954 was offset by an increase in foreign cash items, leaving the total unchanged until 1967 . Since the banks receive interest income on their deposits with foreign banks, this switch increased the banks' earning assets, particularly after 1966.

Column 10 of Table 4:10, which shows the banks' Canadian cash ratio, suggests that there was no basic trend change in the ratio from the 1886-90 period, when it stood at 10.2%, and the 1951-5 period, when it was 9.4%. Prior to that period it had declined from about 16%, and from the 1906-10 period to the 1921-5 period there was again an increase in the ratio.

(2) Call loans, both in Canada and abroad (principally in New York), were much more important in the banks' portfolio prior to the 1931-5 period than from that period onward—with historically high levels in the 1906-30 periods (see cols. 4 and 5, Table 4:8).

(3) The period from 1873 to 1970 was one in which loans (excluding call and day-to-day loans) decreased in relative importance, accounting for 72.8% of total assets in the 1873-5 period and 49.8% in the 1961-5 period, with 50.9% at the end of 1970; and it was a period in which security holdings rose substantially in importance, being negligible in 1873-5 and amounting to 19.0% at the end of 1970. But this switch out of loans into securities was not a steady one, and did not always involve the same types of securities, so a somewhat closer examination is required. From the 1873-5 period to the 1896-1900 period, loans as a proportion of total assets declined by 12.1 percentage points, which was largely accounted for by the 8.5 percentage point increase in security holdings and 5.6 percentage point increase in cash items and call loans (principally the latter). The call loans reflected the increased utilization by the banks of the New York money market for investing short-term funds, and also the developing stock and bond markets in Canada that required financing. The shift into securities was not a move toward increased liquidity, but rather reflected the growing utilization by corporations, municipalities and provinces of the developing new issues market for raising funds. Table 4:9, which outlines the distribution of the banks' holdings of securities in broad categories, makes this quite clear, for it shows that at the end of 1900 federal government securities accounted for only 9% of the total security holdings of the banks, provincial, 16%, railway and other corporate, 51%, and municipal and foreign public, 24%.

This pattern existed until about 1915, with the total of federal and provincial security holdings even declining substantially relative to the total portfolio of securities held. Then two factors caused a permanent change in the chartered banks' investment practices: the First World War financing, which greatly increased the banks' holdings of federal government securities, and the banks' sad (almost fatal in one case) experience with railway financing, which made them shy away from corporate securities in general. As a consequence of these factors the banks' holdings of federal and provincial government securities jumped to 36% of the total by 1920, from 13% in 1915, and their holdings of railway and other corporate securities declined to 13% by 1920, from 54% in 1915 (see cols. 3 and 4, Table 4:9). But equally significant, this trend continued in the 1920s, with federal and provincial securities accounting for 64% of total securities in 1925, railway and other corporate securities, 11%, and municipal and foreign securities, only 25%, the latter down sharply from 1920. Basically this pattern was never altered after that (although it was

Table 4:8 Selected Chartered Bank Assets as a Percentage of Total Assets[1] 1873-1970

	CASH ITEMS AND CALL LOANS							SECURITIES[6]	OTHER LOANS		OTHER ASSETS	
	Cash items			*Call loans*			*Total*					
	CANADIAN[2] (1) %	FOREIGN[3] (2) %	TOTAL (3) %	CANADIAN[4] (4) %	FOREIGN[5] (5) %	TOTAL (6) %	(7) %	(8) %	CANADIAN[7] (9) %	FOREIGN (10) %	TOTAL (11) %	%
1873-1875	8.8	5.4	14.2			2.1	16.3	.8	—	—	72.8	10.1
1876-1880	8.3	8.8	17.1			3.5	20.6	1.2	—	—	65.7	12.5
1881-1885	8.0	8.8	16.8			5.9	22.7	1.6	—	—	65.8	9.9
1886-1890	6.6	6.9	13.5			5.1	18.6	3.0	—	—	68.8	9.6
1891-1895	6.8	8.1	14.9			5.5	20.4	6.4	—	—	64.9	8.3
1896-1900	6.7	7.6	14.3			7.6	21.9	9.3	—	—	60.7	8.1
1901-1905	6.9	3.4	10.3	6.4	6.9	13.3	23.6	9.3	55.9	3.9	59.8	7.3
1906-1910	8.5	3.1	11.6	5.2	8.1	13.3	24.9	7.6	55.5	3.2	58.8	8.7
1911-1915	10.2	4.3	14.5	4.8	6.9	11.7	26.2	6.8	54.0	3.0	57.0	10.0
1916-1920	12.4	3.8	16.2	3.7	6.4	10.2	26.4	15.8	42.3	5.1	47.3	10.5
1921-1925	10.8	3.9	14.7	4.3	7.1	11.4	26.1	16.1	40.2	6.5	46.8	11.0
1926-1930	7.4	4.3	11.7	6.9	7.6	14.6	26.3	15.9	38.9	7.7	46.6	11.2
1931-1935	7.2	4.5	11.7	3.6	2.9	6.5	18.2	30.4	36.2	5.2	41.4	10.0
1936-1940	7.7	5.4	13.1	2.0	1.6	3.6	16.7	42.5	27.4	4.3	31.7	9.1
1941-1945	8.5	5.6	14.1	1.6	1.5	3.1	17.2	51.7	21.2	2.2	23.4	7.7
1946-1950	8.9	3.1	12.0	1.4	.9	2.3	14.3	49.4	25.7	2.6	28.4	7.9
1951-1955	7.9	2.7	10.6	1.6	1.7	3.4	14.0	37.3	35.7	2.6	38.4	10.3
1956-1960	6.2	2.7	8.9	1.9	4.0	5.9	14.8	28.8	41.9	4.2	46.0	10.4
1961-1965	5.5	5.5	11.0	1.9	3.8	5.7	16.7	24.6	42.4	7.4	49.8	8.9
1965	5.5	5.3	10.8	1.8	2.8	4.6	15.4	21.5	45.9	8.7	54.6	8.5

1966	5.6	5.4	11.0	2.0	3.1	4.1	15.1	20.3	45.5	9.2	54.7	9.9
1967	4.9	11.0	15.9	2.0	2.4	4.4	20.3	20.9	46.4	8.4	54.8	4.0
1968	4.6	9.0	13.6	1.9	1.9	3.8	17.4	20.3	45.2	8.0	53.2	9.1
1969	3.9	15.0	18.8	1.2	1.6	2.8	21.6	17.1	44.5	9.0	53.5	7.8
1970	3.6	15.9	19.5	1.9	1.3	3.2	22.7	19.0	41.0	9.9	50.9	7.4

SOURCE: Computed from statistics in C. A. Curtis, *Statistical Contributions to Canadian Economic History* (Toronto: The Macmillan Company of Canada Limited, 1931), vol. II, and *Canada Gazette* (Ottawa: Queen's Printer).

[1]Based on calendar year-end statistics for the periods shown.

[2]Includes specie and Dominion notes until 1913; from 1913 to 1933 includes deposits in Central Gold Reserves and gold and subsidiary coin in Canada; from 1934 to the present includes notes of and deposits with the Bank of Canada.

[3]Until 1912 includes only balances due from banks and agencies abroad, which, however, until 1913 seems to have included at least some call loans; to this in 1913 was added gold and subsidiary coin held abroad; in 1923 holdings of foreign currencies and in 1945 foreign currency items in transit (net). Also after 1944 the item "balances due from banks and agencies abroad" became "deposits with other banks in currencies other than Canadian," and included "Euro-dollar" deposits.

[4]Includes day-to-day loans from 1954 to 1970.

[5]It seems likely that prior to 1900 some foreign call loans at least appeared in the foreign cash item.

[6]Includes Canadian and foreign securities.

[7]From 1954 includes National Housing Act mortgages which in the period 1951-5 accounted for .7% of total assets; from 1956 to 1960, 5.0% of total assets, from 1961 to 1965, 4.0% of total assets, and between 3% and 2% from 1966 to 1970.

Table 4:9 Chartered Bank Holdings of Securities Percentage Distribution 1900-1970 (selected years)

	CANADIAN FEDERAL AND PROVINCIAL GOVERNMENT			OTHER			TOTAL
DEC. 31	FEDERAL (1) %	PROVINCIAL (2) %	TOTAL (3) %	RAILWAY AND OTHER CORPORATE (4) %	CANADIAN MUNICIPAL AND FOREIGN PUBLIC (5) %	TOTAL (6) %	(7) %
1900	9	16	25	51	24	75	100
1915	n.a.	n.a.	13	54	33	87	100
1920	n.a.	n.a.	36	13	53	66	100
1925	n.a.	n.a.	64	11	25	36	100
1935	n.a.	n.a.	83	n.a.	n.a.	17	100
1945	81	7	89	n.a.	n.a.	11	100
1955	70	7	77	n.a.	n.a.	23	100
1965	67	6	73	n.a.	n.a.	27	100
1966	69	5	74	n.a.	n.a.	26	100
1967	70	5	75	n.a.	n.a.	25	100
1968	72	5	77	n.a.	n.a.	23	100
1969	69	5	74	n.a.	n.a.	26	100
1970	73	5	78	n.a.	n.a.	22	100

SOURCE: See source note to Table 4:8.

greatly accentuated by federal government financing during the 1930s depression and the Second World War), for at the end of 1969 federal and provincial security holdings amounted to 74% of the total, and the rest to 26%. In 1925 the latter had been 36%.

It is apparent, therefore, that the steady decline in the relative importance of bank loans among bank assets after the 1911-15 period had its counterpart not simply in an increase in security holdings but in holdings of increasingly more liquid securities. The increase in security holdings prior to the 1911-15 period had been of a quite different character.

Taking all these diverse movements into account, there seems to be little doubt that the banks moved permanently into more liquid assets from the First World War onward. Even in the late 1960s, when there was fairly general agreement in the industry that the banks had reached a minimum liquidity position, they were almost certainly much more liquid than in 1900. If we define the liquidity ratio as Canadian and foreign cash items and Government of Canada securities as a proportion of chartered bank note and deposit liabilities, it stood at about 14% at the end of 1900, and 36% at the end of 1970; if we include foreign call loans and Canadian day-to-day loans, the ratios are 21% and 39%. Or simply as a proportion of total Canadian and foreign assets, all the aforementioned liquid assets amounted to 16% in 1900 and 35% in 1969.

It should be noted parenthetically that in the 1920s (that is, following the substantial increase in their holdings of securities during the First World War), the banks began to develop separate securities departments. Over the years, through their local connections with municipalities, they had become involved in underwriting municipal issues, and also later provincial and corporate issues. Gradually they developed securities-trading facilities, particularly during and after the 1920s, and so in that respect have always competed with the bond dealers. That is, early on in the history of the securities market they became active in buying and selling securities on their own account, in executing orders for clients for a commission especially in the case of stocks, and in underwriting new issues and participating in syndicates formed for selling new issues.

We must now examine what was happening to the chartered banks' structure of liabilities while this move toward increased liquidity was occurring. This, fortunately, is a less complex story, although no less significant for explaining the banks' growth experience.

THE STRUCTURE OF CHARTERED BANK LIABILITIES

Table 4:10 outlines the relative importance from 1873 to 1969 of the various sources of funds of the banks, as revealed by their structure of liabilities. The major changes in sources of funds that it reveals are the following:

(1) complete disappearance of bank notes as a source of funds (these having accounted for 16.3% of total liabilities in the 1873-5 period but then declining steadily until they were abolished completely in 1950 by the Bank Act provisions of 1944);

(2) a remarkable increase in savings deposits as a source of funds, from the 1873-5 period to the 1896-1900 period (from 17.5% to 46.5%) and then no further significant increase, the 1961-5 ratio being 45.6% and the 1970 year-end ratio being 47.4%;

(3) a long-term decline in the relative size of shareholders' capital with capital alone having accounted for 38.1% of liabilities in the

Table 4:10 Selected Chartered Bank Liabilities as a Proportion of Total Selected Liabilities and Chartered Bank Cash Ratios[1] 1873-1970

	CANADIAN NOTES AND DEPOSITS					
	Notes (1) %	*Savings deposits* (2) %	*Demand deposits*[1] (3) %	*Total deposits* (4) %	*Total notes and deposits* (5) %	*Foreign deposits*[2] (6) %
1873-1875	16.3	17.5	28.0	45.5	61.9	—
1876-1880	14.1	19.1	28.2	47.4	61.5	—
1881-1885	15.3	22.4	26.0	48.4	63.8	—
1886-1890	14.0	27.1	25.4	52.6	66.6	—
1891-1895	11.4	35.3	24.2	59.5	70.8	—
1896-1900	12.3	46.5	24.9	65.4	76.1	—
1901-1905	9.6	44.4	20.8	65.2	74.8	5.7
1906-1910	7.8	44.8	23.9	68.7	76.5	6.5
1911-1915	7.4	43.4	27.5	71.0	78.3	6.8
1916-1920	8.5	43.1	28.8	71.9	80.4	9.7
1921-1925	6.8	47.5	24.1	71.6	78.4	11.9
1926-1930	5.8	47.9	24.5	72.4	78.2	12.7
1931-1935	4.7	50.4	22.5	72.8	77.6	12.0
1936-1940	2.9	48.9	27.2	76.0	78.9	12.7
1941-1945	.9	39.0	42.7	81.7	82.6	12.2
1946-1950	.2	49.8	35.3	85.2	85.4	10.6
1951-1955	—	49.8	36.9	86.7	86.7	9.2
1956-1960	—	48.3	32.3	80.6	80.6	13.9
1961-1965	—	45.6	27.7	73.3	73.3	20.3
1965	—	48.0	26.6	74.6	74.6	20.4
1966	—	47.7	26.9	74.6	74.6	20.7
1967	—	50.4[4]	24.5	74.9	74.9	20.8
1968	—	51.1	24.0	75.1	75.1	21.0
1969	—	46.4	21.1	67.5	67.5	28.8
1970	—	47.4	19.0	66.4	66.4	30.0

SOURCE: See source note to Table 4:8.

[1]Includes Government of Canada and provincial government deposits.
[2]This item was not reported prior to 1900.
[3]Excludes rest fund until 1883 and after 1960 includes all "shareholders' equity".
[4]Includes small amounts of debentures from 1967 onward.

Total Can. notes and deposits and foreign deposits (7) %	*Capital and rest*[3] (8) %	CASH RATIOS *Canadian cash items to Canadian notes and deposit liabilities* (9) %	*Canadian cash items (ex. advances) to Canadian notes and deposit liabilities* (10) %	*Canada and foreign cash items (ex. advances) to total notes and deposit liabilities* (11) %
61.9	38.1	15.9	15.9	—
61.5	38.5	15.0	15.0	—
63.8	36.2	12.9	12.9	—
66.6	33.4	10.2	10.2	—
70.8	29.2	9.7	9.7	—
76.1	23.9	11.1	11.1	—
80.6	19.4	9.6	9.6	13.3
83.0	17.0	11.5	11.5	14.5
85.1	14.9	13.6	13.4	17.6
90.3	9.7	16.6	12.7	15.8
90.4	9.6	14.6	12.7	15.6
90.9	9.1	10.3	8.5	12.4
89.6	10.4	9.8	8.1	12.4
91.6	8.4	10.2	10.2	14.9
94.8	5.2	10.8	10.8	15.5
95.9	4.1	10.8	10.8	13.0
95.8	4.2	9.4	9.4	11.4
94.5	5.5	7.8	7.8	9.7
93.5	6.5	7.7	7.7	12.1
95.0	5.0	7.6	7.6	11.8
95.3	4.7	7.7	7.7	12.0
95.8	4.3	6.8	6.8	13.4
96.1	3.9	6.4	6.4	14.7
96.3	3.7	6.0	6.0	20.6
96.5	3.5	5.7	5.7	21.2

1873-5 period and, all shareholders' equity accounting for only 12.1% in the 1961-5 period, much of the decline (i.e. to 9.7%) having occurred by the 1916-20 period;

(4) no significant trend in the proportion of funds coming from demand deposits, these accounting for 28.0% of liabilities in the 1873-5 period and 27.7% in the 1961-5 period, with significant variation from that level occurring during the Second World War and for a period after it, including an interesting move to lower levels in 1967-70;

(5) a build-up of foreign deposits in relation to the other liabilities shown until the 1926-30 period when they amounted to 12.7%, then no further increase in the ratio and even a decline in the first decade after the Second World War, but a remarkable increase (30.0% at the end of 1970) thereafter.

It seems plausible that the decline in equity as a source of funds is a reflection on the one hand of the desire of the banks to maximize existing shareholders' income (including capital appreciation of bank stocks) through increasing the leverage in the banks' capital structure, and on the other hand of a decline in the inherent risks faced by the banks and so a decline in the required equity "cushion." The decline in risk could arise from a number of causes:

(1) a decrease in the size of individual credits to total loans because of bank growth through national economic expansion and because of increased banking concentration through mergers and insolvencies;

(2) increased external supervision by government and from the appearance of the Bank of Canada with its vitally important lender-of-last-resort facilities;

(3) improved internal efficiency in administration and improved information and techniques for appraising credits and making investments; and

(4) the development of a broader securities market which would increase the liquidity of the banks' portfolio.

If the foregoing may be accepted, then it follows that the growth of the banks would depend heavily on the extent to which they could develop a market for their debt instrument. On this point the record of the banks is clear. The most important development favouring their growth was their remarkably successful exploitation of the savings deposit business in the period up to about the turn of the century. We have already seen in Table 4:10 that savings deposits grew much more quickly than other bank liabilities in that period. Table 4:11 below shows that they also grew much more quickly than G.N.P., amounting to about 5% of G.N.P. in 1870 and 24% in 1910.

Table 4:11 further emphasizes the important role that savings

Table 4:11 Major Chartered Bank Canadian Liabilities as a Percentage of G.N.P. 1870-1970 (selected years)

	1870[1] %	1880 %	1890 %	1900 %	1910 %	1920 %	1926 %	1965 %	1969 %	1970
Chartered bank notes in circulation[2]	4.2	3.9	4.1	4.4	3.7	4.1	3.3	–	–	–
Demand deposits[3]	8.0	8.7	7.4	10.0	13.4	13.8	11.8	10.9	9.6	8.8
Savings deposits	4.7	5.9	9.4	17.0	23.8	22.4	26.0	21.3	24.6	24.1

SOURCE: See source note to Table 4:8. Banking figures based on monthly average data.

[1]Because of a break in the available series of banking statistics, the July 31, 1871, figure was used instead of the monthly average for 1870.
[2]Includes notes held by banks.
[3]Includes all federal and provincial government deposits but excludes inter-bank deposits.

deposits played, for it shows that both the banks' notes and demand deposits for the most part grew no faster than G.N.P. from 1870 onward. In other words, as suppliers of media of exchange, the banks had already exhausted their opportunities for growth in excess of the growth of the economy by about Confederation, such growth depending on their supplying savings instruments. When by 1910 they had fully developed their savings deposits business, in that those deposits no longer grew at a rate faster than G.N.P., the growth of bank assets in Canada as a whole was limited to the growth of the economy.

If the development of the savings deposit business after Confederation is the most important development as far as sources of bank funds is concerned, the second most important development is the build-up of their foreign deposits after the 1951-5 period (see Table 4:10), following about thirty-five years of no particular progress in the international area. Apart from the latter, the banks for years introduced no significantly useful innovation into their debt instruments after they made the crucially important decision just after Confederation to enter the savings deposit business and make banking available to the little man and not just to the industrial, commercial and agricultural enterprises of the nation.

Then in the 1960s the banks began a new round of innovation in liability instruments, namely term notes, debentures, and savings plans that may in future prove to be important for their growth and may even help arrest their relative decline in size. This we will discuss again.

THE APPEARANCE OF COMPETITORS

We have already noted that the 44 percentage points decline in the relative size of the banks from 1870 to 1968 was accounted for almost entirely by the relative increase in size of their "distant competitors," not their "near competitors." It is true, of course, that the relative decline of the banks might have been less than it was if they had been able to cause a decline in the relative size of their near competitors after 1870. What happened was that the relative decline of the mortgage loan companies, Quebec savings banks, and Post Office and Government Savings Banks was offset by the appearance of trust companies (after 1880), credit unions and caisses populaires (after 1900), and finance companies (after 1916). To have competed more effectively than they did, the banks would have had to begin issuing debentures and making mortgage loans to compete with mortgage loan and trust companies, to issue short-term notes and enter aggressively and early into instalment financing[38] to compete with finance companies, and presumably to change their public image to compete more effectively with the credit unions and caisses populaires. Also it is possible that had the banks been more aggressive they might have reduced the drift of deposits to the trust companies, credit unions and caisses populaires. The loss of their note circulation after 1934, it is true, was forced on them by legislation. However, even these losses were not very large in relation to the banks' total relative decline. The note circulation they lost was equivalent, in 1968, to about 2.3% of the assets of all financial intermediaries, the demand and savings deposits of trust and mortgage loan companies, about 1.6%, and the deposits of credit unions and caisses populaires, about 2.0% – or roughly 6% in total.[39] Quite obviously one of the most mistaken presumptions of recent years has been that the major reason for the relative decline in the size of the chartered banks has been the activity of their near competitors and the effect on them of legislative restraints.

---

38. This they did in the later 1950s with astonishing speed and success. Whereas the chartered banks provided only 15% of total consumer credit in 1956 and the sales finance companies 26%, only eight years later the banks were providing 30% and the sales finance companies 17%. See also E. P. Neufeld, "The Economic Significance of Consumer Credit," in J. S. Ziegel and R. E. Olley, eds., *Consumer Credit in Canada*, Proceedings of a Conference on Consumer Credit, published by the University of Saskatchewan, Saskatoon, 1966.

39. We assume that, in the absence of legislation abolishing the chartered bank note issue, the banks would have retained their historical share of about 85% of the market for bank notes. For statistics of bank note circulation and deposits see Bank of Canada, *Statistical Summary*, Annual Supplements.

FOREIGN BUSINESS OF THE CHARTERED BANKS

The growth of the chartered banks depends not only on their competitive success in the domestic environment but also on their success in exploiting opportunities abroad. In one respect the chartered banks have always done some foreign business, for they have been the important principals in the foreign exchange business in Canada from the beginning of their existence. Furthermore, they have since the beginning of their operations been the principal source of funds for financing exports and imports. But in addition to this kind of foreign business, the banks over the years have operated abroad in a more direct way. They have utilized foreign capital markets (New York and London) for investing their liquid reserve funds; they have established banking operations abroad in the sense of competing for deposits, making loans and providing other financial services to local customers. This they have done both through establishing branches and subsidiary companies abroad and through agents acting directly on behalf of head office.

The Bank of Montreal opened an agency in New York in 1855, the first foreign agency of a Canadian bank.[40] By 1870 there was only one other Canadian bank with a New York agency – the Bank of British North America (absorbed by the Bank of Montreal in 1918) – but the remarkable opportunities for profitable operations there had begun to be realized. An observer, writing in 1870, described the New York business of these two banks:

> ...The manner in which agencies of Canadian banks came to be established in New York was obviously, in the first instance, to transact the large volume of business between Canada and the States. All Canadian banks have a correspondent in New York on whom they draw, and to whom they remit; and some of them in addition have a broker there, who acts for them in buying and selling exchange and converting American currency into gold. Any bank whose business is large will naturally consider whether they can do the business more economically by establishing an agency for themselves; and the Bank of Montreal and the Bank of British North America both answered this question in the affirmative and have had agencies there for some years.
>
> But once in New York and subjected to the enormous expense which New York business entails, a Canadian bank is naturally led to inquire why they should confine themselves to the business which arises between Canada and New York. Why not take part in the enormous volume of business between New York and Europe, or New York and China, or New York and the interior of the

40. See A. B. Jamieson, *op. cit.*, p. 10.

> States?...The most extensive and important, and also the most steady [business] is the buying and selling of bills on England. The exports of New York all give rise to bills on Liverpool, London, or Glasgow, or perhaps on Paris, which are offered to those in the trade, from day to day. It is a singular fact that the banks of New York do very little of this business, the greater part of it being carried on by a few private firms of vast capital [e.g., Brown Brothers, and Rothschilds], having connections in England, and by the agencies of the two Canadian banks before named.
> ...This...is legitimate banking business, and if managed prudently, ought to yield a steady line of profit.... Connected with this, however, is a facility for entering into transactions of a more speculative character, which are exceedingly tempting to a bold financier. A bank which has undoubted credit in England can use that credit in the way of selling large amounts of bills for gold. This selling may be purely speculative...or it may be that gold is required for use. There are times when gold is very much in request for payment of customs dues (which are payable in gold)....[A] banker who has gold to lend has often the chance of placing it out on the most perfect security, and it is now an established custom to carry on operations in this manner. Gold is lent for a day at a time, at a rate varying according to the demand, from one sixty-fourth of one per cent, to one-half of one per cent, and even higher.... Now the first of these rates amounts to only 6 per cent per annum, but the other amounts to 180%....[The] money deposited as security, and under the banker's control, can also be lent from day to day, and, in fact, is on the security of government bonds, first class railway bonds and such like – the transactions adding again to the banker's profit....
> The other operations of Canadian banks in New York are similar to those they are engaged in here. They grant credits available in China and the West Indies for tea and sugar purchases. They also receive current money on deposit, and lend it in the way previously spoken of, such loans of course involving no speculation in gold; but still subject, if based on stocks, to the action of those that do....[41]

So attractive was this business that by 1874 the Canadian Bank of Commerce and the Merchants' Bank of Canada (absorbed by the Bank of Montreal in 1922) had also established agencies in New York. It was also in the early 1870s that a judicial decision in New York State confirmed that business transacted by agents of foreign banks was not subject to the taxes imposed on domestic banking business – an exemption stemming from an act of 1851.[42] Right up to the present, Canadian banks operating in New York have done so through agents acting for the Canadian head offices of the banks. In

41. See *Monetary Times*, Nov. 4, 1870, or as reprinted in E. P. Neufeld, *Money and Banking in Canada*, pp. 163-6.
42. See E. P. Neufeld, *op. cit.*, pp. 168-79.

other important foreign centres—London, Paris, Chicago and San Francisco—the banks operated through branches.

But it was in the West Indies and in South and Central America that the Canadian banks, at least some of them, experimented with establishing systems of branches abroad. This first arose from the close trade ties that had developed between the port city of Halifax and the West Indies. The entrepôt trade of Halifax, involving U.S. trade as well as trade with the British North American colonies, was important even in the early 1800s. In 1837 the Colonial Bank, a bank operating in Jamaica, appointed the Halifax Banking Company as its agent to facilitate financing of this trade, trade in which the Nova Scotian banks were deeply involved. In 1889 the Bank of Nova Scotia, after repeated urging, was induced to open a branch in Jamaica; and in 1899 the Merchants' Bank of Halifax (later the Royal Bank of Canada) established its first of many branches in Cuba, at Havana. The Canadian Bank of Commerce established a branch at Kingston, Jamaica, and Havana, Cuba, in 1920, and the Bank of Montreal established several branches in Mexico.

In 1907 the chartered banks had 40 branches abroad (excluding 5 in Newfoundland); in 1918 the number was 102; and by 1925, a peak of 175 branches had been established. In 1963 the banks had only 149 branches abroad. Then began a new period of branch expansion, with 189 branches in 1968. The location of these foreign branches at the end of 1927 and again at the end of 1968 is shown in Table 4:12 below.

The activity of the banks in establishing foreign branches suggests that little new was accomplished from the mid 1920s until the early 1960s. Table 4:10, column 6 shows that the build-up of foreign deposits as a source of funds, relative to Canadian sources of funds, also reached its peak in the 1920s—until the sudden growth of the 1960s; and Table 4:8, column 10 shows that the same pattern occurred in the banks' foreign loan business. The most recent growth in the banks' foreign business has centred on their accumulation of U.S. dollar deposits. At the end of 1966 the banks' foreign deposit liabilities amounted to $11,630 million. Of this total, $7,677 million, or 66%, was accounted for by U.S. dollar deposit liabilities standing on the books of the banks' head offices and branches in Canada.[43] But branch banking abroad has expanded, too, with an increase of 40 branches from 1963 to 1968. This increase occurred mainly in Trinidad and

---

43. See Bank of Canada, *Statistical Summary*. For a detailed description of current chartered banking operations in Canada and abroad see J. A. Galbraith, *Canadian Banking* (Toronto: Ryerson Press, 1970).

Table 4:12 Location of Foreign Branches of Canadian Chartered Banks 1927 and 1968

	THE BANK OF MONTREAL		THE ROYAL BANK OF CANADA		THE BANK OF NOVA SCOTIA		THE TORONTO-DOMINION BANK		CANADIAN IMPERIAL BANK OF COMMERCE		BANQUE CANADIENNE NATIONALE		TOTAL	
	1927	1968	1927	1968	1927	1968	1927	1968	1927	1968	1927	1968	1927	1968
Britain	2	2	1	2	1	4	1	2	1	2	—	—	6	12
United States	3	1	1	1	3	2	1	1	4	11	—	—	12	16
France	1	—	1	1	—	—	—	—	—	—	1	1	3	2
Germany	—	6	—	—	—	—	—	—	—	—	—	—	—	6
Bahamas	—	—	—	6	—	6	—	—	—	3	—	—	—	15
Cuba	—	—	55	—	8	—	—	—	1	—	—	—	64	—
Guyana	—	—	—	6	—	1	—	—	—	—	—	—	—	7
Mexico	7	—	—	—	—	—	—	—	1	—	—	—	8	—
South and Central America	—	—	25	20	—	1	—	—	1	—	—	—	26	21
Dominican Republic	—	—	6	12	3	4	—	—	—	—	—	—	9	16
U.S. Virgin Islands	—	—	—	—	—	5	—	—	—	—	—	-	—	5
Puerto Rico	—	—	3	6	2	4	—	—	—	—	—	—	5	10
Trinidad and Tobago	—	—	—	12	—	10	—	—	1	5	—	—	1	27
Jamaica (and Cayman Is.)	—	—	—	12	11	1	—	—	1	9	—	—	12	22
Other West Indies	—	—	12	13	—	7	—	—	1	4	—	—	13	24
Other	—	—	7	1	—	5	—	—	1	—	—	—	8	6
TOTAL	13	9	111	92	28	50	2	3	12	34	1	1	167	189

SOURCE: Dominion Bureau of Statistics, *Canada Year Book*, Queen's Printer, Ottawa.

Tobago, Jamaica and other Caribbean countries, but there were also new branches in California, the United Kingdom and Germany. Earlier the banks had disposed of all their branches in Cuba following the Castro revolution there.

In retrospect it seems unfortunate that the banks were unable for many years to maintain the momentum of the development of their foreign business that had existed up to the mid 1920s. Their surprisingly strategic position in the New York market prior to the turn of the century, had the banks been able to sustain it, could conceivably in the course of time have led to their foreign business being as large as or even larger than their domestic business. Also the Canadian banks' relative inability to adjust to the difficult financial and political environment of South America has meant that indigenous banks have grown up to fill the need there for basic banking facilities. One senses that the Canadian banks over the last forty years have missed important opportunities for rapid development of their foreign banking operations, opportunities open to them because of the venturesomeness of bank officers prior to that period.

RECENT DEVELOPMENTS

Earlier we expressed the opinion that the entrepreneurial spirit of the banks seems to have dimmed in the period after the First World War. However, some evidence of a new aggressiveness began to appear in the late 1950s and in the 1960s. So it is worthwhile to examine the experience of the banks after the Second World War in a more direct way than we have done up to this point.

The relative growth experience of the banks in this period may briefly be recalled. In 1945 the Canadian assets of the banks accounted for 48% of total financial intermediary assets, while by 1968 the figure was 29%; and as a proportion of G.N.P. those assets amounted to 55% in 1945 and 40% in 1970. While this, at first glance, may appear to be a serious deterioration in the banks' relative position, we have seen that most of it represented a reversion to the position the banks occupied prior to the transitory effects of the 1930s depression and war finance that followed it. In the 1960s the banks' assets as a proportion of G.N.P. were running only about 6 percentage points below the level of the 1920s, of which about 3 or 4 percentage points was accounted for by their loss of the note issue. What is left, then, is not a serious deterioration in their growth relative to G.N.P. but rather the suggestion that unless the banks innovate in the area of the savings instruments they supply to the public and in their lending activities they will not be able to grow faster than G.N.P. in future; indeed, they might continue to grow less quickly than G.N.P. as a consequence of the impact on them of innovation by other financial intermediaries. It is within this context that certain recent developments must be seen.

Perhaps the first important postwar change in the activity of the banks came in 1954. The Bank Act of that year permitted the chartered banks to enter the National Housing Act mortgage business, which they did in a remarkably competitive way – until the rates rose above the 6% interest ceiling. The same act permitted the banks to take chattel mortgages as security for loans but not until 1958 did the banks enter aggressively into the consumer instalment credit business. The Canadian Bank of Commerce had first entered this field in 1936, but not until the Bank of Nova Scotia followed in 1958 was a competitive environment created that induced the rest of the banks to follow. The results were dramatic. Whereas in 1952 the banks had supplied about 15% of the consumer credit in Canada, in 1970 they were supplying about 41% of it.[44] In that period the sales finance companies lost their position of dominance in the consumer credit business.

The next major move taken by the banks was the one of bidding for large sums of short-term funds through the introduction of term notes of various kinds. The banks for many years had used the deposit receipt as an instrument for attracting large deposits. These were short-term (usually less than one year to maturity), non-transferable, available only in large denominations and redeemable before maturity. The rate on them was set by the Canadian Bankers' Association, as were all savings deposit rates. But competition for short-term funds from the finance companies, trust companies and corporations issuing commercial paper began to intensify in the 1950s and this competition made the banks' efforts in the short-term market appear very inadequate. In 1960 the Bank of Nova Scotia broke new ground. It introduced transferable term notes of a maturity up to six years and sold them on request either directly or through dealers on commission. Rates reflected changing market rates, and so were not in any way determined by the Canadian Bankers' Association. After that, development came swiftly. The other banks entered the short-term market with a variety of instruments. There are available now the old deposit receipts referred to earlier; there are similar deposit receipts payable in U.S. dollars and the banks have become very active in the "swap" deposit business; there

---

44. See Bank of Canada, *Statistical Summary*, for statistics of consumer credit.

are negotiable, transferable certificates of deposits (i.e. term notes) of one to five years, redeemable only at maturity with interest payable twice yearly by cheque, and usually with a minimum denomination of $10,000; there are non-transferable certificates of deposit with a minimum denomination of $100,000, sold in maturities to fit the requirements of the purchaser, at a rate negotiated with the individual buyer; and there are transferable bearer deposit or discount notes of up to one year to maturity sold at a discount in denominations of $100,000 and not redeemable until maturity. In 1967 the Toronto-Dominion Bank became the first bank to issue debentures, following the changes in the Bank Act of that year that permitted the move.

Most of these moves were designed to make the banks more competitive in the market for large amounts of short-term funds. Other moves were intended to increase the appeal of the banks' facilities to smaller savers—an area where nothing important had happened since the banks began to open savings departments a century ago. Personal chequing accounts were introduced and these were more suitable than either current accounts or savings accounts for the ordinary household; savings certificates in denominations as small as $10 appeared, redeemable at any time with interest included in the redemption value, and not payable in coupons or by cheque; planned savings programs, involving periodic payments, were devised and they included life insurance features; non-chequable savings deposits were offered on which the rate of interest exceeded that on the normal savings account. Savings rates in general became more flexible. As a result of these developments, the banks as a group suddenly had put themselves in a much stronger position in competing for funds. More flexible banking hours also appeared in the 1960s.

In 1962 the banks introduced the bankers' acceptance into the Canadian money market. It is a kind of promissory note (issued usually by a corporation) that is guaranteed or "accepted" by a chartered bank and sold through money market dealers at a discount. Its appeal is that it enables the banks to accommodate their customers even when they are fully loaned up. The banks charge an acceptance fee of ½% per annum or more for taking on the liability involved. The amount outstanding has at times exceeded $200 million but a large proportion of these were held by money market dealers, financed with day-to-day loans obtained from the chartered banks. Until a broader demand for them can be developed, they are unlikely to be an important instrument to the banks.

There have been several other interesting developments in the Canadian banking system. The banks have become quite aggressive in term lending, that is, in making large loans with medium and long terms to maturity to individual borrowers. This has been accompanied by the development of specialized departments (e.g., mining departments) to deal with particular industries in which such loans are made.[45] In this way the banks have resumed a type of activity that around the turn of the century was represented by their holdings of corporation securities.

Through subsidiary companies or through some equity participation in other companies, or even simply by arrangement with other companies the banks have widened the range of their activities. Several of the banks, through interlocking directorships or equity participation, had for many years been associated with trust companies; and in the postwar period all the other large banks followed. So while the banks did not themselves enjoy fiduciary powers, they did put themselves into a position where they would individually have an incentive to provide assistance in trust matters to customers by directing such customers to particular trust companies.

In 1961 the banks co-operated to acquire the charter of the Export Finance Corporation, a company formed in 1959 to finance export trade but which had not become active. However, it ceased operations in 1969. There had been discussion of the adequacy of credit available to finance exports and it is conceivable that the banks acted in response to that discussion when they decided to acquire the Corporation. The Corporation had an issued capital of $10 million, was located only in Toronto, and had a very small staff. Its business was to raise short- and medium-term funds in the international money markets and to use those funds to discount export paper endorsed with full recourse by a chartered bank and/or guaranteed by the Export Credits Insurance Corporation of the federal government. In somewhat the same way as bankers' acceptances, this procedure was to enable the banks to accommodate customers even when funds for lending were scarce. Since the Corporation's assets amounted to only $91 million in 1967 (although in 1966 the figure was $180 million) it was never apparent that it was serving a very useful purpose; and when borrowing rates in international markets rose sharply even its profit position became precarious. So it was phased out of existence beginning in 1969. The banks themselves are continuing to satisfy most of the demand for export credit as they have done for a century and a half, although the federal government's Export Development Corporation is active as well (see below, p. 436).

We have already noted that the banks became increasingly aggres-

---

45. See *Financial Post*, Oct. 28, 1967, p. 4.

sive in their foreign banking business in the 1960s, both in bidding for U.S. dollar deposits abroad and relending them in the international money markets and in establishing new branches. Just how important this has been can be seen by the fact that in 1960 their foreign assets amounted to 19% of their Canadian assets while by the end of 1970 this had increased to 41% – a truly significant development.

The banks had always been forbidden to engage in conventional mortgage lending, but through associating themselves with other companies this had begun to change even before the Bank Act of 1967 permitted them to engage directly in such lending. Kinross Mortgage Corporation was established in 1963 by the Canadian Imperial Bank of Commerce to make mortgage loans, and it has retained an equity interest in that company; the Toronto-Dominion Bank acquired an equity interest in the Canada Permanent Mortgage Corporation; and the Bank of Nova Scotia has an interest in Holborough Investments Limited, which owns the majority of stock in Mortgage Insurance Co. of Canada, a company established in 1964 to insure residential mortgages made by institutional lenders and Central Covenants Ltd.[46] Roymor Ltd. was formed in 1968 by the Royal Bank of Canada and Roy Lea Ltd. in 1969. Their principal business is to purchase first mortgages, mainly residential, from the bank.

The banks have also become interested in companies that provide development capital to new ventures. In 1962 the Royal Bank of Canada, Banque Canadienne Nationale, and several trust companies formed Roynat Ltd., with a capital of $10 million, for the purpose of extending term loans to new and growing companies; the Toronto-Dominion Bank and the Canada Permanent Mortgage Corporation acquired a controlling interest in UNAS Investments Ltd. in 1963, which is a company that provides term loan and equity or venture capital to new companies and to existing ones that appear to have growth potential; the Canadian Imperial Bank of Commerce acquired an interest in Triarch Corporation in 1963, which provides equity and interim mortgage financing, and management services; and the Bank of Montreal and the Toronto-Dominion co-operated with eighteen other financial institutions to form the Canadian Enterprise and Development Corporation in 1962 to provide equity financing and management advice to new companies.

Rather interesting are the steps several of the banks have taken to become more closely associated with the mutual fund business. The Canadian Imperial Bank of Commerce acquired an equity interest in

---

46. See *Financial Post*, March 18, 1967, p. 19.

the Investors Group of which Investors Mutual of Canada is a part; the Toronto-Dominion Bank acquired such an interest in Corporate Investors (Marketing) Ltd. and shares in the Corporate Investors mutual fund are being sold in some of its branches; Royfund Limited, a new mutual fund, was formed in 1967, and its shares are being offered through the branches of the Royal Bank of Canada. Banque Canadienne Nationale in partnership with Trust General du Canada and others introduced a new mutual fund, Canagex Fund, in 1969 which the bank sells through some of its branches.

The banks also introduced credit cards in the late 1960s, the most conspicuous one being Chargex, which is sponsored by a group of them. Such cards enable holders to buy goods and services up to a limit on credit from participating merchants, usually without interest cost for about the first month. The merchant pays a charge based on the value of sales so effected. While the scheme was seen as a further development of the banks' consumer credit facilities, its major long-term significance may be that it makes available the advantages of computerized accounting to ordinary households. Since such credit cards are likely to be essentially a substitute for bank notes (which are all issued by the Bank of Canada) and not significantly for banks deposits, they are not likely to affect unfavourably the chartered banks' sources of funds. Should the banks find ways of inducing the major oil companies and chain grocery stores to use their credit card system, many individuals would be able to have a significant proportion of their total purchases recorded in an exceedingly efficient way.

This trend toward increased diversification of the activities of the banks was further encouraged by the 1967 Bank Act. It, in effect, relieved the banks of the interest rate ceiling on bank loans beginning in 1968; it permitted the banks to issue debentures with a maturity of five years or more up to an eventual amount (spread over ten years) equal to a bank's paid-up capital and rest account; it permitted them to engage freely in conventional mortgage lending (up to 75% of the value of the property involved), excepting only that there is a limit on the rate of accumulation of conventional residential mortgages; and it replaced the 8% ratio of cash to Canadian deposit liabilities with a 12% cash-to-demand-deposit ratio and a 4% cash-to-savings-deposit ratio – which in effect reduced the over-all ratio to about 6½% and so reduced the proportion of assets on which the banks receive no interest income. If the banks take full advantage of these changes, they cannot fail to improve their competitive position, particularly in relation to the trust companies, mortgage loan companies, sales finance companies, credit unions and caisses populaires, small loan companies and money lenders.

The act also required the banks to reduce their holdings of voting stock in trust and loan companies accepting deposits to 10% of the total stock of such companies by July 1, 1971; and it forbade interlocking directorships with such companies. But now that the banks can freely engage in mortgage lending, and can sell debentures, and have begun to compete actively for large and small deposits, it is difficult to see how such restrictions could inhibit their growth. About the only power of importance denied to them is that of engaging directly in fiduciary or trust business. It may be noted that the Bank of Montreal acquired about 10% of Royal Trust Co. shares in 1968. Previously it had had no equity interest in that company, although closely associated with it.

It must also be noted that the 1960s saw greater interest in the formation of new banks than at any time since about the turn of the century. Two received charters – the Bank of British Columbia and the Bank of Western Canada – although only the first one began operations. Other similar ventures have been discussed in public. Appeal to the sentiment of regionalism has featured these newly proposed ventures as well as the successful launching of the Bank of British Columbia, an aspect of which appeal has been the argument that the established chartered banks have not adequately served those regions. The response of the established chartered banks seems to have been to decentralize authority to the regions more than used to be the case and to increase the authority of branch managers generally.

There was also one instance of a non-bank institution becoming part of the chartered banking system. On November 10, 1969, La Banque d'Économie de Québec, one of the two Quebec savings banks in operation, began operations as a chartered bank under the new name of La Banque Populaire, having been granted the necessary charter earlier. However, in 1970 La Banque Populaire merged with La Banque Provinciale du Canada, effective August 3. It is not at all inconceivable that the newly found competitive strength of the chartered banks will encourage other institutions such as trust companies and small loan companies to seek bank charters or to be absorbed by existing chartered banks.

When one considers that the long-term trend has been toward relatively few banks with extensive branch systems, and that the density of branches has been quite stable for many years, not to mention the recent broadening of the activities of existing banks and their willingness to innovate, it is difficult to believe that a significant capital market gap exists that must be filled by new institutions. The more likely development is that of existing non-bank institutions transforming themselves into banks – a development that might well enhance competition and so should be encouraged by the federal government.

There are really two general points that might be made about these postwar developments in the Canadian banking system. First, by finally taking seriously the winds of competition that had begun to develop, by diversifying their activities on their own initiative, and by obtaining exceedingly important changes in the Bank Act, the banks appear to have put themselves in a potentially strong competitive position. Second, many of these postwar developments have begun to transform the local branch into a centre of diversified retail financial services for the man of ordinary means – particularly those relating to consumer credit business, savings plans, savings instruments, and mutual fund facilities. It is entirely sensible, on economic grounds, that the overhead of the branch system should be spread in this way, although it will be exceedingly important for government policy to ensure that competition among the banks is maintained. In future even more financial services – such as more adequate facilities for purchasing securities, for obtaining advice on investments and estate planning and perhaps even for acquiring insurance protection and credit card accounting services – may be developed in the branches in a way that will reduce the cost of those services to the average person. In short, the banks have never developed fully the remarkable potential inherent in their widespread systems of branches. This remains an important challenge for the present generation of bank executives.

Conclusions

This has already been a long discourse. But we would not have achieved our principal objective if we did not now stand back, view the whole history of the banks' development and experiences and the forces behind them, and attempt to provide a comprehensive explanation of their interesting pattern of growth and change in relative size.

First of all, when contemporary legislative restraints on the banks are examined within their institutional context, it is difficult to see how they could have been responsible for the decline in the relative size of the banks up to the 1930s. After that, loss of the note circulation had a small effect on them. But the interest rate ceiling was probably not felt until 1955, by which time most of the relative decline had occurred, and the cash ratio also imposed no restrictions on them, at least not until some time after 1954.

There is, then, the very important question of why chartered bank assets grew much more quickly than G.N.P. until 1910 and, generally speaking, not thereafter. The chartered banks have been the principal suppliers of Canada's media of exchange since they began to issue notes in the 1820s. They enjoyed a legal monopoly of the note issue for some years prior to 1866, and, as we have seen, an effective one until 1934; and ever since the 1850s, when bank deposits seem to have begun to be used increasingly as media of exchange, they have been in a strategic position to supply that form of money. Therefore, any change in the nation's demand for media of exchange is likely to affect the growth rate of the chartered banks.

We saw earlier that until about 1910 bank deposits, particularly savings deposits, grew much faster than G.N.P., but not thereafter. Other data show that money supply (total Canadian bank deposits, notes and coin) did so as well. However, money supply as a proportion of G.N.P. was a little lower in the 1960s than in the 1910-30 period (perhaps four percentage points lower), and the bank asset ratio was running about six or seven percentage points lower—of which about three or four percentage points is explained by the banks' loss of their note circulation. So from 1910 to 1968, taken as a whole, bank assets did not grow more quickly than did G.N.P. and this was probably because the demand for money (as we have defined money) did not increase faster than did G.N.P.[47]

But what caused the pronounced increase in the demand for money and therefore the rapid growth of bank assets up to 1910? Trends after 1910 cast doubt on the proposition that it is explained by rising income and wealth. A more plausible explanation may be found in financial innovation and changes in the financial structure of the nation. It seems that it was in the 1850s that the chartered banks' deposits began to increase faster than their note circulation, which may therefore mark the beginning of increasing acceptance of bank deposits as media of exchange; and it was in the late 1860s that the banks began explicitly to develop their savings deposit business. In 1870, therefore, the bank deposit, both as medium of exchange and

---

47. This conclusion is not altered if we include non-bank deposits in money supply. We estimate that if the deposits of the Quebec savings banks, mortgage loan companies, trust companies, credit unions and caisses populaires, and government institutions are added to our definition of money supply, the money-supply-to-G.N.P. ratio in 1910 was about 49% and in 1965 about 47%.

asset to hold, may in important respects still have been a relatively "unabsorbed" financial innovation. Then came the rapid increase in the density of the banking system through the expansion of branches. This provided the means by which the innovation of the bank deposit was made available to the general public.

But it could not be done quickly. We have seen this in the data on the density of bank branches. In spite of the limitations of the statistics, it can be said with a certain confidence that it was in the period up to 1910 that the banking system expanded so as to approximate its long-term "normal" ratio of population to branches, the same period during which the money supply to G.N.P. ratio and the bank assets to G.N.P. ratio approximately reached their long-term plateau levels. That is, it took branch banking many decades to be developed so as to enable the economy to absorb the financial innovation of the bank deposit, and until it was absorbed the asset-holding of the population was in a state of long-term disequilibrium. Also, until it was absorbed, money supply and total bank assets grew faster than did G.N.P. while after that they did not.

The development of the bank chequing and savings deposits and their increasing accessibility through branch banking probably increased the nation's demand for indirect financial claims relative to direct claims and real property, that is, it increased the relative attractiveness of indirect financing; it probably reduced the relative attractiveness of barter transactions; and it probably replaced less efficient forms of media of exchange. The first two of these influences, for which we have no Canadian quantitative evidence, would have the effect of increasing the demand for money in general (at least if we use the broad definition) and the third would have the effect of increasing the demand for those financial claims that we have defined as money and reducing it for those that are not included in that definition. One striking example of the latter influence at work is the virtual disappearance of the local, non-note-issuing private banker in the period up to the end of the First World War and the decline of the Post Office Savings Bank. We estimate that there were approximately two hundred such local bankers, many of them taking deposits, at a time when there were fewer than five hundred bank branches. By the early 1920s most of them had disappeared, being replaced by bank branches.

It is interesting that the ratio of chartered bank notes to G.N.P., contrary to chartered bank demand and savings deposits, did not increase in the period 1870-1910. This, however, is not surprising since notes were by no means a new instrument in 1870, and their use in contrast to the bank deposit did not depend so much on the density of branches. The greatest thrust of the banks' growth was the growth of their savings deposits. In the 1873-75 period they accounted for 17½% of total chartered bank liabilities, while in the 1896-1900 period the figure was 46½%—after which the ratio changed little. The decision to cultivate the savings deposit was one of the most important ones the banks ever made. Demand deposits grew less quickly up to 1910 than total liabilities, as did chartered bank notes. It should also be noted that the absence of legal restrictions on the size of bank deposit liabilities to bank equity permitted the "leverage" in the banks' capital structure to rise freely, and so adjust quickly to reduced risks of banking brought about by the development of branch banking, improved internal controls and procedures, government inspection and central banking.

There seem not to have been major innovations on the lending side of the banks' operations up to 1910, only the minor ones of engaging in railroad financing through purchasing railroad securities, and increasing their call loan business with the growth of the securities markets. After 1910, and as a consequence of First World War financing, the banks permanently increased their holdings of government securities. But further new changes in their asset structure (ignoring the effects of Second World War financing) did not really occur until the 1950s.

In general, then, the apparent increase in the relative demand for money up to 1910 may possibly be explained by the replacement of inferior (and unrecorded) media of exchange for superior (and recorded) ones in the form of bank deposits; by a relative shift to indirect financing from direct financing because of the increasing availability of a superior indirect financial claim, the bank deposit; and by a relative decline in barter transactions—all of which was made possible by the increasing density of the system of bank branches, the physical means through which the innovations of the chequing and savings bank deposits were finally absorbed by the economy. Until they were absorbed the banks could grow faster than G.N.P., but in the absence of further innovation they could not do so thereafter.

That is, by about 1910 the position of the banks changed fundamentally. The density of their branches had reached its long-term "normal" level, and their savings deposit business had reached maturity in the sense that it no longer grew faster than G.N.P. The slow growth rate of the banks in real terms from just after the turn of the century until the mid 1920s reflected a slow G.N.P. growth rate and the fact that bank asset growth had become locked in with it. Later, when G.N.P. growth rate picked up, so did the growth rate of the chartered banks. But as a proportion of G.N.P. the banks' Canadian assets were no larger (indeed, they were smaller) in 1970 than in 1910.

Until about 1925 there was some indication that the banks would be able to offset their slow Canadian asset growth rate with a faster foreign asset growth rate. Foreign banking business was rapidly developed by a few of the banks, but by the mid 1920s the momentum of that development had disappeared. Not until the late 1950s and early 1960s was it recovered.

For a time this rather ordinary growth experience after about 1910 (or 1906) was hidden by the impact that the 1930s depression had on the banks' competitors, and from 1939 to 1945 by war finance—both transitory factors.

In retrospect, it would seem that the major reasons why the Canadian chartered banks have not grown faster than they in fact have done are the following: they did not attempt to develop liability instruments involving contractual or regular payments by savers, or ones with insurance or pension attributes (thereby losing out to the pension and insurance institutions); they did not develop debenture-like instruments, and did not urge the government (until 1962) to permit them to go into the mortgage loan business (thereby being unable to compete effectively with the mortgage loan and trust companies); they did not persevere with corporate security type of lending after their initial unfortunate experiences; they did not, as a group, enter the rapidly growing personal instalment credit business until long after the finance companies had done so; and they did not maintain the pace of their earlier foreign banking developments for many years after the mid 1920s. Only a very small portion of their relative decline can be explained by the drift of deposit business to other institutions. Their conservative attitude as to what constituted "proper" bank lending was particularly important after about 1910 when they edged persistently toward more liquid assets and when there were extended periods when such assets formed a disproportionately large share of their assets. The entrepreneurial spirit among bankers seems to have dimmed in the period after the First World War.

In the 1950s and the 1960s this began to change. Both new bank liability instruments and new bank assets have appeared, as have new branch services. We have seen that after 1960 Canadian bank assets no longer declined noticeably in relation to G.N.P. or to total financial intermediary assets. If foreign assets are included, bank assets have gained in relative size. If the banks maintain their recent momentum in innovation at home and abroad and utilize fully their newly acquired freedom from statutory restrictions, they should not find it difficult to exceed their growth rate of the past two decades, and reduce that of their near competitors. In this way they may permanently arrest the decline in their relative size that has been such a prominent feature of the capital market over the past century.

5

Savings Banks

The history of savings banks in Canada is interesting, not because these banks have been important, but rather because they have always been relatively unimportant. Yet savings banks have existed in Canada before all other financial intermediaries except the commercial banks and the fire insurance companies. A Montreal savings bank appeared in 1819 and in 1825 New Brunswick introduced legislation to protect savings banks already established and to encourage the establishment of further banks. Until the Province of Canada legislation of 1855[1] the development of savings banks in British North America and the legislation relating to their operations were essentially along the lines of the British trustee savings banks. After that the successful private savings banks – primarily two Quebec savings banks – were soon managed along lines of commercially oriented corporate institutions, apart from the penny savings banks which appeared in the early 1880s. But it was the Post Office Savings Bank, newly formed after Confederation, and the Dominion Government's Savings Bank, inherited from the Maritime provinces at the time of Confederation, that witnessed the most striking developments from Confederation to the turn of the century. In the 1920s several provinces began to establish savings banks without spectacular success. But the early tradition of the trustee savings banks and the government savings banks has most actively been perpetuated by the introduction of the Canada Savings Bonds in 1946, and provincial savings bonds in 1960 and after. The volume of these bonds has now become significant while privately operated savings banks have never been quantitatively important in Canada as a whole, although not unimportant in Quebec.

1. 18 Vic., cap. 96.

Trustee Savings Banks in Canada

Canada inherited the concept of trustee savings banks from the United Kingdom. It was in 1810 that the Ruthwell Savings Bank of Dumfriesshire, Scotland, was established – probably the first regular and carefully organized trustee savings bank in Great Britain.[2] Significantly, it was founded by the Reverend Henry Duncan, for the trustee savings bank system was immediately associated with attempts to improve the position of the poor by encouraging thrift among them. The Edinburgh Savings Bank, formed in 1813 and widely imitated because of its more simplified methods of procedure, was originally called the "Society for the Suppression of Beggars." In 1814 and 1815 such local trustee savings banks were established all over Scotland, and about a dozen in England. Development in England was somewhat slower but by 1817 there were about eighty.[3] The total number in Great Britain exceeded 500 by 1837, reached a peak of 645 in 1861 and has declined steadily since then, with less than 100 in 1960.

Even taking into account the smaller population in Canada, trustee savings banks have never flourished here in the way they did in Great Britain. However, it was the Savings Bank Act relating to English savings banks, sponsored by the Rt. Hon. George Rose and passed by the imperial Parliament in 1817, that strongly influenced Canadian legislative action in the field of savings banks.

The establishment of the Savings Bank of Montreal in 1819, therefore, came remarkably soon after the appearance of such institutions in Great Britain. It was followed about two years later by a Quebec savings bank. Both were in the British tradition of trustee savings banks, and a contemporary almanac even listed them under "charitable institutions."[4] A similar bank, the Home District Savings Bank, was established in Toronto in 1830, some of the records of which still exist. The prospectus of that bank illustrates both the essential character of these early trustee savings banks and their general mode of operation. It reads as follows:

> Home District Savings Bank For the Earnings of Journeymen, Tradesmen, Mechanics, Servants, Labourers, &c. Will Be Open Every Saturday At The Office Of The Treasurer Of The District, Between 11 & 1 o'clock To Commence On Saturday, 5th June 1830.

---

2. See H. Oliver Horne, *A History of Savings Banks* (London: Oxford University Press, 1947), p. 40.
3. *Ibid.*, p. 59.
4. *The Montreal Almanack of Lower Canada Register for 1830*, printed by Robert Armour, 1829.

The object of this Institution, which has been brought forward at the suggestion of His Excellency the Lieutenant Governor, is to receive such small Sums as may be saved by the above description of persons, and to manage the same for the benefit of the Depositors, and thus enable the industrious and frugal, by commencing early in life, with saving only a few shillings weekly, to make a provision for times of need.

General Outline

No sums less than One Shilling and Three pence will be received. When the Deposits amount to Twenty Shillings, and Interest at the rate of Five Per Cent per annum, (being the same allowance which has been promised by the Bank of Upper Canada upon Deposits made by this Institution to a limited extent) will be allowed to commence from the next Quarter day.

The said Quarter days will be 1st of January, 1st of April, 1st of July, and 1st of October.

All Deposits which may be withdrawn will only be allowed Interest to the end of the preceding Quarter.

The Deposits will be lodged in the Bank of Upper Canada by the Collecting Managers, the same day as received, there to remain till required by the Depositors, who may demand the same on any subsequent Saturday, during the hours of business.

In case of the death of a Depositor, the sum due to him or her shall be paid to their representatives.

The undersigned persons have volunteered to become Managers of the Institution, two of whom will be Collectors for six months; the change of these two Collecting Managers to take place on the 1st of January and 1st of July in each year, when the accounts of the Depositors are to be balanced, with the accruing Interest added to the same, and the charge of responsibility will then cease with the two retiring collectors, and devolve upon their successors in office.

JOHN H. DUNN
JOSEPH WELLS
W. W. BALDWIN
ALEXANDER WOOD
F. T. BILLINGS
WILLIAM PROUDFOOT
JESSE KETCHUM
GEORGE MUNRO

Prior to the formation of this bank there was passed in New Brunswick (1825) *An Act to encourage the establishment of Banks for Savings in this Province*[5] the preamble of which read:

Whereas certain Provident Institutions or Banks for Savings have been established in this Province for the safe custody and increase of small savings belonging to mechanics, labourers, servants, and others the industrious classes of His Majesty's subjects; and it is expedient to give protection to such Institutions and the funds

5. 6 Geo. IV, cap. 4—passed March 17, 1825.

thereby established, and to afford encouragement to others to form the like Institutions: –

Much of this preamble is identical to the preamble of the Imperial Act of 1817 already referred to, as are its major provisions. The act went on to provide that existing or new societies operating under the act had to file their rules, orders and regulations with the Clerk of Peace for the County, or City and County; that "... no person or persons being Treasurer, Trustee, or Manager of such Institution, or having any control in the management thereof, shall derive any benefit from any deposit made in such Institution, but that the persons depositing money therein shall have sole benefit of such deposits ..."; that assets of the Institution were to be vested in the name of the Trustees and that the Institution could sue or be sued in the name of the "Trustees" without further description; that the Trustees could pay sums of at least £50 into the Provincial Treasury and receive a Provincial Debenture for it yielding 6%, payable on demand but limited in total to £10,000 (raised in 1841 to £20,000, in 1846 to £30,000 and in 1852 to £50,000); and that they could also invest in any other fund or stock, or upon good and valid security within the Province. Institutions depositing funds at interest with the government had to restrict individual deposits to £50 and to the type of depositor mentioned in the preamble, except friendly societies which could deposit £100. The preoccupation with the lower classes, the voluntary but local management, the deposit at attractive interest with the government and the filing of rules of operation with the Clerk of Peace were very much like the provisions of the Imperial Act of 1817 but the option to invest in non-government securities gave the banks greater freedom than did the provisions of that act.

In 1832 the legislature of Lower Canada passed an act[6] with a title identical to the 1825 New Brunswick act and with a preamble and set of provisions almost identical to it. There was, however, no provision for depositing funds at interest with the government and the trustees could invest in chartered bank stock (but not in private banks) and in other public security but not on personal security. This act remained in force for five years and in 1841 the new Province of Canada passed an act[7] with a preamble identical to the 1832 act and with the major provisions remaining virtually unchanged. However, it was provided that upon the vote of three-quarters of the trustees any profits could be paid to any charitable institutions established by law – a provision which was retained in modified form in the legisla-

6. 2 Wm. IV, cap. 59.
7. 4 & 5 Vic., cap. 32.

tion of 1871 and which is still reflected in one item in the balance sheet of Quebec savings banks.[8] The act was to expire in ten years and in 1851 was continued for another five years.[9] But when in 1855 it was extended for an additional seven years this applied only to banks already in existence[10] and the act which provided for the extension also provided for the establishment of new savings banks along lines which represented a basic departure from the concepts of the trustee savings banks. Before discussing the nature of this departure, we must examine the experience of the trustee savings banks and the legacy they left.

That experience was not a happy one, and in this it was similar to the experience of the same type of banks in Great Britain prior to the 1860s. The government of New Brunswick had to make a grant of £1293-10-10 to the St. John's Savings Bank in 1836 so that losses could be covered, and passed an act[11] requiring a meeting of members and prospective members to be called to choose new trustees and managers and to amend their rules of operation. In 1841 that government obtained the authority[12] to appoint two more inspectors to inspect savings banks, but by 1847 it regarded the trustee savings bank system as a failure and repealed all legislation relating to it[13] except as it related to the St. John's Savings Bank. In its place the act introduced a system whereby "tradesmen, mechanics, labourers, servants, and others of the industrious classes" as well as treasurers of Friendly Societies could deposit their savings with any Deputy Treasurer of the County up to £50 at 5% interest with a minimum deposit of 20 shillings. Deposits were to be received from 10 a.m. to 3 p.m. on the first Monday of the month, and payments would be made during those hours on the first Tuesday of the month. The Deputy Treasurer remitted funds received to the Provincial Treasurer. The only significant savings bank in Nova Scotia was a government institution, the Halifax Savings Bank. It was established in 1832, operated in connection with the Receiver General's Office, was open weekdays except Saturdays, from 10 to 3, and on Dec. 31, 1865, had deposits of $825,000 on which it paid 4% interest.[14] A government savings bank, the Sav-

---

8. When the two banks began operations under charter in 1871 the surplus built up by them as trustee savings banks had to be disposed of. That of the City and District Savings Bank was ascertained to be $180,000 and of La Caisse d'Economie de Notre-Dame de Québec $83,000. Both were placed in poor or charity funds administered by the respective banks with interest distributed annually to charity. The items still appear on the balance sheets.
9. 14 & 15 Vic., cap. 55.
10. 18 Vic., cap. 96.
11. 6 Wm. IV, cap. 52.
12. 4 Vic., cap. 30.
13. 10 Vic., cap. 43.
14. *The Year Book and Almanac of Canada 1867* (Montreal: John Lowe & Co.).

ings Bank of Prince Edward Island, only became active shortly before Confederation; its deposits on Dec. 31, 1864, were $4,864 and a year later $18,346.[15] The Newfoundland Savings Bank was also a government institution established in the 1830s with head office at St. John's and assets by the end of 1864 of $647,659. These developments were a distinct departure from the system of trustee savings banks in that they permanently removed local management and introduced government management in its place; but the automatic use of such funds by government was consistent with the imperial statute of 1817 relating to savings banks. Both characteristics anticipated the Post Office Savings Bank established after Confederation.

The most active and ambitious attempts to establish trustee savings banks occurred in Upper and Lower Canada after the passing of the Savings Bank Act[16] of 1841. That was also a crucial period for the trustee savings banks, because it was one in which they had either to make fundamental adjustments in their operations or gradually disappear. The Montreal Provident and Savings Bank was the first to appear in this period, opening for business on October 1, 1841; and until its insolvency in 1848 – to which we must refer again – it was much the largest savings bank in the Province of Canada with assets in that year of over $800,000. The Hamilton and Gore District Savings Bank was established in January 1846, the Montreal City and District Savings Bank in May 1846, the Quebec Provident and Savings Bank in 1847, La Caisse d'Économie de Québec in May 1848, the Northumberland and Durham Savings Bank (of Cobourg) in June 1850, the London Savings Bank's first statement appeared in 1852, and the Toronto Savings Bank in July 1854. After that the establishment of savings banks ceased, no doubt because of the act of 1855 which required new banks to become established along other than trustee lines – with the very large minimum capital sum of $400,000.

Of the eight banks listed above four were in Upper Canada and four in Lower Canada; the trustee savings banks were not, therefore, essentially a product of French Canada. Even the savings banks in Lower Canada had many English names associated with them, and, as we have already seen, such banks had appeared early in the Maritime provinces and had inherited basic characteristics from English legislation. But only two banks survived and both of these were in French Canada. The experience of these individual banks sheds some light on why this should have been so.

The Home District Savings Bank, which, as we have seen, began operations in Toronto in 1830, was absorbed by the Merchants Bank in 1867 or 1868 with assets of over $200,000. The Montreal Provident

15. *Ibid.*
16. 4 & 5 Vic., cap. 32.

and Savings Bank had a quite different experience. It opened on October 1, 1841, suspended payment on July 24, 1848, and in the interval accumulated assets of over $800,000 – a high rate of growth relative to that of the other savings banks.

General consternation over the failure led to the appointment of a three-man royal commission in 1850[17] to inquire into the affairs and management of the bank and this commission presented a remarkably detailed report and voluminous evidence in 1851.[18] The bank had begun its operations in the spirit of its preamble, which spoke of an institution "wherein the industrious tradesmen, mechanic, and others, might deposit their savings for safe keeping and laying out at interest" and not, in the words of the commissioners, as a "rival or competitor with the chartered Institutions of the Province in the business of banking." The Bank of Montreal even agreed to pay 4% on funds deposited by the savings bank with it. But the practice of the savings bank soon changed in several important respects. First of all, it began to take more deposits from individuals than it was permitted by law to do. Originally it had undertaken to limit a single deposit of any individual to £200 and the total amount on deposit of any individual to £500. But Lord Stanley had objected to the savings bank legislation, including the matter of the large size of deposits that could be made, and thoughts of amending the legislation arose.[19] When Mr. B. Holmes, M.P.P., promised the Montreal Provident and Savings Bank that proposed legislation would not be proceeded with if they altered their rules so as to reduce the maximum size of individual deposit accounts, the bank agreed. However, its rule lowering that amount from £500 to £200 was never deposited with the Clerk of Peace, and was soon persistently violated. Not only were individual deposit accounts accepted that exceeded the £200 and even the £500 limit, but the rule was also circumvented by accepting large deposits in the names of various members of the same family. The commissioners concluded, ". . . there cannot, we think, be the smallest doubt that the law limiting the reception of deposits has been habitually violated in the most flagrant manner. . . ."

Another violation discovered was the failure of the "Director for the day" to check the daily deposit with the chartered bank against

---

17. 13 & 14 Vic., cap. 98.
18. "Report of Commissioners of Inquiry into Montreal Provident and Savings Bank 21st June, 1851," *Journal of the Legislative Assembly Province of Canada, 1851,* vol. 10, Appendix QQ, 1851.
19. Letter of Stanley to Bagot, *Journals of the Legislative Assembly Province of Canada,* vol. 3, 1843, pp. 47-8.

the daily receipts, and the practice of directors' leaving signed blank cheques to be completed by the actuary and treasurer, and the teller, which resulted in substantial loans being made out of cash by the teller to the actuary. The implications of this arrangement have been described graphically by the commissioners:

> ... He could and did borrow from them [the tellers] thousands of pounds at a time; retained the money so long as he pleased, and returned it when he pleased,—or, never returned it at all. If all the funds in the Savings Bank were not sufficient for his wants, he had in his possession blank cheques, signed by a Director, ready to be filled up by himself with any amount he chose, to the extent of the credit of the Savings Bank, at the Bank in which it kept its account; he had Directors at hand sufficiently complaisant to sign these cheques at his requisition to any amount, without asking troublesome questions respecting the purposes for which the money was wanted. Nay more;—if all this was not sufficient, he had Bank stock or other securities, which he could pledge at the General Bank for any further amount he might desire. ... [The] securities which the depositors supposed they had against malversation, had no real existence. ...

This led the bank into suffering severe losses on loans made to the actuary. The commissioners wrote "...The conclusion seems inevitable, that the loss sustained through Mr. Eadie is solely attributable to the Directors' neglect to perform the duties imposed on them by law; and that for the consequences of that neglect, they ought to be responsible."

Many loans were made without adequate security, securities were purchased which under the Savings Bank Act were not eligible, and interest on loans in some cases seems not to have been paid into the bank at all. So the commissioners had to make this final judgment:

> ...We have laid before your Excellency the particulars of a number of loans, on which serious losses have accrued to the Bank, and it is perfectly clear that in the majority of cases, if not in every single case adduced, there has been a gross want of precaution, such as we can scarcely consider any private individual, of ordinary prudence and capacity, would have shown in disposing of his own funds.
>
> ...
>
> ...[About] fifteen thousand pounds of the funds of the Bank is thus shown to have been lost to the institution, owing to the negligence or mal-administration of the Directors of the Bank. These losses, with those on railroad stock... and the large sums locked up in loans of a questionable character, sufficiently account for, and were the prime causes of the suspension of the Bank, and of its inability to meet its engagements. ...

Finally, even after the suspension, some of the large depositors seem to have been treated more fairly than the smaller ones, and the directors in many cases accepted the deposit books in payment of accounts which debtors of the bank had bought at a substantial discount from innocent depositors.

There is little doubt that this default inflicted a severe setback on the development of savings banks. But the implications of this bank's experience for the permanent establishment of savings banks was almost certainly misunderstood at the time. The commissioners significantly pointed out that, with greater prudence over loans made, the bank could have survived in spite of the trade depression which had appeared. Why, it may be asked, did this bank grow as quickly as it did from 1842 to 1847? It appears to have done so precisely because it did begin to deviate from the traditional path of trustee savings banks. It took large deposits, it invested in a relatively wide range of public securities and it ventured into the field of personally secured loans. This was the transition that trustee savings banks had to make to survive. But it did not make the alteration in internal management (including cash control and appraisal of credit risks), and in its capital structure, that the nature of business demanded. It also illustrated a basic weakness of trustee savings banks – the casual approach of management motivated, at best, by charitable rather than pecuniary incentives.

The crucial question after this major default was whether the remaining trustee savings banks would stay within the narrow bounds of traditional concepts and be doomed to eventual disappearance or would make the transition in type of business, internal management and capital structure which would make them commercially viable intermediaries. As it turned out, most of them – indeed all but two of them – were not able to adapt themselves to change and eventually did disappear. This failure resulted partly from the inhibiting aspects both of trustee savings bank concepts and also of the legislation under which they had to operate, and from the later appearance, in the form of building societies and the savings departments of commercial banks, of competitors who were not so inhibited.

The history of the Hamilton and Gore District Savings Bank is rather interesting. It began operations at Hamilton in January 1846, in the spirit of trustee savings banks, accepting deposits of from one shilling to £100; and investing such funds, in the spirit of *Canadian* trustee savings banks in bank stocks and public debentures. However, it did not prosper, its assets in 1855 amounting to only £38,159, and was on the verge of closing down in 1856. Then, curiously enough, it was taken over by the Canada Life Assurance Company, who operated it entirely as a proprietors' enterprise. The savings bank transferred securities – bank stocks at market value and municipal debentures at 2% discount for each year to maturity but not exceeding 20% – equivalent in value to the deposits which depositors agreed to transfer to Canada Life, and any new deposits were taken in the name of Canada Life. This was not Canada Life's first venture into the deposit banking business, for it had accepted such funds as early as 1850,[20] but the rising rates of interest accompanying the real estate boom of the early 1850s led it to move somewhat more aggressively into this field. However, Canada Life's experience with the savings bank was short lived. Former trustees of the savings bank had not been held personally responsible for any deficiency in the amount of securities transferred and some of these apparently had been overvalued. Also Canada Life permitted the actuary of the savings bank to continue the business of the bank in his own office after the transfer of the business. The actuary permitted himself to become heavily indebted to the bank and the security which he transferred to the savings bank proved to be insufficient to cover the deficit.[21] The special auditor investigating the affairs of the company hinted strongly that Canada Life should not be in the savings bank business; the savings bank was then offered to the Bank of Montreal, who refused it, whereupon no further accounts were taken.[22] Such was the somewhat inglorious end to this trustee savings bank, and also in fact to the venture of Canadian life insurance companies into the savings deposit business.

The Home District Savings Bank of Toronto, established in 1830, had assets of only about $200,000 when it was absorbed by the Merchants Bank in 1867. By the terms of Confederation the liabilities of the government savings banks[23] of Nova Scotia and New Brunswick were transferred to the Dominion government and under an act[24] of the new Dominion the business of these banks was continued and expanded by a federal government savings bank managed by the Assistant to the Receiver General. Similarly the St. John's Savings Bank, which had been in operation for about forty years, was declared by an act of 1871 to be a federal government savings bank from July 1, 1867, its deposits in 1871 amounting to $751,

---

20. Canada Life Assurance Company, *Minutes*, July 16, 1850.
21. See the report of the auditor in *Report of the Adjourned Annual Meeting Canada Life Assurance Company*, Oct. 28, 1862.
22. Canada Life, *Minutes of Directors*, Nov. 18, 1862.
23. See below, p. 153.
24. 34 Vic., cap. 6.

789. Its surplus funds were declared to be $39,560.44 and, in harmony with the spirit of trustee savings banks, were placed in the hands of the trustees to be paid over for local purposes or public interest, subject to the approval of the Governor-in-Council.[25]

The first Savings Bank Act of the new Dominion,[26] as a result of the aforementioned settlements, had only the savings banks of Ontario and Quebec to deal with. It gave these banks the alternative of (a) transferring their business to the federal savings bank under the management of the Assistant to the Receiver General, (b) transferring it to a chartered bank, and (c) continuing operations under charter which among other things required them to have a minimum capital of $200,000. The Northumberland and Durham Savings Bank decided to wind up its affairs and in 1868, after eighteen years of operations, its assets totalled only $216,874; its surplus was given over to the trustees to be paid out for local purposes or public interest.[27] The history and fate of the Toronto Savings Bank, opened in 1854, was yet again different. It had remained truly a trustee savings bank and therefore, not surprisingly, its assets in 1868 amounted to only $145,723. When faced with the harsh alternatives of the new Dominion legislation it was argued that under the patronage of His Grace the Archbishop of Toronto it had proved an incentive to save to the industrious poor and a source of assistance to charities in Toronto, and that it would be impossible without injury to change its constitution or wind up its affairs in the prescribed manner. Consequently it was permitted under a special act of Parliament[28] to carry on under the legislation of 1841 and 1864 for a further ten-year period. However in 1879 it was taken over by a new joint stock company formed for that purpose, the Home Savings and Loan Company, a building society or mortgage loan company. This company in turn became a chartered bank, the Home Bank of Canada in 1905, the same bank that failed in 1923 – a sort of financial "Rake's Progress."

The Quebec Provident and Savings Bank also disappeared after 1871; the London Savings Bank, established in 1852, ceased operations before the end of the decade, its assets never having exceeded $30,000; La Caisse d'Économie de St. Roch de Québec suspended payment in 1866; a savings bank in British Columbia (in operation for only a few years, under trustees who deposited funds with the government and having branches at New Westminster, Nanaimo, Yale and Caribou) wound up its affairs in 1872, its place being taken

25. 35 Vic., cap. 9.
26. 34 Vic., cap. 7.
27. See 35 Vic., cap. 9.
28. 35 Vic., cap. 61.

by the Federal Government Savings Bank,[29] and finally, on January 24, 1962, the Premier of Newfoundland announced that the Newfoundland Savings Bank, in operation for 127 years, had been sold to the Bank of Montreal.[30]

The failure of trustee savings banks to become permanently established in Canada did not mean that there existed no economic need for savings institutions at that time. Institutions to provide savers with financial instruments more remunerative than the deposits in chartered banks and to supply the demand for the growing volume of bank stocks, provincial and municipal debentures, and the securities of utilities were necessary. The increasing activity in the formation of trustee savings banks after 1841 and the growth in assets of those that began to escape the restricting confines of the trustee savings bank concepts were evidence of this need. The reason for their failure to meet this need is not difficult to see. The banks that remained true to the original trustee savings bank spirit were too limited in their source of funds ("the industrious poor") and in some cases too limited in their investment of funds to be able to experience great expansion in their operations. Also the voluntary and therefore casual nature of management almost invited abuses, particularly in the way funds were invested, and this deficiency became doubly serious when particular banks began to seek funds somewhat more aggressively and invest those funds in more risky securities than traditional trustee savings banks would have done. In addition, just when these difficulties were becoming evident—highlighted by the insolvency in 1848 of the Montreal Provident and Savings Banks—a new intermediary, the building society, appeared as a potent competitor. This competitor appealed to the small saver without overtones of charity, it pioneered the marvellous innovation of the contractual savings payment, it gave the saver a definite purpose for saving (the purchase of a house), and it could take full advantage of that important instrument, the real estate mortgage.[31] Finally the act of 1855 in the Province of Canada imposing what, for any new local efforts to establish savings banks, were impossibly high capital requirements precluded further experimentation and evolution, particularly since those capital requirements were not at that time imposed on the building societies. But nonetheless it was the trustee savings bank that first recognized the need to provide

---

29. *Canadian Economics,* Papers Prepared for Reading before the Economical Section of the British Association for the Advancement of Science, Montreal, 1884 (Montreal: Dawson Brothers, 1885), pp. 260-1.

30. *Toronto Daily Star,* Jan. 25, 1962, p. 42.

31. See below, pp. 176-9.

facilities to the small as well as the large saver, and recognized that that need might require special facilities. The trustee savings bank also provided the route by which government became involved in providing those facilities—leading later directly to the Post Office Savings Bank and the Government Savings Bank, while the Dominion Government annuity fund and the Canada Savings Bonds are in the same general tradition. In addition, it was the experimentation with trustee savings banks that led to the establishment of two important Quebec savings banks.

Quebec Savings Banks

The two Quebec savings banks, the Montreal City and District Savings Bank and La Caisse d'Économie de Notre-Dame de Québec (since 1944 the Quebec Savings Bank), were the only trustee savings banks of the pre-Confederation period to survive for any length of time. The former is still in operation and the latter became part of the chartered banking system in 1969. When they were established they were not really indigenous institutions, for the legislation under which they operated and the factors which motivated their establishment were clearly in the tradition of the trustee savings banks of Great Britain. The Savings Bank Act of 1841 of the Province of Canada was much like the 1830 legislation of Lower Canada, which in turn was very similar to the imperial savings bank legislation of 1817 and the New Brunswick legislation of 1825. In addition, as we have seen, a number of English-Canadian as well as French-Canadian savings banks were launched under trustee savings bank legislation in Canada. Until the Savings Bank Act of 1890,[32] legislation referred to the "... Savings Banks in the Province of Ontario and Quebec ...". From then on reference to Ontario was omitted.

The Montreal City and District Savings Bank began operations on May 26, 1846, after the Roman Catholic Archbishop of Montreal, His Grace Ignace Bourget, solicited the assistance of seventy-five outstanding citizens to establish an institution to encourage thrift among the common people.[33] La Caisse d'Économie de Notre-Dame de Québec, sponsored by the St. Vincent de Paul Society, began operations on May 21, 1848, and the Archbishop of Quebec was its

32. 53 Vic., cap. 32.
33. See Royal Commission on Banking and Finance, *Hearings*, vol. 17A, p. A1629, brief presented by the Quebec savings banks, May 17, 1962.

patron for some years. Under the Savings Bank Act of 1841 both were permitted to take deposits from individuals up to £500 each; they could pay whatever interest rate they wished; they could invest in provincial or other public securities of the province, and in stock of the chartered banks; and upon a three-quarters vote of the Trustees they could pay profits to any charitable institution established by law. Very different from this act was the Savings Banks Act of 1855. This act contained the following provisions: it prohibited new trustee banks from being formed; it permitted only limited liability joint-stock savings banks with a capital of $400,000 to be established in future; in addition to limiting individual deposits to £500 it also limited deposit liabilities to the size of the paid-up capital or to not more than six times the amount of money or debentures deposited with the Receiver General, whichever was less; it required a deposit of such assets from one-eighth to one-fourth of the capital; it limited the rate of interest to one fixed by the Receiver General; and it provided that the banks could receive special debentures from the government at 2% above the deposit rate for any funds they cared to deposit with the Receiver General. No banks were formed under this legislation but it set the pattern for the new Dominion legislation. However, even before the legislation of 1871 the two Quebec savings banks sought an extension of the powers of the legislation under which they operated—the Montreal City and District Savings Bank in 1862[34] and La Caisse d'Économie de Notre-Dame de Québec in 1866.[35] These special acts had the effect of enabling the banks to take deposits from anyone without limit and of specifically permitting them to make collateral loans to individuals on security of the kind in which the act permitted them to invest. On this latter point the 1841 act had been ambiguous. Loans on real estate were prohibited, as they had been since the dawn of trustee savings banks and as they would be until 1948.

It was the legislation of 1871, *An Act respecting certain Savings Banks in the Province of Ontario and Quebec,*[36] that finally required the trustee savings banks either to obtain a charter and operate as a limited liability joint-stock corporation or to transfer their assets to the government's new savings banks or to one of the chartered banks. The two Quebec savings banks under discussion alone elected to obtain a charter. The act called for a minimum capital stock of $200,000 with shares of at least $400, each director being required

34. 25 Vic., cap. 66.
35. 29-30 Vic., cap. 130.
36. 34 Vic., cap. 7.

to hold at least 25 shares – in complete contrast to the mutual character and voluntary management of the former trustee savings banks. The act of 1911[37] permitted the banks to reduce the nominal value of their shares to $100 and that of 1913[38] made it compulsory, while a further reduction to $10 occurred in 1944[39] and to $1 in 1963.[40] Apart from its capital stock the banks' only source of funds was deposits on which it could pay a rate of interest fixed by the Governor-in-Council – a minimum of 4% and a maximum of 5%. From 1871 to 1967 there were twenty-two acts of the federal Parliament relating to Quebec savings banks and yet the sources of funds permitted to them has remained unchanged – a further characteristic inherited from the very first trustee savings banks and one of importance in explaining the banks' rate of growth over the years. As to the rate of interest to be paid on deposits, the act of 1890[41] eliminated the reference to a minimum rate but left the maximum at 5%, a maximum which was in force until 1954. As we shall see, the powers of the banks to make loans were somewhat restricted for much of their history, so that the matter of a ceiling on their loan rates did not arise. The act of 1948[42] which did give them authority to make unsecured personal loans up to a certain limit, also imposed a ceiling of 6% on their rate of interest or rate of discount. However, as was the case with the banks, this ceiling disappeared after 1967 with interest rate disclosure provisions taking its place. As in previous years there was no ceiling imposed on the rate of interest they could obtain on securities purchased, nor did the ceiling apply to the National Housing Act mortgages which the 1948 act permitted them to make.

The Quebec savings banks always enjoyed considerable freedom in investing funds in bonds and debentures and in making collateral loans, but until 1948 they suffered from being prohibited from making mortgages and personal loans. The prohibition against mortgages is probably of major importance in explaining the relatively slow growth of the Quebec savings banks for, as we shall see again, the two decades after Confederation were ones in which intermediaries catering to mortgage credit demands showed very high rates of growth.[43]

The various acts of Parliament relating to the Quebec savings

---

37. 1-2 Geo. V, cap. 11.
38. 3-4 Geo. V, cap. 42.
39. 8 Geo. VI, cap. 47.
40. 12 Eliz. II, cap. 27.
41. 53 Vic., cap. 32.
42. 11-12 Geo. VI, cap. 65.
43. See below, pp. 200-1.

banks that have been passed since 1871 have introduced numerous detailed changes in the way in which those banks have been permitted to invest the deposits they have accumulated. However, fundamental changes have not been numerous and the most significant changes have occurred since the end of the Second World War. First to be noted is the history of reserve requirements relating to the savings banks. It was the act of 1873,[44] not of 1871, that first introduced the requirement that the banks had to hold 20% of their deposit liabilities in the form of Dominion securities or deposits with a chartered bank. In 1897[45] provincial securities were also eligible for the requirement and in 1900 the eligible list of securities was greatly widened to include the securities of Great Britain and its colonies and possessions, United States federal and state securities, Canadian municipal and Quebec school securities as well as any other security approved by the Treasury Board. In 1913[46] all Canadian school securities were included, and in 1934[47] deposits of the Bank of Canada were added. Finally in 1944[48] there was introduced the requirement that 5% had at all times to be held in the form of Bank of Canada notes and deposits and chartered bank deposits (a provision which still holds), while 15% had to be held in the above forms of cash in excess of the 5% requirement, and Government of Canada and provincial direct and guaranteed securities and municipal securities (although the municipal securities were excluded from 1954 onward). The 1957 act[49] related the reserve requirement to Canadian currency deposit liabilities and the 1967 act[50] confined the reserve securities to Government of Canada and provincial securities payable in Canadian currency—with the general proviso from 1957 onward that " . . . the bank shall maintain adequate and appropriate assets against liabilities payable in foreign currency." So apart from the 5% cash requirement, the liquidity requirement now is again much what it was from 1873 to 1900. It is interesting to contemplate what factors could possibly explain this curious cycle in official liquidity requirements and it is difficult to see what it accomplished.

The Quebec savings banks have, of course, always been permitted to invest their funds in virtually unrestricted amounts in the securities of the various levels of government in Canada, although the

---

44. 36 Vic., cap. 72.
45. 60-61 Vic., cap. 9.
46. 3-4 Geo. V, cap. 42.
47. 24-25 Geo. V, cap. 39.
48. 8 Geo. VI, cap. 47.
49. 5-6 Eliz. II, cap. 12.
50. 14-15-16 Eliz. II, cap. 93.

securities of the *fabriques de paroisse* or syndics, the various religious corporations and institutions for operating hospitals and sanataria were not included until 1944.[51] But in 1890[52] this permission was extended to include any securities the Government of Canada accepted from insurance companies for meeting security deposit requirements, and in 1897[53] began the practice of permitting the savings banks to invest in the bonds and debentures of specifically named types of Canadian corporations—building societies, loan or investment companies and the various utilities. In 1900[54] this was limited to corporations of such groups with a paid-up capital of $500,000. Nothing much then happened until the 1944 act,[55] which added the provision that savings banks could invest in "... any other securities approved by the Treasury Board," and for the first time they were specifically permitted to invest in the bonds and debentures secured by a mortgage of Canadian manufacturing companies, provided such companies had a paid-up capital of $500,000 and a consecutive five-year earned dividend record of at least 4% per annum. Their holdings of such securities could not exceed 5% of deposit liabilities. In 1954[56] all reference to types of industries eligible for investment was dropped, preferred shares were added to bonds and debentures as being eligible, and eligible companies were ones whose common shares were listed on a recognized exchange, who had paid dividends for the past five years, and who had a paid-up capital of $500,000. Also the banks were permitted to buy common shares of chartered banks with the aforementioned dividend record. Holdings of all these corporate securities (including those under the "any other securities approved" category) could not exceed 15% of deposit liabilities. The 1957 act gave them a sort of "basket clause" which permitted them to hold corporate securities not otherwise eligible, provided they were not in default, up to one-half of their paid-up capital and rest fund. This opened the door for holdings of equities in addition to chartered bank stocks. Further liberalization was urged by the Royal Commission on Banking and Finance in its 1964 *Report* (pp. 147-54) and this came in the 1967 act. It greatly simplified matters and broadened the banks' investing powers. It permitted them to invest in the Canadian currency securities and common shares of any company incorporated in Canada up to any amount,

51. 8 Geo. VI, cap. 47.
52. 53 Vic., cap. 32.
53. 60-61 Vic., cap. 9.
54. 63-64 Vic., cap. 28.
55. 8 Geo. VI, cap. 47.
56. 2-3 Eliz. II, cap. 41.

provided the company was not in default on its securities with respect to either principal or interest. Just as the 1897 legislation had specifically recognized that investing in corporate securities was, after all, not undesirable and the 1954 legislation recognized that there was nothing inherently superior about specific industries for the banks' investment purposes, so the 1967 act recognized that a dividend record was a very crude and generally unsatisfactory criterion, and that investing in common stocks was not at all inappropriate for a savings institution. The timid move permitting the banks to hold certain bank stocks in 1954, the further small step represented by the 1957 "basket clause" and finally the giant step of the 1967 act nicely illustrates past caution of the federal government in such matters. It also reflects its past faith in investment prescriptions as a device for protecting the saver, and its sudden change of mind in the matter, now relying heavily on inspection and supervision rather than investment prescriptions to achieve that objective.

Mortgage financing was introduced in 1948[57] and in some respects this represented the most important innovation in the operations of the banks since they were first established. Upon a resolution being passed by the board of directors they were permitted to make National Housing Act mortgages, and conventional mortgages of a residential character up to $100,000 each (changed to 5% of capital and rest paid in 1967) or 60% of the value of the property (75% in 1967), whichever was less, with an over-all limit on mortgage holdings to 5% of deposits. This latter figure was increased to 10% in 1950, 20% in 1954 and 40% in 1957, and the banks requested 60% in their brief to the Royal Commission on Banking and Finance in 1962, which they were granted in 1967.

Finally, the savings banks have since 1871 enjoyed substantial freedom in making collateral loans against a wide range of securities, including Canadian federal, provincial and municipal government securities, British and foreign public securities, chartered bank stocks, stocks of building societies (loan companies), bonds and debentures of institutions and corporations. Permission to make unsecured loans was first granted in 1890[58] but this was restricted to loans to the federal and provincial government, municipal governments, and after 1900[59] to institutions and corporations with paid-up capital of $500,000 and a dividend record of 4% per annum for five years. In 1944[60] all unsecured loans other than those to the federal

57. 11-12 Geo. VI, cap. 65.
58. 53 Vic., cap. 32.
59. 63-64 Vic., cap. 28.
60. 8 Geo. VI, cap. 47.

and provincial governments were restricted to 5% of deposit liabilities, which was raised to 15% in 1957 and left at that figure in the 1967 amendment. In 1967 also the dividend and minimum capital criteria were dropped, being replaced by the same criteria that applied to purchases of corporate securities.

In 1948 for the first time unsecured personal loans were introduced into the act[61] but were limited to $1000 to an individual, which limit was raised to $2000 in 1952, to $5000 in 1957 and to $10,000 in 1967. Commercial lending has been precluded by the banks' not being permitted to make advances on warehouse receipts or on the security of goods or merchandise.

From this summary it is evident that while the liquidity requirements imposed on the Quebec savings banks are as stringent as they ever were, there has been a tendency, greatly speeded up in the period after the Second World War, to increase their freedom in the investment of funds entrusted to them. Indeed, when one considers that in 1967 the banks were permitted (a) to purchase any Canadian currency corporation securities including common stocks of corporations not in default, in unlimited amounts, (b) to make conventional mortgage loans up to 75% of the value of the property, (c) to invest in mortgages up to 60% of their deposit liabilities, and (d) to make personal and other unsecured loans up to 15% of deposit liabilities, then it is clear that restrictions on their lending and investing activity have largely vanished in the postwar years. This, of course, must mean that the Inspector General of Banks, who since 1934 has been responsible for inspecting and supervising the Quebec savings banks, has largely replaced investment prescription as the protector of the depositors of the Quebec savings banks. Deposits, however, are now insured up to $20,000 per depositor.

GROWTH AND RELATIVE SIZE

It is necessary now to examine the actual growth rate experienced by the Quebec savings banks over the years and to attempt to isolate the factors which appear to be important in accounting for it.

Chart 5:1 shows the rate of growth of the assets of the Quebec savings banks in current dollars and the size of those assets relative to the assets of all financial intermediaries in Canada from 1870 to 1968. Immediately apparent is a steady decline in the relative size of the Quebec savings banks and a remarkably stable rate of growth of the banks over much of the period. In 1870 the two savings banks

61. 11-12 Geo. VI, cap. 65.

Chart 5:1—Growth and Relative Size of the Quebec Savings Banks 1870-1970

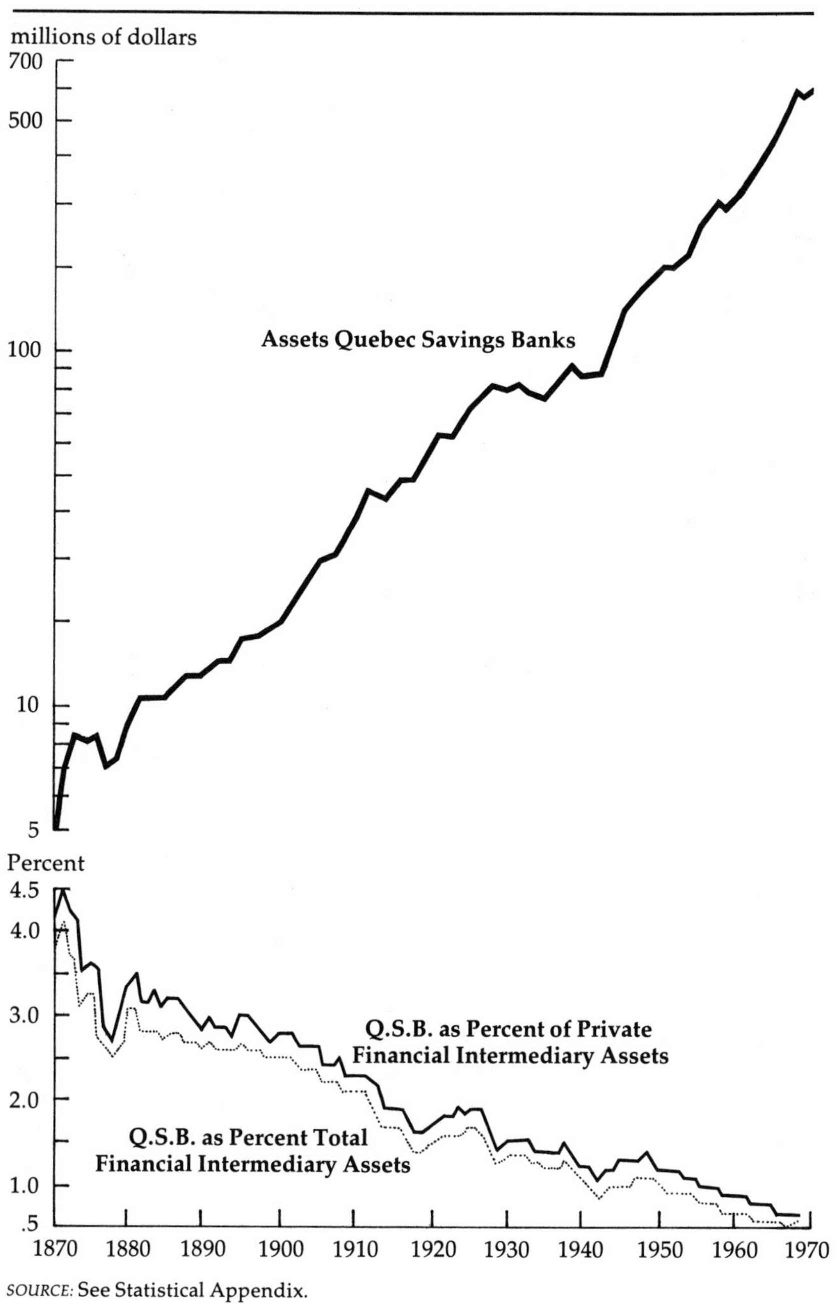

SOURCE: See Statistical Appendix.

accounted for 3.7% of the assets of all financial intermediaries, but by 1900 this had declined to 2.5% and by 1958 to .9%, with a tendency from 1940 onward for the relative size to become stabilized.

As to the banks' rate of growth, four periods are discernible. The period from 1874 to about 1879 was one of difficulty for the Canadian chartered banks in general, with numerous banks in difficulties, and the decline in the assets of the Quebec savings banks correctly indicates that these difficulties extended to them as well. A contemporary newspaper reports that "...The City and District Savings Bank of Montreal, have made a call of five per cent upon the capital of a million. It is understood that this step is mainly in consequence of losses by the break in City Passenger R.R. stock, on which this and other banks had made advances at high valuations, to the syndicate of brokers who failed some months ago."[62] About six months later it was reported that "...the authorities of the City and District Savings Bank of Montreal have taken steps to allay the uneasiness felt regarding that institution by denying that the bank has ever lost anything through their directors; though outside statements are freely made that, at one time, such a loss might have occurred to a very large extent."[63]

But those difficult times passed. From about 1880 to 1927 the assets of the banks in current dollars grew at a steady rate, averaging 4¾% per annum, which, however, was substantially less than the growth rate of the chartered banks which averaged about 6% per annum over that period. From 1927 to 1934, their assets in current dollars declined and then rose at a very slow rate until 1940, a pattern almost identical to that of chartered bank assets. During the war years 1939 to 1945 the assets of the savings banks rose by 54%, and those of the chartered banks by 97%; while from 1945 to 1969 the increases were more nearly the same, the chartered banks' Canadian assets rising by 376% or 6.7% per annum, and the Quebec savings banks' by 326%, or 6.2% per annum. Over the period 1870 to 1969 assets of the two Quebec savings banks rose at an average annual rate of about 4.9%, those of the chartered banks at about 5.8%, and assets of all financial intermediaries combined at 6.8%.

It seems, then, that the pattern of growth of assets of the Quebec savings banks has been similar to that of the chartered banks, that until the end of the Second World War the growth of the savings banks was persistently lower than that of the chartered banks, but that since then a distinct increase in the annual rate of growth of the

62. *Monetary Times*, March 23, 1877, p. 1080.
63. *Monetary Times*, Oct. 5, 1877, p. 419.

savings banks and a slight decline in the growth rate of the chartered banks have combined to reduce the difference between their rates of growth.

It is unlikely that any of these changes are explained by innovations in the sources of funds available to the savings banks, since apart from a small amount of equity capital they have always depended entirely on deposits. At present the banks offer savings deposits, personal chequing deposits, and certificates of deposit which are in effect term deposits. They do not appear to have been under any legal handicap since their formation in competing for deposits.

There have been some changes in the structure of savings bank assets since they were formed. Table 5:1 below shows that until 1900, as far as can be determined from the statistics, the only changes of consequence were a substantial decline in the proportion of assets held in the form of cash (which is a normal development for the period when banking institutions first become established), and a significant increase in holdings of securities (probably municipal securities). This was a period when the Quebec savings banks were active in extending loans to stockbrokers (chartered banks were not permitted to lend against bank stocks but the savings banks were) and this is reflected in the high proportion of secured loans—although of course that figure also included secured loans made to governments and large corporations. It is interesting to notice that after 1900, when the savings banks were given authority to invest in a wide range of public utility securities, there was only a small accumulation of securities in the "other" category, suggesting that the additional freedom to invest was not of major importance to the banks. The major change after 1900 until the late 1920s was the persistent shift away from secured loans to the federal and provincial securities category—a shift that had been legally possible at any time since the formation of the banks.

Holdings of municipal securities have declined steadily in relative importance since 1927, while holdings of federal and provincial securities have done so dramatically since 1945: in that year they accounted for 68% of all assets, whereas in 1970 they accounted for only 15%. The latter decline is not explained only by a readjustment of excessively large holdings of Victory Bonds acquired during the war, for after 1948 the banks were first granted authority to make and hold mortgages, and these increased until by 1966 they accounted for 50% of the assets of the savings banks, and in 1970 the proportion was 54%. Unsecured personal loans, also inaugurated in 1948, do not yet account for a significant portion of the banks' assets. It appears

Table 5:1 Quebec Savings Banks, Distribution of Assets, 1875 to 1970 (selected years)

END OF	1875 %	1880 %	1900 %	1927 %	1940 %	1945 %	1960 %	1965 %	1969 %	1970 %
Cash[1]	23	29	10	12	11	6	8	6	5	5
Government securities	15	18	41	63	77	82	53	28	21	20
– Federal	(n.a.)	(n.a.) }					(12)	5	6	6
			(11) }	(30) }	(50) }	(68)				
– Provincial	(n.a.)	(n.a.) }					(28)	16	9	9
– Municipal	(n.a.)	(n.a.)	(30)	(33)	(27)	(14)	(13)	7	6	5
Other securities	—	—	3	4	6	5	8	7	8	8
Mortgages	—	—	—	—	—	—	20	47	50	54
Secured loans[2]	50	44	41	18	4	4	3	3	3	3
Unsecured loans	—	—	—	—	—	—	2	4	4	4
All other assets	12	9	5	3	2	3	6	6	9	6
TOTAL ASSETS – %	100	100	100	100	100	100	100	100	100	100
– ($mns)	8.3	8.9	20.8	79.0	85.7	143.1	311.4	430.2	541.9[3]	568.5

SOURCE: *Canada Gazette.*

[1]Bank of Canada notes and deposits and chartered bank notes and deposits.
[2]Includes unsecured loans to governments in Canada, and large corporations until 1948 although these appear not to have been important.
[3]On November 10, 1969, La Banque d'Économie de Québec commenced operations as a chartered bank and its assets are excluded.

that mortgage lending is an attractive form of investment for savings banks and that the legal prohibition against it for so many years may well have been detrimental to the banks. As already mentioned, the attractive investment opportunities for a number of decades after the banks were incorporated lay in mortgage financing, and the institutions engaged in it grew at a rapid rate. So great were the opportunities that some of these institutions, as we shall see again,[64] developed new sources of funds for meeting it. The savings banks may not have had the incentive to increase their sources of funds, not being permitted to engage in mortage financing.

In summary, the basis for the growth of the Quebec savings banks has not been the type of credit they extended, for there has never been anything unique about it—except perhaps to a minor extent in their earlier years, when they could make secured loans against the collateral of chartered bank stock and when funds available for that purpose were scarce. Indeed, until 1948 the legal restrictions on mortgage lending probably inhibited the activities of the banks to some extent, although there is little evidence that other legal restrictions on their investment activities were of more than marginal importance to their long-term development.

Nor was there anything unique about the sources of funds of the savings banks after they became chartered institutions. Prior to that they were unique in that they tended to cater to small savers when, for a time, other institutions did not do so; but this was not a type of service that could lead to rapid expansion of assets. Depending on deposits as a source of funds, the banks had to face the increasing competition of the chartered banks, building societies and loan companies after Confederation, as well as the active competition of the Post Office and Government Savings Banks in the period prior to 1900 and the caisses populaires after that. Even the trust companies, which first appeared in the 1800s, soon competed in the same field. By offering competitive rates the savings banks were able to obtain a share of the funds people wished to hold in the form of deposits, but they could not offer them a new form of investment instrument.

Perhaps of major importance in explaining the somewhat modest expansion of the assets of the Quebec savings banks is their decision to limit their operations to the two largest urban areas in the Province of Quebec. The 1944 act defined more clearly than had previously been the case the geographical areas in which each of the banks could operate, dividing the province into the "District of Montreal"

---

64. See below, pp. 194-5.

and the "District of Quebec," and assigning the first to the Montreal City and District Savings Bank and the second to the Quebec Savings Bank. Even so, the former confined itself almost entirely to the island of Montreal—locating 54 of its 55 branches there (1962)—and the latter located all its 19 branches (1962) in the City of Quebec and its suburbs.[65] It does not appear that the banks were ever anxious to extend the area of their operations to other parts of Canada. In the meantime other institutions evolved to fill that gap.

The banks recently argued in favour of being permitted to broaden the services they could offer customers. They had in mind the sale of life insurance, mutual fund shares, real estate investment securities, and trust services. Such an extension would constitute a major change in their ability to compete for funds, perhaps the most significant change since they began operations. But while the 1967 act gave the banks greater freedom in their investment activities, it did not give them these powers, or others that would enable them to offer additional savings instruments. It seemed that if the Quebec savings banks wished to accelerate their growth rate they would have to press for these powers, exercise them, and pursue a policy of greater geographical dispersion of their branch system. Such a policy, of course, would not be easy, given the high density of savings facilities already in existence.

Adjustment, as it turned out, emerged from another direction. In 1969 Les Caisses Populaires Desjardins, Quebec's largest credit union organization, gained control of one of the banks, La Banque d'Économie de Québec, and in that year the latter received a charter enabling it to operate as a chartered bank under the name La Banque Populaire. Then in 1970 La Banque Populaire merged with another chartered bank, La Banque Provinciale du Canada. So disappeared one of Canada's older financial institutions. The remaining savings bank now has legislative authority to operate throughout the province of Quebec.

65. Royal Commission on Banking and Finance, brief presented by the Quebec savings banks, pp. A1631, A1633.

6

The Private Bankers

In the preceding chapters we have referred to the development, and in some instances the disappearance, of chartered banks, joint-stock banks, free banks and savings banks. It remains, however, to describe the character and contribution of the local private banks whose presence was very evident during the late nineteenth century. These local bankers operated extensively in Ontario until after the turn of the century, and to a lesser degree in other parts of Canada, and were engaged in all aspects of the banking business except the issue of demand notes. They are important to this study because of their early activities in bringing financial services to local communities. They also constitute an interesting example of the way certain types of financial institutions have risen to prominence and then, as a result of competitive pressures, have disappeared.

The first private bankers, of course, appeared long before Confederation. Before the appearance in 1817 of Canada's first bank, a bank prepared to accept deposits, issue notes and discount commercial paper, banking in Canada was in the hands of merchants, as we have already seen in chapter 4. This type of private banker, the merchant banker, seems to have disappeared quickly as the merchants, and others, began after 1817 to establish chartered banks. Only one aspect of their banking operation persisted—their custom of extending credit to customers—a practice that drew the ire of financial writers for years.

In the 1830s, as we have already seen, some local private banks established by deed of settlement were organized in Upper Canada but their attempts to issue notes were at first frustrated by the British government and, on March 4, 1837, permanently thwarted by the provincial legislature, which passed an act forbidding such issues by anyone not enjoying legislative authority to do so.[1]

Having been prevented from issuing notes in Upper Canada, the private banker developed in another way. His interest became centred on making loans and discounting paper with funds obtained from his private capital, from deposits and from loans from the chartered banks; he also made collections, traded in foreign exchange, bank and other stocks, debentures, and real estate, and sold insurance; and he arranged mortgage loans and engaged in other financial agency business.

Whereas the merchant banker had arisen because reliable banking institutions as such had not yet appeared in the large commercial centres, the great majority of private bankers arose primarily because of the absence of adequate chartered banking and general financial facilities in the small towns and villages. However, it was probably in the principal cities that the private banker as described above first became clearly identified. The October 1857 issue of the *Canadian Merchants' Magazine and Commercial Review* lists the following under "Private Bankers and Exchange Brokers:"

Montreal – C. Dorwin & Co., St. Francois Xavier Street
Montreal – J. D. Nutter & Co., Place D'Armes
Montreal – Geo. W. Warner, St. Francois Xavier Street
Montreal – D. Fisher, & Co., St. Francois Xavier Street
Montreal – Ewing and Fisher, St. Francois Xavier Street
Toronto – E. F. Whittemore & Co., Toronto Street
Toronto – W. H. Bull & Co., King Street
Toronto – W. B. Phipps, Toronto Street
Toronto – John Cameron, Wellington Street
Toronto – Wm. Weir & Co., Front Street
Hamilton – Hamilton, Davis & Co.
Hamilton – Nelson Mills & Co.
London (C. W.) – B. F. Beddome
Quebec – R. Finn

The W. B. Phipps listed above had been in business for some time before 1857 and remained in business for many years after. This advertisement of his, dated April 1846, suggests that his was a general financial and commercial business.

Goods Sold on Commission
Notes, Debts and Rents Collected
Houses and Lands Sold, Rented, or Let

---

1. Victor Ross, *A History of the Canadian Bank of Commerce* (Toronto: Oxford University Press, 1920), vol. 1, pp. 187-8, and references there cited.

> Bank and Other Stocks Bought and Sold
> Agency Business of all Kinds
> Zealously and Faithfully Attended to.[2]

A greater emphasis on financial matters, and on banking in particular, is indicated by the advertisements of John Cameron and E. F. Whittemore & Co. which appeared in 1856.

> John Cameron, Banker
> Stocks and Money Broker
> Wellington Street Toronto
> Cash advances made on produce
> Provincial and Municipal Debentures Negotiated
> Bank and Other Stocks Bought and Sold
> Money raised upon mortgage securities
> Agents for London Eagle Life Insurance Co.
>
> E. F. Whittemore & Co.
> Exchange Office
> Bills of Exchange, Drafts on New York, American
> Bank Notes and Uncurrent Money bought
> and Sold. Collections made in all cities and
> towns in the United States
> Cash advances . . . on flour, wheat
> and other produce.
> Fire marine and life insurance.[3]

The distinction between private banking and the brokerage business was recognized and made explicit by compilers of the directories as early as 1862, and the names of W. R. Brown, W. H. Bull & Co., John Cameron and W. B. Phipps are listed as private bankers, with Cameron and Brown listed again as brokers.[4] In the year 1868 all the individuals listed as private bankers in Toronto were also listed as brokers: Robert Beatty (who continued in business until the 1890s), Josias Bray, W. R. Brown, C. J. Campbell, Forbes & King, Henry Joseph, H. J. Morse & Co., and W. B. Phipps.[5] So while the distinction between bankers and brokers was made, in practice in Toronto those businesses were closely intertwined.

But the major developments in private banking, in terms of the numbers of such bankers, occurred not in the financial centres, but in the smaller centres of population in Ontario. Adequate statistics of

---

2. *Brown's Toronto City and Home District Directory 1847-8* (Toronto: George Brown Publisher, 1846).
3. *Brown's Toronto General Directory, 1856* (Toronto: W. R. Brown).
4. *Hutchinson's Toronto Directory, 1862-63.*
5. *W. C. Chewett & Cos. Toronto City Directory, 1868-9* (Toronto: W. C. Chewett & Co., 1868).

their number and location are apparently not available until 1885, but one gets the impression that their numbers increased in the 1860s to 1880s, reached a peak in the 1890s and that they had virtually disappeared by the 1920s.

Table 6:1 summarizes our compilation of private bankers operating in Canada in 1885, 1890 and 1895. In those years 147, 189 and 192 respectively have been listed as doing business. This is not an insignificant number when it is remembered that in 1890 there were only 426 chartered bank branches in Canada and that in 1895 there were 530 such branches. It is clear from Table 6:1 that the great majority of these bankers operated in Ontario, and from their addresses that a large proportion of them carried on business in the villages and towns of Ontario. Private bankers also played a part in the development of banking on the prairies and this is reflected in the increase in their numbers in that region to over 30 by 1895; but from the point of view of the history of the institution, the venture out west was the dying gasp of the private banker.

Even before the development of private banking on the prairies, it had appeared on the west coast. The discovery of gold there in 1858 brought the banking facilities of the express companies such as Wells, Fargo and Company. The Victoria agent of this particular company around 1866 was F. Garesche, who joined with A. A. Green to form the private banking firm of Garesche, Green & Co., later Green, Worlach and Co., which operated until liquidated in 1894.[6]

But historically more interesting was Macdonald's Bank, at Victoria, formed by Alexander D. Macdonald in 1859—the first bank west of the Great Lakes to issue notes and take deposits. It operated successfully, even extended its operations to the Caribou district, but the competition from chartered banks was strong and finally in 1864 it suffered a disastrous robbery which it failed to survive. It would in any case have been required to relinquish its note issue or reorganize, for new legislation permitted only chartered banks to issue notes in British Columbia after March 1, 1865.

Among the first private bankers on the prairies was Alloway and Champion, who began operations in Winnipeg in 1879, the year after the Bank of Montreal had opened its first branch in that region. It was purchased by the Canadian Bank of Commerce in 1919, when its assets totalled approximately $3 million, which alone was sufficient

---

6. For private banking in British Columbia see R. Craig McIvor, *Canadian Monetary, Banking and Fiscal Development* (Toronto: Macmillan Company of Canada, 1958), pp. 89-92, and references there cited.

Table 6:1 Private Bankers of Canada

	1885			1890			1895		
	BANKS	KNOWN BRANCHES	TOTAL	BANKS	KNOWN BRANCHES	TOTAL	BANKS	KNOWN BRANCHES	TOTAL
Nova Scotia	3	—	3	3	—	3	3	—	3
New Brunswick	3	—	3	4	—	4	4	—	4
Quebec	7	—	7	9	—	9	9	—	8
Ontario	114	8	122	137	4	141	137	4	141
Manitoba	8	1	9	14	3	17	19	—	19
Northwest Territories	3	—	3	7	5	12	7	7	14
British Columbia	—	—	—	2	1	3	2	1	3
TOTAL	138	9	147	176	13	189	180	12	192

SOURCE: Compiled from data in Rand, McNally & Co., *Bankers' Directory and List of Bank Attorneys*, Chicago, July 1885; *Garland's Banks, Bankers and Banking in Canada*, Mortimer & Co., Ottawa, 1890; *Garland's Banks, Bankers and Banking in Canada*, Mortimer & Co., Ottawa, 1895; and also from contemporary newspapers.

to distinguish it from all other private banks of that period.[7]

At the peak of its development the system of private banks had certain identifiable characteristics. One was its relative freedom from legislative restraints. It is true the private banks had been forbidden to issue notes in Upper and Lower Canada as early as the 1830s and this prohibition became part of the Dominion Bank Act of 1871; and in 1883 they were forbidden by Act of Parliament to use the designation "Bank" or "Banking House" without adding the words "not incorporated." But apart from this they were virtually free agents in their operations, and were not even required to publish financial statements or to submit reports to the government. It was a rare event indeed when in 1886 Loftus Cuddy, Banker, of Amherstburg, Ontario, sent the financial statement of his bank, duly signed by an auditor before a commissioner, to the *Monetary Times* for publication.[8]

In most cases the private bank was without branches. But there were a few exceptions to this. Thomas Fawcett, of London, had under his immediate control, or was associated with, banks at Watford, Wyoming, Arkona and Alvinston, Ontario; furthermore he was associated with the banks of Messrs. Fawcett, Livingstone & Co. at Dresden and Thamesville; and also with the Mitchell Banking Company, the Dresden Banking Co., the Millbrook Banking Co., and with W. O. Smith & Co. at Thornbury. Unfortunately, the "Fawcett Failure" was announced in September 1884. J. A. Halsted & Co. had offices in Mount Forest and Shelburne, Ontario; Wm. Lucas & Co. at Dundalk and Markdale, Ontario; W. H. White at Palmerston and Luther, Ontario; J. W. Scott at Clifford, Palmerston and Listowel, Ontario; and W. Swaisland & Co. at Brantford and Glencoe, Ontario.

A higher proportion of the prairie private bankers had branches than did those of Ontario. Lafferty and Moore had branches at Calgary, Edmonton, Lethbridge, Moosomin, Moose Jaw, Regina and Vancouver; Alloway and Champion at Winnipeg (2), Portage la Prairie and Rat Portage; Le Jeune, Smith & Co. at Calgary, Moosomin and Regina; Allan, Brydges & Co. at Winnipeg and Carberry; and R. Logan & Co. at Glenboro and Carberry.

It is hardly conceivable that the large number of private bankers which operated in Ontario and elsewhere could have become established unless there was a gap in the capital market machinery,

---

7. See *ibid.* and Peter Lowe, "All Western Dollars," *Papers Read before the Historical and Scientific Society of Manitoba, 1945-46,* Winnipeg, 1946, for interesting accounts of the operation of this private banker.

8. It is conceivable that the fact that his ratio of cash to liabilities (excluding capital) stood at 58% influenced his decision! *Monetary Times*, Jan. 14, 1887, p. 818.

and one which they to some extent were able to fill. In the period before Confederation the pervading scarcity of capital encouraged attempts at establishing banks of all sorts, including private banks. The chartered banking system was by no means able to, or in some respects prepared to, provide adequate facilities in that period. Their apparent interest in foreign trade and exchange, probably to the detriment of local trade, is recalled. But the effect which this sometimes had on local banking can best be visualized by recalling the description which a contemporary banker has given of the operations of the Bank of Montreal at that time:

> ... a bank with such command of gold as the Bank of Montreal had in New York at this time [i.e. 1867-8] could make large profits in a perfectly legitimate manner. Gold could be lent from time to time at very high rates of interest. As security for the gold, current funds were generally deposited. These funds were employed again—so I was informed by Mr. King himself—in discounting commercial bills....
>
> To obtain gold necessary for these operations, Mr. King carried out some very drastic measures with regard to the bank's business in Upper Canada. Loans were called in, advances reduced, and accounts closed at nearly every branch in Ontario. At one time a condition almost approaching panic prevailed, owing to the severity of the drain....
>
> It was at this time, and owing to these circumstances, that the Canadian Bank of Commerce started its existence, and rendered important service in filling the void created by the withdrawal of funds by the Bank of Montreal.[9]

But in addition the branch system as such took time to become well established. The failure in 1866 of the Bank of Upper Canada and the Commercial Bank, and the failure of 17 more chartered banks (albeit mostly small in size) from Confederation to the turn of the century, was further evidence that the system of chartered banking was still in a developmental stage.

The chartered banks for years were represented more by local agents than by branches as such and the system of inspection and control even of the branches was rudimentary. As long as this was the case a local private banker was not as different as one might imagine from a locally appointed agent of a chartered bank. There were also numerous local communities, even after Confederation, where no chartered bank agents or branches existed. In 1885, 80 of the 147 private bankers listed in Table 6:1 were operating in centres

---

9. G. Hague, "The Late Mr. E. H. King," *Journal of the Canadian Bankers' Association*, vol. 14, no. 1 (October 1896), p. 24.

where the chartered banks were not represented. Many chartered banks probably were not at that time in a position to carry unprofitable or even low-profit branches in the way they appear to have done in the twentieth century. A writer remarked in 1881 that "while the chartered banks have, in numerous instances, resorted to the policy of closing branches in districts where they did not pay, private institutions, for lending or receiving deposits, have succeeded them in not a few places. . . ."[10]

A succinct rationale for the existence of the private banker was given in 1883 by a financial writer:

> ... The operation of a branch of a chartered bank is ... a somewhat costly business; and unless the trade, and accumulated wealth of the place rises to [a] certain proportion, a branch bank cannot be made profitable. It is here, then, that the legitimate field for private enterprise is found, that is, in those thriving and well situated villages, which have a certain amount of commercial business, and are situated in the midst of a good farming district. A private banker can carry on his business at much less expense than a branch of a chartered bank. He is, moreover, not bound by any restriction as to the rate which he can charge for money, or the kind of security which he can take. He can practically charge what he pleases for the use of money or its transmission from place to place. And although his charges may be considerably higher than those of a banking institution it may be more economical for residents to deal with him, than to incur the risk and expense of dealing with a branch bank, at a distance, perhaps, of ten or twenty miles. These obvious conveniences have given rise to the business carried on in so many parts of the country by private persons, with more or less capital and experience, who open an office, receive deposits, discount notes, and issue cheques, which are received by merchants at a distance much as drafts of banks are received. There can be no possible objection to this business in itself, any more than there can be an objection to a man opening a store, or a law office, or building a saw mill. And if it be alleged that such private bankers enter into competition with the chartered banks in the receipt of deposits, and the discount of bills, it can only be replied that these things are perfectly legitimate in themselves and have always prevailed in one form or other from the earliest beginnings of things amongst us.[11]

These explanations of the existence of the private banker before 1900 also help to account for his disappearance in the several decades after 1900. If a chartered bank branch was in a position to compete, the private banker found it very difficult to survive. His funds frequently were more expensive than those of the chartered banks

10. *Monetary Times*, May 20, 1881, p. 1351.
11. *Monetary Times*, May 9, 1882, pp. 1003-4.

and in many cases he depended heavily on a chartered bank for loans; this in turn meant that he could not compete with the chartered bank in the matter of loan rates. So the persistent expansion of chartered bank branches had its "wearing" effect on the private banker. It is estimated that from 1868 to 1895 407 such branches were added to the system, while from 1895 to 1922 no less than 3,921 additional branches appeared, 1,246 of which were in Ontario. The Post Office Savings Bank, too, expanded its facilities in those years.

This continual growth of economically superior competitors was accompanied, unfortunately for the private banker, by growing evidence of the risks, to customer and banker, inherent in private banking. The risks were those of any small proprietorship, compounded by the special hazards of demand deposit banking. Usually much depended on one man. The general efficiency of the business could therefore be disrupted without warning through death or incapacity. But a major hazard was the temptation placed in the hands of the banker, to engage in speculation and long-term lending. Many were able to resist or survive the consequences of such temptation, as shown by the fact that about 100 of the 147 private banks and branches operating in 1885 were still in operation in 1895. But many others were not able to do so.

These excerpts from contemporary reports in *The Monetary Times* on the failure of private bankers best illustrate the special hazards of private banking before the turn of the century. Nor are they invariably without humour:

March 29, 1878 ...Financial and commercial circles in Halifax are greatly exercised over the failure of the private banking house of Messrs. Almon & Mackintosh, whose suspension was announced on the 18th inst....

...Too much of the firm's means had been locked up by advances on real estate and shipping collateral, which were unavailable when most needed....

Dec. 6, 1878 ...A private banker in Aylmer, Ontario, named Daniel Stewart, is missing, and his affairs are found to be greatly involved....

Stewart had purchased about eighteen patent rights, the majority of them being the invention of one Henry Carter. Through these he had lost $18,000 up to October, 1877. This dabbling in patent rights has been going on for about twelve years, and was, without doubt, the cause of his fall....

Nov. 17, 1882 ...Messrs. James S. McDonald & Co., bankers and

	brokers, Halifax, N.S., are announced in a press despatch to have suspended payment on Wednesday. . . . Speculation in the ranch business in the North-West is said to be the cause of the difficulty. . . .
Feb. 16, 1883	. . . The Mahon Banking Co. of London, Ont., suspended payment on Tuesday last. . . . [The cause appears to have been the character of the retail paper it discounted and its investments in North-west landed properties.]
July 4, 1884	. . . The respectable Toronto firm of Forbes & Lownsbrough . . . whose failure was due to its making advances on Federal Bank stock, has made an arrangement by which the liquidation of the estate will remain in its own hands. . . .
Oct. 3, 1884	. . . A private banker . . . doing business at Wingham and Oakville, was evidently unworthy of the name banker. He was guilty of some very irregular practices and when charged with fraud concealed his books. . . .
July 31, 1885	. . . The assignment of S. Robertson & Son, bankers at Harriston, is announced. It has been explained that the senior partner has not, for some time past, given that attention to the business which it required. . . .
Aug. 21, 1885	. . . The Hamilton Times says that Mr. Chas. Livingstone, formerly of the banking firm of Fawcett & Livingstone, of Dresden, (which has failed) is now editor of the daily Advertiser, published at Honolulu, Sandwich Islands. . . .
Nov. 20, 1885	. . . Messrs. W. Lucas & Co., Markdale have not failed.
July 8, 1887	. . . In 1882 the private banking firm of Fawcett, Livingstone & Co., at Wardsville, was succeeded by John and William Shaw. . . . A day or so ago they absconded, leaving local debts, to a considerable sum, amongst the farming community. A leading bank is also down for a tidy amount which, however is amply provided for by collateral. It is freely whispered that speculating with "bucket shops" is the cause of the trouble. . . .

It was, of course, the failures that attracted attention, but they did reveal the deficiencies of the private banker as an institution. In commenting on the failure in 1889 of W. S. Black & Co., private bankers at Uxbridge, the *Whitby Chronicle* remarked ". . . Surely people must forget themselves to pass the post office savings bank and all the chartered banks and put their few dollars in a private bank. It now appears the Uxbridge people are to receive 38 cents on the dollar of their money back. The half per cent or so they were to receive more than they could draw from a bank proper will now be gone with the principal." In 1898 there was an extended debate in the House of Commons on the operations of the Post Office Savings Bank. In the course of that debate, one member who argued in favour of permitting the bank to offer attractive rates of interest to small savers had this to say in support of his view: ". . .There have been an astounding number of losses through private bankers collapsing. There is hardly a little town in western Ontario which has not in the last few years been the victim of these so-called private banking enterprises; and many people who have been attracted to them by the higher rates of interest they have offered, have been losers to a very considerable extent. . . . If the Government is going to reduce the rate of interest to the extent proposed, it must necessarily follow that poor people will be driven more than ever to deposit in these hazardous banking institutions. . . ."[12]

Without doubt, increasingly more adequate, more efficient and less risky financial facilities, particularly those provided by branch banks, sealed the fate of the private bankers. But it cannot be said that they did not provide useful services in that period of the evolution of the capital market when the branch system of the chartered banks was not yet providing satisfactory facilities to all communities.

---

12. Canada, House of Commons, *Debates*, April 19, 1898, p. 3720.

7

The Building Societies and Mortgage Loan Companies

In 1843 the Trust and Loan Company of Upper Canada was incorporated by special act of the Canadian Parliament for the express purpose of lending money on the security of real property. In 1844 there was formed in Sarnia, Ontario, the Port Sarnia Syndicate which, in 1847, after the passing in 1846 of an act to encourage the establishment of building societies in Upper Canada, became the Port Sarnia Building Society. This was the first of the building societies in Canada. Both kinds of organization were formed to facilitate real estate financing. The latter institution appeared everywhere almost overnight; the former did not. But after several decades of experimentation and innovation some of the building societies evolved into exceedingly successful limited liability joint-stock companies. Mortgage companies in general by the 1880s had experienced phenomenal expansion, accounting for about one-quarter of the assets of all financial intermediaries or about half as large as the chartered banks. Then began their relative decline and by the 1940s their assets were about 2% of the assets of all financial intermediaries. Their growth experience can be seen on Chart 7:1 below. The story of the growth, change and decline of mortgage loan companies is one of the most interesting that the history of Canada's capital market has to tell. The experience of those companies should be of interest to all financial companies, for it illustrates forcibly the great rewards arising from financial innovation and also the severe penalties, in terms of growth, consequent upon a failure to adapt to changing conditions.

Before examining the history of mortgage loan companies and building societies, it is useful to refer briefly to the nature of the financial intermediaries which existed at the time, for there can be

Chart 7:1 — Growth and Relative Size of the Building Societies and Mortgage Loan Companies 1870-1970

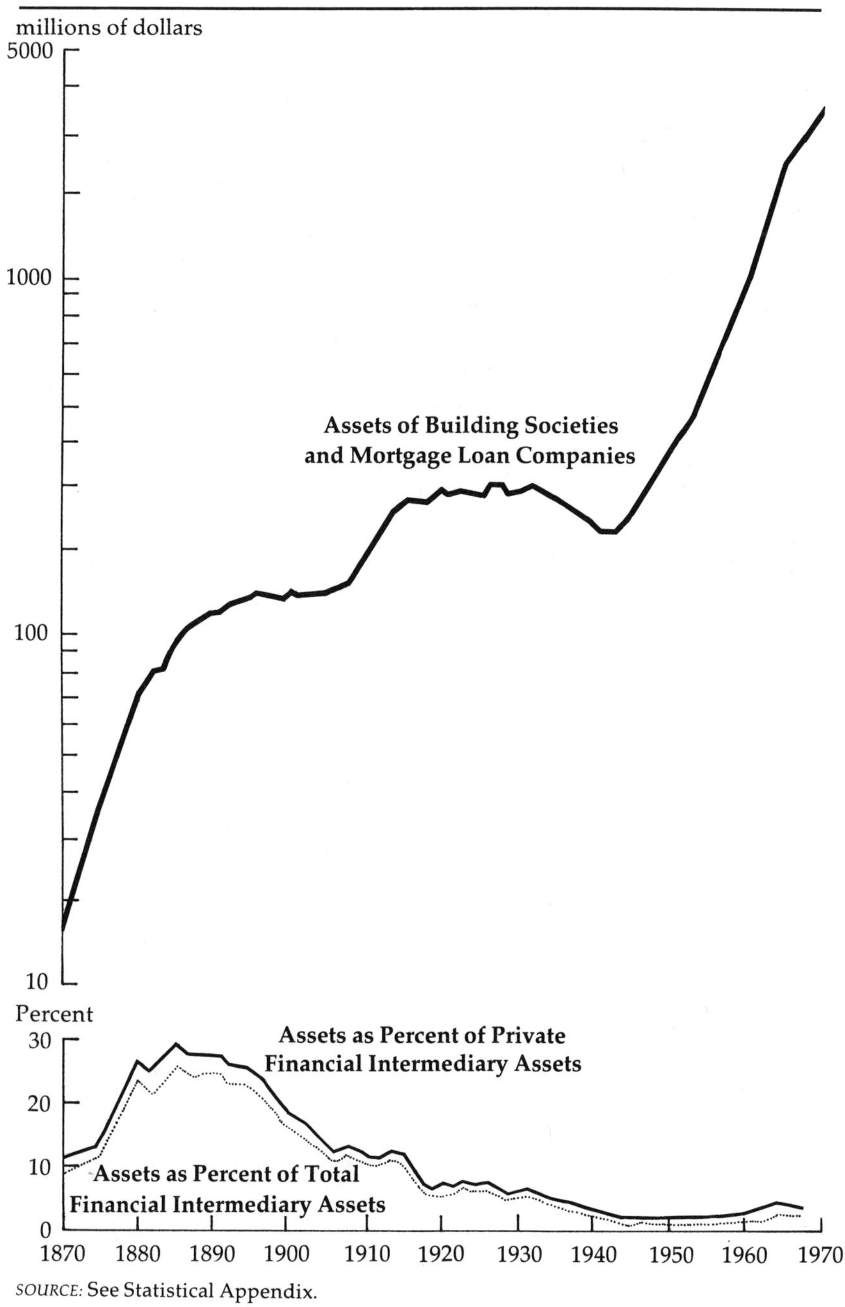

SOURCE: See Statistical Appendix.

little doubt a major gap in the structure of financial institutions assured the eventual success of these newcomers.

When the loan companies and building societies appeared in the 1840s, the chartered banking system had already made substantial strides in its development—the Bank of Montreal had passed its quarter-century mark and experimentation with trustee savings banks was almost as old. Fire insurance companies had been around even longer, and agents of British and American life insurance companies had appeared—although the first Canadian life company did not begin operations until 1847. None of these institutions was designed to mobilize savings for long-term investment. The non-Canadian life insurance companies began, it seems, as exporters of capital collected in Canada. The fire insurance companies then, as now, were not suited for providing large quantities of long-term funds. The trustee savings banks, inhibited by the aura of charity which surrounded their operations, and unsuited without changes in capital structure and approach to management to cope with more venturesome business, failed to fill the gap.

The chartered banks of course dominated the capital market and had made significant contributions to its development. By concentrating on commercial credit, by discounting commercial paper, and by dealing in exchange they began to meet the needs of domestic and international trade. In issuing notes they contributed to the provision of a reliable and convenient currency. By accepting deposits they provided a relatively safe instrument for individual savings. By issuing stock they provided yet another instrument to the saver, and also a useful stock in trade for the first stockbrokers.

In spite of these contributions, obvious and fundamental gaps in the capital market remained, which were left for other institutions to fill. The most obvious one was the provision of longer-term credit for purposes of financing real capital investments and for facilitating the transfer of such assets. The very first charters of the banks prohibited them from lending on "... land mortgage or hypothec, or to purchase such a security on any pretext except as permitted by the charters ...," these exceptions being limited to taking additional security for loans made in the ordinary course of their commercial banking business.[1] While this prohibition was, in practice, not always observed (as became obvious when some banks failed), it was sufficiently stringent to preclude the banks from developing that type of business. The

---

1. A. B. Jamieson, *Chartered Banking in Canada* (Toronto: Ryerson Press, 1953), p. 4.

bank failures themselves appeared to support the view that commercial banks should not "lock up" their funds in long-term credits. Nor could the banks circumvent the regulations by providing loans against collateral other than real estate. Such collateral did not exist in quantity; the most important collateral was land and urban real estate. In any case the demand for commercial credit, as indicated by the high rates of discounts to total assets, was so great that there was no reason for the banks to seek other outlets for lending on a permanent basis.

The scarcity of bank funds was of course a function of the supply as well as of the demand for such funds, and here again the banks faced certain limitations – some self-imposed and others beyond their control. The high proportion of notes in the banks' liabilities made them rather dependent on the quantity of notes they could keep in circulation. This in turn depended on the needs of trade and on their reserves of specie, for they were required to redeem their notes in specie at all times. Their supply of funds was further limited by their relative neglect of the deposit business in the first half of the nineteenth century. And finally, by not cultivating the use of the debenture, they precluded themselves from directly augmenting their reserves of specie and of long-term loanable funds with British capital.

Meanwhile, the demand for long-term credit persisted. The initial purchase of land from land companies, the augmentation of existing holdings and the need to raise capital for improving the land provided a demand for farm mortgages even when the speculative element was absent. Similarly, the growth of urban population provided a demand for housing which at times became intense, and urban commercial property-owners too were anxious to obtain mortgage loans for expansion purposes.

This demand for credit was first catered to by the local invester through barristers and solicitors, somewhat in the same manner as the local private banker provided commercial banking facilities.

But the lawyer acted primarily as a broker between borrower and lender and, of course, as a legal adviser. He could not accumulate large pools of either domestic or foreign savings. He could not provide a convenient credit instrument to people with large and small savings. And certainly he could not tap the vitally needed pools of savings of England and Scotland.

It was in the context of these economic conditions and credit arrangements that in 1843 the Trust and Loan Company of Upper Canada was incorporated and that building societies soon followed.

The Origins of the Industry

Throughout the history of the mortgage lending industry there have been various ways that mortgage loan companies and building societies could legally become established. Prior to Confederation each of the colonies of British North America had building societies legislation under which they could be formed; in addition charters could be obtained through special acts of the local legislatures; and the imperial Parliament could grant royal charters. After Confederation each province as well as the Dominion had jurisdiction over the establishment of such companies and each in turn could, if it wished, use both special acts and general legislation (and this of either a general joint-stock company act or a building society act or a loan company act nature) to incorporate mortgage companies. So the history of legislation governing such companies is somewhat voluminous and complicated. However, it can for our purposes be simplified with justification. First of all, for all intents and purposes, the industry originated and became established in Ontario, so some concentration on developments in that province is justified: in the year 1888, for example, 92% of the assets of 78 loan companies (which represented nearly all of the companies) arose from business in Ontario and, as Chart 7:1 shows, by that year the industry had passed the peak of its rate of growth. Secondly, some forms of building societies were clearly much more important than others. Table 7:1 shows, for example, that in 1888, out of 75 companies, 48 with 58% of the assets of all the companies operated under Dominion and provincial building societies legislation; 11 with 9% of the assets operated under Canadian and provincial joint-stock company legislation; 10 with 18% of the assets operated under private acts of Canadian legislatures; and 6 with 14% of the assets operated under legislation of the imperial government. Also, apart from the companies with royal charters, most others were chartered under legislation of the United Province of Canada, the Province of Ontario, and the Dominion of Canada—although a rash of short-lived companies for which records do not exist appeared in Western Canada after the turn of the century. Finally, legislation of the Dominion of Canada is important in that it tended to establish standards of operations. Emphasis on the growth and development of building societies in Central Canada is therefore necessary, as is emphasis on the development of Ontario and Dominion legislation relating to them.

The Trust and Loan Company was the first Canadian loan company to be formed. Incorporated in 1843 under a special act of the

Table 7:1 Building Societies and Mortgage Loan Companies of 1888

	NUMBER OF COMPANIES	ASSETS	PER CENT OF TOTAL
Operating under Canadian building societies legislation			
Ontario	40	59,898,662	56.0
Quebec	7	2,074,697	1.9
Nova Scotia	1	563,676	.5
	48		58.4
Operating under Canadian joint-stock company legislation			
Dominion	5	5,305,553	5.0
Ontario	6	4,644,722	4.3
	11		9.3
Operating under private acts of Canadian legislatures			
Dominion	8	13,457,647	12.6
Ontario	1	1,708,069	1.6
Quebec (also Ontario)	1	4,526,355	4.2
	10		18.4
Operating under imperial government legislation	6	14,807,496	13.9
TOTAL	75	106,986,877	100.0

SOURCE: Computed from statistics in Dominion of Canada, Department of Finance, *Report of the Affairs of Loan Companies and Building Societies, For the Year 1888*, Queen's Printer, Ottawa, 1889. While the Report probably does not include every mortgage loan company, it does include the great majority of them.

legislature of the United Province of Canada, with headquarters at Kingston and with John A. Macdonald as solicitor, the Trust and Loan Company found it difficult at first to become established. But the purpose of the company, to lend upon real and personal property, by providing a means for tapping the savings of Great Britain, is clearly established in the preamble of its 1843 act:

> ... Whereas, the improvement and advancement of the province are greatly retarded by reason of the deficiency of capital which prevails therein; And whereas the difficulty of ascertaining, with confidence, the money value and legal sufficiency of the security offered by the borrowers, has hitherto, to a great extent, precluded capitalists resident in Great Britain from availing themselves of the opportunities constantly offered in Canada for the profitable investment of Capital; And whereas, such difficulties would, to a great extent, be overcome by the establishment of an Incorporated Joint Stock Company, possessing powers to borrow money on the security of its subscribed Capital and to advance and lend the same, together with such portions of its subscribed Capital as may be paid up, on securities real or personal, in this province....[2]

In order to increase its appeal to British investors the company almost immediately applied for a royal charter, which was granted to it in 1845. Two clauses of its charter are particularly important: the one limiting the rate of interest it could charge to 6%, which doomed its success, and the one which limited its borrowing powers to the amount of the subscribed capital, which gave it some leverage (especially since not all subscribed capital needed to be paid) and which established a pattern that was imitated for many years. After five years of no progress the directors in 1850, and particularly Oliver Mowat, tried again to make it a going concern. In that year a private bill, sponsored by John A. Macdonald, gave it the right to charge up to 8% interest without being subject to the usury laws,[3] and Macdonald undertook a successful mission to London to seek new capital and support for the company.[4] A statement of purpose of the company of 1859 says that it commenced operation in the winter of 1851-2 with a subscribed capital of £500,000, of which £125,000 was paid up, and with the intention of depending on its borrowing powers for additional funds. With two of the most prominent bankers of the City of London, Thomas Baring and George Carr Glyn, as trustees this was not too difficult.

In October 1853 the company exercised its right to increase its subscribed capital to £1,000,000 by issuing an additional 25,000 shares on which £5 per share was paid, thereby also increasing its borrowing potential. In 1858 it received authority[5] to increase its capital to £3,000,000. Although it had authority to lend money to the

---

2. An Act for Incorporating and Granting certain Powers to the Upper Canada Trust and Loan Company 7 Vic., cap. 63, Dec. 9, 1843.
3. 13 & 14 Vic., cap. 138.
4. See Donald Creighton, *John A. Macdonald, The Young Politician* (Toronto: Macmillan Company of Canada, 1952), pp. 57, 58, 162-3.
5. 22 Vic., cap. 132.

provincial government, district councils and other public bodies, it immediately concentrated on mortgage lending. Its balance sheet for December 1857 took this form:

Dr.		
Shareholders' Capital, viz:—		
£5 per share on 25,000 shares	£125,000	
£3 per share on 25,000 shares	£75,000	
Paid in anticipation of calls	£14,362	
		214,362-0-0
Loans on debentures		315,375-0-0
Loan account		21,000-0-0
Income Tax account		2,517-1-4
Sundry creditors in Canada £1,893 10s. 1d. Cy., equal to, at 9½ per cent premium:		1,556-6-1
Reserve Fund account		13,468-6-8
Exchange account		1,241-17-11
Revenue account		9,230-18-1
Suspense account, £1,200 10s. Cy., equal to, at 9½ per cent premium:		986-14-3
		£579,738-5-1
Cr.		
Cash		
At Bankers', in London	1,597-15-4	
Petty Cash	13-14-3	
Petty Cash in Canada £6-14-7 Cr., equal to, at 9½ per cent premium	5-10-6	
Bankers' in Canada, £6,442 19s. 7d. Cy., equal to, at 9½ per cent premium	5,292-12-0	
		6,912-12-1
Investments—		
In London	20,880-0-0	
In Canada, mortgages, Cy.,	£549,056 5s. 6d.	
Montreal Fire Loan	86,932 4s. 9d.	
Municipal debentures	21,485 9s. 9d.	
Total	657,473 19s. 9d.	
equal to, at 9½ per cent premium	540,388 11s. 6d.	561,269-11-6

Sundry debtors in Canada	6,857 19s. 9d. Cy	
equal to, at 9½ per cent premium		5,636-14-0
Ditto in London		65-8-9
Preliminary expense account		5,853-18-9
		£579,738-5-1

Not until 1912[6] was its authorized capital increased, and a 1910 change in its charter[7] which permitted it to borrow money up to four times the amount of its paid-up capital represented no basic change from its earlier policy of requiring only one-quarter of the stock subscribed to be paid for, and borrowing up to the amount of its subscribed capital. However, the change brought its powers roughly in line with those outlined in the Dominion Act relating to loan companies of 1899.[8] The Trust and Loan Company was, for many years, the largest company of the industry, but then it declined in importance and after the Second World War was absorbed by another company.

It may also be noted that several other British companies operating under imperial legislation became important lending institutions—and we do not refer to land companies. The Scottish American Investment Company Limited with headquarters in Edinburgh, was formed in 1873 and operated in Canada until 1900—being one of the smaller British companies. The North of Scotland Canadian Mortgage Company, Limited, of Aberdeen was formed in 1875 for the express purpose of making loans on the security of real estate in Canada and operated in Canada for over half a century. The North British Canadian Investment Company Limited of Glasgow, formed in 1876, was still in operation at the beginning of the First World War.

Under an act of 1874[9] such outside companies were required to be licensed by the Secretary of State to carry on business in Canada, but apart from that virtually no restrictions were imposed on their operations. Restrictions were of course imposed by the charters under which they operated, as we have seen in the case of the Trust and Loan Company.

It is perhaps no accident that these British companies eventually

6. 2 Geo. V, cap. 158.
7. 9-10 Edw. VII, cap. 168.
8. 62-63 Vic., cap. 41.
9. 37 Vic., cap. 49.

disappeared. When interest rates declined toward the turn of the century several of the biggest moved all their operations to Western Canada – the prairies – where interest rates were higher, abandoning their Central Canada operations; and when agricultural settlement reached its maturity, and depression and drought prevailed on the prairies, the one-sided nature of their operations (in a geographic sense) proved to be a weakness. It seems also that control of the operations of the British and Scottish companies remained in the home country, so that management guidance, possibly, may have assisted little in their making adjustments to changing local conditions. The view that British capital market institutions have found it difficult to find a permanent place in Canada is therefore supported in this case, as it was with the British life insurance and fire insurance companies of the 1870s.

The Credit Foncier Franco Canadien has been much more successful than the English and Scottish loan companies in Canada. Just before the Second World War the assets of the Trust and Loan Company and the North of Scotland Canadian Mortgage Company were $8 million and $17 million respectively, those of the Credit Foncier $38 million, which by 1965 had increased to $206 million, while the others by that time had disappeared.

However, much more important for the development of indigenous mortgage loan companies than these outside companies were the building societies, and the companies which evolved from them. The first building society to be formed in Canada and the first mortgage lending institution to be in actual operation appears to have been the Port Sarnia Syndicate, which is still in operation as the Lambton Loan and Investment Company. It appeared even before there was legislation relating to building societies.[10] Robert Skilbeck came to Canada in the 1830s with a background of military service and good education. While still in England he had been an officer of a "terminating" building society and this no doubt influenced him in attempting to mobilize local funds by forming a similar institution in Sarnia. The Syndicate was formed in 1844 and based in Skilbeck's house. Two years later the United Province of Canada passed an act relating to building societies and on March 27, 1847, the Syndicate was granted a certificate of incorporation under the act in the name of the Port Sarnia Building Society. It was a terminable society – which we describe below – of a co-operative nature in which members were required to subscribe to at least one £50 share of stock

---

10. For details of its formation see *One Hundred Years of Service*, The Record of the Lambton Loan & Investment Company, Sarnia, Ontario.

to be paid for, if so desired, by monthly instalments of 5 shillings. A further entrance fee of 2 shillings and a 2-shilling annual management fee were also required to be paid, and when monthly payments and profits amounted to £50 the par value of the share could be withdrawn. Funds accumulated were lent to members by auction and the number of loans, amount lent and the average interest bid from 1847 to 1854 were as follows:

Year	*No. of Loans*	*Amount Lent*	*Average Interest Bid*
1847	10	£500	45.4%
1848	11	£550	39.8%
1849	14	£700	36.4%
1850	12	£600	21.0%
1851	10	£500	12.2%
1852	14	£700	18.7%
1853	10	£500	9.3%
1854	16	£800	10.3%

SOURCE: *One Hundred Years of Service*, p. 15. See fn. 10.

It is interesting that one of the by-laws of the society stipulated that no property be accepted as security for more than two-thirds of its estimated value, a ratio adopted by the Government of Canada in its legislation governing loan companies in 1961 and increased to three-quarters in 1965.[11]

By 1855 the society had reached the stage where, because of the shares having been paid up, it could wind up its business. However, modifications were introduced which permitted it to survive: deposits were accepted with interest; interest was paid on share payments; dividends were paid to shareholders when shares were fully paid; and a fixed rather than tender rate on loans was charged. The name of the company was changed in 1879 to the Lambton Loan and Investment Company and in 1885 the company began to issue debentures for the first time.

The legislation under which the Port Sarnia Building Society was formed was the first general act relating to building societies in British North America—*An Act to encourage the establishment of certain Societies commonly called Building Societies, in that part of the Province of Canada formerly constituting Upper Canada.*[12] However, the first specific act relating to them was one that appeared in the preceding year, 1845, which incorporated the Montreal Building Society.[13] Indeed, the two acts are virtually identical. Just as the Port Sarnia

11. 9-10 Eliz. II, cap. 51, 13-14 Eliz. II, cap. 40.
12. 9 Vic., cap. 90.
13. 8 Vic., cap. 94.

Syndicate can be traced directly to British practice, so the origins of the 1845 Act can be traced to an imperial statute of 1836, *An Act for the Regulation of Benefit Building Societies.*[14] Much of the preamble of the 1836 statute is identical to the Canadian act of 1845, and both carried a vitally important provision which permitted building societies to evade the usury laws, a privilege retained by the societies even when they became limited liability corporations with a permanent capital stock.[15]

As to the background of the British building societies, these first seem to have appeared in 1781 in Birmingham and originally were a device of the middle class to secure a vote by technically satisfying land ownership requirements. Contributions to the society by members soon permitted one of them—chosen by lot—to purchase the required amount of land and the society died when all had purchased land. From this evolved the idea of making contributions to permit individuals to purchase houses.[16]

The preamble of the 1846 Act conveys some impression of the kind of institutions these early societies were intended to be:

> Whereas it is desirable to afford encouragement and protection to the establishment of certain Societies, commonly called Building Societies, for the purpose of raising by small periodical subscriptions a fund to enable the members thereof to obtain unencumbered freehold or leasehold property; And whereas by an Act passed in the eighth year of Her Majesty's reign, certain persons were incorporated as a Society for such purposes in the City of Montreal, by the name and style of the Montreal Building Society, and provisions were made for the conduct and management of that Society, and certain privileges and immunities conferred upon it; And whereas it is expedient to encourage the formation of similar Societies throughout that part of this Province heretofore constituting the Province of Upper Canada, whenever the inhabitants of any particular locality may be desirous of availing themselves of the provisions of this Act; Be it therefore enacted....

Before discussing the details of this act and its results it may be noted that the approach indicated by it was very different from that of the act incorporating the Trust and Loan Company. The latter provided for permanent capital and for the sales of debentures, both

---

14. 6 & 7 Wm. IV, cap. 32.
15. In the cases of the *Canada Permanent Building and Saving Society* v. *Rowell*, 19 U.C. Q.B. 124, and *Canada Permanent Building and Saving Society* v. *Harris*, 26 U.C. C.P. 54, it was ruled that the society could collect its instalments, interest, bonuses, fines and forfeitures notwithstanding the usury laws in existence at that time.
16. See E. S. Watkins, LL.B., "Building Societies," in G. D. H. Cole, ed., *Studies in Capital and Investment* (London: Victor Gollancz, 1935, pp. 176 et seq.).

designed to appeal to "sophisticated" investors in England. The former provided for temporary capital only, and was intended primarily for the small local saver in Canada. This approach proved deficient but it evolved in a way which combined the best of both: an appeal to the British saver *and* to the Canadian saver.

The act provided that twenty or more persons could constitute themselves a building society by filing a declaration to that effect with the Clerk of Peace of their district and by paying him a fee of two shillings and six pence. It also provided for members of the society to purchase a share or shares in the society by instalment (the value of the share not to exceed £100 and the instalment payment not to exceed £1 per month) for the purpose of acquiring funds with which to buy houses. The funds deposited in payment of shares were loaned to members of the society. When total funds deposited and profits on loans were equal to the full value of the shares initially contracted for, the society was terminated and the funds distributed. Generally the life of the society was announced at the time of its formation – usually from ten to fourteen years.

The act permitted the societies to evade the usury laws for it provided

> ... that it shall and may be lawful to and for every such Society to have and receive from any member or members such sum or sums of money by way of bonus or any share or shares, for the privilege of receiving the same in advance prior to the same being realized, besides interest for the share or shares so received or any part thereof, without being subject or liable on account thereof to any of the forfeitures or penalties imposed by any Act or Acts of Parliament, or by any laws in force in that part of the Province heretofore Upper Canada relating to usury.

Thus whenever an amount equal to one or more shares had been accumulated it was possible for the society to lend that sum to a member by permitting him to withdraw the proceeds of his share before actually having paid for them, paying the society the legal rate of interest of 6% plus any additional bonus decided upon. In some cases borrowing members were selected by ballot, in others by rotation, and in still others by auction.[17] The borrowers had to repay the amounts borrowed, including bonus, by regular instalment payments. The societies could not borrow funds and their investments were limited to loans (i.e., advances on shares) on real estate

---

17. See *The Story of the Canada Permanent Mortgage Corporation, 1855-1925* (Toronto: 1925), p. 11.

mortgaged or assigned to the society, although surplus funds could be invested in chartered bank stocks and other public securities of the province.

The unique contribution of this type of financial institution at the time was that it provided savings facilities to the small saver, it committed him to a plan of savings, and it provided funds to the member of modest means for the construction of a house. This is in sharp contrast to the trustee savings banks, which by and large did not lend money to their customers and did not provide contractual savings arrangements.

The act of 1846 was followed by a similar one for Lower Canada in the same year. New Brunswick passed one in 1847,[18] Nova Scotia in 1849,[19] all following the same pattern. But the centre of development of the building societies, and the loan companies which succeeded them, was Upper Canada.

This development in its early stages can only be described as spectacular. A contemporary observer, writing in 1850, observed that the building societies

> ... have continued to increase in public favour, so that there are now, we believe, eight societies in the City of Toronto alone and at least one in almost every county of the Province. The provisions of these societies are generally as follows: — The value of each share £100, and the payments to realize this sum, 10 shillings monthly, with an entrance fee of from 2s. 6d. to 5s. to pay for books, stationery and other preliminary expenses, and 7½d. per month to cover all expenses of management, that the profits may go on accumulating without any deduction. A few of those which have been lately established, have reduced the shares to £50; and one to so small an amount as £12 10s., but the alteration does not seem to be much liked, as the expenses of management are thereby increased without commensurate advantage being gained. The accumulation of profit in these societies is very great, because the whole funds on hand being sold every month at high rates of interest and at a considerable premium, the operation of compound interest upon the increase of the general fund is very effective.[20]

From 1846 to March 1, 1855, there were no less than eighteen declarations of building societies filed in the Office of the Clerk of Peace for the County of York:[21]

---

18. 10 Vic., cap. 83.
19. 12 Vic., cap. 42.
20. *Rowsell's City of Toronto and County of York Directory For 1850-1* (Toronto: Henry Rowsell, 1850), p. xiv.
21. *Monetary Times*, April 2, 1875, p. 1120.

Name	*When Filed*
1. Toronto Building Society	June 13, 1846
2. Farmers' & Mechanics' Society	June 18, 1847
3. Home District Society	Sept. 14, 1847
4. Upper Canada Society	Mar. 28, 1848
5. Peoples Building Society	Mar. 7, 1849
6. Church of England & Metropolitan Society	Feb. 23, 1850
7. County of York Building Society	Mar. 4, 1850
8. Ontario Building Society	Mar. 21, 1850
9. Whitby Building Society	Sept. 10, 1850
10. Commercial Building Society	Jan. 29, 1851
11. Provincial Building Society	Feb. 20, 1851
12. Merchants Building Society	Nov. 24, 1851
13. Provincial Building Society	Feb. 16, 1852
14. Toronto Building Society	Apr. 29, 1852
15. Second Peoples Building Society	Nov. 2, 1853
16. New Provident Building Society	Jan. 2, 1854
17. Provident Permanent Building Society	Jan. 13, 1854
18. Canada Permanent Building Society	Mar. 1, 1855

The Toronto Building Society and the Farmers' and Mechanics' Building Society combined in 1855 to form the Canada Permanent Building and Savings Society. The Commercial also was able to adjust and survive for some years, but the remainder on the list disappeared speedily, some without actually having commenced business, and the rest somewhat ingloriously before the end of their natural life.[22]

Some of the defects of the system of building societies were fundamental; others were less serious. From the point of view of the development of a capital market, the most serious defect was that the societies were temporary, not permanent institutions. Funds available to them were required to be repaid to members when full value for the shares could be realized. In addition, the initial membership and the shares contracted for by it determined the growth of the society over the whole of its life, so that even growth within its temporary period of existence was circumscribed. The structure of the institutions virtually precluded them from achieving economies of scale of operation through branch or agency operations outside their local area. Supply of funds was limited to one source – the instalment payment for shares. Had there been no other defects, these would

22. Joseph D. Ridout, letter to the editor of the *Monetary Times*, April 9,1875, p. 1148.

have been sufficient to force the abolition or evolution of the system of building societies.

But there were other defects. To quote one writer:

> . . . In the early years needy borrowers offered ridiculously high bonuses, but as soon as this class of borrowers was satisfied, the biddings became less spirited, bonuses dropped lower and lower, until finally it became exceedingly difficult to find members willing to borrow even at par. Many had taken shares simply as an investment without any intention of borrowing, others had no security to offer and still others were deterred from borrowing owing to the uncertainty of the terms of repayment. The large bonuses at first freely offered aroused expectations of early termination, but when no bonus could be obtained and it became difficult to invest the funds, fear began to be entertained that subscriptions would be required for a much longer period than was at first announced. Those unfortunate members who had borrowed at high bonuses in the early years became seriously alarmed at the prospect of payments going on indefinitely. It was exceptionally difficult, in fact almost impossible, for a member to sell property that had been mortgaged because no one would buy it subject to the monthly payments, to which there was no defined limit. The directors were equally in the dark as to the duration of the society and consequently were afraid to allow members to commute their future payments lest this might work an injustice to the remaining members.[23]

In fact, because of interest rates made onerous by bonuses and fees, because of the injury to certain members when borrowers defaulted or when other members failed to make their regular payments, and because of mismanagement which resulted from the inexperience of the managers of the hastily formed local societies, the Upper Canada societies acquired an unenviable reputation. Mr. Joseph D. Ridout, a member of one of the first societies and President of the Canada Permanent from 1855 to 1884, wrote in 1875 that ". . . the chief difficulty the . . . [Canada Permanent] . . . had to overcome in its early days, in establishing itself as a high class Provincial monied institution, was the prejudice against the name of Building Society, which the defective system and mismanagement of many of these earlier petty concerns in Toronto and elsewhere had created."[24]

It is not easy to appraise the relative importance of these early terminating societies, but in spite of their numbers one does get the impression that they did not in their "pure" form become quantita-

23. *The Story of the Canada Permanent Mortgage Corporation*, p. 12.

24. Joseph D. Ridout, letter to the editor of the *Monetary Times*, April 9, 1875, p. 1147.

tively important. Several of them did evolve into permanent institutions, and others which called themselves building societies were actually formed after fundamental modifications to the concept outlined above had been made. They are historically important primarily because they constituted the first faltering steps in the direction of establishing reliable indigenous mortgage loan institutions, steps which were facilitated by the ease with which the relevant acts permitted them to be established. It would probably have been very difficult at that time for Canadian institutions to follow the lead of the essentially English Trust and Loan Company, and obtain a charter, sell stock and debentures, perhaps take deposits, and make mortgage loans, even though the building societies were not really important until they evolved into that type of institution.

Transition to Permanent Building Societies

The way in which the transition was made from terminating to permanent building societies is nicely indicated by the formation of the Canada Permanent Building and Savings Society (since 1903, the Canada Permanent Mortgage Corporation) in 1855.

Terminating building societies, as we have seen, originated in Britain. The idea for permanent building societies also originated there. It was discussed in a book published in 1849, which was studied by J. Herbert Mason, who in 1849 became accountant for the Farmers' and Mechanics' Society.[25] In October 1855 that society reached the end of its natural life, and in anticipation of that end Mr. Mason had in the fall of 1854 placed before the officers of the society a draft prospectus and set of by-laws for a permanent society. These were favourably received. At the same time the Toronto Building Society was also about to terminate its existence successfully. The directors of this society indirectly approached Mr. Mason on the matter of the two societies co-operating to form a new society. Co-operation proved to be possible and the declaration forming the Canada Permanent Building and Savings Society was filed with the Clerk of the Peace of the County of York on March 1, 1855. All but one of the directors of the Canada Permanent had been directors of the Toronto and the Farmers' and Mechanics' Building Societies. The president (Joseph D. Ridout) and vice-president (Peter Paterson) of the Canada Perma-

25. *The Story of the Canada Permanent Mortgage Corporation*, p. 17.

nent had held the same offices in the Farmers' and Mechanics', and Mr. Mason, who had in practice been the manager of the Farmers' and Mechanics',[26] became secretary and treasurer of the Canada Permanent and later (1887-1900) president. The directors were for the most part prominent Toronto businessmen, many with financial experience.[27]

This new society represented an important step forward in the evolution of mortgage loan institutions because theoretically its life was perpetual and because it began to accept deposits. Its life was perpetual because of an arrangement whereby a new group of members could begin a new cycle of share payments on the first day of every month, in contrast to the former arrangement whereby a new member, if he wished to join a society after it had begun operations, had to pay up all past instalments. A further improvement was that the duration of share payments was fixed, not indefinite; ultimate share value was £100, instalments were spread over 6 years at 20 shillings a month, and there was a management fee of 1 shilling and an entrance fee of 2s. 6d. per share. Furthermore, only "investing" shareholders shared in the profits; the nominal "borrowing" shareholders did not. It was necessary to retain the fiction that borrowers were shareholders so as to exempt the society's rates on loans (including bonuses and fines) from the usury laws.

In his initial draft by-laws Mr. Mason, following the example of certain English societies, provided for the society to take deposits as well as share payments. It was later reasoned that since the act of 1846 did not specifically prohibit this, it permitted it. In spite of the strenuous opposition of one member of the committee investigating the matter, the plan was adopted and the important feature of Canadian building societies accepting deposits was introduced.[28] Deposits were an important source of funds for the Canada Permanent from its first year of operations.

The next important step in the evolution of these societies came several years later, and also came from the initiative of the Canada Permanent. While the Canada Permanent's arrangement for share payments made it possible for its capital in total to be permanent, in fact it was revolving capital and its permanency depended on a steady stream of new members or of old members subscribing to a new cycle of shares. So the Canada Permanent propounded a system

26. See Joseph D. Ridout, letter to the editor of the *Monetary Times*, April 9, 1875, p. 1147.

27. *The Story of the Canada Permanent Mortgage Corporation*, pp. 22-3.

28. *Ibid.*, pp. 18-19.

for capitalizing shares, and prepared the act of 1859,[29] which permitted it. However, the act provided for capitalization to take place when shares were fully paid up, or due and payable to the holder, so that capitalization of Canada Permanent shares did not begin until 1860. The Freehold Building Society began capitalizing its shares before this date and before its shares were fully paid up, either because it ignored the act of 1859 or because it interpreted it differently from the Canada Permanent.[30] This practice was confirmed by the act of 1865,[31] at the instigation of the Freehold, but it limited such activity to societies with not less than $40,000 paid-up capital and $100,000 subscribed capital. The same act made it possible for building societies to cease issuing terminating stock.

The act of 1859 is an important one, not only because it permitted capitalization of shares, but also because it formally recognized the practice of societies taking deposits and excluding borrowing members from profits. The amount of deposits was limited to "... three-fourths of the amount of capital actually paid in on unadvanced shares, and invested in real securities by such Society."

So by 1859 it was legally possible for building societies to resemble joint stock companies, and some of them did. The one authority which had not explicitly been given them and which they had not assumed without explicit legal authorization was that of issuing debentures. As long as this situation existed, the building societies were denied not merely an additional instrument for gathering savings in Canada (which was not too important, perhaps, since their shares and deposits were readily available to local investors), but also any effective instrument for attracting British funds into their operation, a privilege already enjoyed by the Trust and Loan Company, as we have seen.

In 1862 Mr. Mason, of the Canada Permanent, went to England to negotiate the sale of debentures in that market. His attempt was unsuccessful. There was first of all the question of the society's legal right to issue debentures. The fact that the relevant act did not explicitly forbid the issue of such debentures was apparently not accepted by British capitalists as sufficient, and it proved to be an obstacle to introducing debentures in the same way deposits had been introduced. But this may not really have been the decisive reason for the failure of Mr. Mason's trip. There was also the credit standing of his company; it had no reserve, its capital was still liable

---

29. 22 Vic., cap. 45.
30. Joseph D. Ridout, letter to the editor of the *Monetary Times*, April 9, 1856, p. 1147.
31. Sec. 7, 29 Vic., cap. 38.

to be withdrawn, and its total assets ($718,526.26 on Dec. 31, 1861) were, in London money market terms, still comparatively small.[32] In addition, the aftermath of 1857 and the general disappointment in London over Canadian railroad ventures must have blunted the interest of British capitalists in Canadian ventures.

The introduction of debentures by building societies came eleven years later, in 1873, and as a result of the initiative of the Freehold Permanent Building Society. In that year this society obtained a special act of the Dominion Parliament which permitted it to issue debentures, so long as debenture and deposit liabilities combined did not exceed the amount of principal remaining unpaid on its mortgages and did not exceed an amount equal to twice its paid-up capital.[33] This gave the Freehold a new credit instrument, an instrument which could be sold in Britain; and it increased the borrowing powers of the society from three-quarters of its paid-up capital to twice its paid-up capital. It was an historic innovation.

Small wonder that other societies moved quickly to acquire it. The Canada Permanent prepared an amendment to the general act for submission to the Dominion legislature, and planned to ask for a special act applying only to its own institution if the former failed to receive legislative assent.[34] In the event the Dominion legislature passed "An Act to make further provisions for the management of Permanent Building Societies carrying on business in the Province of Ontario."[35] It was this act that empowered building societies in Ontario to issue debentures (it even outlined the form of a debenture) and thereby opened up the British capital market to them. Societies with a paid-up permanent capital of $200,000 were permitted to have deposit liabilities and outstanding debentures combined up to one and one-third of their paid-up permanent stock; societies with at least $40,000 paid-up capital could have deposits and debentures equal to their paid-up capital.

The act also permitted the societies to invest in Dominion, provincial and municipal securities, as well as in mortgages, whereas previously the provision was that they could "... invest any surplus funds in the stocks of any of the chartered banks or other public securities of the Province. . . ." This move to restrict the investments of the societies may well have been influenced by the severe loss experienced by the Canada Permanent on its holdings of Bank of

---

32. *The Story of the Canada Permanent Mortgage Corporation*, p. 47.
33. *Monetary Times*, May 23, 1873, p. 1036.
34. *Canada Permanent Building and Savings Society Annual Report for the year 1873.*
35. 37 Vic., cap. 50.

Upper Canada stock. Finally, and with some prescience in view of future developments, the act provided for amalgamation among societies.

An important, if somewhat elusive, development within the industry at this time was the establishment of reliable procedures for making mortgage loans. A Scottish-owned company described the process this way in 1876:

> ...The business of lending money on mortgages has been carried on in Canada for over twenty years, and has long been completely organized. The applicant for a loan fills up a printed form, a valuator's report on the property is had, and our advisers and agents consider the proposal. If approved by them the papers are handed to the lawyers, who investigate the title and state of the register. If the title is clear and there is no previous mortgage, which is ascertained by an official search of the Land Registers, the borrower executes the necessary mortgage deed, which the lawyers register, and the money is then paid over, or frequently in instalments, where the money is to be expended on improving a property. The registrar gives the lawyers a certificate that the mortgage has been registered, which is transmitted to us. The deeds are at present deposited with our banker for safe keeping, and a receipt by the banker for the documents is sent to the Head Office in Aberdeen. This explanation will show you the completeness and safety of the system.[36]

The only additional point that should be made is that as time went on all companies began to rely more heavily on their own inspectors for valuing properties, and less so on local agents.

By 1874 the Ontario building societies had in every important respect become loan companies, even though many of them continued to issue terminating stock and some did so exclusively. (Dominion legislation of 1899 and Ontario legislation of 1912 prohibited new companies from issuing terminating stock.) After this, legislative changes of importance involved primarily an expansion of the borrowing privileges of the companies and a relaxation of the provisions outlining the investments they were permitted to make.

It may first be mentioned, however, that the Orton Act of 1880[37] has to this day greatly influenced the type of mortgages that are made. Besides stipulating that mortgages with blended principal and interest must clearly show the principal amount and the interest rate on it, it provided that an individual could redeem any mortgage after

36. North of Scotland Canadian Mortgage Company Limited, *Report of the First Annual General Meeting*, December 29, 1876, p. 7.

37. 43 Vic., cap. 42.

five years on payment of three months' interest. Prior to that mortgages with a maturity much longer than five years had been common. Largely as a consequence of this legislation, the maturity of most mortgage loan debentures came to be five years.

In 1877 three general acts of the Dominion legislature relating to building societies were passed. The first one was the Canadian Joint Stock Companies Act,[38] which included for the first time a whole part (sections 88 to 104) relating only to the formation of loan companies by letters patent. The second and third acts were related respectively to the building societies in the province of Ontario[39] and in Quebec.[40] The significant borrowing provisions of these acts were as follows:

1. *Capital*—In order to borrow money from the public, paid-up capital had to be $100,000 (the 1874 act had stipulated $200,000) and the Companies and Quebec Societies Acts further required that 20% of subscribed capital be paid up.
2. *Deposit liabilities*—If deposits were used to accumulate funds the Companies Act and Quebec Societies Act limited these to the amount of the paid-up capital and cash, and the Ontario Societies Act to the amount of the unimpaired paid-up capital.
3. *Debenture liabilities*—If only debentures were used, the Companies Act and the Quebec Societies Act limited these to four times the unimpaired paid-up capital or the amount of the subscribed capital, at the option of the company.
4. *Debentures and deposits*—If deposits and debentures were utilized, their combined total was limited in all three acts to twice the amount of the unimpaired paid-up capital (with cash deducted from liabilities) and to the amount of unpaid principal on securities held as assets. This also represented a liberalization of borrowing powers, for the 1873 act had stipulated that such liabilities could not exceed the unimpaired paid-up capital by more than one-third.

Further liberalization in Dominion legislation proceeded very slowly. In 1899 the Dominion passed an Act Respecting Loan Companies, which raised borrowing limits to four times the paid-up capital with cash holdings deducted from liabilities; but deposit liabilities were again limited to paid-up capital and cash holdings.

The 1914 Dominion Act respecting loan companies[41] applied to all new federally incorporated mortgage loan companies and it first

38. 40 Vic., cap. 43.
39. 40 Vic., cap. 49.
40. 40 Vic., cap. 50.
41. 4-5 Geo. V, cap. 40.

introduced the provision that companies could borrow an amount equal to four times the paid-up capital and reserve and raised paid-up capital requirements from $100,000 to $250,000. In 1927[42] it became 6 times the paid-up capital and reserve, in 1948[43] 10 times the paid-up capital and reserve, in 1958[44] 12½ times the paid-up capital and reserve, and the industry asked this to be raised to 15 times in its submission to the Royal Commission on Banking and Finance. In 1965[45] it became 15 times a company's excess of assets over liabilities instead of 12½ times its capital and reserve. Separate limits on deposits disappeared in 1922.[46] This steady increase in permitted "leverage" reflected a basic trend in most financial intermediaries. However, in the case of the chartered banks there were no effective legal restraints to slow it down, whereas in that of the mortgage loan companies there were.

Legislation in Ontario relating to provincially incorporated companies was not very different from federal legislation. Borrowing privileges of up to three times the paid-up capital and not exceeding unpaid principal of securities held as assets appeared in 1884,[47] which was changed to reserves plus 4 times unimpaired paid-up capital in 1912; to 4 times unimpaired paid-up capital and reserves plus cash in 1921; raised to 8 in 1927, to 10 in 1949, to 12½ in 1959.

Prior to 1874, as we have seen, investment powers of building societies or loan companies were fairly broad—extending to the only readily available common stock of the time, that is chartered bank stock. From then until 1899 legislation restricted them to Dominion, provincial, municipal and school securities besides mortgage loans and loans against securities eligible for investment. In 1899 Dominion legislation again permitted investment in chartered bank stock and even in securities of all Canadian and provincially incorporated companies (excluding bills of exchange and promissary notes)—a very extensive liberalization (one also found in the Ontario legislation of 1912). Then with the 1914 act,[48] and as had happened in 1910 in the case of life insurance companies, and in 1897 with the Quebec savings banks, began a period of considerably more detailed prescription of securities that could be held, too numerous to mention here. However, a few highlights may be mentioned, the 1922 act being of

42. 17 Geo. V, cap. 61.
43. 11-12 Geo. VI, cap. 57.
44. 7 Eliz. II, cap. 35.
45. 14 Eliz. II, cap. 40.
46. 12-13 Geo. V, cap. 31.
47. 47 Vic., cap. 29.
48. 4-5 Geo. V, cap. 40.

particular importance. Many of the provisions resembled the ones governing life insurance company investments. The regulation that investment in common stocks had to be confined to companies with a dividend record of 4% for seven years and other securities of Canadian corporations with a dividend record of 4% for five years came in 1922;[49] a type of provision (e.g., 6% dividends for three years) introduced in Ontario in 1919.[50] The same act included the provision that not more than 30% of the common stock and 35% of the total stock (changed later also to 30%) of any one company could be held. It also introduced the provision that mortgage loans up to 60% of the value of a property might be made (changed in 1961 to 66⅔% and in 1965 to 75%); and it prescribed a minimum liquid-asset-to-deposit ratio of 20% (introduced in Ontario in 1946) which is still in force. Assets qualifying for the requirement have changed somewhat and now include primarily cash, deposits with chartered banks, federal and provincial government securities, certain municipal securities and demand loans against any of these securities.

From 1914 to 1922 there was a provision that securities of chartered banks and Canadian corporations were limited to 25% of the company's assets; in the 1948 act[51] it was re-introduced in changed form, now relating only to common stocks and limiting these to 15% of the book value of all of a company's funds. In 1961 liberalization again held sway when a sort of "basket clause" was introduced which permitted companies to invest in any securities not previously eligible (excluding mortgages and real estate), up to 15% of a company's unimpaired paid-up capital and reserve. Ontario introduced a similar provision in 1959. This process of liberalization was pursued further in 1965,[52] the change again resembling closely the changes that were made in life insurance legislation. Mortgage lending up to 75% of the value of properties, instead of 66⅔%, was now permitted; common shares with a five-year instead of a seven-year dividend record of at least 4% were now eligible investments, and in addition also eligible were the common stocks of companies with an earnings record that would have permitted such a dividend payment, whether it was paid or not. Finally, total holdings of common stocks could now amount to 25% of the book value of a loan company's funds instead of 15%.

It is obvious from the foregoing that the general trend of Ontario legislation has been the same as that of the federal government,

---

49. 12-13 Geo. V, cap. 31.
50. 9 Geo. V, cap. 42.
51. 11-12 Geo. VI, cap. 57.
52. 13-14 Eliz. II, cap. 40.

sometimes anticipating it, at other times following it. There are, however, a number of differences in detail which we need not examine here.[53]

When the implication of these changes in legislation may have been for the growth of mortgage loan companies we shall consider after we have examined their actual and relative growth since 1870.

Growth and Development

RATE OF GROWTH, RELATIVE SIZE AND NUMBER OF COMPANIES

An examination of Chart 7:1 and Table 7:2 permits us to obtain an over-all impression of the growth experience of building societies and mortgage loan companies in Canada since 1870. The figures are all based on companies in actual operation whose assets have been tabulated on an annual basis. It is clear that the period prior to about 1891 constituted the "golden years" of those companies. The assets of the tabulated companies grew by about 11¼% per annum from 1870 to 1891 and accounted for about 24% of the assets of all financial intermediaries recorded—a ratio not exceeded by any other non-bank intermediary until the life insurance companies did so in the 1920s. The decade of the 1870s was particularly important for the establishment of loan companies, with 63 new ones appearing (see Table 7:3) and only 9 disappearing and almost a doubling in the average size of assets per company. "The rapid increase in the number of these companies, and the large aggregate of capital they control, is one of the most noticeable features of recent Canadian finance," noted the *Monetary Times* in 1878.[54] From about 1891, except for the decade prior to 1914, the industry experienced remarkably little growth until after 1944. Consequently, companies diminished steadily and dramatically in relative importance until by 1944 their assets comprised only 2% of the assets of all financial intermediaries recorded in this study. After the Second World War the assets of the companies again began to grow and did so at a slightly higher rate than the assets of all financial intermediaries combined,

53. But see Dominion Mortgage and Investment Association, *Submission to the Royal Commission on Banking and Finance*, 1962, Appendix 6.

54. *Monetary Times*, Feb. 1, 1878, p. 898.

Table 7:2 Growth and Relative Size of the Building Societies and Mortgage Loan Companies 1870-1968

	1870-1891 %	1891-1902 %	1902-1914 %	1914-1944 %	1944-1968 %
Average annual growth rate — current dollars[1]					
— Mortgage loan companies	11¼	¾	5¼	0	10¾
— Chartered banks	4½	6¾	8	5	7
— Total private financial intermediaries	6¼	5¾	8	5¼	8¾
— Total financial intermediaries	6½	5¾	8	5¾	9
Assets as a proportion of assets of all financial intermediaries — end of period					
— Mortgage loan companies	24	14	11	2	3

SOURCE: See Statistical Appendix.

[1]To nearest ¼%.

Table 7:3 Number of Tabulated Building Societies and Mortgage Loan Companies and Average Size of Assets 1870-1900

	NO. OF COMPANIES, END OF PERIOD	NEW COMPANIES DURING THE PERIOD	COMPANIES DISAPPEARED DURING THE PERIOD	AVERAGE ASSETS PER COMPANY, END OF PERIOD (MILLIONS OF DOLLARS)
1870	28	—	—	$ .5
1871-1875	61	34	1	.6
1876-1880	82	29	8	.9
1881-1885	83	14	13	1.2
1886-1890	88	17	12	1.4
1891-1895	95	15	8	1.4
1896-1900	86	4	13	1.6

SOURCE: See Statistical Appendix.

the former mounting to an average annual growth rate of 10¾%, and the latter 9% from 1944 to 1968; but their assets remained small as a proportion of the assets of all financial intermediaries, and former glories remained irretrievably lost. Indeed, the growth rate itself is in one respect overstated, for it includes the growth of investment contract companies, which, as we note later, are not strictly loan companies. If their assets are excluded the 1944-68 growth rate is slightly lower.

It is interesting to observe the appearance and disappearance of these companies during the period of their greatest development and the early period of their relative decline. Table 7:3 shows that by 1889 there were 82 tabulated compared with 28 a decade before, and that the most rapid rate of formation had occurred by then. It also shows that, in addition to assets of the industry growing through an increase in the number of companies, they grew through an increase in the average size of the companies, and that as the appearance of new companies levelled off, the disappearance of old companies increased through mergers, amalgamations and liquidations. The total number of companies continued to increase right up to and perhaps even after the growth of the industry had come to a halt: in 1895 a peak of 95 tabulated companies was reached whereas their assets had begun to level off long before that and had virtually ceased to rise by about 1892.

After the turn of the century the number of companies that disappeared began persistently to exceed new companies and by 1965 only 36 companies could be tabulated and in 1969, 33. In this period some loan companies disappeared by merging with or being transformed into trust companies, as well as through amalgamations and liquidations. The shift toward trust companies to some extent resulted from subtle developments within legislation governing the latter. When trust companies first appeared in the 1880s their borrowing powers reflected official attempts to differentiate between them and those of mortgage loan companies and banks, for they were not permitted to issue debentures and take deposits. However, by the 1920s their Guaranteed Investment Certificates had in every practical, if not legal, sense become a substitute for debentures, and they had acquired the right to take deposits. In addition, they enjoyed fiduciary powers on which they could build their estates, trusts and agency business. In effect, therefore, they had all the powers of loan companies and some powers that loan companies did not have.[55]

55. See below, pp. 293-300, for a detailed account of these developments.

A rather remarkable aspect of the history of these companies is the relatively orderly nature of their disappearance. In the period prior to Confederation most of the small, local terminating building societies did vanish rather ingloriously, giving their successors a somewhat beclouded public image. But few of the important permanent building societies and joint-stock loan companies which succeeded them did so. As early as 1874 the *Monetary Times* reported that "... the suspension or insolvency of a Canadian building society is something wholly unknown; certainly the public outside the stockholders have suffered in no single instance."[56] In 1914 Hume Cronyn, a leading figure in the industry, wrote that ". . . after an experience of seventy years no loan company whose business was confined to mortgage lending has failed to meet all demands, and among those few companies who through gross mismanagement or worse have collapsed, not one had in any sense contributed to its down-fall through overborrowing."[57]

The principal reason why the mortgage loan companies were so generally successful in honouring their liabilities to the public probably was that they largely confined their activities to mortgage lending and seldom became promoters of risky ventures, and because they were required to maintain a very high equity-to-debt ratio. As we shall see again, the factors explaining the decline in importance of mortgage loan companies may have been that they were required to be too conservative in their borrowing operations.

Another reason for their orderly disappearance was that, being generally in a sound financial position, individual companies could be merged with or their assets sold to other mortgage companies without difficulty. By 1960, for example, the Huron and Erie Mortgage Corporation merged with or acquired the assets of nine other companies, and the Canada Permanent Mortgage Corporation thirteen other companies. In some cases companies with whom these two merged had themselves earlier merged with other companies.

STRUCTURE OF ASSETS AND LIABILITIES

The nature of the assets and liabilities of the building societies since 1863 are outlined in Table 7:4. This gives us an impression of the changing character of the sources of funds of those companies and the relatively unchanging character of the investment of those funds by the companies. The early building societies confined themselves very largely to mortgages, for this was the purpose of their being

56. *Monetary Times*, May 29, 1874, p. 1224.
57. Hume Cronyn, "Canadian Loan and Savings Companies," *The Scottish Bankers' Magazine*, July 1914.

established; and Table 7:4 shows that during the years 1863 to 1875 mortgages accounted for over 85% of the assets of the companies and societies – a period in which many terminating or partially terminating societies were still present and were still in the process of evolving into permanent societies or loan companies. Also the unusually high return on mortgages encouraged the companies to maximize their holdings of them, as they did until the 1890s. Then, with the slowdown in the growth of the companies after 1890, their holdings of mortgages in relation to total assets declined to around 80%; in 1895 the ratio was about 79%, as it was in 1968, and only during the years affected by Second World War financing did it fall below 70%. At the same time it is apparent that for a decade or two prior to the First World War, when the industrial corporation came to the fore in Canada, the loan companies increased their holdings of corporation securities, but then tended to lose interest. It is quite conceivable that the new trend in legislation which began in 1914 and featured limitations on corporate securities that could be held by the loan companies prevented the companies from evolving out of mortgage loan companies into investment funds.

The type of mortgage financing engaged in by the industry has changed since the period of its greatest development. The early building societies seem to have concentrated on financing on the security of residential and other urban real estate. When these evolved into the more flexible forms of permanent building societies and loan companies, the emphasis shifted in response to demand, to providing long-term credit to farmers, a form of financing which soon predominated. One loan company described its operations of 1876 in this way:

> ... The great bulk of our money goes to improve the land we hold in security. Sometimes, however, a farmer with a fully improved farm bonds it for the purpose of buying another farm, or a piece of unimproved land, for a son he has to start in the world, or it may be to increase his own holding. . . . Perhaps I ought also to refer to another idea which occurred to me in travelling through Ontario. Seeing the people settled on their own land, rapidly reclaiming it and increasing its value, it seemed to me that the farmers in Ontario will by-and-by become so rich that they will not require our money. Should this prove to be the case, we must just make up our minds to move further westward, and in Manitoba, when intersected by the great railway running across the continent, I believe we shall find an outlet for our money for as long a period as it is any use thinking about at present.[58]

58. North of Scotland Canadian Mortgage Company Limited, *Report of the First Annual General Meeting*, December 29, 1876.

Table 7:4 Assets and Liabilities of Building Societies and Mortgage Loan Companies Registered in Ontario,[1] Percentage Distribution 1863-1968

	LIABILITIES TO SHAREHOLDERS			LIABILITIES TO PUBLIC						
					DEBENTURES					TOTAL ASSETS OR LIABS. %
	PAID-UP CAPITAL	OTHER[2]	TOTAL	DEPOSITS	PAYABLE IN CANADA	PAYABLE ELSEWHERE	TOTAL	OTHER	TOTAL	
1863	65.4	11.7	77.1	19.8	—	—	—	3.1	22.9	100
1867	65.3	n.a.	n.a.	17.9	—	—	—	n.a.	n.a.	100
1870	60.3	n.a.	n.a.	25.9	—	—	—	n.a.	n.a.	100
1875	50.3	19.1	69.4	25.0	—	3.9	3.9	1.7	30.6	100
1880	35.8	10.8	46.6	17.1	.4	33.5	33.9	2.8	53.4	100
1885	34.2	9.7	43.9	16.8	4.7	32.8	37.5	1.8	56.1	100
1890	28.9	10.5	39.4	15.8	7.1	35.5	42.6	2.2	60.6	100
1895	28.1	9.4	37.5	12.7	7.7	36.2	43.9	5.9	62.5	100
1900	27.7	13.9	41.6	15.0	12.0	29.7	41.4	1.6	58.0	100
1905	27.9	11.8	39.7	15.7	15.1	27.4	42.5	2.1	60.3	100
1910	25.5	11.7	37.2	12.5	14.0	34.2	48.2	2.1	62.8	100
1915	22.2	14.2	36.4	11.3	12.7	38.7	51.4	.9	63.6	100
1920	23.8	16.4	40.2	13.9	n.a.	n.a.	43.9	2.0	59.2	100
1925	20.6	22.9	43.5	14.0	n.a.	n.a.	41.3	1.2	56.5	100
1930	16.0	13.2	29.2	16.2	32.9	13.3	46.2	8.5	70.9	100
1935	16.1	11.5	27.6	15.1	37.3	13.2	50.5	6.8	72.4	100
1940	16.9	13.1	30.0	17.1	37.9	11.8	49.2	3.2	70.0	100
1945	15.2	14.1	29.3	24.2	35.6	7.2	42.8	3.7	70.7	100
1950	11.4	12.3	23.7	32.4	38.8	3.2	42.0	1.8	76.2	100
1955	7.2	10.4	17.7	31.2	47.3	1.5	48.9	2.3	82.4	100
1960	5.4	8.7	14.1	22.8	59.6	1.6	61.2	1.9	85.9	100
1965	4.4	6.6	11.1	25.4	54.3	.6	54.9	8.6	88.9	100
1968	3.6	7.9	11.5	22.4	n.a.	n.a.	59.1	7.0	88.5	100

SOURCE: For the year 1863 Province of Canada, *Municipal Returns*, 1863.
1867-1885, Canada, Department of Finance, *Report of the Affairs of Building Societies Loan and Trust Companies*, 1912, pp. VIII-XI.
1890-1968, Province of Ontario, *Report of the Registrar of Loan and Trust Corporations*, Annual.

[1]1867-1885 includes several companies not registered in Ontario and years prior to 1880 exclude U.K. loan companies. Excludes "investment contract" companies.
[2]Essentially reserve fund and contingency reserve, balance of profit and loss account, investment reserves and dividends unpaid.

		SECURITIES								
MORTGAGES	CASH	DOMINION & U.K. DIRECT & GTD.		PROVINCIAL & GTD.	MUNICIPAL	TOTAL GOV'T BONDS	CORPORATION BONDS	STOCKS	TOTAL BONDS & STOCKS	OTHER
85.7					.3	n.a.		—		13.2
87.5	5.6		n.a.		.7	n.a.		—	n.a.	n.a.
93.1	3.3		n.a.		.5	n.a.		—	n.a.	n.a.
91.6	3.2		n.a.		.7	n.a.		—	n.a.	n.a.
80.9	6.4		.5		1.8	n.a.		—	2.3	8.1
85.5	2.8		.5		1.6	n.a.		—	2.1	7.5
85.0	2.5		n.a.		.8	n.a.		—	n.a.	n.a.
79.0	3.0		n.a.		1.5	n.a.		—	n.a.	n.a.
77.7	2.4		.7		2.1	n.a.		7.0	9.8	10.1
79.5	2.8		—		2.0	n.a.		11.5	13.5	4.1
80.6	3.5		—		2.0	n.a.		10.6	12.6	3.3
78.1	5.9		.7		1.6	n.a.		9.4	11.7	4.2
71.3	4.8		5.5		5.2	13.7	3.0	4.3	18.0	5.8
71.2	5.4		7.4		3.4	14.6	3.8	3.6	18.2	5.1
78.4	3.0		4.3		1.7	8.4	2.4	3.8	12.2	6.5
74.1	3.0		7.3		1.0	10.0	1.7	4.7	14.7	8.2
69.6	4.0		9.2		1.4	11.5	.9	5.1	16.6	9.8
51.5	3.5	27.6		3.2	1.2	32.0	1.6	6.5	40.1	4.9
68.9	4.2	13.3		2.1	.9	16.3	.3	6.8	23.4	3.5
75.2	2.6	10.7		2.0	1.3	14.0	.8	4.1	18.9	3.3
79.4	1.6	6.9		1.3	.8	9.0	2.0	4.3	16.6	2.4
80.3	2.9	n.a.		n.a.	n.a.	8.1	n.a.	3.7	11.8	5.0
79.5	1.5	n.a.		n.a.	n.a.	5.5	1.5	3.8	10.8	8.2

This is about what happened. An informed observer wrote in 1921:

> ...Up to 1890 the demand for farm mortgage loans in Ontario had absorbed a large share of the available funds of lending societies. A prospectus issued by the Canada Permanent Building Society in 1867 states that five-sixths of the loans of that society were made upon improved farms, but after 1900 the demand for farm mortgage loans in Ontario rapidly diminished owing to the improved financial standing of the farmers themselves and the fact that the lending of monies of individuals was very largely directed to this form of investment. It was at this time, therefore, that the lending companies turned to the Western Provinces....[59]

The fillip given the mortgage loan companies by the opening up of the prairies is suggested by the higher rates on mortgages there as compared with those in Ontario.[60] But basic changes in the demand for mortgage money of the loan companies were only temporarily delayed. They came with a vengeance through the effects of the completion of prairie settlement, the gradual retirement by farmers of outstanding mortgage debt, the debilitating experience of the 1930s with its drought, depression and defaults, and finally the growing participation and eventual monopolization of both federal and provincial governments of financing on the security of farm land – a trend that was signalled by the formation of provincial lending agencies after the turn of the century and particularly by formation of the Canadian Farm Loan Board by the federal government in 1927.[61] This disappearance of the demand for a type of credit that had been very important to the companies for many decades was a major blow to their growth rate. They had to develop other business to take its place – seldom an easy task – and by the period after the Second World War farm mortgage lending had become a minor part of their business.

Sources of funds for the companies have changed materially over the years. First, shareholders' equity, which accounted for about 70% of the funds in 1875, accounted for only about 11% of the liabilities of the companies in 1968. It had declined to about 40% by 1890 and remained at about that level until the middle 1920s. The depression for obvious reasons reduced it further but it was in the period after the Second World War that the companies, taking advantage of the

---

59. V. Evan Gray, M.A., LL.B., "Mortgage Lending Institutions in Canada," in *Loan and Trust Corporations' Statements for the Year ended 31st Dec. 1920*, printed by order of the Legislative Assembly of Ontario, p. 229.

60. See Table 7:5 below.

61. See chapter 13.

less restrictive borrowing provisions of the legislation under which they operated, permitted their equity to decline materially. This long-term decline in the relative size of equity is similar to the decline in the equity of the chartered banks and appears to be a common feature of the development of financial intermediaries in general. The fact that legislation may have impeded that natural development in the case of loan companies is therefore of special interest to us and we shall return to it again.

This relative decline in shareholders' funds was of course matched by an increase in borrowed funds of the companies. The early Canadian building societies were not legally permitted to take deposits until 1859, although several of them did so before then; but none of them issued debentures before they were legally permitted to do so in 1874. English joint-stock loan companies, of course, were permitted to sell debentures long before 1874 and did so. For Canadian companies deposits were the only important source of funds prior to 1874, and these amounted to about 20% to 25% of their total funds. After 1874 debentures almost immediately became as important a source of funds as equity capital (and much more profitable for shareholders), as can be seen in Table 7:4. In 1968 they accounted for 59% of the companies' liabilities, as against 11% for shareholders' funds and 22% for deposits. The importance of the debenture after 1874 was not just that it gave the companies a new instrument to offer to savers, but that it provided the companies with a route into the English and Scottish capital markets at very favourable cost to them.

Let us examine that new source of funds further. In 1874, the year after it had been granted special permission to issue debentures, the Freehold Loan and Savings Company of Toronto sold $100,000 debentures, at 6% interest and having five years to run, in England through the firm of A. R. McMaster & Brothers of London; these were the first Canadian building society debentures issued.[62] Another company soon after sold debentures through agents in Glasgow and Edinburgh[63] and thereby began the long and remarkable marketing of Canadian loan company debentures in Scotland. How this was done was described by the Ontario Registrar of Loan Corporations in 1921:

> ... The sale of the securities, that is to say, of the debentures of loan corporations, has been largely done through investment agencies. This is particularly the case in Scotland. As you know, there are in Scotland, well established investment agencies usually Solicitors or

62. *Monetary Times*, Oct. 2, 1874, p. 375.
63. *Monetary Times*, Dec. 11, 1874, p. 658.

> Writers to the Signet, whose offices are maintained through succeeding generations, and which control the investments of very large accumulations of wealth. The Canadian loan companies which seek British monies have operated almost exclusively through these agencies by payment of a commission for monies secured. This commission has, I believe, been steadily maintained at a rate of 1 percent for five years, or a proportionate amount for a shorter term on the proceeds of all debentures sold either original or renewals. The sale of currency debentures locally has been chiefly done through the offices of the companies themselves, through paid solicitors and by payment of commissions to general investment agents. In every case the lending company has borne the expense of these commissions.[64]

Until about the turn of the century, when debentures were supplying a significant portion of the companies' funds, four-fifths or more of those debentures were sold elsewhere than in Canada—primarily in England and Scotland. There is no doubt that the introduction of the sterling debenture by the loan companies was the major innovation in their sources of funds that permitted them to attain a high rate of growth and unusual prominence prior to the turn of the century. However, the success of that innovation lulled the companies into a false sense of security, for during that period they did not really develop their local market for debentures and the statistics suggest that they permitted their deposit business to drift. At the same time developments beyond their control were soon to reduce the U.K. market for their debentures. The *Monetary Times* remarked as early as 1877 that "... deposits have not been so much sought by these Companies since they acquired the right to issue debentures."[65] A chairman of one of the companies points out in his annual address even in 1876 that "... The Company's debentures, as you are aware, are the source of our money-making power..." and he also pointed out "... there is one item of decrease, but it is an item in which Directors desired a decrease—that is, the deposits. As we stated on a former occasion, it is looked upon as generally safer for the Company not to depend upon having money on deposits which might be called up in time of panic suddenly, but to have it on debentures running for fixed periods of years, and, I am happy to say, we are able to obtain our money in that way on very favourable terms."[66]

As for the virtual disappearance of the U.K. market for Canadian mortgage loan company debentures, this arose largely because of the

---

64. V. Evan Gray, *op. cit.*, p. 232.
65. *Monetary Times*, April 20, 1877, p. 1204.
66. *Monetary Times*, Jan 21, 1876, p. 830.

closing of the interest rate gap between the two countries. Table 7:5, column 5 shows that the gap between sterling loan company debentures and U.K. Government consols was 2.75% in 1873; by 1883 it had narrowed to 1.77%, by 1895 to 1.24%, by 1914 to less than 1% and by 1920 the gap had almost vanished. This, of course, reflected the effect on U.K. interest rates of war finance as well as the secular decline in interest rates in Canada. Obviously U.K. investors would not be interested in loan company debentures under those circumstances. At the same time Canadian loan companies could not increase their yield profitably because of the decline in mortgage loan rates that had occurred. Column 6 of Table 7:5 shows that by the turn of the century the gap between yield on Ontario mortgages and cost of sterling debenture money had fallen below 2%, which, since the "normal" gap is more like 2% to 2¾%, may be regarded as being small. Looked at in another way, by about the turn of the century the average cost of Canadian debenture money was about as low as that of sterling debenture money so that not only was there little incentive for U.K. investors to buy the latter but there was also reduced incentive for Canadian companies to sell them. There apparently was even an incentive for Canadian companies to speed the shift out of sterling debentures into Canadian debentures. One writer pointed out in the 1920s that

> . . .The effect of the World War was not only to discourage new borrowings from Great Britain, but also to encourage paying off maturing debentures, this in view of the decline in sterling exchange which enabled the loan corporations to pay off their indebtedness to Great Britain at a profit although there was a decline also in the Canadian exchange. Some of the loan corporations took advantage of the situation to the extent of going into voluntary dissolution. . . . It will be noted that the borrowings from Great Britain are being replaced to a greater extent every year by borrowing from the Canadian public, but it has obviously been of great advantage to have British loans, to the extent possible, during the transition.[67]

So in the 1920s the loan companies began to concentrate on sales of debentures in Canada, and they also began to pay more attention to deposits as a source of funds. In 1968 Canadian debentures accounted for 59% of the liabilities of companies registered in Ontario, debentures sold elsewhere were negligible in amount, and deposits at 22% of liabilities were relatively larger than they had been over the six decades from the 1870s to the 1940s (see Table 7:4).

---

67. Emil Sauer, *Canadian Loan Corporations* (Washington, D.C.: U.S. Government Printing Office, 1929), p. 9.

Table 7:5 Comparison of Yield on Canadian Mortgages and Loan Company Debentures with Yield on U.K. Government Consols 1873-1920 (selected years)

	U.K. GOV'T CONSOLS % (1)	STERLING LOAN COMPANY DEBENTURES % (2)	ONTARIO MORTGAGES % (3)	MANITOBA MORTGAGES % (4)	2-1 (5)	3-2 (6)
1873	3.25	6.00	9.00	—	2.75	3.00
1876	3.17	5.75	8.50	—	2.58	2.50
1880	3.06	5.00	—	—	1.94	—
1881	—	—	—	9.50	—	—
1883	2.98	4.75	7.75	—	1.77	3.00
1885	3.02	—	7.50	—	—	—
1886	—	—	—	8.50	—	—
1889	2.64	4.25	—	—	1.61	—
1890	—	—	—	8.00	—	—
1895	2.39	3.63	—	—	1.24	—
1897	2.26	—	6.50	—	—	—
1898	2.28	3.75	—	7.50	1.47	—
1900	2.53	—	6.25	—	—	—
1902	2.66	4.00	5.75	7.50	1.34	1.75
1904	2.84	4.25	5.75	7.50	1.41	1.50
1906	2.85	4.25	6.25	7.50	1.40	2.00
1908	2.90	4.25	6.25	7.50	1.35	2.00
1910	3.10	4.25	6.25	7.50	1.15	2.00
1912	3.30	4.25	6.50	7.50	.95	2.25
1914	3.35	4.25	6.50	8.00	.90	2.25
1916	4.33	4.75	6.50	8.00	.42	1.75
1918	4.40	5.50	7.00	8.00	1.10	1.50
1920	5.41	5.50	6.75	8.00	.09	1.25

SOURCE: Columns 2, 3 and 4 from "Report of the Registrar of Loan Corporations for the Year Ended 1920," *Ontario Sessional Papers*, Part III, vol. LIII, 1921, pp. 242-3. Relates to the experience of one major company. Columns 3 and 4 refer to average interest earned.

INVESTMENT CONTRACT COMPANIES

Our data of total assets of mortgage loan companies include the assets of what Ontario has called "investment contract" companies and the Dominion Bureau of Statistics, "savings certificate" companies. This, on balance, is an appropriate classification because of their mortgage lending activity, but in fact such companies pioneered a new type of debt instrument and so must be examined separately.

The first of them was Investors Syndicate Limited, which was formed in Winnipeg in 1940 as Investors Syndicate of Canada and which has always accounted for most of the assets of investment contract companies. At the end of 1967 it, together with its associated company the Western Savings and Loan Association, had 82% of the assets of that group of companies. There were eight companies in total, belonging to six organizations, in 1969. In addition to the two companies referred to above, there were First Investors Ltd. and Associated Investors Ltd. operating as associated companies out of Edmonton, Savings and Investment Corporation of Quebec City, Keltic Savings Corporation Ltd. and Service Investments Corporation Ltd. of Halifax and Commonwealth Savings Plan Ltd. The latter was in financial difficulties in 1969.[68] Total liabilities under investment contracts amounted to just over $400 million at the end of 1967 and the funds so accumulated were invested primarily in mortgages but in debentures as well.[69]

The new savings contract or certificate that these companies pioneered in Canada is, in a sense, a cross between a mortgage loan company debenture and a mutual fund share, and also resembles some life insurance contracts. They are sold essentially through the direct appeal of salesmen, and all salesmen selling them also sell mutual funds. All companies issuing them also offer mutual funds. Savers can acquire the certificates either through regular monthly instalments or through making a lump sum payment. Significant amounts of them seem to have been sold to lower income groups.[70]

Certificates carry a guaranteed annual rate of return and usually also an additional return based on the company's profits, although there is no legal obligation on the company to pay the latter. All such returns are left with the company until maturity of the certificate and

---

68. For this and other information on investment contract companies see *Report of the Canadian Committee on Mutual Funds and Investment Contracts*, Provincial and Federal Study, Queen's Printer, Ottawa, 1969.

69. *Ibid.*, p. 652.

70. *Ibid.*, pp. 648-9.

earn the guaranteed annual rate of return. For example, if a saver purchases a $10,000 twenty-year certificate and pays for it in monthly instalments, at the end of twenty years he may have paid, say, $7,200; the guaranteed annual rate of interest on the sums paid in and on annual interest received of say 3% will raise this to the face value of $10,000 and additional annual accumulated credits out of profits and interest on such credits will raise this to say $11,300—the final redemption value of the certificate. So on the one hand it is a fixed interest instrument and on the other hand the rate of return may be affected by the profits of the company. However, profits for distribution may have arisen only because of a relatively low guaranteed interest element in the contract since the funds themselves, as noted above, are invested essentially in fixed interest instruments. It is essentially accurate to regard those savings certificates as fixed interest debt instruments. At maturity the certificates may be redeemed but optional settlements, the most important one being an annuity, are also offered. If an investor wishes to terminate his contract before maturity he may do so at a cash surrender value outlined in the contract. The contract may also convey certain other benefits such as loan privileges, insurance benefits and mutual fund conversion rights.

All investment contract companies operate under provincial legislation. In five provinces they operate under legislation designed specifically for them; in the others they are subject to securities legislation administered by securities administration—including in Manitoba, from where the largest of them operates. Control emphasizes the importance of ensuring that the companies will be able to meet their liabilities as indicated by both cash surrender values and maturity values of the contracts outstanding. Companies are restricted in the type of investments they are permitted to make.

What rate of return a company promises will depend on the accumulation rate permitted by administrators for determining outstanding liabilities (i.e., the lower the permitted rate, the lower the rate that can be guaranteed); on salesmen's commission and administrative expenses; and on actual return on investments. The simple way for a company to play it safe is to be conservative with respect to the guaranteed return and rely on the system of additional credits to increase the rate of return. This is what the companies have done and in some cases additional credits account for half of the total return to certificate holders.[71]

As noted above, investment contract companies are distinguishable from other financial intermediaries primarily in the nature

71. *Ibid.*, p. 659.

of the savings instrument they offer and not in their investment practices. Their survival in their present form will therefore depend heavily on how attractive those savings instruments continue to be to savers. Since they are essentially debt instruments it might, at first glance, seem a simple task to compare the rate of return they offer with that offered by the debt instruments of all the other financial intermediaries, e.g., deposits, debentures, guaranteed investment certificates, Canada Savings Bonds and other bonds. However, accurate comparison is made difficult by the detailed characteristics of the savings certificates relating to additional credits, prepayment arrangements, death and disability benefits, loan privileges and optional settlements. The companies themselves have argued that their important service to savers is not the rate of interest they can offer but the inducement they give to individuals to embark on a savings program.[72]

Judged by rate of return realized, it would seem that the certificates of investment contract companies have not been attractive relative to other readily available debt instruments. A recent study outlines the average theoretical return and the average actual return as a percentage of amounts paid on a sample of contracts issued by one company in February 1957 and August 1962, from date of issue to the end of 1967. It shows that for the most part actual returns were very small or even negative in some cases and that actual returns were very different from theoretical returns. For example, the actual annual return on 325 contracts with a 20-year term, after running for 10 years, was .24% while the theoretical return (including declared additional credits) was 9% or more.[73] The study concluded that "... the discrepancy between the theoretical return under instalment investment contracts and the returns actually attained is sufficient to justify a rejection of the argument that these contracts force their holders to save and therefore provide them with a benefit. ..."[74]

It would seem that the investment contract companies have grown essentially because they have been able to sell a fixed interest savings program to savers who are not sensitive to interest return. Such insensitivity may be explained either by absence of information with respect to rates of return on savings certificates and alternative debt instruments, or by the possibility that some savers place a certain value on the other non-quantifiable benefits that go with entering into such a savings program. To the extent that it is the former, the

---

72. *Ibid.*, pp. 667-8.
73. *Ibid.*, pp. 674-5.
74. *Ibid.*, p. 677.

outlook for the future growth of investment contract companies is not bright since interest rate information is improving steadily.

RECENT DEVELOPMENTS

While we have made passing references to the experiences of the mortgage loan companies after 1944, it is perhaps worthwhile to examine that experience in a more direct way and to summarize it. First of all it may be recalled that the growth rate of the mortgage loan companies from 1944 to 1968 exceeded that of the total of all financial intermediaries combined. At the same time the number of companies declined further in this period. In 1947 the federal Superintendent of Insurance included 40 federal and provincial loan companies in his statistics of such institutions, but by 1961 the number had declined to 24. There then began a period of increased interest in the formation of such companies, so that in 1965 the total was 36. But this trend was short-lived, for in 1969 there were 33.

There has been no change in the traditional interest of the companies in mortgage financing in the postwar period, although the shift away from farm mortgages that had begun in the 1930s, and probably even in the 1920s, was fully completed. Until 1961 the companies were permitted to make conventional mortgage loans up to 60% of the value of a property, but this was then changed to 66⅔% and in 1965 to 75%. Restrictions on investments in corporation securities were also eased substantially so that if they now wish to do so the companies can greatly increase their activity in this area—similar to that of the decade or two prior to the First World War and prior to the restrictive legislation of 1914. There is no indication, however, that this will happen.

It will be noted from Table 7:4 that from 1960 to 1968 there was a noticeable increase in the item "other" liabilities, rising from 1.9% of total liabilities in the former year to 7.0% in the latter. More detailed data reveals that this was accounted for largely by an increase in the use of borrowed money by several loan companies, including Kinross Mortgage Corporation. The latter is a corporation through which the Canadian Imperial Bank of Commerce engages in the conventional mortgage lending business, so that the "borrowed money" really represents a channelling of the bank's deposits into mortgages. With the 1967 changes in the Bank Act, the bank could, of course, engage in the mortgage business directly. For these reasons, Kinross is not really in the tradition of the older mortgage loan companies, but rather illustrates the new sources of competition faced by the older companies.

Conclusions

We can now summarize specifically our view as to why the building societies and mortgage loan companies experienced such a varied history of growth and of changing relative importance. The forces behind the period of expansion up to 1891 were the successful evolution of terminating building societies into permanent societies and so the successful emergence of loan companies; the development of standard and reliable procedures for valuing real estate and land; the unusually strong demand for mortgage money, particularly farm mortgage money, as reflected in high interest rate levels in Canada for much of that period (a demand prolonged by the opening up of the prairies); the development of the sterling debentures and the resulting decline in borrowing costs relative to lending rates; and finally, the absence until the later part of that period of competitors in mortgage lending.

However, as that period of expansion progressed and the period of relative decline began, a number of forces were beginning to work against the companies: the gap between borrowing costs in the United Kingdom and lending costs in Canada narrowed substantially,[75] reducing the importance of the unique advantage the companies enjoyed in having access to the United Kingdom capital market; the opportunities for making farm mortgages were diminishing; the life insurance companies began in the 1880s to enter a period of greatly increased relative importance (their assets equalling loan company assets by about 1902) and the trust companies (with virtually all the advantages of loan companies and one or two unique ones as well) appeared in force at about the turn of the century—and both these institutions began to compete in the mortgage field.

In retrospect the loan companies seem to have made two major mistakes which weakened their ability to withstand new competition and other adverse forces: they failed to develop adequately their sources of funds in Canada during those years when United Kingdom funds were so easy to obtain, leaving a vacuum filled by the chartered banks, life insurance companies and trust companies; and they concentrated too heavily and too long on farm mortgage financing at a time when such financing was declining greatly in importance and when the financing of urban property (including corporate industrial property) was becoming increasingly important. Furthermore, it is possible that the 1914 legislation prohibited them from

---

75. See above, p. 212.

evolving into investment companies at a time when such companies were just beginning to appear.

Their failure to develop adequately Canadian sources of funds may also have been in part because of restricting legislation. The loan companies, as we have seen, not only were restricted in the amount they could borrow in relation to their paid-up capital and reserve but, until the 1920s, were faced with an even more restrictive limit on the amount of their deposit liabilities; and while it is difficult to know what effect this had, it is the case that the companies complained about it at the time. Hume Cronyn, a senior executive in the industry, pointed out in 1918 that Canadian companies were limited in borrowing up to the amount of their reserves plus four times the paid-up capital, while some equivalent institutions in the United States, while denied the privilege of taking deposits, could borrow up to fifteen times their paid-up capital and reserves combined.[76] Also the chartered banks, not being so restricted, went much further much sooner in reducing their ratio of paid-up capital and reserve to total liabilities than did the loan companies. Finally, there seems to have been a certain sentiment against loan companies taking deposits.[77] This sentiment was based on the view that the maturity of assets and of liabilities should be about equal, and it rested on the assumption that savings deposits were not long-term funds. This gave the banks ample opportunity to develop the savings deposit business, when loan companies might have done so. The return of the loan companies to a rate of growth comparable to all other intermediaries combined after the Second World War, occurred in a period when the limitations on the amount of borrowed funds were eased and when there was a substantial decline in their ratio of equity to total liabilities. It was also a period when restrictions on their investments were eased, but in view of their historic emphasis on mortgage financing this was not an important change – apart from increasing the loan-to-property-value ratio to 75%.

The major new threat to the future growth of the old type of mortgage loan companies is likely to be the chartered banks and to the investment contract companies the increasing awareness among small investors of alternative savings instruments bearing higher rates of return. The banks, having been given powers to sell debentures in limited amounts and make conventional mortgage loans, can now more or less do everything the loan companies can do, either directly or through associations with separate mortgage lending

76. *Monetary Times*, Jan. 4, 1918, p. 86.
77. *Monetary Times*, May 16, 1879, pp. 1418-9, and Feb. 18, 1881, p. 961.

companies. This is an old story, as we have seen, for prior to the turn of the century the life companies had invaded their mortgage business, then came the trust companies which invaded both their mortgage business and their debenture market, and now the banks are able to do as the trust companies did earlier. There is no better illustration of the way competition in the capital market emerges from structural changes in existing institutions and from the emergence of new institutions, than the experience of the building societies and mortgage loan companies.

8

Insurance Companies and Societies

Over the past century and a half, life insurance companies in Canada have become major accumulators and distributors of the nation's savings. Among financial intermediaries, only the chartered banks' assets exceed those of the life companies, whose assets in Canada are about equal in amount to the personal savings deposits of the chartered banks. Obviously the "product" which the life companies have had to offer has proved to be attractive to savers. And this is why a study of the growth of the Canadian capital market must examine closely the growth of life insurance companies in Canada.

It might have been otherwise if the experiment with assessment life insurance in the late nineteenth century had been successful. But, as we shall see, it was not successful and the universal adoption of the policy of accumulating reserves to provide for the liabilities of future policy benefits created the connecting link between the popularity of life insurance and the growth of the assets of life insurance companies.

Life Insurance in Canada Before Confederation

Life insurance was introduced into Canada by British companies. Prior to agents' being established in Canada, some Canadians held policies of British companies, principally those of the National Loan Fund Life Assurance Society. In 1846 the Scottish Amicable Life Assurance Society opened an office, and in 1847 so did the Colonial Life Assurance Co. (a subsidiary of the Standard Life Assurance Company of Edinburgh which was absorbed by the Standard in

1865). In 1851 came the agents of the Liverpool and London and Globe Insurance Company and the Royal Insurance Company. Others soon followed.

But until the appearance of the Canada Life Assurance Company in 1847 there was no active Canadian life insurance company. As we have seen, all policies were being written by agents of United Kingdom and United States companies, in whose countries life insurance had been in existence for many years. The first American life insurance contracts became effective on May 22, 1761, and were written by the *Corporation for Relief of Poor and Distressed Presbyterian Ministers and of the Poor and Distressed Widows and Children of Presbyterian Ministers* (still in existence and, mercifully, known as the Presbyterian Ministers' Fund). These contracts actually predated by one year the incorporation of the "Old Equitable of London" – the Society of Equitable Insurance on Lives and Survivorship.[1]

While a number of profit-oriented life insurance companies were formed in the United Kingdom before 1847, the Canada Life was among the first so formed in North America. Several institutions similar to the Presbyterian Ministers' Fund were formed in the United States before 1800. In addition the Insurance Company of North America was established in 1792, but it apparently issued its last life policy in 1817; the Pennsylvania Company for Insurances on Lives and Granting Annuities was formed in 1809, but ultimately became a trust company; and the Girard Life Insurance, Annuity and Trust Company of Philadelphia was incorporated in 1836 but by 1900 had withdrawn entirely from the life insurance business.

It was after this that the modern United States life companies really began to appear: the New England Mutual Life Insurance Company (1835, but not fully organized until 1843); the New York Life Insurance Company (1841); the Mutual Benefit Life Insurance Company of New York (1842); the State Mutual Life Insurance Company of Massachusetts (1844); Mutual Benefit (1845); and the Connecticut Mutual (1846). The Canada Life Assurance Company was formed under Deed of Settlement dated August 21, 1847, and issued its first policy on November 9 of that year, remarkably soon after the important U.S. companies had first appeared.

Before examining this company more closely, we may note that its formation did not represent the first attempt to establish a life company in Canada. The British American Fire & Life Assurance Co., the first fire insurance company of Upper Canada, was incorporated on February 13, 1833, but seems never to have exercised its right to issue

---

1. See Alexander Mackie, *Facile Princeps*, Presbyterian Ministers' Fund, 1956.

life policies.[2] In 1835 influential promoters in Upper Canada sponsored the formation of the Life Insurance and Trust Company, patterned on the New York Life and Travel Company. The relevant act passed the Assembly of Upper Canada, was reserved by the governor, and was refused assent by the imperial government. This company sought three distinct types of power: to effect life insurance, to receive deposits, and to accept and execute trusts.[3] When one traces the notable success in future decades of deposit banking, of the life insurance industry and of the trust company business, it is interesting to reflect on the opportunities which were lost by the promoters of this company when royal assent was denied their venture. The reason given by Lord Glenelg, the Colonial Secretary, for refusing assent provides an interesting example of the nature of British influence on the early formation of financial institutions in Canada. He felt that a company should not mix life, deposits and trustee business.

Promoters of Canada Life eleven years later were more successful, and the first formal steps for establishing that company were recorded in this way:

> At a Meeting held in the News Room of the Mercantile Library Association, in Hamilton, on Tuesday evening the 3rd November, 1846, pursuant to a circular generally distributed and called for the purpose of considering the propriety of forming a Provincial Life Assurance Society, Mr. Sheriff Thomas being called to the Chair and Mr. Thomas Simons appointed Secretary, and the Chairman having then stated the objects of the meeting it was moved by H. C. Baker Esq. seconded by G. S. Tiffany Esq. and resolved, "That viewing life insurance as a most important benefit, if not a duty that we owe to ourselves and families; and well aware that this advantage can at present be attained only at a needless sacrifice, we resolve that steps shall be immediately taken to obtain a charter and to form a Society, for the assurance of lives, granting annuities and transacting all business based upon the chances of Life, upon the Mutual principle to be called the *Canada Mutual Life Assurance Society*, and to be organized in Hamilton.[4]

The moving spirit behind the formation of the Canada Life was Hugh C. Baker. Baker was interested and experienced in finance. Not only was he manager of the Bank of Montreal at Hamilton, but he was also an original director of the Hamilton and Gore District Sav-

2. See William McCabe, "The History of Life Insurance in Canada," *Canada, An Encyclopaedia of the Country* (Toronto: Lippincott Publishing Company, 1899), vol. 5, p. 325.
3. *Ibid.*, p. 326.
4. Canada Life Assurance Co., *Minutes*, November 3, 1846.

ings Bank founded in 1846, and a publication (*circa* 1851) lists him as being president of two local building societies and secretary of another.[5] These building societies also were new financial ventures. In addition Baker is credited with having had considerable mathematical ability, and was interested in actuarial science. It was this kind of person, then, that was forced to travel to New York, an arduous journey at the time, in order to satisfy the requirements of one of the foreign life companies operating in Canada when he applied to it for life insurance. He took steps to form the Canada Life soon after that journey and the reference in the resolution to "needless sacrifice" can be understood in the light of it. But it must also be remembered that the scientific basis for life insurance was well built by 1847, that United States and United Kingdom companies were being formed in rapid succession, and that British companies made an extra charge on Canadian policies to compensate for what they regarded as an extra climatic risk – all additional reasons why it is not too surprising that a Canadian life insurance company appeared on the scene at that time.

The individuals who were present at the organizational meetings, or otherwise supported the venture, included a number of barristers, one or two doctors, a number of merchants, the Clerk of Peace, the City Clerk, the Sheriff, and such notable personages as Sir Allan MacNab, the Honourable Adam Fergusson and Judge O'Reilly.

It is interesting that the sponsors attempted to establish the company on the mutual principle, a principle which, while it was introduced into Canada with the incorporation of the Mutual Life of Canada as early as 1869, did not become general among life insurance companies until at least a hundred years later.

The sponsors' application for incorporation was refused on third reading and this over the mutual principle. A company without a guarantee of capital was not acceptable to members of the legislative council. Rather than wait until another charter could be obtained, the sponsors decided to begin operations under a Deed of Settlement or Co-Partnery. This they did and their Deed was dated August 21, 1847. Capital of the company was £50,000, 500 shares at £100 each; subscriptions for shares were taken at the Bank of Montreal; 63 shareholders, mostly from Hamilton, subscribed for the 500 shares and paid 1% down, and Hugh C. Baker with 30 shares was the largest shareholder. Baker was elected president and also was appointed manager and actuary of the company.

Policy No. 1 of the company was dated Nov. 9, 1847, and insured

---

5. W. H. Smith, *Canada: Past, Present and Future* (Toronto: circa 1851), vol. 1.

the life of Hugh C. Baker for £500 on the whole life plan. In the meantime a charter was again applied for and was secured on April 25, 1849.

The early years of the operations of the Canada Life are of interest to us because that company was the only Canadian life company in business until 1871 (when the Sun Life Assurance Company of Canada began operations under a charter granted in 1865). But they also are of interest because they illustrate forcibly that selling insurance is one problem and investing the proceeds wisely is another, a fact which has occupied the attention of Canadian life companies, supervisory authorities and even economists to this day. Finally, those years are important to our discussion because of the contributions which the company made at that time to the development of the capital market in general.

Selling insurance: Because of the advanced state of actuarial knowledge and of experience with life insurance in the United Kingdom, it does not appear to have proved to be a difficult task for the company to actually commence business. The Carlisle mortality tables (compiled in 1815 on the experience of two parishes in the town of Carlisle, England) were adopted, and the temporary policy adopted was the one of the National Loan Fund Life Assurance Society of London. Mr. George W. Burton was appointed solicitor to the company in October 1847, a judicious move in view of the many minute legal problems which arose from the company's life and investment contracts. The prospectus published in 1849 indicates the variety of methods of insurance which were known to and made available by the company:

> The participation scale, or scale with profits; the non-participation scale, or scale without profits; the half credit system, under which, for a term of years, a reduced premium rate is charged; the decreasing temporary assurance system, which is peculiarly adapted to borrowing shareholders and building societies; endowment assurances; endowment assurances for children, with or without return of the whole premium paid theron, in case of death occurring before the age is attained, or the endowment is made payable; assurance on joint lives, either upon the death of the first assured, or on the death of the longest liver; immediate annuities, payable during the remainder of life or deferred annuities to commence at a given age and to continue thereafter during life on the payment either of a fixed sum or of an annual premium....

In addition to having a sophisticated product to sell, the company (like all life companies) had an effective story with which to sell it.

The first resolution of the sponsors, as we have seen, regarded life insurance "as a most important benefit; if not a duty that we owe to ourselves and family." The Hon. Adam Fergusson, in moving the adoption of the second annual report of the company, was able to dwell on similar sentiments. In later years agents of all companies developed the art of selling, around the theme of loved ones, death and thrift, to a wonderful degree of sophistication. But the theme itself was always there and it immediately provided the company with a unique attraction for the saver. The company had, however, to compete with United States and English life companies.

The Canada Life appears to have decided at the outset that it would appeal more to the "lower orders of society" than had the English companies. Besides appointing a number of agents (at Woodstock, Port Sarnia, Paris, Colborne, Brantford, Montreal, Quebec, etc.) within a few months of becoming established, the company appointed a general agent, George W. Baker, brother of the president, to carry the story of life insurance to the people. In addition the company initiated a reduced scale of premiums, which it was able to do because existing scales of English companies were based on an expected 3¼% return on investments whereas in Canada current rates were much higher than that—well in excess of the legal rate of 6%. By April 30, 1850, it had 473 policies outstanding representing $814,903 insurance in force. By 1855 the amounts were 1,307, $2,349,609; in 1860, 1,807, $3,365,407; in 1865, 2,453, $4,013,268; and in the year 1870, 4,270, $6,404,437. In the latter year the company's insurance in force represented about 15% of life insurance in force in Canada, the 85% being divided among twenty-four British and United States companies. The Canada Life in that year led all those companies in amount of insurance in force in Canada, premium income in Canada, and number of new policies written in Canada. In the matter of selling insurance the company had made relatively steady and satisfactory progress.

Investing funds accumulated: Investment of the funds accumulated was another matter, for in this the company encountered serious, almost fatal, difficulties.

When the company received the 1% payment on its capital stock it no doubt wished to invest it in sound, relatively liquid yet remunerative securities. It chose bank stocks, which, among securities locally available, most nearly met those requirements. The following constitute the first recorded purchases by the company, of each of the various types of securities in which it invested during 1847, 1848 and 1849.

Date		No.	Security	Par value	Purchase price
1847	Nov. 23	22 shares	Bank of Upper Canada	£220-0-0	£268-8-0
	Dec. 20	8 shares	Bank of Montreal	400-0-0	422-0-0
1848	Feb. 28	5 shares	Gore Bank	50-0-0	50-0-0
	July 27	Mortgage	(Sir Allan MacNab's property)	361-14-1	327-5-0
	Sept. 18	20 shares	Provincial debentures	100-0-0	98-10-0
	Nov. 23	2 shares	District of Gore debentures	50-0-0	38-0-0
	Nov. 27	1 share	District of Wellington debentures	10-0-0	8-15-0
1849	Mar. 17	1 share	Dundas & Waterloo Road debentures	129-0-0	113-10-5
	May 23	1 share	City of Hamilton debentures	100-0-0	80-0-0
	Dec. 12	1 share	Government debenture	50-0-0	40-0-0

Purchase of the mortgage on Sir Allan MacNab's property "in rear of the market place" in Hamilton was actually ratified by the board on July 18, 1848. That mortgage was brought to the attention of the board by a barrister and solicitor, as was so often the case in future years. In the period 1848-50 the company purchased many of the small provincial debentures (£2, £5) of about one year to maturity with interest at 6% at an average price of about 98, which the Province of Canada was forced to issue to finance its requirements. The company bought numerous Gore district and Wellington district debentures, which also came in small denominations (£5, £10, £25, etc.), had from two to ten years to run to maturity and in most cases yielded the company from 10% to 12%. In effect the company began its investment activities by buying bank stocks, by accumulating the small debentures which had originally been tailored for the local individual investor and by buying outstanding mortgages.

The way the investment policy of the company developed can best be seen by referring to the percentage composition of the assets of the company. From 1847 to 1852 the company shifted out of its liquid assets, cash and bank stocks, into more remunerative investments. By 1852 it had a portfolio which included mortgages (9%) and a variety of municipal debentures (totalling 56%), and in addition a few bank stocks and provincial debentures.

But after 1852 an economic boom developed which was accompanied by land and urban real estate speculation and high commodity prices (from 1852 to 1857 a price index of fifteen food products rose by 69%). The boom was based on railroad construction financed heavily with British capital, an increase in urban population and the Crimean War. An auditor who was appointed in 1862 to appraise the position of the Canada Life after the "bubble" had burst explained that "in the years 1854, 1855, and 1856 an immense expenditure on the construction of various railways caused an extraordinary influx of capital, and a consequent sudden rise in the value of real estate until that was supposed to be the most eligible investment for capital so that parties, deemed the most prudent in the community, were carried away with the prevailing mania."[6]

Among those parties was the management of the fledgling Canada Life. With real estate values rising, the demand for mortgage money seemed limitless and interest rates on mortgages rose to 16% and beyond. The Canada Life bought outstanding mortgages until by 1856 they formed about 56% of the company's assets as compared with 9% in 1852. The company used every means at its disposal to take advantage of the high interest rates on mortgages: it virtually ceased its purchases of municipal debentures; in many cases it paid for mortgages with its own acceptances or certificates of deposits and, as we shall see, it even acquired a savings bank so as to augment its resources with funds deposited in that institution.

Prosperity persisted until late 1857, although some commodity prices had weakened as early as 1855. Inevitably real estate values dropped sharply. In addition, the year 1857 saw crises in the British and United States capital markets, and the realization that British capital invested in Canadian railroads was going to experience disappointing returns caused an abrupt change of sentiment towards Canada among British capitalists. A process of severe economic and financial adjustments in Canada began in 1858 and persisted until about the year of Confederation.

By February 1858, the Canada Life began to experience defaults in its mortgages and these mounted as the months went by. Defaults on debentures held by the company—those of the City of Hamilton, and of Dundas, Caledonia and Renfrew—added to its difficulties, as did the loss from the operations of the savings bank. Public discussion, which was sharply critical of the affairs of the company and its management and which extended even to the legislature, persisted for some months. Management decided that an independent auditor's report would be desirable and an auditor was appointed. This report, to which reference has already been made, commented on the mortgage business of the company during the period of inflation.

> Looking to the magnitude of the Company's transactions in mortgages and real estate during the period of inflation, it could

6. *Report of the Adjourned Annual Meeting, Canada Life Assurance Company*, October 28, 1862, Appendix.

> scarcely be expected that all their operations would have a satisfactory result, when heavy losses on similar investments were sustained by every institution in the province. At the same time, your auditors must say that, in some cases of importance, a great want of business caution has been manifested; for example, the purchase of a mortgage representing $20,000, on a farm of 80 acres in the vicinity of Hamilton, on which a probable loss of 50% may be estimated; also the purchase of a mortgage on a certain mill property, amounting to nearly $12,000 which will entail the loss of about 80%; these, with many smaller sums, swell the total loss to a considerable amount. The fact of mortgages made for large sums and sold to pay an exhorbitant interest, should have suggested the strictest enquiry into the value of the property, as well as the means of the nominal owner to redeem it, previous to its purchase by the Company. In justice to the present management, it should be stated that these investments were all made previous to their appointment.[7]

The reference to the change in management should be explained. The president, Hugh C. Baker, died in 1859. A new general manager had therefore to be found. Mr. A. G. Ramsay, secretary of the Scottish Amicable Assurance Society of Glasgow, was induced to come to Canada to assume that position in 1859.

The period of readjustment for the company which began in 1857 lasted until about 1867, during which time its assets showed little growth. But the asset structure began to show a better balance, with mortgage holdings declining substantially and holdings of municipal debentures rising once more as a proportion of total assets. In addition, when A. G. Ramsay became manager in late 1859 he immediately introduced a new mortgage investment policy. Instead of purchasing mortgages, he relied heavily on the company's making its own mortgages at 8%, frequently with life insurance on the unpaid balance, and after a more careful inspection of the real estate property than had previously been the case. The stipulated rate of 8% was possible because of the relaxation of the usury laws in 1858.

When it is remembered that the company had begun operations just a few years prior to the beginning of the inflationary period, and that institutions such as the prestigious Bank of Upper Canada and also the Commercial Bank failed to survive the readjustment, it appears remarkable that it did survive and that its name soon became a household word throughout Canada.

The savings deposit business of the company: Under its charter the company was permitted to accept deposits, and this it began to do as

---

7. *Ibid.*

early as 1849, although at first it did not attach much importance to its savings branch. In its 1852 annual report, however, the company expressed the view that "the time has ... now arrived when this branch may be safely extended, and it is the intention of the directors to take an early opportunity of making public the highly favourable terms upon which they are prepared to receive deposits at interest." The demand for funds soon became intense, as we have seen, with rates of return unusually tempting. This led the directors of the Canada Life to purchase the Hamilton and Gore District Savings Bank, a local bank operating under the Savings Bank Act and formed in 1846. (Of the nine original directors of that institution, at least five were associated with the formation of the Canada Life.)

That savings bank, as most others of its kind, had not prospered satisfactorily, and in 1856, when it was about to cease operations, the Canada Life took the opportunity to acquire it. New deposits were to be taken in the name of the Canada Life and the approval of existing depositors was to be obtained for transferring their deposits to the Canada Life, with an offsetting transfer of securities for any deposits that were shifted to the Canada Life. A 2% discount for each year to maturity, with a maximum of 20%, was permitted on municipal debentures transferred, and bank stocks were to be valued on an actual offer of sale. Any untransferred deposits on December 31, 1856, were to be transferred to the Canada Life *en bloc* on that date together with sufficient securities to cover the liability.

But the venture soon encountered difficulties. First of all, the scarcity of money resulted in some unusual drafts on the savings bank, which it met by overdrawing its account with the Bank of Montreal. Then, with the collapse of real estate values, it soon became clear that the assets of the institution were insufficient to cover its liabilities; a short-fall of about $30,000 resulted, which was met by the shareholders.[8] Unfortunately, the company had not obtained the personal liability of the bank's trustees in the event of such a short-fall. Finally, the new institution was not well supervised; the actuary of the savings bank was permitted to continue the business of the bank in his office even after the transfer of assets and liabilities had been effected. So the auditor's report to which reference has already been made posed the fundamental question: "Whether an institution like the Canada Life Assurance Company should connect itself with a savings or other bank, liable to be run upon, and its character jeopardized by an idle or malicious rumour. It seems to be generally conceded that such institutions should be kept apart, and left to work out

8. See Canada Life Assurance Co., *Annual Report*, 1862.

their objectives separately.... In the present state of mind... [we recommend]... the shareholders to dissolve the existing connection so soon as suitable arrangements for the transfer can be made."

The company approached the Bank of Montreal about a possible transfer of its savings business, but that bank declined the offer. On November 18 the board of the company agreed to decline all new accounts. On April 30, 1863, the savings bank was closed and shortly thereafter absorbed by the Commercial Bank. Thus ended the company's deposit business.

Had the company had a happier experience with its savings deposit business, it is conceivable that it could have become an integral part of the life insurance industry in Canada—just as it has of the business of the chartered banks and trust companies. It might, in other words, have provided an opportunity for savings institutions to develop more independently of the chartered banks than they were to do. The great popularity of savings deposits in future years suggests that had this happened life insurance companies would be even more important in Canada than they now are.

Contributions to the capital market: There can be little doubt that the Canada Life's most important contribution to the development of the capital market was that when it began to accumulate life insurance funds it also, in contrast to the British and United States companies, began to channel those funds entirely into Canadian securities. This had the effect of reversing the anomalous position of Canada's (apparently) being an exporter of capital as far as life insurance companies were concerned and, equally significant from our point of view, it provided an institutional demand for a wide range of Canadian credit instruments.

The latter point warrants elaboration. During the 1850s the banks of Ontario and Quebec were preoccupied with discounting notes and bills, these constituting about 80% of their total assets. Their interest in securities was at that time incidental to their discount operations. The building societies and loan companies, on the other hand, concentrated primarily on mortgage lending. The Canada Permanent Building and Savings Society, in its first annual report in 1856, shows 79% of its funds invested in mortgages. The nineteen building societies and loan companies reporting to the Dominion government in 1867 had 88% of their assets in the form of mortgages. These companies were established first to satisfy the demand for loans on mortgages, and the task of seeking funds was in that sense a secondary matter.

The position of the Canada Life was different. Its unique characteristic in the capital market arose not from the type of credit it supplied but rather from the type of liability, i.e. life contract, it offered. This not merely permitted it to approach the matter of investment of funds from a broad point of view, but made it almost inevitable that it would do so. The result was that its interest in credit instruments was much broader than that of the building societies and loan companies and of the banks. Its interest was centred much more on marketable credit instruments than was that of the other financial institutions and so provided a new kind of institutional demand for those securities. This somewhat broader interest in investments must also have had the effect of improving the flow of funds between different credit instruments.

How this occurred in practice has already been referred to, particularly with reference to the types of securities purchased by the company in the first few years of its existence and the move to a more balanced portfolio after a period of over-investment in mortgages. Almost from the beginning, in its purchases both of the small denomination debentures and of outstanding mortgages, it improved the marketability of instruments designed for the local individual investor.

It also helped pave the way for the placing of larger issues at lower cost. On March 18, 1862, the board approved the purchase of the whole of a new issue—$40,000 Victoria debentures. As early as October 24, 1865, the board approved of a tender being made for the £12,500 Montreal Harbour debentures at 7¾%, and from then on the company periodically tendered for a variety of new issues. These developments may be viewed as the beginning of the local institutional market for new issues, that is, the beginning of the domestic new issues market as we know it today.

Over the years 1850 to 1867 the company purchased a wide variety of Ontario county, township, city, town and village debentures. In addition it bought City of Montreal, Montreal Harbour, Hamilton and Brock Road Company, and government sterling debentures. In 1854 it purchased £1,770 Hamilton Gas Light Company debentures and in the years 1862 to 1864 it also purchased stocks of the various Canadian banks. It is interesting that in March 1867 it subscribed for $10,000 of the capital stock of the new Canadian Bank of Commerce, and that in 1870 it began to make substantial loans to stockbrokers against debentures and stocks. Between 1867 and 1870 there is growing evidence that the prominent brokers of the day (e.g., Pellatt and Olser, MacDougall and Davidson) offered sizable blocks of debentures to the company.

So by 1870, through its demand for a wide variety of marketable securities, through its contribution to placing new issues, and through its assistance to the financing of inventories of securities, the Canada Life had participated actively in and contributed materially to the development of a more efficient and more institutionalized capital market. In 1870 it was joined by another Canadian company – the Ontario Mutual Life Insurance Company (incorporated in 1869), now the Mutual Life Assurance Company of Canada, and in 1871 by the Sun Mutual Life Insurance Company (incorporated in 1865), as the Sun Life then was called. In terms of laying the foundations for accumulating funds and investing them, much had been accomplished by the time of Confederation through the efforts of the Canada Life and the agents of the British and United States companies. By Confederation there were about twelve non-Canadian companies operating in Canada, a fact that was soon to influence government action concerning life insurance companies. However, up to Confederation there had been no specific legislation relating to life insurance business, even though there was fire insurance legislation. Furthermore, the assets in Canada of life insurance companies in 1870 amounted to only about 2% of total financial intermediary assets, which was smaller than those of fire insurance companies. Finally, the good reputation of the industry had not at all been established. It may therefore be said that in these important respects the industry was in its infancy at the time of Confederation.

Developments After Confederation

All this changed in the period after Confederation. By about 1906 life insurance companies were the second largest private financial intermediary (only the chartered banks being larger), a position they have occupied ever since. On the other hand, before the end of the 1930s they had begun a period of relative decline in terms of size of assets. Significant developments occurred in their sources of funds and, in one instance, in the investment of those funds. To cope with the complexity of developments in the industry we will discuss them in this order: (1) government supervision, (2) growth of the industry, (3) assets, (4) liabilities, (5) recent developments, (6) conclusions.

GOVERNMENT SUPERVISION

It is to be noted that after Confederation all foreign life insurance companies, as well as life companies incorporated under Dominion legislation, operated under federal government supervision. In addition, the provinces were seen to have the power to incorporate local life companies, and while some provincial companies appeared after Confederation, their business has never exceeded 10% of that of the federally registered companies. Furthermore, fraternal benefit societies offering life insurance protection to members began to appear under both federal and provincial legislation in large numbers in the 1870s and 1880s, but they were even smaller in total than the provincial life insurance companies. Finally, from about the 1870s until the 1920s there were a number of assessment life insurance companies, as distinct from the "old line" life insurance companies; but their inherently actuarily unsound method of operation, and the impact on them of new restrictive legislation, caused their disappearance. Much of our discussion will be confined to the federally registered companies, which comprise most of the life insurance industry in Canada.

For many years controversy surrounded the matter of constitutional jurisdiction over insurance companies in Canada, so a brief initial comment on it may be useful. The British North America Act gave such jurisdiction to both the federal government and the provinces, although insurance as such is not even mentioned in the act. For many years it seems to have been accepted that provincially incorporated companies could operate only locally, but the question as to whether any aspects of the operations of federal life insurance companies were subject to provincial jurisdiction arose early. Ontario appointed an Inspector (later Superintendent) of Insurance and Registrar of Friendly Societies in 1879 and by an 1881 decision of the Judicial Committee of the Privy Council (*Citizens Insurance Co.* v. *Parsons*) the province was confirmed in its view that it could control life insurance contract provisions including those of federal companies under the "property and civil rights" clause of the B.N.A. Act. Another Privy Council decision some years later permitted provincially incorporated companies to operate in other provinces under provincial licences.

Subsequent developments and legal decisions were such as to create the present arrangement whereby

> the Federal Government is responsible for the registration and supervision of all Dominion, British and foreign insurance companies and fraternal benefit societies operating in Canada, especially from the point of view of solvency while the provincial governments are responsible for provincially-incorporated companies and societies along with legislation respecting policy provisions, licensing of agents and brokers, and other matters of a more local nature.[9]

9. Superintendent of Insurance for Canada, *Submission to the Royal Commission on Banking and Finance*, Ottawa, 1962.

However, as we will see, provincial life companies have remained relatively unimportant.

The first general legislation affecting life insurance companies in Canada was the Dominion Insurance Act assented to May 22, 1868. There was little that was surprising about the act, its provisions reflecting earlier non-life insurance legislation. All companies (except provincial companies operating solely within the province of incorporation) had to obtain a licence from the Minister of Finance, and had to deposit $50,000 (rising to $100,000 for non-Canadian companies) for each line of insurance (except combination of life and accident, and fire and inland marine, for which one deposit was sufficient). New Brunswick as early as 1856 had required outside fire insurance companies to register or obtain a licence, as did the Province of Canada from 1860 onward, which also required a $50,000 deposit.[10]

The 1868 act also required companies to submit an annual statement to the government, which had first been a feature of the charter of the British America Fire and Life Assurance Company granted in 1833. Mutual companies did not have to make a deposit assigned specifically to their Canadian business, and there was no provision for government inspection.

Pressure for such inspection began to appear. It seems to have arisen because of the scandalous behaviour of a number of British and United States companies and also because some of the American states were already providing working examples of how such supervision would operate.

Commenting on English insurance companies, an observer wrote in 1869:

> It is high time that something were done to remedy existing abuses. Not long ago a witness in a court of justice ... was compelled to admit that his occupation had been the formation of assurance companies, and that he made a treble profit, for he had obtained something as their founder, a salary as manager, and a percentage when they were in liquidation.... [It] would appear that during the past twenty-five years, 355 assurance companies have been founded, that of these 328 have ceased to exist. Last year 30 were projected and 17 became bankrupt.[11]

---

10. For many of the details included here see G. D. Finlayson, "Sixty Years of Insurance Legislation and Administration," *Monetary Times*, vol. 78, pp. 212-20; A. D. Watson, "The Development of Life Insurance in Canada," Government of Canada, *Canada Year Book*, 1933, pp. 937-44; "Insurance in Canada During the Depression and War Periods," Government of Canada, *Canada Year Book*, 1947, pp. 1064-9; Superintendent of Insurance, *Submission*.
11. *Monetary Times*, April 1, 1869, pp. 517-8.

On the U.S. situation:

> A good deal of distrust has arisen from the failure of two or three American life companies, which no doubt has affected all, more or less.... [We] predicted the collapse of many of the smaller young offices, hatched into life by the hot-bed process, and forced on the American people by means fair or foul, to the serious detriment of life insurance, and to the probable future disgrace of everyone associated with them. These predictions are now being fulfilled and the work has only begun. Probably a score, at least, have yet to follow in the footsteps of the Great Western Mutual and the Farmers' and Mechanics'....[12]

The attempt in 1871 to introduce stricter control into Canadian legislation, indeed control very similar to that contained in legislation of 1875, was defeated, apparently as a result of pressure from the industry, for it was reported that

> Very considerable changes have been made in the Banking and Insurance Bills since their introduction. This remark applies particularly to the latter measure, nearly all the principal features of which were strongly opposed by the officers of the leading companies doing business in Canada, who mustered at the Capital in strong force. The Committee on Banking and Commerce, to the surprise of the Minister of Finance, struck out nearly all its principal clauses. The Bill as amended, contains little else than the two clauses providing for the winding up of insolvent companies. The most obnoxious features to the companies—such as compelling them to make deposits sufficient in amount to re-insure their entire annual business, the proposed system of inspection, and the necessity of making deposits for Canadian policy holders only—were all swept away by the Committee.[13]

Following the example of a number of American states, Canadian critics argued that a government insurance commissioner should be appointed. In December 1872 and January 1873 the *Monetary Times* wrote a series of editorials on it, in one of which it went to the heart of the matter:

> It is scarcely necessary to repeat what is so well known, that an insurance company, more especially a life company may be hopelessly bankrupt for a series of years, and yet pay all its current losses and expenses. When the fact is at last discovered it is always after the mischief is beyond remedy. ... It is not a sufficient answer ... to say ... that policy-holders should investigate and make themselves acquainted with the position of an office to whose charge

12. *Monetary Times*, Feb. 3, 1871, p. 485.
13. *Monetary Times*, April 4, 1871, p. 688.

> they have committed their funds. The large majority of them are not capable of making an intelligent investigation. . . .
>
> Had we an Insurance Commissioner armed with the necessary powers and guided by the well-established principles of life insurance, we should not have such an institution as the Citizens Insurance Company of Montreal flaunting its delusive announcements in the face of the public—advertising to the world a million dollars of capital when it really has not $10,000 paid up in cash. . . .
>
> A salutary effect of wise governmental supervision would be to impart greater confidence in Canadian companies by giving the public the fullest and most satisfactory assurance of their soundness. . . . It is well known with what rapidity the business of life insurance has grown amongst us even though the policies have been sent from abroad; but had we once impressed on the public mind the fact that home companies were as successful, as safe, and as liberal as the best of those organized and conducted in other countries, and which now carry out of Canada such large sums annually, the result would be a more general resort by our people to the benefits of life insurance. . . .

Facing continuing public pressure of this kind, it is not surprising that the government revived earlier attempts at supervision, this time successfully so, in the form of two acts of Parliament, one in 1875[14] and one in 1877.[15] These acts established most of the enduring principles of insurance supervision in Canada:

(1) The first act established a Superintendent of Insurance in the Department of Finance (which was changed in 1910 from a branch to a separate Department of Insurance, but was still under the Minister of Finance); while the second act extended the powers of the Superintendent to include supervision of life as well as other insurance companies.

(2) Companies had to maintain assets in Canada sufficient to cover their obligations in Canada—a fundamental principle to this day. This provision applied to new business only.

(3) Annual statements of companies had to be published by the government so that they would be available to the public.

(4) The Superintendent was to make an annual examination of each company and report to the Minister on his findings.

(5) Companies had to show actuarial reserve liabilities on their statements at least equal to policy-holders' claims.

(6) The acts prescribed mortality tables and a rate of interest (at that time 5%) to be used to compute the companies' liabilities to policy-holders.

The first Superintendent of Insurance, J. B. Cherriman, who was

---

14. 38 Vic., cap. 20, and 38 Vic., cap. 21.
15. 40 Vic., cap. 42.

Professor of Mathematics and Natural Philosophy at the University of Toronto, emphasized at the time "that there should be no secrecy of the affairs of an insurance company, that the directors are only trustees or agents for the disposition of the money entrusted to them by the ensured, and the ensured has the right to know what is done with the money so entrusted."[16] This led him to emphasize *publicity* and *solvency*. This emphasis has not changed over the years. In his 1962 Submission to the Royal Commission on Banking and Finance (pp. 41-2), the Superintendent of Insurance wrote:

> the main purposes of the legislation and of the Departmental examination of companies in implementation of that legislation, have been to ensure that each and every company licensed or registered with the Department is in a sound condition.... In the main, these purposes have been attained by requiring (1) the maintenance in Canada by all out-of-Canada companies of adequate assets and of records and accounts of their transactions; (2) the placing of sound values on the assets of all companies; (3) the proper determination of the liabilities of all companies; (4) the regular examination of the records and accounts of companies to see that these requirements are met by companies on a continuing basis; and (5) the publication of a detailed annual report on all companies, giving full information for the insuring public and affording a basis for informed criticism within the industry itself.

Foreign companies must deposit the requisite securities with the Minister of Finance, or a trust company as approved by the minister, while Canadian companies make only nominal deposits but must hold all their assets, except those necessary for carrying on operations abroad, under their own control.

One important consequence of the new legislation of the 1870s was the withdrawal from Canada of a number of British and United States companies because they refused to make the necessary deposits to cover their Canadian businesses. This left a vacuum which new Canadian companies quickly filled, so that whereas in 1870 Canadian companies did 15% of the business, in the 1960s they did over 60%. British companies, as we shall see, recovered hardly at all from their incredibly foolish decision to withdraw in the 1870s.

After establishing the principles of government supervision and the machinery for applying them in the 1870s, federal government legislation concerned itself largely with life company investments—excluding that pertaining to assessment companies and fraternal benefit societies. There was also perennial discussion of federal-

---

16. Quoted in Superintendent of Insurance, *Submission*, p. A26.

provincial jurisdiction in matters of life insurance, which we will not review here.[17]

Until 1899 investment powers of life insurance companies were not stipulated in the general act, but were outlined in the individual company charters. The act of that year[18] did outline general investment powers, but not until the act of 1910[19] were wider powers of individual companies repealed. Still, the 1899 legislation provided the format for subsequent legislation relating to investments with its practice of defining eligible investments. It permitted the companies to invest in a broad range of Canadian and foreign government securities, and in many corporate securities (debentures, bonds and stocks) without specific limits. Such corporations were not even required to have a dividend record, apart from steam railway companies which, for their bonds and debentures to be eligible life company investments, had to have paid dividends for two years prior to their securities' being purchased. Land, except for actual use or occupation, could be held for only twelve months.

Soon after this legislation appeared, the life insurance industry in the Western world came in for close public scrutiny, including the Canadian companies. It began in New York State with the "Armstrong Committee," or Joint Committee of the Senate and House, which revealed serious irregularities in the industry during its hearings. Its report was published in February 1906. This investigation prompted an investigation of the industry in the United Kingdom by a Select Committee of the House of Lords, which in turn led to the appointment of a Royal Commission on Life Insurance in Canada in February 1906. The Report and Evidence of that Commission focussed attention, among other things, on some of the curious investment practices of the life companies at that time and led to the more specific statutory prescriptions relating to investments contained in the act of 1910.

We cannot examine the Royal Commission material in detail and will merely quote several passages from the *Report* of the Commission to illustrate the investment abuses that had developed. These relate to the operations of the Canada Life and Sun Life, since they were the two largest Canadian life companies at the time, accounting for over half of the assets of the Canadian companies.

> The absolute control, real or potential, residing in the president and general manager [Mr. G. A. Cox], and in which his stockholding and

17. See Superintendent of Insurance, *Submission*, pp. A53-71, for a discussion of the matter.
18. 62-63 Vic., cap. 13.
19. 9-10 Edw. VII, cap. 32.

offices secure him, have to a marked extent influenced the investments of the company, which have been made to serve not only the interests of the Canada Life Assurance Company, but also his own interests and the interests of other institutions in which he was largely concerned.... The Central Canada Loan and Savings Company, in which there is a large independent shareholding, is under Mr. Cox's control to such an extent that to use his own language, we are to treat it as being himself. This company has been very largely interested in the promotion of enterprise of a more or less speculative nature, the success of which largely depends upon facilities for carrying and marketing the stocks and bonds of those enterprises. Mr. Cox has, from time to time, as he frankly stated, brought about the investment in securities of this description, of the funds of the Canada Life Assurance Company, in aid of transactions in these securities on his own part and on the part of other institutions which he controls.... Upon one occasion... when he was himself ... largely concerned in maintaining the market price of a security of this description, he made use of the funds of the company to purchase the security for the express purpose of strengthening or upholding its market price....[20]

It is to be observed that the management of this company [Sun Life] have had differences with the Department as to their investments, and as to the classification of accounts and other matters of detail. The company has constantly adhered to its own view without regard to the view of the Department....

It was disclosed in the evidence that the company invested in the securities of a certain undertaking, and portions of these securities were handed over to certain members of the board on the same terms as the company acquired its holdings. It is reasonably clear that by this transaction the members of the board so obtaining these securities did so on more advantageous terms than would have been possible for them as individuals.... It had to be conceded that, if the investment had turned out to be an undesirable one, it would have been impossible to enforce ... any obligation to take any share in the venture.[21]

The Sun Life by 1906 was well on the way with its policy of emphasizing common stock investments, a policy that reached its extreme stage in the late 1920s. The commissioners clearly disapproved of this, offering the view that "the propriety of continuing to permit investment in ordinary unsecured stocks may properly be questioned." They seem to have felt that such investments were too risky for funds held in trust.

While many of the commission's recommendations (which, by the way, were similar to those of the Armstrong Committee) were never adopted, there is little doubt that its detailed investigation of individual companies had a salutary effect on them, and that it was

20. Royal Commission on Life Insurance, *Report*, 1907, p. 14.
21. *Ibid.*, pp. 19-20.

directly or indirectly responsible for the changes introduced in the 1910 legislation.[22] The more important changes were: (a) establishment of a separate Department of Insurance to improve government supervision of the industry, (b) cancellation of special investment powers contained in individual life company charters, (c) submission by companies of a biannual statement outlining details of securities bought and loans made; (d) stricter eligibility provisions relating to corporate securities which permitted purchase of debentures of corporations with three-year default-free records, preferred stocks of corporations having paid (or parent company having paid) regular dividends for the last five years, and common stocks of corporations (up to 30% of the stock or of any stock issue of any company) having paid regular dividends of at least 4% for seven years, and mortgages, etc., up to 60% of the value of the real estate covered; and (e) prohibition against underwriting, except to protect investment, and against the promotion of any other company by a company or its officers. The act also required companies to publish many standard guarantees and provisions in their policies (a requirement which was repealed in the 1932 legislation).

In the 1917 legislation[23] the corporation debenture eligibility rule was changed to include only companies having paid regular dividends on their preferred or common stock for five years preceding purchase of the debentures. By an act of 1924[24] no par value shares were eligible if dividends of $4 had been paid on them for seven years. Three years later it was stipulated[25] that payment of dividends of $500,000 or over in one year would be regarded as equivalent to 4%, and so would meet the eligibility requirement.

It is to be noted that up to this point there were no restrictions on the proportion of funds that could be invested in particular types of securities, and since there had been a number of years of prosperity, many corporation securities were in fact eligible under the dividend performance rule. The Sun Life, meanwhile, continued full speed to invest in common stocks – particularly U.S. common stocks. By 1930 about half of its assets were in common stock form. The Superintendent of Insurance in his 1928 *Report* commented that Canadian laws were freer regarding Life company investments than U.S. laws, that Canadian companies had been very active in purchasing preferred and common stocks, and that in view of their price fluctuation, statutory limits on the proportion of funds invested by life com-

22. 9-10 Edw. VII, cap. 32.
23. 7-8 Geo. V, cap. 29.
24. 14-15 Geo. V, cap. 50.
25. 17 Geo. V, cap. 59.

panies might be introduced. In 1930 he recommended a 25% limit, and he also recommended that the $500,000 clause relating to dividends be repealed.

By this time the 1929 stock market collapse had occurred and the Western world was moving deeper into economic depression. What effect all this had on the Sun Life, with its heavy common stock investments, has never to our knowledge been revealed in detail. The Superintendent of Insurance has commented that the company was "seriously embarrassed."[26] These developments lay behind the legislation of 1932.[27] The act at first stipulated that investments in common stocks be limited to 25% of total assets, but at the request of the life insurance companies this was changed to 15%, at book value. Companies with more than that amount were not to purchase any stocks until the 15% requirement had been met. The $500,000 dividend clause was removed, and the 4% or $4 rule on no par value shares was retained. No basic changes were introduced until 1948, although a number of minor alterations did appear.

In 1948 the "basket clause" was first introduced, which permitted life companies to make loans and investments, not otherwise eligible and subject only to minor minimum conditions, such as default-free record, up to 3% of a company's ledger assets. This was changed in 1961 to 5%. The 1961 legislation[28] also permitted life companies to lend up to 66⅔% of the value of real estate, a figure that had been at 60% since 1910; it increased the permissible amount of investment in real estate or leaseholds for the production of income to 10% from 5%. Finally, in 1965[29] the "basket clause" limit was raised to 7%; mortgage lending up to 75% of the value of the real estate involved was now permitted; the permitted amount of holdings of common stocks was increased to 25% of the book value of a company's assets; and the seven-year record of dividend payments for common stocks to be eligible was reduced to five years and was broadened to include companies with earnings available for the payment of such dividends, whether they paid them or not. While life companies still could not hold more than 30% of the common stock of a company, they could buy any amount of particular issues, and the 30% rule now did not apply to investments in foreign life companies, Canadian non-life insurance companies or real estate companies.

To complete this description of the legislation governing life com-

---

26. Superintendent of Insurance, *Submission*, p. A83.
27. Separate acts were passed for the Canadian and British companies, 22-23 Geo. V, cap. 46, and for foreign companies, 22-23 Geo. V, cap. 27.
28. 9-10 Eliz. II, cap. 13.
29. 14 Eliz. II, cap. 40.

pany investments, it may be noted that life companies also enjoy great freedom in the purchase of Canadian and other government securities—national, provincial or state, and municipal—including securities of the International Bank for Reconstruction and Development; they may purchase bonds of corporations with earnings over the past ten years equal to ten times its interest payments on non-current debt (with annual earnings at least equal to 1½ times such annual interest payments in at least four of the five years); they may purchase bonds and equipment trust certificates secured by a wide range of real and financial assets and contracts; and they may make collateral loans against securities regarded as eligible for investment.[30]

We may make the general point that until the legislation of 1932 the legislative prescriptions relating to investments could hardly be regarded as being restrictive. The restrictions then introduced were subsequently relaxed to where, by 1965, they again could not be regarded as being inhibiting; and, excepting only the Sun Life which had to alter its asset structure, it is doubtful whether the restrictions of 1932 altered the way the companies invested their funds.

As for the record of government supervision of the industry over almost a full century, it must in many respects be regarded as a remarkably good one. The early emphasis on publicity of life company operations still seems sound, as do the other principles recently outlined by the Superintendent.[31] The technique of the basket clause overcomes the major limitations inherent in prescribing in detail what constitutes eligible investments for life companies. However, there have been times when the Department seems to have adopted a somewhat restricted view of what constituted appropriate life company investments, which may have influenced the industry in an indirect way. This seems to have arisen essentially from its interpretation of the meaning of "trust" in the sentence, "the life insurance companies hold the policyholders' funds in trust." This point we will return to again when examining actual investment practices of the life companies.

THE GROWTH OF THE INDUSTRY

Number and relative size of types of companies: As we noted earlier, at the time of Confederation the life insurance industry was in its infancy, accounting for about 2% of financial intermediary assets. It

30. For full details see 13 Eliz. II, cap. 40, s. 63.

31. See above, p. 237.

was also dominated by non-Canadian companies. In 1869 there was only one Canadian company underwriting life insurance and its net insurance in force accounted for 15% of the net insurance of federally registered companies. The remainder belonged to the thirteen British companies (46%) and the nine American companies (39%), as can be seen in Table 8:1. Then came the impact of the short-sighted reaction of a number of British and U.S. companies to the new legislation, which helped vault Canadian companies to the fore in the industry. British companies took especial exception to the act of 1868 (and the act of 1871), which required them to deposit with the Receiver General at least $50,000, rising to $100,000, in stated securities for the protection of Canadian policy-holders. Non-Canadian companies took equally strong exception to the more stringent legislation of 1875, which required them to maintain assets in Canada at least equal to their total liabilities in Canada. As a consequence a number of British and United States companies withdrew, some of them returning in later years, but in the meantime leaving Canadian companies with an open field. By 1885 there were ten Canadian companies and they had 50% of the insurance in force of the federal companies; the British companies had 17% and the U.S. companies 33%. At about this time the U.S. companies stabilized their position and in 1969 the non-Canadian, non-British companies (mainly, but not entirely, U.S.) had about 26% of the business of the federal companies and 24% of all insurance in force in Canada (see Table 8:1). But the British companies did not maintain their share, and by 1935 had only about 2% of the life insurance in force. After that they recovered and in 1969 had about 5%. The Canadian federal companies had 69% of the federal company insurance in force and 63% of all insurance.

Contrary to the experience of the banking industry, the life insurance industry has seen a steady increase in the number of companies in business. There were 10 Canadian federally registered companies in 1885, which increased to 22 by 1905, and to 28 by 1925, at about which level it remained until after the Second World War. Then came another period of expansion, and in 1969 there were 44 Canadian federally registered companies. In that year there were also 14 British and 69 other (mainly U.S.) companies. No Canadian life companies have been liquidated, only fourteen have disappeared after having had their business reinsured with other Canadian companies, and one was merged with another company. No Canadian policy-holder has lost money in a Canadian company, and only small sums were lost in the failure of the British Medical and General in 1878, a British company, and of the Atlantic Mutual Life Insurance Company in

Table 8:1 Life Insurance in Canada: Number of Companies and Relative Size of Types of Companies 1869-1969 (selected years)

	Number of institutions								Net insurance in as % of total fed-			
	FEDERALLY REGISTERED COS.				PROV.	FRATERNAL SOCIETIES			FEDERALLY			
	CAN.	BRITISH	OTHERS	TOTAL[1]	COS.	FED.	PROV.	FOREIGN[5]	CAN. $MN	%	BRITISH $MN	%
1869	1	13	9	24	n.a.	n.a.	n.a.	n.a.	5	15	16	46
1875	7	16	13	36(2)		n.a.	n.a.	n.a.	22	26	19	22
1885	10	18	12	40(13)		n.a.	n.a.	n.a.	75	50	26	17
1895	11	14	14	39(12)		n.a.	n.a.	n.a.	188	59	34	11
1905	22	14	16	52(12)		n.a.	n.a.	n.a.	398	63	49	7
1915	26	15	17	58(13)		n.a.	n.a.	n.a.	830	63	58	5
1925	28	15	16	59(13)		9	n.a.	15	2673	64	109	3
1935	27	14	20	61(19)		7	n.a.	24	4165	67	123	2
1945	28	12	17	57(11)		15	n.a.	28	6441	66	184	2
1955	32	14	34	80(9)		16	n.a.	30	17,401	68	692	3
1960	36	15	47	98(8)		16	n.a.	30	30,418	68	1555	3
1964	39	16	57	112(5)		15	n.a.	33	43,209	69	2706	4
1965	40	16	58	114(5)		14	n.a.	33	47,900	69	3071	4
1968	43	14	65	122(2)		14	n.a.	32	64,410	69	4518	5
1969	44	14	69	127(1)		14	n.a.	32	70,761	69	5096	5

SOURCE: Canada, Department of Insurance, *Report of the Superintendent of Insurance*, Annual, Queen's Printer, Ottawa.

[1]Figures in parentheses indicate the number of companies in the total figure not writing new insurance, all of which are British and foreign companies.
[2]Figure for 1916.
[3]Excludes all fraternal societies and provincial companies prior to 1915 figure.
[4]Includes assessment assurance which the fraternal benefit societies were writing at the time with little legislative restraint.
[5]Writing life insurance.

1877 and the Globe Mutual Life Insurance Company in 1879, both U.S. companies.

The absence of mergers among Canadian companies is partly explained by the nature of Canadian legislation and by the predilections of the Department of Insurance. Since 1910 Canadian life companies have been prohibited from buying the shares of another life company, with the exception of the 1965 legislation[32] which permitted them to invest in life companies incorporated abroad and so permitted them to establish foreign subsidiary companies. It is true that

32. 14 Eliz. II, cap. 40.

force in Canada and erally registered cos.				Total federally registered companies								Total insurance in force in
REGISTERED COS.				PROV.		FRATERNAL SOCIETIES						
OTHERS		TOTAL		COS.		FEDERAL		PROV.		TOTAL		
$MN	%	$MN	%	$MN	%	$MN	%	$MN	%	$MN	%	$MILLIONS
14	39	36	100	n.a.								36[3]
44	52	85	100	n.a.								85
49	33	150	100	n.a.								150
97	30	319	100	n.a.								319
189	30	630	100	n.a.								630
424	32	1312	100	13[2]	1	99[2]	8	336[2,4]	26	435[2]	33	1760
1377	33	4159	100	53	1	187	4	116	3	303	7	4515
1971	31	6259	100	88	1	158	3	74	1	232	4	6579
3127	32	9751	100	213	2	246	3	133	1	379	4	10,343
7359	29	25,452	100	1173	5	366	1	325	1	691	3	27,316
12,676	28	44,649	100	2304	5	702	1	286	1	988	2	47,942
16,756	27	62,672	100	3934	6	904	1	462	1	1366	2	67,973
18,685	27	69,656	100	4508	6	963	1	539	1	1502	2	75,666
24,285	26	93,213	100	6141	7	1410	1	861	1	2271	2	101,625
26,928	26	102,785	100	6978	7	1613	1	850	1	2463	2	112,226

under the 1910 legislation companies were permitted to purchase the whole business of another company with the approval of the Treasury Board. But this has largely been nullified by the policy of the Department of Insurance. For example, in his 1962 *Submission* the Superintendent of Insurance explained:

> The policy up to date ... has been against agreements of this kind in the case of life companies unless necessary or desirable to protect the interests of policyholders. This policy has been based upon the view that there have not been too many Canadian life insurance companies in the field and it is desirable to retain the identity of those already operating, particularly having regard for the difficul-

> ties and waste inherent in the launching of new companies. If the number of federally-incorporated life companies were to decrease materially, it is likely that this would be followed by a wave of new companies being incorporated, either federally or provincially. With this prospect, it seems better to see the present companies continue in existence.

This stands in sharp contrast to the policy that has been pursued by the government with regard to the chartered banks, where mergers have been permitted until only nine institutions remain.[33] It is not evident that the Superintendent has come to his view after determining what constitutes the economically optimum-sized life company.

Relative size of individual companies: It is interesting to examine what has happened to the relative size of individual *Canadian* federally registered companies over the years. Table 8:2 shows the relative size of assets, both in and out of Canada, of these companies for selected years from 1880 to 1969. The most striking developments were the relative decline in size of the Canada Life, which in 1900 accounted for 38% of total assets of Canadian companies and in 1968, 8%; and the increase and subsequent relative decline in the size of the Sun Life, whose assets amounted to 18% of the total in 1900, 39% in 1930 and 23% in 1969. In 1900, the five largest companies accounted for 84% of the assets of the Canadian companies, while in 1969 the five largest companies accounted for 63%. In 1900 the remaining 16% was divided among 13 companies; while in 1969 the remaining 37% was divided among 38 companies. So among Canadian companies there has always been a relatively high degree of concentration and a relatively long "tail" of small companies.

Foreign control and mutualization: Until 1929 all Canadian federal life companies were controlled in Canada.[34] In that year a small Canadian company passed into the hands of British investors. Not until 1954 were there other cases of foreign takeovers, and by 1961 seven more companies had been acquired by non-Canadian interests. In that period there was a real possibility that some of the larger companies might also be sold to foreign insurance interests. This threat led to a change in the Canadian and British Insurance Companies Act that (1) required a majority of the whole board of directors of every federally incorporated insurance company to be Canadian citizens ordinarily resident in Canada; (2) authorized the board of directors of federally incorporated life companies to disallow the transfer of shares out of

---

33. See below, pp. 97-100.
34. See Superintendent of Insurance, *Submission*, pp. A98-9.

Table 8:2 Relative Size of Assets of Individual Canadian Federally Registered Life Insurance Companies 1900-1969 (selected years)

	1900 %	1920 %	1930 %	1945 %	1960 %	1965 %	1969 %
1. Acadia Life	—	—	—	—	—	...	...
2. Alliance Mutual Life	—	—	—	—	.4	.4	.5
3. Allstate Life of Canada	—	—	—	—	—	...	...
4. Assurance—Vie Desjardins	—	—	—	—	.1	.2	.3
5. British Pacific Life	—	—	—	—	...	...	...
6. Canada Life	38.1	18.1	12.5	9.6	8.3	8.4	8.1
7. Canadian Premier Life	—	—	—	—	...	...	.2
8. Canadian Reassurance	—	—	—	—	...	...	.1
9. Commercial Life	—	...	.1	.1	.1	.1	.1
10. Confederation Life	13.1	6.5	5.4	6.0	5.4	5.1	4.9
11. Continental Life (Zurich Life)	—	.7	.6	.4	.5	.5	.4
12. Co-operative Life	—	—	—	—	.1	.2	.2
13. Crown Life	—	.8	1.0	2.3	3.8	4.2	4.5
14. Dominion Life	.9	1.5	1.7	2.0	2.3	2.3	2.3
15. Dominion of Canada General	—	—	...	.1	.2	.2	.2
16. Eaton Life	—	...	.2	.4	.4	.4	.3
17. Equitable Life of Canada	—	—	—	.5	.4	.5	.5
18. Excelsior Life	.7	1.5	1.2	1.0	1.4	1.4	1.5
19. Family Life	—	—	—	—	—	...	...
20. Fidelity Life	—	—	—	.1	.1	.1	.1
21. Great West Life	1.6	8.9	8.5	7.1	9.0	9.2	9.2
22. Imperial Life	1.9	4.6	4.2	3.7	3.4	3.4	3.2
23. Income Disability	—	—	—	—	—	—	...
24. Life of Alberta	—	—	—	—	...	...	...
25. Laurier Life	—	—	—	—	—	...	...
26. London Life	1.7	3.1	4.3	6.6	9.2	9.8	10.1
27. Manufacturers Life	3.8	7.9	7.2	9.1	11.2	12.4	12.6
28. Maritime Life	—	—	...	.2	.2	.2	.2
29. Monarch Life	—	.4	.7	.7	.9	1.0	1.0
30. Montreal Life	—	—	.4	.4	.5	.5	.4
31. Mutual Life of Canada	8.7	10.1	7.7	7.8	7.8	7.8	7.7
32. National Life	.2	1.2	.7	.5	.8	1.1	1.4
33. North American Life	6.7	4.8	3.0	2.8	3.9	4.2	4.4
34. Northern Life	.4	.9	.6	.5	.6	.6	.6
35. North West Life	—	—	—	—	—	—	...
36. Principal Life	—	—	—	—	—	—	...
37. Sauvegarde Life	—	.5	.3	.3	.6	.6	.6
38. Sovereign Life	—	.4	.4	.4	.5	.4	.4
39. Sun Life	17.6	27.3	39.0	37.1	27.7	24.5	23.1

Table 8:2 (continued)

40. Toronto Mutual Life	—	—	—	.1	.1	.1	.1
41. United Investment Life	—	—	—	—	—	—	...
42. Wawanesa Mutual Life	—	—	—	—	...	...	...
43. Western Life	—	.1	.1	.1	.1	.1	.1
44. Westmount Life	—	—	—	—	—	...	.1
45. Federal[1]	2.1	—	—	—	—	—	—
46. Home[1]	.5	—	—	—	—	—	—
47. Royal Victoria[1]	.5	—	—	—	—	—	—
48. Temperance & General[1]	1.6	—	—	—	—	—	—
49. Capital[1]	—	.2	.2	—	—	—	—
50. Saskatchewan[1]	—	.1	.1	—	—	—	—
51. Security[1]	—	.1	—	—	—	—	—
52. Travellers[1]	—	.2	—	—	—	—	—
53. Columbia[1]	—	—	...	—	—	—	—
54. Royal Guardians[1]	—	—	.1	...	...	—	—
Two largest—	55.7	45.4	51.5	46.7	38.9	36.9	35.7
Five largest—	84.2	72.3	74.9	70.7	65.4	64.3	63.1

SOURCE: Canada, Department of Insurance, *Report of the Superintendent of Insurance*, Queen's Printer, Ottawa, Annual.

[1]Companies no longer in operation.

Canada; and (3) permitted federally incorporated life companies to mutualize if they so wished. The latter move resulted in five companies with about 25% of the insurance of the federal companies becoming mutualized. In 1965 the federal government amended the insurance acts so as generally to limit total foreign ownership of federally incorporated Canadian life insurance companies in future to 25%, and ownership by any one foreign shareholder and his associates to 10%.

The concept of the mutual company is an old one, arising out of the benevolent character of early experiments with life insurance. In Canada the first mutual company was the Mutual Life, incorporated in 1869, but a number of the other early companies considered the mutual type organization when they were first organized. However, the failure in the 1870s of several large U.S. mutual companies, partly, it was thought, because of the absence of the cushion of equity capital, tarnished the name "Mutual." The North American Life Insurance Company dropped the word from its corporate title in 1882.

The possibility of using mutualization as a technique for frustrating changes in ownership was raised by the Superintendent of Insurance in his 1927 *Report*, at a time when the stock markets were very active and when he thought that there was a danger of life companies' passing into "undesirable" hands. This, in the event, did not happen and nothing was done until the 1957 legislation already referred to.

Today the mutual companies constitute a significant portion of the Canadian life insurance industry. The full implications of this for the control and direction of mutual companies have probably not yet been clarified. The impossibility of policy-holders' participating in any effective way in choosing directors tends to make boards of directors self-perpetuating. Also, since security analysts have no real interest in mutual companies, there is no group that examines the relative efficiency of individual companies. The performance of boards of directors is not challenged since the Department of Insurance is interested essentially in solvency, not efficiency. It is conceivable that some independent, but public-oriented, organization could assume the role of appraising the performance of mutual and other life insurance companies using efficiency criteria, for the guidance of prospective policy-holders.

Competitors of the federally registered companies: The federally registered companies have always dominated the life insurance business in Canada and in 1969 accounted for 92% of the insurance in force in Canada. In that year the insurance in force of fraternal benefit societies was only 2% of federal insurance, and that of provincial companies was 7% (see Table 8:1). However, the provincial companies have grown in number and size since the end of the Second World War, to the point where the importance of competent provincial inspection of their operations has obviously increased greatly.

Table 8:1 shows that in 1915 the figure for insurance in force of fraternal benefit societies was very large, one-third the size of the federal companies. In fact, that figure includes assessment insurance in force of assessment companies and fraternal societies, a form of insurance that proved to be actuarially unsound and subsequently disappeared. The appeal of assessment insurance, as explained by its promoters, was that it could provide life insurance at lower cost. Typically the scheme involved enrolling a certain number of young members, imposing a uniform and low assessment, and making additional assessments in the event of excessive deaths or loss of funds. The major problem was that as the average age of the members increased, so did the deaths, and additional assessments multiplied, which led younger members to default, since they could then obtain cheaper insurance in "old line" companies. When that happened the assessment companies soon became insolvent.

That type of insurance was first offered in volume in Canada by the fraternal benefit societies in the 1870s. Fraternal benefit societies as such seem to have had their origin in orders and societies that existed centuries ago. Societies providing voluntary relief existed in ancient Greece and Rome. In England guilds, fraternities and monasteries dispensed assistance to the poor and the sick in the thirteenth and fourteenth centuries. When the structure of guilds and of monasteries crumbled, no important organized bodies interested in the plight of the poor and sick remained. The poor laws began to appear in the seventeenth century but with limited effectiveness. It was in this general period that many "self-help" fraternities and societies—secret because they were forbidden by law—began to be formed. Members made contributions and received benefits. In time these included medical, sickness, funeral, disability, financial distress and endowment (i.e. life insurance) benefits.

These societies began to be formed in British North America as well. Endowment benefits seem to have been offered by the Canadian Order of Odd Fellows from 1852 but not until the 1870s did the following appear: the Knights of Pythias, Masonic Mutual Benefit (which failed in 1870), the Ancient Order of Foresters, Sons of England and the Odd Fellows Relief, Sons of Scotland, Royal Arcanum, Canadian Order of Foresters, United Workmen.[35] In the 1880s appeared the Catholic Mutual Benefit Association, the Independent Order of Foresters, the Orange Mutual, the Select Knights, Knights of Maccabees, Catholic Foresters, Home Circle, Royal Templars of Temperance, Canadian Relief Society and Chosen Friends. Ontario passed an act in 1892 relating to insurance companies that also covered fraternal societies and required them to make public returns. In 1898 the Quebec government did so as well, and it included a minimum rate that had to be charged by such societies. The federal government, curiously enough, did not pass such legislation. It did, however, pass legislation in 1885 relating to assessment companies, at the time sometimes also called "mutual" or "co-operative" companies, which had begun to appear and which offered life insurance similar to that offered by the fraternal benefit societies. Such insurance was typically sold to low-income people, who were unable to appreciate the basically precarious nature of the companies selling it. The 1885 act, among other things, required such companies

35. See John Ferguson, M.A., M.D., "Fraternal Insurance and Sick Benefit Societies," *Canada, An Encyclopaedia of the Country*, pp. 339-47.

to make a deposit of $50,000, to use the words "assessment system" on their written material and to indicate that they were not required by law to maintain reserves. An act of 1894 forbade them to issue annuities or endowment insurance and required new assessment companies to have at least five hundred members before being licensed. And the 1910 Insurance Act prohibited any new assessment companies from being formed. Actually by 1910 all the assessment companies as such had vanished.

In the meantime, since there was no fraternal benefit legislation, some of these societies had begun to operate under federal assessment company legislation. By 1917 all Canadian fraternal benefit societies had begun to operate on an actuarially sound basis, but not so the U.S. societies operating in Canada under provincial licences.[36] This resulted in further legislation in 1919 which required rates on new insurance to be sufficient to provide the benefits promised, and required all societies to attain over-all solvency by March 31, 1925. Not only did this result in a transformation of many of the societies but, as Table 8:1 shows, it also resulted in a sharp decline in the relative size of the insurance they had in force. With this decline, the federally registered life insurance companies had the life insurance field largely to themselves.

It may be noted in passing that the number of fraternal benefit societies, as well as their size relative to the life insurance companies, has remained relatively constant over the last decade and a half (see Table 8:1). Of $2,463 million fraternal life insurance in force in 1969, $1,299 million was accounted for by federally incorporated Canadian societies, $314 million by federally registered foreign societies, and $850 million by provincially incorporated Canadian societies. Of the $1,299 million insurance of federal societies, 51% was accounted for by the Artisans and 43% by the Independent Order of Foresters—which by an exceedingly wide margin are the two largest societies in Canada.[37]

But the strongest competition for the federal life companies after the Second World War has come not from competitors writing insurance (principally the provincial life companies), but from competitors offering long-term savings, including retirement plans—especially the mutual funds, trusteed pension plans, and now the Canada and Quebec pension plans. We will see later that some changes are appearing in the Canadian life insurance industry that reflect the challenge of this kind of competition.

---

36. See Superintendent of Insurance, *Submission*, pp. A29-31.

37. See Ontario, *Annual Report of the Superintendent of Insurance for the Province of Ontario.*

Growth rate and relative size of federally registered companies: Charts 8:1 and 8:2 give a comprehensive visual impression of the growth experience of these companies since 1870. Chart 8:1 shows the growth of their assets in Canada and their premium income in Canada in current dollars, while Chart 8:2 makes the asset growth trend more meaningful by comparing it with the growth of G.N.P. and of total financial intermediary assets, and by showing those assets on a per capita constant (1935-9) dollar basis.

From about 1870 to 1900 the companies grew much faster than did all other financial intermediaries combined; they grew faster than did G.N.P. and, using per capita constant dollars as the criterion, their growth rate was very high by historical standards – reaching about 11% per annum as compared with the 1870-1968 average of 5.1% per annum. (Table 8:3 gives some of the actual figures on which Charts 8:1 and 8:2 are based). The current and constant dollar growth rates for 1870 to 1900 were each 12%, compared with the long-term average of 9% and 7%, respectively.

Then from about 1900 to 1920 the companies made almost no further progress (using the criteria of Chart 8:2), although their current dollar and constant dollar annual average growth rates were 8% and 3%. However, from about 1920 to 1935 the companies again experienced growth rates similar to the 1870-1900 period, their assets in Canada rising much faster than G.N.P. (partly because of a depressed G.N.P. after 1930), or than the total of all financial intermediary assets; and in constant dollar per capita terms they rose by 10% per annum. In 1934 the assets in Canada of these companies amounted to a peak of 30% of all financial intermediaries. It had been a period of most unusual development and growth.

But after about 1935 the industry slipped in relation to other intermediaries and in relation to G.N.P. From 1945 to the present its assets in Canada have grown less than those of all other intermediaries or even of all other private intermediaries (see Table 8:3, cols. 4 and 5), and less than G.N.P. From 1926 to 1930 total premium income and annuity considerations of all companies and societies in Canada amounted to 4.5% of personal disposable income. The ratio then rose because of the depressed income levels of the 1930s, declined after 1933 to a level of 3.5% by 1950, rose to 4.0% by 1964 and then declined again, standing at 3.6% in 1968. This shows that the growth of the industry has come to be limited to the growth rate of the national income aggregates and it may possibly not even maintain that rate. The industry, in other words, seemed to have reached – perhaps even over-reached – its maturity by the early 1930s.

Chart 8:1—Total Assets and Premium Income in Canada of Federally Registered Life Insurance Companies 1870-1969

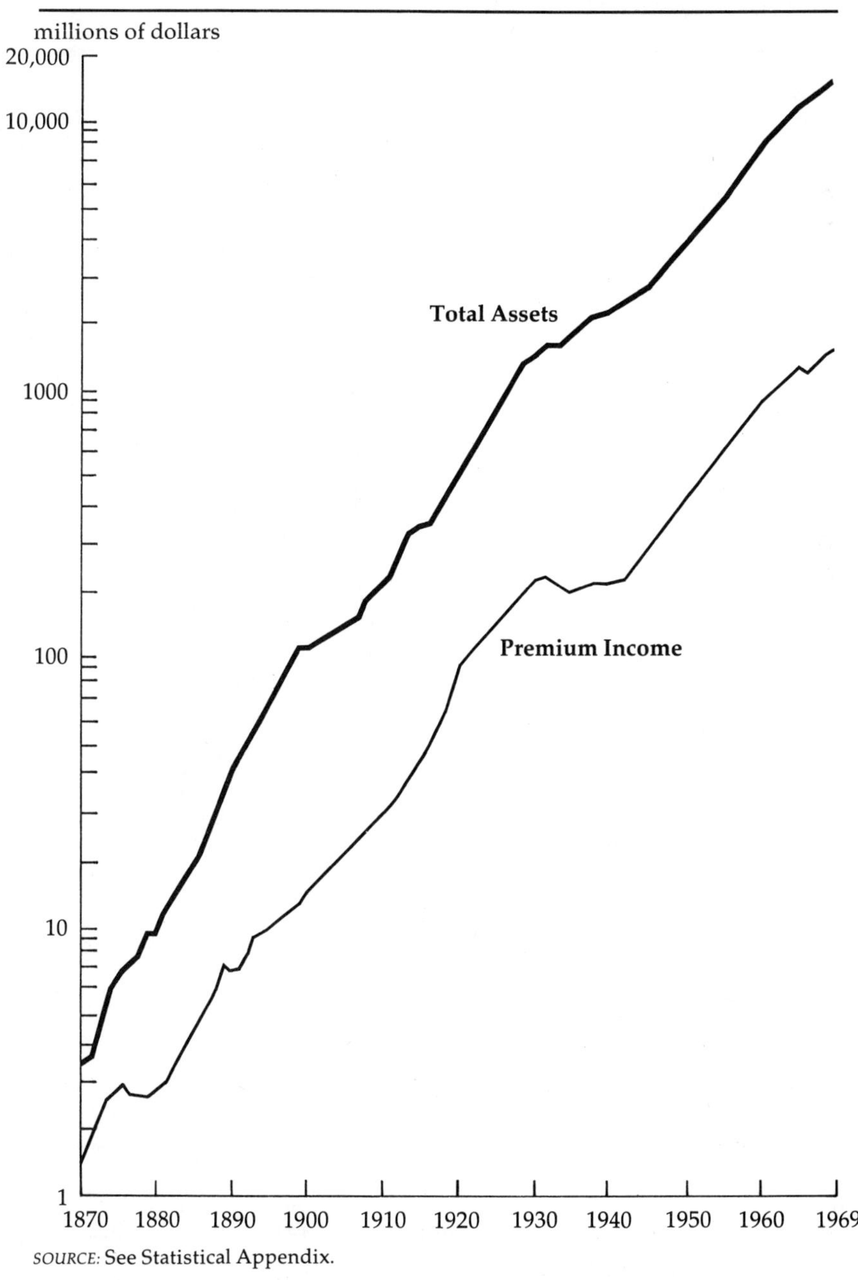

SOURCE: See Statistical Appendix.

Chart 8:2—Relative Size of Assets in Canada of Federally Registered Life Insurance Companies and Total Per Capita Assets in Constant Dollars 1870-1969

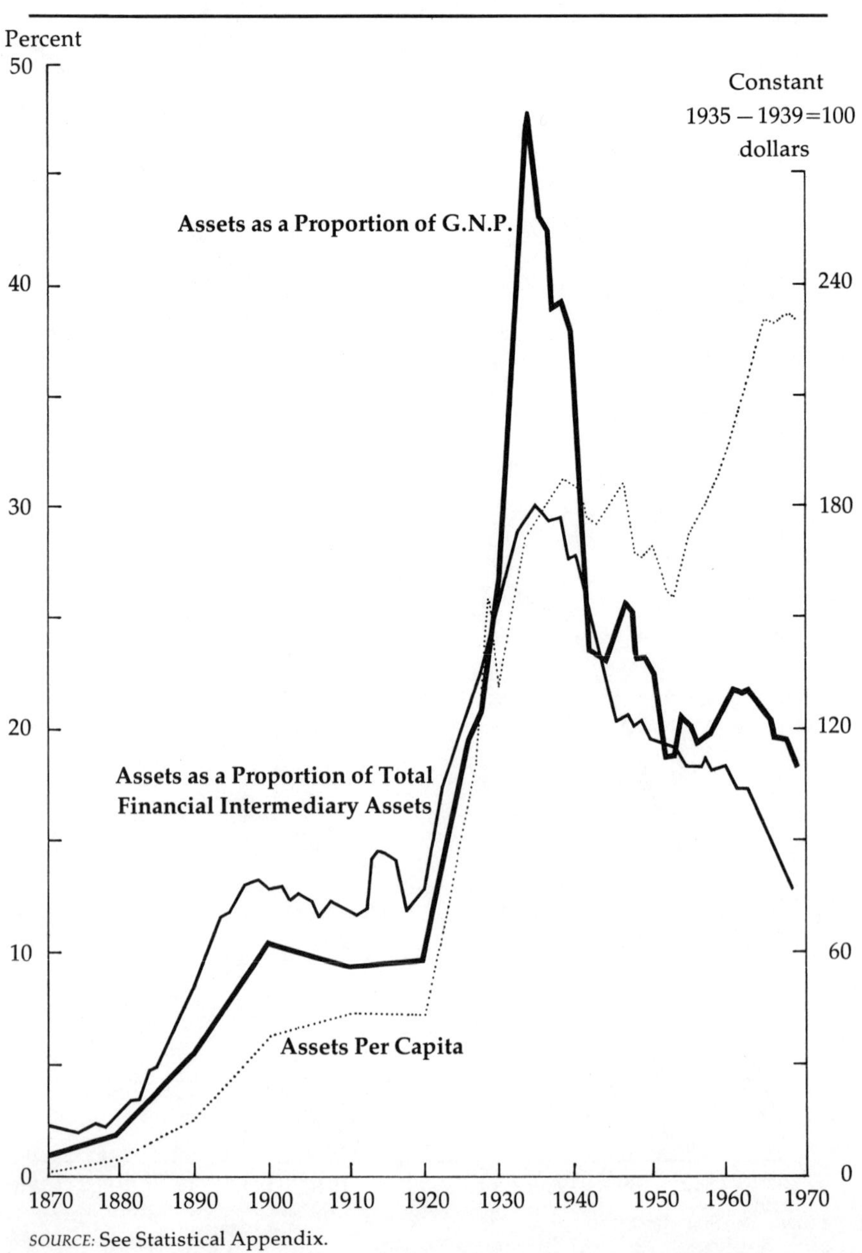

SOURCE: See Statistical Appendix.

Foreign business of federally registered companies: A word now about the foreign business of the Canadian federally registered companies, which is not included in the preceding figures. From about 1890 to 1910 these life companies greatly expanded their foreign operations, their assets outside of Canada rising to 22% of total assets. Then by 1920 (see Table 8:3, col. 7), partly as a result no doubt of the war, this figure had declined to 12%. But, as in the case of their domestic business, the 1920s was a period of great expansion in the foreign business of the Canadian companies, their assets outside of Canada rising to 32% of the total by 1930, and to 41% by 1945. After that it declined again, and in 1968 was 28%. It is quite apparent that for a long period the life companies greatly augmented their domestic growth rate by extending their operations abroad.

Sun Life Assurance Company of Canada decided in December 1879 to make an attempt to establish agents in the British West Indies.[38] Relative absence of competition there seemed to be the attraction, and contrasted with the intense competition in Canada.[39] The Manufacturers Life followed in 1893, Confederation Life in 1902, Imperial Life in 1907, North American Life in 1908, and a few others later on.

Canadian companies also moved into the United States. Canada Life began operations in Michigan in 1889,[40] and Sun Life in 1895.[41] Even before that Sun Life had sent representatives on a remarkably audacious trip around the world to establish agents. In 1891 one of them established connections in Japan, visited China, the Straits Settlements, India and Ceylon, and appointed agents at Singapore, Colombo, Bombay and also Jerusalem. Soon after, agents were established in Japan and Java. Then in 1893 the company established itself in the United Kingdom, in spite of a legal battle with the Sun Life Assurance Society over the use of its name and emblem (it retained the former but relinquished the latter).

By 1900 six Canadian companies were operating abroad, their foreign premium income amounting to 21% of their total premium income. About 70% of it was accounted for by Sun Life, which astonishingly enough was receiving almost half of all its premium income from foreign business.[42]

---

38. George H. Harris, *The President's Book* (Montreal: privately published, 1928), p. 88.
39. See C. V. Callender, *The Development of the Capital Market Institutions of Jamaica*, Institute of Social and Economic Research (Jamaica: University of West Indies, 1965).
40. See *Monetary Times*, Nov. 22, 1889, p. 621.
41. See Harris, *op.cit.*, p. 122.
42. See *Report of the Superintendent of Insurance for Canada for the Year Ended December 31, 1900* (Ottawa: Queen's Printer, 1901), p. xci.

Table 8:3 Growth Rate and Relative Size of Federally Registered Life Insurance Company Assets 1870-1968 (selected periods)

	Average annual growth rates of assets in Canada: based on:			Size of assets in Canada in relation to:[1]			Foreign business of Canadian federally registered companies
	CURRENT DOLLARS (1) %	CONSTANT (1935-39) DOLLARS (2) %	CONSTANT DOLLARS PER CAPITA (3) %	ALL FINANCIAL INTERMEDIARIES (4) %	ALL PRIVATE FINANCIAL INTERMEDIARIES (5) %	GROSS NATIONAL PRODUCT (6) %	ASSETS OUTSIDE CANADA AS A PROPORTION OF TOTAL ASSETS (7) %
1870	—	—	—	2	3	1	—
1870-1900	12.2	12.4	11.0	13	15	10	4
1900-1920	8.4	3.4	.9	13	15	10	12
1920-1935	8.5	11.5	9.8	29	33	43	32
1935-1945	4.6	1.5	.6	20	25	24	41
1945-1968	7.0	3.4	1.0	14	18	19	28
1870-1968	8.8	7.1	5.1	—	—	—	—

SOURCE: See Statistical Appendix for life insurance asset figures. For gross national product, implicit price index and population data see footnote to Table 3:2.

[1] As at end of period shown.

By 1920 there were ten Canadian companies in foreign fields (eight if Newfoundland is excluded), but only Sun Life and Manufacturers Life had ventured beyond the West Indies and Central and South America and the United States. Sun Life accounted for 61% of the foreign premium income and annuity considerations received, and 60% of its total income came from foreign countries. Next in size of foreign business was Canada Life, whose foreign income was about one-third as big as that of Sun Life. A few more Canadian companies began operations outside Canada in the 1920s, so that by 1930 there were fourteen in all operating abroad. However, Sun Life and Manufacturers Life continued to spread themselves much more widely around the globe than did the others, and those two companies and Canada Life and Confederation Life accounted for about 95% of the net foreign premium income and annuity considerations received by Canadian federal companies in 1930. Sun Life alone accounted for 71% of such income and in that year it received 80% of its premium and annuity income from outside Canada. It is difficult to avoid commenting parenthetically that the growth and development of Sun Life up to 1930, and in another sense after 1930, may well constitute the most remarkable of any financial intermediary in Canada's history, with only the early history of the Bank of Montreal and the later history of the Royal Bank standing comparison to any extent.

The depression of the 1930s, the Second World War, and the emergence in many countries of independent economic and political nationalism after that war changed the foreign business of the few Canadian life companies that had been engaged in it for several decades. In 1969 the foreign premium income and annuity considerations received by all Canadian companies amounted to 38% of their total premium and annuity receipts, whereas in 1930 it had been 48%. The companies ceased doing business in many of the countries where they had operated for years, including the following: British Honduras, Costa Rica, Cuba, Guatemala, Haiti, Honduras, Mexico, Nicaragua, Panama, El Salvador, St. Pierre and Miquelon, Argentina, Colombia, Guyana, Peru, Burma, Ceylon, China, Cyprus, Hong Kong, India, Indonesia, Malaysia, Pakistan, Singapore, Syria, Thailand, Egypt, Kenya, Malawi, Rhodesia, Tanzania, Uganda and Zambia. Some but not all of the Canadian companies also withdrew from the Bahamas, the Dominican Republic, Israel, the West Indies, Netherlands Antilles, the Philippines and Surinam. The companies, however, for the most part did continue to operate in the United States and its possessions, the Bahamas, Bermuda, the West Indies, the United Kingdom, Ireland and South Africa; one company also continued to operate in Venezuela, another in Malta, one in West Germany, and another in Southwest Africa. One wonders whether the companies would not have been able to sustain their operations abroad more successfully had they been permitted by Canadian legislation to establish foreign subsidiary companies—a type of organization that might have become more integrated with the local environment than did the agency arrangement that existed. Apart from political and social adjustments, the natural tendency of this head office type of organization to export capital from their foreign operations—(just as the early British companies had done in Canada before Confederation), was bound to meet opposition in countries that suffered from a shortage of capital for purposes of economic development.

LIFE COMPANY ASSETS

In recent years the investment practices of the life insurance companies have been the most controversial aspect of their operations. This controversy has centred on their lack of interest in equity investments. The controversy acquired an extra edge to it in the 1950s, as Canadians began to become concerned over foreign ownership of Canadian business, for it was thought that the problem had arisen partly because of the conservative investment practices of the life companies. Our immediate task is to describe the investment practices of the life companies over the past century, which will also serve the purpose of indicating what the companies have regarded as being appropriate investment policy; to refer again to what the Superintendent of Insurance has regarded as appropriate investment policy; and finally to comment in a general way on appropriate life company investment policy.

Table 8:4 shows the percentage distribution of assets of federally registered Canadian life insurance companies for selected years from 1850 to 1969. A number of generalizations may be made about the asset behaviour of these companies.

(1) From the earliest years the companies have depended heavily on real estate mortgages and bonds for investing their funds. In 1881 they accounted for 73% of total assets, in 1911 70%, in 1932 a low of 50% and in 1969 78%.

(2) While holdings of bonds in total have fluctuated substantially, there has been no basic change in trend. But there was a shift out of municipal into corporate bonds as the latter began to appear in volume just prior to the turn of the century, and into provincial bonds as these began to appear in volume in the 1920s.

(3) In periods of prosperity there usually has been a shift out of bonds into mortgages (excluding war periods).

(4) In the period of historically rapid growth of life companies just prior to the turn of the century the companies for a time shifted heavily into mortgages and out of municipal bonds. They also rapidly built up their holdings of corporate bonds, and stocks, and engaged actively in collateral lending.

(5) In the period of slower growth that followed, ending at just about the close of the First World War, the companies shifted into Government of Canada bonds (as a result of war financing), their holdings of mortgages declined (relatively speaking from prior to the turn of the century), and their holdings of corporate bonds also tended downward. Their collateral loan business vanished permanently, almost certainly because of the uncomfortable publicity it received during the Royal Commission hearings of 1906. Holdings of foreign assets rose, reflecting the increased foreign life business in which the companies were becoming engaged.

(6) The period of unusual growth from the end of the First World War until the 1930s saw the decline in bond holdings which is normal for periods of prosperity, but it also saw a quite abnormal increase in holdings of common stocks – more particularly U.S., not Canadian, stocks. Life company holdings of foreign common stocks amounted to about 2% of total assets in 1921, while in 1932 they amounted to about 15%. Furthermore, this resulted almost entirely from the investment behaviour of one company, the Sun Life Assurance Company, which in 1930 had just over half of its assets in common stocks.[43] The investment behaviour of the remainder of the companies was along traditional lines.

(7) After that period the whole industry, including Sun Life, followed a traditional investment pattern, holdings of common stocks amounting to 4% of total assets in 1969 or roughly the same as in 1901. Sun Life held 9% of its assets (book value) in common and preferred stocks in 1964, whereas in 1930 it held 56%. Since it was a period of prosperity there was again the shift out of bonds into mortgages by the industry as a whole. Indeed, in 1969 their mortgages amounted to 43% of total assets, a figure higher than any since the turn of the century.

What is quite apparent is that if the common stock activities of Sun

---

43. See W. C. Hood, *Financing of Economic Activity in Canada* (Ottawa: Queen's Printer, 1958), p. 334.

Table 8:4 Asset Distribution of Canadian Federally Registered Life Insurance Companies[1] 1850-1969 (selected years)

	1850 %	1860 %	1870 %	1881 %	1891 %	1901 %	1911 %	1921 %	1927 %	1932 %	1941 %	1951 %	1961 %	1964 %	1965 %	1969 %
Cash	12	1	7	3	2	2	1	1	1	1	2	1	1	1	1	1
Bonds																
1. Canadian bonds																
a) Government of Canada	—	—	5	—	—	—	—	12	5	4	15	15	5	3	3	2
b) Provincial	6	—	—	—	—	1	—	2	4	4	8	4	7	7	7	6
c) Municipal	43	25	35	41	15	15	12	15	12	8	5	4	5	5	5	3
d) Corporation		1	—	1	3	13	12	8	9	8	9	13	11	12	12	12
e) Total	49	26	40	42	18	29	24	38	29	23	37	37	28	27	27	23
2. Foreign bonds																
a) Government				—	1	1	1	3	5	4	13	12	5	6	6	3
b) Corporation	—	—	—	—	—	3	11	5	4	4	10	14	13	10	10	9
3. Total bonds	49	26	40	42	19	33	36	46	38	30	60	63	46	43	42	35
Collateral loans			1	—	11	6	1	—	—	—	—	—	—	—	—	—
Policy loans			3	9	8	10	12	13	14	18	9	5	5	5	5	7
Mortgages																
Canadian	9	52	32	31	43	—	—	—	—	20	12	17	30	32	33	33
Other	—	—	—	—	—	—	—	—	—	1	—	3	7	8	9	9
Total	9	52	32	31	43	29	34	25	24	20	12	20	37	40	42	43

Stocks																
1. Canadian																
Preferred	—	—	—	—	—	n.a.	n.a.	n.a.	n.a.	1	—	1	0	...	...	...
Common	4	—	2	2	3	n.a.	n.a.	n.a.	n.a.	4	2	1	1	2	2	3
Total	4	—	2	2	3	6	5	3	4	5	2	2	1	2	2	3
2. Other																
Preferred	—	—	—	—	—	n.a.	n.a.	n.a.	n.a.	1	1	2	1	1	1	1
Common	—	—	—	—	—	n.a.	n.a.	n.a.	n.a.	15	7	2	3	3	3	4
Total	—	—	—	—	—	1	2	2	12	16	8	4	4	4	4	5
3. Total	4	—	2	2	3	7	7	5	16	21	11	6	6	6	6	8
Real estate	—	11	13	4	8	8	4	4	3	4	3	2	3	3	3	4
Other assets	26	10	2	9	6	5	5	5	5	6	4	3	2	2	2	4
TOTAL	100	100	100	100	100	100	100	100	100	100	100	100	100	100	100	100

SOURCE: *Report of the Superintendent of Insurance,* 1928, p. xxxii for 1881-1927 figures, and relevant annual reports thereafter for 1923-69 figures. Book value figures.

[1]Up to and including 1870, figures relate to the Canada Life Assurance Co. and should only be regarded as providing a general indication of its asset distribution.

Life from about 1890 to 1930 are excluded, then the industry can be seen to have shown very little change in its interest in common stocks over the whole of its long history. That interest has been minimal. It is difficult to believe that the restrictive legislation of 1932 had any effect other than that of requiring Sun Life to fall into step with the rest, and it is even more difficult to believe that the 1965 increase in the basket clause and in the minimum ratio of permissible common stocks to total assets will, by themselves, lead to a greater interest by the companies in common stocks. What would have to change first would be the basic view of life company investment committees and investment officers as to what constitutes appropriate life company investment policy.

Not only have the great majority of the Canadian life companies maintained only small proportions of common stock in their portfolios, but the view has also existed in the industry for over half a century that U.S. stocks in any case are more attractive, on the whole, than Canadian stocks – a view expressed by Sun Life before the 1906 Royal Commission and referred to by the Superintendent of Insurance in his 1962 *Submission*. This has led life companies actually to hold more U.S. stocks than Canadian stocks. It is not apparent that past stock market experience supports this view, and in any case the matter is largely irrelevant to the basic question of whether or not the companies should hold significant amounts of common stocks.

The companies have also argued that investment in common stocks is minimized because they must compute their liability under each policy in a way that fixes that liability for the whole life of the policy, while the value of their assets fluctuates with the market. A severe decline of the latter, even if temporary, could wipe out reserves and make a life company technically insolvent. We shall return to this matter when discussing the nature of life company liabilities, but may point out that since there are substantial differences even among Canadian companies as to the proportion of assets held in the form of stocks, it is not the only explanatory factor. We shall also see that recent changes in asset valuation procedures have reduced the problem of short-term fluctuations in security prices. At the same time it must be noted that British companies operating in Canada which have greater flexibility in controlling their liabilities hold more common stocks than Canadian companies.

The views of Canadian life companies concerning common stock investments, in their fundamental aspects, came to be very similar to those of the Superintendent of Insurance, particularly after the change in Sun Life investment policy since the 1930s. However, they do seem to have drifted slightly apart since 1961, for in that year the life companies proposed that the 15% limit on common stock holdings be increased (perhaps to help the non-resident companies that already held a fair proportion of stocks); that they be permitted to use amortized values for valuing Canadian, U.S. and U.K. municipal securities as they were permitted to do for the national government securities of those countries and for Canadian provincial securities; and that they be permitted to average their common stock values over a three-year period.[44] Such suggestions the Superintendent of Insurance opposed in his 1962 *Submission* to the Royal Commission on Banking and Finance.

Let us examine the views of the Superintendent more closely. In his 1962 *Submission* he referred with approval to the views on investments that the first Superintendent expressed in 1875, for he said of his distant predecessor:

> On the question of investments, his recommendations were equally sound. He said it must be observed that a life company is not in the position of a commercial institution where a high rate of interest can be made with a certain amount of risk. The all essential principle of a life company is security and no speculative employment of the funds entrusted to it can be sanctioned (p. A26).

The Superintendent also quoted with apparent approval the 1906 Royal Commission *Report*:

> the Commission has stated very fully its conviction that all accumulated funds belonging to policyholders are essentially trust funds. It necessarily results that permissible investments should be confined within such boundaries as may be appropriately delimited for the investment of that class of funds. Speculative investments ought to be excluded . . . (p. A37).

Finally the Superintendent in 1962 clearly indicated that by risky investments he had in mind common stocks subject to wide fluctuations in price, and incidentally, he also suggested that his view on investments had wide support in the industry, which is true:

> many life insurance companies do not feel that common stocks are a suitable investment medium for life insurance funds. . . . Certainly, if a life company does invest heavily in common stocks, it exposes itself to the wide fluctuation of the market and if it should suffer embarrassment as a consequence, the criticism of policyholders would be loud, sharp and prolonged. It is impossible to satisfy all critics and the first duty of life companies is to their policyholders (p. A79).

---

44. See *Submission of the Canadian Life Insurance Officers Association to the Royal Commission on Banking and Finance*, hearing held at Ottawa, July 9, 1962, vol. A21, p. A7.

The view of the Superintendent, therefore, has been that life companies hold money in trust for policy-holders, that this means that they should ensure that liabilities can be met in current dollars, and that as a consequence securities subject to wide market fluctuations should be avoided.

This view suffers from a narrow interpretation of the word "trust." First of all, life companies, particularly since they accumulate individual savings as well as sell protection, are little different from any other financial intermediary. They all hold funds in "trust." The question is, how should that trust be honoured? Is it sufficient merely to ensure return of the principal in current dollars plus a modest rate of interest? Surely the objective of the life company should be to maximize its return on funds entrusted to it (a return adjusted for normal capital loss experience), by operating along the whole spectrum of securities available. Such maximization involves selecting an appropriate portfolio of fixed interest securities with a suitable maturity structure and an appropriate portfolio of equity investments including common stocks. Because economic conditions can change, rigid rules of thumb in investment policies are not desirable. It would, for example, have been misguided investment policy for the life companies to have made efforts to acquire long-dated fixed interest securities in much of the period after the Second World War. Their shift out of low-yielding Government of Canada bonds into mortgages in that period seems entirely appropriate, a judgment confirmed by the rates of return experienced by the companies. For example, the Canadian Life Insurance Officers Association, using the experience of a sample of companies, has estimated that in each year from 1951 to 1960 inclusive their rate of return after investment expenses on mortgages was greater than on bonds.[45]

However, they have also estimated that in nine out of ten of those years the net rate of return on common stocks (an asset of which they held only very small amounts) was greater than on any other securities they held.

Only if one were to assume that there would be another great depression would it become rational for life companies to avoid common stocks. And this really takes us to the heart of the matter. Life company and Department of Insurance attitudes toward common stocks were formed in a period of our history (i.e., up to the turn of the century) when goods and service prices were remarkably stable, that is, when the real value of fixed-interest securities was not in jeopardy; when the nature of the business cycle was not at all under-

45. *Ibid.*, p. A107.

stood; and when techniques for controlling it were virtually non-existent. The crucial question that life companies must answer for themselves is whether those attitudes remain relevant in the post-1930s, post-Keynesian, inflation-oriented world in which they now operate. Our own view is that it is not sensible to operate financial intermediaries on the assumption that there will be another depression, for this would lead to misallocation of the nation's funds through overly conservative investment policies, and would eventually impede the growth of life insurance companies.

The basic issue therefore is, what constitutes a "balanced" asset structure for life insurance companies? Precision is not possible in this area, but it is difficult to believe that it does not contain more equities—whether in common stock or other form, or whether Canadian or foreign in national origin—than have been found in the asset portfolios of the average Canadian company.

LIFE COMPANY SOURCES OF FUNDS

The basis for accumulation of funds: Life companies, like other financial intermediaries, accumulate funds by offering their liability instruments to the public—mainly life insurance and annuity contracts; and individuals normally make equal annual payments (level-premiums) for their rights under those contracts. Just how this leads life companies to accumulate large sums of money has been clearly described by them:

> The regular methodical purchase of level-premium plans of life insurance by millions of Canadians is the basis for the accumulation of funds in the companies.
>
> Under level-premium plans the amount of the annual premium remains unchanged throughout the premium-paying period although the probability of death of the insured person increases as time goes on. In the early years of a level-premium policy, the likelihood of death is low in relation to later years and the premiums paid for a block of like policies exceed death claims. In the later years of the block of policies, the premiums paid are less than the amounts necessary to meet the claims that come with advancing years and rising mortality or the maturity of the policy.
>
> When a level-premium plan is issued, a fund or reserve must be accumulated in the early years to meet the rising level of claims that will occur during the later years of such policies. These reserve requirements lead to the accumulation of personal savings through life insurance.
>
> The extent to which reserves are built up varies with the type of level-premium plan. Term life insurance covers the possibility of death during the limited term of the policy while a straight life policy is based on the certainty of the death of the insured and the cer-

> tainty that the death benefit must be paid. A five-year or longer term policy would be written on a level-premium plan but the short duration and the very nature of such a policy would not require a reserve accumulation during the five years or other terms of nearly the size that would be necessary under a straight life policy that would be expected to carry on many years until the death of the insured. In turn, the rate of reserve accumulation under an endowment policy is greater than under straight life or other so-called life policies since the payment of the endowment benefit is due either at the end of a specific period of, say, 20 years or at the death of the insured if earlier.
>
> There are, of course, other factors affecting the rate of accumulation of funds in the companies, for example, the rate of investment earnings, the extent of cash withdrawals in the case of policies having reserves and the degree to which beneficiaries leave policy proceeds (including policyholder dividends) on deposit with the company to earn interest.[46]

Valuation of liabilities and assets: As we shall see, it has become a cardinal rule of life insurance company operations in Canada that companies at all times have assets to cover their liabilities to policy and annuity contract holders. To estimate what those liabilities are requires estimating future premiums to be paid; interest likely to be earned so as to arrive at an estimate of the present value of future premiums; and the mortality rate, so as to estimate the present value of claims that are likely to be encountered. The companies for many years have used contracts in which the premiums are set and fixed for the life of the contract and in which non-forfeiture provisions provide strong protection to the policy-holder. These features, for which the companies themselves are responsible, give them little flexibility in changing the value of their liabilities under varying economic circumstances. (Guaranteed policy loan rights of policyholders may also inhibit the companies since their asset structure must always permit them to honour such rights). Other features that result in rigid liability valuation have been introduced by legislation, namely the prescribed rate of discount for computing the present value of future premiums and the mortality tables for computing death claims. Because of all these features the companies, having little flexibility in changing their liabilities, have argued on the one hand that their assets must largely be confined to ones that change little in value and on the other hand that asset valuation procedures for smoothing out temporary fluctuations should be permitted. Such procedures, as we shall see, have recently been adopted.

The only significant move toward flexibility on the liability side

---

46. *Ibid.*, pp. A37-38.

was the introduction in 1961 of section 81(5) of the Canadian and British Insurance Companies Act, which permitted life insurance companies to establish separate funds to be used for the purpose of issuing policies for which the reserves, and therefore the benefits payable, vary according to the market value of the assets in the fund. Policies issued under this provision have largely been confined to group schemes, and their growth for some time was quite disappointing, but recently has accelerated. The important point to note at this stage is that they provide the companies with the means to experiment with more flexible contracts, thereby partially removing the complaint that conservative investment policies are forced on them by rigid liability valuations.

While we discuss the life companies' investment powers and policies later, it is convenient at this point to refer to recent innovations in the valuation of their assets. Valuation procedures are important to the companies because of the rigidity of their liabilities — as already noted. A sharp variation in asset values, even though temporary, might wipe out the capital (if a joint-stock company), surplus and reserves of a company, leaving insufficient assets to cover actuarial liabilities. This would cause the company to be declared insolvent, even though it suffered from no real "cash-flow" problem and even though the price fluctuation was temporary.

The first attempt to soften the harshness of this possibility came as a result of the effect of the First World War on security prices.[47] This involved the companies' obtaining permission from the Minister of Finance, under unusual circumstances, to use prices higher than those existing in the market. These special "authorized" values were used during and just after the First World War and during the depression of the 1930s.

Apart from this provision the companies for many years had to show assets at market value. However, the Department of Insurance had successfully encouraged the companies first to show assets at the lower of book (i.e. cost) value or market value; and then it encouraged them to always show their assets at book value, adjusting for any deficiency between book and market value by altering an investment reserve established for that purpose.

In spite of opposition from the Superintendent of Insurance, who persistently favoured the use of market values, the companies in 1950[48] were permitted to use amortized values for holdings of Government of Canada, provincial, United Kingdom and United States

---

47. See Superintendent of Insurance, *Submission*, p. A88.
48. 14 Geo. VI, cap. 28.

government bonds. Notwithstanding strong representation from the industry, the use of amortized values has not been extended.

However, in 1965 an important change in valuation procedures was adopted. Prior to that date assets not shown on an amortized value basis had to be valued at market prices and were shown at book value, with any deficiency between market and book values accounted for by an investment reserve adjustment. After that the companies were permitted to modify market values of such assets so as to smooth out depressed asset prices over a three-year period. An example will show how this is to be done. Suppose in year one the book and market values of a company's total non-amortizable assets are 100, and in year two their market value drops to 90. The companies need not value their assets in year two at 90, but rather at 100–(100–90) (1/3)=96.67. In year three, if there is no further change in market value, it would be 96.67–(100–90) (1/3)=93.34 and in year four 93.34–(100–90) (1/3)=90. If there were further changes in market value after the first year, the calculation each year would involve subtracting from the values shown on the books in the preceding year one-third of the difference between market and book values for the year in question.

With this change, together with the use of amortized values as outlined above, and the use in a serious emergency of "authorized" values, it can no longer be said that asset valuation imposes a significant handicap on life insurance companies operating in Canada.

Types of funds accumulated: Table 8:5 provides an outline of the broad categories of Canadian life insurance company liabilities. As in the case of most financial intermediaries, paid-up capital has declined steadily in relative importance. Combined paid-up capital and surplus (i.e., excess of assets over liabilities excluding paid-up capital) declined in relative size until the 1930s but has since increased again—no doubt partly because of the experience of the companies during the depression. The amount of liabilities represented by actuarial reserves for contracts in force has declined steadily in relative size, from 90% in 1900 to 74% in 1969. The main point to be noted is that the deposits left by policy-holders with federal Canadian life insurance companies have grown to significant size, accounting for about 8% of the total liabilities of the companies. However, since 1945 the growth of these deposits has been no greater than the growth of all life company funds combined. We may conclude that, while the largest proportion of the funds accumulated by the life insurance companies arises from payments for life insur-

Table 8:5 Structure of Liabilities of Federally Registered Canadian Life Insurance Companies 1900-1969 (selected years)

	Capital stock and surplus						Actuarial reserve for contracts in force		Deposits		Other liabilities		Total
	Capital stock paid		Surplus		Total								
	$MNS	%	$MNS	%	$MNS	%	$MNS	%	$MNS	%	$MNS	%	$MNS
1900	2.4	4.0	2.6	4.4	5.0	8.4	53.4	89.8	n.a.	—	1.0	1.7	59.5
1920	6.2	1.5	31.3	7.5	37.5	9.0	359.5	85.6	2.2	.5	20.8	5.0	420.0
1930	11.1	.7	60.7	4.0	71.8	4.7	1259.3	83.3	37.4	2.5	142.9	9.4	1511.4
1945	11.9	.3	131.2	3.8	143.1	4.1	2725.4	79.0	280.6	8.1	300.7	8.7	3449.8
1960	18.1	.2	512.9	6.0	531.0	6.2	6787.2	78.8	651.2	7.6	641.1	7.4	8610.5
1965	19.6	.2	800.6	6.6	820.2	6.8	9279.2	76.7	960.8	7.9	1036.6	8.6	12,096.8
1969	25.3	.2	1061.8	7.0	1087.1	7.2	11,234.9	74.2	1171.3	7.7	1650.1	10.9	15,143.4

SOURCE: Canada, Department of Insurance, *Report of the Superintendent of Insurance*, Annual.

ance and annuity contracts, some of the funds have come to them because the companies have successfully persuaded policy-holders to leave deposits with them. This, by the way, is an example of how even life insurance companies compete *directly* with banks, trust and mortgage loan companies, credit unions and caisses populaires and others for funds.

We must now examine in greater detail the changing nature of the funds received by the companies from premiums and annuity considerations.

Table 8:6 shows the premiums and annuity considerations received by all federally registered life insurance companies from various types of contracts, and it also shows each as a proportion of the total of such funds received. It reveals several quite interesting changes. Prior to the 1930s almost all funds received arose from the insurance, not the annuity, business, and only a minute portion of those funds came from group insurance business. We examine the history of pensions and annuities in chapter 13, and need not repeat it here. However, it may be noted that the Canadian life insurance companies offered individual annuities from the beginning of their operations in Canada before Confederation, although for many decades they did not develop that business in any significant way. When the federal government introduced its annuity program in 1908, it did so in part because it was dissatisfied with the progress the life insurance companies had made in the field.[49] Then in 1923 the life companies began to offer group annuities, an important departure from past practices in view of the later importance of such contracts. In the 1950s the companies also began to offer a "deposit administration contract". Under it contributions of employers and employees are not used immediately to purchase a paid-up annuity, as is the case with the aforementioned group annuity plans, but are invested until needed to purchase an annuity for the employee when he retires. In contrast with the group annuity plans, under such contracts the employer and not the life company assumes responsibility for the adequacy of the fund to meet future pensions, but it is an arrangement particularly suited to cases where there are no employee contributions and it is simple to administer. Finally, and as already noted, in 1961 at the request of the industry, federal insurance legislation was amended to permit life companies to offer pension plans with unrestricted investment of funds in equities provided that such assets (called "segregated funds") were separated from the other assets of the company.[50] In 1969 no less than thirty-one Canadian

49. See below, pp. 444-5.
50. For further details see below, pp. 278-9.

companies, three British and two United States companies were offering such plans, and their segregated funds grew from $45 million in 1962, to $61 million in 1964, $312 million in 1968 and $438 million in 1969.[51]

After 1930, and particularly after 1945, annuity business grew substantially in relative importance, and group business—both in life and in annuity form—increased greatly in importance. In 1969, as Table 8:6 shows, of the total premiums and annuity considerations received, about 17% came from annuity business (it was about 23% in 1964); and just over 30% of all funds received came from group contracts, about 11½% from annuities and 18½% from group insurance—the latter being mainly term insurance.

These are not the only changes in the liabilities of the life companies that have occurred since the 1930s. Table 8:7 shows the relative importance of the various types of insurance contracts in force which were subsumed under the term "ordinary" insurance used in Table 8:6, and it also shows the relative size of the various types of annuity contracts in force. Group annuity contracts, which accounted for about 38% of the total in 1930, accounted for about 88% of the total in 1969. As for the types of life insurance, term insurance accounted for about 5% of ordinary insurance in 1930, but by 1969 it accounted for about 34%. In the 1920s term insurance had actually declined in importance—probably because of the sharply reduced competition from the assessment life companies after the First World War (see above, p. 251). This shift into term insurance, both in the form of individual policies and in the form of group life insurance, has important implications for the relative size of life insurance companies as financial intermediaries. As we have already seen, premium income per $1,000 of term insurance is much smaller than on ordinary life and endowment insurance; and so a shift toward term away from life and endowment reduces the rate of growth of the life company assets. For example, consider Table 8:8, which shows the ratio of premium income to insurance in force and the ratio of premium income plus annuity considerations to insurance in force for selected years from 1880 to 1969. Apparently from 1880 until about 1930 (the long period in which the life companies experienced high absolute growth rates and high growth rates in relation to other intermediaries) premium income remained at 3% to 3½% of insurance in force, while after that it declined steadily, standing at 1.2% in 1969. In other words, it took more than twice as much insurance in force in 1969 to generate the same premium income as in 1930. Furthermore, column

51. See *Report of the Superintendent of Insurance for Canada for the Year Ended December 31, 1969*, vol. 1, p. 33A.

Table 8:6 Net Insurance Premiums and Annuity Considerations Received by All Federally Registered Life Insurance Companies on Canadian Business[1] 1900-1969 (selected years)

	Insurance premiums								Annuity			
	ORDINARY	%	GROUP	%	INDUSTRIAL	%	TOTAL	%	ORDINARY	%	GROUP	%
1900	14,453	96.3	—	—	553	3.7	15,006	100	—	—	—	—
1920	77,276	85.5	652	.7	12,288	13.6	90,218	99.8	206	.2	—	—
1930	174,820	78.5	5,136	2.3	40,567	18.2	220,523	99.0	1,647	.7	518	.2
1945	198,698	68.7	14,152	4.9	48,325	16.7	261,176	90.4	14,296	4.9	13,608	4.7
1960	583,716	64.4	106,378	11.7	38,581	4.3	728,676	80.4	32,223	3.6	145,636	16.1
1965	759,238	61.2	173,163	13.9	29,745	2.4	962,148	77.5	62,249	5.0	216,999	17.5
1969	919,620	62.5	274,257	18.6	24,423	1.7	1,218,300	82.8	81,730	5.6	170,936	11.6

SOURCE: Canada, Department of Insurance, *Report of the Superintendent of Insurance*, Annual.

[1] In thousands of dollars.

5 of that table shows that increased income from annuities was not sufficient to offset this trend, for it shows the ratio of premium income and annuity consideration to insurance in force standing at 3.4% in 1930 and 1.4% in 1969.

One final aspect of the development of life insurance must be noted: its annual growth rate and the "density" of policies in force. Table 8:9 gives some indication of both. First of all, the figures for growth of life insurance in force on a per capita constant dollar basis outline the same periods of high and low growth rates as did the assets in Canada figures. From 1870 to 1969 the average annual growth rate was 4.6%, the figure for 1870-1930 being 5.8%, and from 1930 to 1969, 2.8%. With a rate of 4.1% from 1945 to 1969, life insurance in the postwar period has been rising at less than its long-term growth rate, even though the individual amount of insurance carried (in constant dollars) has continued to climb. Also to be noted is that from 1945 to 1969 federally registered life company assets in Canada (using constant dollar per capita figures) rose by only 1% annually on the average, whereas life insurance in force rose by 4.1%. This is once more a reflection of the fact that there has been a substantial shift toward individual and group term insurance and that the growth of life insurance company assets has slowed down for that reason.

considerations			Total							
INDUSTRIAL	TOTAL		ORDINARY		GROUP		INDUSTRIAL		TOTAL	
%	%		%		%		%		%	
—	—	14,453	96.3	—	—	553	3.7	15,006	100
206	.2	77,482	85.7	652	.7	12,288	13.6	90,422	100
2,165	1.0	176,467	79.2	5,654	2.5	40,567	18.2	222,688	100
27,904	9.7	212,994	73.7	27,760	9.6	48,325	16.7	289,079	100
177,860	19.6	615,940	67.9	252,015	27.8	38,581	4.3	906,537	100
279,248	22.5	821,488	66.2	390,163	31.4	29,745	2.4	1,241,396	100
252,666	17.2	1,001,350	68.1	445,193	30.3	24,423	1.6	1,470,967	100

Table 8:9 shows the number of ordinary and industrial policies in force per thousand of population. In 1900 the number was 75 and in 1930 it was 659, from which level the number subsequently retreated. Group insurance may, of course, explain some of that decline after 1930. But it also seems plausible that by the 1930s the companies had probably sold insurance to about as large a proportion of the population as would buy it, and that thereafter it was a matter mainly of maintaining that proportion and of trying to sell more insurance to that part of the population that already had some. In other words, it may be that until about 1930 an unexploited insurance market still existed, while after that it did not exist to any important extent.

The only significant diversification of the life insurance companies beyond the life and annuity business has been their development of the group (and to a minor extent, individual) personal accident and sickness insurance business. Table 8:11 on p. 286 shows that in 1969 their net premiums written amounted to $350 million, compared with only $69 million for the fire and casualty insurance companies, so in that area of private insurance they have come to dominate the field. The companies have, however, suffered substantial underwriting losses in their non-life business.

We may conclude our discussion of the life companies' sources of

Table 8:7 Analysis of Ordinary Life Insurance and Annuities in Force in Canada of Federally Registered Life Insurance Companies[1] 1920-1969 (selected years)

	Ordinary life insurance in force							Annuities in force									
	LIFE		ENDOWMENT		TERM AND TEMPORARY ADDITIONS		TOTAL	ORDINARY		GROUP		SETTLEMENT		DISABILITY		TOTAL
	$MNS	%	$MNS	%	$MNS	%	$MNS	$MNS	%	$MNS	%	$MNS	%	$MNS	%	$MNS
1920	1,899	70.4	567	21.0	233	8.6	2,699	—	—	—	—	—	—	—	—	—
1930	4,007	75.4	1,029	19.4	282	5.3	5,317	1.6	25.4	2.4	38.1	1.2	19.0	1.1	17.4	6.3
1945	n.a.	n.a.	n.a.	n.a.	n.a.	n.a.	n.a.	27.7	35.0	43.8	55.4	5.1	6.4	2.5	3.2	79.1
1960	22,374	55.5	7,646	19.0	10,294	25.5	40,314	60.7	8.2	658.4	89.4	13.8	1.9	3.3	.4	736.2
1965	31,644	54.8	8,866	15.4	17,183	29.8	57,693	77.7	7.5	941.8	90.6	16.3	1.6	4.0	.4	1,039.8
1969	40,232	52.8	9,710	12.7	26,263	34.5	76,205	108.5	9.6	998.3	88.3	19.1	1.7	5.1	.4	1,131.0

SOURCE: Canada, Department of Insurance, *Report of the Superintendent of Insurance*, Annual.

[1]Based on gross amounts.

Table 8:8 Size of Premium Income, and Annuity Considerations in Relation to Net Insurance in Force of Federally Registered Life Insurance Companies 1870-1969 (selected years)

	Premium income (1) 000's	Premium income and annuity considerations (2) 000's	Life insurance in force (net) (3) 000's	1 ÷ 3 % (4)	2 ÷ 3 % (5)
1870[1]	1,500	1,500	42,400	3.5	3.7
1880	2,721	2,721	91,272	3.0	3.0
1900	15,006	15,006	431,069	3.5	3.5
1920	90,218	90,424	2,657,025	3.4	3.4
1930	220,523	222,695	6,492,283	3.4	3.4
1945	261,176	289,220	9,752,282	2.7	3.0
1960	728,677	906,537	44,648,974	1.6	2.0
1965	962,148	1,241,396	69,655,958	1.4	1.8
1968	1,164,978	1,437,815	93,212,695	1.2	1.5
1969	1,218,300	1,470,967	102,785,116	1.2	1.4

SOURCE: Canada, Department of Insurance, *Report of the Superintendent of Insurance*, Annual.

[1]Average for the years 1869, 1870 and 1871.

funds by making the following points: (1) Prior to the 1930s the life insurance companies in Canada grew rapidly because they were for years faced with a partially unexploited market for insurance, as well as because population and income were rising, and because term insurance was still relatively unimportant. (2) After 1930 the proportion of the population entering into *individual* contractual arrangements with life companies probably could no longer increase and the people in it turned increasingly to term insurance. Group insurance, which is essentially term insurance, became popular, and to some extent may have displaced ordinary insurance. In consequence, there was not only slower growth of total insurance per capita, but also a shift toward a type of insurance that generated reduced premium income for the companies. Hence an historically slow growth rate of life insurance company funds resulted. (3) The aforementioned trends after 1930 were partially offset by innovations in instruments

Table 8:9 Growth Rates of Life Insurance in Force and Number of Policies of Federally Registered Companies 1870-1969 (selected periods)

	Average annual growth rate of life insurance in force (constant dollars) (per capita)	Number of policies [1,2]			
		Ordinary insurance	Industrial	Total	Total per 1000 of population
1870-1880	6.3				
1880-1900	7.3	251,639	144,601	396,240	75
1900-1920	2.0	1,253,764	2,319,860	3,573,624	418
1920-1930	10.1	2,448,681	4,282,747	6,731,428	659
1930-1945	.8	3,679,951	4,141,632	7,821,583	573
1945-1969	4.1	8,857,900	1,383,731	10,241,631	486
1870-1930	5.8				
1930-1969	2.8				
1870-1969	4.6				

SOURCE: Canada, Department of Insurance, *Report of the Superintendent of Insurance*, Annual.

[1]Excludes group insurance, of which at the end of 1965 and 1969 there were 45,173 and 48,809 policies in force, under which 19,947,539 and 26,320,533 certificates were in force. In 1930 there were 335 such policies.

[2]End of period figures.

offered, or at least by greater exploitation of existing instruments. Until 1945 deposits supplied an increasing proportion of funds, although after that they barely maintained their relative size. Also, the development of the annuity business, especially group annuity business, particularly after 1945, generated an increasing proportion of the life companies' total funds. And the group business as such also developed greatly after the 1930s.

These innovations, however, were insufficient to overcome the combined effect of slower real growth rates per capita of insurance in force and the shift of insurance sales within ordinary insurance and through group insurance toward term insurance policies. Consequently, after the 1930s and even after 1945 the growth of life insurance company assets in Canada was less than that of other financial intermediaries and less than the growth of G.N.P. To improve on that record in future would require the companies to be more successful than they have been over the last three decades in persuading individuals that the insurance policies and annuity contracts offered by them are desirable savings instruments as well as desirable instruments for providing protection and minimal security.

This conclusion provides an appropriate transition to a discussion of recent developments.

RECENT DEVELOPMENTS

There is considerable essentially non-statistical evidence that the kinds of issues discussed in the preceding section have already begun to influence the operations of the life insurance companies. For this reason, it seems worthwhile to examine developments after the Second World War more closely than we have done up to this point. We have already seen that in this period the assets in Canada of life insurance companies grew less quickly than did G.N.P., and premium income and annuity considerations no faster than personal disposable income. Their assets also grew more slowly than the assets of all other financial intermediaries or private intermediaries combined. Particularly to be noted is that, whereas from 1945 to 1968 the life companies' assets in Canada as a proportion of total financial intermediary assets declined 6.8 percentage points, those of the trusteed pension funds increased about 6.1 percentage points and those of mutual funds increased 3.3 percentage points – these two probably being the two closest private sector competitors of the life companies. In order to compete effectively with them the life insurance companies might have been expected to (a) develop and market effectively their annuity instruments, and (b) introduce an equity element into their assets so as to provide contract holders with more protection against inflation than had been customary in the past.

Their annuity business has indeed been developing. In 1969 it provided about 17% of the income from net insurance premiums and annuity considerations of federally registered companies, compared with 10% in 1945 (see Table 8:6). However, not until 1961 did the companies request and receive permission to sell plans and policies in which the contract holders' benefits (and so the companies' liabilities) vary with the value of specifically segregated assets. Such segregated funds are not limited in the amount of their investment in common stocks. By 1969 thirty-six federally registered companies were offering variable annuities (mainly for groups, but individual annuities also) and had established segregated funds. The combined assets of Canadian companies in such funds totalled $410 million in 1969, of which 45% was in the form of stocks. Yet the companies are facing stiff competition in the annuity business. While they received 17% of their premium and annuity income from annuity business in 1969, it had been about 23% in 1965. Looked at in another way, until about 1964 the life companies increased their share of funds flowing into pension plans, as did the trusteed pension funds, at the expense of the federal government annuity scheme.[52] After 1964 the trusteed pension funds continued to gain, the federal government annuities continued to lose, and the life company annuities about held their own. Additional competition for all private pension schemes, including life company annuities, has since 1965 come from the Canada and Quebec pension plans.[53] In the area of their equity products the companies of course continue to face the strong competition of the mutual funds. The recent legislation permitting them to own subsidiary mutual fund companies may be of marginal benefit to them.

A further adverse factor for the life insurance companies was the imposition on them of the federal corporation income tax in 1969, the full consequences of which are not yet clear. The companies have also been fearful of the trend across Canada of permitting individuals to be licensed to sell both life insurance and mutual fund stock—referred to as "dual licensing"—although its consequences too are not certain.

Rather less enthusiastic than their venture into policies with variable benefits has been their use of the investment freedom contained in the basket clause, which was introduced in 1948 and put at 3% of

---

52. See below, Table 13:6, p. 450.
53. See below, pp. 447-54.

the book value of total ledger assets (this was raised to 5% in 1961 and to 7% in 1965). By 1957 the Canadian companies had only 1.7% of their assets in the "basket," which was also the 1965 level, and by 1969 this had increased only to 2.5%.

An interesting change was the one in the 1965 legislation that permitted life companies to hold more than a 30% interest in real estate companies. This has enabled them to participate in the equity of companies formed specifically for developing property, and several of the larger companies have already taken advantage of the provision. It is quite conceivable that the larger life companies, with their large pools of funds, would be making a more distinct contribution to the capital market in providing equity capital of this kind than they would by merely buying well-known common stocks, a field already well served by the mutual funds; and that they would find relatively more attractive equity investment opportunities in this area than in the area of listed equities. Because of the large amounts of funds required for individual projects of that kind and because of the new internal expertise required for engaging in such real estate development financing, it may have to be confined to the larger companies and the ones among them that are prepared to make the effort to enter quite new investment activity.

Some life insurance companies are also offering individual life insurance policies in which the benefits, as in the case of the group scheme referred to earlier, are related to the value of the company's segregated assets. In February 1967 the National Life Assurance Company of Canada introduced an equity life insurance policy. It is essentially an ordinary life policy but with half the related assets invested in common stocks, and without the normal borrowing privileges. If the earnings of those assets, including capital appreciation, exceed the company's regular net interest earnings, an extra dividend is credited to the equity policy-holder; and that dividend together with the regular one is used to buy additional paid-up insurance. If stock prices decline, the extra dividend could be negative, and if this is greater than the regular dividend, the amount of coverage and related cash surrender values would decline. In brief, this novel credit instrument combines protection, interest income and capital appreciation in one package. Other companies have followed this lead. Some of these policies began to resemble mutual fund shares and so provincial securities commissions began to argue that they should be made subject to securities regulations. Ontario and Quebec adopted the criterion that policies would be exempt from such regulations if at least 75% of premiums paid in were guaranteed to be paid out either at maturity or at death.

CONCLUSIONS

The growth of life insurance in Canada to the point where life companies became the second largest financial intermediary in Canada (a point reached by about 1906) is one of the major events in the development of the Canadian capital market. Until the 1930s life company assets in Canada grew faster than G.N.P. and faster than the assets of all other financial intermediaries. It is true that there was a period of slower growth from about 1900 to 1920 but this was a temporary interruption to a growth trend that did not end until the 1930s – an interruption caused possibly by the adverse publicity surrounding insurance companies over part of that period, the massive diversion of individual savings into War Bonds, the temporary diversion of insurance selling efforts as a result of the war, and the "destruction" of insurance in real value terms by inflation.

The substantial increase in the number of individual policies per thousand of population until the end of the 1920s suggests that in that period the growth of the industry benefited greatly from the sale of insurance to a still not fully exploited market. It benefited also from the relative unimportance of term insurance. Government supervision helped ensure against life company failures, and legislation relating to investments gave the companies a substantial degree of freedom – sufficient to permit the Sun Life to invest half of its funds in common stocks. However, with the exception of the Sun Life, the industry had firmly established its conservative attitude toward common stocks long before the legislation of 1932 – an attitude that had the full support of the Superintendent of Insurance and one that seemed to be entirely vindicated by the depression of the 1930s. Expansion of foreign business up to the end of the 1920s was an outstanding feature of the growth of Canadian companies – although only a few companies were active in this development.

After the 1920s the basic position of the life insurance companies changed. They grew persistently less than did financial intermediaries in total and less than G.N.P.; their assets in Canada on a constant dollar per capita basis and their premium and annuity income as a proportion of personal disposable income have shown no increase in the period after the Second World War. At the same time, insurance in force in per capita constant dollar terms continued to increase, although at a reduced rate.

Probably the two most important reasons for this reduced growth were (a) the relatively complete exploitation of the insurance market by the end of the 1920s – since individual policies per thousand of population ceased to grow, and (b) the shift toward term insurance, by individuals and through group insurance. The latter meant that it took more than twice as much insurance in force in 1969 to generate the same premium income as it did in the years prior to the 1930s. The Canadian life companies' foreign business did not provide the impetus to growth after the 1930s that it did before the 1930s but remained very important to them.

To some extent they softened their relative decline by developing their deposit business and their annuity business. Their major failure was waiting so long to devise means whereby they could offer instruments that would provide some protection against inflation and meet the competition that was beginning to emerge. By not introducing group variable annuities until 1961 they lost business to the very rapidly growing trusteed pension funds administered by trust companies (see below, p. 452), and by not generally developing individual variable annuities they left an open field to the mutual funds. Their attitude toward common stocks, as indicated by their investment practices, remained as conservative as it always had been, which, no doubt, explains their lack of enthusiasm and initiative in introducing the innovations referred to above. It is difficult to believe that the legislative restrictions under which they operated played an important part in their relative decline—particularly since changes were usually introduced soon after the industry asked for them. Following the legislative changes of 1965, not even a hypothetical case could be made for arguing that legislative restraints seriously inhibited the activities of the companies. It was in the 1960s that the life companies began to appreciate the nature of the competition that they were facing and began to adjust to meet it.

For the nation, perhaps the most important long-term problem in the industry is the one of devising means to appraise the economic efficiency of mutual life companies, which, because they hold no interest to investment analysts and to investors, are not now being scrutinized on efficiency grounds. It is not at all inconceivable that the character of the Department of Insurance—so long oriented toward accounting matters—will have to change so as to cope with the full economic implications of a heavily mutualized insurance industry.

For the industry the challenge will be to retain its past share of the business of accumulating and distributing the nation's savings in the face of strong competition from mutual funds, trusteed pension plans and compulsory national pension plans. It is not clear that this can be done without the introduction and exploitation of further new savings instruments, new investment practices, and new marketing procedures. At present the life insurance industry, like the chartered banking system, seems to have reached maturity in that its growth is not greater than the national economic aggregates and in some respects is less. Recent indications, in the form of experimentation of individual companies with new types of policies and annuity contracts and new forms of investments such as real estate development projects, and a generally more open-minded approach to equities, suggest that the industry will make at least some of the necessary adjustments. That there is ample room for individual companies to reap the rewards of innovation seems to be quite certain.

Fire and Casualty Insurance Companies

Fire and casualty insurance provides protection against specific risks and generally excludes a savings element. For these reasons the amount of funds accumulated through such business is not large and the financial intermediation activity of the companies is thereby limited. But they do accumulate some funds to meet claims and they do invest such funds in financial assets and so constitute a part of the financial system. For this reason we will examine briefly their development.

Marine and transit insurance appeared long before fire insurance. Florentine families used it at the beginning of the fourteenth century.[54] The great fire of London of 1666 demonstrated the need for fire insurance, and in 1667 there was founded the Fire Office (later Phoenix), in 1681 the City of London's Mutual Fire Insurance Scheme, and in 1684 the Friendly Society. Others soon followed. The first real mutual company was formed in 1696 (later known as Hand-in-Hand), and Lloyd's Coffee House, which was later to become a powerful insurance group, opened in 1688. Fire insurance protection also appeared in Hamburg in 1677 and in Paris in 1750. By 1720 a number of the well-known names in British fire insurance had appeared—the Sun Insurance Office (1710), the Union Society (1714), the Westminster Fire Office (1717), the Crown (1718) and the London Assurance Corporation (1720), and the Royal Exchange Assurance Corporation added fire to its business in 1720. Fire insurance companies developed somewhat later in the United States. Mutual fire insurance companies were formed in 1752, 1768 and 1784, but in 1792 appeared the Insurance Company of North America. English companies had offices in the United States as well.

---

54. Much of our historical data are from the useful sketch of the history of fire insurance and the detailed discussion of its development and nature in Canada by Gérard Parizeau, *Traite d'assurance contre l'incendie au Canada*, les presses de l'Ecole des Hautes Etudes Commerciales, Montreal, 1961.

It is at this point that the development of fire insurance in Canada may be examined. Fire insurance seems not to have existed during the French régime. A 1790 prospectus of the Phoenix Company of London advertising its fire insurance facilities was directed toward inhabitants of the Canadas, Nova Scotia and the United States. In 1804 it opened an agency in Montreal and one in Halifax in 1805. Then appeared the first "Canadian" company. In 1809 a group of individuals of Halifax formed the Nova Scotia Fire Association, a mutual organization, which in 1819 was incorporated as the Halifax Fire Insurance Company. The second Canadian company was the Quebec Fire Assurance Company, which was unsuccessfully launched as a mutual organization in 1816, and then reorganized as a general insurance company. It began to operate successfully in 1818 and in 1829 it was incorporated as a joint-stock company. The Montreal Insurance Company appeared at about the same time, but subsequently ceased operations. In 1821 an American company, the Aetna Insurance Company of Hartford, opened an office in Montreal and introduced some new methods into the business, while the Hartford Fire Insurance Company opened offices in Canada in 1836. The British American Assurance Company, the first company formed in Ontario, appeared in 1833, and in the mid 1830s there appeared a large number of local mutual fire insurance companies in Upper and Lower Canada. So by the end of the 1830s Canadian fire insurance companies had become well established. The Western Assurance Company, which was subsequently to become very important in the industry, was organized in 1851. In 1875 there were 27 companies operating under federal registration in Canada, of which 11 were Canadian, 13 British and 3 American.

Casualty or accident insurance began to be written by existing insurance companies and also by companies formed specifically for that purpose. Apparently the first licence in Canada for writing accident insurance was issued in 1868 to the Travelers Company of Hartford, Conn., and the first Canadian company to take out a licence for such insurance was the Citizens, in 1893, which also did a life insurance business.[55] The first purely accident company licensed in Canada was the Accident Insurance Company of North America, in 1874, and in 1880 the English company the London Guarantee entered the field. In 1897 there seem to have been 13 companies licensed, 8 Canadian, 1 American and 4 British. Today almost all fire insurance companies also write casualty insurance.

---

55. For these details see *Accident Insurance in Canada, Canada: An Encyclopaedia*, ibid., pp. 347-8.

Statistical data relating to fire and casualty insurance are available from 1869 onward. Table 8:10 summarizes some of that material. A characteristic of the industry for many years was a steady increase in the number of companies. There were 27 federally registered companies writing fire and casualty insurance in 1875 and 331 in 1945. However, since 1955 the number of such companies has declined dramatically, numbering 264 in 1969; thus the industry is undergoing substantial change. Table 8:10 shows that non-Canadian companies have always dominated the field, accounting for more than 50% of net premiums written. Foreign ownership in the industry at present is substantially greater than implied by net premiums written by non-Canadian companies, because of foreign ownership of Canadian companies. Net premiums written by foreign-controlled Canadian companies and non-Canadian companies amounted to 82% in 1969.[56]

Data for provincial companies are not available in detail. However, it is apparent that federally registered companies have always dominated the field. In 1931 provincially licensed companies accounted for 12.5% of net premiums written by fire and casualty companies; in 1945 the figure was 9.6% and in 1969 9.7%. Assets of federally registered and Ontario fire and casualty companies increased faster than G.N.P. until the early 1960s and at about the same rate as total financial intermediary assets until the 1930s (see Table 8:10). For the past century casualty insurance has grown at a faster rate than fire insurance. In 1875 fire insurance premiums written amounted to 96% of the total and casualty premiums 4%, while in 1969 fire premiums were 18% and casualty premiums were 82% (see Table 8:10). The rapid rate of growth of casualty insurance is only part of the explanation, the other reason being the relatively slow growth of fire insurance since the turn of the century. Before 1900 net fire insurance premiums written grew at a substantially faster rate than did G.N.P. almost certainly because of an increase in the proportion of real properties covered by such insurance and also by an upward drift in insurance rates. After 1900 they grew at a rate less than G.N.P., probably because of the persistent tendency of the cost of insurance to fall. In 1900 $100 of fire insurance on the average cost about $1.25, while in 1967 it cost less than $.50. Better fire protection and more fireproof structures reduced fire risks, thereby reducing insurance rates, which in turn slowed the growth of premiums written and so

---

56. *Report of the Superintendent of Insurance for Canada for the Year Ended December 31, 1968*, vol. 2 (Ottawa: Queen's Printer), p. 5A.

Table 8:10 Fire and Casualty Insurance 1870-1969 (selected years)

	Number of federally registered companies[1]				Assets[2]			Net premiums written by federally registered companies					
	CANADIAN NO.	U.K. NO.	OTHER NO.	TOTAL NO.	$ MNS.	% OF G.N.P.	% OF TOTAL F.I. ASSETS	CANADIAN %	U.K. %	OTHER %	TOTAL $ MNS.	% FIRE	% CASUALTY
1870	5	12	3	20	4.5	1.0	3.2	28	62	10	1.9	100	—
1875	11	13	3	27	8.4	n.a.	3.4	46	46	8	3.7	96	4
1880	9	15	4	28	9.1	1.6	3.1	36	56	8	3.6	96	4
1890	12	28	8	48	17.4	2.2	3.5	24	66	10	6.2	93	7
1900	14	26	9	49	27.6	2.6	3.3	19	67	14	9.4	88	12
1910	46	25	27	98	58.9	2.6	3.3	29	50	21	24.0	78	22
1926	54	65	125	244	162	3.1	3.6						
1937	66	72	193	331	217	4.1	3.2	27	35	38	77.1	55	45
1945	69	77	185	331	320	2.7	2.3	28	28	44	127.6	46	54
1950	81	89	186	356	551	3.1	2.7	30	28	42	303.3	38	62
1955	95	95	209	399	920	3.3	3.0	36	24	40	517.7	28	72
1960	88	77	147	312	1388	3.7	3.1	37	23	40	788.4	25	75
1965	87	63	133	283	1949	3.6	2.6	44	18	38	1176.7	19	81
1966	86	59	134	280	2163	3.5	2.7	46	17	37	1320.0	18	82
1967	86	60	132	277	2304	3.5	2.6	47	16	37	1466.9	18	82
1968	86	54	132	272	2516	3.5	2.5	47	15	38	1566.6	18	82
1969	85	50	129	264	2758	3.5	n.a.	47	15	38	1727.2	18	82

SOURCE: *Report of the Superintendent of Insurance for Canada*, Queen's Printer, Ottawa, Annual.

[1]Excludes companies writing life insurance.

[2]Includes federally registered and Ontario company assets. See Statistical Appendix.

Table 8:11 Types of Casualty Insurance and Marine Insurance 1969

	Net premiums written	
I **Casualty insurance**	$MNS.	PERCENT OF TOTAL
Non-life insurance companies		
Aircraft	15.5	1.5
Automobile	729.9	68.8
Boiler and machinery	16.2	1.5
Credit	1.3	.1
Earthquake	.2	...
Explosion	...	...
Forgery	.2	...
Guarantee fidelity	8.5	.8
Guarantee surety	20.6	1.9
Hail	4.2	.4
Inland transportation	13.3	1.3
Liability – public	69.3	6.5
Liability – employer	8.6	.8
Livestock	.6	...
Mortgages	.6	...
Group personal accident and sickness (ex. life cos.)	30.6	2.9
Individual personal accident and sickness (ex. life cos.)	38.9	3.7
Personal property	80.8	7.6
Plate glass	4.2	.4
Real property	5.9	.6
Sprinkler leakage	...	...
Theft	11.4	1.1
Title	.1	...
Weather	...	...
Windstorm	.6	...
Sub-total	1061.5	100
Life insurance companies		
Group personal accident and sickness	311.2	
Individual personal accident and sickness	38.5	
Total casualty insurance	1411.3	
II **Marine insurance**	20.4	

SOURCE: *Report of the Superintendent of Insurance for Canada for the year ended December 31, 1969*, Queen's Printer, Ottawa, pp. 2B-73B.

Table 8:12 Assets of Fire and Casualty Insurance Companies 1966-70

	1966 %	1968 %	1969 %	1970 %
Cash and demand deposits	5.6	4.4	4.3	4.3
Canadian securities				
Government of Canada	25.7	21.4	21.7	18.6
Provincial	17.6	19.2	17.7	19.0
Municipal	6.7	6.4	6.0	6.4
Sub-total	(50.1)	(47.0)	(45.4)	(44.0)
Short-term paper and term deposits	1.3	2.4	3.4	3.9
Corporate bonds, debentures and collateral loans	10.6	11.8	12.5	14.0
Mortgages	1.0	1.3	1.2	1.4
Preferred and common shares	12.0	13.9	14.0	14.0
Investments in and advances to subsidiaries	—	.4	.5	.2
Foreign securities	4.2	3.0	2.7	2.6
Amounts due from other insurance companies agents and uncollected premiums	n.a.	11.5	11.4	11.5
Real estate	n.a.	1.8	1.5	1.5
All other assets	n.a.	2.4	3.1	2.6
	100	100	100	100

SOURCE: Dominion Bureau of Statistics, *Financial Institutions — Financial Statistics*, Queen's Printer, Ottawa, quarterly.

of fire insurance company assets. Without their casualty business, fire insurance companies would have grown at a substantially slower rate than they did, an interesting example of successful innovation. In this respect it may be noted that in 1969, of 264 federally registered companies writing fire or casualty insurance or both (excluding life insurance companies), no less than 220 in fact wrote both types and only 7 wrote fire insurance only.

Since 1900 casualty insurance net premiums have increased on the average at about 19-20% per annum and since 1945 at about 13-14% per annum. The relative importance of the various types of casualty insurance behind this growth experience is shown in Table 8:11. Two points stand out. First, automobile insurance dominates the field, accounting for 69% of net premiums written by the non-life companies in 1969; and second, the field of group personal accident and sickness insurance, which is by a substantial margin the second largest type of casualty insurance, has essentially been lost by the companies under discussion through the activities of life insurance companies. Marine insurance is not an important area of insurance activity in Canada, as Table 8:11 shows.

Because of the importance of automobile insurance to private fire and casualty insurance companies, the introduction of minimum compulsory nationalized car insurance in Saskatchewan and Manitoba could constitute a development of some significance were it to become a national trend.

The fire and casualty insurance companies invest their funds in relatively liquid financial claims. This is because the policies they issue are short-term in nature, normally for three years, and because the claims against particular companies can vary quite substantially from year to year, much more so than in the case of life insurance companies. Table 8:12 shows their asset distribution in recent years — earlier detailed data not being available.

9

The Trust Companies

The unique contribution to the financial system of the trust companies is their provision of a variety of executor, administrator and trustee services. They are unique among the financial institutions in this respect because banks, life insurance companies and loan companies are not permitted to act in a fiduciary capacity. The earliest Canadian trust company legislation emphasized these services. It also loosely circumscribed the holding of real estate by them, and expressly forbade them from engaging in the "business of banking." Had the trust companies remained as "pure" as this, they would be of rather less significance to this study and to the capital market than they in fact are. The decisive change occurred when the trust companies, in addition to managing estates, trusts and agencies funds, were permitted to accept funds in exchange for their own credit instruments—the trust deposit, the deposit receipt and the guaranteed investment certificate. This enabled them to become active in the accumulation of savings, and to exercise wide judgment (within the limits of the relevant statutes) in the distribution of savings. We shall see that the way this activity has developed has made the trust companies' borrowing and lending activities little different from those of the mortgage loan companies and the savings business of the chartered banks.

In general, the Canadian trust companies are important to a study of the development of the capital market not merely because of the trustee and other services they provide in managing new and outstanding security issues, but also because they have developed into important financial intermediaries. The business of the trust companies can be divided into two parts for purposes of discussion: the business arising from the company funds (essentially shareholders' equity) and guaranteed funds (arising from deposits taken and certificates issued), which is really the business that makes trust companies financial intermediaries; and the estates trusts and agencies business, in which there is a small element of financial intermediation but which pertains mainly to services rendered for which a fee is charged.

The Emergence of Trust Companies

To say that the trust companies are unique among financial institutions in that they provide trustee and executor services is not to suggest that those services were not being provided before the trust companies appeared in the 1880s. They were provided by many individuals who frequently were also accountants, auditors, lawyers and general financial agents. Therefore, when trust companies began to emerge, they were able to operate successfully not because they were superior to existing financial institutions but rather because they were superior in many respects to individual executors and trustees. By also assuming banking and loan company functions they gained added strength without really contributing anything unique to the capital market, a point to which we will return.

The superiority of the trust companies over individual trustees, executors and administrators arises primarily from the large volume of their business, which permits them to develop a certain expertise in all of the many facets of the business, and from their permanent corporate status, which enables this expertise to be available whenever it is needed. An individual executor may be ill or dead when his services are required, or he may have moved, or his relationship with the testator may have undergone subtle changes, or through ignorance or irresponsibility he may delay settlement of an estate or delay taking action to protect the interests of the estate. In many cases an individual simply may not have friends (or relatives) whom he cares to trust with the settlement of his estate. The services of a trust company preclude or overcome some of these difficulties entirely, and others to some extent at least. Considerations such as these help to explain the initial appearance and success of trust companies.

But there were other reasons as well. In addition to serving individual clients, a trust company may serve corporations as transfer agent and registrar for securities issues, and as trustee under bond issues; or even as liquidator, receiver or assignee where corporations have failed to meet their obligations. The growth of new domestic securities issues, particularly corporation issues, increased the need for services of this kind at about the time when the trust companies began to appear.

The basic idea of a "trust" is a very old one, being evident in eleventh-century England in the legal institution of the "use," in the sense of property being conveyed to a grantee "to the use" of another. For several centuries the carrying out of the "use" depended on the conscience of the "Transferee to uses," for, not having a writ to fit the case, the common law did not enforce it. Abuses in the employment of the use lead to the Statute of Uses of 1535, which was intended to abolish the use but which, through exceptions arising from judicial decisions, became the basis for certain surviving uses. These survivors became known as "trusts," and they form the basis for the law of trusts. So the trust was English in origin, and not surprisingly was introduced from there into the United States and the British Commonwealth, including Canada.[1]

Corporate trustees, however, did not emerge first in England, possibly because of the prevailing view that to execute a trust required a conscience and that abuse of a trust required punishment—a view that could not easily accommodate the idea of a legal entity acting as trustee.

The concept of the corporate trustee is essentially a North American one, although even before the first one appeared in 1822 the "Agency Houses" in India had transacted business somewhat similar to that of trust companies. The first corporation to obtain a charter that included power to engage in trustee business was the Farmers' Fire Insurance and Loan Company, incorporated February 28, 1822, under the authority of the Legislature of the State of New York. Its charter was amended on April 17, 1822, to include trustee powers, for it had become evident that in order to properly serve its clients resident outside of New York City it would need to have trustee powers. In 1836 the Pennsylvania Company for Insurance of Lives and Granting Annuities of Philadelphia, which had been incorporated in 1812, secured trust company powers; and in 1853 the first company to transact trust company business exclusively was formed—the United States Trust Company of New York. By 1850 there were about fifty trust companies in the United States, some of which also operated as savings banks and provided safety deposit facilities. The trust company charter at that time specifically included such banking func-

1. See G. G. Bogert, "Trust," *Encyclopaedia Britannica*, 1962, vol. 22, pp. 516-19; Ernest Heaton, *The Trust Company Idea and Its Development* (Toronto: Hunter Rose Co., 1904).

tions; and, as we have seen, in some cases corporate trustee facilities were provided by life insurance companies. The banking functions of trust companies became increasingly important until those companies were in fact commercial banks. The banks regarded them as being in a privileged position because of the favourable tax treatment they received and because they did not have to hold reserves, and also felt that they were a threat to the stability of the banking system. In 1908 New York brought the trust companies under the same law as the banks; in 1913, with the passing of the Federal Reserve Act, the fiduciary powers enjoyed by trust companies were extended to the commercial banks, and trust companies were permitted to become members of the federal reserve system. In this way the two became blended into one system.[2] As an example of this change, the Farmers' Fire Insurance and Loan Company referred to earlier became the City Bank Farmers Trust Company and was owned by the First National City Bank of New York; later it was amalgamated with the latter, becoming the bank's trust division. We will see that in Canada the development of the trust companies has been somewhat different; they have survived as more distinct entities than those in the United States.

It is rather interesting that the first attempts to establish a corporate trustee in Canada apparently came almost as early as in the United States. In 1835 the Assembly of Upper Canada, with general support from both houses, passed an act incorporating a Life Insurance and Trust Company modelled on the New York Life and Trust Company, which had been incorporated in 1830. The governor reserved the bill, and in the event, assent of the imperial government was refused. The Colonial Secretary, Lord Glenelg, thought that abuses would arise from mixing life insurance, deposit, and trust business, and in the matter of a corporation engaging in trust business he had this to say:

> The Courts by which the trusts are to be delegated to this Company are not invested with any summary jurisdiction over the corporate body, its officers or its funds. The property of infants and of absentees, of married women and of lunatics, would be thus committed to functionaries not amenable to the summary orders of the tribunals from which their power is to be derived, nor bound to render to them any account of the administration of the trust funds. In every case of alleged breach of trust, legal proceedings must be instituted, the nature of which is not at all explained, and the success of these proceedings must depend upon the solvency of a body virtually irresponsible for their conduct. . . .[3]

---

2. See B. F. Hoselitz, "Trust Company," *Encyclopaedia Britannica*, 1962, vol. 22, pp. 519-22.
3. See above, p. 222, and reference there noted.

The Colonial Secretary also pointed out that (a) the proposed paid-up capital of $120,000 was inadequate security for those dealing with the company; (b) the company was in any case exempt from special security for the discharge of trusts; and (c) there was no Court of Equity in the province, as there was in England, where individuals could seek relief for neglect or breach of trust. So assent was refused and for over thirty years no progress was made in the development of corporate trustees in Canada.

The next significant date in the development of Canadian trust companies was March 2, 1872, when the Ontario legislature gave its assent to a bill incorporating Canada's first trust company, the Toronto General Trust Company. On the same day it also passed a bill extending trust company powers to a loan company which had been formed in 1869.

This loan company, the Ontario Trust and Investment Society, in 1869[4] had been empowered to acquire, hold, and dispose of stocks, bonds, and debentures, and take deposits up to a combined total equal to its paid-up capital. But in addition it was given very rudimentary trust powers in that it could

> act as an agency, and may hold, invest and deal with such moneys, mortgages, securities or debts as shall, from time to time, be transferred or delivered to the company, upon trust or as agents, and may exercise all the rights which parties so transferring or delivering the same might or would exercise; and the company may give such guarantee as may be agreed on for repayment of principal and interest, or both, of any such moneys, mortgages or debts.

However, in 1872 an amendment to that act gave the company explicit fiduciary powers.

The relevant clause was identical to the one in the act of that same date which incorporated the Toronto General Trust Company.[5] A petition for incorporating the General Trust Co. of Ontario was read in the Ontario legislature on December 20, 1871. The bill for incorporating the company, now referred to as the General Trusts Company of Ontario, received first reading on January 26, 1872. An amended bill, in which the company's name was changed to "Toronto General Trusts Company," was reported on February 13, 1872. It received the Royal assent on March 2, 1872. It stated that the companies were authorized

> to take, receive and hold all estates and property, real and personal which may be granted, committed, transferred, or conveyed to them

4. 34-35 Vic., cap. 68.
5. 34-35 Vic., cap. 83.

> with their consent, upon any trust or trusts whatsoever, (not contrary to law) at any time or times, by any person or persons, body or bodies corporate, or by any court of the Province of Ontario, and to administer, fulfill, and discharge the duties of such trusts for such remuneration as may be agreed on: and they are also authorized to act generally as agents or attorneys for the transaction of business, the management of estates, the collection of rent, interests, dividends, mortgages, bonds, bills, notes and securities for money and also to act as agents for the purpose of issuing or countersigning the certificates of stock, bonds or other obligation of any corporation, association, municipality, and to receive and manage any sinking fund therefor, on such terms as may be agreed upon.
>
> The said company are also authorized to accept and execute the offices of executor, administrator, trustee, receiver, assignee (other than under any Act relating to insolvency,) guardian of any minor, or of confinement of any lunatic....

In addition the act incorporating the Toronto General Trust limited its real estate holdings to its office requirements, and authorized it "... to invest any moneys forming part of their capital or reserve, or accumulated profit in such securities, real or personal, as the directors may from time to time deem expedient; provided nothing in this Act shall authorize the said company to engage in the business of banking." The company was required to submit an annual return to the provincial government. Its capital was $200,000 with $50 shares, and the company had the right to increase it to $500,000; shareholders had to be given an opportunity to buy new stock on a *pro rata* basis.

The company, however, was not really organized and did not begin business until 1882. The Hon. Edward Blake was its first president, and J. W. Langmuir left the service of the Province of Ontario to become its manager.

In the first year of its operation the company was appointed trustee for the High Court of Justice for Ontario, and was appointed to the management of lunatic estates. On May, 1882, its first advertisement announced that the company had $300,000 in trust funds for investment in straight loans on real estate.

Other trust companies were formed within a few years, the earlier ones being:

Name	*Year*	*Charter*
Grey and Bruce Trust & Savings Co.	1887	Ontario
The Montreal Trust Co.	1889	Quebec
Imperial Trust Co.	1889	Dominion
The Royal Trust Co.	1892	Quebec
Eastern Trust Co.	1893	Dominion
Canada Trust Co.	1893	Dominion

General Trust Corp. of Ontario	1894	Ontario
The London & Western Trusts Co. Ltd.	1896	Ontario
The Trusts & Guarantee Co. of Toronto (later Crown Trust Company)	1897	Ontario
The National Trust Co. of Ontario Ltd.	1898	Ontario

As is apparent from this tabulation, most of the trust companies formed operated under provincial charters and, contrary to the case of banks and life insurance companies, a significant portion of the industry has always been composed of provincially incorporated companies. Since the trust companies began by emphasizing their "estates, trusts and agencies" business, provincial incorporation is not surprising. Such business falls in the provincial sphere under the "property and civil rights" clause of the British North America Act. But, as we shall see, in later years their financial intermediation business grew in importance, and since such operations quickly cross provincial boundaries, federal incorporation, one would have thought, would have had advantages. It is possible that the difficulty of federal incorporation, since a special act of Parliament was required in each case, partially explains the importance of provincial companies over the years. If so, then the future should be different from the past, for the federal Trust Companies Act was amended in 1970 to permit incorporation of trust companies by letters patent as an alternative to incorporation by special act.

In at least three cases trust companies from the very beginning were closely associated with individual chartered banks, although not always through equity participation on the part of the latter: the Royal Trust with the Bank of Montreal, the Montreal Trust with the Royal Bank of Canada, and the National Trust with the Canadian Bank of Commerce. These associations proved lasting and after the Second World War the other large chartered banks also aligned themselves with individual trust companies. However, the Bank Act of 1967 forbade interlocking directorships between banks and trust companies and limited a bank's holding of the voting stock of a trust company to 10% of the total of such stock from July 1, 1971, onward.

Legislative Influences on Trust Companies

The pioneer legislation under which trust company powers were granted to the Toronto General Trust and the Ontario Trust and Investment Society, and to which reference has already been made, has three significant aspects. First, it was remarkably comprehensive in its summary of the trustee, executor and agencies functions to be enjoyed by the companies; second, it attempted to fit trust companies into the capital market without encroaching on the business of the banks, loan companies and life insurance companies; and third, it attempted to provide protection for the customers of the trust companies.

With respect to the first of these aspects, a summary of such powers enjoyed by the trust companies today indicates that there have been no important additions since the first Ontario legislation. Companies generally enjoy the power

(a) to receive property granted to them by persons, corporations or courts, upon any trusts not contrary to law;
(b) to hold property in safe-keeping;
(c) to act as agents in management of property and collection of rents, interest, dividends, etc.;
(d) to act as corporation agents (transfer agencies, etc.);
(e) to act as executor, administrator, receiver, liquidator, custodian, trustee in bankruptcy, guardian of infant's property, committee for estates of mentally incompetent, etc.;
(f) to invest trust moneys;
(g) to guarantee investments;
(h) to perform all acts necessary in dealing with property;
(i) to own real estate necessary to carry on their business;
(j) to charge remuneration for their services.[6]

The second important aspect of early legislation was that it attempted to enforce specialization onto the trust companies by prohibiting them from engaging in the business of banking and insurance and by attempting to withhold from them certain powers enjoyed by the loan companies. The act incorporating the Toronto General Trust stated categorically that "... nothing in this Act shall authorize the said company to engage in the business of banking," but it did not define what was meant by the "business of banking." Early Dominion government legislation was more explicit. For example, acts incorporating the Union Trust Corporation of Canada in 1884,[7] the Imperial Trusts Co. of Canada in 1887,[8] the General Trust Corporation in 1894,[9] and the Dominion of Canada Trusts Co. 1895[10] all stated that

6. See Winslow Benson, *Business Methods of Canadian Trust Companies* (Toronto: Ryerson Press), p. 3.
7. 47 Vic., cap. 100, assented to April 19, 1884.
8. 50-51 Vic., cap. 115.
9. 57-58 Vic., cap. 115.
10. 58-59Vic., cap. 84.

> Nothing in this Act shall be construed to authorize the Corporation to issue any note payable to the bearer thereof, or any promissary note intended to be circulated as money or as the note of a bank, or to engage in the business of banking or insurance.

In addition, the above paragraph in the Act incorporating the Dominion of Canada Trust Co. in 1895 has added to it the clause, "...and the company shall not have power to issue debentures." This, of course, was an important source of funds for the loan companies.

The act of the Quebec legislature incorporating the Royal Trust and Fidelity Company in 1892[11] emphasizes again the conscious attempts made to prohibit the trust companies from engaging in the business of banking. The initial act stated that "...the said company shall have power to receive money on deposit, and to allow interest on the same...," and also "...to lend money to any company, partnership or person, or corporate body, upon such terms as are deemed expedient, upon the security of real estate, ground rents, public securities of Canada, or any of the Provinces thereof, or on the securities or debentures of any municipal or other corporation issued under any statutory authority, or upon the security of stocks, shares or goods, warehoused or hypothecated with the company." Had these provisions not been objected to, they would have given the company almost all the important powers enjoyed by banks except the authority to issue bank notes. But objection did arise, and an amending act in the same year repealed the paragraph permitting the company to receive money on deposit, and amended the direct lending powers of the company so that it was confined to making loans on the security of real estate. The company was permitted, however, to take funds on trust and to guarantee repayment of principal and payment of interest, and it was permitted to issue bonds or debentures up to three-quarters of its paid-up capital.

These early experiments with trust company legislation indicated that when the federal and provincial authorities said that they wished to preclude those companies from engaging in banking they seemed to mean that they wished to preclude them from (a) issuing bank notes, (b) borrowing funds through taking deposits, and (c) making short-term loans. As the number of trust companies multiplied, the need for general legislation governing them became more obvious, and it was this general legislation which clarified the views of the authorities relating to trust company business, and particularly their views on the authority of trust companies to take deposits.

---

11. 55-56 Vic., cap. 79; as amended, 55-56 Vic., cap. 80.

Ontario passed the first general act respecting trust companies.[12] It prohibited trust companies from issuing debentures, but was silent on the matter of deposits. However, this omission was remedied by its "Act respecting Loan and Trust Corporations,"[13] which clarified the matter for all time. It stated that:

> 17. (1) A trust company incorporated under the law of Ontario shall not borrow money by taking deposits or by issuing debentures or debenture stock, and Letters Patent incorporating any such company shall expressly prohibit it from doing so (See Order in Council of 28 Oct., 1907.)
>
> (2) Where money is entrusted to the company for the *bona fide* purpose of its being invested by the company as trustee for, or as agent of the person by whom it is entrusted, the guarantee by the company of the repayment of the same or of the payment of the interest thereon at such rate as may be agreed on on fixed days shall not be deemed to be money borrowed by the company by issuing debentures within the meaning of subsection 1.

In other words, companies could take deposits as long as they were regarded as funds taken in trust with repayment and interest guaranteed and, preferably, were not called deposits; and similarly, they could take funds in trust for longer periods and issue an instrument which outlined their guarantee, as long as they avoided the name debenture. To the saver, and to the capital market generally, however, the differences in practice between a trust company deposit and a bank deposit, and between a loan company debenture and a guaranteed trust certificate, were negligible. Striking similarities between the trust companies and the banks and loan companies were inevitable, the moment the trust companies were permitted (a) to take funds in trust, (b) to pay a pre-determined rate on those funds, (c) to pool all such funds for investment purposes and (d) to retain the profits from the investments made, after payment of interest.

The 1921 act amending the Ontario Loan and Trust Corporation Act reiterated that trust companies could not "borrow" by taking deposits or selling debentures, but could take such funds "in trust"; in addition, it was less shy over the word "deposit" than previous acts had been. It stated that trust companies could ". . . receive deposits of money repayable upon demand or after notice and bearing such interest as may be agreed upon between the company and depositor and the company shall be entitled to retain the interest and

12. 60 Vic., cap. 37.
13. 2 Geo. V, cap. 34.

profit resulting from the moneys in excess of the amount of interest payable to depositors."

This is also essentially the way the act reads at present, although since it now states that trust companies may take deposits "at such rates and on such terms as the company may from time to time establish," such companies now have the same flexibility as banks in deciding the rate to be paid on deposits.

The general trust company legislation of the Dominion and of the province of Quebec developed in a similar fashion. Early Quebec legislation[14] distinguished between borrowing funds and holding funds in trust in this way, and does so to this day:

> 7. (1) Subject to any provision to the contrary contained in a special charter, no company shall borrow money by receiving deposits or by issuing bonds or debentures by whatever names such bonds or debentures may be described.
>
> (2) Whenever money is entrusted to a company for the *bona fide* purpose of having such money invested by the company in its capacity of trustee or agent, the fact of the company guaranteeing the payment of such money or of the interest thereon at an agreed rate of interest at fixed dates shall not constitute a loan or an issue of bonds or debentures forbidden by subsection 1 of this section.
>
> (3) A company may however, borrow or issue bonds or debentures to an amount of not more than seventy five per cent of its paid-up capital, in order to erect buildings for its own use, in whole or in part.

The Dominion Act respecting trust companies (passed in 1914)[15] stipulated that trust companies could not borrow by the issue of bonds or debentures; but it was reticent about referring specifically to deposits, indicating only that trust companies could "... receive moneys in trust for investment and allow interest thereon for a reasonable time until invested." The act also restricted the sum of a trust company's borrowing and its funds under guarantee, to an amount not exceeding five times the company's paid-up capital and reserve—increased in 1931 to seven times, in 1947 to ten times, in 1958 to twelve and a half times, in 1965 to fifteen times "the excess... of assets... over liabilities," and in 1970 to twenty times that amount.

As early as 1921, however, the federal government became more specific about the matter of deposits, for in that year it passed an act which permitted the Canada Trust Company[16] ". . . to receive

14. R.S.Q. (1909), cap. 7096a; 3 Geo. V, cap. 44; R.S.Q. (1925), cap. 248.
15. 4-5 Geo. V, cap. 45.
16. 12-13 Geo. V, cap. 67.

money on deposit in trust and allow interest thereon from the time of deposit at such rate as may be agreed upon between the Company and the depositor." This paragraph became part of the Trust Companies Act in the following year[17] and has remained so essentially without amendment.

The trust companies incorporated by the provinces of Ontario and Quebec and by the federal government have always dominated the field, so that a detailed review of the trust company legislation in the other provinces is unnecessary.

In general it may be said that if one ignores the fine legal distinction between "borrowed funds on deposit bearing interest," and funds on deposit "held in trust" bearing interest – a distinction without economic significance – then Canadian trust companies have in a significant way always been in the business of banking. This is true even more so today, for the banks now are also denied the right to issue notes, while the trust companies have branches and offer chequing privileges, also engage in short-term financing through their purchases of commercial and finance company paper, and have begun to make personal loans under a basket clause. The relative importance to them of this business will be discussed in a moment.

It may also be said that, since the trust companies have been permitted to issue guaranteed investment certificates and have been permitted to invest in real estate mortgages, they have thereby always encroached on the business of the loan companies.

What then has made the trust companies unique? In contrast to developments in the United States, chartered banks in Canada have never been given trustee powers, and the trust companies until recently were not permitted to make unsecured loans. In short, their uniqueness has always rested on statutory restrictions, and without these it is at least questionable whether they would have survived as a distinct type of organization, or would even have appeared in the first place. Their services, in other words, might have been provided by departments of life insurance companies or chartered banks.

There is no doubt that the original intentions of the authorities have been frustrated, and this because those intentions were unrealistic, even confused. The trust companies have become much more flexible in their financial operations than was originally envisaged. It is this flexibility, together with their legal monopoly of corporate trustee powers, that lies at the root of the long-term success of trust companies.

---

17. 12-13 Geo. V, cap. 51.

Growth and Development

NUMBER OF COMPANIES AND BRANCHES

Because not all provinces, over the years, have required provincially incorporated trust companies to report annually to a central authority, there does not exist a complete record of the number of trust companies in existence. However, the federal Superintendent of Insurance, in his annual report on *Loan and Trust Companies*, has for some time included aggregate data on provincial companies using information voluntarily supplied to him, and he has kindly made available to us information that has enabled us to compile the data shown in Table 9:1. It shows that in 1947 there were 60 trust companies of which 45 were provincially incorporated and accounted for 76% of total assets (company and guaranteed funds). The number of companies declined until by 1958 there were only 48 in total. Then began a period of expansion lasting to 1965, similar to that which occurred among the life insurance and mortgage loan companies, so that by 1965 there were 65 companies, 57 of which were provincially incorporated. But by that year the latter accounted for only about 66% of total assets. Much of this decline since 1947 was accounted for by the merger in 1961 of the Toronto General Trust Co., an Ontario company, with the Canada Permanent Trust Company, a federal company.

For there to be any significant and sudden further increase in the relative size of the federal group of companies would require a shift into the federal field through merger or re-incorporation of one or more of the larger provincial companies, namely, the Royal Trust Co., the Montreal Trust Co., and the National Trust Co. (see Table 9:3). After 1962 the relative size of the provincial group, largely through the appearance of new companies, actually tended to increase, and since provincial companies account for two-thirds of the industry in terms of size of assets, the importance to the nation of provincial supervision of trust companies is clearly illustrated. At the same time provincial companies may no longer gain relative to federal companies. Table 9:1 shows that since 1965 the number of provincial companies has declined, in part almost certainly because some of the provinces found that their lax control legislation invited questionable activities among new companies and they therefore took remedial action. Also a 1970 amendment to the federal Trust Companies Act will make it easier for companies to acquire federal charters, as it permits companies to be incorporated by letters patent—a much simpler process than by special act of Parliament.

The increase in the number of companies in recent years has been

Table 9:1 Federal and Provincial Trust Companies in Canada Assets,[1] Total Number and Relative Size 1939-1969

	Federal			Provincial						Total		
				FEDERALLY SUPERVISED			PROVINCIALLY SUPERVISED					
	Number	Assets $ mns	Percent of total	Number	Assets $ mns	Percent of total	Number	Assets $ mns	Percent of total	Number	Assets $ mns	Percent of total financial intermediary assets
1939		47.2	20.3		9.0	3.9	n.a.	175.9	75.8		232	3.0
1946		71.3	23.3		14.6	4.8	n.a.	219.5	71.7		306	2.0
1947	15	79.4	23.8	9	15.6	4.7	36	237.9	71.4	60	333	2.1
1948	14	91.4	24.9	9	16.2	4.4	36	258.9	70.5	59	367	2.1
1949	15	101.6	25.8	8	14.8	3.8	36	277.6	70.4	59	394	2.1
1950	13	105.1	23.8	8	16.0	3.6	34	319.8	72.5	55	441	2.1
1951	12	105.9	23.3	8	16.1	3.5	34	332.8	73.1	54	455	2.1
1952	12	120.2	25.2	7	15.9	3.3	34	340.4	71.4	53	477	2.1
1953	11	123.4	25.2	7	16.6	3.4	35	350.1	71.4	53	490	1.9
1954	11	152.0	23.9	8	18.1	2.8	35	466.8	73.3	54	637	2.3
1955	10	172.4	24.0	7	19.0	2.6	36	525.5	73.3	53	717	2.3
1956	10	187.9	25.2	7	19.1	2.6	35	538.0	72.2	52	745	2.3
1957	11	196.0	24.9	7	19.2	2.4	35	569.9	72.5	53	786	2.3
1958	10	257.0	26.5	7	18.3	1.9	35	695.1	71.6	52	970	2.5

1959	10	280.4	26.0	5	20.8	1.9	33	777.8	72.1	48	1079	2.6
1960	10	346.0	26.5	5	22.3	1.7	34	937.5	71.8	49	1306	2.9
1961	10	552.0	34.3	5	27.3	1.7	34	1029.2	64.0	49	1608	3.2
1962	10	670.3	35.1	5	34.8	1.8	37	1202.0	63.0	52	1907	3.5
1963	9	836.8	35.6	6	43.4	1.8	41	1467.8	62.5	56	2348	3.9
1964	8	1006.5	34.6	8	59.0	2.0	47	1843.0	63.4	63	2909	4.4
1965	8	1163.5	33.4	8	74.7	2.1	49	2244.3	64.4	65	3483	4.7
1966	9	1260.5	32.0	9	92.0	2.3	47	2581.5	65.6	65	3934	4.9
1967	9	1418.5	32.8	9	105.9	2.4	46	2803.2	64.8	64	4328	4.9
1968	9	1538.5	31.5	10	128.4	2.6	44	3222.4	65.9	63	4889	5.0
1969	10	1797.5	31.4	10	163.4	2.8	41	3763.1	65.7	61	5724	n.a.

SOURCE: Superintendent of Insurance, Department of Insurance, Ottawa, and Statistical Appendix.

[1]Company and guaranteed funds.

accompanied by a substantial increase in the number of branches. While comprehensive statistics of trust company offices are not available, we have estimated their number (see Table 9:2). The figures show that, whereas in 1952 there were just under 200 offices, and only about 200 in 1958, by 1963 the number had increased to about 300, then to over 450 in 1965 and in excess of 500 by 1967.

In spite of the large number of trust companies, and the intensive activity in establishing new ones, much of the business remains concentrated in relatively few institutions. Table 9:3 outlines this in detail. It shows that the two largest companies in the estates, trusts and agency business—the Royal Trust Co. and the Montreal Trust Co.—have persistently accounted for over 50% of such business both before and after 1945.

The large group of trust companies included in the "all other" category in Table 9:3 accounted for about 17% of fiduciary business in 1969 and 18% in 1945, which is another measure of the relatively unchanging character of the concentration of such business in the industry.

Financial intermediary business of the trust companies, as indicated by their company and guaranteed funds, is spread more evenly among the companies. The two largest companies over the years—and they were not the same two companies throughout the period shown in Table 9:3—accounted for about 31% of the total in 1969, which was bigger than in 1939 or in 1926, and there has indeed been a tendency toward increased concentration in recent years. The share of the "all other" group was 30% in 1969, down from 46% in 1939. Relative shares of individual companies in both types of business have changed, however, as can readily be seen in Table 9:3, reflecting in some cases growth through merger and in others presumably superior or inferior business performance, although as the note to Table 9:3 explains, differing subsidiary relationships between trust and mortgage loan companies necessitates taking care when comparing the size of companies.

We must now examine the nature of the trust companies and their business in greater detail.

ESTATES, TRUSTS AND AGENCY BUSINESS

Growth and development: We have seen that a number of Canada's major trust companies were established in the two decades before the turn of the century. There is little doubt that the emphasis of their operations in the early years was on the unique area of their business. Table 9:4 shows the growth of company, guaranteed, and

Table 9:2 Number of Trust Company Offices 1952-1971[1]

	BRANCHES	HEAD OFFICES	TOTAL	NUMBER OF COMPANIES NOT INCLUDED	GRAND TOTAL
	(1)	(2)	(3)	(4)	(5)
1952	133	40	173	13	190
1954	133	44	180	10	190
1956	137	45	182	7	189
1958	149	36	185	16	201
1960	172	37	209	12	221
1963	240	45	285	11	296
1964	322	50	372	13	385
1965	387	55	442	10	452
1966	429	56	485	9	494
1967	470	57	527	7	534
1968	468	56	524	7	531
1969	450	52	502	9	511
1970	436	50	486	n.a.	n.a.
1971	442	44	486	n.a.	n.a.

SOURCE: Compiled by the author from data in the *Directory of Canadian Trust Companies,* printed by the Trust Companies Association of Canada for the years 1963 onward; and from data in the *Monetary Times,* for years prior to that. Figures of branches are as of various dates of the year, in recent years, as of May.

[1] For various reasons these data should only be regarded as approximations. Column (4) was computed by taking the difference between our compilation of trust companies and that of the Superintendent of Insurance as shown in Table 9:1. The companies included in the latter's compilation but not in ours are probably mainly local, one-office type institutions – hence the justification for adding column (4) to column (3) to obtain a grand total of offices. However, this obviously leaves room for error, as does the fact that the Superintendent's compilation is as at the end of the year and ours is not. Also, the implicit assumption in column (3) that a head office also contains a branch may not be true in all cases. Finally, agencies have been excluded.

estates, trusts, and agencies funds of trust companies registered for operation in Ontario over the years 1900 to 1968. While problems of valuation necessitate caution in the use of figures for estates, trusts and agencies assets, those figures probably do reflect broad trends in the development of the trust companies. Table 9:5, in turn, shows the percentage distribution of the various types of guaranteed and company funds of trust companies. It is apparent from these tables that

Table 9:3 Concentration of Assets Among Trust Companies 1926-1969 (selected years)

	1926 %	1939 %	1945 %	1950 %	1955 %	1960 %	1965 %	1966 %	1967 %	1968 %	1969 %
ESTATES, TRUST AND AGENCY FUNDS											
Royal Trust Co.	42.7	28.7	27.6	27.9	28.6	30.5	27.4	27.4	27.9	38.3[1]	38.9[1]
Montreal Trust Co.	19.4	31.8	29.7	25.1	23.2	22.6	24.7	25.3	26.3	22.0	19.8
National Trust Co.	16.2	10.4	9.5	9.8	9.4	9.7	8.8	8.8	9.5	8.0	7.4
Canada Permanent Trust Co.[2]	1.1	1.8	2.2	2.3	2.6	2.7	8.2	8.0	12.4	10.1	8.8
Chartered Trust & Executor Co.[2]	1.1	0.7	0.9	1.2	1.8	1.8	5.3	3.9	—	—	—
Eastern Trust Co.[2]	—	2.1	2.3	2.5	2.7	2.8	—	—	—	—	—
Toronto General Trust Co.[2]	16.2	8.1	8.1	8.0	8.1	7.0	—	—	—	—	—
Canada Trust Co.	1.4	1.0	1.1	3.2	4.4	5.4	6.3	6.4	7.1	6.1	6.0
Guaranty Trust Co.	—	0.2	0.6	1.2	1.5	2.0	2.0	2.1	2.2	2.0	1.9
All other	1.9	15.2	18.0	18.7	17.7	15.4	17.2	18.0	14.6	13.5	17.2
TOTAL	100.0	100.0	100.0	100.0	100.0	100.0	100.0	100.0	100.0	100.0	100.0
Two largest	62.1	60.5	57.3	53.0	51.8	53.1	52.1	52.7	54.2	60.3	58.7
Four largest	94.5	79.0	74.9	70.8	69.3	69.8	69.1	69.5	76.1	78.4	74.9
COMPANY AND GUARANTEED FUNDS											
Royal Trust Co.	8.1	6.5	8.2	9.1	13.8	16.0	13.0	14.3	16.4	19.8	19.4
Montreal Trust Co.	14.6	13.2	11.0	13.3	10.4	10.9	10.6	10.1	10.3	9.6	8.3
National Trust Co.	14.1	12.8	10.2	8.7	9.4	9.2	9.1	8.9	9.7	9.4	8.8
Canada Permanent Trust Co.[2]	5.9	1.2	0.8	1.0	0.6	0.3	4.4	4.6	13.9	12.3	11.1

Chartered Trust & Executor Co.[2]	1.2	2.3	3.3	4.4	4.1	3.8	8.8	7.8	—	—	—
Eastern Trust Co.[2]	—	3.2	4.3	3.9	3.6	3.5	—	—	—	—	—
Toronto General Trust Co.[2]	16.4	10.6	9.0	7.8	8.2	6.6	—	—	—	—	—
Canada Trust Co.	4.4	4.1	3.2	5.0	5.4	7.1	5.6	5.6	6.4	6.8	6.5
Guaranty Trust Co.	0.2	0.5	1.8	5.0	5.9	7.9	11.3	11.2	12.6	11.9	10.8
All others	35.0	45.6	48.2	41.7	38.5	34.6	37.2	37.4	30.7	30.2	35.1
TOTAL (Dom. and Provincial)	100.0	100.0	100.0	100.0	100.0	100.0	100.0	100.0	100.0	100.0	100.0
Two largest	28.7	26.0	21.2	22.4	24.2	26.9	24.3	25.5	30.3	32.1	30.5
Four largest	42.7	43.1	38.4	38.9	41.8	44.0	44.0	44.5	53.2	53.6	50.1

SOURCE: Data for individual companies from Ontario, *Report of the Registrar of Loan and Trust Corporations*, Queen's Printer, Toronto, annual; total figures from Canada, *Report of the Superintendent of Insurance, Loan and Trust Companies*, Queen's Printer, Ottawa, annual, and D.B.S., *Financial Institutions Financial Statistics*, Queen's Printer, Ottawa, quarterly.

Statistical problems arise because some trust companies are subsidiaries of mortgage loan companies and so show unconsolidated accounts whereas other trust companies have loan company subsidiaries and show consolidated accounts. In 1969, for example, the Canada Permanent Trust Company had company and guaranteed funds of $642 million while the Canada Permanent Mortgage Corporation had assets of $687 million. Also in 1969 the Canada Trust Company had company and guaranteed funds of $374 million; its parent, the Huron & Erie Mortgage Corporation, had assets of $607 million; and also two of its own subsidiaries, Waterloo Trust and Halton & Peel Trust, were not consolidated with Canada Trust and they had assets of $187 million and $98 million respectively.

[1]Comparison is invalidated because the company reported on a market value basis.

[2]The Chartered and the Eastern Trust merged in 1965 and the resulting company merged with the Canada Permanent in 1967, while the Toronto General merged with the Canada Permanent in 1961.

Table 9:4 Assets of Trust Companies Registered in Ontario 1900-1969 (selected years)

(THOUSANDS OF DOLLARS)

	Company funds (1)	Guaranteed funds (2)	Total (3)	Estates, trust & agency funds (4)	(4)÷(3) (5)
1900	–	–	3,869	13,373	3.5
1905	–	–	14,019	38,686	2.8
1910	–	–	10,812	132,416	12.3
1915	–	–	28,326	350,248	12.4
1918	26,058	45,677	71,735	483,178	6.7
1920	31,280	36,154	67,434	575,259	8.5
1923	35,181	48,969	84,150	766,328	9.1
1925	36,141	57,462	95,603	871,451	9.1
1930	60,849	147,472	208,321	1,867,622	9.0
1935	55,177	130,708	185,885	2,243,024	12.1
1940	58,893	135,844	194,737	2,439,188	12.5
1945	66,091	176,285	242,376	2,753,477	11.4
1950	72,730	319,719	392,449	3,262,472	8.3
1955	87,784	577,358	665,142	4,416,447	6.6
1960	115,565	1,110,317	1,225,882	7,068,901	5.8
1965	240,558	2,924,080	3,164,638	11,922,153	3.8
1966	269,254	3,280,101	3,549,355	12,704,096	3.6
1967	272,223	3,593,924	3,866,147	13,670,003	3.5
1968	370,867	4,121,865	4,492,732	17,859,760	4.0
1969	381,995	4,813,622	5,195,617	20,251,358	3.9

SOURCE: Ontario, *Report of the Registrar of Loan and Trust Corporations*, Toronto, Annual.

as of 1915 the trust companies had not yet built up their guaranteed business, but that as a proportion of company and guaranteed funds, their estates, trusts and agencies business had virtually reached its historical peak – the latter amounting to twelve times the former. Their early emphasis on fiduciary business is not surprising for it was in that area, and particularly in the area of corporate trusteeships, that an obvious need existed. The period up to the First World War was one which saw a spectacular acceleration in the formation of

Table 9:5 Liabilities of Canadian Trust Companies, Percentage Distribution 1915-1970 (selected years)

	Company and guaranteed funds										
	Loans			Deposits and certificates					Shareholders equity[2]	Other	Total
				Deposit and demand certificates			Deposit receipts and guaranteed certificates				
	FROM BANKS	OTHER	TOTAL	CHEQUABLE	NON-CHEQUABLE	TOTAL		Total			
	(1)	(2)	(3)	(4)	(5)	(6)	(7)	(8)	(9)	(10)	(11)
1915	5	1	6	n.a.	n.a.	n.a.	n.a.	10	84	n.a.[1]	100
1918	4	—	4	n.a.	n.a.	n.a.	n.a.	55	36	5	100
1920	2	1	3	n.a.	n.a.	n.a.	n.a.	55	37	5	100
1923	n.a.	n.a.	6	n.a.	n.a.	12	46	58	35	1	100
1925	n.a.	n.a.	6	n.a.	n.a.	14	48	62	31	1	100
1930	n.a.	n.a.	5	n.a.	n.a.	17	54	71	23	1	100
1935	2	2	4	n.a.	n.a.	27	41	68	27	1	100
1945	4	1	5	n.a.	n.a.	31	37	68	24	3	100
1950	2	—	2	n.a.	n.a.	38	40	78	18	2	100
1955	1	...	1	n.a.	n.a.	38	46	84	13	2	100
1960	1	...	1	n.a.	n.a.	32	57	89	9	1	100
1965	...	1	1	16	16	32	58	91	7	1	100
1966	...	1	1	14	14	28	62	90	8	1	100
1967	...	1	1	13	14	27	63	90	8	1	100
1968	...	1	1	12	13	25	65	90	8	1	100
1969	...	...	...	8	16	24	67	91	7	1	100
1970	...	...	...	6	16	22	68	90	7	3	100

SOURCE: See Table 9:3.

[1] Apparently included in guaranteed funds.
[2] Essentially paid in capital and reserve funds.

public industrial corporations requiring such services.[18] Also, as we have seen, it took several decades to completely clarify the companies' legal position in financial intermediation, and it may have been that the close relation between some of the trust companies and the banks discouraged the former from developing a "banking" business. In this respect it is interesting that it was not the trust companies that were closely associated with banks that first built up the deposit business, but rather the smaller companies.[19]

While the relative size of estates, trusts and agencies funds declined in the 1920s as the companies' intermediary business expanded, this trend was interrupted by the depression of the 1930s and the Second World War. Even in 1945 those funds were about eleven times the size of company and guaranteed funds. However, after that and particularly after about 1950, the downward trend in their relative size was resumed. In 1965 and after they were only about four times as large as company and guaranteed funds, although in absolute terms they grew persistently, amounting to about $20 billion in 1969 compared to $3 billion in 1950.

Appropriate net profits figures for judging the relative contribution of the fiduciary business to the companies' total profits are not available, but there is little doubt that the financial intermediary (i.e., company and guaranteed) business has developed to the point where the industry depends on it for its survival as a significant segment of the economy.

This is not to suggest that the estates, trusts and agencies business is unimportant to the industry—although it certainly is to a number of smaller individual companies within the industry. The Royal Commission on Banking and Finance found certain areas of it to be quite profitable.[20] Perhaps just as important, by having a monopoly of the corporate trustee business the trust companies are able to differentiate themselves from other institutions—a useful "marketing" characteristic. For these reasons loss of their monopoly of the corporate trustee business through, say, the chartered banks acquiring such power could be a serious matter for the long-term prospects of the trust companies.

It is difficult to describe succinctly the nature of the estates, trusts and agencies business because of the unique aspects of each individual estate, trust and agency arrangement, and the reader is referred

---

18. See below, p. 475.
19. See I. M. Drummond, *Capital Markets in Australia and Canada*, doctoral thesis, Yale University, 1959, p. 102n.
20. *Report of the Royal Commission on Banking and Finance* (Ottawa: Queen's Printer, 1964), p. 197.

elsewhere for details of this type of business.[21] But several general points may be made.

A trust is a legal relationship in which, usually, the legal title and possession of property is vested in a trustee who deals with it as his own, but where beneficial ownership belongs to the beneficiaries of the trust. The trustee normally receives a stated fee for his work, he may not acquire trust property himself, he must observe the terms of the trust and is held personally responsible for so doing, and he must keep trust property separate and identifiable.[22] (Under Quebec civil law these generalizations would have to be modified.)

The trust companies tend to view their activities as being divided into the "personal trusteeship," which includes the bulk of their estates, trusts, and agencies business; "corporate trusteeship," which involves the trust company in the new securities issue market; and the "collective trusteeship," which includes the exceedingly important activities of the companies as financial intermediaries.

Personal trusteeships: Most of this business involves the trust company in the administration of estates as a result of its having been named "executor" in a will, and also "trustee" where there is a continuing trust. Besides managing the assets, the trustee must somehow reconcile the conflict of interest between the "life tenants," who receive the income of the assets for life, and the "remaindermen," who receive what is eventually left over. Provincial law governs the matter of wills, the devolution of estates, legal responsibilities of executors and administrators, and the matter of fees for such services.

In addition to administrating estates under the wills or "testamentary trusts" referred to above, the trust companies also manage property under "living trusts," that is, under trust arrangements that come into force during the settler's lifetime. There are also "life insurance trusts," where a fund provides for the payment of such insurance; "business insurance trusts," where partners, for example, take out insurance on each other with proceeds held in trust to enable surviving partners to purchase the interest of the deceased; and "escrow agreements," where property is held in trust until a transaction is completed.

The investment powers of trust companies in individual trusteeships are derived from the wills, or other documents, that appoint the trust company as executor or trustee. If it is simply an agency

21. See Benson, *op.cit.*, and The Trust Companies Association of Canada, *Submission to the Royal Commission on Banking and Finance*, July 1962.

22. See The Trust Companies Association of Canada, *Submission*, pp. A25-26.

agreement, then the principal usually retains investment powers. If the relevant documents do not outline investment policy, then provincial legislation governing trustee investments applies. In past years the majority of trustee documents gave the trustee investment powers as outlined in the provincial Trustee Acts, and in the Canadian and British Insurance Companies Acts, but the trend seems to have been toward giving trust companies greater freedom in investing funds held in trust. Such funds have increasingly been invested in stocks. Actual distribution of estates, trusts and agency assets as of December 31, 1961 and 1969, for companies licensed to do business in Ontario was as follows:

	$ millions		Percent of total	
	1961	1969	1961	1969
Real estate	301.5	619.1	3.9	3.1
Mortgages and agreements for sale	642.0	2481.2	8.3	12.2
Bonds	5514.8	6981.2	71.5	34.5
Stocks	980.2	9173.5	12.7	45.3
Sundry	224.2	692.0	2.9	3.4
Cash	50.4	304.4	.7	1.5
	7713.1	20251.4	100.0	100.0

SOURCE: The Trust Companies Association of Canada, *Submission, ibid.*, p. A.95, and Ontario, *Report of the Registrar of Loan and Trust Corporations*, Business of 1969, Toronto, Sept. 1970.

Special mention should be made of the Common Trust Funds. In 1950 and 1952 Ontario introduced legislation that permitted a trust company to establish such funds. Small estates can buy units in such a fund, thereby achieving greater asset diversification and higher net yields than would otherwise be possible.

The growth of trusteed pension funds in recent years has further expanded the operations of trust companies under personal trusteeships and, by the way, brought the trust companies into direct competition with the annuity business of the life insurance companies. When a Canadian employer wishes to establish a pension he may establish an "insured" plan or "deposit administration" plan offered by a life insurance company or a "trusteed" plan administered through trustees. It is the latter that involves the trust companies, although the management of such plans may also be undertaken by a group of individuals or a "pension fund society" incorporated for that purpose. Investment policy of trusteed pension funds is decided by the employer and his decisions are embodied in the trust document appointing the trustee. Investment powers of trust companies managing pension funds are restricted by provincial pension acts and regulations, although in most cases trust companies have unrestricted investment powers with respect to the pension funds they manage. Until 1955 individual trust companies administered each pension fund separately but then some began the practice of pooling some of the smaller pension funds under their administration, for investment purposes. Indeed, a number of trust companies have established several types of pooled funds, referred to, for example, as "pooled pension" or "retirement savings" equity fund, bond fund, mortgage fund, etc. The income of the individual pension plans is then invested in the units of the various funds, although some trust companies invest such income in the investment funds that they also operate and that closely resemble mutual funds. A large number of trust company pooled pension funds appeared in 1957 and after, following extension in 1957 of federal tax benefits to pension payments of self-employed individuals provided they were invested in what began in that year to be called "Registered Retirement Savings Plans."

The trust companies have been quite successful in the pension fund business as outlined in chapter 13. In 1969 trusteed pension plan assets totalled $10,003 million. Of this amount, $3,630 million, or 36%, was managed by trust companies, which constitutes a valuable addition to their trustee business. Of the $3,630 million, $1,833 million was in the form of individually managed pension funds, $464 million was pooled, and $1,333 million was a combination of both,[23] so the practice of pooling has become quite important since 1955.

Corporate trusteeships: The issue of securities by a corporation almost always requires the services of a trustee, and the trust companies have come to dominate this corporate trustee business. When a corporation engages in secured borrowing, the relevant mortgage conveys the property to the trustee for the benefit of the holders of the security. Even when no collateral is involved, the trust deed of a new issue frequently contains covenants protecting the holders of existing securities issues of the corporation and the trustee must ensure that these are being observed. In the case of defaults on debts, the trustee immediately must use discretionary judgment for protecting the position of creditors. In addition, a corporate trustee may be

---

23. D.B.S. *Trusteed Pension Plans Financial Statistics* 1968 (Ottawa: Queen's Printer, 1969).

asked to call and supervise meetings of shareholders for changing trust deeds, and to hold shares in trust or in escrow. Finally, a trust company is usually appointed agent for transferring shares from one owner to another, and it provides services relating to dividend disbursements, mailing annual statements and reports of corporations, tabulation of proxies, scrutinizing meetings of corporations, and changing the capitalization (e.g., redemption of preference shares) of corporations.

We turn now to an examination of the trust companies' "collective trustee" business, or, more generally, its activities as a financial intermediary involving the accumulation and disposition of its company and guaranteed funds.

FINANCIAL INTERMEDIARY BUSINESS

Growth rate and relative size: Chart 9:1 shows the growth rate of trust company assets acquired with company and guaranteed funds and it also shows the size of those assets relative to total financial intermediary assets. Evidently the companies had three periods of rapid growth, both in an absolute sense and a relative sense: from their formation up to 1913, from 1921 to 1930 and from 1943 to the present. Table 9:6 shows that in those periods the growth of their assets in current dollars ran well ahead of their 1900 to 1968 annual average of 9½%; and that in each of those periods they grew faster than all intermediaries combined, all private intermediaries combined, or all "close" competitors combined, or than the assets of the chartered banks. However, the periods of slow, or no, growth from 1913 to 1921 and from 1930 to 1943 had the effect of greatly diminishing the relative size of the trust companies from what they would otherwise have been. What is perhaps surprising is that not until the 1960s had the trust companies regained the relative size they had acquired by 1930 and subsequently lost. Only after 1964 did they begin to exceed their 1930 relative size in relation to total financial intermediary assets and only after 1962 did they do so in relation to total private assets. For example, in 1930 their assets were 4.4% of total financial intermediary assets, the same as in 1964; and in 1930 their assets amounted to 4.7% of private financial intermediary assets while in 1962 the figure was 4.5%. Also, in 1930 their assets were equal to 7.6% of their "close" competitors' assets, while in 1962 it was 7.3%. However, in 1930 their assets were equal to 9.5% of the "Canadian" assets of the chartered banks, while in 1962 they were 11.6% and in 1968 17.1%. Their relatively greater growth compared with that of the chartered banks should be considered in association with the factors explaining the slow growth of the latter, which we have examined in

Chart 9:1 – Growth and Relative Size of Canadian Trust Company Assets (Company and Guaranteed Funds) 1900-1970

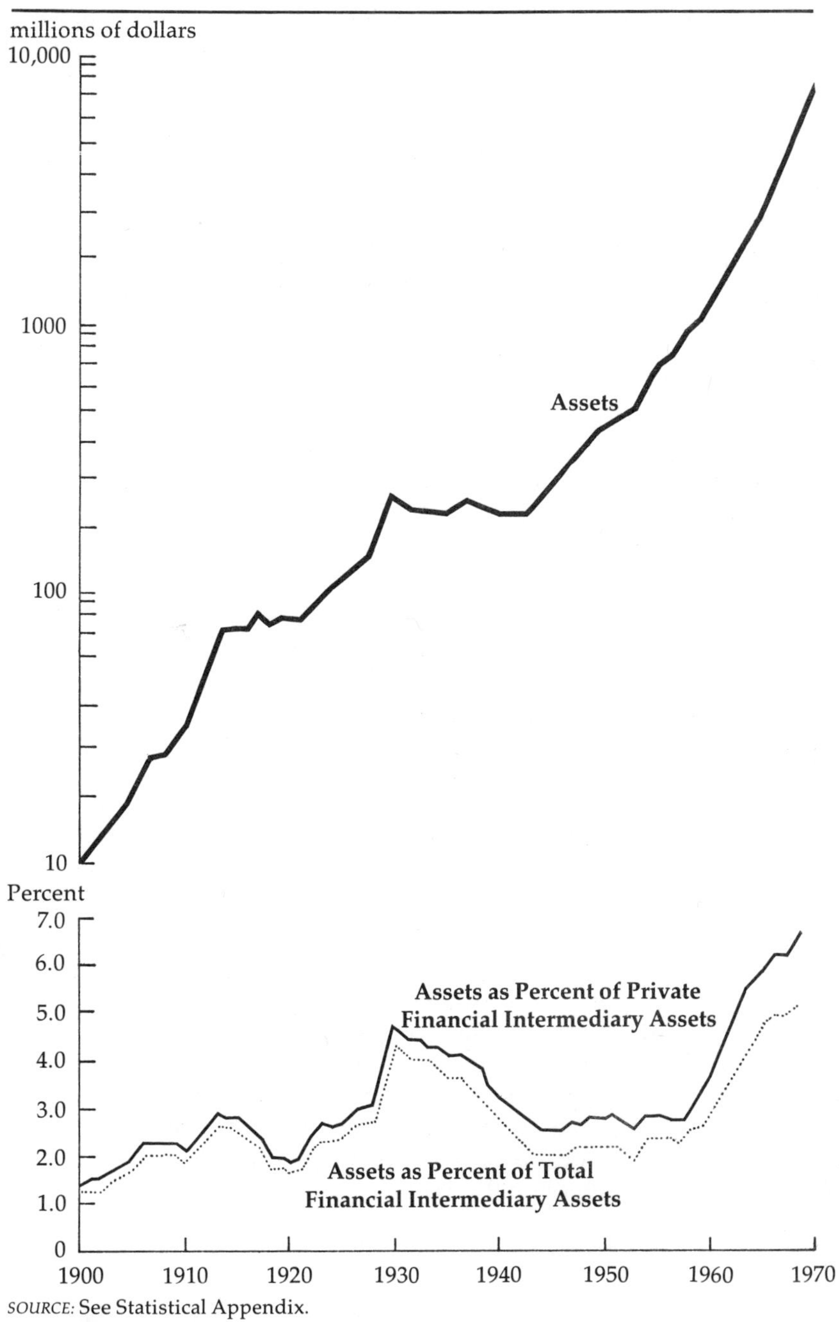

SOURCE: See Statistical Appendix.

Table 9:6 Growth and Relative Size of Canadian Trust Company Assets (Company and Guaranteed Funds) 1900-1968 (selected periods)

	1900 to 1913 %	1913 to 1921 %	1921 to 1930 %	1930 to 1943 %	1943 to 1968 %	1900 to 1968 %
Average annual growth rates						
Trust Company assets – current $	15¼	1¼	15¾	0	13	9½
Trust company assets as a proportion of:[1]						
– All financial intermediary assets	2.6	1.7	4.4	2.1	5.0	
– Private financial intermediary assets	2.9	1.9	4.7	2.6	6.5	
– Close competitors' assets[2]	3.4	2.2	7.6	3.5	10.6	
– Chartered banks' "Canadian" assets	4.6	2.9	9.5	4.8	17.1	

SOURCE: See Statistical Appendix.

[1]As at end of period.
[2]Includes chartered banks, Quebec savings banks, mortgage loan companies, consumer loan companies, credit unions and caisses populaires, government savings banks and Bank of Canada.

chapter 4. Before we consider specifically the possible reasons for the trust companies' alternating periods of high and slow growth, we must examine the structure of their assets and liabilities.

Structure of assets and liabilities: Tables 9:5 and 9:7 outline the structure of the trust companies' liabilities and assets for the period 1915 to 1969. The 1915 figures clearly show that the first period of rapid growth of the trust companies was based on the growth of their estates, trust and agencies business, and on the capital stock funds required to support that business. Tables 9:4 and 9:5, for example, show that in 1915 estates, trusts and agencies funds were twelve times the size of company and guaranteed funds and that of the latter, 84% was accounted for by "shareholders' equity." Furthermore, of the remaining 16%, a surprisingly large amount came from bank loans – a reflection of the close relationship between several of the larger trust companies and the banks.

After that initial period the importance of their financial intermediary business increased rapidly, although conditions during the years of the First World War greatly diminished the growth of the trust companies. By 1930 their guaranteed investment certificates and deposit receipts had been fully developed and amounted to 54% of their company and guaranteed funds, while shareholders' equity now only accounted for 23% of such funds. This again illustrates the general phenomenon of increasing leverage that typically accompanies a financial intermediary as it moves from the phase of initial development to maturity. Table 9:7 shows that from the earliest years the trust companies favoured investment in mortgages. These accounted for 52% of total funds in 1925, 45% in 1930 and 58% in 1970. By 1930 the companies had not yet fully developed their deposit business, but deposits did account for 17% of total company and guaranteed funds, and that business was growing. Essentially, therefore, in the 1920s the trust companies moved heavily into the intermediary business, competing especially with the mortgage loan companies in the accumulation of funds through the development of their guaranteed investment certificates and deposit receipts, and through their mortgage lending activities; and by so doing they successfully took advantage of the potential market strength gained through having a monopoly among financial institutions of the trustee business. That is, their intermediary business, which essentially was no different from that of the mortgage loan companies, was built on the base of their fiduciary business, which they had built up in their earliest period of growth and which was not open to the mortgage loan companies. It is not surprising, therefore, that a number of mortgage loan companies were transformed into trust companies in the 1920s. However, it does raise the pertinent question of what would happen to the trust companies if their fiduciary base was weakened through fiduciary powers' being granted to the chartered banks, a question to which we will return.

Several important developments in the companies' structure of assets and liabilities occurred in the period after the Second World War, as can be seen in Tables 9:5 and 9:7. Loans from banks virtually disappeared as a source of funds; deposits and demand certificates, which for years had grown faster than the companies' total funds, continued to do so until about 1950, but ceased doing so thereafter, and their relative size declined substantially after about 1955; guaranteed investment certificates and deposit receipts, which had suffered somewhat in the 1930s, once more began to grow in relative size until by 1970 they accounted for 68% of total company and guaranteed funds – a record level (see Table 9:5). Therefore, it was the

Table 9:7 Assets of Canadian Trust Companies, Percentage Distribution 1915-1970 (selected years)

		Securities excluding shares											
	Cash	Government of Canada	Provincial	Sub-total[1]	Municipal	Corporate and other	Total	Mortgage loans and sale agreements	Collateral loans	Canadian common and preferred shares	Real estate and equipment	Other	Total
	%	%	%	%	%	%	%	%	%	%	%	%	%
1915	5	n.a.	n.a.	1	1	31[3]	33	28	n.a.	n.a.	11	23[2]	100
1918	5	n.a.	n.a.	9	5	10	25	42	14	4	5	5	100
1920	4	n.a.	n.a.	9	7	5	21	46	12	4	5	8	100
1925	3	n.a.	n.a.	7	7	5	19	52	15	2	5	4	100
1930	4	n.a.	n.a.	7	5	4	16	45	26	2	4	3	100
1935	5	9	2	11	7	5	23	44	13	4	8	3	100
1945	6	40	5	45	3	4	53	23	7	6	3	2	100
1950	6	34	9	44	6	7	56	26	4	5	2	1	100
1955	5	21	13	34	7	11	51	32	5	3	2	2	100
1960	3	21	8	29	5	16	50	37	4	3	2	1	100
1965	3	11	6	17	4	13	33	56	3	2	1	2	100
1966	2	10	6	17	3	14	34	55	3	2	1	2	100
1967	2	10	7	17	3	15	35	55	3	2	1	2	100
1968	2	10	6	16	2	16	34	55	3	2	1	3	100
1969	4	10	5	15	2	14	30	57	3	2	1	3	100
1970	5	8	5	13	2	14	29	58	3	2	1	2	100

SOURCE: For the years 1965 and after based on data in Dominion Bureau of Statistics, *Financial Institutions Financial Statistics;* for the years 1935 to 1960, from Bank of Canada, *Statistical Summary, Annual Supplement;* for the years 1915 to 1930, from Ontario, *Report of the Registrar of Loan Corporations,* Toronto, Annual, which in 1935 included companies that accounted for 85% of the assets of the companies included in the 1935-60 data.

[1]From 1915 to 1930 includes United Kingdom government securities.
[2]Apparently includes collateral loans.
[3]Includes stocks.

latter that provided the greatest thrust, from the sources-of-funds point of view, to the growth of the trust companies after the Second World War.

The principal changes in their structure of assets after 1945 were the decline in their holdings of Government of Canada securities from 40% of total assets in 1945 to about 10% after 1965 – almost the same as the figure prior to the Second World War; and the increase in mortgage loans from 23% in 1945 to 58% by 1970 – a proportion well in excess of the one for 1935 and even of that of 1925, which was 52%. In addition, the companies' collateral loans never recovered the relative size they had in the 1920s; but their holdings of corporate and other non-government securities increased in relative importance up to about 1960 – partially a reflection of their activity in the short-term paper market.

Recent developments: Developments within the trust company industry after the Second World War were among the most significant in the Canadian capital market, and therefore justify closer attention. These developments included their relatively high rate of growth; the move of additional companies into close relationships with the chartered banks and some for the first time into close relationships with finance companies and real estate brokerage firms; the development of new services such as pooled trust and pension funds and investment fund facilities; innovation in the establishment of branches, particularly shopping-plaza and supermarket branches; and emphasis on better service to the customer in the form of more convenient business hours than those of the chartered banks. Also, there appeared developments, in particular the financial difficulties of one prominent trust company, the British Mortgage and Trust Company, and the 1967 revision of the Bank Act, which cast a shadow over the possibility of the trust companies' maintaining their previous rate of growth.

Table 9:1 shows that until about 1958 nothing unusual happened to the growth rate of the trust companies in the sense that trust company assets grew at about the same rate as total financial intermediary assets. The total number of trust companies even declined and the number tabulated by the Superintendent of Insurance reached a low of 48 in 1959. But beginning in 1958 trust companies grew much faster than total financial intermediary assets; and after 1959 began a period in which new companies appeared in rapid succession – a total of 65 were tabulated in 1965, or 17 more than in 1959, and virtually all were provincially incorporated. After 1965 the number of trust companies, and especially trust company branches (see Table 9:2), began to decline—a reflection of some retrenchment in the industry.

Tables 9:5 and 9:7 show clearly that the foundation for the trust companies' high growth rate was funds obtained from the rapid growth of guaranteed investment certificates and deposit receipts (i.e., not from demand liabilities) and channelled into mortgage loans. Accompanying the growth was an expansion not just in the number of trust companies but also in the number of branch outlets. In 1967 there were over five hundred offices compared with just over two hundred in 1960. The National Trust Co. apparently opened the first shopping-plaza trust company branch in Canada, in Hamilton in 1961, and the Chartered Trust Co. soon followed, as did others.[24] In 1963 a new company experimented with branches in supermarket stores.[25] In all cases the hours of service were more favourable than those of the banks, although as time went on the banks too began to stay open longer.

The trust companies began to offer a few new services to the public in the 1960s. In 1963 the Metropolitan Trust Co. and United Dominions Investments Limited announced a plan under which they would provide a sort of combined first and second mortgage financing in one loan agreement,[26] and a similar plan was announced by the Royal Trust Co. and Industrial Acceptance Corporation in March 1964. This innovation was soon adopted by other institutions. The Guaranty Trust Co. announced in October 1967 that it would start making personal loans under the basket clause provisions of trust company legislation.[27] The Trust Companies Association had asked for specific authority to make such loans in 1966, but had not done so in their 1962 *Submission* to the Royal Commission on Banking and Finance. Also the Mercantile Bank made an arrangement with a group of local Ontario trust companies in 1967 whereby the latter would channel personal loans to the bank.[28] The 1970 federal Trust Companies Act expanded the trust companies' ability to make personal loans.

In 1964 a trust company acquired a major real estate brokerage company.[29] But perhaps the most conspicuous extension of the business of the trust companies was their move into the mutual fund

24. See *Globe and Mail*, Toronto, Jan. 31, 1961, p. 27.
25. See *Financial Post*, Toronto, Oct. 26, 1963, p. 9.
26. See *Financial Post*, Toronto, Mar. 16, 1963, p. 10.
27. See *Globe and Mail*, Toronto, Oct. 4, 1967.
28. See *Globe and Mail*, Toronto, Sept. 26, 1967.
29. See *Financial Post*, Toronto, Jan. 23, 1965.

business. Such funds had enjoyed unusually rapid growth in the postwar period.[30] The Canada Trust Co. (a subsidiary of Huron and Erie Mortgage Corp. of London, Ontario) set up its investment fund in June 1959, and the Montreal Trust Co. followed in February 1961. By 1969 eleven trust companies were offering funds to the public, and many of them operated several different kinds of funds. The total assets of those funds in 1969 amounted to $211 million or 6% of total mutual fund assets in Canada. They make no acquisition or "loading" charge, whereas 10% is common among ordinary mutual funds.

All these developments suggest that there was considerable initiative among at least some of the trust companies in the 1950s and 1960s in the development of a number of aspects of their business.

But what aspects of the competitive environment in the capital market help explain the high rate of development of the trust companies as financial intermediaries? It is our view that the major forces explaining it are not exclusively related to their mode of operation, but are partly related to the legislative restraints on the chartered banks. This could have important implications for the future of trust companies in Canada.

First of all, we saw in chapter 4 that the density of chartered bank branches was lower in the postwar years than in the period back to 1910,[31] and it might conceivably be that this created a gap in the provision of local financial services—one that was filled by trust company branches and also by small loan company branches[32] and credit unions and caisses populaires. It is also possible that the density of chartered bank local services was below optimum through their practice over much of the postwar period of adhering to 10 A.M. to 3 P.M., Monday to Friday banking hours, and this gap the trust companies filled by staying open longer and by opening on Saturdays. Also we noted earlier[33] that the chartered banks were exceedingly late in providing attractive rates for longer-term savings, which, after about 1955, might have become a serious matter because of the rapid increase in interest rates and the continuation (until 1967) of the 6% interest rate ceiling on non-instalment loans of the chartered banks. This gap the trust companies filled, as can be seen by the rapid growth of their guaranteed investment certificates. Finally, the chartered banks were denied the conventional mortgage business until 1967, while the trust companies saw this type of lending expand faster than any of their other lending activities. The only

30. See below, p. 368.
31. See below, p. 102.
32. See below, p. 349.
33. See above, p. 129.

restriction of consequence on the trust companies that the banks did not face was the prohibition on unsecured lending – apart from the use of the basket clause. A certain business lethargy on the part of the banks together with certain legal restrictions on the banks' operations may, therefore, have played a significant part in the acceleration of the growth of the trust companies after 1958. This does not provide a very secure base for the continued rapid growth of the trust companies. The banks now are offering much more attractive interest rates and a greater variety of savings instruments to small savers than they used to do, they have more flexible banking hours, they are not inhibited by any interest rate ceiling and they are free to make conventional mortgage loans.

Further development of their savings deposits and certificates and their debentures could remove whatever remaining advantage the trust companies might still enjoy in accumulating funds of small savers. It therefore seems that the trust companies face a future of intensive competition in their intermediary business. There are likely to be a number of mergers among trust companies as a result of this competition, and the survival of even the larger trust companies as a significant force in the financial intermediary business may well depend on their willingness and ability to become chartered banks, in the sense of obtaining bank charters while retaining their fiduciary powers. Were the banks to be given fiduciary powers before the larger trust companies had been given the legislative authority and the time to, in effect, become chartered banks, it is difficult to see how the trust companies could survive as distinct entities. The British and United States pattern might then emerge in which the banks handle corporate trustee business in departments established for that specific purpose.

For a period it seemed that a growing corporate relationship between banks and trust companies would be the form that evolution would take, but this is no longer certain. We have already seen that for many years there had been close business ties (including in some cases, ownership ties) between the Royal Trust Co. and the Bank of Montreal, the Montreal Trust Co. and the Royal Bank, and the National Trust Co. and the Canadian Imperial Bank of Commerce. In 1960 the Bank of Nova Scotia acquired a large majority of the shares of the Chartered Trust and Executor Co.,[34] an interest that was perpetuated when the Eastern Trust and the Chartered Trust companies merged in 1965; while in 1961 the Toronto-Dominion Bank became one of the largest shareholders of the company formed out of the

34. See *Financial Post*, Toronto, Nov. 15, 1961.

merger of the Canada Permanent Trust Co. and the Toronto General Trust Co. Then in 1967, when this merged company and the Eastern and Chartered Trust Co. merged (the new company being called the Canada Permanent Trust Co.), the Bank of Nova Scotia owned 17.1% (11.5% directly) and the Toronto-Dominion Bank 14.9% of the resulting companies.[35] As a result of all these developments, by the end of 1967 the four largest trust companies, accounting for almost half of the trust companies' financial intermediary business (which in its details was much like chartered banking), were closely tied to the five largest banks. But then came the 1967 Bank Act. It prohibited directors of chartered banks from being directors of trust companies, and individual chartered banks from owning more than 10% of the voting stock of a trust company effective July 1, 1971. While the trust companies have maintained that their association with the banks has not inhibited them in competing with the banks, it did begin to seem that such competition would be more permanently assured if the association were broken.

But this view assumes that the trust companies can survive and develop further in the face of chartered bank competition. To facilitate this the policy of governments and the actions of trust company management in the next decade may need to be directed toward encouraging the growth of trust companies to optimum size, through mergers if necessary and through permitting some trust companies to become chartered banks in the full sense of the term while permitting them to retain fiduciary powers. The long-term decline in the importance of mortgage loan companies and the early history of savings banks in Canada are a reminder that a failure to make adjustments could lead the trust companies to a similar fate as far as their financial intermediary business is concerned.

35. See *Financial Post*, Toronto, Nov. 11, 1967.

10

Sales Finance and Consumer Loan Companies

Consumer credit is by no means a new form of credit. Centuries of preoccupation with and discussion of usury and the usury laws reveal the conspicuous presence of credit granted to individuals for non-business purposes. What is of more recent origin is the emergence of financial intermediaries with the primary objective of satisfying the demand for consumer credit. This chapter concentrates on those intermediaries, namely, the instalment finance companies and consumer loan companies, but it does this within the context of the development of consumer-credit-granting institutions in general.

Structure of the Consumer Credit Industry

The financial intermediaries dispensing consumer credit other than the sales finance companies and consumer loan companies are the chartered banks, Quebec savings banks, credit unions and caisses populaires, life insurance companies (through their policy loans), very recently some of the trust companies through their basket clause investment provisions and retail merchants themselves.

Table 10:1, which outlines the relative size of consumer credit supplied by the various institutions, shows clearly that significant structural changes have occurred in the consumer credit industry since the end of the Second World War. Retail dealers and motor vehicle dealers, who on their own account supplied 32% of total consumer credit in 1948, only supplied 6% in 1970, a decline of 26 percentage points, and this was because of a massive shift of such credit into specialized financial institutions. Until 1956 the shift was largely toward the sales finance companies, for their share of total credit rose from 8% in 1948 to 26% in 1956—18 percentage points—and those years were in fact the best years of their growth. From 1948 to 1956 credit supplied by the consumer loan companies (small loan companies and money lenders) gained 5 percentage points, amounting to 12% of the total in the latter year, the share of the credit unions increased only marginally, that of the chartered banks declined slightly and the relative size of life insurance policy loans declined substantially from the high levels created during the depression years of the 1930s.

After 1956 the pattern changed markedly. The share of the sales finance companies declined steadily, amounting to only 10% in 1970—or 16 percentage points lower than in 1956; that of the chartered banks increased to 41%—a remarkable rise of 26 percentage points, which left them as the dominant force in the consumer credit industry; credit unions and caisses populaires increased their share until 1967, it amounting to about 13% in 1970, and the consumer loan companies have more than held their own, their share in 1970 amounting to 15%. The relative decline in the size of consumer credit supplied by the sales finance companies since the late 1950s raises questions concerning their future role in the capital market. Before considering this and other questions, however, we will examine the history of their emergence, growth and development and that of the consumer loan companies.

Sales Finance and Consumer Loan Companies

ORIGINS

Consumer credit may conveniently, if not entirely accurately, be regarded as taking two major forms: direct credit in the form of cash loans not specifically related to the prior purchase of some consumer good or service; and indirect credit in the form of an arrangement allowing an extended time for the payment, usually in instalments, for specific consumer items already purchased. The first type of credit, which has existed since antiquity, led in Canada to the formation of small loan companies and money lenders who have dealt directly with small borrowers; the second, which is of more recent origin, led to the formation of instalment finance companies, who discount or purchase the instalment paper of dealers and merchants, and thus deal only indirectly with the small borrowers when the loan is granted. Consumer credit for some purposes may also usefully be

Table 10:1 Consumer Credit in Canada: Balances Outstanding by Type of Lender 1948-1970

	Sales Finance Companies	%	Consumer Loan Companies				Chartered Bank Loans	%	Quebec Savings Banks	%	Life Insurance Policy Loans	%	Dept. Stores	%	Furniture & Appliance Dealers	
			Instalment Credit	Cash Loans	Total	%									Instalment Credit	Charge Accounts
1948	70	8.4	—	64	64	7.6	154	18.4	—		158	18.9	70	8.4	34	17
1949	116	11.8	—	77	77	7.8	173	17.6	—		167	17.0	84	8.5	48	20
1950	202	16.5	—	93	93	7.6	224	18.3	—		178	14.6	94	7.7	62	25
1951	186	15.7	—	114	114	9.6	204	17.2	—		199	16.8	77	6.5	43	22
1952	373	23.0	—	148	148	9.1	242	14.9	2	0.1	213	13.1	140	8.6	86	25
1953	516	26.1	3	173	176	8.9	308	15.6	3	0.2	225	11.4	167	8.4	111	26
1954	492	23.0	6	209	215	10.1	351	16.4	2	0.1	240	11.2	186	8.7	134	23
1955	599	23.8	6	273	279	11.1	441	17.5	2	0.1	250	9.9	226	9.0	149	26
1956	756	26.3	13	343	356	12.4	435	15.2	3	0.1	270	9.4	244	8.5	163	26
1957	780	26.2	15	347	362	12.2	421	14.1	4	0.1	295	9.9	262	8.8	169	26
1958	768	23.6	19	382	401	12.3	553	17.0	6	0.2	305	9.4	282	8.7	170	27
1959	806	21.8	38	446	484	13.1	719	19.5	6	0.2	323	8.8	314	8.5	173	29
1960	828	20.6	45	504	549	13.6	857	21.3	6	0.1	344	8.6	368	9.2	170	25
1961	757	17.5	35	559	594	13.8	1030	23.9	9	0.2	358	8.3	401	9.3	168	26
1962	801	16.9	52	662	714	15.0	1183	24.9	13	0.3	372	7.8	427	9.0	167	27
1963	874	16.6	55	755	810	15.4	1432	27.2	14	0.3	385	7.3	456	8.7	168	30
1964	1035	17.1	54	850	904	14.9	1793	29.6	15	0.2	398	6.6	508	8.4	169	32
1965	1131	16.3	67	976	1043	15.0	2241	32.3	16	0.2	411	5.9	565	8.1	176	33
1966	1184	15.7	74	1089	1163	15.4	2458	32.5	16	0.2	450	6.0	599	7.9	181	35
1967	1105	13.2	78	1225	1303	15.6	2980	35.6	17	0.2	486	5.8	606	7.2	180	37
1968	1125	11.7	96	1417	1513	15.8	3673	38.3	21	0.2	553	5.8	632	6.6	173	39
1969	1264	11.6	107	1675	1782	16.4	4157	38.3	24	0.2	660	6.1	693	6.4	174	40
1970	1129[1]	9.9	— [2]	1733	1733	15.2	4663	40.9	22	0.2	745	6.5	708	6.2	170	39

SOURCE: Bank of Canada, *Statistical Summary*, Annual Supplement and Monthly.

[1] Excludes loans for financing passenger cars used for commercial purposes.
[2] This item now included under sales finance companies.

classified into "point-of-purchase" or "vendor" credit and "cash loan" credit, the first referring to credit supplied or arranged by the merchant selling the particular good being financed, and the second referring to credit arranged and supplied by specialized financial institutions themselves.

While the individual's desire for personal cash loans has always been explained by a wide range of personal circumstances, it was the growing importance of consumer durable items that encouraged the growth of instalment credit. It is recorded that as early as 1807 the New York furniture house of Cowperwait & Sons introduced instal-

Total	%	Motor Vehicle Dealers	%	Sub-total	%	Other Retail Dealers: Instal-ment Credit	Other Retail Dealers: Charge Ac-counts	Other Retail Dealers: Total	%	Oil Com-pany Credit Cards	%	Credit Unions & Caisses Popu-laires	%	Total
51	6.1	20	2.4	587	70.3	33	161	194	23.2	n.a.	—	54	6.5	835
68	6.9	26	2.6	711	72.2	37	174	211	21.4	n.a.		63	6.4	985
87	7.1	38	3.1	916	74.9	45	190	235	19.2	n.a.		72	5.9	1223
65	5.5	29	2.4	874	73.7	25	211	236	19.9	n.a.		76	6.4	1186
111	6.8	26	1.6	1255	77.3	51	223	274	16.9	n.a.		94	5.8	1623
137	6.9	18	0.9	1550	78.3	54	247	301	15.2	n.a.		129	6.5	1980
157	7.4	15	0.7	1658	77.6	57	270	327	15.3	n.a.		151	7.1	2136
175	7.0	19	0.8	1991	79.1	62	270	332	13.2	20	0.8	174	6.9	2517
189	6.6	22	0.7	2275	79.3	63	280	343	12.0	26	0.9	226	7.9	2870
195	6.6	23	0.8	2342	78.7	77	267	344	11.6	32	1.1	258	8.7	2976
197	6.1	18	0.6	2530	77.9	78	285	363	11.2	35	1.1	320	9.8	3248
202	5.5	17	0.5	2871	77.8	84	299	383	10.4	40	1.1	397	10.8	3691
195	4.8	16	0.4	3163	78.7	81	300	381	9.5	43	1.1	433	10.8	4020
194	4.5	17	0.4	3359	77.8	85	308	393	9.1	47	1.1	516	12.0	4315
194	4.1	18	0.4	3722	78.4	84	316	400	8.4	49	1.0	579	12.2	4750
198	3.8	18	0.3	4187	79.4	87	329	416	7.9	53	1.0	614	11.7	5270
201	3.3	18	0.3	4872	80.5	88	332	420	6.9	59	1.0	705	11.6	6056
209	3.0	20	0.3	5636	81.2	85	337	422	6.1	72	1.0	813	11.7	6943
216	2.9	17	0.2	6103	80.8	90	338	428	5.7	88	1.2	937	12.4	7556
217	2.6	18	0.2	6732	80.3	94	351	445	5.3	104	1.2	1094	13.1	8375
212	2.2	16	0.2	7745	80.7	98	371	469	4.9	131	1.4	1247	13.0	9592
214	2.0	16	0.1	8810	81.2	104	388	492	4.5	153	1.4	1401	12.9	10856
209	1.8	14	0.1	9215	80.9	103	401	504	4.4	186	1.6	1493	13.1	11398

ment credit.[1] Other furniture companies followed and the practice spread to other cities in the United States and began to include other goods, particularly household furnishings. Two household items that were soon being purchased with instalment credit were sewing machines and pianos, the first through the Singer Sewing Machine Company from about 1850, and the second from the 1880s on.[2] How-

1. See Evans Clark, *Financing the Consumer* (New York: Harper & Brothers Publishers, 1920), pp. 19-20.
2. *Ibid.*, p. 20.

ever, it was the emergence of the low-priced automobile that caused instalment credit to assume significant proportions and that gave an incentive for the formation of separate companies providing such credit. Until about 1910 automobiles were purchased essentially by the wealthy for cash. In that year there were only 8,967 motor vehicles registered in Canada, which, however, was already a substantial increase from 1904 when the number was 535. After 1910 and with the popularity of the model T Ford the increase in the number of cars purchased was rapid, 89,944 motor vehicles being registered in 1915, 407,064 in 1920 and 836,794 in 1926. Not surprisingly, it was in this period that the sales or instalment finance companies first emerged in Canada. In the United States they appeared only a few years earlier. The Fidelity Contract Corporation was established in 1904 (later called the Bankers Commercial Corporation) to discount retail piano paper; the Commercial Investment Trust Corporation and National Bond and Investment Company appeared in 1908, the Pacific Finance Corporation in 1910 and the Commercial Credit Company and Northern Finance Company in 1912.[3] Apparently L. F. Weaver of San Francisco began to buy automobile instalment paper in 1913, the first company in the United States to do so, and from about 1915 existing companies purchased automobile paper covering all makes of cars. Scores of new companies soon began to appear. The National Association of Finance Companies estimated that there were 1,297 such companies in 1928.[4]

It would seem that the sales finance industry first emerged in Canada in 1916. In that year the Guaranty Securities Corporation (later the Continental Guarantee Corporation of Canada Limited) appeared and its first transaction involved financing the sale of a truck chassis by the Ford Motor Company of Canada, Limited.[5] A branch office of General Motors Acceptance Corporation (G.M.A.C.), a New York company, was opened in Toronto in 1919[6] (General Motors Acceptance Corporation of Canada Limited was incorporated in 1953). In 1919 also Commercial Credit Company Limited was formed; it was acquired by Continental Guarantee Corporation of Canada Limited in 1924, the latter having been acquired by Commercial Credit Company of Baltimore the year before. Continental Guar-

3. Wilbur C. Plummer and Ralph A. Young, *Sales Finance Companies and Their Credit Practices* (New York: National Bureau of Economic Research, 1940), pp. 33-4.
4. *Ibid.*, p. 34.
5. See F. N. Cooper, "50 Years of Finance History," *Motor in Canada*, June 1966, p. 19.
6. See Federated Council of Sales Finance Companies, *Submission to the Royal Commission on Banking and Finance*, hearings held at Ottawa, September 24, 1962, vol. 37A, p. A14. (Hereafter *Submission*.)

antee was changed to Commercial Credit Corporation of Canada Limited in 1934 and to Commercial Credit Corporation Limited in 1947. The first Canadian-sponsored finance company, Traders Finance Corporation Limited, was incorporated in Manitoba in 1920 and in Ontario in 1923, and these two were merged under a Dominion charter in 1926. Canadian Acceptance Corporation Limited, a U.S.-financed company, was established in 1922. Industrial Acceptance Corporation Limited, Canada's largest finance company, began in 1923 as a Canadian branch of a South Bend, Indiana, company of the same name. It became Industrial Acceptance Corporation of Canada Limited in 1925 and Industrial Acceptance Corporation Limited in 1928, and in 1930 the company passed into Canadian ownership and control,[7] where it has remained. The three largest companies in the 1960s (which accounted for about two-thirds of the industry's business at that time) were ones that had appeared by 1923 – I.A.C., Traders and G.M.A.C. Of twenty-seven companies surveyed in 1961, whose receivables accounted for about 94% of the total for the industry tabulated by the Dominion Bureau of Statistics, five had appeared prior to 1930, one in the period 1930-9, three from 1940-9, and eighteen after 1950. The industry also includes a large number of local, exceedingly small sales finance companies, which were not included in the 1961 survey, but which would have raised the total of all companies in operation in 1961 to about 175.[8]

The variety of companies engaged in discounting instalment contracts is so great that it is not easy specifically even to define the industry. There are first of all the large independent Canadian companies – mainly Industrial Acceptance Corporation, Laurentide Financial Corporation and the Traders Group Limited; then there are the "captive" or subsidiary companies of U.S. automobile companies – General Motors Acceptance Corporation, Ford Motor Credit Company of Canada and Chrysler Credit Canada; there are also other foreign but independent companies such as Canadian Acceptance Corporation (U.S.), Avco-Delta Corporation Canada Limited (U.S.), Commercial Credit Corporation Limited (U.S.), Union Acceptance Corporation Limited (France), and United Dominions Corporation (Canada) Limited (U.K.). There are, furthermore, as noted earlier, a large number of small independent provincially incorporated Canadian companies. Finally there are Canadian finance companies that are subsidiaries of merchandising and manufacturing companies – including subsidiaries of the large Canadian and U.S. farm machine-

---

7. See *Submission*, p. A14.
8. See *Submission*, p. A15.

ry companies. The latter group of wholly owned subsidiaries are not included in the statistics of sales finance companies of the Dominion Bureau of Statistics.

The sales finance companies have always been relatively unregulated, operating not under special legislation but rather under ordinary federal and provincial company legislation. (However, in late 1968 the federal government first introduced a bill that is designed to regulate them.) There are virtually no restrictions on the type of lending and investing they can engage in, although not until after about 1957 was there any significant tendency for them to diversify their activities. As for borrowing powers, the legislation is not quite clear but the industry seems to have believed that it does not have the power to engage in taking deposits. In fact, as we shall see, most sales finance companies have never sought funds from small lenders, confining themselves to taking bank loans and selling normal security issues and finance company paper. This, in itself, is probably a major reason why closer regulation of the industry did not develop. Trust deeds covering the notes, debentures and other debt that the sales finance companies issue place limitations on their borrowing activities, so that in effect control is exercised by the market through the requirements of underwriters and investors.[9] These requirements, as Table 10:6 shows, have led to a ratio of equity capital to total liabilities of about 11% for the ten largest companies, and in fact it tends to be higher for the companies that are not subsidiaries of U.S. automobile companies.

Following the bankruptcy of Atlantic Acceptance Corporation in 1965 and Prudential Finance Corporation in 1966, pressure mounted to improve provincial government regulation of finance companies. The latter company, operating under Ontario law, began to issue short-term notes to the general public in 1961, and when it failed over eight thousand relatively small investors lost some of their savings.[10]

One consequence of those failures was that the large and reputable sales finance companies (the ten largest of which account for over 80% of the industry), particularly the independent Canadian ones, greatly increased the amount of statistical information relating to their operations that they made available to investors and to the general public.[11]

---

9. See *Report of the Royal Commission on Banking and Finance* (Ottawa: Queen's Printer, 1964), p. 214.
10. *Financial Post*, April 1, 1967, p. 30.
11. *Financial Post*, April 2, 1966, p. 7. One of the best examples of this development is in the Industrial Acceptance Corporation Limited Supplement to its Annual Report, first published in March 1966.

The origin of the consumer loan companies—referred to as small loan companies when federally incorporated and money lenders when provincially incorporated—is both more simple and more complex than that of the sales finance companies. Local, unregulated money lenders have probably been present in Canada from the days of the first settlements. The abolition of the usury laws in 1858 removed virtually all legislative restraints on interest rates. Not surprisingly, complaints of unscrupulous lending practices began to attract political attention. In 1906 the Parliament of Canada passed the Money-Lenders Act,[12] which was designed to limit the cost of small personal loans. The act proved not to be effective for achieving that objective, as the Superintendent of Insurance has explained:

> Its main defect lay in the fact that "interest" was not defined and could not be held to include ancillary expenses, especially in view of the conflicting references to 12% per annum for interest alone in section 6 and to 12% for both interest and expenses in section 7. . . . Other reasons for the ineffectiveness of the Money-Lenders Act were that no licensing or supervision of money lenders was required, no one was charged with the responsibility of enforcing its terms, and borrowers were reluctant to incur the publicity and expense of taking remedial action themselves.[13]

Because the act did not require money lenders to be licensed, the business of making personal cash loans continued to be carried on largely by unlicensed provincially incorporated companies, partnerships, and individuals, without any meaningful regulation.

The first important change occurred in 1928 when Central Finance Corporation was incorporated under a private act of the federal Parliament. It was Canada's first federally incorporated small loan company, lending money on personal security and chattel mortgages. Because there was no general legislation covering the operation of such companies, it was in some respects made subject to the Loan Companies Act, including particularly the provision that a licence had to be obtained from the Minister of Finance, and for this reason it became Canada's first registered small loan company. Maximum interest and expense charges were stipulated and the company was prohibited from taking public deposits or selling debentures to the public. Beginning as a Canadian-owned company, it was acquired by Household Finance Corporation, a U.S. company, in 1933, and in

---

12. 6 Edw. VII, cap. 32.

13. See evidence of K. R. MacGregor, Superintendent of Insurance for Canada, *Proceedings of the Special Joint Committee of the Senate and House of Commons on Consumer Credit*, June 2, 1964, p. 17.

1939 changed its name to Household Finance Corporation of Canada.

The second small loan company, the Peoples Thrift Corporation, was incorporated in 1928 also but was never organized. In 1930 Industrial Loan and Finance Corporation was incorporated and organized, became Community Finance Corporation in 1951 and ceased operation in 1966. It was followed in 1933 by the Discount and Loan Corporation, a subsidiary of Beneficial Industrial Loan Corporation, a U.S. company, which changed its name to Personal Finance Company of Canada in 1944 and finally to Beneficial Finance Company in 1956. While a few others were incorporated, it was not until 1947 that another company began operations – Canadian Acceptance Company, a subsidiary of Canadian Acceptance Corporation, a sales finance company. Laurentide Finance Company of Vancouver and Brock Acceptance Company of Winnipeg were organized in 1960. As a result of these developments there were five federally incorporated small loan companies in operation in 1969.

The unsatisfactory operation of the Money-Lenders Act of 1906 led to the Small Loans Act of 1939[14] and it was under this act that the aforementioned small loan companies operated. The act also applied to all other money lenders (excluding chartered banks and pawnbrokers)[15] who made personal cash loans of $500 or less (changed to $1,500 in 1956) and charged in excess of 1% per month for such loans. Maximum loan charges including all expenses and interest were stipulated.[16] Within a year of the act's coming into force, no fewer than sixty-five provincial companies, partnerships and individuals became *registered money lenders* under the act.

The act did not apply to money lenders making only loans in excess of the stipulated size and therefore some subsidiary companies (e.g., Household Finance Corporation Limited) were formed for the purpose of making such loans. This has meant that the regulations have not applied to all personal cash loans, and that the data on small loan companies and money lenders in the Superintendent's reports do not encompass the whole industry.[17] Nor does the act

---

14. 18-19 Geo. V, cap. 77. It was based on the sixth draft of the Uniform Small Loans Act of the United States. For this and many other details see J. S. Ziegel, "The Legal Regulation of Consumer Credit," in J. S. Ziegel and R. E. Olley, eds., *Consumer Credit in Canada*, proceedings of the Conference on Consumer Credit, Saskatoon, May 2-3, 1966, published by the University of Saskatchewan, pp. 70-82.
15. Pawnbrokers are regulated under the federal Pawnbrokers Act.
16. The 1956 amended act permitted 2% per month for loans not exceeding $300; 1% per month for loans larger than that, up to $1,000; and ½% per month for loans exceeding $1,000.
17. In 1967, for example, assets of registered consumer loans companies totalled $1,043 million, whereas assets of consumer loan companies compiled from tax returns totalled $1,216 million, so that the former constituted about 86% of the industry. See Tables 10:7 and 10:9.

cover "purchase credit," and so it is not concerned with the business of the sales finance companies. The latter exclusion is rather surprising in view of the importance of small loans made in the form of instalment "purchase credit," and the absence of any significant economic distinction between "cash loans" and "purchase credit." The matter arose in this way when the Small Loans Act was being debated by the Banking and Commerce Committee in 1938:

> MR. COLDWELL: In these general discussions of the small loan business will the committee have the power or the opportunity of including in its investigation automobile loans and small loans of that type?
>
> HON. MR. DUNNING: This is not comprehended in the reference.
>
> MR. COLDWELL: Oh, is it not? I had hoped we might have some opportunity of going into that.
>
> MR. FINLAYSON [Superintendent of Insurance]: I think the term small loans limits the investigation to companies whose business is the making of small loans, direct from lender to borrower. I think there is a distinction between the small loan companies and companies whose business is the financing of commercial paper. I think the latter come in another field.
>
> HON. MR. DUNNING: That would open up the whole field of instalment credit buying, a very attractive field; but I am afraid we would lose ourselves in the woods if we got away from the specific thing which we can deal with.
>
> MR. VIEN: It would be altogether too much involved for the committee to deal with it concurrently with small loans and the Companies Act. That is a totally different field.
>
> HON. MR. DUNNING: You get into the field of Chattel securities and mortgages, a provincial question. . . .
>
> MR. COLDWELL: Very high rates of interest are charged, and it is comparable to the small loan business in some respects.
>
> HON. MR. DUNNING: In basis they are similar.[18]

And so attention was concentrated entirely on the small loan companies and money lenders, and it was to these institutions that the new act applied, the instalment finance companies continuing to operate under ordinary company legislation although subject to provincial conditional-sale agreements legislation as well. However, in November 1968 a bill respecting investment companies was introduced into the federal Parliament by the government, which would specifically regulate federal sales finance companies.

---

18. Canada, House of Commons, Standing Committee on Banking and Commerce, *Minutes of Proceedings and Evidence Respecting Small Loan Companies*, No. 1, February 17, 1938, pp. 8-9.

OWNERSHIP AND BUSINESS TIES

The preceding discussion has shown that U.S. participation was important at the very beginning of the industry. This participation has persisted. Table 10:2 shows the trend in the total assets of the ten largest sales finance companies operating in Canada and the relative size of the assets of the three Canadian companies and the seven foreign subsidiaries among them. Until 1964 the three Canadian companies were very successful in retaining their share of the business, with their assets accounting for 73% of the assets of the ten largest companies – almost certainly a postwar high figure. After that they lost ground and in 1968 their assets were down to about 57% of the total. In 1969 a proposed takeover of Traders Group Limited by a large United States company was prevented by intervention of the federal government. Had it not been prevented, the share of assets of the ten largest sales finance companies belonging to Canadian companies would have declined by about 17 percentage points – to 40% or less from 57% in 1968. From now on, the shift to foreign ownership in the industry, if it occurs at all, presumably will occur through the relatively more rapid growth of foreign companies than Canadian companies.

That this is occurring is strongly suggested by the fact that the seven largest foreign companies have, since 1964, been growing more quickly than the three largest Canadian companies. And while ownership information is not available for the companies not included in the ten largest grouping, it is fairly certain that the Canadian companies are losing ground there as well. The bankruptcy in 1965 of Atlantic Acceptance Corporation, a Canadian company, seems to have made it more difficult for the smaller, that is Canadian, finance companies to obtain funds from the short-term money market because of the suspicion surrounding the quality of their short-term paper. Even the larger companies have had to reduce their dependence on short-term funds. But in addition to that both the Ford Motor Company and Chrysler Corporation have recently formed their own finance company subsidiaries, the former in 1962 and the latter in 1966.[19] For all these reasons the trend has begun to be toward increased foreign ownership of the sales finance business in Canada.

Foreign ownership is also important among the money lenders and small loan companies, in part because a substantial portion of that industry is composed of subsidiaries of sales finance companies. Among the federally incorporated small loan companies, two companies accounted for 93% of the total loan balances at the end of 1969 as

---

19. Ford Motor Credit Company of Canada and Chrysler Credit Canada Limited.

Table 10:2 Canadian and Foreign Ownership of Ten Largest Sales Finance Companies 1953-1969

	Three Canadian companies[1]	Seven foreign companies[2]	Assets of ten companies	Assets of ten companies as a proportion of total industry
	PERCENT OF TOTAL	PERCENT OF TOTAL	$MNS.	ASSETS
1953	63	37	839	97
1954	62	38	764	98
1955	66	34	914	96
1956	63	37	1224	98
1957	65	35	1286	98
1958	67	33	1237	98
1959	67	33	1463	98
1960	67	33	1628	93
1961	72	28	1582	91
1962	70	30	1809	91
1963	69	31	2101	89
1964	73	27	2383	86
1965	70	30	2773	88
1966	61	39	2809	88
1967	60	40	2821	89
1968	57	43	3108	92
1969	54	46	3553	90

SOURCE: First three columns based on data obtained from the Federated Council of Sales Finance Companies and annual reports of the three Canadian companies. The fourth column utilizes our estimate of total industry assets as outlined in the Statistical Appendix, and should be regarded only as an approximation.

[1]Includes Industrial Acceptance Corporation, Traders Group Ltd. and Laurentide Financial Corporation Ltd.

[2]Includes Canadian Acceptance Corporation Ltd. (U.S.), General Motors Acceptance Corporation of Canada Ltd. (U.S.), Avco-Delta Corporation Canada Ltd. (U.S.), Commercial Credit Corporation Ltd. (U.S.), Union Acceptance Corporation Ltd. (France), Redisco of Canada Ltd. (U.S.), United Dominions Corporation (Canada) Ltd. (U.K.).

shown in the federal Superintendent's report,[20] Household Finance Corporation of Canada with 61% and Beneficial Finance Co. of Canada Ltd. with 32% – both being U.S.-owned. And of the ten largest money lenders, which at the end of 1969 accounted for 97% of

20. *Report of the Superintendent of Insurance for Canada, Small Loan Companies and Money-Lenders* (Ottawa: Queen's Printer, Annual).

total small loan balances as shown in the Superintendent's report, eight were foreign-owned and their balances represented about 60% of the assets of this group. The remaining 40% of balances of Canadian money lenders were accounted for by those of Niagara Finance Company Limited, a subsidiary of Industrial Acceptance Corporation, and Trans Canada Credit, a subsidiary of Traders Group Limited—both parent companies being important in the sales finance industry. What this really means is that if Industrial Acceptance Corporation and the Traders Group Limited were to become foreign-owned, the Canadian ownership element in both the sales finance industry and the consumer loan industry would become insignificant.

The close relationship between sales finance companies and money lenders is important for the operation of both. How close this relationship is, is indicated by the fact that most of the ten largest sales finance companies have small loan or money lender subsidiaries, and these account for a significant portion of the total assets of small loan companies and money lenders. For the finance companies this relationship has meant that they have been permitted to enter the rapidly growing field of cash personal loans, and for the money lenders and small loan companies the arrangement has given them a new source of funds—loans from the parent companies. The consumer loan companies are closely restricted in their source of funds, while the sales finance companies are not, as we shall see below.

GROWTH AND DEVELOPMENT OF SALES FINANCE COMPANIES

Growth experience: Chart 10:1 shows the rate of growth of sales finance and consumer loan companies and Chart 10:2 outlines the relative growth of assets of those financial intermediaries. The sales finance companies experienced rapid growth in the 1920s, then a sharp decline in the early 1930s as sales of cars collapsed, followed by a recovery that ended in 1941 when wartime controls halted the production of cars for domestic purposes. From 1945 to 1956 the sales finance companies grew at a much faster rate than the total of all financial intermediaries, as well as faster than the total of all private intermediaries and of all their "near competitors." It was also a period when their share of total consumer credit increased significantly (see Table 10:1) Those were the "golden years" of their growth and development. From 1956 to 1965 the industry did not grow much faster than financial intermediaries in general and after that it began to grow less quickly than all the others combined.

Chart 10:1 – Assets of Sales Finance and Consumer Loan Companies 1926-1970

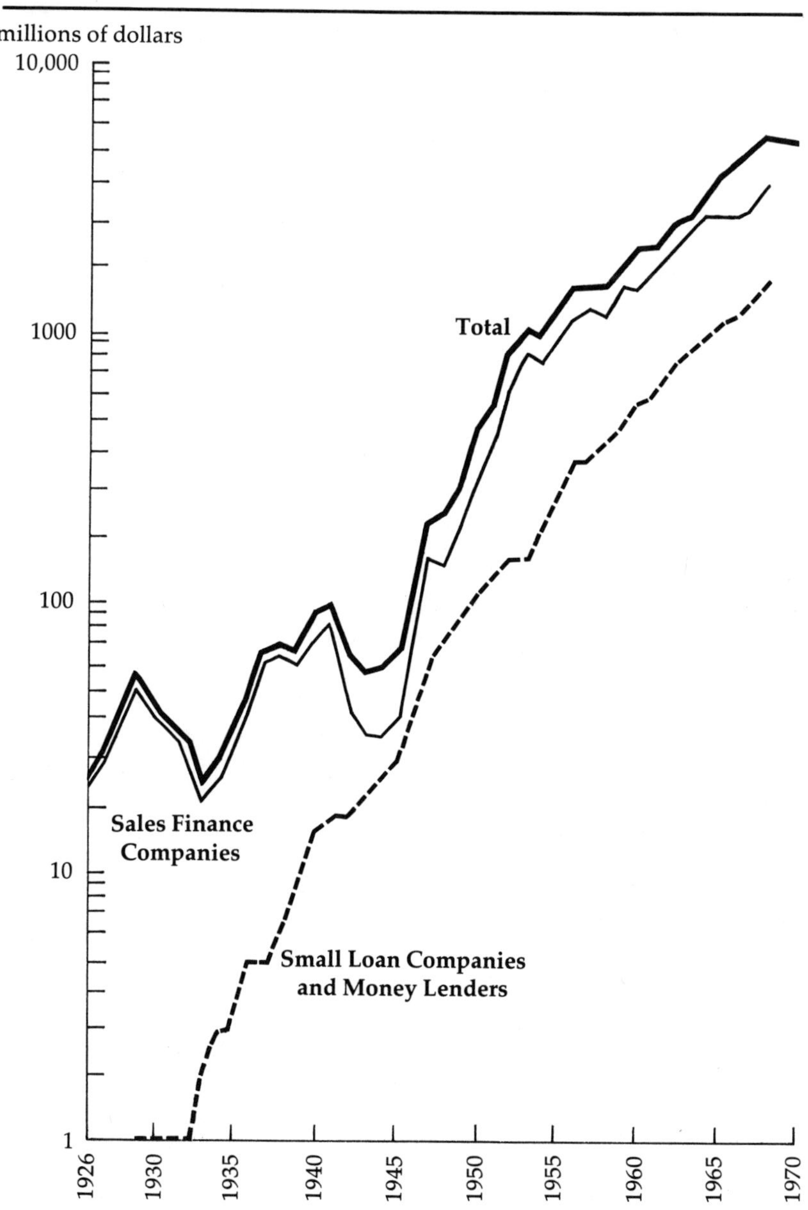

SOURCE: See Statistical Appendix.

Chart 10:2 — Relative Size of Assets of Sales Finance and Consumer Loan Companies 1926-1968

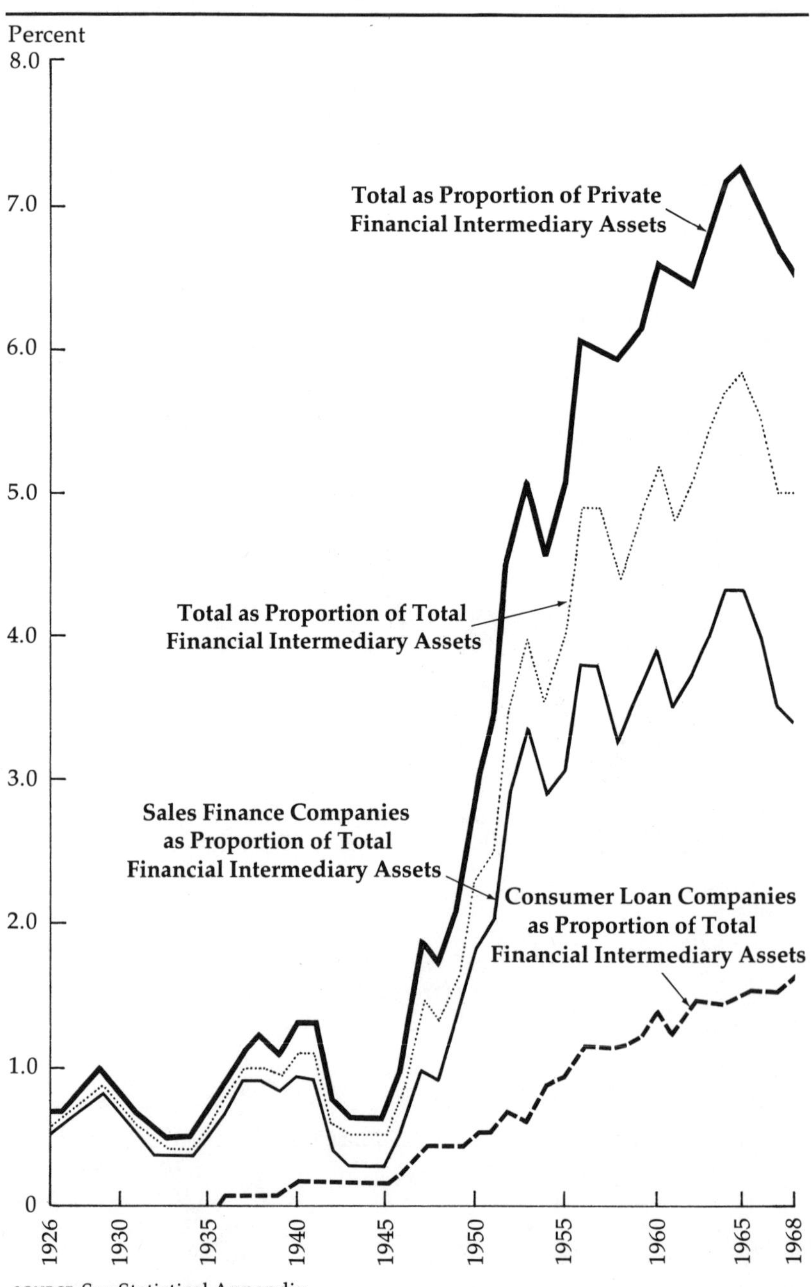

SOURCE: See Statistical Appendix.

The period of rapid growth of the sales finance companies after the Second World War can, in a general way, be explained by three influences: the high rate of growth of G.N.P. and personal disposable income; the expansion of the volume of consumer credit at a faster pace than G.N.P. and personal disposable income; and the success of the sales finance companies in increasing their share of the consumer credit business. From 1948 to 1958 G.N.P. increased by 125% (personal disposable increased by 112%), total consumer credit by 289%, and consumer credit supplied by sales finance companies by 997%. Roughly two-thirds of the growth of the sales finance companies from 1948 to 1958 is explained by the increase in their share of the total consumer credit business.

No special comment need be made on the rapid growth of G.N.P. and personal disposable income, but the growth of consumer credit substantially in excess of those aggregates is interesting. Table 10:3 shows the ratio of consumer credit outstanding to personal disposable income from 1948 to 1970, for both Canada and the United States. Both countries saw that ratio rise substantially from 1948 to 1958 – the Canadian rose by 84% – and both saw the rise continue thereafter but at a slower pace, with the Canadian ratio increasing by 53% from 1958 to 1970. While appropriate Canadian data are not available to test the hypothesis with confidence, it would seem fairly certain that the growth of total consumer credit in excess of aggregate personal disposable income arose in large part because of an increase in the number of people using such credit, with other influences such as an increase in personal net worth, a shift from non-recorded to recorded consumer credit, and conceivably some increase in the ratio of personal debt to net worth also being partly responsible for it. The slowing down in the rate of expansion of consumer credit after about 1958 in relation to income is probably an indication that maturity is gradually being approached in this area – maturity in the sense of all individuals' using consumer credit to their individual "optimum" levels. It is rather reminiscent of the approaching maturity in the life insurance industry in the 1920s,[21] and has the same implication for the future growth of consumer-credit-oriented institutions as the former did for the growth of the life insurance industry.

There remains the most significant development of all – the relative increase up to about 1957 in the share of consumer credit supplied by the sales finance companies. While this kind of question can more fully be answered when we discuss the changing structure of the assets and liabilities of the companies, one point already noted

---

21. See above, p. 252.

Table 10:3 Consumer Credit Outstanding as a Proportion of Personal Disposable Income, Canada and the United States 1948-1970

Year	Canada %	United States %	Year	Canada %	United States %
1948	7.5	7.6	1959	14.9	15.3
1949	8.3	9.2	1960	15.5	16.0
1950	9.6	10.4	1961	16.5	15.9
1951	8.0	10.0	1962	16.7	16.6
1952	10.0	11.5	1963	17.3	17.7
1953	11.6	12.4	1964	18.7	18.3
1954	12.4	12.6	1965	19.4	19.1
1955	13.5	14.1	1966	19.1	19.1
1956	13.9	14.4	1967	19.6	18.7
1957	13.5	14.6	1968	20.7	19.2
1958	13.8	14.2	1969	21.5	19.4
			1970	21.3	18.5

SOURCE: Based on statistics in Dominion Bureau of Statistics, *National Accounts Income and Expenditure*, Bank of Canada, *Statistical Summary*, and United States, Council of Economic Advisers, *Statistical Indicators*.

may be recalled. Table 10:1 shows that from 1948 to 1957 the sales finance companies increased their share of the consumer credit business by 18 percentage points, from 8% to 26%, while the biggest losers were the retail dealers, whose share declined by 12 percentage points. Consumer loan companies gained 5 percentage points, chartered banks lost 4 percentage points and life insurance policy loans lost 9 percentage points. It is safe to generalize that increased efficiency explains this shift to specialized consumer credit institutions and that the sales finance companies (and consumer loan companies) benefited most because (a) they were there first and so received the rewards of innovation, (b) the chartered banks showed almost complete indifference to this area of rapidly growing credit demand and (c) the caisses populaires and credit unions were only just beginning to be aggressive in that area.

After about 1957 conditions became much less favourable for the sales finance companies. This was not essentially because of any substantial slowdown in the growth of consumer credit, although for reasons already noted, some slowdown did begin to occur. The major development was the reduction in the sales finance companies' share of the total credit—which by 1970 had declined to about 10% from 26% in 1957. The banks' share rose from 14% in 1957 to about 41%, following their decision in 1958 to enter the field, and the share of the caisses populaires and credit unions also increased. From 1958 to 1969 G.N.P. rose by 129%, total consumer credit by 234%, and consumer credit supplied by sales finance companies — 66%. Had consumer credit grown at the same rate as in the 1948-59 period and had the sales finance companies simply maintained their 1957 share of the market, their consumer credit outstanding at December 31, 1969, would have been about $3,700 million instead of $1,264 million. The short fall is roughly explained to the extent of 63% by the decline in the companies' share of the market, the remainder accounted for by a slower growth of G.N.P. and a slowdown in the growth of consumer credit relative to G.N.P. Just as the sales finance companies had displaced the inferior credit arrangements of the retail dealers, so now the chartered banks were rapidly proving to be superior to the sales finance companies. A more dramatic structural change in the capital market would be difficult to find, and it was accompanied by painful internal readjustment within even some of the larger sales finance companies.

Why should the banks have proven to be such strong competition for the sales finance companies? In part this was because the sales finance companies encountered difficulties of their own, as we shall see. But there appears to have been one other influence at work—the shift in demand from "point-of-purchase" consumer credit to "cash loan" credit. Table 10:4 shows the relative size of consumer credit classified in this way. It appears that point-of-purchase credit has decreased in relative importance ever since 1953 and cash loan credit has increased in relative importance since that date. While data to conclusively prove the point are not available, it seems apparent that consumer borrowers have found cash loan credit to be more attractive—possibly because of a combination of cost and convenience—than point-of-purchase credit. It may be that as the income and the net worth of individuals increase, and especially as credit rating services become more comprehensive and efficient, there is less need for credit grantors to tie funds borrowed to purchase of specific items. It may also be that there are advantages to borrowers on grounds of sensible personal asset management not to do so. That is, it makes sense for individuals to regard their borrowing requirements as determined by the net effect of all their financial transactions, just as companies do, and not by individual transactions. It is more efficient to have one loan to meet total borrowing require-

Table 10:4 Point-of-Purchase and Cash Loan Credit as a Proportion of Total Consumer Credit[1] 1948-1970

Year	Point-of-purchase credit %	Cash loan credit %	Year	Point-of-purchase credit %	Cash loan credit %
1948	48.5	51.5	1960	46.7	53.3
1949	51.3	48.7	1961	42.7	57.3
1950	53.6	46.4	1962	40.9	59.1
1951	50.0	50.0	1963	39.3	60.7
1952	57.0	43.0	1964	37.9	62.1
1953	57.7	42.3	1965	35.8	64.2
1954	55.4	44.6	1966	34.5	65.5
1955	54.7	45.3	1967	30.7	69.3
1956	55.5	45.5	1968	28.0	72.0
1957	55.5	45.5	1969	27.3	72.7
1958	51.8	48.2	1970	24.1	75.9
1959	48.8	51.2			

SOURCE: See Table 10:1.

[1]Under point-of-purchase consumer credit is included the credit extended by sales finance companies, department stores and other retail dealers, oil company credit cards and instalment credit of consumer loan companies, while cash loan credit includes the cash loans of consumer loan companies, chartered banks, credit unions, life insurance companies and Quebec savings banks.

ments than to have more than one loan, and the former is possible with cash loan credit but frequently not with point-of-purchase credit. The shift in demand to the former was painful to the sales finance companies, who were largely dependent on the demand for the latter through automobile dealers and consumer durable goods merchants; and it was exceedingly beneficial to the banks, who, through their system of branches, were in an ideal position to supply directly the demand for cash loan credit. The impact on the sales finance companies of this shift in demand was softened to some extent by the growth of their consumer loan subsidiary companies.

We must now examine the operations and experiences of the sales finance companies as they are revealed in the structure of their assets and liabilities.

Assets: The sales finance industry was born when the automobile emerged, and over the years the financing of passenger cars and commercial vehicles has remained of pre-eminent importance to the companies. The structure of assets of the ten largest sales finance companies from 1953 is shown in Table 10:5. Until about 1957 passenger cars and commercial vehicle receivables accounted for about 55% or more of their assets, other retail business about 20%, and wholesale receivables about 16%. Then began the period of slow growth for the companies. The share of their assets accounted for by passenger car receivables began to decline and this reflected the aggressive entry of the banks into that business. As the competitive pressure of the banks emerged, the sales finance companies began to seek new lending opportunities. Some companies began to make real estate loans, and capital loans to automobile dealers for improving their premises increased in relative importance. But the greatest activity is reflected in the item "investments in subsidiary and associated companies," for it increased from 4% of total assets in 1957 to 21% in 1969. That activity included the formation or expansion of subsidiaries engaged in making cash personal loans, commercial loans and mortgages, residential mortgages, and home improvement loans, entering into leasing arrangements, selling insurance, and owning rental property. However, this diversification, as we have already seen, was insufficient to sustain the growth rate of industry.

In part this was because the companies encountered problems in their sources of funds in addition to increased competition in the consumer credit market, as an analysis of their liabilities will show.

Liabilities: Table 10:6 outlines the liability structure of the ten largest companies from 1953 onward. While comprehensive data are not available for the years prior to 1953, it is quite apparent that until about 1951 the companies depended mainly on loans from the chartered banks and long-term debt in the form of secured notes and debentures. Traders Finance Corporation, for example, showed bank loans as constituting 42% of its year-end liabilities in the period 1926–30 and 59% in the period 1936–40 – both being periods of expanding business. In the period 1945 to 1950 Industrial Acceptance Corporation showed 49% of its liabilities as being in the form of bank loans. In the early years equity capital provided a significant proportion of total funds, as is always the case with financial intermediaries in the early years of their development, but this proportion declined as the companies became established.

A major change in their sources of funds began in 1951 when the companies for the first time began to issue short-term notes, or finance company paper, which, incidentally, gave powerful impetus to the development of a short-term money market in Canada. Placed

Table 10:5 Structure of Assets of the Ten Largest Sales Finance Companies 1953-1969 (selected years)

(PERCENTAGE DISTRIBUTION)

	1953	1955	1957	1960	1963	1964	1965	1966	1967	1968	1969
Assets											
Cash	3.2	2.2	3.3	1.9	1.2	1.4	.8	1.4	.9	.8	1.4
Marketable securities				5.8	3.2	3.4	2.1	2.0	2.2	1.6	1.6
Notes and accounts receivable											
Retail	78.0	77.5	75.2	68.3	62.5	64.6	61.1	57.6	56.3	54.4	53.7
Of which: passenger cars	45.8	46.9	44.8	34.9	30.8	32.2	30.6	29.9	n.a.	n.a.	n.a.
: commercial vehicles	13.7	16.4	9.5	8.4	7.6	7.8	7.4	7.7	n.a.	n.a.	n.a.
: sub-total	59.5	57.2	54.4	43.3	38.5	39.9	38.0	37.7	n.a.	n.a.	n.a.
: other retail	18.5	20.3	20.9	24.9	24.1	24.6	23.1	19.9	n.a.	n.a.	n.a.
Wholesale	16.1	16.0	15.9	14.6	14.7	11.1	16.1	13.4	15.2	17.5	14.8
Real estate loans					.4	1.2	1.7	1.6	1.4	1.7	1.6
Capital loans to dealers	.3	.6	.5	.7	.7	.7	.7	1.2	1.1	1.1	1.0
Other accounts receivable	.2	.4	.4	.4	.6	.4	.5	1.2	2.6	3.1	4.2
Total receivables	94.8	94.5	92.0	83.9	79.0	78.0	80.0	75.1	76.6	77.7	78.4
LESS: Provision for doubtful accounts	1.0	1.0	.9	.9	.8	.8	.7	.8	.7	.8	.7
Net receivables	93.8	93.5	91.1	83.0	78.2	77.2	79.3	74.3	75.9	76.9	77.6
Investments in subsidiary & associated companies	2.2	3.5	4.4	8.2	16.5	16.8	16.7	21.3	19.8	19.7	21.3
Other assets	.9	.9	1.2	1.0	1.2	1.4	1.4	1.7	2.1	1.0	1.0
Total assets	100.0	100.0	100.0	100.0	100.0	100.0	100.0	100.0	100.0	100.0	100.0

SOURCE: Federated Council of Sales Finance Companies. End-of-fiscal-year figures.

Table 10:6 Structure of Liabilities of the Ten Largest Sales Finance Companies 1953-1969 (selected years)

(PERCENTAGE DISTRIBUTION)

	1953	1955	1957	1960	1963	1964	1965	1966	1967	1968	1969
Liabilities											
Bank borrowings	22.8	18.9	12.1	10.0	8.4	6.6	9.8	8.2	6.5	6.1	7.2
Other demand loans			.1	.1	.1	...	...	.3	.1	.2	3.6
Short-term notes	25.3	26.0	31.8	30.1	31.2	35.3	28.2	23.9	21.0	24.8	22.3
Long-term notes – more than 2 years to maturity when issued	16.7	17.0	17.7	20.6	22.3	23.7	22.0	24.1	39.9	36.1	34.9
Bonds and debentures	12.4	13.7	15.0	15.4	12.9	11.2	10.4	12.3			
Total debt	77.2	75.6	76.7	76.2	74.9	76.8	70.5	68.8	67.5	67.3	68.0
Advances from parent or associated companies	.7	—	—	.6	.6	.5	6.6	7.2	7.3	8.0	8.6
Other liabilities	12.2	12.0	12.2	11.5	12.1	11.1	11.9	11.8	13.1	13.3	12.2
Shareholders' equity											
Preferred stock	2.2	2.2	2.3	2.1	2.3	2.2	2.7	3.1	2.9	2.6	2.4
Other shareholders' equity	7.8	10.3	8.8	9.5	10.1	9.4	8.3	9.1	9.2	8.8	8.8
Total capital accounts	10.0	12.5	11.1	11.7	12.4	11.6	11.0	12.2	12.1	11.4	11.2
TOTAL LIABILITIES AND CAPITAL	100.0	100.0	100.0	100.0	100.0	100.0	100.0	100.0	100.0	100.0	100.0

SOURCE: Federated Council of Sales Finance Companies.

directly with investors or through investment dealers, finance company paper varies in maturity from a few months to several years and the interest rate on it is very sensitive to short-term market conditions. Table 10:6 shows that within two years, that is by 1953, this paper accounted for 25% of the funds of the ten largest companies, rising to 32% by 1957 and to a high of 35% in 1964. When first introduced, finance company paper was advantageous to the companies because it was a less costly form of credit than bank loans. Then in the credit squeeze of the 1953–7 period of expansion its advantages were even more apparent, for the banks began seriously to reduce the credit lines of the finance companies. There can be little doubt that the innovation of the finance company paper materially contributed to the rapid growth of the sales finance companies up to about 1958.

After about 1958 two developments relating to sources of funds aggravated the position of the sales finance companies at the very time that they were beginning to experience strong competition from the banks in the extension of consumer credit. First, possibly because the banks now clearly were their competitors, the finance companies saw a further and permanent decline in the relative importance of bank loans as a source of funds. Second, short-term notes as a source of funds suffered because of the financial difficulties in 1965 of Atlantic Acceptance Corporation and several other smaller companies. This development forced some companies, particularly the independent Canadian companies, to depend less on short-term paper and more on longer-term debt, and to increase the ratio of equity to debt—all of which almost certainly increased the cost of funds to them from what it would otherwise have been. The impact on the companies of these developments was severe, and in some respects permanent, forcing even the larger ones to introduce extensive changes in their operations. One financial paper reporting in 1967 on the internal change taking place within the Traders Group Limited began its article by remarking that "any finance company executive will tell you the past two years have been the most difficult in his career. Ever since the 1965 collapse of Atlantic Acceptance Corporation made investors wary of finance companies, these firms have had difficulty getting their raw material—money."[22] The years 1965 to 1968 were indeed difficult ones for the industry, and saw the disappearance not only of Atlantic Acceptance, but also of Prudential Finance Corporation and Alliance Credit Corporation. Even Laurentide Financial Corporation, one of the larger companies, received an injection of $9

22. *Financial Post*, Oct. 14, 1967.

million equity capital from its major shareholder—Power Corporation of Canada.[23] Retrenchment in lending was industry-wide and many branches were closed.[24]

When these adverse developments in sources of funds were occurring, it became evident that the sales finance companies as a group had not developed sources of funds similar to those available to their near competitors, that is, deposits and small debentures for sale to the general public. The company acts under which they operate do not specifically permit the finance companies to take deposits, but in addition we have found little evidence that the large and reputable companies seriously sought powers to develop a broader source of funds.

Summary and conclusions: Up to 1958 the high rate of growth of the sales finance companies was the result of: (a) the high rate of growth of the economy; (b) the even higher rate of growth of consumer credit as an increasingly larger proportion of the population began to use it; (c) the fact that the sales finance companies were first to take advantage of the economies that specialized consumer credit institutions have over non-specialized institutions; (d) the absence of any significant shift of demand from point-of-purchase to cash loan credit; and (e) source of funds innovation by the sales finance companies in the form of the development of finance company paper. From 1958 onward their relatively slow rate of growth was the result of: (a) the decision of the banks to enter into the consumer credit field; (b) the growing preference of the consumer borrower for cash loan credit; (c) the loss, in a relative sense, of bank loan accommodation by the finance companies; (d) the set-back to finance paper caused by bankruptcies in the industry; (e) to a small extent, the approach to long-run equilibrium of the stock of consumer credit; and (f) the failure of the sales finance companies to develop lending areas to fully replace consumer credit business they lost, and their failure to find competitive sources of funds to replace bank and money market accommodation lost. The foreign companies survived all these developments better than the Canadian companies did. For some companies the impact of developments after 1957 was softened somewhat by their having consumer loan company subsidiaries. The fundamental forces that lay behind the slow growth of the sales finance companies have not yet worked themselves out, and so a further relative decline in the size of those companies, accompanied by mergers

23. *Financial Post*, March 2, 1968, p. 15.
24. *Financial Post*, Feb. 26, 1966, p. 7.

and insolvencies, may be expected over the next decade. Individual companies in the industry may, however, recognize the winds of change, adjust to them, as some have already tried to do, and thereby sustain comparatively satisfactory growth rates. But as an industry the "golden years" are gone.

GROWTH AND DEVELOPMENT OF CONSUMER LOAN COMPANIES

Growth experience: The growth experience of the federally registered small loan companies and the provincial money lenders is shown in Charts 10:1 and 10:2. Being less dependent on car sales, the growth of these consumer loan companies continued uninterrupted through the period of the Second World War, and at a rate very similar to that of the sales finance companies. When the growth of the sales finance companies began to falter after 1957, that of the consumer loan companies was reasonably well sustained. Their share of total consumer credit reached a new high in 1969 (see Table 10:1), whereas that of the sales finance companies began to level off in 1957 and declined sharply thereafter, their share in 1969 being no better than it was in 1949. The consumer loan companies benefited from the shift in consumer preference from point-of-purchase credit to cash loan credit.

Expansion of the consumer loan company business is reflected in the growth of their branches (see Table 10:7). In 1954 they had 540 branches and fifteen years later they had 2,197; the former figure was equivalent to 13% of the number of chartered bank branches, and the latter figure to 36%. They aggressively developed the market for small cash credit at a time when the banks largely ignored it. However, after 1958 the consumer credit granted by the banks increased at a substantially faster pace than did that of the consumer loan companies and the latter began to feel the competitive strength of the banks.

One interesting development, as Table 10:7 shows, is the more rapid growth from 1951 to 1968 of the registered provincial money lenders than of the registered federal small loan companies, following a period that included the war years, when the opposite was the case. In 1951 the provincial licensees had 31% of the total assets of all licensees, whereas in 1968 they had 60%. But in 1969 they declined noticeably and seventeen money lenders ceased operations. By 1960 the provincial companies had more branches than the federal companies. Quite obviously the role of provincial financial institutions is not a small one.

Table 10:7 Number of Registered Consumer Loan Companies in Canada and Their Branches[1] 1940-1969

	Small loan companies			Money lenders			Total		
	Companies NO.	Branches NO.	Proportion of total assets %	Companies NO.	Branches NO.	Proportion of total assets %	Companies NO.	Branches NO.	Assets $ MNS.
1940	3		41	65		59	68		17
1945	3		53	51		47	54		30
1950	4		69	56		31	60		88
1951	4		70	57		30	61		105
1952	4		66	59		34	63		134
1953	4		64	58		36	62		155
1954	4	360	65	61	180	35	65	540	172
1955	4	448	60	66	254	40	70	702	209
1956	4	471	56	70	311	44	74	782	262
1957	4	468	61	75	316	39	79	784	327
1958	4	469	61	76	368	39	80	837	409
1959	4	475	57	77	447	43	81	922	489
1960	5	510	53	75	511	47	80	1021	549
1961	5	541	53	76	607	47	81	1148	589
1962	7	584	52	80	739	48	87	1323	677
1963	7	622	51	79	866	49	86	1488	736
1964	7	652	47	78	1040	53	85	1692	797
1965	6	695	45	83	1283	55	89	1976	900
1966	5	721	43	78	1265	57	83	1994	995
1967	5	759	42	71	1304	58	76	2063	1043
1968	5	782	40	69	1362	60	74	2144	1133
1969	5	795	50	52	1402	50	57	2197	1485

SOURCE: Canada, Department of Insurance, *Report of the Superintendent of Insurance of Canada, Small Loan Companies and Money-Lenders*, Queen's Printer, Annual.

[1]These companies are the ones licensed under the Small Loans Act (Statutes of Canada, 1939, cap. 23, as amended in 1956 by cap. 46). They exclude consumer loan companies not charging in excess of 1% per month and up to 1957 also companies confining themselves to making loans in excess of $500, and after 1957 companies making only loans in excess of $1500. They seemed to account for about 87% of the assets of consumer loan companies operating in Canada in 1969.

In spite of the large number of companies in the industry, a relatively small number account for most of its loans. In 1960, 1966 and 1969 the asset distribution among the larger companies was as follows:

Table 10:8 Relative Size of the Ten Largest Consumer Loan Companies 1960, 1966, 1969

	1960 %	1966 %	1969 %
Household Finance Corporation of Canada Limited[1]	37	29	30
Beneficial Finance Company of Canada Limited[1]	15	15	17
Niagara Finance Company Limited	15	13	12
Seaboard Finance Company of Canada Ltd.	3	7	9
Avco Finance Ltd.[2]	3	6	4
Trans Canada Credit Corporation Limited	8	5	6
G.A.C. International Finance Corporation Limited[3]	—	4	5
Associate Finance Company Limited	—	4	5
Union Finance Company Limited	1	2	2
Citizens Finance Company Limited	2	2	2
Sub-total	84	85	92
All other (47 licensees in 1969)	16	13	8
TOTAL	100	100	100

SOURCE: See Table 10:7, except that the "large loans" in Canada of Household Finance Corporation of Canada Limited have been added to its assets, using data supplied by the company, which removes the major deficiency of data in the aforementioned table, as far as the comparisons in this table are concerned.

[1]Small loan companies, the other eight being money lenders.
[2]Until 1967, Crescent Finance Corporation Ltd.
[3]Until 1966, Atlantic Finance Corporation Ltd.

The ten largest companies accounted for 92% of total assets in 1969, which was more than in 1960, but the three largest accounted for 59%, which was significantly lower than in 1960 when it was 67%.

Assets and liabilities: Essentially the consumer loan companies confine themselves to the personal loan business and they obtain funds for lending mainly from their parent companies and from the banks. Table 10:9 shows that accounts receivable represented 96% of their assets in 1969. Accommodation from parent companies is not explicitly shown in that table, for such data are not available, but the items short-term loans, debt due to individual shareholders, and shareholders' equity, which account for over two-thirds of the funds of the companies, are the ones through which such accommodation is made available.

In 1968, 56% (in value) of the loans reported to the Superintendent of Insurance were secured by chattel mortgages and 44% were unsecured, and the shift has been toward the latter. Loans of $500 or less accounted for 16% of the value of total loans outstanding, those from $500 to $1,000 for 51%, and those of $1,000 to $1,500 for 33%. When one sees the size of these loans it is apparent why the consumer loan companies have had to develop a nation-wide system of branches.

For loans of up to $1,500 the rates of interest charged are controlled by the maximum charges on the unpaid balance, being as follows:

Size of Unpaid Principal Balance $	*Maximum Percent Charge Per month*
0 – 300	2
300 – 1000	1
1000 – 1500	1/2

If a loan of $500 or less is made for a period longer than twenty months and a loan of $500 or more is made for a period longer than thirty months the maximum charge is 1% per month.

The simple liability structure of the consumer loan companies is dictated by the Small Loans Act, which says that a licensee ". . . shall not issue any bonds, debentures or other securities for money borrowed, nor shall it accept deposits."[25] Some of the companies have in effect broadened their borrowing powers through their affiliation with sales finance companies.

Now that the chartered banks are aggressively competing in the small cash loan business with the consumer loan companies, it may be wondered how the latter will sustain their growth. It seems that the loan companies specialize in the riskier small loan business, where they can charge higher rates of interest. However, now that there is no ceiling on rates that the banks may charge, it is conceivable that in time they too will move aggressively in that direction. While we know little about the economics of running a branch in Canada, it may be that the cost of making loans from a chartered

25. Strictly speaking, this provision legally applies only to the small loan companies, but in practice it apparently has been made to apply to money lenders as well.

Table 10:9 Assets and Liabilities of Consumer Loan Companies 1965-1968

	1965		1966		1967		1968	
	$ MNS.	%	$ MNS.	%	$ MNS.	%	$ MNS.	%
Assets								
Cash, securities, advances	18.1	1.7	13.6	1.1	19.2	1.6	19.5	1.8
Accounts receivable	1014.7	95.7	1204.3	96.6	1119.4	92.0	1044.7	95.7
Other	27.1	2.6	29.0	2.3	77.8	6.4	27.1	2.5
TOTAL	1059.9	100.0	1246.9	100.0	1216.4	100.0	1091.3	100.0
Liabilities								
Bank loans	75.9	7.2	50.5	4.1	63.2	5.2	36.1	3.3
Short-term loans	336.0	31.7	419.2	33.6	416.4	34.2	437.5	40.1
Due to shareholders and affiliates	287.4	27.1	362.2	29.0	314.1	25.8	286.4	26.2
Net long-term debt	203.9	19.2	210.7	16.9	190.4	15.7	127.8	11.7
Other liabilities	59.1	5.6	75.0	6.0	91.4	7.5	73.2	6.8
Shareholders' equity	97.4	9.2	129.3	10.4	140.8	11.6	130.3	11.9
TOTAL	1059.9	100.0	1246.9	100.0	1216.4	100.0	1091.3	100.0

SOURCE: Dominion Bureau of Statistics, *Corporation Financial Statistics*, Annual.
These data include some consumer loan companies that are not registered under the Small Loans Act.

bank branch, with its broad range of financial services, is less than that for loans made from a consumer loan company branch. Also the cost of funds of a bank, because of its deposit business, is lower than the cost of funds of a consumer loan company. Because of this it may well be that if the consumer loan companies wish to maintain their relative position among their competitors they will have to broaden their sources of funds (somehow overcoming legislative restraints), increase the financial services offered through their branches, and diversify their lending activity.

11

Mutual Funds, Investment Trusts and Development Companies

The term "investment companies" is commonly used when referring to mutual funds or "open-end" funds, which first appeared in Canada in 1932, and to investment trusts or "closed-end" funds, which appeared about three decades earlier. Both types of investment companies are financial intermediaries, for they sell their own securities to individuals and groups or institutions and they use the proceeds to acquire other financial claims. What they have in common, and what distinguishes them from most other financial intermediaries, is that the claims they sell are almost entirely equities, thereby making the supplier of funds an owner or shareholder and not a creditor of the company; and the claims that they buy are almost entirely equities, thereby giving their shareholders a convenient entry into an equity or common stock portfolio. The investment companies, in other words, are unique essentially because they provide a convenient means for individuals and groups to enter into the stock market in a diversified way and to obtain the services of professional equity investment managers.

The principal difference between open-end and closed-end companies lies in the way their shares are bought and sold. The mutual funds will usually at all times sell shares (treasury shares) to the public, in blocks or on a periodic investment plan basis and at a price equal to the per share net asset value of the fund, plus (usually) an initial acquisition charge; and they at all times stand ready to redeem the shares at the net asset value price. The closed-end companies, or investment trusts, sell issues of shares and debentures to the public only periodically, and do not undertake to redeem the stock; so a shareholder if he wishes to dispose of his stock must sell it to another investor—usually through the stock exchange—just as would a shareholder of any other joint-stock company, with the cost limited to the normal stock brokerage commission. As a result, whereas the share price of a mutual fund is always equal to its current net asset value, that of a closed-end fund can be less than, equal to, or more than its net asset value depending on expectations as to the future prospects of the fund. Actually, almost all closed-end Canadian investment funds have persistently carried a market price below the break-up value of the securities owned by them, a feature that may well have worked to the detriment of the closed-end funds.[1]

It may also be noted at the outset that there are several different types of closed-end investment companies. There is the normal closed-end investment fund that holds a diversified portfolio of shares of relatively well-established companies and does not seek to control them; there is the investment holding company that seeks to control or at least influence the management policies and the operations of the companies whose shares it holds; and since the Second World War there has been a third type, which we will refer to as the investment development company and which specializes in sponsoring and assisting new companies, or companies that appear to have potential but have not yet become well established.

There are, of course, great differences between individual mutual funds, but these arise essentially out of the character of the equities that they hold, as we shall see. However, it should be noted that several companies have emerged that, in their operations, may be viewed as part mutual fund and part mortgage loan company. These are what we refer to as "investment contract companies"; the oldest of these, and the one that dominates the area, is Investors Syndicate Ltd., formed in 1940. Because they concentrate on investments in mortgages we have discussed them in chapter 7, although since their method of raising funds is in some respects similar to that of the mutual funds we might have discussed them here.

The Emergence of Investment Companies

The investment trusts, or closed-end funds, originated in the United Kingdom in the 1860s. However, La Société Générale de Belgique, which was formed under another name in 1822, later acquired some of the characteristics of an investment company, [2] as did the International Financial Society of London, formed in 1863, and the Conti-

1. See *Financial Post*, "Survey of Investment Funds 1969," p. 29.
2. For details of the early United Kingdom, United States and Canadian investment companies see Hugh Bullock, *The Story of Investment Companies* (New York: Columbia University Press, 1959).

nental Union (an English company), formed in 1864. In 1868 there was formed in London the Foreign and Colonial Government Trust, whose prospectus stated that it would provide "the investor of moderate means the same advantage as the large capitalist, in diminishing the risk of investing in Foreign and Colonial Government Stock, by spreading the investment over a number of different stocks"—which is a good description of an investment company even today.[3] It seems to have been the first investment trust. The trust deposited with a banking house eighteen different issues of fifteen foreign governments (including, incidentally, one Nova Scotia issue), against which it issued a fixed number of 6% £100 certificates priced at £85 to yield 7%. A sales charge of almost 3% was made and management expenses were limited to 1/4% of the proposed £1,000,000. Substitution of securities was not permitted and profits (after interest) and expenses, together with proceeds from called securities, were placed in a sinking fund and used to redeem certificates by lot. However, all certificate holders were entitled to a share of the profits when the trust was finally terminated.

Eighteen similar trusts were formed before 1875, and in 1873 appeared the first of the subsequently prominent Scottish investment trusts—the Scottish American Investment Company, formed by Robert Fleming and specializing in holdings of American railroad bonds. The Joint Stock Companies Act of 1862 and 1867 permitted the formation of limited liability companies for dealing in market securities, so while some of the companies actually were common law trusts (hence the name "investment trusts"), others were limited liability companies. After the 1870s almost all the British trusts assumed the latter form, selling common stock instead of certificates, and were referred to as "investment trust companies." They also began to introduce "leverage," that is, to add to their assets with *borrowed* funds. (In the United States the term "investment trust" was generally accepted until 1940, at which time the Securities and Exchange Commission indicated its preference for the term "investment companies.") At the time of the First World War there were about one hundred British investment trust companies. Another round of expansion occurred in the 1920s. However, all the companies formed until the 1930s were of the closed-end type—that is, ones that sold issues only infrequently and were not self-liquidating in character.

It is not easy to identify the first United States investment company. Some of the early life insurance companies and building and loan associations had some of the characteristics of diversified investment companies, as had holding companies, which, however,

---

3. Quoted in Bullock, p. 2.

were formed for purposes of controlling corporations whose shares were acquired. In 1893 the Boston Personal Property Trust was formed, which eventually clearly became a closed-end investment company. The Railway and Light Securities Company, formed in Boston in 1904, was possibly the first investment company with leverage. The Alexander Fund, started in 1907, is of interest because it had some mutual fund characteristics. It sold units (since it was not incorporated), and if such units went to a premium, new purchasers of them would pay the current price, while redemption at current asset value was provided for. Prior to 1921 there were formed a number of companies that in subsequent years evolved into closed-end funds. But in 1921 appeared the International Securities Trust of America, which from the beginning was a true closed-end investment company and which ushered in the period of rapid investment company formation of the 1920s, culminating in explosive growth from 1927 to 1929 and then widespread collapse and bankruptcy. A compilation of the dates of formation of American investment companies that existed as of December 31, 1929, shows the magnitude of their development:

Table 11:1 Formation of American Investment Companies Prior to 1930

Year of formation	Number of companies formed
1920 and before	13
1921	1
1922	5
1923	4
1924	14
1925	26
1926	24
1927	89
1928	130
1929	203
Total as of December 31, 1929	420

SOURCE: Compiled from data in Bullock, *ibid.*, pp. 199-211. It should be noted that many of these companies, perhaps even half of them, were really holding companies.

Almost all of the companies formed were closed-end companies and many were leveraged. When many of them collapsed after 1929, it was found that the leveraged companies suffered most, and that many of the companies had engaged in grossly fraudulent activities. The reputation of all investment companies suffered severely, and when the companies began to recover in the late 1930s and after the Second World War, it was the open-end companies that dominated the field, not the closed-end ones. We have already noted that one U.S. company formed in 1907 had some mutual fund characteristics. The first true open-end fund was probably the Massachusetts Investors Trust, formed in 1924, and a few others were formed after that; but it was not until the 1930s that the mutual funds began to appear in significant numbers.

This summary of developments in the United Kingdom and the United States helps to place Canadian developments in historical perspective. Prior to the turn of the century there was great activity in the formation of mortgage loan and trust companies in Canada,[4] and while they were not entirely forbidden to hold securities, legislation governing them was generally biased in favour of their confining their activities to mortgage lending and trust business. Possibly the first, and certainly the oldest surviving, closed-end fund was the Debenture and Securities Corporation of Canada, formed in Toronto under special act of the Parliament of Canada in 1901. The act permitted it to "... lend money on, or purchase, sell and deal in stocks, bonds, debentures and obligations of municipal and other corporations secured by mortgage or otherwise; or Dominion, provincial, British, foreign and other public securities."[5] Other companies were also given such powers soon after, but they did not long survive. A holding company, Yucatan Power Company (soon changed to Mexican Consolidated Electric Co. Ltd.) was formed in 1906, and when years later the Mexican government acquired its tramway properties it became an investment company, since 1958 under the name Magnum Fund Limited. It is this kind of transformation, it may be noted in passing, that makes it very difficult to compile statistics that distinguish between holding companies and investment companies; and it is made even more difficult because in some cases a company may be a holding company (i.e., may exercise management control) with respect to some of the stocks it holds and not others.

In 1920 began what was to be a distinct trend in the formation of closed-end investment companies in Canada during that decade—the sponsoring of such companies by investment dealers. Nesbitt, Thomson & Co., a Montreal firm, in that year formed Canadian Pulp

4. See above, chapters 7 and 9.
5. 1 Edw. VII, cap. 94.

& Power Investments, Ltd.; in 1925 it formed Power Corporation of Canada Ltd.; in 1927, Foreign Power Securities Corporation, Ltd.; and in 1929, Great Britain and Canada Investment Corporation Ltd. Both American and British capital, as well as Canadian capital, was involved. Wood, Gundy & Co. in 1927 formed Hydro-Electric Bond & Share Corporation and also Investment Bond and Share Corporation, with Sir Herbert Holt, president of the Royal Bank of Canada, as president of both as well as of London Canadian Investment Corporation, which was formed by Wood, Gundy in 1928. Their fourth closed-end investment company was formed in 1929, Consolidated Investment Corporation of Canada. Foreign as well as Canadian capital was used in the formation of some of these funds.

Some of the above-mentioned companies had holding company characteristics – that is, they were designed partially to exercise control over or at least influence the management of some of the companies whose stock they held. Some also were heavily leveraged. Not so the first closed-end fund sponsored by the Right Honourable Sir Arthur Meighen. In 1926 the Meighen group formed Canadian General Investment Trust, Ltd., which soon had a very diversified portfolio (over four hundred securities in 1930) and which issued only share capital. The group formed three other companies along similar lines, called Second, Third, and Fourth Canadian Investment Trust, Ltd. in 1927 and 1928. Cochrane, Hay & Co., another investment dealer, formed two companies, Economic Investment Trust, Ltd. in 1927 and Dominion-Scottish Investments Ltd. in 1929. Several closed-end funds were formed for the purpose of holding only foreign assets, thereby receiving favourable tax treatment, including Hydro-Electric Securities Corporation, which appeared in 1926, and International Holding & Investment Co. Ltd., formed in 1927. Table 11:2 shows the year of formation of fifty closed-end companies, including holding companies, that existed at the end of 1929, and confirms that as in the United States the period of great activity in the formation of closed-end investment companies was 1927 to 1929. The stock market crash of late 1929 and the succeeding prolonged depression decimated the investment companies.

All the Canadian investment companies formed in the 1920s and before were of the closed-end type. The first Canadian open-end company, or mutual fund as they came to be called after the 1930s, was Canadian Investment Fund, Ltd., organized in 1932 under a federal Companies Act charter by one of the prominent American pioneers in the establishment of investment companies, Calvin Bullock. In 1931 Corporate Investors Ltd. was formed, also under a federal charter, but when it began operations in 1932 it did so as a closed-end fund. As early as 1934[6] it considered transforming itself into a mutual fund but decided against it. It took that step in 1938. Another company, Commonwealth International Corporation, which also began operations as a closed-end fund in 1932, transformed itself into a mutual fund in late 1933 and began operations as such in 1934. These were the first three mutual funds organized in Canada and all of them are still active. The period of rapid expansion of mutual funds, as we shall see, did not begin until about 1950.

Table 11:2 Formation of Canadian Investment Companies Prior to 1930

Year of formation	Number of companies formed
1924 and before	2
1925	1
1926	3
1927	14
1928	9
1929	21
Total as of December 31, 1929	50

SOURCE: Essentially from Bullock, *ibid.*, pp. 221-2. Relate only to companies that existed as of December 31, 1929.

A majority of the closed-end companies operate under the federal Companies Act, while most of the remainder operate under companies legislation of the provinces of Ontario and Quebec. Mutual funds accounting for about 75% of Canadian mutual funds assets (in 1968) operate under federal companies legislation, about 9% under provincial companies legislation, and 17% (including all funds sponsored by trust companies) under trust deeds or declarations of trust. Incorporated funds sell "shares," while those operating as trusts sell "certificates." All funds are subject to the regulations of securities commissions of the provinces in which they sell their shares and certificates.

It has become common for a sponsor or sponsoring group to offer more than one mutual fund, and to provide management services for

6. Minutes of Directors, March 15, 1934.

a fee to the individual funds. Such "management companies" are legally separate from the funds but the officers of the funds are frequently also officers of the management companies. In 1968 the eight most important mutual fund management companies were responsible for from two to five funds each. Agreements between funds and management companies outline the services that the latter will provide to the former and the fees to be received for such services.

Table 11:3 shows that while the closed-end investment companies emerged first, the mutual funds, beginning right after the Second World War, grew at a faster rate and by 1955 greatly exceeded the closed-end funds in dollar value. By 1969 they were over three times as large in dollar value as closed-end investment companies, holding companies, and development companies combined, their assets amounting to about $3242 million.

Table 11:3 Relative Size of Groups of Canadian Investment Companies 1929-1969 (selected years)

	1929 %	1939 %	1946 %	1950 %	1955 %	1960 %	1965 %	1968 %	1969 %
Closed-end companies									
Investment companies	71	59	54	44	21	15	12	10	11
Holding companies	29	28	35	27	18	14	14	10	9
Development companies	—	—	—	—	...	1	3	3	4
TOTAL: %	100	87	89	71	39	30	29	23	24
($ Mns.)	(189)	(79)	(132)	(145)	(332)	(396)	(809)	(1025)	(1015)
Mutual funds									
Canadian	—	13	11	29	34	45	69	76	75
Non-resident-owned	—	—	—	—	27	25	2	1	1
TOTAL: %	—	13	11	29	61	70	71	77	76
($ Mns.)	—	(12)	(16)	(59)	(501)	(942)	(2012)	(3423)	(3242)
TOTAL: %	100	100	100	100	100	100	100	100	100
($ Mns.)	189	91	148	204	833	1338	2821	4448	4257

SOURCE: Compiled from data in Financial Post, *Survey of Industrials, Survey of Investment Funds* and company annual reports.

Growth and Development

CLOSED-END INVESTMENT COMPANIES AND HOLDING COMPANIES

Of the 50 closed-end funds, including holding companies that existed at the end of 1929, about 30 had been formed in 1928 and 1929 (see Table 11:2). It is not surprising, therefore, that most of them failed to survive the stock market crash of 1929 and the depression of the 1930s. For the year 1939 we were able to compile 23 companies. The number has changed from year to year after that, as funds were formed for various purposes or were merged with other funds. But the essentially static nature of the closed-end funds as a group is indicated by the fact that their number fluctuated between about 20 and 30 from 1946 to 1968, well below their 1929 level. Table 11:4 shows that the only company of significant size in 1969 that emerged after the 1930s was the holding company Argus Corporation. In 1929 the closed-end funds accounted for about 3.5% of total private financial intermediary assets, while in 1968 they accounted for 1.2%, whereas mutual funds, which did not exist in 1929, accounted for 4.5% of private intermediary assets in 1968. It would seem that investors have found the mutual funds to be superior to closed-end funds as a vehicle for acquiring a diversified investment portfolio.

It is not immediately apparent why only two holding companies of significant size should have emerged in Canada – Power Corporation, formed in 1925, and Argus Corporation, formed in 1945.[7] But it may be that the holding company's contribution, i.e., the injection of managerial technology and talent into corporations, is being satisfied as efficiently or possibly more efficiently by other organizations, particularly by the business management consulting firms. If the latter were the case, then one would not expect the performance of companies in a holding company group to be better on the average than those not in such a group, and therefore similarly so for the holding company itself. This would of course discourage the formation of holding companies. However, we are not able to test this hypothesis here. We noted earlier that the market value of the shares of closed-end companies, including holding companies, has in Canada been substantially below the per share break-up value of the assets they own. Obviously an investor is not under those circumstances likely to be interested in purchasing the new equity issues of such funds, and this, in turn, would discourage the growth of closed-end funds.

---

7. It may be noted that a few other funds are emerging that may become quite important in future. There are CEMP Investments Limited, a private fund based on family wealth, and also Canadian Pacific Investments Limited, which manages the investments of the Canadian Pacific Railway.

Table 11:4 Assets of Individual Closed-End Funds Ranked by Size as of 1970

(MILLIONS OF DOLLARS)

Closed-end investment companies	Year of establishment of: Original co.	Present co.	Net assets in 1970
Canadian General Investments Ltd.	1928	1930	92.1
United Corporations Ltd.	1929	1933	71.2
Hambro Corporation of Canada Limited	1929	1971	29.3
Third Canadian General Investment Trust Ltd.	1928	–	28.2
Economic Investment Trust Ltd.	1927	–	24.4
Great Britain & Canada Investments (1968) Ltd.	1929	1968	21.7
Toronto and London Investment Co. Ltd.[1]	1843	1951	19.5
Dominion and Anglo Investment Corporation Ltd.	1928	–	18.9
Magnum Fund Ltd.	1906	1958	18.3
Canadian & Foreign Securities Co. Ltd.	1926	–	15.0
Dominion-Scottish Investments Ltd.	1929	–	13.8
Sub-total			352.4
Fifteen other companies	–	–	57.7
			410.1
Holding companies[2]			
Power Corporation of Canada Ltd.	1925	–	181.6
Argus Corporation Ltd.	1945	–	161.4
F-I-C Fund Inc.	1962	1966	13.2
Central Fund of Canada Ltd.	1961	–	2.4
Total			358.6
TOTAL			768.7

SOURCE: Based on data in Financial Post, *Survey of Investment Funds, 1970.*

[1]In 1843 the incorporated mortgage company the Trust and Loan Co. was formed (see above, pp. 180-4), whose assets were acquired in 1951 by the company shown in the table.
[2]UNAS Investments Ltd. is discussed under development companies (see p. 365).

But it is not at all clear why such a discount from break-up value exists. Is it because investors believe that the managerial impact of a closed-end fund will actually make a company worse off than it would be without it? Is it because the closed-end funds are not able to distribute tax-free capital gains? Is it because Canadian funds, in contrast to U.S. funds, are not permitted to buy in their own shares?[8] Or is it simply that, in the absence of any evidence to the contrary, investors believe that companies in a closed-end fund will on average perform about the same as those represented in a mutual fund portfolio and that, given that, the liquidity characteristics of the mutual funds become decisive in turning investor preferences in their favour?

The structure of assets and liabilities of closed-end investment companies is exceedingly simple, with most of the assets composed of Canadian common shares and most of the liabilities being accounted for by shareholders' equity. In 1970, for example, 79% of their assets were Canadian common shares and 92% of their liabilities were shareholder equity. About half of the paid-in capital is in the form of preferred shares, so there is more leverage among the companies than Table 11:5 suggests.

CLOSED-END INVESTMENT DEVELOPMENT COMPANIES

There seems to have been recurring concern over the years as to the adequacy of medium- and long-term credit facilities for new or small and relatively undeveloped companies with growth potential. This concern was expressed in the United Kingdom by the Macmillan Committee of 1931 and the term "Macmillan gap" is frequently used to describe the phenomenon. It was a concern that led to the formation in 1944 by the federal government of the Industrial Development Bank as a subsidiary of the Bank of Canada, and a number of the provinces have also introduced loan schemes for assisting industrial development.[9]

What interests us at this point is the emergence of private financial intermediaries that specialize in providing equity and other finance and managerial assistance to such companies. It is not an easy task to compile a definitive list of these companies, for they have tended to come and go and change their character. But a few have emerged to prominence and these we will briefly examine here. The size of their assets for selected years from 1953 onward is shown in Table 11:6.

Charterhouse Canada Ltd. of Toronto appeared in 1952, as a subsidiary of a British company, and has always emphasized the

8. For some discussion on these points see *Foreign Ownership and the Structure of Canadian Industry*, Report of the Task Force on the Structure of Canadian Industry (Ottawa: Queen's Printer, January 1968), pp. 279-82.

9. See below, p. 430.

Table 11:5 Closed-End Investment Companies Assets and Liabilities, Percentage Distribution 1963-1970 (selected years)

Assets	1963	1965	1967	1968	1969	1970
Cash	.5	1.6	1.1	5.2	1.3	1.1
Canadian bills, notes and bonds	5.4	5.8	4.0	3.6	5.0	6.8
Canadian mortgages	—	.2	.1	.1	.2	.1
Canadian preferred shares	7.1	7.0	8.5	5.5	6.3	5.3
Canadian common shares[1]	79.8	77.3	77.4	74.0	72.4	81.3
Foreign bonds, notes, etc.	—	.1	.2	.5	.3	.3
Foreign shares	5.7	7.2	7.7	8.2	5.1	4.4
All other	1.2	.8	1.0	2.8	9.4	.7
TOTAL	100	100	100	100	100	100
Liabilities						
Short-term loans	4.9	3.2	5.8	1.0	2.3	3.7
Accounts payable	.5	.6	.9	2.1	.6	.6
Long-term debt	7.9	5.9	4.2	3.1	3.3	2.8
Other debt	.2	.2	.1	.1	.9	.2
Shareholders' equity:						
Paid-in capital	44.6	46.5	44.0	47.8	48.3	50.3
Retained earnings	41.9	43.6	45.0	45.9	44.6	42.4
TOTAL	100	100	100	100	100	100

SOURCE: Dominion Bureau of Statistics, *Business Financial Statistics* and *Financial Institutions Financial Statistics*. Based on values at cost. Excludes holding companies.

[1] Includes equity in subsidiary and affiliated companies.

provision of mid-term and long-term capital to small and medium-sized businesses. It takes a substantial minority equity position in the companies which it finances and retains an interest in the companies as long as its unique services are needed. A number of the companies which it has financed have subsequently become public companies and have had their stock listed on the stock exchanges. Generally Charterhouse does not invest in natural resource companies, public companies and speculative companies. Its loans would average about $250,000 each.

UNAS Investments Ltd. of Toronto was formed in 1952 as United North Atlantic Securities Ltd. by British and Continental European merchant banking interests. N. M. Rothschilds of London are still

Table 11:6 Assets of Investment Development Companies 1953-1970 (selected years)

(MILLIONS OF DOLLARS)

Name of company	Year established	Assets					
		1953	1960	1965	1968	1969	1970
Charterhouse Canada Ltd.	1953	.1	4.0	5.7	9.4	11.2	10.3
UNAS Investments Ltd.	1953	2.5	3.4	16.2	17.5	20.2	16.3
Canadian Enterprise Development Corporation Ltd.	1962	—	—	5.5	7.6	7.5	8.7
Roynat Ltd.	1962	—	—	51.2	101.1	110.0	138.2
TOTAL		2.6	7.4	78.6	135.6	148.9	173.5

SOURCE: Annual reports of the individual companies. Fiscal year end dates were used and these vary from one company to another.

shareholders, the Toronto-Dominion Bank also has an interest in it, and Canadian capital in general is predominant in the company. It operates as a closed-end investment company but specializes in investing in securities of companies with growth potential, particularly those of medium size which have not yet reached the point where funds from the general public are readily available. It emphasizes equity participation, it does not require voting control, but it normally is represented on the boards of the companies in which it invests. Its investment in a company would range from $250,000 upward, and no industry is excluded from consideration.

Canadian Enterprise Development Corporation Ltd. (C.E.D.) of Montreal was formed in 1962 with a capital of about $5 million by a fairly large group of Canadian institutional investors. These in 1968 included two Canadian chartered banks, twelve life insurance companies, two investment dealers, one sales finance company, one trust company, one mortgage loan company, and seven others. It is modelled on the American Research and Development Corporation of Boston, which is one of its shareholders, as are equivalent institutions of the United Kingdom and France. C.E.D. is a shareholder of those foreign institutions as well. Its essential purpose is to provide unsecured capital in the form of notes, preferred stock and common stock of companies with the potential for substantial growth. Such companies may be either old or new. Most of its investments have been on a minority equity basis, and in fact it does not usually seek control. However, it does provide counsel and non-financial assistance as well as funds. In its first six years it invested in 27 companies.

The largest of the companies listed, Roynat Ltd. of Montreal, was formed in 1962 by two Canadian chartered banks and three Canadian trust companies. Its purpose is to provide a readily available source of term financing to medium-sized Canadian businesses in virtually all areas of the economy, except land development and rental real estate. It aims to provide a company with its total term financing requirements by purchasing its mortgage bonds, income bonds, debentures, or preferred or common stock, or a combination of these. Financing of up to $1 million or more, for periods up to 15 years, are arranged. Roynat does not confine its activities to new companies, or even to companies that have experienced difficulty in obtaining term financing, but rather it operates competitively in the term financing field in general. This distinguishes it from the companies discussed above and helps explain its exceedingly rapid rate of growth.

There are a few other institutions that take a specialized interest in the development of new or small industrial companies, but their approach is more that of an industrial conglomerate organization than a financial intermediary. Two examples of this would be Toromont Industrial Holdings Limited and Canadian Corporate Management Company Limited, each of which has acquired control of a number of relatively small industrial enterprises.

MUTUAL FUNDS

Growth rate and relative size: Mutual funds as a group have experienced a remarkably high rate of growth in the period after the Second World War. Chart 11:1 shows that their period of rapid growth began in 1949. Changes in the total number of mutual funds we have compiled confirm that timing in their growth pattern. Table 11:7 shows that in 1946 there were about 8 funds, in 1950 15, in 1960 65, and in 1970 149 funds. The total number of funds has not yet levelled off, nor has the rate of growth of their assets. From the year that the funds began to grow rapidly they have exceeded the growth rate of all other financial intermediaries.[10] Their assets in 1970 were almost $3 billion. This unusually rapid growth justifies our examining somewhat more closely the inherent nature of the unique contribution of the mutual funds and their method of operation.

When most individuals contemplate adding common stocks to their portfolio, they face several important problems. First, their knowledge of stocks is limited, and it is likely to remain so since they do not have the time to master required analytical techniques and to study complex data. Second, since the sums they wish to invest are frequently quite small, they would have to confine themselves to relatively few stocks, which reduces the extent to which they can spread the risk of investing in equities. Third, human nature being what it is, their investment in stocks would probably not be orderly and might well be quite sporadic. Now when an individual buys shares in a mutual fund he is in fact buying a part of the diversified portfolio of the fund, which removes the problem of risk inherent in holding a small number of stocks. Also, if it can be assumed that the expertise of the group managing the fund is greater than his own, he is acquiring access to useful portfolio management services, thereby freeing his own time for his own career or pleasure. Finally, since funds generally offer plans that involve regular or instalment purchases of shares, he can add to his holdings of equities in an orderly way, and without time-consuming contemplation every time he does. There seems little doubt that the unique contribution of the mutual funds, and therefore the reason for their growth, was that they provided a convenient and attractive way for individual inves-

---

10. See above, p. 68.

Chart 11:1 — Growth and Relative Size of Mutual Fund Assets 1933-1970

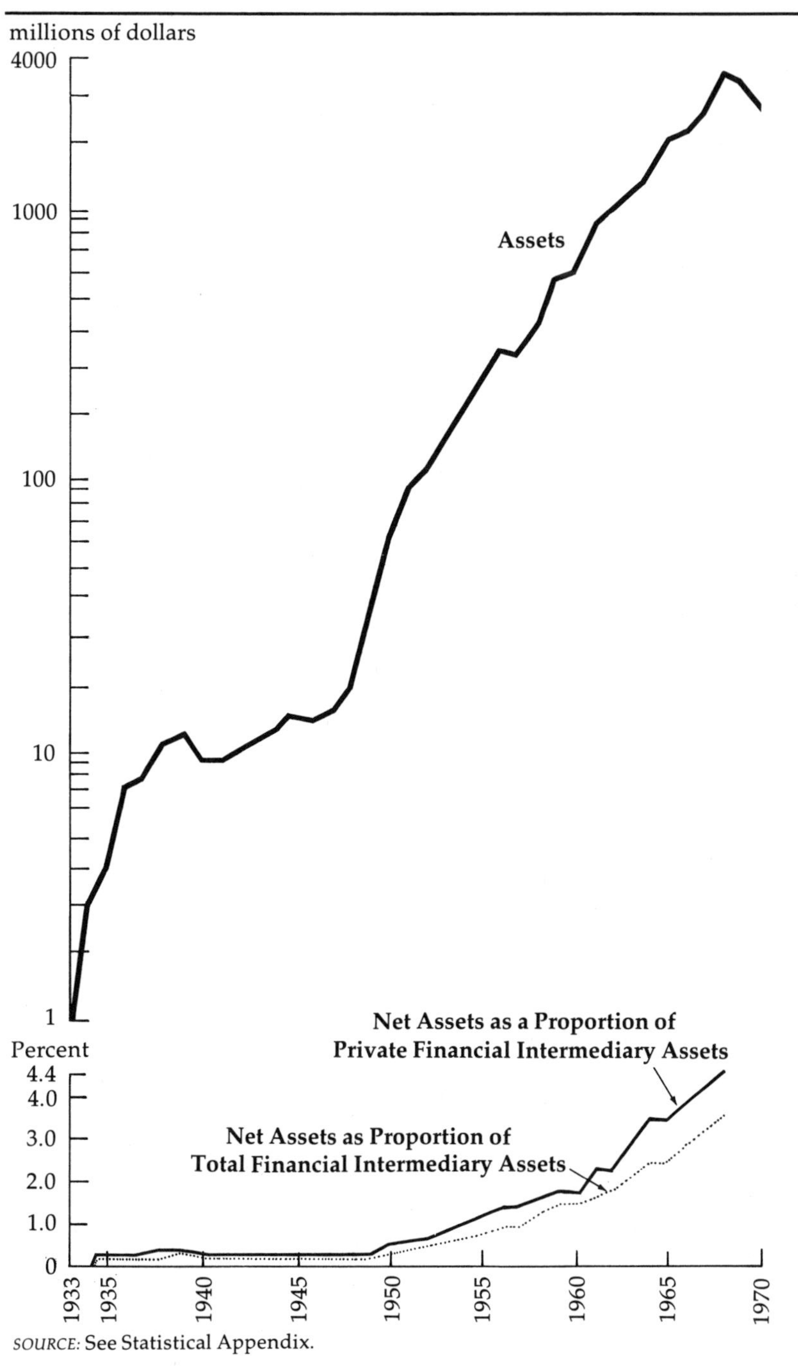

SOURCE: See Statistical Appendix.

Table 11:7 Number of Mutual Funds in Canada 1932-1970

1932	1	1951	18	
3	2	2	20	
4	2	3	25	
5	2	4	33	(1)[1]
6	2	5	37	(5)
7	2	6	43	(7)
8	3	7	50	(8)
9	7	8	54	(8)
1940	7	9	61	(9)
1	7	1960	65	(10)
2	7	1	74	(11)
3	7	2	73	(11)
4	8	3	72	(10)
5	8	4	88	(4)
6	8	5	98	(3)
7	9	6	114	(3)
8	10	7	121	(3)
9	13	8	132	(3)
1950	15	9	134	(3)
		1970	149	(3)

SOURCE: Compiled by the author from data found essentially in Financial Post, *Survey of Industrials* and *Survey of Investment Funds*. Different sections (e.g. income, equity) within one mutual fund are treated as separate funds.

[1]Bracketed figures refer to the number of special non-resident–owned funds included in the total shown.

tors to enter the stock market. To this was added their door-to-door type of retail sales organization, which undoubtedly speeded the rate at which individuals took advantage of the unique services offered by this new type of financial intermediary. Their system of periodic payments and their approach to selling is, of course, nothing new, having been used by life insurance companies in Canada for over a hundred years.

How unusual is the rate of growth of mutual funds? Over the period 1950-68, in constant dollars, they grew at an average annual rate of about 21%. The mortgage loan companies experienced a period of rapid growth from 1870 to 1880 and that growth in constant dollars was about 18% per annum. The life insurance companies grew rapidly from 1880 to 1900, with an annual rate of about 13%. The sales finance companies experienced an annual growth rate of about 20% from 1948 to 1958. So, viewed as a new financial intermediary, the growth rate of mutual funds should not be regarded as unusual. They are still benefiting from a "once-for-all" adjustment that individuals are making in their asset portfolios, and the closer that adjustment comes to being over, the slower will be the growth rate of mutual funds.

Types of funds: The aggregate figures of mutual fund assets hide the great diversity of funds that now exists. This diversity is so complex that a detailed classification is not very useful. Funds vary from holding all equities, to holding equities and bonds and mortgages, to holding bonds and mortgages, and to holding all bonds and all mortgages. In the case of all equity funds, they may differ in that some hold shares of a great diversity of companies, some concentrate on particular industries; some tend to concentrate on speculative situations with the prospect of greater return and also greater risk, some hold only shares of other funds; some hold only foreign equities and some are owned entirely by non-residents. Needless to say, funds also differ in that some are better managed than others, for there are substantial differences in return to investors among the funds.

Table 11:8 provides a very general classification of funds, and enables us to make several general points. First, bond or fixed-income funds have remained insignificant in size; most of the growth is accounted for by funds investing heavily or entirely in equities. Second, while still relatively small, there has been a marked increase in the absolute size of the speculative funds. Third, the balanced funds (i.e., those holding bonds and equities in significant proportion) have declined in relative size. Fourth, the trust company funds, which first began to appear in 1959 and most much later than that, had net assets in 1969 of $210.6 million, or 6.3% of Canadian mutual fund assets. Fifth, the non-resident–owned funds shown have vanished to insignificance, having earlier been almost as large as the Canadian-owned funds. These funds were created essentially because in 1954 U.S. tax laws were altered to permit such funds to be taxed at the capital gains rate, not at the income tax rate, provided they reinvested all their earnings. When this favoured tax treatment was withdrawn, interest in these funds declined sharply, and all but three changed their domicile from Canada to the United States.

Table 11:8 Relative Size of Various Types of Mutual Funds 1957-1969 (selected years)

		1957 %	1960 %	1964 %	1969 %
I Canadian mutual funds					
Fully managed and	%	45.0	44.3	43.3	51.6
common-stock funds	$ mns.	137.1	269.9	737.5	1729.0
Specialty funds	%	6.5	8.3	12.7	11.3
	$ mns.	19.7	50.4	216.4	377.2
Balanced funds	%	48.4	46.7	39.5	20.7
	$ mns.	147.4	284.5	672.0	691.3
Speculative funds	%			—	8.2
	$ mns.	—	—	.2	274.5
Bond funds	%	.2	.3	.4	.1
	$ mns.	.6	2.1	7.1	5.0
Trust company—	%		.1	2.4	.9
bond funds	$ mns.	—	.9	40.6	31.0
Trust company—	%		.1	1.7	5.4
equity funds	$ mns.	—	.7	29.5	179.6
Mortgage funds	%				1.8
	$ mns.		—	—	60.7
Total	%	100	100	100	100
	$ mns.	304.8	608.5	1703.3	3348.3
II Non-resident–owned	%	95.3	14.8	3.9	1.5
funds[1]	$ mns.	290.4	89.8	65.6	50.2

SOURCE: Based on data in Financial Post, *Survey of Investment Funds*. Excludes funds investing only in shares of other funds.

[1]As a percentage of Canadian mutual funds assets.

Assets and liabilities: Table 11.9 helps to confirm points already made about the mutual funds industry. Their almost total reliance on equity capital as a source of funds is indicated by the relative size of shareholders' equity, which usually accounted for about 98% of their liabilities. The emphasis on equities as investment is also shown, for preferred and common shares amounted to 79.7% of assets in 1963, 82.8% in 1967 and 82.9% in 1970. Rather conspicuous is the dramatic shift toward holdings of foreign equities away from Canadian equities, the latter amounting to 46.9% of assets in 1970, compared with 63.3% in 1963, and the former increasing to 36.0% by 1970 from 16.4%

Table 11:9 Canadian Mutual Funds Assets and Liabilities, Percentage Distribution 1963-1970 (selected years)

	1963 %	1965 %	1967 %	1968 %	1969 %	1970 %
Assets						
Cash	1.3	2.9	3.0	5.3	5.4	4.1
Canadian bills, notes and bonds	16.2	16.0	11.0	7.7	9.3	8.2
Canadian mortgages	.6	.8	.4	.3	.3	.3
Canadian shares:						
Preferred	7.0	7.0	5.5	5.0	5.4	6.5
Common	56.3	51.4	40.1	31.5	35.1	40.4
Foreign securities:						
Fixed interest	1.1	.3	.9	1.3	1.9	2.5
Preferred and common shares	16.4	20.1	37.2	46.2	39.5	36.0
All other	1.2	1.5	1.9	2.7	3.1	2.0
TOTAL	100	100	100	100	100	100
Liabilities						
Short-term loans	.2	...	...	.2	...	...
Accounts payable	.8	.6	1.7	3.5	1.7	2.1
Other	.1	.1	...	...	.1	...
Shareholders' equity:						
Paid-in capital	91.8	90.4	84.7	79.3	82.0	89.3
Retained earnings	7.1	8.8	13.5	17.0	16.2	8.6
Total	98.9	99.2	98.2	96.3	98.2	97.9
TOTAL	100	100	100	100	100	100

SOURCE: Dominion Bureau of Statistics, *Balance Sheets, Selected Financial Institutions* and *Financial Institutions Financial Statistics.* Based on values at cost.

in 1963. While some of this shift may be transitory, not all of it is. Some of it probably reflects a general shortage of equities in Canada,[11] and also total absence of equities of certain industries not found in Canada.

Operating characteristics and performance: Mutual fund shares are sold either directly to individuals by salesmen of the fund, through salesmen of a separate selling company that has entered into a distribution agreement with the fund, or through stockbrokers. Funds spon-

11. See below, p. 511.

sored by trust companies are sold only through the branches of the companies. One fund, Royfund Ltd., is distributed essentially only through the branches of the Royal Bank of Canada; another fund, Corporate Investors Ltd., is offered both directly and through the offices of the Toronto-Dominion Bank. Management of the assets of the fund is done either internally, that is, by the fund itself, or, as noted earlier, by a separate management company with which the fund has a management agreement.

Most funds sell shares to investors in lump sums and under periodic investment plans involving regular, usually monthly, purchases. They also make arrangements for investments in funds to serve as registered retirement savings plans under the Income Tax Act; and they usually offer facilities to investors for regular monthly or quarterly withdrawals from the funds invested. While the inherent nature of the mutual fund share undoubtedly explains why mutual funds have grown to significance, the speed with which they have done so is at least partly accounted for by the marvellous selling device of the periodic payment and by the aggressiveness of the field sales force—both of which had been used many decades earlier by the life insurance companies when they experienced their period of rapid growth.

Mutual fund shares are purchased at an "offering price" which is equal to the per share net asset value of the fund plus, usually, an acquisition charge ("loading charge"). The net asset value is equal to the market value of the fund's assets minus its liabilities. A few funds, instead of having a "loading charge," make a charge when shares are liquidated. Other funds, particularly those operated by trust companies, have no acquisition charge at all. However, the presence or absence of a loading charge is not in itself a useful indication of the attractiveness of a fund, for this will depend also on the costs of operating the fund and on the market performance of the securities it holds. It is more satisfactory to regard the attractiveness of a fund as depending on the income and the capital appreciation (or depreciation) of the fund, *minus* the following three cost items: acquisition or sales charge, management fee paid to the management company, and costs of administration including custodian charges. It can therefore easily be seen that, hypothetically, a "no load" fund might be very unattractive, because of poor market performance of its assets, or because of high management fees and costs of administration. In 1969, for example, the net asset value per share varied greatly among the 121 funds examined, the poorest showing a decline in value of 40% and the best showing a gain in value of 12%. Administrative expenses, as a proportion of net assets, varied from 2.30% to .23%. Loading or acquisition charges varied from zero to the figure common for many funds of about 8½% offering price, which is roughly 10% of net asset value per share. It is apparent that fund performance can overwhelm the cost items as a factor determining the attractiveness of a fund. A recent study suggests that investors do react to fund performance, at least to some extent, when choosing which fund to buy.[12]

In most cases an investor can sell his shares back to the fund at a price equal to the current per share net market value of the assets of the fund without notice and without charge, although in a few cases a transaction charge is levied at the time of sale. Management companies that operate more than one fund usually permit an investor to shift from one fund to another without any, or any significant, charge. Most funds also permit an investor to withdraw funds with the option of re-acquiring the investment in the fund at some future date without an acquisition charge. A requirement of the Canadian Mutual Funds Association is that member funds permit periodic deposit investors to rescind their contract at any time within 30 days of entering into an agreement and to have refunded all sales charges.[13]

We have noted that a mutual fund enables an investor to acquire the services of professional investment management. Such services would, of course, be valuable only if professionally managed funds performed better than funds managed by the individual (both net of costs involved). Recent attention has turned to testing this hypothesis and to determining whether funds behaved better than stock market indexes. A Canadian study came to the conclusion that funds do better than individuals would.[14] But scrutiny of fund performance is likely to persist, for other studies have questioned the superiority of performance of professionally managed funds.

Competition in the industry: If competition in the industry is effective, one would expect that the industry would tend toward a position where the net return to the buyer of the funds would be maximized. This in turn would occur because of the tendency for excessive profits and other income to employees and managers of the funds to vanish (i.e., excessive in relation to what they would be in a competitive environment in the long run), for high costs arising from inefficiency in the use of administrative resources to disappear, and for poor performance funds to be replaced by good performance funds.

---

12. See G. D. Quirin and W. R. Waters, *A Study of the Canadian Mutual Funds Industry* (The Canadian Mutual Funds Association, 1969), paper 3.

13. For detailed discussion of these matters see Quirin and Waters, *ibid.*, paper 6.

14. See Quirin and Waters, *ibid.*, paper 11.

Statistical data, however, do not permit one to test for the degree of competitiveness in these ways, and it is therefore necessary to rely on an examination of developments in the industry to form a judgment.[15]

The increase in the number of funds available to investors, as shown in Table 11:7, suggests persistent competition through ease of entry into the industry. However, since individual management companies in some cases sponsor more than one fund, it is useful to examine the degree of concentration of assets under the control of the major management companies. Table 11:10 shows that in 1969 the eight largest management companies accounted for 79% of industry assets, compared with 95% in 1957; and the largest company, which in 1969 had 31% of industry assets, had accounted for 42% in 1957.

Table 11:10 Concentration of Mutual Fund Assets in the Largest and the Eight Largest Management Companies 1957-1969

	Percent of industry assets	
	Largest company[1]	Eight largest
	%	%
1957	42	95
1958	40	95
1959	44	93
1960	45	92
1961	44	90
1962	43	86
1963	42	85
1964	41	83
1965	37	82
1966	36	81
1967	34	79
1968	31	80
1969	31	79

SOURCE: For the years 1957-67 see Quirin and Waters, *ibid.*, Table 2-3; figures for 1968 and 1969 computed by the author.

[1]The largest management company throughout the period was the Investors Group.

15. See *ibid.*, for a detailed study of the industry, including a discussion of competition in the industry.

The trend apparently has been toward diffusion of assets among the companies in the industry. There has also been some change in the companies that account for the eight largest. Table 11:11 shows the eight largest management companies in the year 1969. Of these, four had also been among the eight largest in 1957, one had almost been, one moved from eighteenth to second place in that period, and two were new in that period.

Another aspect of the unfolding competitive environment in the industry is the entry of other financial intermediaries into it. We have seen that the first mutual fund appeared in 1932. Excluding funds sponsored by trust companies, their assets totalled $3,188 million in 1970. In 1959, the Canada Trust Co. became the first trust company to sponsor a mutual fund, and by 1970 all the larger trust companies were doing so with assets of about $164 million. In the 1950s the trust companies began to establish pooled investment funds and registered retirement pension funds for individuals and groups. The assets of the equity funds of this type amounted to about $570 million in 1969. Following a change in legislation in 1961, federally registered life insurance companies were permitted to establish segregated pension funds and invest such funds entirely or partly in equities. Their equity funds amounted to about $177 million in 1969. Two chartered banks began offering a mutual fund through their

Table 11:11 Relative Size of Mutual Fund Assets of the Eight Largest Management Companies 1969

Management companies	Assets 1969 $Mns.	%	Companies ranked by size of assets 1968	1957
The Investors Group	1039	31	1	1
United Funds Management Ltd.	459	14	2	18
A.G.F. Management Ltd.	332	10	3	9
Canadian Funds Management Co. Ltd.	262	8	4	—
Calvin Bullocks, Ltd.	172	5	5	2
Capital Management Ltd.	171	5	6	7
Mutual Funds Management Corporation Ltd.	119	4	7	3
Canadian Security Management Ltd.	66	2	8	—
	$2694	79		

SOURCE: See Table 11:9.

branches in the mid 1960s as well. It was in this way that competition from other institutions began to emerge in a fairly direct way, attracted by the relatively high growth rate of the mutual funds industry. There is no doubt that the structure of the mutual funds industry will continue to undergo change, and it is even possible that this change will be as great as occurred in the consumer credit industry. The facilities of the trust companies and banks may suit those investors who do not require the inducement of a personal call to buy fund shares and who wish to transact much of their financial affairs in one place. The facilities of the life insurance companies may appeal to investors who wish to combine life insurance with retirement plans and who value, or are motivated by, a personal call or solicitation. Such developments will provide strong competition for the other mutual funds in the years ahead.

Regulation of the industry: Mutual funds, as we noted earlier, may be incorporated under the federal or provincial Companies Acts, or may be established as trusts under either federal or provincial trustee regulations. There is no special provincial or federal legislation governing the operations of mutual funds. The Companies Acts impose no investment restrictions on funds, and while trustee legislation does, it is routine to insert in trust deeds a clause that exempts trustees from those restrictions. Since the mutual funds issue securities, they are of course subject to the Securities Acts of the provinces—there being no federal Securities Act—and the rulings of the provincial securities commissions that administer those acts. A fund must obtain approval of its prospectus covering its issues of shares and must abide by laws governing the distribution of new issues. This means, among other things, that funds sold nationally face ten different sets of regulations relating to the sale of their shares, with differences between them frequently difficult to understand on rational grounds.

In practice, securities commissions seem to have concerned themselves not with restrictions on investments, but rather with such other matters as methods of distribution and the magnitude of management fees stipulated.

This somewhat loose legislative control over mutual funds has recently attracted the attention of the federal and provincial governments and also the industry itself. The latter formed a trade association, the Canadian Mutual Funds Association, in 1962 and the association began to impose constraints on its members. However, not all the funds are members, and the association does not extend to the trust company funds, so that self-regulation of the industry is not entirely complete. The major constraints imposed by the association are that members are *not* permitted to (a) borrow or pledge more than 10% of their assets (which severely limits the leverage of the funds); (b) engage in short sales or margin transactions; (c) hold more than 10% of their consolidated assets in securities of one issue or invest more than 10% of the securities of one issue, except government securities, other mutual funds, wholly owned subsidiaries and a few others; (d) invest in the shares of the management company, underwriter, or distributor of the fund; and (e) issue share-purchase warrants.[16]

In spite of this trend toward self-regulation of the industry, together with the disclosure approach to regulations implicit in the prospectus requirements, the federal and provincial authorities seem to have concluded that special legislation concerning it may be desirable. They also concluded at a federal-provincial conference on securities regulation in 1966 that co-operation in the matter was necessary, and so together they formed a Canadian Committee on Mutual Funds and Investment Contracts which was to determine whether additional legislation was necessary. That committee published its voluminous report with many detailed recommendations in 1969.[17] If out of this investigation comes some kind of joint or common federal-provincial legislation, or common regulatory agency, it would not only simplify the presently confused legislative framework facing the industry, but would hold out the hope of attaining common financial and securities legislation in future years.

---

16. *Ibid.*, paper 12.

17. *Report of the Canadian Committee on Mutual Funds and Investment Contract Companies* (Ottawa: Queen's Printer, 1969).

12

Caisses Populaires and Credit Unions

The feeling that commercially oriented financial intermediaries do not provide sufficiently satisfactory borrowing and savings facilities to people of modest means has been vocally expressed by various groups for many decades. We have already seen how concern over the need to encourage thrift among the poor led to extensive but unsuccessful experimentation in Canada before Confederation with trustee savings banks,[1] the emphasis there being on savings facilities, not borrowing facilities. Then in the 1840s came the building societies, where the emphasis was more on providing borrowing facilities, although periodic and regular saving was also a feature; but the purpose of the borrowing was largely confined to acquiring a house. In any case the experiment, for various reasons, failed and the societies evolved into mortgage loan companies that were entirely commercial in nature.[2] But in important respects they were spiritual forerunners of the caisses populaires and credit unions that came later, as were a few of the private banks.[3] With the formation at the time of Confederation of the federal government's Post Office Savings Bank and the acquisition by the federal government of the trustee savings banks run by the Maritime Provinces prior to Confederation, and, even more important, following the decision of the banks at that time to develop savings departments, the savings facili-

---

1. See above, chapter 5.
2. See above, chapter 7.
3. The Farmers' Bank of Rustico in Prince Edward Island, for example, was organized among farmers in 1864 and operated successfully as a kind of credit union for almost three decades. See National Association of Canadian Credit Unions, *Brief to the Royal Commission on Banking and Finance*, hearings held at Ottawa, July 13, 1962, p. A272.

ties available to low-income people soon became quite satisfactory.

Concern after that seems to have been focused more on facilities for borrowing than for saving. The two complaints that repeatedly emerged were that loans for low-income people were available only at usurious interest rates or were not available at all. Efforts to meet these complaints took two lines: regulations affecting the operation of existing financial institutions, and the formation of new institutions.

The first of these approaches centred largely on interest rate regulation. As we have discussed elsewhere,[4] efforts at controlling interest rates on small loans were completely ineffective until the appearance of the small loans legislation of 1939, and recurring charges were made that extortionist interest rates were being levied. It was precisely this that led to the second approach being taken to solve the problem—the formation of new institutions in the form of caisses populaires by the French-speaking Canadians of Quebec, and credit unions in the English-speaking communities of the nation.

Origins of Caisses Populaires and Credit Unions

The co-operative people's banks, and credit unions, and caisses populaires all have a common origin—the co-operative movement, and particularly the principles of co-operation as applied to lending and borrowing.[5] Robert Owen succeeded in forming a consumer's co-operative among the unemployed weavers of Rochdale, England, in 1844, and throughout western Europe there appeared at that time numerous articles and pamphlets on the concept of co-operatives. Of particular interest was one called "Credit Unions and Loan Unions," written by Victor Huber, that appeared in Germany. The idea that co-operative principles could be applied to borrowing and lending, as well as to buying and selling, was emerging and was soon being tested in Germany. Friedrich Raiffeisen, mayor of the village of Flammerfeld in southern Germany and a religious man, was deeply moved by the poverty of his rural people and by the impact on them of usurious loan charges. In December 1849 he started a co-operative

4. See below, chapter 15.

5. There is an extensive bibliography on co-operatives and credit unions. See Jack Dublin, *Credit Unions* (Detroit: Wayne State University Press, 1966), chap. 9, and bibliography on pp. 173-5. Numerous submissions to the Royal Commission on Banking and Finance came from credit union and caisses populaires organizations and these provide a wealth of detailed information on the operations of these institutions in Canada.

loan bank. It was philanthropic in nature, however, since the funds came from a few wealthy members and not from the ordinary farmers of the community. This approach was not successful and in about 1864 he established a credit society which was "a true co-operative institution of mutual self help in the provision of credit.... [Like] Huber, Raiffeisen considered the credit union far more than a mere credit co-operative. It was pre-eminently a moral and spiritual force."[6] This was the "Raiffeisen bank," which was to influence greatly the development of the credit union movement in many countries, including Canada. The Raiffeisen societies in Germany, Switzerland and the Netherlands have largely retained their original characteristics, for they remain small, rural and genuinely co-operative institutions.[7]

Another influence emerged from the experiments of Herman Schulze, mayor of Delitszch in the Rhineland, who was usually referred to as Schulze-Delitszch. He established a loan bank in 1850 for the urban workers—mechanics, craftsmen and small tradesmen. From the beginning his "People's Banks" were much more businesslike than the Raiffeisen societies. Funds were obtained by selling shares with an attractive rate of return to anyone, member or nonmember, who would buy them and by taking deposits from anyone; employees and officers were paid; only productive loans were made and these only to members; if necessary, funds were borrowed from commercial banks; high entrance fees were charged and members bought high-price shares with instalment payments; and unlimited liability of members was imposed. Schulze-Delitszch is recognized as the founder of urban credit unions, while Raiffeisen worked in rural areas, where he established hundreds of societies.

In France and Belgium the People's Banks have become state-controlled institutions specializing in short-term and long-term small business finance, and they receive a substantial portion of their funds from the state. In Italy, Germany and the Netherlands they do the same kind of business but are private banks approximating more the mutual type of institution than the co-operative type. This contrast between the evolution of the Schulze-Delitszch People's Banks and the Raiffeisen societies is worth recording because in essence it represents the two options to future development that face the credit unions in Canada today.

---

6. See John G. Perold, *Credit Union History*, Workers' Educational Association of Canada, Toronto, mimeographed, 1943.

7. See Gilles Mercure, *Credit Unions and Caisses Populaires*, working paper prepared for the Royal Commission on Banking and Finance, Queen's Printer, Ottawa, 1962, pp. 1-4.

The early developments in Germany attracted attention in a number of countries. Luigi Luzzatti modified German practices (low entrance fees, low-priced shares, unsecured loans, reserve fund, democratic control, limited liability) and began the urban credit union movement in Milan, Italy, in 1866; and he encouraged Leon Wollemborg to develop rural credit unions.[8] Henry Wolff was writing about co-operatives in Great Britain, and Charles Gide and others were doing the same in France. In Canada Alphonse Desjardins, a graduate of Lévis College, Quebec, became interested in the European credit union experiments when he was a Hansard reporter in the House of Commons in the 1880s. He corresponded with Luzzatti, Wolff, Gide and others and in 1900 introduced the caisses populaires or credit unions into North America with his "Caisse Populaire de Lévis." He described the circumstances in this way:

> It was the deplorable revelations brought about by law suits in Montreal and elsewhere, where poor borrowers had been obliged to pay to infamous usurers rates of interest amounting to several hundred per cent for most insignificant loans, that induced the writer to study carefully this problem with a view to finding out the best possible solution. The experience offered, above all by Germany, soon enlightened him.
>
> After 15 long years of constant study, at last believing that he had acquired the necessary theoretical knowledge and being induced to do so by many of the leaders of the movement in Europe, he undertook the establishment of the new system. Aided by the devoted zeal of a certain number of citizens – the parish priest and several members of the Catholic Clergy of the locality – he succeeded in founding in Lévis, Canada, the first bank of this type ever organized on this continent.
>
> The Lévis Co-operative People's Bank was organized on December 6, 1900 but for one reason or another did not begin its business until January 23, 1901.
>
> The first instalment paid was a dime and the total of the first collection amounted to only $26.40....
>
> What a comforting sight it is to see an honest workingman, or a settler coming to honor his signature.[9]

So Desjardins started the first Canadian credit union. He also played an important and direct part in establishing the first one in the United States, the credit union of St. Marie Parish of Manchester, New Hampshire, in 1909, and in obtaining the first credit union legislation in the United States, that of the state of Massachusetts. He

8. See Jack Dublin, *op. cit.*, pp. 145-6.
9. Alphonse Desjardins, *The Co-operative People's Bank, La Caisse Populaire*, Russell Sage Foundation, New York, August 1914, pp. 27-9.

also helped organize some of the very first credit unions in Ontario.[10]

Desjardins selected different aspects of the various European approaches to credit unions when he formed his first credit unions. From Raiffeisen he took the "bond of association" concept as the basis for organizing a local caisse populaire—the common bond in his case being the parish. From Italy came the system of "honour loans," limited liability, democratic control and unpaid committees. His emphasis on thrift and "self-help" may have come partly from the New England mutual savings banks. Shares were of small denominations, usually $5 payable in instalments and withdrawable on short notice. Both borrowers and savers were in practice members, the latter perhaps because limited liability necessitated that the caisses populaires depend largely on their members for funds. The co-operative character of the new institutions was to be preserved by the policy of one member one vote and by the emphasis on non-profit objectives, or in Desjardins's words:

> ... the people's bank is above all an institution aiming at the betterment of its members rather than at mere profits—an association of honest individuals rather than one of mere funds like a joint-stock company.

Members elected officers at a general meeting, and three committees of officers were actively in charge—board of administration, credit committee, and board of supervision which checked loans and audited accounts.

At first development was slow. The absence of legislation covering the operation of caisses populaires meant that Desjardins had to assume large personal liability in pursuing his objective of limited liability for the members.[11] Only two other local caisses were established before the province of Quebec in 1906 passed the Syndicates Act (covering co-operative societies) that Desjardins had drafted. While provinces did not, and do not, have the authority to incorporate banks, they were able to incorporate societies doing business only with their members. By 1910 there were about 50 caisses and by 1920 there were 113, with a membership of 32,000 and assets of $6.3 million.[12]

Desjardins attempted to obtain federal credit union legislation in 1907, and a bill passed the House of Commons but was defeated by

---

10. See Ontario Credit Union League Limited, *Brief to the Royal Commission on Banking and Finance*, hearings held at Toronto, April 12, 1962, p. A700.

11. See Mercure, *op. cit.*, pp. 8-20, for a brief account of the history of the caisses from which we have taken some of the material that follows.

12. See Table 12:1.

one vote in the Senate after both the Banking and Commerce Committee and the Justice Department reported the opinion that it was outside federal jurisdiction. During the sessions of 1909-10 and 1910-11 private members' bills on co-operative credit societies were introduced but failed to pass the House of Commons, and similar bills brought in by the Solicitor-General in 1913 and in 1914 received only first reading. [13]

Interest in co-operative credit was maintained because of concern over the state of agricultural credit. In 1913 the Saskatchewan Agricultural Credit Commission was appointed, and it, together with an American commission, studied credit organizations of Europe. Then in 1923 Dr. H. M. Tory, President of the University of Alberta, was authorized by the Minister of Finance to inquire into provincial systems of agricultural credit. He reported in 1924, and submitted a supplementary report in 1925 in which he said,

> I am of the opinion that the development of co-operative organizations is the proper way to proceed and for the following reasons: —
> 1. It will give the farmer himself the experience which will teach him how to use money advantageously and in a business way.
> 2. It will, if successful, lead ultimately to financial independence by putting him in relation to a self-supporting institution through which capital can be commanded.
>
> I am further of the opinion that the organization, supervision and control of this type of credit should be left to the provinces. Dominion supervision would be difficult and expensive.[14]

In accepting this opinion, the federal government missed the opportunity to become an influential force in the regulation of what was later to become an important type of financial intermediary in Canada. The field was left to the provinces. It is true that in 1953 the federal government passed the Co-operative Credit Association Act, which facilitated credit union pooling on the national level and established that provincial centrals of credit unions and caisses populaires, both of which we will examine later, were constitutional and could be registered under federal legislation. But this organization has constituted a relatively insignificant incursion of the federal government into the field of co-operative credit, and the thrust of development has remained in the provincial sphere.

Ontario was the first province outside of Quebec to introduce such legislation. In 1922 it passed the Co-operative Credit Societies Act,

---

13. See "Co-operative Credit," *Canada Year Book* (Ottawa: King's Printer, 1925), pp. 711-12.
14. *Ibid.*, p. 712.

but because of some abuse of the provisions the Ontario government, after a period, refused to issue further credit society charters.[15] Leadership for the formation of credit unions in English-speaking parts of Canada then passed to Nova Scotia. In 1930 the Extension Department of the St. Francis Xavier University, Antigonish, Nova Scotia, was organized and it soon became internationally famous for its work in co-operative organization. In 1932 Nova Scotia passed the Credit Union Societies Act, which became a model for the other provinces. Prince Edward Island and New Brunswick each followed with one in 1936, Manitoba and Saskatchewan in 1937, Alberta and British Columbia in 1938 and Ontario in 1940.

Legislation governing the operations of credit unions and caisses populaires vary from province to province. Generally speaking, a small group of people, usually about ten, having a common bond of occupation or association or a well-defined neighbourhood may apply for a credit union charter. In Quebec there is no grant of a charter, but incorporation comes through deposit of a memorandum of association and by-laws with municipal and provincial officers. Quebec membership is restricted to persons, associations and corporations within a territory outlined in the by-laws and not exceeding the boundaries of a city or provincial electoral district.

Once this is done, a board and officers are elected, committees formed, and facilities arranged for (frequently in the premises of the business or institution concerned if occupation is the common bond), and, within the limitations of provincial legislation and of charter or memorandum of association and by-laws, the new credit union or caisse populaire becomes a going concern. Voluntary assistance plays a continuing and important part in the operation of most locals, and their dominant characteristics are their local autonomy, bond of association, spirit of mutual assistance, non-profit emphasis, and their co-operative organizational and operational concepts and methods, including one member one vote.

Legislative controls relating to permissible investments, sources of funds, rates of interest, reserve funds, auditing and supervision also vary from province to province, and we need not detail them here.[16] Some generalizations can, however, be made. Both secured and unsecured lending is permitted, giving the locals great leeway in this area, and they enjoy similar leeway in most provinces in purchasing

15. See Perold, *op. cit.*
16. For a 1962 summary of these provisions as they relate to credit unions see National Association of Canadian Credit Unions, *Brief to the Royal Commission on Banking and Finance*, hearings held at Ottawa, July 13, 1962, pp. A276-401. However, some provincial legislation has been amended since 1962.

securities. Interest rates on loans are generally limited to 1% per month, although in British Columbia federal Small Loans Act rates apply, and the maximum rate on "large" loans is 1½% per month. Locals across the country may raise funds by selling shares and taking deposits from members; and, subject to limits expressed in terms of a percentage of assets or capital, they may supplement the funds of their members by borrowing from non-members, including financial institutions. Minimum legal liquidity requirements exist only in a few provinces; their purpose is to ensure that cash withdrawals can always be met. Most provinces require that some portion of annual net income be retained as a reserve. Distribution of the remainder again varies between the provinces, each deciding in its own way how much should go as a rebate to borrowing members and how much should go as an extra dividend to shareholders, and how much should be allocated for "educational purposes."

Subsequent analysis will show that there are substantial differences between the operations of the caisses populaires and the credit unions in Canada. But both encountered the problem of how to operate as local, independent organizations when for many reasons economies could be effected by banding together. The solution was for local credit unions and caisses populaires to form regional leagues, or associations, or unions, to further their common interest. These included promoting desired credit union legislation, organizing credit union locals, assisting locals in the supervision of their accounting, providing officer and member education and a ready source of supplies, and also establishing, either as a department of those regional leagues or as separate corporate entities, central organizations—commonly referred to as *centrals*—for receiving surplus funds from member locals, lending emergency funds to them, clearing cheques and providing other financial services to their members.

In Quebec the initial unifying influence of Desjardins gave way in the 1920s to the formation of four regional unions—in Quebec, Montreal, Trois-Rivières and Gaspé—and most caisses affiliated themselves with one of the regional organizations. The regional unions began to act as banker to the local caisses, and as a cheque-clearing house, and encouraged development of the movement in general. These four regional unions in 1932 formed La Fédération de Québec des Unions Régionales des Caisses Populaires Desjardins. The Quebec government immediately gave the federation authority to supervise its members and a subsidy to finance that activity. In some cases non-financial local co-operative societies were also members of these centrals. The present structure was attained in the period

1935-45. By that time a network of caisses reflecting the network of parishes had emerged fully; about a dozen very large caisses existed; six additional regional unions, making ten in all, were formed and all were members of the federation.

Supervision of the whole system became more efficient. However, some of the older caisses began to object bitterly to the attempts of the federation to raise standards and eliminate questionable practices. In 1945 the president of the federation took about a dozen of the caisses around Montreal out of the federation and formed a new one — La Fédération de Montréal. Mercure described the situation this way in 1962:

> The birth of the Fédération de Montréal was accompanied by much politicking from both sides, and by byzantine quarrels on fine points of the Desjardins doctrine allegedly betrayed by this or that man. This merely confused the only real issue which was an honest difference of opinion about the limit of the authority of the Federation over its autonomous affiliates. Naturally, the new Federation formed by this splinter group was a weak organization of strong members; this without inconvenience for a while; but they started founding new caisses after 1954-55 — and have found now that they would like to have firmer control over these newcomers. So there is nothing anymore to keep apart the two groups, but for the bitterness left over from their quarrel of the past.[17]

But the two groups are still apart, so there are eleven central societies of caisses populaires in Quebec, ten linked to La Fédération de Québec des Unions Régionales des Caisses Populaires Desjardins, and one operated as a department of La Fédération de Montréal.

French-speaking communities outside of Quebec have also formed caisses populaires and central organizations, although the way they operate is in many cases more akin to the "English" credit unions than the caisses populaires of Quebec. In Ontario there are three such centrals, and in Manitoba and New Brunswick one each.

The credit union, as distinct from the caisse populaire movement, has also evolved a system of centrals. These centrals in some provinces are the co-operative credit societies formed by the local provincial credit unions, and in others are departments of Credit Union Leagues formed by the locals. In the provinces of Newfoundland, Prince Edward Island, Nova Scotia, New Brunswick, Manitoba, Saskatchewan, Alberta and British Columbia, the local credit unions are organized around one provincial central, while in Ontario there are two and in Quebec three centrals. In 1968 there were twenty-nine centrals in Canada.

---

17. See Mercure, *op. cit.*, pp. 12-15, for this and preceding details.

Specialized financial institutions have been formed by the credit unions of some provinces to provide additional services. CUNA Mutual Insurance Society, incorporated in the United States in 1935, was registered in Canada in 1942, and locals began to insure their members on a group basis based both on share holdings and outstanding balance of loans. The locals were pioneers in this field, and only many years later did the chartered banks begin to offer such insurance arrangements. A Co-operative Fire and Casualty Company was also formed with the assistance of credit unionists. In 1952 the Co-operative Trust Company Ltd. was formed in Saskatchewan to provide state administration and trustee and guarantor services, and to make long-term mortgage loans to credit unions. It also acts as administrator of the Family Farm Credit Act, under which loans are granted to assist family farms.[18] In 1962 La Société de Fiducie du Québec (Quebec Trust Company) was incorporated, and was acquired by the Desjardins movement in 1963. It provides personal, corporate and other trust services, as well as services related to the management and transfer of property, and it operates guaranteed deposit and other investment funds. The latter also acquired control of the Quebec Savings Bank, obtained a chartered bank charter for it, renamed it the People's Bank and then saw it merged with the Provincial Bank of Canada, in which it also had made a significant investment. This tie between the Desjardins movement and a chartered bank may yet prove to be the route by which the caisses populaires locals are integrated into a full-fledged banking system.

Landmark Credit Limited was incorporated in 1962 in Ontario for the main purpose of supplying second mortgage money to credit union members, and in 1965 the Landmark Savings and Loan Association was formed in Ontario to take over and expand the growing first mortgage business of the former.

A national organization under federal charter, designed to serve as banker to the provincial centrals (and also other types of co-operative societies), began operation in 1954, as the Canadian Co-operative Credit Society; but its success as a national central has been limited since only four provincial centrals became members of it. There is also the Credit Union National Association (CUNA) organized in the United States in 1934, which has become an international association of the state, provincial or regional leagues, federations, societies, or centrals, and to which some of the Canadian centrals belong. The names of some of its departments reflect its services to the member leagues and federations: advertising and promotion; credit union

18. See Canada, Department of Agriculture, Economics Branch, *Credit Unions in Canada*, 1963 (Ottawa: Queen's Printer, 1964), pp. 6-7.

executive services; education; data processing; management consultant; legislative; insurance services; organization expansion; personnel; publications; research and economics.[19] Affiliates of CUNA supply materials (CUNA Supply Co-operative) and insurance (CUNA Mutual Insurance Society) to unions and members.

As a result of all these developments the structure of the co-operative credit movement as related to Canada is of the following nature:[20]

1. Local caisses populaires and credit unions.
2. Centrals
   - (a) Newfoundland
     - —The Terra Nova Co-operative Credit Society Ltd.
   - (b) Prince Edward Island
     - —Share and Loan Department, P.E.I. Credit Union League, Ltd.
   - (c) Nova Scotia
     - —Deposit and Loan Department, Nova Scotia Credit Union League
   - (d) New Brunswick
     - —Central Credit Department, New Brunswick Credit Union Federation Ltd.
     - —Caisse Centrale, La Fédération des Caisses Populaires Acadiennes Ltée.
   - (e) Quebec
     - (1) Affiliated with La Fédération des Caisses Populaires Desjardins, Lévis,
       - —Union Régionale des Caisses Populaires Desjardins de Trois-Rivières
       - —Union Régionale des Caisses Populaires de Gaspé
       - —La Caisse Centrale Desjardins de Montréal
       - —La Caisse Centrale Desjardins de Sherbrooke
       - —Union Régionale des Caisses Populaires de Rimouski
       - —La Caisse Centrale Desjardins de l'Ouest-Québecois
       - —Union Régionale de St-Hyacinthe des Caisses Populaires Desjardins
       - —La Caisse Régionale Desjardins de Joliette
       - —Union Régionale de Caisses Populaires de Chicoutimi
       - —Union Régionale des Caisses Populaires Desjardins

19. See Dublin, *op. cit.*, p. 95.
20. See Canada, Department of Agriculture, *Credit Unions in Canada*, 1963, pp. 4, 5.

(2) Not affiliated with above
- La Fédération de Montréal des Caisses Desjardins

(3) Credit Union Leagues
- La Ligue des Caisses d'Économie du Québec
- Quebec Central Credit Union
- Fédération des Caisses d'Économie du Québec

(f) Ontario
- Central Credit Department, Ontario Credit Union League
- Ontario Co-operative Credit Society
- La Caisse Régionale de Cochrane et Temiskaming Ltée.
- La Caisse Régionale de Nipissing-Sudbury
- La Fédération des Caisses Populaires Canadiennes-Françaises de l'Ontario Ltée.

(g) Manitoba
- Co-operative Credit Society of Manitoba Ltd.
- La Centrale des Caisses Populaires du Manitoba Credit Union Society Ltd.

(h) Saskatchewan
- Saskatchewan Co-operative Credit Society Ltd.

(i) Alberta
- Credit Union Federation of Alberta Ltd.

(j) British Columbia
- British Columbia Central Credit Union

3. National Organization and Membership*

The Canadian Co-operative Credit Society
- B.C. Central Credit Union
- Co-operative Credit Society of Manitoba Ltd.
- Ontario Co-operative Credit Society
- Saskatchewan Co-operative Credit Society Ltd.

4. International

Credit Union National Association

(One credit union league or society from each province except Newfoundland was a member. No caisses populaires leagues were.)

*Excluding non-financial members such as co-operative retail organizations.

Growth and Development

RELATIVE SIZE AND RATE OF GROWTH

Charts 12:1 and 12:2 show that the growth to prominence, both absolutely and relative to financial intermediaries in general, of the caisses populaires and credit unions really began in the early 1940s. In 1940 their assets accounted for .3% of total financial intermediary assets and for .4% of total private financial intermediary assets, with the equivalent figures growing to 1.7% and 2.1% by 1950, to 3.3% and 4.2% by 1960, and 4.2% and 5.6% by 1968. Whereas the caisses populaires and credit unions had 179 locals and 46,000 members in 1930, in 1968 they had 4,861 locals and 4,632,000 members (see Table 12:1 below). Their development after the Second World War was one of the more important events in the Canadian capital market during that period.

Their rate of growth, however, did not remain constant, and the experiences of the caisses populaires and of credit unions have not been identical. Table 12:1 shows that the peak growth rate of caisses populaires and credit unions, in terms of growth of members, of locals, and of assets, occurred in the decade ended 1945, with particularly high growth rates of members and locals (31% and 33% annually respectively) in the first half of that decade and of assets in the last half (42% annually). After that, growth rates declined. The growth of members for the caisses populaires became stabilized at around 8% per annum, there has been hardly any increase in the number of locals after 1965, and assets which had grown at about 12-14% per annum until 1968 dropped to 9%. The credit unions did not slow down to those growth rates until the 1960-4 period, and their growth of assets remained slightly higher than those of the caisses populaires but their growth rate also declined noticeably in 1968. Both caisse populaire and credit union assets were growing substantially faster than total financial intermediary assets up to 1967. And both continued to experience an increase in membership well in excess of the growth of Canada's population, the ratio of members to population reaching 23.5% in 1969.

One of the most apparent and persistent differences between the caisses populaires and the credit unions was the relative size of their individual locals. For example, in 1968 the locals of the former had assets, on the average, of about $1,385,000 and about 1,800 members, while the average credit union had assets of only $525,000 and about 600 members. The principal reason for this difference appears to rest in the concept of "bond of association" that each has adopted. The caisses populaires from the beginning adopted the parish as the common bond, and the parish, in addition to its impor-

Chart 12:1 – Growth of Assets of Caisses Populaires and Credit Unions 1935-1970

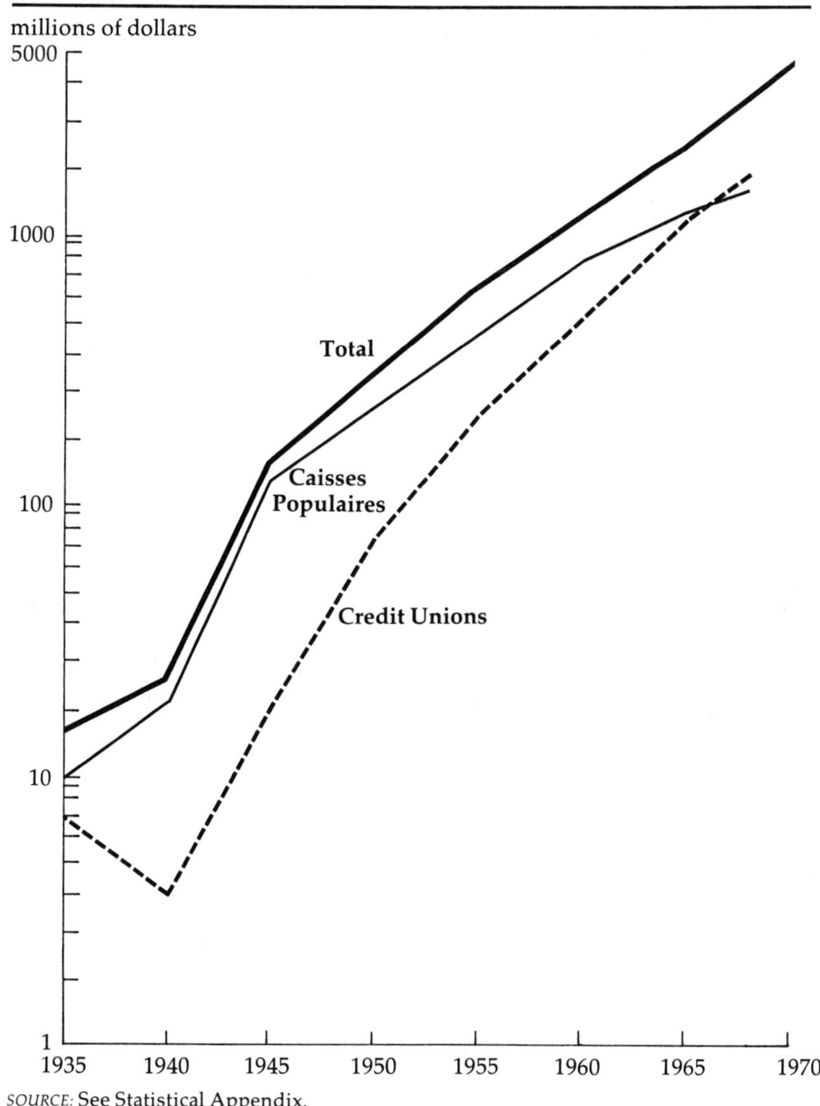

SOURCE: See Statistical Appendix.

tant religious and social aspects, had explicit geographical or territorial attributes. These geographical attributes were ideal for developing a retail financial outlet of efficient size. Not so the credit unions

Table 12:1 Caisses Populaires and Credit Unions: Members, Locals, Assets 1910-1969 (selected years)

	QUEBEC CAISSES POPULAIRES *Members*			*Locals*			*Assets*			*Members*		
	No. (000)	Per cent of total	Annual growth rate[3] %	No.	Per cent of total	Annual Growth rate %	$mns.	Per cent of total	Annual growth rate %	No. (000)	Per cent of total	Annual growth rate %
1910	n.a.	n.a.	—	50[1]	100	—	.2	100	—	—	—	—
1920	32	100	—	113	100	8.5	6	100	—	—	—	—
1930	45[1]	98	3.5	150[1]	84	2.9	11	100	6.3	1	2	—
1935	47	90	.9	239	86	9.8	10	100	−1.9	5	10	—
1940	119	59	20.4	549	47	18.1	21	84	16.0	82	41	75.0
1945	389	66	25.2	912	41	10.7	125	86	42.9	202	34	19.8
1950	619	60	9.7	1088	37	3.6	235	75	13.5	417	40	15.7
1955	883	51	7.4	1161	28	1.3	406	62	11.5	848	49	15.2
1960	1268	50	7.5	1249	27	1.5	724	56	12.3	1286	50	8.6
1964	1704	50	7.7	1315	27	1.3	1147	52	12.2	1714	50	7.5
1965	1857	51	9.0	1325	27	.8	1308[1]	51	14.0	1820	49	6.2
1966	2037	53	9.7	1325	27	.0	1477	50	12.9	1823	47	.2
1967	2215	51	8.7	1322	27	−.2	1686	50	14.2	2093	49	14.8
1968	2402	52	8.4	1331	27	.7	1844	50	9.4	2230	48	6.5
1969	n.a.	n.a.	n.a.	n.a.	n.a.	n.a.	n.a.	n.a.	n.a.	n.a.	n.a.	n.a.

SOURCE: For period 1910-50 from Gilles Mercure, *Credit Unions and Caisses Populaires, ibid.*, and Queen's Printer, Ottawa, and Queen's Printer, Quebec. Later figures from Canada, Department of Agriculture, *Credit Unions in Canada*, annual, D.B.S., *Credit Unions*, annual, Quebec Bureau of Statistics, *Caisses Populaires 1953-1962*, April 1964, and *Quebec Year Book*, annual. Not all inconsistencies between these various sources of data have been reconciled, but they are not significant.

[1]Estimate.
[2]Including caisses populaires outside of Quebec.
[3]All annual growth rate figures in this table refer to average annual growth rates for the period bounded by the year against which the rate is shown and the preceding year shown.

of Ontario and Quebec. Their common bond was frequently not explicitly geographically oriented, but rather, following the practice of the U.S. credit unions, was based on occupation or place of work or association. This tended to limit the size of credit union locals and so inhibited their development into efficient organizations.

Table 12:2, which gives some provincial data, illustrates this point, although the data do not distinguish between caisses populaires and credit unions. It shows that in Quebec, where the density of local members to population was by far the highest of any province

CREDIT UNIONS[2]						TOTAL						
Locals			Assets			Members			Locals		Assets	
No.	Per cent of total	Annual growth rate %	$ mns.	Per cent of total	Annual growth rate %	No. (000)	As percentage of population %	Annual growth rate %	No.	Annual growth rate %	$ mns.	Annual growth rate %
—	—	—	—	—	—	—	—	—	50[1]	—	—	—
—	—	—	—	—	—	32	—	—	113	8.5	6	—
29	16	—	—	—	—	46	—	3.7	179	4.7	11	6.3
38	14	—	—	—	—	52	—	2.5	277	9.1	10	−1.9
618	53	30.5	4	16	—	201	1.8	31.0	1167	33.3	25	20.1
1307	59	16.1	21	14	39.3	591	4.9	24.6	2219	13.7	146	42.3
1877	63	7.5	77	25	29.7	1036	7.5	11.9	2965	6.0	312	16.4
2939	72	9.4	247	38	26.3	1731	11.1	10.2	4100	6.7	653	15.9
3359	73	2.7	575	44	18.4	2554	14.2	8.1	4608	2.4	1299	14.7
3555	73	1.4	1066	48	16.7	3418	17.6	7.6	4870	1.4	2213	14.2
3614	73	1.7	1234	49	15.8	3677	18.6	7.6	4939	1.4	2542	14.9
3609	73	−.1	1449	50	17.4	3860	19.3	5.0	4934	−.1	2926	15.1
3589	73	−.6	1681	50	16.0	4308	21.0	11.6	4911	−.5	3367	15.1
3530	73	−1.6	1855	50	10.4	4632	22.3	7.5	4861	−1.0	3699	9.9
n.a.	n.a.	n.a.	n.a.	n.a.	n.a.	5003	23.5	8.0	4769	−1.9	4064	9.9

(44%), the proportion of locals that were community-based was also very high (86%), and its average assets per local were almost the highest of any province, that is, $1,142,000. Saskatchewan, with the second highest density and the highest average assets per local, had community-based locals amounting to 84% of the total. Ontario has a density of only 12%, its community-based locals are only 17% of its total number of locals, and its average assets per local are much below the national average. The growth of membership in Ontario has also been below the national average.

Chart 12:2 — Relative Size of Assets of Caisses Populaires and Credit Unions 1915-1968

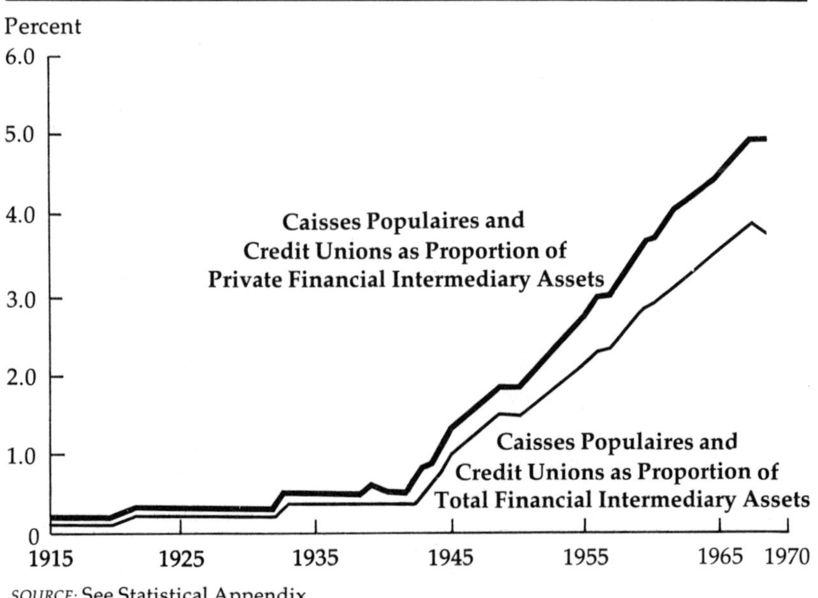

SOURCE: See Statistical Appendix.

In general it would seem that the failure of the credit union movement to become more territorially oriented in the highly populated parts of the country has limited its appeal and inhibited its evolution into more efficient-sized units, whereas the Quebec caisse populaire movement with its parish base has been much more successful.

STRUCTURE OF ASSETS

A comparison of the structure of assets of the caisses populaires and credit unions reveals that they pursue quite different lending practices. A major difference is that the caisses populaires place less emphasis on making personal loans to members and more on making mortgage loans, particularly residential mortgage loans, and on buying securities than do the credit unions. The motivation of the credit union was much more that of providing loans to its members — in its early years emergency or distress loans and later loans for purchasing consumer durable goods — than of being a "thrift" orga-

Table 12:2 Provincial Comparison of Credit Unions and Caisses Populaires 1965, 1968

	Members to population %		Assets of locals per local members $		Average assets per local ($000)		Growth of local membership 1968 %	Common bond basis of locals percentage distribution: Rural community %		Urban community %		Occupational %		Other %	
	(1)		(2)		(3)		(4)	(5)		(6)		(7)		(8)	
	1965	1968	1965	1968	1965	1968		1965	1968	1965	1968	1965	1968	1965	1968
British Columbia	14	16	683	867	617	1095	17.1	25	—	20	—	41	—	14	100
Alberta	8	9	555	745	214	375	9.2	37	35	11	11	22	36	30	18
Saskatchewan	25	31	1090	1280	872	1349	6.7	79	80	4	4	9	9	8	7
Manitoba	15	18	725	884	410	657	5.6	40	44	3	4	29	29	28	23
Ontario	11	12	671	808	379	424	4.7	8	—	3	9	59	60	30	31
Quebec	35	44	694	761	911	1142	7.9	46	45	34	41	20	14	—	—
New Brunswick	16	17	287	358	169	237	4.3	54	53	15	15	24	24	7	8
Nova Scotia	11	12	350	437	167	257	.2	48	48	19	20	28	27	5	—
Prince Edward Island	8	9	301	404	77	150	2.6	82	78	18	22	—		—	—
Newfoundland	1	1	199	275	21	21	5.0	12	—	71	85	17	14	—	1
Northwest Territories	—	1	—	192	—	21	9.2								
Canada	19	22	691	799	582	761	5.9	33	29	17	21	35	26	15	24

SOURCE: Canada, Department of Agriculture, *Credit Unions in Canada*, annual, and D.B.S. *Credit Unions*, annual, Queen's Printer, Ottawa.

Table 12:3 Distribution of Assets, Caisses Populaires and Credit Unions[1] 1953-1968 (selected years)

	1953			1955			1960			1964	
	C.P. %	C.U. %	TOTAL %	C.P. %	C.U. %	TOTAL %	C.P. %	C.U. %	TOTAL %	C.P. %	C.U. %
Cash	14.4	2.1	10.4	16.2	8.6	13.4	17.9	6.4	12.8	16.4	6.0
Loans }	46.2	82.9	28.6	47.9	77.0	28.7	48.6	79.8	32.9	13.0	64.4
Mortgages }			29.6			30.2			29.6	40.3	15.0
Investments	36.1	9.0	27.3	32.4	12.7	24.9	29.3	11.7	21.4	26.3	12.0
Other	3.3	6.0	4.1	3.5	1.7	2.8	4.2	2.1	3.3	4.0	2.6
Total—%	100	100	100	100	100	100	100	100	100	100	100

SOURCE: See Table 12:1.

[1]Quebec caisses populaires data are shown in the first column of each year and the second column includes caisses populaires outside of Quebec.

nization for its members, whereas the opposite was the case with the caisses populaires. This will be seen more clearly when we examine the liability structure of the two institutions. The lending activity of credit unions is simplified by their emphasis on making loans to members, that is, to individuals about whom they already have information relating to credit worthiness, whereas a significant portion of the funds of the caisses populaires is allocated to non-member borrowers. Table 12:3 shows that in 1968 the caisses populaires had only 20% of their assets in loans, compared with 54% for the credit unions, and data for the latter even include caisses populaires outside Quebec. As a result only a small proportion of the members of caisses populaires are normally borrowers, whereas a much higher proportion of credit union members are borrowers at any one time.[21] The caisses populaires had 35% in mortgages compared with 25% for the credit unions; they had 23% in investments while the credit unions had 13%; and they held much more cash (17%) than did the credit unions (5%). It must be noted, however, that over the last decade the caisses populaires have reduced the proportion of funds invested in securities and mortgages and have increased the proportion in loans, while the credit unions have done

21. See Royal Commission on Banking and Finance, *Report* (Ottawa: Queen's Printer, 1964), p. 159.

	1965			1966			1967			1968		
TOTAL %	C.P. %	C.U. %	TOTAL %	C.P. %	C.U. %	TOTAL %	C.P. %	C.U. %	TOTAL %	C.P. %	C.U. %	TOTAL %
11.4	16.6	6.2	11.1	16.6	5.0	10.9	16.2	5.0	10.6	17.0	5.2	11.1
37.8	15.6	59.8	38.8	17.6	56.8	37.0	18.5	56.1	37.3	20.0	54.1	37.1
28.1	38.4	17.4	27.4	36.7	21.9	29.4	35.5	22.1	28.8	35.3	24.6	29.9
19.4	25.3	13.6	19.1	24.6	13.4	19.0	25.4	13.6	19.5	23.3	12.5	17.9
3.4	4.1	3.0	3.6	4.5	2.9	3.7	4.4	3.2	3.8	4.4	3.6	4.0
100	100	100	100	100	100	100	100	100	100	100	100	100

the opposite, so that the differences in their lending practices are not as great now as they were. If we recall the rapid growth of consumer credit[22] and the attractive rates of interest to be earned in that field, it seems that the credit unions, with their heavy emphasis on personal lending, have pursued quite appropriate lending policies, and that the caisses populaires may to some extent have missed a valuable opportunity by not cultivating this business earlier.

There are several reasons why the caisses populaires did not develop their personal loan business earlier. At the very beginning of their operation, loans for "productive" purposes were emphasized and loans for ordinary consumption expenditures were refused.[23] At the same time Desjardins felt it was quite appropriate for a local caisse to make mortgage loans and also loans of 5, 10, 15, 20, or more years to maturity repayable in annual instalments,[24] including loans in the form of serial municipal debentures. The Quebec civil code also made it difficult to engage in chattel mortgage financing, which would discourage lending for the purchase of durable consumer goods. Also, the practice of not permitting the credit committees of caisses populaires to delegate the power to approve loans discour-

22. See chapter 11.
23. See Mercure, *op. cit.*, p. 7.
24. See Desjardins, *op. cit.*, p. 40.

aged the examination of large numbers of small loans.[25] But the personal loan business of the caisses populaires has now begun to increase in relative importance and probably will continue to do so.

The relatively greater cash holdings of the caisses populaires is explained by the greater importance of their highly liquid deposit liabilities, including chequing deposits, and the illiquid character of their assets. With relatively more long-term assets and relatively more short-term liabilities, it is not surprising that the caisses populaires maintain larger cash reserve ratios than do the credit unions. One important part of the long-term assets of the Quebec caisse populaire locals is their holdings of securities, particularly those issued by Quebec municipalities and school boards. Their investments amounted to $430 million in 1968 and they were probably the largest buyers of local government securities in Quebec. Most of the actual acquisition of securities is effected by the centrals for the local caisses.

These generalizations hide substantial differences in lending practices between the different provinces and between locals within a given province. The locals operate independently of each other, and the legislation under which they operate gives them ample opportunity to pursue different lending practices. In British Columbia, for example, a few locals emphasize medium- and long-term loans to fishermen, whereas many locals in Canada will lend only for short term. In Saskatchewan farm financing is important, as it is in the Maritimes, and Saskatchewan locals also frequently make business loans, whereas this is not common generally among credit unions. Some locals will charge the legal maximum rate of 1% per month, paying out surplus after dividends on shares and interest on deposits, in the form of a patronage dividend; whereas others will charge less, particularly on certain loans, and pay no patronage dividend. Some caisses populaires in Quebec have greatly increased their unsecured personal lending business while others have not.

STRUCTURE OF LIABILITIES

The differences between the sources of funds of the caisses populaires and credit unions are just as striking as the differences in their utilization of funds just discussed. The credit unions depend heavily on "shares" as a source of funds. Such liabilities amounted to 62% of their total liabilities in 1968, whereas shares accounted for only 11% of caisses populaires liabilities (see Table 12:4). The main

25. See Mercure, *op. cit.*, p. 132.

source of funds for the caisses populaires was deposits and these were 83% of their liabilities in 1968, in sharp contrast to the credit union figure of 24%. Credit unions are more inclined to supplement their funds with loans than are the caisses populaires, who studiously avoid such activity. Both hold about the same reserves and retained earnings, roughly 6% or 7% of total liabilities. The credit unions with place of employment as the common bond, for example those of Ontario, have had one significant advantage in the accumulation of funds of members, namely the payroll deduction. The Ontario Credit Union League has put it this way:

> One of the greatest incentives for saving in the credit union is the privilege of payroll deduction for credit union purposes, which has been granted by many industries to the credit union operating in their plant or business. It provides a painless way for the member to save by adding regular and specified sums to his credit union share account. In addition, it makes for regular repayments to the credit union of the money that the member has borrowed from his credit union.[26]

These important payroll deduction facilities are not available to other financial intermediaries, thereby giving the credit unions a unique advantage.

The encouragement of the deposit business by the caisses populaires began in the early years of their existence. Desjardins explained in 1907 that he soon realized that purchasing shares only did not suit members who would soon require the use of their funds, so he began taking deposits. As time went on, it was thought that holding of large numbers of shares by caisses populaires members should actually be discouraged, possibly so as to prevent individual members from dominating the operation of the locals (through threat of making large withdrawals) and to help maintain the dividend rate. Consequently a fee of 2% or higher is charged for each subscription of new shares and a limit is placed on the number of shares an individual member can hold. A great majority of the members of the caisses populaires hold only one qualifying share, holding virtually all their funds in the form of deposits.

The credit unions, in contrast, have never depended primarily on deposits as a source of funds. In 1968 they accounted for 24% of total liabilities compared with 13% in 1964 and 21% in 1953.

However, the differences between shares and deposits, as here

---

26. See *Brief to the Royal Commission on Banking and Finance,* hearings held at Toronto, April 12, 1962, p. A705.

Table 12:4 Distribution of Liabilities, Caisses Populaires and Credit Unions 1953-1968 (selected years)

	1953			1955			1960			1964	
	C.P. %	C.U. %	Total %	C.P. %	C.U. %	Total %	C.P. %	C.U. %	Total %	C.P. %	C.U. %
Shares	6.5	69.8	27.2	6.6	67.6	29.7	6.3	74.2	36.8	8.2	72.3
Deposits	87.1	21.0	65.5	86.9	22.9	62.7	87.4	15.4	55.1	85.6	13.2
Loans and other debts	.5	n.a.	n.a.	.4	3.9	1.7	.5	5.8	2.8	.4	7.5
Retained earnings and reserves	5.8	n.a.	n.a.	6.0	5.7	5.9	5.8	4.6	5.3	5.7	7.0
Total	100	100	100	100	100	100	100	100	100	100	100

SOURCE: See Table 12:1.

used, should not be exaggerated. One writer has described them this way:

> The shares of credit unions and caisses populaires are a subordinated claim against the assets of the societies, after all other liabilities have been fully paid; in that respect, they are like what is usually named a share. Otherwise they are like deposits: they are issued and redeemed on a day-to-day basis at the request of the shareholders; they are entitled to a dividend that, even if it is somewhat uncertain like the dividends of companies, is rather stable and is subject to some ceiling.[27]

It would seem that the shares of caisses populaires and credit unions are quite similar to investment certificates and non-chequable savings or term deposits of trust companies and banks, and that their deposits are rather like the chequable savings and current account deposits of the banks.

OPERATIONS OF CENTRAL ORGANIZATIONS

While the locals in all provinces have formed one or more central organizations, these institutions have developed much further in some provinces than in others. For example, in 1969 all central credit

27. Mercure, *op. cit.*, p. 74.

	1965			1966			1967			1968		
Total %	C.P. %	C.U. %	Total %	C.P. %	C.U. %	Total %	C.P. %	C.U. %	Total %	C.P. %	C.U. %	Total %
39.1	8.9	65.3	38.5	9.6	67.1	38.1	10.5	64.9	37.7	11.0	61.6	36.4
50.8	85.2	20.1	51.0	84.4	18.2	51.6	83.7	21.9	52.8	83.0	24.2	53.5
3.8	.4	7.6	4.2	.5	7.2	3.8	.4	7.0	3.7	.4	7.4	3.9
6.3	5.5	7.0	6.3	5.5	7.5	6.5	5.4	6.2	5.8	5.6	6.8	6.2
100	100	100	100	100	100	100	100	100	100	100	100	100

unions made loans of $437 million, of which 58% were accounted for by Saskatchewan even though Saskatchewan locals accounted for only 10% of assets of locals in Canada; while Quebec centrals accounted for only 6% of central loans even though their locals had 54% of total assets of locals in Canada. Percentage distribution of central loans among the rest of the provinces in 1968 (with percentage of total local assets in brackets) was as follows: British Columbia 20% (8%), Alberta 5% (3%), Manitoba 3% (4%), Ontario 7% (19%), New Brunswick ¼% (1%) and Nova Scotia ½% (1%). Figures for Prince Edward Island and Newfoundland were negligible relative to the other provinces. However, since local co-operatives other than credit unions and caisses populaires are also members of the centrals —accounting for about one-fifth of the membership of the latter— these statistics can give only tentative indications of the degree of centralization.

The essential purpose of the provincial centrals, which is to accept surplus funds from and provide an emergency source of funds for the locals, is reflected in the structure of their assets and liabilities. In 1970, as Table 12:5 shows, 84% of the liabilities of provincial centrals were deposits of its member locals and 8% were share subscriptions of its members. But there are substantial differences in operation of the various provincial centrals. The eleven caisses populaires centrals of Quebec act as intermediaries between the local caisses and the chartered banks in the clearing of cheques, and between the local

Table 12:5 Distribution of Assets and Liabilities, Central Caisses Populaires and Credit Union Organizations 1955-1970 (selected years)

	1955 %	1960 %	1965 %	1968 %	1969 %	1970 %
Provincial Centrals						
Liabilities						
Shares	15	16	12	10	7	8
Deposits	79	75	72	77	78	84
Other	6	9	16	13	15	8
Assets						
Loans and mortgages	20	23	35	39	37	29
Investments	61	51	49	40	43	44
Other	19	26	16	21	20	27
Total – %	100	100	100	100	100	100
Total – $ millions	77.4	176.3	357.3	520.0	562.3	658.2
National Central (Canadian Co-operative Credit Society)						
Assets – $ millions	.1	.1	1.2	.5	.6	n.a.

SOURCE: See Table 12:1.

caisses and the bond market in bond transactions.[28] They also receive and manage the liquid reserves of the locals, investing them in bank deposits and securities. Strangely, they engage in very little lending activity with their member locals, pursuing a conservative tradition in such matters that has existed for many years.

The credit union centrals differ from the Quebec caisses populaires centrals in that they engage actively in making loans to members. While not all centrals provide the same range of services, as a group they engage in the following activities: receive term and demand deposits from members, which include credit union locals and other co-operatives, and make loans to them; clear cheques for their members; grant mortgage loans to individuals; and, where they have grown to important size, generally act as a unifying influence on the financial operation of the locals. As we have already noted, several

28. See Mercure, *op. cit.*, pp. 18-19.

closely affiliated companies have appeared that provide trustee and mortgage loan facilities to credit union members.

The only national central, the Canadian Co-operative Credit Society, was established in 1954 under the Federal Co-operative Credit Associations Act. Its primary credit union function is to receive deposits from its provincial central members and extend credit to them. However, only four out of the twenty-eight centrals have become members and, as Table 12:5 shows, its assets have remained small.

Conclusions

Reflecting on all of the foregoing discussion, we may ask, what explains the high relative rate of growth of the caisses populaires and the credit unions? It was not really that they introduced unique credit instruments or provided unique types of credit. There is little doubt that non-quantifiable influences played an important part. Disenchantment with the borrowing and savings accommodation available to individuals of modest means and small businessmen certainly existed when they first began to emerge in a significant way, for those were the days of the great depression. The appeal of a co-operative "non-profit," self-help type of organization was, in itself, a strong one in those groups, and the unique organizational structure of the caisses populaires and credit unions was able effectively to realize the potential in it. That appeal and that organizational structure were the important unique contributions of the caisses populaires and credit unions, ones which perhaps more than anything else explain why they emerged and began to grow to prominence.

But there was undoubtedly more to it than that. They were for a long period able to offer distinctly better rates to small borrowers and savers than the other financial institutions. Better lending accommodation was particularly important to the credit unions, for, contrary to the caisses populaires, they emphasized personal lending. The credit unions emerged at a time when the local bank branches did not really cater to the borrowing needs of individuals, and also at a time when institutionalized consumer credit was beginning to grow rapidly. The local credit union in many cases was able, therefore, to provide credit of a kind that the banks were not providing. Furthermore, being limited generally by law to charge no more than 1% per month and usually charging less, particularly after allowing for dividends and insurance benefits, they were exceedingly competitive with the institutions that were providing such credit—the sales finance and consumer loan companies. Also, their intimate knowledge of the character of their borrowing members and the strong moral pressure on members to repay loans (since they were borrowing the funds of other local members) may have given them a lower loss experience than that of private companies, thereby again enhancing their competitive position. Volunteer labour, free or low-cost premises in many cases, and exemption from corporation income tax further reduced the costs of both credit unions and caisses populaires, although it has been estimated that the latter is not an important influence.[29] Their daily hours of service were also more convenient than those of the banks. All the influences that drew borrowing customers to them also probably attracted savings, because to some extent the two are almost certainly functionally related. And while they did not generally offer substantially higher savings rates, they probably did so in some communities, particularly over the many years when the savings rate on bank deposits was kept at a low level, and especially in communities without trust and loan company branches. For many locals it seems more accurate to say that their rates were regarded as being about competitive with those available elsewhere. Payroll deduction facilities almost certainly enhanced the accumulation of savings through credit unions.

The unusually rapid development of the credit unions in Saskatchewan and the caisses populaires in Quebec merit special comment. The one thing they have in common is the preponderance of community- or territory-based locals, and it seems therefore that they received important benefits from evolving an organizational form that was superior to that of areas depending essentially on occupation or association as the common bond. Both also seem to have enjoyed particularly friendly local political climates. In Saskatchewan the Co-operative Commonwealth Federation (C.C.F.) party formed the provincial government for the first time in 1944, and true to its name it actively encouraged the co-operative movement, even forming a special department of Co-operation and Co-operative Development. The Quebec government was the first of any government in Canada to pass co-operative legislation, and the caisses populaires may well have had a special appeal in that province for, apart from the two Quebec savings banks, they were the

29. The Royal Commission on Banking and Finance argued that since their dividends are really interest, only the absence of a tax on their retained earnings gives them a competitive advantage, and this they estimated would amount to only about .1% to .25% of their assets.

only type of financial intermediary that was essentially indigenous to and wholly owned within the province. Prior to the 1920s the ratio of population to chartered bank branches was lower in Quebec than in Canada generally, but this was not the case thereafter, so it is not immediately apparent that the caisses populaires movement expanded because of an inadequate number of banking outlets, although it would require more detailed information than this to be certain on that point.

Up until the most recent statistics, the caisse populaire and credit union movement was doing well. Its membership was increasing faster than the population and until 1967 its assets were rising faster than those of most other financial intermediaries. However, some environmental conditions unfavourable to them have developed. The entry of the banks into personal lending has not only made that kind of credit available in some six thousand additional outlets in Canada and at rates that are close to those of the locals (which is a strong new competitive factor for the credit unions); but also all across the country the banks, trust companies and others have become exceedingly competitive in their bid for savings. In this environment the credit unions and caisses populaires do not have the competitive edge in interest rates on loans and savings that they used to have, and their financial advantage may now be limited largely to lower administrative costs (if they are lower) arising from volunteer labour and subsidized facilities.

In Quebec the ratio of members to population is now relatively high, which may mean that future growth will depend more on the success of the caisses in inducing members to deposit a larger proportion of their savings with them than in the past. This may be difficult to do. There is also the unanswered question of the effect that affluence will have on an institution that still bases its appeal at least partly on the virtues of self-help and mutual assistance and its operations partly on voluntary assistance, subsidized facilities and privileged payroll deduction facilities.

Within the context of this changing environment will the organizational structure remain adequate to meet competition? In Quebec and some parts of the country where the locals are community-based there is no reason why they should not, provided the unifying influence of the centrals is increasingly felt, permitting if necessary the long-term evolution of something more akin to a system of branches perhaps than a system of independent locals. We have already noted the interesting potential in the link that exists between the Desjardins movement in Quebec and one of the chartered banks. The closest parallel at present might be with sections of the retail food and the retail automotive and hardware industries, where local franchised outlets are independently owned and operated but within the context of the strong centralizing influence on operations and policy of one central organization. In this way all the new technology necessary for efficient financial operation could be utilized by the movement. But in areas where the locals are not now community-based and assets per local are relatively small, including particularly Ontario, long-term changes necessary for improving the relative position of the credit unions and perhaps even for maintaining their present position are more difficult to envisage.

That some of the environmental changes may already have begun to have an effect is suggested by recent information on the growth of credit union and caisse populaire assets. These grew by about 10% annually in 1968 and 1969 compared with 15% from 1964 to 1967. Canadian assets of the chartered banks increased by about 11% in 1968 and 1969. Also in 1968 assets of locals increased less quickly than total financial intermediary assets, which was the first time that this had happened. In the next decade or two the provincial supervisory authorities and the central organizations may have to concern themselves much more with the problem of maintaining a healthy movement than they needed to do in the past two decades of unusual and uninterrupted expansion.

13

Government Financial Intermediaries and Pension Plans

Government Financial Intermediaries

We noted in chapter 1 that in the hypothetical business world that economists technically refer to as a "perfectly competitive economy" there would not be much justification on economic grounds for the existence of government financial intermediaries.[1] It would be an economy in which competition would allocate factors of production to their most productive uses and would maximize their income; output produced would accurately reflect the relative preferences of consumers; costs of production would be minimized; and the income and costs referred to here would include both private and social income and private and social costs.

In this kind of economy the capital market too would be achieving maximum efficiency through competition, in the sense that it would operate to achieve efficiency of resource allocation not just in the rest of the economy but also within its own operations. The financial intermediary and brokerage institutions would be of "optimum" size and this size would be such as to ensure that conditions of perfect competition would prevail in the capital market. There would be a division of the financial capital allocation function between direct and indirect financing and between internal and external financing

1. I am indebted to Mr. E. J. Doak for assisting me in accumulating some of the material for this chapter. He subsequently completed a Ph.D. thesis in the field for the University of Toronto entitled *Financial Intermediation by Government: Theory and Canadian Experience Since 1867*. It constitutes the most detailed study available on government financial intermediation in Canada and includes not only a fairly detailed description of the operations of some of them but also an analysis of the extent to which they achieved their objectives.

that would equalize marginal costs of these different forms of financing. Types of primary and indirect securities issued would reflect perfectly the portfolio preferences of investors and this would also lead to a minimization of cost of capital to borrowers given those preferences. It is apparent that in this kind of capital market, government intervention could not be justified on grounds that it would achieve a more economically efficient allocation of resources.

Such intervention by government, it would seem, could only be justified for two reasons: to achieve objectives other than those automatically achieved by the "perfect" economy described above, and to correct resource and income allocation defects arising from the fact that the economy in reality is not perfectly efficient but rather suffers from imperfections or rigidities.

Given these grounds for government intervention, the question arises as to the form that such intervention should take. As far as intervention in the capital market is concerned it can take the following broad lines: making available information that will keep participants in the capital market better informed; prescribing rules of operations for capital market participants, including the provision of incentives for certain kinds of operations; and forming government financial institutions. A rational government in particular cases presumably would choose whichever one of these approaches would most efficiently achieve its desired objective. Such a government would know that in some instances these approaches are substitutes for each other in the achievement of desired objectives.

Our concern at the moment is to examine the history of Canadian governments with respect to the third approach—specifically, the history of government financial intermediation. The other approaches have, of course, been explored in discussing the statutory rules under which financial institutions and other capital market participants operate.

No further general comment need be made at this stage about the use of government intermediaries for achieving "non-economic" objectives, but it is useful to note what kinds of capital market imperfections might call for corrective measures. If the optimum size of a certain type of intermediary was such as to approximate monopoly conditions, either because of the risks inherent in the operation or because of diminishing marginal administration costs, then government would have to decide whether regulation or government ownership was the best approach to meeting the imperfections. Furthermore, it might be that there are "credit gaps" in the capital market in the sense that private institutions are not extending credit to all individual borrowers, or types of borrowers, or borrowers in certain regions of the country, with the required relative credit worthiness. This could arise because they are underestimating that credit worthiness; because the size of the amounts of capital required involves them in risks that they are not prepared or in a position to take; or because, in appraising credit worthiness, and specifically, the net rate of return borrowers may expect to realize from using borrowed funds, they are not in a position to take account of the net social rate of return in cases where net private and net social rates of return are not identical. It might also be that there are "gaps" in the capital market in the sense that the portfolio preferences of savers are not adequately reflected in the savings instruments made available by private institutions. We would expect one or a combination of these reasons to lie behind the formation of government financial intermediaries, or at least to be used by governments in rationalizing their formation.

GROWTH AND RELATIVE SIZE

A complete record of all cases of government financial intermediation would be very difficult to compile. This is because every loan scheme introduced by the federal government and the ten provincial governments would have to be regarded as a financial intermediary, as would all their contributory plans such as superannuation funds. We have, however, compiled data for all the important ones and we estimate that these would account for more than 90% of the assets or liabilities of government financial intermediaries.

Chart 13:1 and Table 13:1 provide a relatively comprehensive perspective on the rate of growth and relative size of government financial intermediaries in total, and individually, and by major type of lending activity. The chart shows that not until the 1930s was there any significant increase in the size of government financial intermediaries relative to total financial intermediary assets. In 1870 they accounted for 8% of such assets and also in 1930, with fluctuations as high as 11% both before the turn of the century and during and after the First World War. However, with the formation of the Bank of Canada in 1934, their relative size began to increase. By 1940 it was 14% of total intermediary assets, and by 1945 it was 20%. In much of the post–Second World War period the ratio did not rise very rapidly, standing at 21% in 1950 and 22% in 1960. But a further period of more rapid acceleration in relative size emerged in the 1960s and by 1968 the ratio had increased to 23%. An increase in the relative size of

Chart 13:1 – Government Financial Intermediary Assets 1870-1968

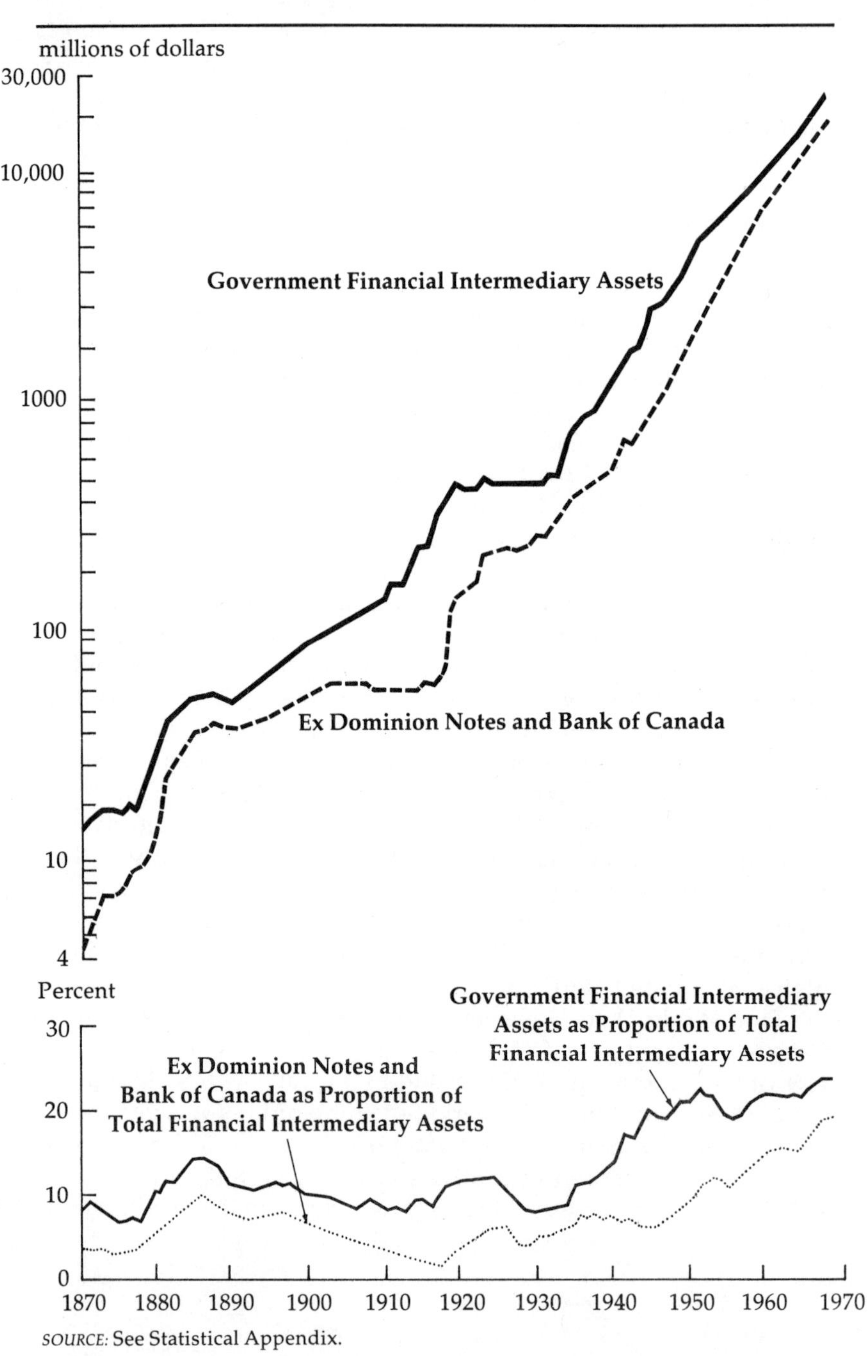

SOURCE: See Statistical Appendix.

government intermediaries from 8% to 23% in less than four decades represents a rapid and significant inroad of the public sector into the intermediation process.

The largest part of the increase, as Table 13:1 shows, is accounted for by federal government financial intermediaries. Provincial intermediary assets rose to considerable relative significance in the 1920s, accounting for 26% of government financial intermediary assets in 1930. But then the interest of the provincial governments in intermediation schemes diminished, while that of the federal government increased, so that even in 1960 provincial government intermediary assets were only 6% of total government intermediary assets. After that it increased sharply, standing at 18% in 1968, although it must specifically be recognized that this was largely because we have classified both the Caisse de Dépôt et Placement du Québec (the repository of Quebec Pension Plan funds) and the Canada Pension Plan as provincial intermediaries.

Table 13:1 also outlines the various types of government financial intermediaries that emerged and indicates roughly the timing of their changing growth rates relative to government intermediary assets in total, while the Statistical Appendix provides data on an annual basis of the changing size of these government intermediaries relative to total financial intermediary assets. Using these data a number of general points may be made. At the time of Confederation the note issue accounted for about 70% of government intermediary assets. Then began a period of rapid growth for the federal savings institutions, which in 1890 accounted for 72% of government intermediary assets and resulted in the latter category's rising distinctly more rapidly than private financial intermediary assets (see Chart 13:1). After that the federal savings banks levelled off in relative size, and gradually declined to insignificance. The Dominion Note Issue again emerged as the predominant government intermediary even before First World War financing, and in 1920 it accounted for 67% of government intermediary assets. Thereafter it declined steadily in relative size.

The period from the end of the First World War to 1930 saw several important developments in government financial intermediation: the emergence of provincial government intermediaries of significant size, mainly in the form of savings banks, agricultural loans, and housing loans; the increase to significant size of the federal government's annuity, insurance and pension account; the sharp decline in relative and absolute size of federal government intermediary assets in total, largely because of an absolute, not just relative, decline in the Dominion Note Issue; and the rise to some significance of government farm lending activity, both provincial and federal.

Table 13:1 Relative Size of Various Government Financial Intermediaries 1867-1968 (selected years)

(MILLIONS OF DOLLARS AND PERCENTAGE DISTRIBUTION)

	1867		1880		1890		1900		1910	
	$	%	$	%	$	%	$	%	$	%
I. By level of government										
1. Federal	6.0	100.0	30.0	100.0	55.0	100.0	84.6	100.0	151.2	100.0
2. Provincial	—	—	—	—	—	—	—	—	—	—
Total $mns.	6.0		30.0		55.0		84.6		151.2	
II. By type										
1. Monetary										
a) Dominion Note Issue	4.3	71.7	14.2	47.3	15.6	28.4	28.4	33.6	90.7	60.0
b) Bank of Canada	—	—	—	—	—	—	—	—	—	—
2. Savings banks										
a) Federal	1.7	28.3	15.8	52.7	39.4	71.6	56.1	66.3	58.0	38.4
b) Provincial	—	—	—	—	—	—	—	—	—	—
Total	1.7	28.3	15.8	52.7	39.4	71.6	56.1	66.3	58.0	38.4
3. Annuity, insurance, pensions										
a) Federal Annuity	—	—	—	—	—	—	—	—	.8	.6
b) Federal Insurance & Pensions	—	—	—	—	—	—	.1	.1	1.7	1.0
c) Provincial Insurance & Pensions[1]	—	—	—	—	—	—	—	—	—	—
d) Canada Pension Plan	—	—	—	—	—	—	—	—	—	—
e) Caisse de dépôt	—	—	—	—	—	—	—	—	—	—
Total							.1	.1	2.5	1.6
4. Agricultural loans										
a) Veterans loans	—	—	—	—	—	—	—	—	—	—
b) Farm Credit Corp.	—	—	—	—	—	—	—	—	—	—
c) Provincial loans	—	—	—	—	—	—	—	—	—	—
Total	—	—	—	—	—	—	—	—	—	—
5. Industrial loans										
a) Industrial Development Bank	—	—	—	—	—	—	—	—	—	—
b) Provincial industrial loans	—	—	—	—	—	—	—	—	—	—
Total	—	—	—	—	—	—	—	—	—	—
6. Other										
a) C.M.H.C.	—	—	—	—	—	—	—	—	—	—
b) E.C.I.C.	—	—	—	—	—	—	—	—	—	—
c) C.D.I.C.	—	—	—	—	—	—	—	—	—	—
d) Provincial–misc.	—	—	—	—	—	—	—	—	—	—

SOURCE: See Statistical Appendix.
[1]Excludes plans under trusteed arrangements.

1920		1930		1940		1946		1950		1960		1967		1968	
$	%	$	%	$	%	$	%	$	%	$	%	$	%	$	%
434	93.9	340	73.6	1001	85.8	2688	93.1	4020	93.7	9124	93.5	17766	85.0	19282	82.0
28	6.1	122	26.4	165	14.1	198	6.9	272	6.3	635	6.5	3141	15.0	4237	18.0
462		462		1166		2886		4292		9759		20907		23519	
312	67.5	175	37.9	—	—	—	—	—	—	—	—	—	—	—	—
—	—	—	—	627	53.8	1949	67.5	2350	54.8	3044	31.2	4412	21.1	4636	19.7
39	8.4	25	5.4	22	1.9	36	1.2	37	.9	29	.3	19	.1	—	—
2	.5	39	8.4	45	3.8	89	3.1	122	2.8	167	1.7	260	1.2	294	1.3
41	8.9	64	13.8	67	5.7	125	4.3	159	3.7	196	2.0	279	1.3	294	1.3
10	2.2	23	5.0	156	13.4	357	12.4	620	14.4	1199	12.3	1326	6.3	1325	5.6
4	.9	57	12.3	108	9.3	170	5.9	359	8.4	2756	28.3	6374	30.5	7084	30.1
—	—	5	1.1	13	1.1	24	.8	39	.9	175	1.8	373	1.8	406	1.7
—	—	—	—	—	—	—	—	—	—	—	—	1353	6.5	2108	9.0
—	—	—	—	—	—	—	—	—	—	—	—	419	2.0	684	2.9
14	3.1	85	18.4	277	23.8	551	19.1	1018	23.7	4130	42.4	9845	47.1	11607	49.4
69	14.9	54	11.7	36	3.1	108	3.7	189	4.4	166	1.7	383	1.8	423	1.8
—	—	6	1.3	38	3.3	22	.8	27	.6	164	1.7	955	4.6	1085	4.6
13	2.8	58	12.6	103	8.8	83	2.9	93	2.2	229	2.3	431	2.1	460	2.0
82	17.7	118	25.6	177	15.2	213	7.4	309	7.2	559	5.7	1769	8.5	1968	8.4
—	—	—	—	—	—	16	.5	31	.7	107	1.1	341	1.6	379	1.6
—	—	—	—	—	—	—	—	3	.1	42	.4	259	1.2	242	1.0
—	—	—	—	—	—	16	.5	34	.8	149	1.5	600	2.8	621	2.6
—	—	—	—	14	1.2	25	.9	395	9.2	1642	16.8	3567	17.1	3961	16.8
—	—	—	—	—	—	5	.2	12	.3	17	.2	357	1.7	357	1.5
—	—	—	—	—	—	—	—	—	—	—	—	32	.2	32	.1
13	2.8	20	4.3	4	.3	2	.1	15	.3	22	.2	46	.2	43	.2

After 1930 and continuing on until the 1960s, federal government intermediary assets grew rapidly until they accounted for about 94% of government intermediary assets. The reasons for this are quite clear: the accelerated growth of the federal government's annuity business and its insurance and pension accounts, and the rapid growth of the government's new housing loans as indicated by the growth of the assets of Central Mortgage and Housing Corporation formed in 1945. For example, from 1930 to 1960 the relative size of federal government financial intermediaries increased from 74% to 94%, or 20 percentage points, while over that period the federal government's annuity, insurance and pension accounts increased by 23 percentage points and C.M.H.C. by 17 percentage points, with declines occurring in the relative size of the federal and provincial governments' savings banks, agricultural loans, and Bank of Canada. The Bank's rapid growth in relative size before and during the Second World War proved later to be transitory, for thereafter it declined steadily in relative size just as did the chartered banks. It should also be noted that the period after 1930 saw the beginning of the entry of federal and provincial governments into industrial lending.

After 1960 the relative size of provincial government intermediaries increased as a consequence mainly of the introduction of a national pension plan. But the main trends in the growth of government intermediaries were the same as they had been, namely, a continuing decline in the relative size of the Bank of Canada and the government savings banks and a further increase in the relative size of the general area of annuities insurance and pension accounts, industrial loans, and farm lending by the Farm Credit Corporation. Of total government financial intermediary assets of $23,519 million in 1968, 49.4% was accounted for by the annuity insurance and pension accounts; 19.7% by the Bank of Canada; 16.8% by the Central Mortgage and Housing Corporation; 8.4% by agricultural loans; 2.6% by industrial loans; and 1.5% by the Export Credits Insurance Corporation. Pensions, money supply, housing, and farm loans—that, essentially, is what government intermediation consists of in the Canadian capital market.

CHRONOLOGY OF DEVELOPMENT

The aggregate data we have just examined hide much of the unfolding character of government intermediation activity. Further details of the history of the development of government financial intermediaries are therefore necessary for a more complete understanding of the role of government financial intermediaries in Canada.

Federal savings banks: Probably the first important government involvement in financial intermediation in Canada occurred in the Maritime Provinces when they were still British colonies. They became involved in the formation of government savings banks – an aspect of the trustee savings bank development. This we have already discussed.[2] Briefly, the Nova Scotia government started the Halifax Savings Bank in 1832, Newfoundland opened the Newfoundland Savings Bank in 1834, and, after repealing legislation relating to the discredited trustee savings banks, New Brunswick in 1847 introduced a system whereby low-income people as well as treasurers of local friendly societies could deposit up to £50 at 5% interest with the Deputy Treasurer. Prince Edward Island introduced a government savings bank shortly before Confederation. There is little doubt that these savings institutions were intended primarily to encourage thrift among low-income people by providing them with convenient facilities for investing small savings. The presumption, in other words, was that there existed a gap in the capital market with respect to the accumulation of small savings. Since the chartered banks were not then much interested in the savings deposit business, and the local building societies and trustee savings banks were finding it very difficult to become firmly established, there is indeed a strong possibility that such a gap did exist. Under the terms of the British North America Act the new federal government assumed all the liabilities of and management responsibilities for the government savings banks in Nova Scotia, New Brunswick and, from 1873 onward, Prince Edward Island, and also the Saint John Savings Bank. The federal government operated these savings banks through the Department of Finance and opened another one in Winnipeg in 1871, one in Toronto in 1872, and one each in Victoria, Nanaimo and New Westminster, British Columbia, in 1873. In addition to these government savings banks the federal government in 1868 began operating a post office savings bank in Ontario and Quebec.[3] The formation of the post office savings bank was not the consequence of overwhelming public demand. There was public awareness of the success of the British Post Office Banks and several individuals had privately urged the Canadian Government to adopt the system.[4] The resulting legislation received little attention, and when it was presented to Parlia-

---

2. See chapter 5 above.
3. See *Canadian Economics,* Papers Prepared for Reading Before the Economical Section of the British Association for the Advancement of Science, Montreal, 1884 (Montreal: Dawson Brothers, Publishers, 1885), chapters 19 and 20, which discuss the formation of the Government Savings and the Post Office Savings banks.
4. *Ibid.,* p. 244.

ment it formed part of a plan for a uniform postal system. The size limit on one person's deposit was fixed at $1,000 and this provision was introduced, it would seem, in order to protect the deposit business of the banks.

For a period the government and post office banks experienced rapid growth, as we have already seen, and in 1888 their deposits amounted in size to about 69% of the savings deposits of the chartered banks. It is quite possible that part of this growth is explained by the absence of completely adequate savings facilities, as noted above, and the fact that the ratio of chartered bank branches to population had not yet risen to its long-run "normal" level might be taken in support of this view.[5] However, there were a number of local private bankers and local mortgage loan companies that were also providing savings facilities,[6] so that the changing density of chartered bank branches is not a completely adequate index of the density of savings facilities. There is some evidence that the final surge of substantial growth of the government's savings institutions, that is in the 1880s, depended on the government's allowing a rate on deposits in excess of current market rates. Up to 1880 the chartered banks offered 4% (and some 5%) on savings deposits but then as interest rates fell generally this was reduced to 3%.[7] The government savings institutions, which had also been offering 4%, did not reduce their rate in 1880. Almost immediately the deposits of the government savings institutions began to grow at an accelerated pace, increasing from $11 million in 1879 to $43 million in 1888. In 1889 they reduced their rate to 3½% and promptly began to decline in relative size. Before the turn of the century the rate was reduced again to 3%, and at that rate the chartered bank deposits, with their attribute of easy transferability, were probably regarded as a superior savings instrument. The growing reputation of the banks for financial solvency probably also made the government savings institutions increasingly less necessary, in the eyes of the saving public. While slipping steadily in relative importance from 1888 onward, it was not until 1968 that the federal government finally abolished its post office savings institution, the latter having absorbed the government savings banks in 1929. It stands as an example of how such institutions tend to live long after there is any identifiable justification for their existence.

Government note issue and Bank of Canada: We have seen that the federal government savings banks had developed their roots in the pre-

---

5. See above, pp. 101-2.
6. See above, pp. 168-9.
7. See *Canadian Economics, op. cit.*, p. 245.

Confederation period. The only other important government financial intermediary that pre-dated Confederation was the Provincial Note Issue introduced in 1866, which became the Dominion Note Issue after Confederation. During the French régime paper money in the form of playing cards was circulated successfully for a period, and other early attempts at issuing paper money were also made.[8] But attempts on the part of government to wrest from the chartered banks some or all of the intermediation process involved in circulating paper medium of exchange were first made in 1841. Following the union of the provinces of Upper and Lower Canada, the governor, Lord Sydenham, attempted to establish a government-controlled bank of issue that would have a monopoly of the note issue. He was probably heavily influenced by his close association with the "currency school" group[9] in England, but supporters of the plan also favoured it because of the contribution it would make to improving the government's finances. Chartered bank opposition and political division was sufficient to defeat the proposal. The Free Banking Act of 1850 first associated government directly with the note issue, for under it banks would receive notes from the government by depositing securities with the government. Only a few small banks operated under the plan and essentially it was a failure. Then in 1866 the Minister of Finance, A. T. Galt, succeeded in having enacted the Provincial Notes Act. Under it a government note issue not to exceed $8 million was provided for and incentives were offered to the banks to relinquish voluntarily their note issue. The financial needs of the government seem to have been paramount in the introduction of the plan. As it turned out, only the Bank of Montreal relinquished its note issue, and this only temporarily. From the beginning of the issue until it disappeared in 1934 with the formation of the Bank of Canada, the Dominion Note Issue, in spite of being increased regularly, did not constitute more than about 15% of the nation's total note issue, the remainder being that of the chartered banks.[10]

In 1934 the Bank of Canada was formed. By that time the consensus of opinion internationally seems to have been that central banks should have a monopoly of the note issue. So Bank of Canada notes begin to replace not only outstanding Dominion notes, but also chartered bank notes, and by 1950 the Bank's monopoly of the note issue was complete. This acquisition of the note issue monopoly was one reason why the Bank of Canada was larger in relative size than the note issue it replaced, and in recent years, as Table 13:2 shows, over

8. See above, p. 37.

9. See C. A. Curtis, "History of Banking in Canada," in E. M. Rosengren, ed., *Readings in Money and Banking* (Toronto: University of Toronto Press, 1947), p. 18.

10. See above, p. 108.

half of the Bank's liabilities have been in the form of notes held by the general public. But there was another important reason as well. Under the 1934 banking legislation the banks were required to maintain a cash reserve ratio, and cash had to be in the form of Bank of Canada notes and deposits. Previously, while the banks had held some Dominion notes, they had also held large amounts of gold and New York call loans. Table 13:2 shows that about one-third of the Bank's liabilities are in the form of notes held by the chartered banks and chartered bank deposits with the Bank of Canada. The acceleration in the Bank's relative size as a result of monetary expansion in the Second World War was short-lived, however, for while its assets accounted for 5.7% of financial intermediary assets in 1938 and 12.9% in 1946, in 1968 the figure was 4.6%.

We need to make only a brief reference to the distribution of the Bank's funds. The Bank has in fact confined itself essentially to holding Government of Canada securities as Table 13:2 shows. Because of this it may be said that the Bank is indeed fulfilling the wishes of Francis Hincks (of the 1840s) and A.T. Galt (of the 1860s) and others who wished to see a government monopoly of the currency for purposes of providing assistance to the national finances. The only exception of importance to this generalization is the Bank's financing of the Industrial Development Bank—its wholly owned subsidiary which in 1970 accounted for about 9% of its total assets.[11]

Annuities, pensions and superannuation funds: We will be referring to the activities of governments in this area of the capital market when we discuss trusteed pension plans.[12] Here we may note that the Government of Canada introduced a pension plan for its civil servants in 1870. More significant, from the point of view of the role of government intermediaries, was the introduction by the federal government in 1908 of government annuities. The government, not wishing to introduce an old-age pension plan, felt that low-income people should themselves be encouraged to save and provide for their old age; but it also concluded that existing institutions, particularly the life insurance companies, were not providing necessary facilities in an adequate way.[13] Therefore it introduced annuities. However, by

---

11. The large decline in foreign assets by 1940 is explained by the transfer of the nation's gold and foreign exchange reserves from the Bank of Canada to the Exchange Fund Account. Also, from 1935 to 1947 the Bank held some provincial securities, but never thereafter.

12. See below, p. 442.

13. See below, p. 444.

Table 13:2 Bank of Canada Assets and Liabilities 1935-1970 (selected years)

(PERCENTAGE DISTRIBUTION)

	ASSETS				LIABILITIES						TOTAL	
					NOTES IN CIRCULATION		DEPOSITS			OTHER		
Dec. 31	*Government of Canada securities*	*Industrial Development Bank*	*Foreign assets*	*Other*	*Held by banks*	*Held by other*	*Government of Canada*	*Chartered banks*	*Other*		*$mns.*	*% of total financial intermediary assets*
1935	37.1	—	60.6	2.3	13.2	19.2	5.8	59.0	.3	2.5	308	4.9
1940	91.3	—	6.1	2.6	15.7	41.8	1.7	34.7	1.5	4.6	627	7.8
1945	90.7	.5	7.7	1.1	8.0	47.6	7.5	25.7	1.5	9.7	2032	14.4
1950	82.6	1.1	15.3	1.0	9.8	48.3	1.1	24.6	8.8	7.4	2350	11.4
1955	90.4	1.3	4.4	3.9	11.1	55.3	3.4	21.0	1.3	7.9	2620	8.6
1960	88.4	2.9	2.6	6.1	10.8	56.9	1.2	21.8	1.1	8.2	3044	6.8
1965	86.4	6.1	1.1	6.4	9.7	54.4	2.9	26.1	.9	6.0	3956	5.4
1968	83.8	7.6	2.3	6.3	12.3	57.4	1.0	24.0	.8	4.5	4636	4.6
1969	83.0	8.3	3.3	5.4	11.1	59.4	1.7	22.6	.9	4.3	4888	n.a.
1970	78.5	8.7	3.6	9.2	9.7	57.5	4.2	21.8	.7	6.1	5405	n.a.

SOURCE: Bank of Canada, *Statistical Summary*.

1930, that is, after twenty-two years, the outstanding annuities amounted to only $21 million. Quite obviously demand for them had been grossly over-estimated. Then sales increased, and the annuities outstanding amounted to $140 million in 1940, $288 million in 1945 and $930 million in 1955 after which their growth again decelerated. A rate of 4% was for the most part permitted in computing the value of the annuities until 1948, which from the late 1930s was above competitive market rates. As was the case with the government savings banks in the 1880s, it would seem that a major reason explaining the high growth rate was the attractive price offered, that is, a price that did not reflect current rates of interest in the market. This was also the conclusion of a 1962 royal commission.[14] The commission found that the annuity program had been very costly to the government and was inferior in some respects to other programs available, so it recommended that it be discontinued. This the government began to do in 1967. Therefore, apart from the early years when the program may have served the purpose of encouraging the life insurance companies to speed the development of their annuity business (and possibly also the more dubious one of quieting demands for an old-age pension plan), it is difficult to see that it served any useful purpose at all. Indeed, if the income groupings of the purchasers of annuities were known, they might even reveal that the subsidy element in the scheme tended to redistribute income to higher income groups.

We have seen that another source of retirement funds for the government sector has been provincial government employee pension plans. These did not begin to appear in large number until the 1920s. Then one province after another began to introduce them. There appeared public service superannuation funds, teachers' superannuation funds, similar funds for government crown corporations, and recently also superannuation funds for members of the provincial legislative assemblies. Some provincially sponsored insurance plans also appeared. The western provinces introduced crop insurance plans, Saskatchewan in 1945 entered a general insurance business as well, and then came hospital and medical insurance plans. Finally in 1965 all provinces except Quebec entered the National Pension Plan, and Quebec introduced its own plan, which was generally consistent with the former. Contrary to a number of the previously mentioned plans, some of which were on a "cash" basis and others of

---

14. See *Report of the Royal Commission on Government Organization* (Ottawa: Queen's Printer, 1962), vol. 3, pp. 286-8, and Arthur Pedoe, *Life Insurance, Annuities and Pensions* (Toronto: University of Toronto Press, 1964), p. 146.

which were not properly "funded" and so did not generate large stocks of financial assets, the national and Quebec pension plans are generating substantial amounts of surplus funds and these are all channelled back to the provinces.

Agricultural loans and provincial savings institutions: While the federal and provincial governments had made special loans to the private sector of the economy from time to time, such as the railway loans and relief loans, the first sustained government lending programs involved provincial government loans to farmers. At first these schemes were completely insignificant in size. One of the first schemes must have been the Ontario Tile Drainage Loan program which was introduced in the late 1870s and is still in existence. A variety of grain, dairy, agricultural co-operative and elevator company loans appeared even before the First World War. But the decisive entry of government into farm credit programs did not occur until Manitoba made the move in 1917, closely followed by most of the other provinces.[15] In 1913 the Saskatchewan Commission on Agricultural Credit recommended in support of a government role in the provision of agricultural credit, which was a sort of straw in the wind. Then in 1917 the following provincial actions were taken:[16] (1) Manitoba passed the Rural Credits Act which provided for the formation of local rural credit societies for making short-term loans to farmers; funds came from the farmer subscribers and from the province. (2) Manitoba created the Manitoba Farm Loans Association to act as the medium between the government and farmer borrowers in extending long-term loans to the latter; funds came from the province and also from bonds sold by the association itself, and from capital stock purchased by the government and borrowers. (3) Saskatchewan passed "An Act to provide for Loans to Agriculturists upon the Security of Farm Mortgages" which was very similar to the Manitoba scheme except that all funds were to be raised by the sale of provincial bonds. (4) Alberta passed three acts, the Live Stock Encouragement Act, the Co-operative Credit Act, and the Farm Loan Act, the first providing for loans for the purchase of livestock, the second (following Manitoba closely) for the formation of local rural credit socie-

---

15. See W. T. Easterbrook and H. G. J. Aitken, *Canadian Economic History* (Toronto: Macmillan Co. of Canada, 1956), pp. 506-13, for a survey of farm credit, and also generally W. T. Easterbrook, *Farm Credit in Canada* (Toronto: University of Toronto Press, 1937), and V. C. Fowke, *Canadian Agricultural Policy: The Historical Pattern* (Toronto: University of Toronto Press, 1946).
16. See W. J. Jackman, "The Growth of Rural Credit in Canada," *Monetary Times*, Jan. 6, 1922, vol. 68, pp. 68-70.

ties for short-term lending, and the third for providing long-term loans. (5) British Columbia passed the "Land Settlement and Development Act" which provided for a Land Settlement Board for extending short- and long-term loans to farmers and which was to assume the functions of the Agricultural Credit Commission that had earlier been established. Actually British Columbia had an Agricultural Credit Act as early as 1898; and New Brunswick and Nova Scotia had passed "land settlement" legislation in 1912 and Ontario in 1916, for purposes generally of encouraging farmers to stay on the farm. The federal government embarked on land settlement loans for soldiers in 1919 (and again under the Veterans' Land Act after the Second World War).

Ontario took the decisive step into agricultural credit operations in 1920. The Ontario Farm Loans Act of that year was patterned on the Manitoba Rural Credits Act, and the Agricultural Development Act provided for mortgage loans similar to those offered under the Manitoba Farm Loans Act.

Interestingly enough, both the Ontario and the Manitoba ventures into savings banks arose from their desire to obtain funds for financing the aforementioned farm loan schemes. Under the Ontario Agricultural Development Act the Provincial Treasurer was empowered to establish savings offices throughout Ontario and pay over the funds to the Agricultural Development Board as needed for making farm loans. This was the principal reason for establishing what became known as the Province of Ontario Savings Office. In the case of Manitoba, the rural credit societies at first received loans from the banks at 6% to finance their operations, but when in early 1920 the banks raised the rate to 6½% the provincial government opened its Provincial Savings Office to obtain funds for rural credit loans.[17] The Ontario office is still in operation while the Manitoba Savings Office was closed in 1930. For the sake of completeness it should also be noted that Alberta had passed a Provincial Savings Certificate Act in 1917 to make available to small investors a relatively attractive savings instrument and to provide the government with funds at lower cost than available elsewhere. Then in 1938 the Alberta government introduced its Treasury branches which are still in operation as savings institutions.

What, it may be asked, lay behind this wave of provincial agricultural loan schemes? A contemporary, and probably somewhat biased, observer wrote as follows in 1922:

> The original plea was to help farmers in outlying and unorganized districts where credit was not available at any price, due either to

---

17. *Ibid.*, p. 67.

> weak financial position of borrowers, the very liberal exemption laws, or to great distance from any bank or financial institution. On the above grounds the movement had the co-operation and assistance of bankers, but it soon resolved itself into a matter of cheap money and plenty of it. . . .[18]

The writer, in other words, implies that the schemes were rationalized as necessary for closing a "credit gap" but soon became vehicles for providing subsidized funds. Another contemporary observer, however, noted that ". . . in all countries banking systems are not adapted to the special conditions of agriculture, and, consequently, there have come into operation institutions for meeting these requirements."[19] That is, he accepts the credit gap argument. Writing more recently, two economic historians have generally supported the latter view.[20] The fact is that the Canadian banks originated as commercial banking institutions and only through amendments to the Bank Act over the years was farm demand for credit accommodated, which presumably could mean that prior to those amendments farm credit was not adequate. This then could explain the widespread agitation among farmers in Canada for more adequate *short-term* lending facilities.

Their agitation for long-term loan facilities had slightly different roots. Until the First World War the aggressive activities of the mortgage loan companies, using both domestic and British capital, seem to have made long-term farm credit quite readily available, even too readily available at times. Then the First World War cut off the foreign supply of funds. This was followed by debt moratorium legislation in Ontario, Manitoba, Saskatchewan and British Columbia which protected borrowers against foreclosures, a move that shook the confidence of institutional lenders in farm mortgage credit. It was further shaken when the federal government introduced a scheme in 1915 to permit banks to make loans for emergency seed grain purchases, loans that enjoyed precedence over all other farm debt. In this environment it is understandable that farmers might be worried about the adequacy of private sources of long-term credit.

The assets of provincial agricultural loan schemes rose to about $87 million by 1934 but then levelled off as write-offs became numerous and even in 1950 they only amounted to about $93 million. However, long before 1934 many of the provincial schemes were experiencing losses and were being curtailed, including those of Manitoba and Saskatchewan, while the Alberta mortgage lending plan was never

18. O. A. Harper, "Provinces' Invasion of the Banking Field," *Monetary Times*, Jan. 6, 1922, vol. 68, p. 23.
19. Jackman, *op. cit.*, p. 67.
20. See Easterbrook and Aitken, *op. cit.*, p. 511.

important. Ontario ceased making mortgage loans after 1934.[21] It was in this context of emerging failure among the provincial schemes that the federal government formed the Canadian Farm Loan Board in 1927, which began operations in 1929. The provinces welcomed the move, although it must be noted that in 1936 Quebec formed its Farm Credit Bureau which, in the post–Second World War period, was to become the largest provincial farm credit institution.

The Canadian Farm Loan Board—renamed the Farm Credit Corporation in 1959—received its funds from the Government of Canada and made loans for the purchase of land, farm equipment, and livestock, for farm improvements, for debt refinancing and for covering operating expenses. Until the mid 1950s the Canadian Farm Loan Board proceeded at a relatively leisurely pace. Its loans outstanding in 1939 were $33 million and in 1950 they were $26 million. Then began a period of accelerated growth, with loans rising to $117 million in 1960, and to the very large amount of $1,036 million by 1969.[22] By the latter year, when provincial farm loan schemes had assets of approximately $450 million, the Farm Credit Corporation had established itself not only as the pre-eminent government farm lending agency, but also as the principal source of long-term farm credit in the country, private and public institutions included. The corporation in its 1968-9 annual report pointed out that it had 67,108 mortgages outstanding, which was equal to about one-quarter the number of all commercial farms in Canada, and that its provision of low-cost credit had been a factor putting upward pressure on land prices.

One reason for the accelerated growth of the corporation may have been the evidence that the provinces were again becoming restless over the adequacy of farm credit facilities. In consequence a number of important provincial agricultural schemes suddenly rose to prominence. The Quebec Farm Credit Bureau had been established in 1936 for making low-interest loans to farmers for consolidating debts, acquiring land and making improvements. It had assets of $26 million in 1939, $52 million in 1950, and $169 million in 1968. The Ontario Junior Farmer Establishment Loan Corporation was established in 1952 for "making loans to assist young qualified farmers in the establishment, development and operation of their farms." The interest income of the corporation has not been sufficient to meet its cost of funds and administrative expenses, so a subsidy is involved. It had assets of $103 million in 1968.

---

21. See Easterbrook and Aitken, *op. cit.*, p. 512.
22. Farm Credit Corporation, *Annual Report 1968-69*, p. 27.

Manitoba established its Agricultural Credit Corporation in 1959 for the usual purpose of assisting farmers in acquiring land and making improvements, and also for the purchase of cattle. Its assets in 1968 were $31 million. Interest rates are low and not sufficient to meet its cost of funds and administrative expenses. Alberta established a Farm Purchase Revolving Fund at about the same time and by 1967 had made advances of $20 million. In 1952 there was formed in Saskatchewan the Co-operative Trust Company for making long-term mortgage loans and acting in a fiduciary capacity generally. The Saskatchewan government helps the company in making long-term farm mortgage loans by guaranteeing the securities it sells to obtain the required funds. Nova Scotia, New Brunswick, Prince Edward Island and Newfoundland all have farm settlement or development loan schemes, and in addition, after the Second World War, developed fishermen loan schemes.

There was one significant difference between development after the Second World War and that during the 1920s: the emphasis of government agricultural loans after 1945 was concentrated essentially on long-term lending whereas in the 1920s it included both short- and long-term loans. This suggests that governments no longer believe that a gap exists in the short-term agricultural credit area, but that they do believe it exists in the long-term credit field. In part this may be because of government loan plans under which governments provide whole or partial guarantees for short- and medium-term loans to farmers extended by private institutions, particularly the chartered banks. The most important of these plans is that of the federal Farm Improvement Loans Act of 1944, under which the chartered banks (recently extended to include also trust, loan and insurance companies, credit unions and caisses populaires) make loans of up to ten years, up to an individual limit of $25,000 (or up to $15,000 for land purchases), for purchasing livestock, land, machinery and equipment, and for making general improvements, with a government guarantee for up to 10% of losses incurred. Such loans amounted to over $300 million in 1970. The banks also had outstanding at that time over $700 million in other agricultural loans, some of which were made under various provincial guarantee loan schemes. These include the Manitoba Agricultural and Development Act; the Ontario Junior Farmer Establishment Act; the Quebec Farm Improvement Act; the New Brunswick Farm Loans Act; and the British Columbia Distress Area Assistance Act.[23]

---

23. See "Credit on the Farm: The Banks' Part in Financing Agriculture," Canadian Bankers' Association, *Bulletin*, vol. 12, no. 3, September 1969.

Why the sustained activity of government intermediaries in long-term farm lending? That it might be explained by a "credit gap" among private lenders need not be discarded out of hand. The mortgage loan companies seem not to have been anxious to enter the field following their experience with farm mortgages in the 1930s and before. But there was another factor at work. Lending rates offered by the government schemes involved government subsidies from the beginning, thereby discouraging the activities of private lending agencies. The presence of subsidies is possibly explained by political considerations, although in theory they might also be justified on economic grounds if they accelerated trends regarded as being desirable—as, for example, the transition from small to large farms. Whatever the forces at work, by the late 1960s long-term farm lending was almost entirely the preserve of government lending agencies with the federal Farm Credit Corporation dominating the field.

Industrial lending programs: Just as the inter-war period was one in which government-sponsored farm credit was introduced and became firmly established, so the post–Second World War period was one in which federal and provincial governments embarked in a sustained way on lending to private industry. Interest of local governments in encouraging industries to locate in their area has, however, been present for a very long time. Governmental assistance for railway-building, for example, has a long history predating Confederation. Then from the 1870s onward there emerged strenuous efforts on the part of local communities to attract industries by offering financial incentives of one kind or another. In view of a recent resurgence in this kind of activity, in the form of both federal and provincial development schemes and the activities of local government industrial development commissioners, it may be interesting to quote a few of the many contemporary press reports on industrial location incentives from the 1870s to the 1890s:

> . . . A matting factory has been established in Cobourg, with a bonus of $5,000 from the town and the Norval woollen factory has been removed to Cobourg, getting $2,500 bonus. . . .[24]

> . . . Mr. Heale, of Utica, N.Y. has accepted the inducements offered by the Ottawa Corporation, viz., a lease of land for ninety-nine years, exemption from taxes for ten years and a bonus of $10,000, and is going to erect a woollen factory which will employ not less than one hundred hands. . . .[25]

24. *Monetary Times*, March 16, 1877, p. 1052.
25. *Monetary Times*, Nov. 22, 1878, p. 655.

> ... Brampton offers to Mr. Vogelsang, button manufacturer a bonus to remove his works thither from Berlin. ...[26]

Just how widespread this practice was even by 1879 is suggested by the following news item:

> ... Complaint is made by the Sarnia Observer that that town forms the only exception to the prevailing fashions of towns and villages in Western Ontario endeavouring to secure the establishment of manufacturers in their midst. ...[27]

Nor was the practice confined to the many towns and cities of Ontario:

> ... The municipal electors of Longueuil have decided ... to grant a $10,000 bonus to Messrs. H.R. Ives & Co. of Montreal for the purpose of securing the establishment of a foundry in their town. ...[28]

> ... The council of St. John's, Que. passed a by-law loaning Mr. Bowles $3,000 for ten years without interest, to rebuild his pottery in that place. ...[29]

> ... The council of Lachine has voted a bonus of $5,000 to the Dominion Barbed Wire Company, which is shortly to open a branch in that town. ...[30]

The inducements that were offered, it can be seen, included grants of land, bonuses, loans and tax exemptions. The spectacle of municipalities using taxpayers' money to bid industries away from each other became increasingly difficult to justify and the activity began to die away. In recent times the inducements offered by municipalities have tended to concentrate on making available well-serviced and conveniently located industrial sites, as well as publicizing generally the advantages offered by the local community to new industries. However, heavily subsidized government loan programs for industry have not disappeared. They have shifted from the municipalities to the provinces and the federal government. The loan programs associated with the provinces have tended to concentrate on location incentives, while those of the federal government have tended to concentrate on assisting small industries regardless of loca-

26. *Monetary Times*, March 21, 1879, p. 1174.
27. *Monetary Times*, April 18, 1879.
28. *Monetary Times*, April 21, 1882, p. 1289.
29. *Monetary Times*, May 26, 1882, p. 1443.
30. *Monetary Times*, April 17, 1885, p. 1193.

tion. The federal government, however, has introduced various plans for influencing industry location by providing tax incentives.

We may now examine some of these developments in more detail. There were almost no provincial and federal government industrial loan programs prior to the Second World War. British Columbia had an Industrial Development Fund for several decades before that but it remained insignificant in size and finally disappeared entirely. Unquestionably the most important development occurred in 1944 when the federal government introduced the Industrial Development Bank, taking the legal form of a subsidiary of the Bank of Canada. Its assets in 1970 amounted to $498 million, larger than the assets of all provincial industrial loan schemes combined (see Table 13:1), and as Table 13:3 shows, they consisted almost entirely of loans. Since the powers of the Industrial Development Bank were broadened in 1960 it has been permitted to lend to virtually any kind of business. Nor are its operations confined to particular geographical regions. The basic criterion it is to use is that it should provide fixed-term capital to businesses, particularly small enterprises, that may reasonably prove to be successful, but only if such businesses are unable to obtain financing on reasonable terms and conditions elsewhere. Thus it is designed specifically to fill a presumed credit gap in the capital market, one involving medium- and long-term loans to small and medium-sized businesses. It has obtained all its funds from the Bank of Canada, through the sale of shares and bonds and debentures to the Bank, and is specifically forbidden to go into the deposit business.

Measured by rate of return (i.e., net income after losses) on shareholders' equity, which has averaged only about 3%, the Industrial Development Bank has not been a successful institution – in spite of not paying taxes and receiving funds from the Bank of Canada at attractive rates. It can of course be argued, quite properly, that before one could conclude that these results imply a misallocation of the nation's resources, one would have to consider the success of the bank's borrowing customers. This would involve access to internal information of the bank. Considering the large size of the bank's operations, it is no longer of indifference to the nation whether or not its operations result in resource misallocation, and a detailed examination of its economic performance utilizing internal information would be entirely appropriate.

The provinces, with the exception of British Columbia, have all introduced schemes for extending financial assistance for industrial development purposes. However, as Table 13:1 shows, the combined total of their assets in 1968 was not yet equal to the assets of the Industrial Development Bank of the federal government. New-

Table 13:3 Industrial Development Bank Assets and Liabilities 1945-1970 (selected years)

	Assets			Liabilities			Customers on books
Sept. 30	Loans	Other	Total	Capital and reserve	Bonds and debentures	Other	
	%	%	$MNS.	%	%	%	
1945	9.9	88.1	10.1	100.0	—	—	80
1950	70.4	29.6	31.1	87.5	—	12.5	490
1955	95.7	4.3	46.0	71.7	20.7	7.6	693
1960	96.5	3.5	106.8	39.1	59.6	1.3	1967
1965	97.4	2.6	262.0	23.5	74.6	1.9	6962
1966	97.7	2.3	305.1	21.7	76.3	2.0	7870
1967	98.1	1.9	340.8	20.9	77.0	2.1	8595
1968	97.9	2.1	378.9	20.1	77.5	2.4	9512
1969	98.9	1.1	423.0	19.1	78.3	2.6	10629
1970	97.8	2.2	498.0	17.0	79.1	3.9	12285

SOURCE: Industrial Development Bank, *Annual Reports,* and Bank of Canada, *Statistical Summary.*

foundland has had a variety of industrial development arrangements and in 1967 formed the Newfoundland Industrial Development Corporation; Nova Scotia introduced the Nova Scotia Industrial Loan Fund in 1944, and in 1958 the Nova Scotia Industrial Estates Ltd., the latter now being one of the larger provincial government industrial lending agencies; New Brunswick formed its Industrial Development and Expansion Board in 1956 and its Development Corporation in 1959; Prince Edward Island Industrial Enterprises Incorporated appeared in 1966; the very important General Investment Corporation of Quebec—also among the largest of the provincial agencies—was incorporated in 1962; the Ontario Development Corporation appeared in 1966; the Manitoba Development Fund, another relatively large provincial agency, was formed in 1948; the Saskatchewan Industrial Development Fund was formed in 1951, but it has been phased out, its place taken by the Saskatchewan Economic Development Corporation, formed in 1963; the Alberta Industrial Development Corporation was formed in 1947, and the Alberta Commercial Corporation and Alberta Investment Fund in 1963.

We cannot examine here the performance of these lending agencies. Indeed, appraising their economic success or failure would require internal data that are not publicly available. Yet there is no doubt that between them all there must by now exist substantial experience in Canada relating to government financial assistance to industry. What is not known is whether this experience argues in favour or against the perpetuation of provincial government industrial financing schemes.

We may briefly describe a few of these lending agencies. The Nova Scotia Industrial Estates Ltd. is wholly owned and financed by the province. It assists industrial development principally by financing up to 100% of the construction and expansion of secondary manufacturing plants. These plants may be owned by and leased from I.E.L. with an option to buy, or may be purchased with I.E.L. providing first mortgage financing. I.E.L. also finances up to 60% of the cost of installed machinery and has an agreement with most municipalities to impose lower taxes for up to ten years. On March 31, 1969, its assets totalled about $66 million. Included in that total was a $16 million investment in Clairtone Sound Corporation Ltd., a corporation with large accumulated operating losses. Its investment of $16 million in trouble-ridden Deuterium of Canada Ltd.—a company that is to manufacture heavy water—was taken over by the province. Up to 1970 I.E.L. had assisted in the establishment or expansion of sixty-one plants, including those producing metal containers, hardboard, cement, batteries, electronic equipment, automobiles, foundry products, carpets, boats, textiles, heavy water and food products.[31]

The General Investment Corporation of Quebec is a joint public and private venture in that (in 1970) 33% of its shares with a cost value of $10 million were owned by the province and the remainder by the public. Its assets in 1970 exceeded $49 million. As in the case of most of the provincial industrial development agencies, its primary objective is to assist in the formation and development of industrial enterprises in its province. But it is different from most of the others in its emphasis on inducing the people of Quebec to participate in the equity financing of such development and in its readiness to acquire a controlling interest in industrial projects. G.I.C. has been interested in a variety of fields, including shipbuilding, dredging, railroad cars, turbines, boilers, sawmill equipment, heavy machinery, vegetable canning, car assembly, particle board, veneer, garments and hosiery.[32]

---

31. See *Prospectus* for Province of Nova Scotia $20,000,000. 9¾% Twenty-Five-Year Sinking Fund Debentures, March 19, 1970, pp. 15-17.
32. General Investment Corporation, *Financial Statements,* and *Prospectus* for Quebec Hydro-Electric Commission $60,000,000 9¼% Debentures, March 3, 1970, p. 29.

Ontario had guaranteed loans under its Economic Development Loans Guarantee Act through the Ontario Development Agency formed in 1963, but in 1966 it formed the Ontario Development Corporation to give direct assistance to industries that are promising but cannot obtain funds on reasonable terms and conditions elsewhere. Loans to industries locating or located in certain designated areas may be forgiven in whole or in part. The institution has a capital of $7 million, all supplied by the province. In addition to giving assistance by way of loans, guarantees or purchase of shares and other securities, it provides a range of technical, business and financial advice. Its activities seem to have been quite limited.

The Manitoba Development Fund was formed in 1959 for the usual purpose of assisting new and expanding industries in the province that cannot obtain funds on reasonable terms elsewhere. Its capital of $5 million was provided entirely by the provincial government and it also obtains advances from the government. Assets have exceeded $30 million.[33] It has been criticized for not making public the details of its lending activity.[34]

The Saskatchewan Economic Development Corporation was also formed as a provincial crown corporation in 1963 and gradually replaced the Industrial Development Fund established in 1948. Its basic purpose is to provide mortgage funds to industry and certain specialized and intensive agricultural operations, such as hog and poultry raising, in cases where normal borrowing from established institutions is not possible.[35] Its assets have exceeded $13 million.

The insistence of these institutions that assistance from them is available only when normal sources of funds are not obtainable is rather interesting. Since their customers for the most part are also ones that are eligible in principle for Industrial Development Bank loans, it means either that there is duplication of facilities or that loans are made to borrowers that the I.D.B. would not regard as being credit-worthy. The expanded activities of the I.D.B. in recent years probably restrained the growth of these provincial agencies.

In general, sources of short-, medium- and long-term funds for new and expanding small (and some not so small) industrial and commercial businesses in Canada are now quite numerous. Some private development companies[36] specialize in the field, and other private institutions, including particularly the chartered banks and sales finance companies, also are in it. The federal government has been quite aggressive here as well, through the I.D.B., with a view to

33. See Manitoba Development Fund, *Annual Reports*.
34. See *Financial Post*, April 8, 1967, p. 10.
35. Government of Saskatchewan, Treasury Department Memo, April 21, 1967.
36. See above, pp. 364-8.

closing gaps left by the private institutions, while almost all the provinces have also entered the field presumably to close gaps left by the I.D.B. and the private institutions. It is not too likely that many gaps remain. But unfortunately intensive appraisal of the usefulness of the government lending agencies is not possible without detailed internal information.

Housing mortgage loans: The federal government's entry into the financing of residential construction began in 1918 when, under the War Measures Act, it made $25 million available to the provinces for re-lending to municipalities for housing purposes. About six thousand houses were built through this form of assistance in the 1920s and early 1930s. However, the Dominion Housing Act of 1935 was the first general housing legislation and it in effect gave the federal government a continuing role in the financing of residential construction. Under it and under the National Housing Acts of 1938 and 1944, most of the government's assistance to residential construction took the form of joint lending with private lending institutions on the basis of one-quarter and three-quarters respectively. Central Mortgage and Housing Corporation, a federal crown corporation, was formed in 1945 to administer the government's activities under the National Housing Act. In 1954 the joint loan scheme was discontinued, its place taken by a scheme involving loans advanced wholly by private institutions (those referred to as "approved lenders," and including particularly life insurance, trust and mortgage loan companies and the chartered banks), but with payment guaranteed through insurance with C.M.H.C. Mortgages on both new and existing homes may be covered. The corporation also makes mortgage loans directly to borrowers when private funds, in its judgment, are not in adequate supply, and it is this direct lending activity that essentially accounts for the rapid growth of C.M.H.C. assets since 1957, with funds supplied entirely by the federal government. Table 13:4 shows that from 1960 to 1970 C.M.H.C. supplied, on the average, about 17% of all funds for new housing, other public funds supplied 2%, and private funds supplied 81%. Of the latter, N.H.A. guaranteed loans supplied 18%. So through direct lending and through its guarantees, C.M.H.C. was associated with about 35% of new-house financing from 1960 onward, which underscores the position of dominance it has come to occupy in the financing of new housing in Canada.

In addition to its ordinary direct lending and loan guarantee activity, C.M.H.C. makes loans to limited-dividend companies and non-profit corporations on low-rental housing projects; to universities

Table 13:4 Sources of Funds for New Housing and Assets of Central Mortgage and Housing Corporation 1951-1970 (selected years)

	Public funds			Private funds					Total funds for new housing	Assets of C.M.H.C.	
	C.M.H.C. loans	Other	Total	Institutional N.H.A.	Institutional Conventional	Owners' equity	Other	Total			
	%	%	%	%	%	%	%	%	$Mns.	$Mns.	% of Total Financial Intermediary Assets
1951	11.0	6.8	17.8	16.6	7.4	28.8	29.3	82.2	782.1	395	1.9
1955	1.4	2.1	3.5	33.6	11.8	18.7	32.4	96.5	1675.1	481	1.6
1960	18.2	2.4	20.6	12.1	20.1	17.8	29.4	79.4	1492.9	1642	3.6
1961	18.7	1.6	20.3	26.0	16.8	15.5	21.3	79.7	1469.3	2002	4.0
1962	12.5	2.0	14.5	24.5	25.3	20.2	15.4	85.5	1533.8	1999	3.7
1963	8.8	2.3	11.1	20.6	33.4	15.0	19.9	88.9	1628.5	2070	3.5
1964	15.4	1.5	16.9	15.0	34.9	13.4	19.9	33.1	1971.8	2281	3.5
1965	15.4	1.4	16.8	13.9	36.4	14.2	18.7	83.2	2177.7	2574	3.5
1966	22.3	1.9	24.2	9.2	28.7	21.2	16.6	75.8	2150.3	2879	3.6
1967	32.8	1.6	34.4	10.2	24.6	18.2	12.6	65.6	2346.9	3567	4.0
1968	14.4	1.6	16.0	25.6	29.6	19.8	9.0	84.0	2770.9	3961	3.9
1969	12.2	2.9	15.1	20.4	30.6	16.7	17.2	84.9	3338.9	4428	n.a.
1970[1]	18.9	1.8	20.7	22.9	18.0	16.1	22.3	79.3	3002.7	4981	n.a.
1960-1970 Average	17.2	1.9	19.1	18.2	27.1	17.1	18.4	80.9			

SOURCE: Central Mortgage and Housing Corporation, *Canadian Housing Statistics*.

[1]Preliminary.

and certain schools, co-operatives, charitable corporations, training hospitals, provincial and municipal agencies, and student housing; also to provincial and municipal sewerage corporations. It provides insurance for home improvement loans and guarantees returns on moderate rental housing projects; it buys and sells mortgages and acts as a sort of lender-of-last-resort to approved lenders; it assists in urban renewal projects; it makes long-term loans to provinces and municipalities for public housing projects; it constructs, owns and manages housing projects for the federal government and on its own account; and it engages in and encourages research into the technical, economic and social aspects of housing.[37]

It must be noted that all the provinces have agencies for administering the joint federal-provincial housing and land assembly projects, and most of them also have quite separate housing legislation which includes assistance to housing. Relative to C.M.H.C., these programs are still quite small and we have not included them in our tabulations. However, the Ontario Housing Corporation Ltd. is the most important one of them, and it was announced in the Ontario budget of March 31, 1970, that the Ontario government would establish a $50 million capital fund under the O.H.C. to provide first and second mortgage financing to purchasers of new homes at rates the same as those charged by C.M.H.C. The corporation had been formed in 1964, but prior to this announcement it had concerned itself primarily with the development of public housing. Its assets were mostly composed of such public housing, which it rented to low-income families. The 1970 announcement would have the effect of making it a financial intermediary as well as an owner of real estate.

Export Development Corporation: During the Second World War the federal government had developed a detailed system of control over the country's foreign trade and capital flows.[38] As part of its broader program for facilitating the transition of the economy from wartime to peacetime conditions it established the Export Credits Insurance Corporation (E.C.I.C.) in 1944, which, however, was from the beginning regarded as a permanent feature of the government's approach to assisting exporters. It was under the direction of a Board of Directors composed of eight senior government officials, and there was an Advisory Council appointed from the private sector by the cabinet. The role of E.C.I.C. was to provide insurance for exporters against

37. See Central Mortgage and Housing Corporation, *Annual Report*, 1968, pp. 44-5.
38. See Dominion Bureau of Statistics, *Canada Year Book*. 1945, pp. 477-84.

non-payment arising from insolvency, exchange restrictions, political instability and other similar occurrences. The view that government must provide insurance to exporters against a wide range of essentially "political" risks had already been reflected in the export insurance facilities of a number of other countries.

Until 1961 E.C.I.C. confined itself essentially to providing insurance. Its consumer goods and general commodities policies insured an exporter's entire export sales for one year; its capital goods policies covered individual sales of capital goods such as locomotives, ships and heavy machinery; and its service policies covered engineering, construction, technical and similar services contracted for by foreign buyers from Canadian firms and individuals. Usually 90% of the value of the contracts was covered and the term extended up to five years. In cases where the Minister of Industry, Trade and Commerce feels that a business transaction should, in the national interest, be insured and yet would involve the corporation itself in too high or too large a risk, the corporation may enter into such a contract of insurance at the government's risk.[39] There were fifteen amendments to the Export Credits Insurance Act of 1944 up to 1969, which generally extended the scope and flexibility of the operations of E.C.I.C. In 1961 E.C.I.C., with cabinet approval, was empowered to lend money at long term in order to facilitate the export of capital goods and related engineering services. This move generally increased its role as a financial intermediary (see Table 13:5). All funds, including equity capital, required by the E.C.I.C. came directly from the Government of Canada, as do those of the new E.D.C. Loans for a long while were made at 6%, which in view of market rates was a subsidized rate. Subsidized export insurance and financing has become common among exporting countries, and the potential danger exists that it will degenerate into simply another form of artificial stimulus to trade. This danger, however, is somewhat lessened by the existence of the Union d'Assureurs des Crédits Internationaux (i.e. Berne Union), of which E.C.I.C. was a member. Formed in 1943, it is an association of export credit insurers which concerns itself with the orderly development of international credit insurance and acts as a forum for exchanging ideas and experiences among its members.

From 1966 onward E.C.I.C. could extend unconditional guarantees to Canadian chartered banks that agreed to provide non-recourse financing to insured exporters who sold capital equipment abroad on medium-term credit.

---

39. See *Canada Year Book*, 1969, pp. 1020-1.

Table 13:5 Assets and Underwritings of Export Credits Insurance Corporation 1945-1969 (selected years)

	ASSETS		RISKS UNDERWRITTEN ANNUALLY
	Insurance account $MNS.	*Long-term financing account* $MNS.	$MNS.
Dec. 31			
1945	5.1	—	13
1950	11.5	—	33
1955	14.6	—	48
1960	17.0	—	101
1962	19.1	57.7	146
1964	21.0	217.3	346
1966	22.0	262.5	208
1968	22.5	334.8	341
1969 (Sept. 30)	22.3	361.1	175

SOURCE: Export Credits Insurance Corporation, *Annual Reports*.

In spite of the growth and development of E.C.I.C., the government began in 1967 to be concerned over its adequacies, and commissioned J. Douglas Gibson to investigate and report upon export credit insurance and financing in Canada. The study found that export insurance and financing facilities were more adequate in some other countries than in Canada and recommended changes, including the formation of a new institution with broader responsibilities and a different administrative structure, to be called the Export Development Corporation.

This corporation began operations in October 1969, with a capital and surplus of $50 million instead of the $20 million of the E.C.I.C. and with liabilities under insurance to businesses in Canada permitted up to ten times the amount of capital and surplus as before. Loans to foreign buyers and guarantees for such loans were increased to a limit of $800 million instead of $500 million, and E.D.C. was given complete discretion up to $600 million—a flexibility its predecessor did not enjoy. A board of twelve members is responsible for the affairs of the corporation, with four chosen from the private sector, an arrangement which in effect replaces the old Advisory Council. In addition to the powers enjoyed by E.C.I.C., E.D.C. can insure any person or institution (not just an "exporter") engaged in an export transaction; it can also insure costs of an export transaction incurred abroad, such as installation charges; it can insure export sales of a foreign affiliate to a foreign buyer, if Canadian trade is thereby facilitated; it can provide some insurance for Canadian investments made abroad. Finally E.D.C. will be able to rediscount export paper generated by Canadian financial institutions, which could increase the liquidity and hence the attractiveness of such paper and encourage private institutions to engage in export financing. The rediscounting facility in effect replaced the intended activity of the Export Finance Corporation sponsored jointly in 1961 by the chartered banks[40] which was never really successful and passed out of active operation in 1969.[41]

With the formation of the E.D.C. with its broadened powers, the federal government reconfirmed its intention of staying permanently in the business of insuring and financing Canadian export trade.

Deposit insurance corporations: In 1967 the Government of Canada introduced its Canada Deposit Insurance Corporation (C.D.I.C.), Ontario introduced the Ontario Deposit Insurance Corporation (O.D.I.C.) and Quebec formed the Quebec Deposit Insurance Board (Q.D.I.B.). All were designed to protect depositors against loss through the bankruptcy or insolvency of certain financial institutions that solicit deposits from the general public. The United States had had its Federal Deposit Insurance Corporation since 1935, its introduction prompted by the massive bank failures of the early 1930s. Deposit insurance is a means for providing a degree of protection for depositors, particularly those with relatively small deposits, and by so doing it also tends to diminish the risk of a "run on the banks." Furthermore, by offering deposit insurance, the insuring government institution is often able to exercise a degree of supervision or surveillance over financial institutions that might not otherwise be possible. The financial difficulties of the British Mortgage and Trust Corporation, an Ontario company, and of other trust and loan companies in 1965 and after, made it seem that deposit customers of non-bank financial institutions needed more protection than they were getting, and that the institutions themselves would have to be more carefully supervised. Actually the very introduction of deposit insurance is a recognition of the fact that supervision cannot provide complete protection to customers of financial institutions.

---

40. See above, p. 130.

41. For a general review of the E.D.C. see R. G. P. Styles, "Export Development Corporation," *The Canadian Banker*, October 1969, pp. 16-19.

The Ontario Deposit Insurance Corporation Act became law on February 9, 1967, eight days before the federal legislation.[42] Soon after the federal legislation was passed, the Ontario act was amended so as to require all Ontario corporations that were eligible for federal deposit insurance to be insured by the C.D.I.C. This has meant that the O.D.I.C. has not developed into an important institution. It may be noted, however, that the O.D.I.C. provides for insurance of deposits, which are defined to include some certificates and debentures, up to $20,000 with a premium of one-thirtieth of 1% of insurable deposits paid by the insured institution; it may borrow up to $250 million from the Ontario government to support the obligations of insured institutions; and, if the government orders it, the corporation can take over the administration of a member institution whose financial condition is regarded as being unsatisfactory.

The C.D.I.C. provides insurance up to $20,000 per depositor with respect to all deposits of member financial institutions. All of the federally incorporated private financial institutions that take deposits must be covered by insurance, which includes the chartered banks, Quebec Savings Bank, and many trust and mortgage loan companies. Provincial trust and loan companies may apply for membership in C.D.I.C. if the province of incorporation so consents. The term "deposit" is interpreted broadly for insurance purposes, and includes not just deposits but also deposit receipts, certificates and debentures (excluding chartered bank debentures) involving money repayable on demand or notice or on a fixed date not more than five years after the money is received. But deposits not payable in Canada or not payable in Canadian currency cannot be insured. Member institutions pay a fee of one-thirtieth of 1% of insurable deposits.

Another important role of the C.D.I.C. is to act as lender-of-last-resort to its member institutions. It can obtain up to $500 million from the federal government for making loans to members that are temporarily in financial difficulties and are unable to obtain funds elsewhere. It may be noted that companies operating under the proposed federal Investment Companies Act, and particularly sales finance companies, are also eligible for such assistance, even though they are not eligible for deposit insurance. The chartered banks, of course, already have lender-of-last-resort facilities at the Bank of Canada, as do money market dealers, and all institutions making N.H.A. mortgage loans can use such mortgages as collateral for

---

42. For an interesting and detailed discussion of Canadian deposit insurance see *Report of the Study Committee on Financial Institutions*, Government of Quebec, June 1969, chap. 7.

obtaining temporary funds from C.M.H.C. Thus, with the emergence of C.D.I.C., lender-of-last-resort facilities have become quite extensive in the Canadian capital market.

The Quebec Deposit Insurance Board is a much more important institution than the O.D.I.C., mainly because the Province of Quebec has actively sought to maximize the amount of insurable deposits in Quebec that are insured through it rather than through C.D.I.C. No institutions in Quebec, except the chartered banks, may solicit deposits unless they hold a Board permit, and individuals are not permitted to solicit them at all. Problems of conflicts in jurisdiction between C.D.I.C. and Q.D.I.B. arise out of this Quebec legislation because some provinces, as well as the federal government, require that all the insurable deposits of financial institutions incorporated by them be insured by the C.D.I.C. – including deposits taken in Quebec. If neither the C.D.I.C. nor the Q.D.I.B. had relented, some institutions would have had to pay double premiums, that is, a premium to each jurisdiction. An accommodation is being worked out, which will possibly require all institutions operating in Quebec to obtain permits from the Q.D.I.B. but exempt them from paying premiums on deposits taken in Quebec if they are already covered by the C.D.I.C.

The Q.D.I.B. insures deposits up to $20,000; it also defines deposits broadly, but excludes issues of instruments registered with the Quebec Securities Commission other than those of trust and loan companies; it may make advances of up to $250 million to member institutions, with funds obtained from the Quebec government; and it can receive loans of up to one year from the C.D.I.C. against sufficient security.

CONCLUSIONS

It has been estimated that since 1867 about 168 government financial intermediaries – which includes loan schemes – have appeared, of which about one-third have vanished. The life span of the ones that vanished averaged 21 years. Some seem to have lived much longer than was justified by objective operating criteria. Many of them seem to have failed to meet the objectives which they were designed to meet. The subsidization of operations, even where it was intended that no subsidies should be provided, was common and there was also displacement of private intermediary activity by subsidized public intermediary activity. It has been concluded that ". . . if there is to be any improvement . . . in the future government must (1) establish explicit goals for these institutions, (2) develop explicit criteria . . . for appraising their operations, and (3) establish procedures that will lead to constant appraisal of their operations."[43] Our findings are consistent with the above and we endorse those conclusions. We have formed several additional impressions on government financial intermediation that may be noted. First, loan schemes seem to be a fairly convenient device for creating the political impression that decisive action is being taken, including particularly where on economic grounds no such action should be taken. Second, the apparent conflict that this involves can in some cases conveniently be minimized through restraining the growth of the intermediary. Third, the long average life of government intermediaries frequently seems to be explained not by their economic contribution, but rather by the continuing importance of the non-economic objectives they were designed to serve, and especially by the almost complete absence of objective analysis of their operations. Finally, it may be that one of the most valuable aspects of government intermediary operations is that they provide some quantitative evidence of the existence or non-existence of "gaps" in the private sector of the capital market, and encourage private financial institutions to be aware of them.

But the fact remains that if economic efficiency in financial intermediation is of continuing importance to the nation, as it surely must be, then more attention must be directed toward appraising the operations of government financial intermediaries than has been the case in the past.

Pension Plans

DEVELOPMENT

History: Pension plans as a group have been among the fastest-growing financial intermediaries in Canada after the Second World War, reflecting widespread desire to enjoy a guaranteed level of income after retirement. This desire is itself explained by the increased urbanization of society, increased life expectancy and decreased working-life expectancy, and the desire for "independence" from children at old age. As we shall see, all this has been encouraged by favourable tax treatment.[44] The development has featured the growth

43. Doak, *op. cit.*, chap. 4.
44. See Daniel M. Holland, *Private Pension Funds: Projected Growth*, National Bureau of Economic Research, Occasional Paper 97, 1966, pp. 1-2.

of group pension plans, with contributions in Canada typically but not invariably coming from both employees and employers, and plans arranged for individuals, particularly self-employed individuals. The need to build up a fund that will generate income sufficient to pay future pension rights under a plan is, of course, the reason why pension plans have become important financial intermediaries. Pension plans at first will accumulate more funds than they pay out, and those with continuously expanding membership will continue to do so. This, however, assumes that the plans are fully or partially "funded," meaning that at any given time there are pension fund assets that fully or partially counterbalance the pension rights earned by that time. The change in size of those assets will depend on the relative sizes of the flows into and out of the fund – with the flows in being the contributions of employers and employees plus income earned on assets owned by the fund, and the flows out of the fund being benefits paid including withdrawals and costs of administration. Many funds are not fully funded and their assets, of course, grow less quickly than they would if they were fully funded. The size of the contribution is most commonly related to size of salary and the benefits are most commonly related to years of service and some average of salary earned – frequently now the average of the last five years.

In Canada private pension plans have taken the form of annuity contracts with life insurance companies, until recently also annuity plans offered by the federal government under the Government Annuities Act of 1908, and trusteed pension plans. The trusteed pension plans are ones under which invested accumulated contributions are held in trust against future payments under the plans. These trust funds are held and managed by trust companies, by individual trustees, or by a pension fund society formed under provincial or federal pension fund societies legislation.

Pension plans as such have a long history. Grants of freehold land to soldiers of ancient Rome were an early form of them, and there were even rough attempts made at that time to calculate the value of a life annuity. Edmund Halley provided a fairly accurate mortality table in 1693 and showed how to deduce the value of annuities from it.[45] The British government, under the Life Annuity Act of 1808, began to offer life annuities. In both the United Kingdom and the United States the annuity business was developed by life insurance companies. While the term "annuity" first meant a payment made annually, over the years it has come to mean any series of periodical

45. "Annuity," *Encyclopaedia Britannica*, 1962, vol. 2, p. 2.

payments made at regular intervals. The growth of labour unions in the late eighteenth century was in part related to the desire to obtain retirement, accident and death benefits, and in the United States the first significant superannuation scheme for a union appeared in 1908.[46]

In Canada the first important pension payments were probably those made to retiring soldiers of the British regiments.[47] Annuity plans were introduced into Canada by the British and United States life insurance companies, and when Canada's first life insurance company, the Canada Life Assurance Company, was formed in 1847 it began to offer "immediate annuities, payable during the remainder of life or deferred annuities to commence at a given age and to continue thereafter during life on the payment either of a fixed sum or of an annual premium," in the words of its 1849 prospectus.

The federal government's Superannuation Act of 1870, which provided for pensions for its civil servants, was one of the earliest systematic arrangements for retirement, while the contributory pension plan introduced in 1874 by the Grand Trunk Railway for clerical and indoor staff was possibly the first pension plan in private industry,[48] excluding a variety of *ad hoc* and informal arrangements for long-term employees. The chartered banks began to introduce contributory pension plans in the two decades before the turn of the century.

In spite of these developments, the prevailing opinion at the turn of the century was that individuals themselves should plan for their old age. And yet this opinion was not reflected in any significant growth of the annuity business of the life insurance companies. This was one of the main reasons why the federal government introduced annuities under the Government Annuities Act of 1908—just one hundred years after the British government had done so. Its preamble states that "it is in the public interest that habits of thrift be promoted and that the people of Canada be encouraged and aided thereto so that provision may be made for old age, and expedient that further facilities be afforded." The Minister of Finance, in answering criticisms that the scheme would compete with life insurance companies and so should not be advertised aggressively, said, "Though the

---

46. See H. Robert Bartell, Jr., and Elizabeth T. Simpson, *Pension Funds of Multiemployer Industrial Groups, Unions and Nonprofit Organizations* (National Bureau of Economic Research, 1968), Occasional Paper 105, pp. 1-2.
47. See H. Weitz, "Old Age Security in Canada," in Dominion Bureau of Statistics, *Canadian Statistical Review*, August 1967, p. i.
48. *Ibid.*

insurance companies have always been authorized to carry on annuity business, the annuities carried by these companies in Canada number only 1,321 and the average is only $270. . . . They do not make any effort to press that business."[49] In 1919 the principle was established that up to a point employees could deduct contributions to pension plans from their taxable income and that a pensioner's benefits under a pension plan constituted taxable income. In 1938 the Income Tax Act was amended to permit employers to deduct pension plan contributions for past service benefits from taxable income, and in 1941 this was specifically extended to include contributions for future service benefits.[50] In 1957 the limited privilege of deducting pension contributions from taxable income was extended to self-employed individuals when paid into accredited plans referred to as Registered Retirement Savings Plans. Prior to that time the term "approved" plans had been used. This development encouraged life insurance companies, trust companies and the federal Annuities Branch to adjust their plans for individuals in ways that made them eligible for being classified as registered plans. Favourable tax treatment undoubtedly encouraged the growth of pension plans.

Life annuities: It was noted earlier that for many decades the life insurance companies did not develop the annuity business in a significant way. The year 1923 marks a change in this respect for it was in that year that the first insured group pension plan was written in Canada.[51] Under such an insured plan, when an employee premium is paid the insurance company guarantees an amount of pension which will be available at retirement and will be paid monthly over his lifetime. For the employer such an insured plan had the great advantage of simplicity, for it relieved him of much of the administrative details of operating it, including the investment of funds, and yet offered a guaranteed benefit. In the 1950s the life insurance companies began offering a "deposit administration contract" under which contributions of employers and employees are not used immediately to purchase a paid-up annuity, as under group annuity plans, but rather are deposited and invested until needed to purchase an annuity for the employee when he retires. This represented a compromise with the previous "fully insured" plan,

---

49. Canada, House of Commons *Debates*, June 18, 1908, p. 10851.

50. See L. E. Coward, "History of Pensions in Canada," *Financial Post*, Nov. 23, 1963, p. P-5.

51. See E. S. Jackson, "Insurance Company Functions in the Pension Field," *Financial Post*, Nov. 23, 1963, p. P-17.

for under it the employer assumes responsibility for the adequacy of the fund; but it is well suited for cases where there are no employee contributions and it is simple to administer.

A more significant compromise with the "fully insured" plans occurred in 1961 when, at the request of the industry, federal life insurance legislation was amended to enable life companies to offer pension plans involving unrestricted investment of pension funds in equities, provided that such assets—commonly referred to as "segregated funds"—were segregated from the ordinary life and annuity assets of the company. The segregated assets are held in a variety of "pooled segregated funds" or "pooled investment funds" —e.g., equity fund, fixed income fund, mortgage fund, U.S. equity fund, bond fund—and investment in those funds is through purchasing units of the funds. From this innovation have emerged several types of pension arrangements. Some individual employers have their own separate fund managed by a life insurance company, in which there are segregated assets. Some employers with a deposit administration contract have part of their contribution invested in a pooled segregated fund and share in the performance of the pooled fund. The annuities received under these plans vary with the value of the assets of the fund. And apart from the mortality element which is guaranteed, they resemble the pooled equity funds of the trust companies in which the employer is responsible finally for the fund's being sufficient to cover benefits stipulated in the pension plan. In addition to these group plans with variable benefits, some companies have established variable annuities for individuals, and in such cases it is the individual who carries the risk for the absolute size of the benefits ultimately received. Some insurance companies, instead of offering a combination of guaranteed group annuity, deposit administration contract, and equity fund, offer participation in more than one fund, e.g., equity fund, mortgage fund, bond fund, which can provide roughly the same kind of pension product.

The variable benefit group and individual annuities of the life insurance companies provided a means whereby savings in the form of pension payments could be invested in common stocks and thereby provide protection against inflation. Their development was prompted by the spectacular growth of the mutual funds, and by the equally spectacular growth of trusteed pension plans, both of which were accommodating public desire to have some pension funds and long-term savings invested in common stocks.

Trusteed pension funds: The trusteed pension funds seem to have appeared first in the 1920s. The system involves payment of contributions to a trustee—trust company, group of individuals, or pension fund society—and management of the funds by the trustee. The trustee is given varying degrees of discretion in investing the funds, but he does not guarantee the adequacy of the fund. On retirement a member of such a plan is paid his pension by the trustee out of the fund, or the trustee may purchase an annuity for him.[52] The trust companies have taken a leading role in the development of trusteed pension plans. Until 1955 they administered the assets of each plan separately. But even before that, the federal and Ontario trust companies were permitted to establish pooled trust funds, the first such fund apparently appearing in 1952.[53] In 1955 they began the practice of pooling some of the pension funds in their trust, for investment purposes, thereby permitting greater diversification of investments and achieving lower administration costs for the smaller group pension funds and those of individuals. In essence the trust companies have established various kinds of pooled registered retirement savings funds—equity, bond, mortgage, etc.—and the income of the pension plans is used to purchase units of these funds. In some cases the trust companies invest the accumulated savings of the individual and pooled registered retirement savings funds entirely in the units of the mutual or investment funds that they also sponsor. The year 1957 saw the introduction of a large number of these trust company pooled pension funds, no doubt in part because of the extension in that year of tax benefits to pension payments of self-employed individuals.

Universal pensions: No mention has yet been made of universal pension plans sponsored by governments. In 1927, under the Old Age Pension Act, means test pensions for people aged seventy years and over were introduced. The cost was shared by the federal government and the provinces but the plan was administered by the provinces since pensions were a provincial matter under the British North America Act. Following an amendment to that act permitting the federal government to enter the field, the Old Age Security Act was passed in 1951 and it introduced universal old-age pensions for everyone meeting residence requirements without a means test. Benefits were changed in various years, but by 1970 benefits were available to everyone aged sixty-five and over and the plan had a

---

52. For a concise description of pension plans see W. C. Hood, *Financing of Economic Activity in Canada* (Ottawa: Queen's Printer, 1958), pp. 367-79, and Arthur Pedoe, *Life Insurance, Annuities and Pensions* (Toronto: University of Toronto Press, 1964), pp. 337-62.

53. See Hood, *op. cit.*, p. 317.

built-in cost-of-living adjustment. An amendment to the act in 1966 provided for a guaranteed income supplement to pensioners with little or no income other than their old age pension. For our purpose the important point about this plan was that it was on a pay-as-you-go basis financed through corporation and personal income taxes. This, of course, meant that it did not acquire a pool of assets and so did not become a financial intermediary.

However, in 1965 appeared the Canada Pension Plan and the Quebec Pension Plan, which introduced universal retirement pensions into Canada, as well as certain disability, widows', orphans' and death benefits. The Quebec Plan was formed as a consequence of Quebec's taking advantage of a provision in the Canada Pension Plan Act permitting provinces to establish their own plans providing certain requirements were met. The plans are compulsory for virtually all employed people; they are contributory, with contributions and benefits related to earnings; they have a built-in cost-of-living adjustment for both contributions and earnings; and the scale of contributions and level of benefits are such that the plans will generate a surplus of funds for some years to come. All the funds accumulated are made available to the provinces, with each province's share determined by the relative size of contributions of its residents to the plan. A province obtains its money by selling a non-marketable bond to the Pension Fund on which it pays interest, while any money left in the fund is invested in Government of Canada securities. The Province of Quebec itself manages funds collected under the Quebec Pension Plan through the facilities of its Caisse de Dépôt et Placement du Québec. The latter need not confine its investments to securities of the Province of Quebec and so, in contrast to the Canada Pension Plan, it at least has the possibility of pursuing rational portfolio management policies.

Regulation: We have already noted that pensions were a provincial matter under the terms of the British North America Act. Through amendments to that act the federal government was able to enter the field of universal old age and retirement benefits. The annuities sold by the life insurance companies are, of course, regulated through life insurance legislation, and this means that a large portion of that pension business is under the supervision of the federal Superintendent of Insurance. It is also true that until 1957 the federal government exercised some indirect control over private pension plans by requiring them to conform to certain standards if income paid into them was to be deductible for income tax purposes. But the constitutional difficulties inherent in this indirect control caused the federal government to discontinue it in 1957. Control of some kind, however, was clearly necessary and Ontario took the lead by appointing the Ontario Committee on Portable Pensions in 1960. This led to the Pension Benefits Act of Ontario of 1963, an act designed to improve private pension plans in operation in the province. It was in fact a pioneering act for Canada as a whole. It improved the portability of such pensions by establishing minimum "vesting" privileges (that is, the right of an employee to take with him some or all of his benefits in a plan, based on his own contributions and those of his employer, when changing jobs); it required that all plans had to be fully funded by 1990; it established rules for the investment of pension funds; and it required that employees be informed of their pension rights and benefits. The portability element as well as other aspects made it desirable that there be uniformity in provincial pension legislation. Therefore, an inter-provincial conference was convened by Ontario in 1964, and from it came a draft of uniform pension legislation. Ontario amended its act to comply, and Quebec did the same by passing its Supplemental Pension Plans Act in 1965. Several other provinces followed; it was one of the few instances of co-operation between provinces in the matter of financial legislation.

GROWTH AND RELATIVE SIZE

The growth of the major types of pension plans is shown on Table 13:6. Over the period 1950 to 1968 the total of pension plans shown there (excluding the Canada and Quebec pension plans) grew at an average annual rate of 14%, with trusteed plans growing by 14% annually, life insurance company group annuities by 16% and federal government group annuities by 6%. The trusteed pension funds, with 71% of pension funds in 1969, have about maintained their relative size since 1950. The life insurance group annuities reached their peak in relative size in 1964 with 25% of total pension fund assets, and they have essentially maintained it, in part because of the introduction of pension plans based on segregated funds. However, the federal government group annuities declined steadily in relative size, from 17% in 1950 to 4% in 1969. In 1967 the federal government finally decided to cease selling its annuities, and this, it can be seen, came after some years of lacklustre growth. The trusteed pension plans obviously have for many years been the dominant form of pension plan, although the life insurance company group annuities have become important as well. In 1968 trusteed pension plan assets amounted to 8.9% of total financial intermediary assets (see Chart 13:2) or $8,972 million, an amount exceeded only by the total assets of

Table 13:6 Assets of Pension Plans in Canada 1950-1969 (selected years)

(MILLIONS OF DOLLARS; PERCENTAGE DISTRIBUTION; RATE OF GROWTH)

	Trusteed pension plans		Life insurance companies				Federal government group annuities		Total		Canada and Quebec pension plans	Grand total	
			Group annuities		*Segregated funds*								
	$	%	$	%	$	%	$	%	$	ANNUAL GROWTH %	$	$	ANNUAL GROWTH %
1950	875[1]	68	190[2]	15	—	—	225[2]	17	1290	16.0	—	—	
1957	2460	66	756	20	—	—	495	13	3714				
1958	2791	66	894	21	—	—	525	12	4210	13.4	—	—	
1959	3200	66	1062	22	—	—	560	12	4822	14.5	—	—	
1960	3583	67	1208	22	—	—	600	11	5391	11.8	—	—	
1961	4036	67	1397	23	...	...	610	10	6043	12.1	—	—	
1962	4530	67	1606	24	...	...	625	9	6771	12.0	—	—	
1963	5127	68	1818	24	...	...	623	8	7568	11.8	—	—	
1964	5766	68	2049	24	58	1	615	7	8488	12.2	—	—	
1965	6541	68	2333	24	94	1	634	7	9602	13.1	—	—	
1966	7250	69	2491	24	139	1	644	6	10524	9.6	719	11243	17.1
1967	8068	70	2692	23	194	2	636	5	11590	9.9	1605	13195	17.4
1968	8972	70	2891	23	259	2	635	5	12857	10.9	2595	15452	17.1
1969	10003	71	3062	22	401	3	634	4	14100	9.7	3730	17830	15.4

SOURCE: Dominion Bureau of Statistics, *Trusteed Pension Plans Financial Statistics* and *National Income and Expenditure Accounts*; *Report of the Superintendent of Insurance for Canada*, various years; Canada, Department of Labour, Industrial Pensions and Annuities Branch.

[1]Estimate as reported in Royal Commission on Banking and Finance, *Report*, 1964, pp. 238, 257.
[2]Approximation only as estimated by the author.

Chart 13:2 — Growth and Relative Size of Trusteed Pension Plans 1950-1969

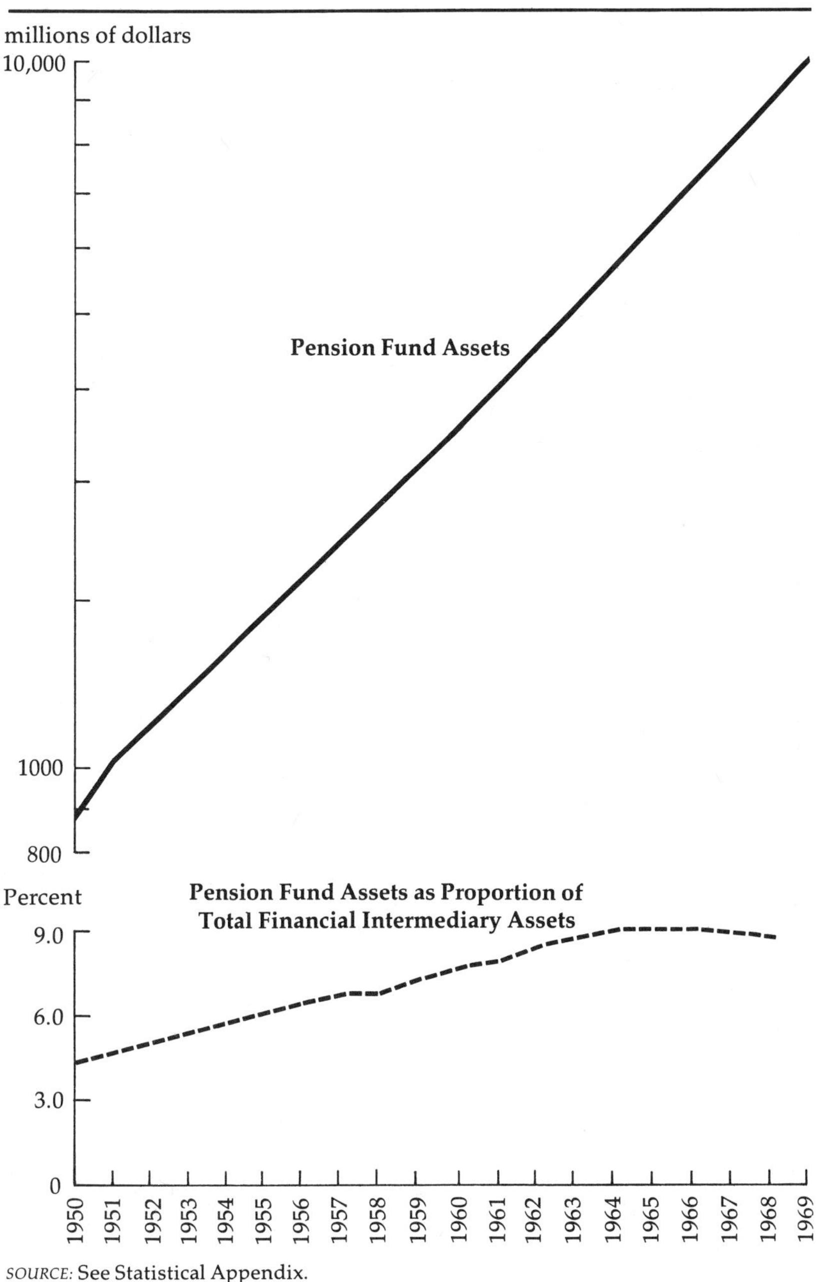

SOURCE: See Statistical Appendix.

the chartered banks and the life insurance companies among the major types of private financial intermediaries.

However, Table 13:6 also shows that in only three years of operation, the Canada and Quebec pension plans amassed assets of over $2½ billion and have therefore become major competitors in the pension field. To what extent their growth will diminish the growth rate of the trusteed pension plans and the annuity business of the life insurance companies remains to be seen. In this respect two points should be noted. First, supplemental pension plan benefits are likely to be sought by many who enjoy basic benefits under the national plans, and this will provide support for the trusteed and insured plans. Second, it would seem that the Canada and Quebec pension plan assets will grow very quickly in the early 1970s, their growth rate will then diminish and by the mid 1980s it will become negative.[54] This means that as time goes by the Canada and Quebec pension plan funds will diminish in relative importance as accumulators of savings so that, given a constant rate of saving, this will work to the benefit of the growth rate of other financial intermediaries, including probably the private pension funds. It may be noted from Table 13:6 that in the years immediately prior to 1965 the pension funds shown there grew at an annual rate of about 12½% and after 1965, when the national plans came into operation, their growth rate declined to about 9½-10%. At the same time total pension funds, including the national pension plans, increased from the former rate of growth of 12½% to over 16%. This leads to the general impression that about one-third of the growth of the national pension plans came at the expense of the private plans, and two-thirds came from an acceleration in the flow of savings into pension plans.[55] That the national plans did slow the growth of the private plans is also apparent by the increase in cash withdrawals from trusteed pension plans that began in late 1965.[56]

The growth of the private plans in terms of number of funds and number of plan members is shown in Table 13:7. Of the private plans there shown, the trusteed funds accounted for 70% of all individual members in 1969 compared with 60% in 1960, while the proportions accounted for by both life company annuities and

---

54. Cf. *Financial Post*, Jan 9, 1965, p. P-19.
55. To what extent that two-thirds is explained by a slowdown in the growth of other financial intermediaries or in the growth of direct financing, or by an increase in the rate of savings, is an interesting question, but we cannot explore it here.
56. See Dominion Bureau of Statistics, *Trusteed Pension Plans Financial Statistics*, 1967, p. 10.

Table 13:7 Private Pension Plans: Number of Funds and Plan Members 1960-1969

	Trusteed pension funds		Life insurance		Federal government group annuities		Total	
			Group annui-ties	*Segre-gated funds*				
No. of funds	No.		No.		No.		No.	Percentage increase
1960	1139		6,564		1556		9,259	n.a.
1961	1362		7,305		1513		10,180	+ 9.9
1962	1546		8,276		1437		11,259	+10.6
1963	1804		9,276		1365		12,444	+10.5
1964	2118		10,048	92	1312		13,570	+ 9.0
1965	2997		10,866	160	1267		15,290	+12.7
1966	3467		11,459	246	1416		16,588	+ 8.5
1967	3789		11,718	413	1398		17,318	+ 4.4
1968	4065		12,891	571	1365		18,892	+ 9.1
1969	4072		13,209	822	1110		19,213	+ 1.7
Plan members	No.	Percent of total	No.	Percent of total	No.	Percent of total	No.	
1960	1,001,066	60.5	469,339	28.4	185,000	11.2	1,655,405	n.a.
1961	1,077,119	61.5	501,060	28.6	174,000	9.9	1,752,179	+5.8
1962	1,126,634	61.7	536,886	29.4	161,090	8.8	1,824,610	+4.1
1963	1,253,437	63.6	560,539	28.5	155,586	7.9	1,969,562	+7.9
1964	1,332,391	64.9	570,925	27.8	149,026	7.3	2,052,342	+4.2
1965	1,467,424	67.0	580,984	26.5	141,579	6.5	2,189,987	+6.7
1966	1,554,891	69.4	563,579	25.1	122,576	5.5	2,241,046	+2.3
1967	1,603,079	69.1	598,427	25.8	116,892	5.0	2,318,398	+3.5
1968	1,655,962	69.5	616,911	25.9	111,503	4.7	2,384,376	+2.8
1969	1,719,423	70.4	616,312	25.2	105,187	4.3	2,440,922	+2.4

SOURCE: Dominion Bureau of Statistics, *Trusteed Pension Plans*, various years.

government annuities declined over that period. It may also be noted that from 1960 to 1965 the number of members in the individual plans grew annually at a rate in excess of 4% per annum, whereas in 1966 it increased by only 2.3%, in 1967 by 3.5%, in 1968 by 2.8%, and in 1969 by 2.4%. It is likely that this slowdown is related to the introduction of the Canada and Quebec pension plans, and it may mean that the peak rate of growth of the private pension plans has already been passed.

The number of trusteed plans in 1960 was 1,139 (see Table 13:7). Of that number, 80% were accounted for by corporate trustees (i.e. trust companies), 17% by individual trustees, and 3% by pension fund societies. In 1969, with 4,072 funds, the equivalent ratios were 74%, 24% and 1%, with a further 1% accounted for by a combination of corporate and individual trustees. Apparently there has been some relative shift of plans away from corporate trustees toward individual trustees. This, however, is not the case when assets managed rather than number of plans managed are used as a measure of size. In 1960 corporate trustees managed about 33% of trusteed pension plan assets, and individual trustees about 55%, while in 1969 the former managed 36% and the latter 51%. The pension fund societies have not become important as managers of pension funds.

ASSETS AND INCOME OF TRUSTEED PENSION FUNDS

In 1957, as Table 13:8 shows, the trusteed pension funds invested 6.8% of their funds in preferred and common stocks and pooled pension and mutual funds, whereas in 1969 they invested 32.3%. This substantial shift into equities, and out of government bonds, was the most significant change in the investment practices of pension fund trustees. The table also shows that there has been a shift into foreign stocks as well as into Canadian stocks. The preference for equities probably explains in part the higher growth rate of trusteed pension funds after 1965 compared with the life insurance group annuities. It is true, of course, that the life insurance companies have begun to offer group and individual variable annuities based on common stocks but this has been a relatively recent development. At the same time, that development is understandable considering the shift of trusteed funds into equities.

These aggregate statistics of the asset distribution of trusteed pension funds hide substantial differences between the trusteed funds of various types of organizations. Table 13:9 shows that trusteed pension funds of the municipal and provincial crown corporations and agencies, including the "educational" grouping, had not shifted as heavily into equities or pooled pension and mutual funds by 1969 as

Table 13:8 Assets and Income of Trusteed Pension Funds, Percentage Distribution 1957-1970 (selected years)

ASSETS	1957	1960	1963	1966	1968	1969	1970
Canadian securities							
Government of Canada	19.6	18.1	11.3	6.7	5.5	5.0	4.3
Provincial	33.5	30.8	32.5	30.6	28.3	27.1	26.8
Municipal	11.3	10.8	10.5	9.4	7.9	7.2	6.9
Corporate and other bonds	15.8	17.2	15.4	15.0	14.1	13.3	14.1
Preferred and common stocks	5.7	7.2	10.1	13.6	16.1	17.9	18.9
Foreign securities							
Bonds	.4	.1	.1	.1	.1	.2	.1
Preferred and common stocks	.5	.6	1.9	3.2	5.7	6.4	5.4
Other assets							
Mortgage loans	7.2	8.3	9.3	9.3	8.6	8.6	9.2
Cash	2.5	1.9	1.1	1.6	1.2	1.1	1.2
Investment in pooled pension funds and mutual funds	.6	2.9	5.6	7.6	8.1	8.0	7.7
Other assets	2.8	2.1	2.2	2.9	4.4	5.2	5.4
Total	100	100	100	100	100	100	100
INCOME							
Employer contribution		41.8	40.0	40.4	41.8	39.6	40.5
Employee contribution		29.1	28.4	24.5	23.0	24.7	24.4
Investment income		27.6	29.9	32.6	32.3	31.8	33.6
Other		1.5	1.7	2.5	2.9	3.9	1.5
Total		100	100	100	100	100	100

SOURCE: Based on data in Dominion Bureau of Statistics, *Trusteed Pension Plans Financial Statistics*, annual.

had others, although data for preceding years confirm that they too were holding more equities than they used to do. Their funds were heavily invested in provincial and municipal bonds, and the question naturally arises of whether there was not a conflict of interest involved to the detriment of sound pension portfolio management, and so to the detriment of the financial interests of members of those plans and the economic interests of the nation.

Considering now sources of funds, we find from Table 13:8 that the

Table 13:9 Trusted Pension Funds by Type of Organization, Percentage Distribution of Assets 1969

Type of organization	BONDS				FUNDS		COMMON AND PREFERRED STOCKS	MORTGAGE	OTHER
	Government of Canada	*Provincial*	*Municipal*	*Other*	*Pooled pension*	*Mutual*			
Municipalities and their enterprises	2.2	43.4	32.9	6.6	2.0	.6	4.7	3.7	3.8
Provincial crown corporations and agencies	8.7	60.6	5.5	9.1	.4	.1	8.7	4.2	2.7
Federal crown corporations and agencies	14.8	13.8	1.5	8.1	.9	2.1	26.0	27.4	5.4
Religious and charitable	13.6	18.4	8.3	20.8	1.6	—	21.1	11.2	5.0
Educational	1.4	72.8	4.5	3.1	2.5	.1	3.0	1.1	11.5
Health	1.1	9.3	4.9	17.6	11.3	—	44.4	3.9	7.5
Trade and employee associations	7.9	10.5	4.8	13.1	40.2	1.5	14.6	1.1	6.3
Co-operatives	1.9	13.7	8.9	25.6	22.8	2.5	17.4	3.9	3.3
Industry	3.8	13.5	5.0	17.8	11.6	.3	33.4	8.1	6.4
Other	23.6	1.2	2.3	2.2	22.3	—	5.7	.5	42.2
Total	5.5	27.1	7.2	13.5	7.'5	.5	24.3	8.6	5.8

SOURCE: Dominion Bureau of Statistics, *Trusteed Pension Plans, 1969*.

trusteed pension plans receive about 40% of their income from employer contributions, 25% from employee contributions, and 32% from investment. The latter has been increasing and employee contributions have been declining in relative size in recent years, while the share of employer contributions has remained relatively unchanged. In a sense, this development constitutes a tendency to move in the direction of United States pension fund practice, where employee contributions are unimportant.

CONCLUSIONS

In a relatively short period of time pension funds in Canada have become major repositories of the nation's savings. If all such funds, including those operated by the federal and provincial governments, are tabulated, they appear to amount to about one-fifth of total financial intermediary assets in Canada. How efficiently those funds are being used has become a matter of importance. The changing structure of assets of the trusteed funds suggests that market influences do affect the way those funds are allocated, and the high proportion of such funds under corporate trustees does increase the chances that rational portfolio management will prevail. It would seem that the greatest risk of misallocating pension funds lies with funds closely aligned with governmental authorities. In this respect the problems posed are similar to those posed by the operations of government financial intermediaries.

14

Brokers, Dealers, and Securities Markets

At the beginning of this study we indicated that the major functions of a capital market are first, accumulating funds from those in surplus and distributing them to those in deficit, and secondly, facilitating changes in ownership of the outstanding securities that this process inevitably creates. Past chapters have essentially been concerned with that first process, for the growth and development of financial intermediaries is really the story of the growth and development of capital market institutions specializing in accumulating and distributing surplus funds.

The capital market institutions and institutional arrangements designed for making markets in securities have not yet been discussed, and so tracing their growth and development is our immediate task. There are really three aspects to that development: the evolution of credit instruments, of specialized brokerage-type institutions, and of organized trading arrangements. We will attempt to trace the emergence of the major types of credit instruments and of the stock exchange brokers and investment dealers that specialize in trading securities and underwriting securities issues. We will also outline the development of the market arrangements that facilitate this change in ownership of securities: stock exchanges essentially for transferring equity securities, bond markets for transferring bonds and debentures, and money markets that specialize in short-term debt instruments.

Earlier we discovered that the growth of financial intermediaries was a steady one extending over many decades and that dividing that growth into periods—such as pre–First World War and post–First World War—for reasons other than mere exposition could hardly be supported by the evidence. The history of the growth of the volume of credit instruments and the growth of Canadian institutions which specialize in trading such instruments is slightly different—but only in degree. The period from about 1896 to 1920 saw rapid developments in the volume of credit instruments in the Canadian market and in brokerage and underwriting institutions. The sudden growth, through the merging of smaller private businesses, of the Canadian public industrial corporation well before the First World War, the deflection of Canadian government (federal, provincial, and municipal) borrowing from the London to the Canadian markets, the large volume of governmental financing as such even before but especially during the First World War, and the general wave of economic prosperity that began several years before the turn of the century—all these combined to increase greatly the volume of securities in the Canadian market and so to provide new opportunities to new institutions. The bond dealer, specializing in underwriting stocks, bonds and debentures, in promoting mergers, and in trading in bonds and debentures, quickly became highly specialized as a result of these developments. The view that the Canadian capital market had little history prior to the First World War is explained by past concentration of attention on the sudden growth in the volume of bonds available to Canadian financial houses during the war. But prior to that period the growth of industrial financing was in full stride, and over the decades the major forms of credit instruments were being developed and were growing in volume, as were trading institutions and financial intermediaries. To that earlier period we now turn.

The Pre-Confederation Period

CREDIT INSTRUMENTS

The earliest significant attempts to develop indigenous credit instruments were those relating to the provision of adequate media of exchange, and these included the French use of card money and the merchants' "bons."[1] In 1761 Nova Scotia, following a summer of drought, found it necessary to provide relief for the impoverished people in Halifax and, having insufficient funds, was obliged to borrow £850 currency against the security of treasury notes bearing the legal maximum interest rate of 6%.[2] Having been introduced in that

1. See above, p. 37.
2. See Victor Ross, *A History of the Canadian Bank of Commerce*, vol. 1, appendix I (Toronto: University of Toronto Press, 1920).

way, these treasury notes were sold repeatedly over the years. Beginning in 1813, some of them evolved into small denomination, non-interest bearing, and reissuable notes – in fact, paper currency – but other issues of interest-bearing notes and certificates were also available. They were all of short-term maturity and closely resembled currency, even though they provided a rate of return to the holder.

The Army Bills issued by the British colonial authorities during the War of 1812-14 also were a cross between currency and investment securities. Their convenient denomination and convertibility into cash or bills of exchange made them acceptable as currency and yet, since denominations of $25 and over bore interest, they were also a convenient and reliable form of investment. However, they soon disappeared through redemption.

But their place as investment securities was soon taken by the first debenture issue of Upper Canada in 1821, from which time such debentures have always been in existence. A special committee on arrearages of militia pensions reported on March 28, 1821, that militia pensions outstanding of £23,858-6-8 could not be paid because of the delay in Upper Canada's receiving its share of the duties paid at the port of Quebec, and recommended that because of the distress occasioned by non-payment of the pensions the government should borrow sums necessary to meet the charge "on debentures bearing interest and payable in three yearly periods by equal instalments, to be secured on the duties to be received from Lower Canada."[3]

Consequently the First Debenture Act[4] was passed on April 14, 1821, and it authorized an issue up to £25,000 in the form of three debentures, of one, two and three years to maturity with interest at the legal maximum rate of 6% payable twice a year. The lieutenant-governor reported later that he "was gratified in finding that the negotiation of the loan was immediately effected within the Province."[5] Debentures amounting to £20,000 currency were granted to Messrs. Clark and Street, Merchants, on September 15, 1821, and since these merchants took sizable amounts of later debenture issues as well, they may well have constituted Canada's first underwriters of securities. Additional debentures under the First Debenture Act were granted to the new Bank of Upper Canada in July and September of 1822. It is interesting to note that chartered bank participation in new government financing has been a feature of the Canadian approach to underwriting from the beginning.

Government revenues continued to prove disappointing and gov-

---

3. *Journal of the House of Assembly of Upper Canada*, March 28, 1821.
4. 2 Geo. IV, cap. 24.
5. *Journal of the House of Assembly of Upper Canada*, November 21, 1821.

ernment ventures into improvement of the waterways soon reached huge proportions, so that by 1833 there had been about twenty debenture issues in Upper Canada amounting to £255,800, of which only £52,666-13-4 had been redeemed.[6] Advances to the Welland Canal Company, and to companies sponsoring the building of the Port Hope Harbour, the Cobourg Harbour and the Desjardins Canal, and payments for construction of the Burlington Canal, Kettle Creek Harbour and Oakville Harbour, and for roads and bridges, as well as for war losses, had in a decade made the Upper Canada government a major borrower. Indeed, we shall see that it had reached an amount that local sources of funds could not begin to meet.

During that decade the largest amount of debentures was granted to the Bank of Upper Canada, a large number to Messrs. Clark and Street, and smaller amounts to Christopher Widmen, the Canada Company, the Hon. Wm. Allen, George Jacob, J. G. Bethune and Andrew Drew. The debentures issued were of various denominations, some small enough to appeal to relatively small savers, and of both a serial and a fixed dated kind. A straight twenty-year debenture issue was sold to the Bank of Upper Canada in 1827, but most were of shorter maturity than that. The importance of the Bank of Upper Canada in this early financing is explained by the fact that it was the government's fiscal agent, and the government had invested £25,000 currency in the bank, holding 2,000 of its shares.

The weight of financing induced the receiver-general to seek external funds. In a letter to the lieutenant-governor dated December 23, 1833, he says that in an attempt to sell debentures recently authorized to be issued he had inserted a notice of intended loans and invitations to tender in both provincial and United States newspapers, without much success. In addition, a Commissioner for the Improvement of the St. Lawrence had visited the United States and could find no capitalist willing to invest in the loan. The receiver-general's view was that while some debentures had been sold in the province, the interest rate stipulated was too low for both the province and the United States.

He then sent a letter to several respectable houses in London, including Messrs. Barings and Brothers and Messrs. Thomas Wilson & Co., and while Barings initially declined on the grounds that the interest rate was too low, the stage was soon set for the pattern of financing that persisted for many years.[7]

---

6. *Journal of the House of Assembly of Upper Canada*, 1833-4 Session, Appendix pp. 122-9.
7. See *Journal of the House of Assembly of Upper Canada*, 1833-4 Session, Appendix pp. 113-16.

The position was this. Capital in Canada was scarce, and financial intermediaries, apart from the chartered banks, who were more interested in commercial business, had not developed to mobilize efficiently the savings that did exist. The legal rate of interest of 6% on debentures held little attraction in any case, and interest rates in the United States suggested that capital was scarce there as well. Interest rates were much lower, and capital much more plentiful, in Great Britain, so it was inevitable that appeals would be made to that market. Appeals to the United States capitalists were not fruitful and these had to wait at least half a century to be successful, that is until a fundamental structural change in U.K., U.S., and Canadian interest rates had occurred.

So in 1835, about two years after initial approaches, the Province of Upper Canada raised a loan of £400,000 in the London market through Messrs. Barings and Messrs. T. Wilson & Co. As with the first debenture issue, interest on it was to be secured by the duties levied at the port of Quebec. Wilson's failed in 1837 but within less than two weeks Sir George Grey, under-secretary at the Colonial Office, had, through George Carr Glyn, arranged for Messrs. Glyn to assume Wilson's obligations respecting the Upper Canada financial agency. When the Canadian receiver-general reached London he found that he had new agents. Glyn's and Barings therefore were the financial agents for Canada from June 1837 to December 1892, when the Bank of Montreal was granted the agency.[8] Prior to Confederation political and economic instability on several occasions caused doubt to be cast on the soundness of Province of Canada securities, and the financial agents in London had to provide active support for them.

By January 1, 1841, the total funded debt of Upper Canada was £1,026,222, of which 81% was in sterling and the remainder in currency. The funded debt in Lower Canada was much smaller, only £93,975, most of this having arisen from enlarging and improving the harbour at Montreal and for completing the Chambly Canal. The large proportion of sterling debt meant, of course, that underwriting and brokerage intermediaries in Canada did not develop as fast as they would have done had it been currency debt sold in Canada.

This rapid development of provincial borrowing, particularly in Upper Canada, was greatly accelerated by an act of 1849[9] introduced

8. For an interesting article on the early experiences of the London agents see "The Canadian Financial Agency," *Three Banks Review*, London, March 1961.

9. 12 Vic., cap. 29, 1849.

by Francis Hincks, which permitted the government to make loans to railway companies on terms that were easy, and made easier by new legislation two years later. Also, the Municipal Loan Fund introduced in November 1852,[10] which began operations in 1853 in Upper Canada and in 1854 in Lower Canada, gave a large number of municipalities the ability to become large borrowers. Municipal financing as such had begun before this. In 1835 the City of Toronto sold a £5,000 6% issue.[11] Under the Municipal Loan scheme municipalities could apply for a loan for a specific purpose, and when it was approved by the governor-in-council, the receiver-general could issue debentures in the amount of the loan and these could be sold by the municipality; alternatively, the government could sell them and remit the proceeds to the municipality.[12] Initially no provincial guarantee was involved and the only advantages were those attaching to the pooling of municipal resources to back municipal debentures, and the advantages of a large issue of Municipal Loan Fund debentures over the small issues of many individual municipalities. Later, when default on payments began, the provincial government became directly involved. By 1858, when the active operation of the Fund was about over, almost $10 million had been borrowed by municipalities ($2.3 million in Lower Canada), much of it for making advances to railroads. The results of this venture can best be understood from contemporary comments.

> The refusal of the municipalities to acquit their indebtedness to the Municipal Loan Fund, and even to make an effort to pay a portion of it, involves the moral guilt of repudiation, and sets a contaminating and corrupting example to private persons. . . .
>
> The great error was in allowing municipalities to contract more debt on the credit of this Fund than they had a reasonable prospect of being able to pay. . . . At first the Government merely undertook to administer the Fund, without guaranteeing the bonds issued on its credit. Investors did not always note the distinction; they sometimes looked on the issue as one for which the Government was responsible. To save its honour the Government had eventually to incur an obligation on which it had not counted at the outset; and the time came when the holders of Municipal Loan Fund debentures were permitted to exchange them for Government securities. . . . A law was passed to relieve . . . [the municipalities] . . . by

10. 16 Vic., cap. 22.
11. See D. G. Fullerton, *The Bond Market in Canada* (Toronto: Carswell Co. Ltd., 1962), p. 69, and A. M. Hillhouse, *Municipal Bonds*, 1926.
12. For details see Albert Faucher, "Le Fonds D'Emprunt Municipal Dans Le Haut-Canada 1852-1867," *Recherches Sociographiques*, 1, janvier-mars 1960.

> diminishing the annual payments; but its necessary and fatal effect was to increase the amount of the debt. There sprung up a sort of tacit understanding not to pay; not openly to repudiate, but to do so practically. The effect was to throw upon the whole country the burthen of the debts of particular municipalities. . . .[13]

The larger cities such as Montreal, Quebec, and Toronto had begun to issue their own debentures while the Maritime Provinces, like the Province of Canada, began to place issues in London.

The foregoing suggests that during the half-century before Confederation there was seldom a period when an ample supply of government securities for investment did not exist in Canada. After Confederation these securities began to reap the benefits of better financial management on all levels of government, whereas before the financial solvency of governments frequently could not be taken for granted.

We have seen that supplies of government securities increased rapidly after 1820. The only important private security which enjoyed a similar growth and an acceptable credit standing was the stock of the chartered banks. The securities of individuals or small private companies, such as discounted paper and promissory notes and chattel and real estate mortgages, which did exist were insufficiently homogeneous (then as now) to permit the development of organized markets in them. While promissory notes and discounted paper benefited from the growth of the chartered banks, mortgages had by and large to wait for the development of the non-bank institutional investors, which did not really begin until the late 1840s and took several decades after that to move into full stride.

The non-government securities that might have enjoyed sufficient homogeneity to permit the development of an active market in them were those of incorporated companies. However, a general Companies Act which accepted the principle of limited liability was not passed in the Province of Canada until 1850 and required further development to be adequate in all cases, and while institutions and utilities such as banks, canals, railroads, bridges, and toll roads were able to obtain limited liability charters through special acts of Parliament, the sentiment of the time was against freely granting such privileges to trading and manufacturing concerns.[14] But perhaps

---

13. *Monetary Times*, Dec. 20, 1872, p. 494.
14. For a detailed account of the birth of Canadian company law see A. W. Currie, "The First Dominion Companies Act," *The Canadian Journal of Economics and Political Science*, August 1962.

even more important, the growth of the supply of industrial securities was limited by the character of Canadian business until almost the turn of the century. After that the transition from local private companies, through the formation of new limited liability companies and the purchase and merging by them of the small companies into large industrial corporations, became very rapid.

The growth of the utility companies, particularly canal and railroad companies, was of course substantial from the 1820s onward. However, these resulted much more in the growth of government securities than in the growth of corporation securities. The disappointing profit experience of such companies caused them to depend heavily on government assistance, and restricted the volume of their own securities that they could sell, which in turn restricted the development of an active trading market in them. A few utilities did establish a record of profits which caused their stocks to begin to be traded before Confederation, but the vast majority of them did not gain that degree of respectability.

It was primarily the chartered banks that were able, long before Confederation, to develop a good record of profits, to create a feeling of confidence in their operations, and to win the approval of large numbers of local investors. This enabled brokers in bank stocks and markets in bank stocks to develop. By the 1870s they were joined by the mortgage loan companies – which by then had rid themselves of the inhibiting aspects of the early building societies – for by then they also began to experience substantial and sustained profits. Next, as we have seen, came the industrial securities. But also, throughout this period, government notes and debentures were available to investors and brokers.

The remarkable position enjoyed by bank stocks in the early development of the Canadian financial market can be seen in a number of ways. For example, many of the new financial institutions when first formed, and so in need of instruments in which to invest their paid-in capital, for short and long periods, invested such funds to a substantial degree in bank stocks. This was the case with the Canada Life Assurance Company (1847), the Montreal City and District Savings Bank (1846), and the Quebec Provident and Savings Bank (1847). Two years after formation the Canada Permanent Building and Savings Society pointed out in its annual report that "As affording an additional safeguard against the possibility of inconvenience in the event of an unusual demand being made on the funds of the Society, it has been deemed expedient to invest a portion of the money deposited for accumulation, in a security readily available at any time, and accordingly 176 shares in the stock of the Bank of Upper Canada have been purchased for, and are held by the Society."[15] As early as 1832 a resident of Upper Canada wrote to a friend in Ireland that "All the spare cash I had, I have invested in bank stock, in the bank of Upper Canada. It is a decided fact that this stock pays regularly twelve per cent and is as safe as in the Bank of England."[16]

So prior to Confederation the securities available for investment that were outside the highly speculative range were the direct and guaranteed debentures of the provinces and municipalities, and the stocks of the chartered banks and a handful of utilities. It was to these that the fledgling non-bank financial intermediaries – the Trustee Savings Banks, the building societies, and the life and fire insurance companies – had to turn to invest their funds. The assets of several of them for selected years, shown below, indicate this quite clearly and are rather interesting in themselves.[17]

Assets of St. Lawrence Inland Marine Company 1845

480 shares Gore Bank	£ 6000- 0- 0
200 shares Commercial Bank	5000- 0- 0
80 shares City Bank of Montreal	2000- 0- 0
40 shares Montreal Bank	2000- 0- 0
88 shares Bank of Upper Canada	1100- 0- 0
Bills receivable net	3384-12-10½
Cash	681-11- 2½
Company boats	174- 4- 6
Unsold damaged property	529- 1- 5

Assets of Montreal and Provident Savings Bank 1848

Bank stocks	£27,890-13-11
City of Montreal Corporation Bonds	1,555- 9- 9
Road Trust Bonds Guaranteed by Province	1,029-12- 9

15. *Report of the Directors of the Canada Permanent Building and Savings Society for the Year Ending January 31st, 1857.*

16. Thomas Radcliff, ed., *Authentic Letters from Upper Canada* (Toronto: Macmillan Co. of Canada, 1953), p. 72.

17. As reported in Province of Canada, *Sessional Papers.*

Loans with personal security on:	
Bank stocks	10,137- 4- 2
Champlain and St. Lawrence Railroad stock	5,600- 0- 0
Lachine Railroad stock	353-13- 1
City of Montreal and St. Ann's Market Bonds	4,770-10- 3
Fabrique Bonds	1,950- 0- 0
Montreal Road Trust Bonds	100- 0- 0
City of Montreal Water Works' Bonds	9,962-11- 6
Balances with banks	74- 5- 0
Interest accrued	188- 6- 3
Furniture	207-12- 9

Assets of Quebec Provident and Savings Bank 1848

Bank of Montreal stock	£ 3,000- 0- 0
Quebec Bank stock	2,100- 0- 0
City Bank of Montreal stock	4,025- 0- 0
Banque du Peuple stock	1,900- 0- 0
Commercial Bank stock	1,000- 0- 0
Deposited at interest	4,145- 4- 7
Secured by bank stock	1,947-10- 0
Vested in or loaned on public security	17,551-13- 0
Accrued interest	1,585-15- 9

Assets of Montreal City and District Savings Bank 1848

Bank stocks	£25,437- 7- 7
City Corporation Bonds	3,594-10- 5
Road Trust Debentures and Government Debentures Guaranteed	1,065-12- 5
Collateral loans	5,591-12- 2
Balances due by other banks	64-11- 5
Cash on hand	2,743-12- 7
Furniture	169-15- 3

Assets of Canada Life Assurance Company 1849

Bank stock at par	£ 410- 0- 0
Provincial debentures at par	442-10- 0
Road company debentures at par	129- 0- 0
Municipal debentures at par	1,302-10- 0
Mortgages on real estate at par	1,032- 5- 1
Cash	547-14- 6
Premiums secured on policies	1,484- 1- 0
Accrued interest	61-10- 0
Furniture, etc.	56- 4- 5

Over the first four years of its operations, from 1847 to 1851, the Canada Life Assurance Company purchased stock of the Bank of Upper Canada, Bank of Montreal, Gore Bank, and debentures of the Province of Canada, of the districts of Wellington and Gore, of the Township of Walsingham, of the City of Hamilton, and of the Town of London. It is interesting to note the substantial accumulation by Canada Life in those early years of exceedingly small-denomination municipal debentures obviously originally designed for small individual holders, for it so clearly illustrates the transition from direct financing of borrowers by savers to indirect financing through the accumulation of savings by financial intermediaries. The advantages to borrowers and savers of the transition assured its permanency.

UNDERWRITERS, BROKERS AND STOCK EXCHANGES

With the rapid growth of bank stocks, the persistent issuing of provincial and municipal debentures, and the appearance of stocks and debentures of a few utilities, it was inevitable that underwriting and trading activity would begin to emerge. However, since the large proportion of debentures were sterling issues designed to draw funds from the London capital market, their appearance did not involve much underwriting in Canada. They were handled in London by merchant banking institutions, and prior to Confederation no Canadian institutions, not even the chartered banks, engaged in underwriting activity there. It is true that Canadian financial institutions, such as the Bank of Upper Canada, the Bank of Montreal and the Canada Life Assurance Company, began to purchase all or parts of new debenture issues, but apparently not for purposes of reselling. The Bank of Upper Canada as fiscal agent of the province made direct purchases, and when in late 1863, as a result partially of this bank's financial difficulties, the Bank of Montreal became the fiscal agent it began its new role by buying debentures of the financially hard-pressed province.[18] It had as early as 1841 made loans to the province and in that year also purchased £10,000 of Montreal Municipal Bonds.[19] In addition to direct purchases, the system of tendering for municipal issues at least in Upper Canada was well established even prior to Confederation. The methods of acquiring debentures, the characteristics of the debentures acquired and the nature of the municipal securities business in general are indicated by the following example from the *Minutes* of the investment committee and board of directors of the Canada Life Assurance Company:

July 15, 1854—"reconsidered the proposed purchase of the Grimsby debentures and agreed to buy them at a rate to yield 10% interest from this date paying £750 in cash and certificates of deposits bearing interest at 6% and payable by instalments through twelve months for the balance."

July 16, 1856—"Mr. Osborne's offer of £2,000 debentures of the village of St. Mary's payable May 1866 was considered and it was agreed to recommend their purchase at 20% discount with current interest. . . ."

September 23, 1856—"the by-law of the municipality of St. Mary's having been reported invalid it was agreed to recommend the advance of the sum £636.18.0 proposed to have been made in cash upon the debentures, provided the municipality would secure by collateral means the delivery of valid debentures as soon as a new by-law could be passed. . . ."

March 9, 1857—"agreed to purchase the following lot of city [Hamilton] debentures—of £500 each payable in 2 to 8 years from 8th October 1856 with interest compounded half yearly, issued under an approved by-law and at the price and terms offered viz. £300 with accrued interest, £1,000 by acceptance with interest at forty days, £1,000 at eighty, the balance in cash."

August 20, 1861—"Question as to action of Board about overdue Hamilton debentures was postponed."

March 4, 1862—"The directors were prepared to purchase $10,000 Harbour of Montreal 8% bonds at the market quotation of 106."

March 18, 1862—"The board approved of taking the whole issue of Victoria debentures $40,000, at such a rate as should yield 7%,—that being the same rate as they had agreed to purchase $20,000 of this issue on the 11th February last."

July 22, 1862—"It was decided to put the City of Hamilton coupons

---

18. See Merrill Denison, *Canada's First Bank* (Toronto: McClelland & Stewart, 1967), vol. 2, p. 130.
19. *Ibid.*, p. 9.

due the first July in suit." [Similar problems were being encountered with other municipal issues.]

October 24, 1865 — "The board approved of a tender being made for the $12,500 Montreal harbour debentures at 7¾%."

December 25, 1865 — "Montreal Corporation bonds — the manager was authorized to tender for $40,000; to pay 7¾% over."

January 9, 1866 — "The manager reported the non-acceptance of the company's tender for Montreal bonds."

So it would seem that by Confederation the main characteristics of the municipal securities business had appeared in Upper Canada. There were both serial and sinking fund municipal debentures, and institutional investors had emerged as buyers of them. The smaller municipalities, as well as some of the larger ones, seem generally to have sold their debentures through direct negotiations, but other larger issuers were already calling for tenders. Post-Confederation developments were to involve essentially a refinement of these trends and the appearance of specialized investment dealers who engaged in underwriting and distributing new issues.

Even these in some respects had begun to appear prior to Confederation in the form of stockbrokers and stock exchange arrangements. Such institutions had already come a long way in other countries. The Brussels Stock Exchange had its roots in the thirteenth-century markets of Bruges and Antwerp, and the latter city began issuing bonds at the end of the Middle Ages, thus creating a need for securities-trading arrangements.[20] Germany, Italy, France and England saw the emergence of similar market activity in the sixteenth and seventeenth centuries. The development of joint-stock companies and government-funded debt — as in England in the seventeenth century — provided the impetus for the formation of securities markets. The "stock jobbers" of London who began to raise government funds, through long-term debt issues, formed a "club" in 1762 and the London Stock Exchange, legally constituted under Deed of Settlement, began operations in 1802. The War of Independence in the United States led to a large funded debt, and the formation of the Bank of the United States in 1791 added another financial instrument. It was in that environment that the New York Stock Exchange was formed in 1792.

In the 1830s and 1840s firms began to appear in Toronto and Montreal that traded in stocks and bonds, along with other commission business such as wholesale food, collection of rents and debts, and

20. For brief historical details see David E. Spray, ed., *The Principal Stock Exchanges of the World* (Washington, D.C.: International Economic Publishers Inc., 1964).

real estate. We have already examined them in our discussion of the emergence of private bankers.[21] Gradually there began to emerge brokers that specialized increasingly in the sale of securities, and these began to arrange meetings to effect security transactions. In Montreal a small group of brokers was meeting regularly as early as 1832, the year in which £59,000 capital for the St. Lawrence Railway was subscribed for in Montreal.[22] In 1842 a Board of Stock and Produce Brokers was formed in Montreal. Then in August 1852 there appeared in the Toronto press a notice to the effect that a Toronto Stock Exchange was being formed.[23] However, the degree of order this created in securities trading apparently was limited, for one writer commented on the Toronto Stock Exchange at the turn of the century in this way:

> Previous to July, 1865, Toronto had a Board of Brokers which had its officers and regular meetings, and which furnished a report of the state of the market. Unfortunately it became a Board in nothing but the name. There were brokers, and plenty of them, but each constituted a Board in himself—each making the best bargain he could, obtaining the greatest amount of profit possible on each transaction. It opened the way for irregular, and, if anyone was so disposed, for dishonest dealings, where one of the parties in a transaction was not fully posted on the state of the market.[24]

A change for the better seems to have occurred in 1865 when a committee of the Exchange was formed to issue authorized weekly lists of stocks, the first one of which appeared on December 1st of that year.[25] Trading meetings were held in various member offices. What the nature of the early stock lists were we have already seen.[26]

Montreal brokers in 1863 formally formed a Board of Brokers and began keeping official minutes. In that year the Board also outlined commissions, listing fees and rules governing membership. At first the Board met daily between 12:00 and 12:30 in the office of the Board's honorary secretary, but in 1866 they rented an office especially for such meetings. Montreal listings in those early years were larger in number than those of the Toronto Stock Exchange, but for a period both increased only at a slow rate. The Toronto Exchange listed 15 issues in 1857 and in 1865 it listed only 18; however, by 1872

---

21. See above, pp. 165-7.
22. See Carl Bergithon, *The Stock Exchange*, privately published, Montreal, 1940, p. 11.
23. Toronto *Globe*, Aug. 14, 1852, p. 39.
24. *The Annual Financial Review, Canada*, July 1901, vol. 1.
25. *Ibid.*, and Bergithon, *op. cit.*, p. 12.
26. See above, pp. 44-7.

this had increased to 34 issues. The Montreal Exchange showed 20 issues in 1857, and 63 in 1874.[27] Throughout that period the major listings were the chartered banks, but there were also fire insurance companies, gas utilities, railroads, mining companies, and government and county debentures. At the time of Confederation there were about a dozen stockbrokers listed in a Toronto directory, and Montreal had at least that many.

This survey of developments before Confederation suggests that significant stages in the evolution of the capital market emerged in that early period. Municipal debenture financing was well established, as was provincial debenture financing, and the instruments that they were issuing already reflected the early stages of the emergence of demand from institutional investors. The U.S. market had been investigated and had been found to be unreceptive to Canadian issues. London financing had clearly emerged in response to the inadequacy of domestic savings, and English underwriting houses were handling the Canadian issues in London. Chartered bank stock had developed into a respectable savings instrument—although still subject to a not insignificant risk of bankruptcy in individual cases—as had a few utilities; and there was also a readily available supply of small- and large-denomination municipal and provincial debentures, at least in Upper Canada. A number of brokers were operating actively in both Montreal and Toronto, and organized although unincorporated stock exchanges had emerged in both centres. These brokers were selling stocks and bonds to institutional and individual investors. All this had happened in five decades preceding Confederation. Most of the developments after Confederation were an elaboration of trends that had emerged before Confederation, although some were quite new. To these developments we now turn.

Confederation to the Turn of the Century

BASIC TRENDS

The development of the capital market in this period can best be understood if it is placed within the context of certain over-all economic and financial trends of the time. First, while there were a number of years of slow growth in that period, it was one in which real G.N.P. almost tripled in size and output per worker increased by

---

27. See above, pp. 44-7.

over 50 per cent.[28] Capital spending increased at about the same rate as G.N.P., government spending more quickly, and consumer spending less quickly, and there was a persistent foreign trade deficit until 1894.[29] Interpreted in terms of its implications for the capital market, this meant that there was probably an increasing rate of domestic savings in that period, providing increasing opportunities for the domestic placement of savings instruments; nonetheless, there was probably a shortage of domestic savings relative to demand. This gap was filled by foreign capital inflow and provided opportunities for financial institutions able to develop such foreign business. A rough measure of the need for foreign capital inflow is indicated by the fact that from 1868 to 1893 Canada had a deficit-on-merchandise-trade account in all but two years, and one that in total amounted to $330 million.[30] It must also be noted for future reference that the year 1896 marked the beginning of an acceleration of economic activity that ran well into the new century.

The second major point to be made is that it was a period in which there was a strong interest rate incentive to obtain funds from the United Kingdom. For much of the period the gap between Canadian and British interest rates was relatively wide, even though Canadian interest rates declined steadily until they reached their low point in 1896. But, as the turn of the century approached, this gap reached the vanishing point and removed much of the former incentive, while at the same time improving the relative attractiveness of the United States as a source of capital.[31]

Third, the period from Confederation to the turn of the century was one in which financial intermediaries grew steadily in relative importance[32] and provided an increasing demand for domestic securities as well as an increasing supply of very acceptable equities. With these broad developments in mind we may now examine the period in detail.

CREDIT INSTRUMENTS

Government: Data on the volume of government bonds issued in the four decades after Confederation are sadly deficient, but Tables 14:1

28. See O. J. Firestone, *Canada's Economic Development 1867-1953* (London: Bowen & Bowen, 1958), p. 66.
29. *Ibid.*, p. 72.
30. See M. C. Urquhart and K. A. H. Buckley, eds., *Historical Statistics of Canada* (Toronto: Macmillan Co. of Canada, 1965), p. 173.
31. See below, pp. 555-67.
32. See above, pp. 54-9.

Table 14:1 Bonded Indebtedness of Canadian Governments 1867-1933 (selected years)

	1867	1895	1914	1933[1]
Government of Canada	71	225	303	3657
Provincial governments	n.a.	29	132	1279
Municipal governments	n.a.	n.a.	442	1173
Total	n.a.	n.a.	877	6109
Ontario municipal governments	n.a.	53	195	—

SOURCE: Ian M. Drummond, *Capital Markets in Australia and Canada 1895-1914*, unpublished Ph.D. thesis, Yale University, May 1959, p. 11, and M. C. Urquhart and K. A. H. Buckley, eds., *Historical Statistics of Canada*, pp. 204, 210, 211.

[1]Net direct and guaranteed funded debt.

and 14:2, together with other information, permit us to make several reliable generalizations. First, federal government debt expanded quite steadily from Confederation to the First World War, almost all of which was sterling debt. Second, municipal bonded debt also increased and was much larger in volume than that of the provinces. It would seem that a not insignificant portion of this debt was placed in Canada. Third, provincial bonded debt amounted to only about $31 million in 1890 (see Table 14:2), of which $21 million was

Table 14:2 Funded Debt of Canadian Provinces 1890-1925 (selected years)

(MILLIONS OF DOLLARS)

	1890	1900	1910	1920	1925
Alberta	—	—	—	42.0	81.5
British Columbia	1.7	8.0	10.8	34.1	76.4
Manitoba	3.4	4.9	13.4	49.7	66.7
New Brunswick	2.2	3.0	6.0	20.7	32.3
Nova Scotia	2.1	3.8	8.3	17.2	38.7
Ontario	—	—	17.5	98.4	277.0
Prince Edward Island	—	.2	.8	.7	1.9
Quebec	21.4	35.1	25.7	40.7	81.9
Saskatchewan	—	—	—	36.7	50.5
Total	30.9	55.1	82.4	340.3	706.9

SOURCE: *The Monetary Times Annual*, Jan. 7, 1927, vol. 78.

accounted for by the Province of Quebec; Ontario did not begin to have a net funded debt until after the turn of the century. We shall see, however, that selling the Quebec issues did involve historic stages in the development of the Canadian capital market. While most of the provincial debt was sold in London, some was also sold in New York and Paris, and when Ontario began to borrow seriously after the turn of the century it was the first among the provinces to develop a successful local market for its securities.[33] Fourth, there was a massive increase in the volume of provincial and municipal financing over the period 1895-1914, for their bonded indebtedness seems to have increased about four-fold over those years. This acceleration was significant in that it greatly expanded the opportunities for the development of specialist bond houses.

Corporations: There can be little doubt that the major development in credit instruments over the 1867-1900 period was the emergence of the securities of industrial corporations. Table 14:3 gives a general indication of the timing and magnitude of this development, for it shows the authorized capital of new joint-stock companies incorporated by the provinces of Quebec and Ontario and by the government of Canada over the period 1870-1910. It seems that there was no

Table 14:3 Authorized Capital of New Joint-Stock Companies 1870-1910 (selected years)

(MILLIONS OF DOLLARS)

	QUEBEC	ONTARIO	GOVERNMENT OF CANADA
1870	1.2	n.a.	n.a.
1875	1.3	n.a.	n.a.
1880	2.0	7.3[1]	1.9
1885	1.4	7.9	2.1
1890	1.2	26.5	7.3
1895	2.6	11.3	6.3
1900	12.8	78.9	9.6
1905	5.7	78.9	99.1
1910	28.4	225.0	458.4

SOURCE: Government of Canada, Ontario, and Quebec *Sessional Papers.*

[1]1881.

33. See Drummond, *op. cit.*, pp. 124-5.

great shift from the unincorporated to the incorporated form of business organization prior to 1885, but that by 1890 such a movement was under way and by 1910 had reached explosive proportions. That was a period of mergers, of the takeover of family enterprises by new corporations, and of rapid industrial development. A by-product of that development was the rise to predominance of industrial securities and with it new opportunities for underwriters and brokers, the total number of which increased rapidly up to the First World War. It must also be noted in passing that this was the period when a quite new corporation security first appeared—the "preferred stock." Federal legislation permitted its introduction in 1899.

While these new credit instruments were entering the market in volume, the older instruments that had already been important prior to Confederation continued to grow as well, although at a less rapid pace. In 1870 the paid-up capital of the chartered banks had amounted to about $34.2 million, while in 1900 it was $67.1 million, an average annual increase of about 2¼%—a rough indication of the change in the supply of bank stocks. In 1900 the paid-up capital of the sixteen Canadian life insurance companies was $2.4 million, whereas in 1870 there had been only the Canada Life Assurance Company. Mortgage loan companies had a paid-up capital of about $8 million in 1870 and one of over $30 million in 1900, and an annual average growth rate of about 5% (some of them, however, were foreign companies). It was also a period when several financial intermediary claims first appeared, particularly the mortgage loan company debenture and the trust company guaranteed investment certificate and deposit, while others rose to new prominence, i.e., the life insurance policy claim and the chartered bank savings deposit. While available statistical data do not permit us to estimate the relative size of the stocks of these various financial claims at the turn of the century, it does seem that by that time much of the innovation in types of financial claims had occurred. The new claims that were to appear after 1900 were closed-end and mutual fund shares, credit union and caisses populaires shares, commercial paper of corporations, short-term paper of sales finance companies, government-guaranteed residential mortgages, and the demand securities of governments, particularly the Canada Savings Bonds.

THE STOCK MARKET

In 1872 the Montreal Board of Brokers began calling itself the Montreal Stock Exchange and in 1874 it applied for a charter and became legally incorporated under Quebec law. D. L. Macdougall was the first chairman, and other members included Charles Geddes, Col. Ford, J. W. Taylor, George W. Simpson, T. M. Taylor and H. S. Macdougall. Of the 63 issues listed on the Montreal Exchange in 1874, there were 21 bank stocks, 9 government and municipal bonds and debenture issues, 4 railroad issues, 3 mining issues, 3 navigation company issues, 2 telegraph company issues, 1 gas company issue, 10 industrial company issues, 3 financial company issues and 7 assorted bond and stock issues. The par value of the entrance fee to the Board had earlier been set at $1,000, but in 1877 a seat sold for $2,900; in 1882 one sold for $2,820 and another for $3,250; in 1883 the price for a seat was $5,750.[34] By 1901 the highest price received was about $12,000 and the number of members was forty.[35] However, not until 1904 did the Exchange have its own building. Besides the "regular" board of the Montreal Stock Exchange, there was an "open" board used by brokers who were not members of the former.

The 1865 improvements in the organization of the Toronto Stock Exchange still seem to have left a loose and casual stock trading arrangement, for in 1871 there was a reorganization that led to an exchange with daily meetings, daily lists and a common meeting place. A contemporary newspaper described it this way:

> We are glad to learn that the stock brokers of Toronto have organized a stock exchange, of which the following firms are members: Pellatt & Osler, Campbell & Cassels, Blaikie & Alexander, Philip Browne & Co., H. J. Morse & Co., Forbes & Lownsbrough, W. B. Phipps, Wm. Paterson & Co., Hime & Baines, Robert Beatty & Co., Hope & Temple, H. Joseph, Clarke & Fields, Edgar J. Jarvis. At a meeting held on the 2nd inst., Mr. W. G. Cassels was elected President, and Mr. W. Hope Secretary-Treasurer. Suitable rooms have been secured over the Dominion Bank, and it is expected that operations will commence forthwith. The institution is to have daily meetings at 11:30, the proceedings of which will be in most respects similar to those of the stock exchanges of the principal cities on the continent. The membership fee is fixed at $250. A code of rules and regulations has been drawn up and adopted. A daily list will be issued showing the quotations of banks and other shares. Such a price current will have the advantage of being quite reliable, since it will be based on all the transactions of the market, and not compiled by an individual or firm. This exchange will be the means of saving much valuable time which is now lost for the want of a common place and hour of meeting. It cannot be doubted that Toronto has acquired sufficient importance as a stock and share market to justify such an organization, and to give good hope of its success.[36]

34. See *Monetary Times*, May 23, 1879, p. 1445; July 28, 1882, p. 100; July 6, 1886, p. 8.
35. See *The Annual Financial Review*, Canada, July 1901, p. 2.
36. *Monetary Times*, Sept. 8, 1871, p. 187.

While London remained the dominating influence on Canadian markets until after the turn of the century, New York was also exceedingly important and, what is more, had telegraph connections with Canada. Toronto received reports on the New York stock and gold quotations every twenty minutes, which were delivered by telegraph messenger boys.

The improvement in organization seems to have survived and to have led finally in 1878 to the incorporation under a special act of the Province of Ontario of the Toronto Stock Exchange. Its twenty-one members were W. Alexander, P. S. Barnston, W. J. Baines, R. Beatty, James Browne, Philip Browne, Ewing Buchan, C. J. Campbell, W. G. Cassels, W. G. Cassels, Jr., R. Cochran, H. R. Forbes, C. S. Gzowski, Jr., H. L. Hime, W. Hope, W. Kirsteman, Jr., Herbert Mortimer, E. B. Osler, H. Pellatt, W. A. Phipps, and R. H. Temple.[37] A scale of broker's commission was also established in 1878, which was ½% on stocks and debentures, and ¼% for transactions over $2,000.[38] In 1881 the Exchange, now with thirty members, moved into its first permanent trading quarters, the new and cumbersome Phelps-type ticker tape machines were installed in some brokers' offices, and the Toronto market for the first time was linked directly to the New York Stock Exchange.[39] Opening of transatlantic cables in 1886 helped open up a market for Canadian securities in Europe, some of which were listed on the London, Paris and other exchanges. In 1891 a faster ticker, the Wirsching type, was introduced. In 1895 an even better one, the Bury, made its appearance and its greatly enhanced speed of operation established a firm basis for future operations of the Exchange. It provided a continuous link with the New York market, although it was not operated directly but rather from the telegraph office which received quotations by Morse. The Montreal Stock Exchange saw similar developments. It is obvious from all this that data transmission technology had gone a long way before the turn of the century, a technology that was essential for increasing the efficiency of stock trading.

The mining boom that developed in the 1890s, especially in the Rossland, British Columbia and Rainy River areas, greatly increased the demand for venture capital and the supply of mining stocks.[40] The regular exchanges in Toronto and Montreal did not accommodate that development and so in 1896 the Toronto Stock and Mining Exchange with twenty-five members and a price of $25 per seat was

---

37. *Monetary Times*, June 7, 1878, p. 1438.
38. See Huntly W. McKay, "The Stock Exchanges in Canada," in Spray, *op. cit.*
39. See *Globe and Mail*, Oct. 15, 1952.
40. See *ibid.*, and Bank of Nova Scotia, "The Stock Market in Canada," *Monthly Review*, September 1960.

formed, followed in 1897 by a rival, the Standard Stock and Mining Exchange. The two exchanges merged under the name of the latter in 1899, applied for and received an Ontario charter in 1909, and remained active until 1934 when it merged with the Toronto Stock Exchange. These initiatives led to Toronto's being the principal centre for trading in mining stocks, at a time long before it began to exceed the Montreal Stock Exchange in trading in industrial stocks.

In 1900 the Toronto Stock Exchange moved into larger quarters, thirty-five of its forty members were active and the last seat sold attracted a price of $3,000. Seats on the Montreal Exchange, as we have seen, had sold for about $12,000, and it is certainly true that at the turn of the century Montreal continued to be the principal Canadian stock exchange centre, as it had been from the beginning.

Actual trading until about the turn of the century was based on the old "call" system. A contemporary observer described the trading in Toronto in this way:

> Until about 1900, there were actual "seats" on the Exchange. Against three walls were arranged individual small desks and each member was armed with a book and pencil. Starting at 10 o'clock, the secretary would mount to his desk and proceed to "call" the listed stocks from "A" on, allowing an interval to secure a "bid and asked" and to permit of trades, which each member would note in his book for the information of his office. When the "call" was over, open trading would be permitted until time for the next "call."[41]

It will be noted that from the very beginning of the exchanges, bonds and debentures were listed on the exchange board and traded, and such trading reached a peak in 1919 with $71.6 million traded on the Montreal Stock Exchange and $60.5 million on the Toronto Stock Exchange.[42] The bond business, however, as we shall see, was in fact beginning to shift away from the stock business before the turn of the century, and this occurred not through any forced separation of bond and stock trading, but rather through the emergence of bond underwriting houses and investment dealers.

UNDERWRITERS, INVESTMENT DEALERS AND THE BOND MARKET

We have seen that the Canadian balance of merchandise trade in the three decades after Confederation was such as to require a sub-

---

41. E. Gordon Wells, "The Stock Exchange and 'The Street,'" *Canadian Banker*, Spring 1951, pp. 123-4.
42. "Growth of Investment Business and Investment Organization," *Monetary Times Annual*, January 7, 1927, vol. 78, p. 129.

stantial capital inflow and that there was a strong interest rate incentive to obtain that capital through the sale of securities in the United Kingdom. It has been estimated that in 1900 there was $1,232 million foreign capital invested in Canada, of which $1,050 million was British, $168 million was U.S. capital, and $14 million was other foreign capital.[43] The greatest proportion of this represented sales of bonds abroad, and so gives an indication of the important underwriting opportunities provided by Canadian borrowers in the London market.

The first Canadian financial institution to seize that opportunity was the Bank of Montreal. In 1870 it opened an agency in London for purposes of developing and facilitating its foreign business, investing its surplus funds and providing for the transfer of its stock and for payment of its dividends to English investors.[44] However, the agency soon provided a base for developing a London underwriting business in Canadian issues. It was in 1874 that the bank first became an underwriter, or investment banker, as such. It participated with Morton, Rose & Co. in underwriting an £800,000 sterling issue for the Province of Quebec; it soon followed this with a £750,000 City of Montreal issue, and then a £500,000 subscription to a Dominion of Canada loan. In 1876 it bought the remaining £111,000 of the City of Montreal issue and also formed a syndicate with the Imperial Bank of Toronto to purchase £100,000 worth of City of Toronto bonds. A Toronto press comment on the latter indicates clearly how this activity of the Bank of Montreal was beginning to direct attention to emerging Canadian underwriting activity:

> TORONTO DEBENTURES. The tender made by the Bank of Montreal to take $537,217.60 renewal debentures of this city at 99 52.100 cents in the dollar has been accepted by the Finance Committee of our City Council. This tender was the highest made. . . . Some two years ago ninety-seven and one-half cents in the dollar was paid by the same bank for Quebec Government debentures which are now worth about 103. We understand that the Toronto debentures will shortly be placed on the market at a similar rate . . . and in future it would be better in selling our securities to give them if possible to a leading Canadian institution rather than place them in the hands of private bankers or capitalists in England to negotiate them.[45]

---

43. See F. A. Knox, "Canadian Capital Movements and the Canadian Balance of International Payments, 1900-1934," in Herbert Marshall, Frank A. Southard, and Kenneth W. Taylor, *Canadian-American Industry* (New Haven: Yale University Press, 1936), pp. 298-9.
44. See Denison, *op. cit.*, vol. 2, p. 172.
45. *Monetary Times*, May 5, 1876, p. 1267.

In 1877, jointly with the Merchants Bank, the Bank of Montreal underwrote and distributed successfully a $200,000 Province of Quebec debenture issue and decided to join a London syndicate to underwrite the balance of the issue amounting to $400,000. All this activity arose from the entry of Quebec into railway building.[46]

In February 1879 occurred an event of great importance for the history of the Canadian bond market, for in that month the Bank of Montreal agreed to negotiate the sale of a $3,000,000 Province of Quebec bond issue, payable either in sterling or in United States dollars. The bank then formed a syndicate in New York (it had had an agency there since 1858) in which its participation was $400,000, and the issue was successfully placed. Not only was this the first Canadian issue sold in New York, and so the beginning of what many years later became a dominant trend, but it was also apparently the first foreign issue sold there on its merits. One contemporary New York newspaper columnist said:

> The point is this: these bankers have outbid the London bankers who wished to take the loan, and are about to try the first experiment in placing a foreign loan in this country on its merits. Efforts have been made in past times to sell in this market such bonds as those of Mexico, but only as a means of turning political sympathy into something tangible.

After the issue was sold another newspaper reported: "It should go on the record that the first foreign loan ever offered in New York was successful beyond expectation."[47] A Canadian paper also read appropriate historical significance into the event, for it reported as follows:

> Recently, in noticing the abundance of capital in the United States seeking investment at low rates of interest, we raised the question whether the state of things might not have some effect on the rate of interest here. But we did not then foresee that the time was so near at hand when negotiations for a loan for a Canadian Province would be set on foot in New York. The first foreign loan ever negotiated in New York . . . was begun to be negotiated by the Bank of Montreal, Kulba Hoel & Co. and Winslow, Lanier & Co., acting as agents for the Province of Quebec. . . . financial agents of the highest standing regarded New York as an eligible market in which to negotiate a Provincial Canadian Loan. . . .
>
> Hitherto Canada, as a borrower, has practically been confined to

46. *Ibid.*, pp. 184, 185.
47. *Ibid.*, pp. 186, 187.

> the English market; and it cannot but be an advantageous circumstance if she is hereafter to have a choice of markets in which to borrow.[48]

The Bank of Montreal became Canada's first underwriter of significant size, and other banks soon engaged in that activity as well—predating by many years the underwriting activity of the investment dealers. Their lead in underwriting was maintained for many years and the banks have never vacated the field. On January 1, 1893, the Bank of Montreal became fiscal agent for the federal government in London, succeeding the English merchant banking houses of Glyn, Mills, Currie & Co., and Baring Brothers, and in the fall of 1894 it underwrote a £2,250,000 Dominion of Canada issue. How extensively the Canadian banks succeeded in acquiring the business of underwriting Canadian government issues has been accurately documented. In referring to the years 1895-1915, a period which saw a huge expansion in provincial debt issues, Professor Drummond found that in addition to handling all of the ten Dominion Government loans,

> [the] Bank of Montreal also handled all Ontario's London loans, most of Quebec's, and New Brunswick's single issue. The Canadian Bank of Commerce shared in the business of issuing provincial loans. It inherited the London business of British Columbia when it absorbed the old Imperial Bank of British Columbia in 1901, and it also handled most of Saskatchewan's and Manitoba's issues. These two large Canadian banks handled most of the provincial issue business. The occasional provincial loan passed through Lloyds Bank, Parr's Bank, and the National Provincial Bank. These British firms handled £4,191,000 in provincial issues during our period. However, the issues through Canadian banks were nearly three times as large.[49]

The Province of Quebec revealed ingenuity in ways other than its pioneering New York issue in its efforts to place new issues. In June 1880 it placed a $4,000,000 issue in Paris through Paris bankers. "France was a place not generally looked to as likely to afford loans to any Canadian Province," commented a Canadian financial paper.[50] In July 1882 the Quebec government called for tenders in Canada on a $1,500,000 loan, one-half of which was apparently taken up by M. Wurtele and the other by L. J. Forget, stockbrokers in Montreal.[51] This represented not just an important attempt to sell bonds to Cana-

48. *Monetary Times*, March 14, 1879, p. 1146.
49. Drummond, *op. cit.*, p. 53.
50. See *Monetary Times*, June 25, 1880, p. 1525; July 9, 1880, p. 39; Nov. 5, 1880, p. 525.
51. *Monetary Times*, Nov. 10, 1882, p. 519.

dian investors, but also an instance of brokers moving in the direction of becoming bond underwriters of importance, for it was reported that "Forget & Co., it is said, have deposited $30,000 as a guarantee that the contract will be completed."[52]

The timing of the Province of Quebec's very interesting innovations in the international marketing of its issues (in London, New York, Paris and Canada) and the extent of its borrowing by the turn of the century is indicated by the following data of its unmatured funded debt as of June 30, 1899:[53]

Date of issue	*Where payable*	*Amount outstanding*
1st May 1874	London	$2,726,306.67
1st May 1876	London	3,111,746.67
1st Nov. 1878	London or New York	2,698,000.00
1st July 1880	London or Paris	2,226,986.68
1st July 1882	London	1,788,897.67
1st July 1882	Quebec	780,500.00
1st Jan. 1888	London or Paris	3,224,653.33
1st March 1894	London or Montreal	2,537,966.67
30th Dec. 1894	Paris	5,332,976.00
1st May 1896	London or Montreal	292,000.00
1st April 1897	London or Montreal	1,360,000.00
1st April 1897	London	9,048,725.03
		$35,128,758.72

There were instances of other Canadian provinces selling issues in Canada. In November 1884 it was reported that:

> A five per cent loan of the Province of Nova Scotia, to the amount of $400,000 has been placed in the Province at $106 to $107. Parties in England tendered for the loan at 108, but were unable to make good their offer, and Provincial subscriptions were fallen back upon with the above result. It may be considered a good sale for the Province.[54]

Relationships were also developing between Canadian brokers and London financial institutions. For example, in June 1887 the press noted that "The province of Manitoba has negotiated its new loan of one million dollars with A. T. Drummond of Montreal, who has, we understand, taken it for a London, England syndicate."[55]

---

52. *Ibid.*
53. *Monetary Times*, 1899-1900, vol. XXXIII, p. 240.
54. *Monetary Times*, Nov. 1884, p. 610.
55. *Monetary Times*, June 24, 1887, p. 1529.

The marketing of municipal government issues became increasingly sophisticated as well, in the period from Confederation to the turn of the century, and throws considerable light on the way domestic underwriters emerged. A distinction may be made between the sale of debentures of the larger cities and those of the smaller cities, towns and municipalities. The larger cities such as Toronto, Montreal, Quebec, Hamilton, Ottawa, Kingston, Windsor, London, Galt, Guelph and Winnipeg typically invited tenders by newspaper advertisements and by about 1880 such advertisements were drawing a remarkably broad response. This response is illustrated in the following newspaper reports of 1880:

> Debentures of the city bridge over the Red River, at Winnipeg, were tendered for by parties in Montreal, Toronto, Buckingham, St. Paul, and Winnipeg. They were sold to Crawford Livingstone, of Minnesota, at 91⅝.[56]

> That the credit of Montreal stands well with capitalists, is shown by the tenders sent in for a new Municipal loan of $200,000 at 5 per cent. Tenders for supplying the above loan were opened last Saturday, when it was found that nineteen applicants tendered $1,785,000 at prices varying from par to 2 per cent. premium. The offer made by the Bank of British North America of $100,000 at 1½ per cent. premium, and $100,000 at 2 per cent. premium, was accepted. The tenders were all from Canadian capitalists. . . .[57]

The following comment on an 1879 Toronto issue illustrates how London and New York underwriters and Canadian brokers and chartered banks had by that time all become a part of the process surrounding the marketing of such prominent issues:

> Two amounts have been offered and taken at fair terms. Messrs. Morton, Bliss & Co. of New York and London, bid 97½ for $784,837 consolidated loan, and Messrs. James & Philip Browne, of Toronto, offered 56½ cents above par for $45,000 out of $83,991 of the local improvement issue. The first tender was accepted, and the other conditionally on the whole amount being taken by the Messrs. Brown [sic], they having expressed the desire that in case their tender were accepted they should have the option of taking the balance. . . .
>
> It is the opinion of some experienced people that better could have been done for the city of boldly offering the loan on the London market under the auspices of say Morton, Rose & Co., or the Bank of Montreal. . . .[58]

---

56. *Monetary Times*, April 9, 1880, p. 1196.
57. *Monetary Times*, July 2, 1880, p. 8.
58. *Monetary Times*, June 27, 1879, pp. 13-14.

The marketing of issues of small municipalities was quite another matter and in the several decades after Confederation the following description, written from memory in the 1920s by an experienced investment dealer, would seem to be accurate:

> It used to be that a municipal treasurer, when he wanted to borrow $10,000 or $15,000 by the issue of debentures, would get the by-law passed and the debentures printed and signed on rather poor paper, and most of the debentures filled in with pen and ink, put them under his arm and come to Toronto and try and negotiate a sale with the banks or some other people who were known to be buyers. When he made this deal with the banker or broker, of which latter there were perhaps three in the City of Toronto, he would go over to the solicitor and make a declaration required by the solicitor, the solicitor would give his legal opinion and the man would get his cheque and the deal was closed. . . .[59]

The records of the Canada Life Assurance Company support this description and shed light on the emerging bond business of brokers. In the 1850s Canada Life purchased a wide variety of Ontario county, township, city, town and village debentures, as well as Montreal and provincial government debentures. This continued in the 1860s but now there is explicit evidence of recurring deals with brokers—John Riddell's name appeared first in 1862 in such transactions and continued to appear until the mid 1880s; the name of the firm of Pellatt and Osler, formed in 1867, first appeared in 1868; that of MacDougall & Davidson in 1869; Campbell and Cassells and W. Hendrie in 1873. From about 1883 onward there was a noticeable increase in the number of relatively small municipal issues acquired by Canada Life through direct tenders, probably a reflection of the increasing interest by banks, mortgage loan companies, life insurance companies and brokers in this business, and probably marking a significant improvement in the machinery for marketing these new issues. The demand for municipal debentures by the mortgage loan companies becomes increasingly evident around 1880. Ontario registered mortgage loan companies doubled their holdings from 1875 to 1880 although in absolute terms these were not large.[60] One issue of the *Monetary Times* of 1882 shows six prominent mortgage loan companies advertising for debentures,[61] and other companies did so in subsequent issues. Some of them began to develop a securities business, in addition to buying securities as an investment.

---

59. C. H. Burgess, "Growth of Government and Municipal Financing in Canada," *Monetary Times Annual*, January 7, 1927, vol. 78, p. 156.

60. See below, p. 207.

61. *Monetary Times*, July 7, 1882.

It would seem, then, that by the middle 1880s the development of a bond market in Canada had gone a fair distance. By that time a large number of even very small municipalities were successfully placing debentures by well-advertised public tender; brokers were active in that business and had connections with London financial houses; banks, life insurance companies and mortgage loan companies were active buyers; the banks, particularly the Bank of Montreal, were firmly established in underwriting Canadian government, provincial and large city debentures in London, and had begun to test the New York market. All this activity may well have meant that Canadian investors were absorbing about as large a volume of bonds as relative attractiveness would permit. After the mid 1880s the major developments were the acceleration in the volume of debenture issues and the "explosion" in the flow of new corporate issues referred to earlier, the emergence of the specialized investment or bond dealers and active bond trading, the utilization of the London market by even small municipalities, and the emergence of New York as a major source of funds for Canadian borrowers.

The emergence of specialized bond dealers was an important aspect of the development of underwriting facilities in Canada. They emerged both as quite new institutions, taking advantage of the acceleration in the volume of government and corporate issues that were coming to market in the 1890s, and through the transformation of stockbrokers and mortgage loan companies into investment dealers that carried on an extensive bond business as well as a stock brokerage business. Also, it became quite common for individuals to leave a particular investment house and form a new one.

We have already referred to a number of stock brokerage firms that were also doing a bond underwriting business in a small way, some even before Confederation. Because of this it is not possible to identify a particular firm as being Canada's first bond dealer. In fact, stock and bond firms have always been closely intertwined in Canada as they are today. However, houses concentrating heavily on the bond business did emerge and the following comment on the origin of the bond underwriting business, while probably not entirely accurate, does shed light on the beginnings of one of the very first bond houses in Canada.

> The bond business in Canada had its start within the walls of the University of Toronto. About fifty years ago the Bursar of the University of Toronto was Mr. George A. Stimson. At that time the University had modest sums from endowments for investment, and when a local municipality or township wished to borrow money to build a school, or to put in a bridge or do other necessary works, it

> would pass a by-law and the treasurer of the municipality would come into Toronto to see if the University had any money to invest. He might then go to the Canada Life, which was at that time located in Hamilton, and to one or two of the banks. . . . To save the local treasurer the trouble of making this tour and, incidentally, to make himself some additional income, Mr. Stimson offered to canvas the various buyers on behalf of the borrower and, as a result of his success at this, later began his bond firm.[62]

The firm of G. A. Stimson was formed in the 1890s and was active in the bond business until the 1920s. In 1883 Hanson Brothers, a Montreal brokerage firm, was formed; it developed into a prominent bond house and remained so until it succumbed in the depression of the 1930s. In 1889 A. E. Ames, a few months after marrying the daughter of the prominent financier G. A. Cox, left his position as manager of the Ontario Bank at Lindsay to form his own private banking and brokerage house in Toronto. Nine years later Ames accepted subscriptions for two new companies—the Imperial Life Assurance Company and the National Trust Company, and in 1899 the company established itself in investment banking by underwriting its first industrial issue—$300,000 of Dunlop Tire & Rubber Goods Company 7% Preferred Stock. Others soon followed, including issues of Carter-Crume Company (now part of Moore Corporation, Limited), Wm. A. Rogers Limited, and City Dairy Company (now part of the Borden Company).[63] In 1903, when the market slumped, the company had to suspend payment. It was reorganized under a Dominion charter, ultimately paid off its creditors including depositors, and then in 1908 began to develop its bond business, starting with a successful tender for a $15,000 Town of Windsor issue that year.

The Central Canada Loan and Savings Company occupies an important place in the development of the Canadian bond market. It was formed in 1884 by G. A. Cox. E. R. Wood, who was undoubtedly the most influential high-grade bond man in Canada before the 1920s, joined that company in its founding year. Another future bond man of importance, J. H. Gundy, also received his early training with Central Canada Loan and Savings. In its early years the company operated essentially as a mortgage loan company, but it was formed at a time when such companies were beginning to be interested in bonds and when the volume of bonds was about to

62. W. P. Scott, "The Underwriting and Sale of Investment Bonds," in J. F. Parkinson, ed., *Canadian Investment and Foreign Exchange Problems* (Toronto: University of Toronto Press, 1940), p. 162.

63. See *A.E. Ames & Co. Limited*, 1889-1949, privately published, 1950.

increase rapidly. Gradually it developed a quite active bond business. One circular shows it offering for sale the following bonds: Dominion of Canada, Government of Newfoundland, provinces of Ontario, Nova Scotia, and Quebec, cities of Toronto, London, Ottawa, St. Thomas, and Quebec, towns of Stayner, Brockville, Cobourg, Aylmer, and Mattawa, village of East Toronto, townships of Logan, Elliee, Manvers, Essa, and Dover, and school districts of Neepawa and Loretta, Manitoba. It also was underwriting bonds of the Toronto Electric Light Company. The volume of this business seemed by the turn of the century to justify formation of a separate company.

So in March 1901, under the initiative of E. R. Wood, application was made for an Ontario charter for the Dominion Securities Corporation Limited, essentially a subsidiary of Central Canada Loan and Savings. Its authorized capital was $1,000,000, of which $300,000 was subscribed. The largest shareholder was Central Canada Loan and Savings with $115,000, while H. M. Pellatt had $80,000 and E. R. Wood $50,000. E. R. Wood was president until G. A. Cox took over the position in 1903, but Wood took up the position again in 1912; F. W. Baillie was managing director; E. R. Peacock was general manager; G. H. Wood, who came from the Firm of G. W. Wood & Son, Bond Brokers, was secretary; G. A. Morrow was treasurer; and J. H. Gundy was accountant. All members of this group were to remain influential in the bond market for many years, but not all with Dominion Securities. In 1905 J. H. Gundy and G. H. Wood left the company to form Wood, Gundy & Company. These three houses, A. E. Ames and Company Limited, Dominion Securities Corporation Limited, and Wood, Gundy & Company Limited, which were to become the three largest bond underwriting houses in Canada, had therefore emerged by 1905. The basic bond business opportunities that lay behind their emergence, and that of others previously mentioned, had appeared well before the turn of the century.

A large number of other underwriting houses soon appeared, but one requires explicit recognition, for it made a unique contribution. This was Royal Securities Corporation. In 1899, Max Aitken, later Lord Beaverbrook, at the age of twenty became secretary to John P. Stairs of the firm of William Stairs, Son & Morrow, of Halifax, Nova Scotia. Stairs had wide financial and commercial interests, including the Union Bank of Halifax and the Nova Scotia Steel Company.[64] Aitken was soon involved in effecting a merger between the Union Bank of Halifax and the Commercial Bank of Windsor, and in a finan-

64. See F. A. Mackenzie, *Beaverbrook* (London: Jarrolds, 1931), pp. 30-44.

cial reorganization of the Nova Scotia Steel Company. In these ventures he revealed his unusual talents. As a consequence of this, in 1902 a group of wealthy individuals who were associated with Stairs decided to form a holding and investment company, Royal Securities Corporation, for Aitken to operate. Soon he was involved in establishing electric traction companies in the West Indies. Aitken transferred Royal Securities to Montreal in 1906 and it almost immediately became the leading underwriter of industrial issues arising from mergers, reorganizations, and new ventures—many of which were initiated by Aitken. These included among others the Porto Rico Railway Co.; the Canadian Power and Calgary Power Companies; the Standard Ideal Co. of Port Hope; the Robb Engineering Company; the Cape Breton Trust Company; The Montreal Trust and Deposit Company; the Camoguey Electric and Traction Company. He merged the Rhodes Curry Co., the Dominion Car and Foundry Co., and the Canadian Car Co. to form the Canadian Car and Foundry Company with a capital of $20 million. He formed the Western Canadian Power Co. in 1909, which acquired Slave Lake Power Co. Ltd.; he formed Steel Co. of Canada with a nominal capital of $35,000,000 and under it amalgamated Hamilton Steel and Iron Co., Montreal Rolling Mills Co., Canada Screw Co., Dominion Wire Manufacturing Co., and Canadian Nut and Bolt Co.; and then the most spectacular and notorious move of all—the merging of thirteen cement companies to form the Canada Cement Company.

E. R. Wood must be considered the pre-eminent person in the development of the high-grade bond business, and particularly with reference to the underwriting and mass distribution of such securities. But Max Aitken was unquestionably the dominant personality in the development of that part of the securities market that is concerned with the financing of industrial reorganization and of large new ventures.

There is no doubt that by the turn of the century the earlier dominance of the banks in underwriting had to a certain extent been diminished by the operations of brokers specializing in the bond business, and that the number of potential tenderers for bond issues had become large. A contemporary report on the placement of a Montreal issue at that time illustrates the degree of development of the market at that time:

> There was a warm discussion in the Montreal City Council on Monday over the recent issue of the city's 3½ per cent bonds to the extent of $3,000,000 to the Bank of Montreal at a shade over par. It appears that the Bank of Nova Scotia, Messrs. Burnett & Co. and others desired to tender but were not allowed. And now that it is

> reported that the purchaser has made a good profit out of the bonds some of the council are indignant. The method pursued was, as Alderman Rainville explained, that the finance committee asked only four people to tender – the Bank of Montreal, the Bank of British North America, Mr. R. Wilson-Smith and Messrs. Hanson Brothers, thinking it better to confine the tenders to a limited number of undoubted parties than to solicit tenders from some scores of firms or institutions. . . .[65]

Developments in the Twentieth Century

BASIC TRENDS

The period after the turn of the century was one of cataclysmic developments, in particular, two world wars, the severe and prolonged depression of the 1930s, and then a period of unprecedented prosperity after the Second World War. In spite of these changing conditions several generalizations relevant to most of the period can be made, and these are useful in acquiring initial perspective on Canadian capital market developments in the twentieth century.

The first general point is that the Canada–United States–United Kingdom interest rate pattern that began to emerge before 1900 became permanently established after that. Interest rates in those countries reached a low in 1896 or 1897.[66] However, from 1867 to 1897 Canadian and United States interest rates declined more than United Kingdom rates, which gradually began to increase the relative attractiveness of the United States as a source of funds for Canadian borrowers. We have already seen that the first Canadian bond issue was sold in the New York market in 1879 and that by 1900 about 14% of foreign capital invested in Canada was United States capital. Then from 1897 to 1920 the truly decisive changes in the international interest rate structure occurred, with U.K. rates rising more than Canadian rates and Canadian rates more than United States rates. For example, over that period the yield on U.K. Consols increased by 139%, from 2.26% to 5.41%; the yield on Province of Ontario bonds in Canada increased by 83% from 3.25% to 5.95%; and the yield on the five best United States railway bonds increased by 40%, from 3.64% to 5.10%. As a consequence of these developments the United Kingdom no longer constituted an attractive source of funds, while at the same time a permanent gap was established between Canadian and

---

65. *Monetary Times*, 1899-1900, vol. XXXIII, p. 49.
66. For details see below, pp. 555-67.

United States interest rates that made the latter an attractive source of funds for Canadian borrowers. This pattern has persisted right to the present.

The second major point is that there was in fact a persistent increase in the proportion of total foreign investment accounted for by U.S. investment. Table 14:4 shows that U.S. investment amounted to 14% of the total in 1900, 23% in 1914, 50% in 1922, 60% in 1939, 70% in 1945, 76% in 1950 and 81% in 1967.

Thirdly, it was a period in which Canadian investors greatly increased their proportion of purchases of new bond issues. From 1904 to 1914, as Table 14:4 shows, they seem to have purchased less than 25% of such issues (although the figures are very approximate); during the First World War (that is, from 1915 to 1920) this increased to 67%; in the 1930s it rose to 83%; from 1946 to 1950 it was 93%; and after that it declined slightly (see also Table 14:10 on page 510).

Fourthly, until the 1930s, U.S. investors took an increasing share of total Canadian bond issues, as did Canadian investors, which offset the disappearance of U.K. bond purchases. But during the 1930s the proportion of new bonds going to U.S. investors dropped very sharply and stayed low. It is also the case that after the 1930s non-resident investment declined steadily as a proportion of G.N.P. but increasingly took the form of direct investment (see Table 14:4). Data on direct investment prior to 1926 are not available, but it does seem that it had become increasingly important even before then; U.K. investment in 1900 seems to have been largely portfolio investment and by 1926 direct investment amounted to 30% of non-resident investment. In the case of U.S. capital invested in Canada by the year 1926, 45% was direct investment, whereas only 13% of U.K. capital was in the form of direct investment, which strongly argues that with the emergence of U.S. investment there was also an acceleration of investment in direct form.[67] One prominent Canadian bond dealer who began his career before the turn of the century made the following comment in 1927 when discussing the emerging inflow of U.S. capital around the turn of the century:

> While the British investor, in the main, was content with the lower interest and the greater security afforded by the purchase of such securities as government, municipal and corporation bonds, American investors were more inclined to the policy of establishing industries and developing natural resources, retaining the junior securities. . . .
>
> The Canadian factories of many of the American manufacturers

67. For data on direct investment see Urquhart and Buckley, *op. cit.*, p. 169.

Table 14:4 Foreign Investment in Canada and Domestic and Foreign Sales of Canadian Bonds 1900-1970

Year	Total non-resident investment						Origin of total non-resident investment			Period	Sales of Canadian bonds			
	DIRECT		PORTFOLIO		TOTAL						TOTAL	SOLD IN CANADA	SOLD IN U.S.	SOLD IN U.K.
	$MNS.	%	$MNS.	%	$MNS.	%GNP	U.S. %	U.K. %	OTHER %		$MNS.	%	%	%
1900					1232		14	85	1					
1905					1540		19	79	2					
1910					2529		19	77	4					
1913					3746		21	75	5					
1914					3837		23	72	5	1904-1914	2186	17.7	9.1	73.2
1916					4323		30	66	4					
1918					4536		36	60	4					
1920					4870		44	53	3	1915-1920	3428	67.0	29.6	3.4
1922					5207		50	47	3					
1924					5616		55	42	3					
1926	1782	29.7	4221	70.3	6003	116.6	53	44	3					
1930	2427	31.9	5187	68.1	7614	133.1	61	36	3	1921-1930	5491	57.6	40.6	1.8
1933	2352	31.9	5013	68.1	7365	210.9	61	36	3					
1939	2296	33.2	4617	66.8	6913	123.0	60	36	4	1931-1939	6314	83.3	13.5	3.2
1945	2713	38.2	4379	61.7	7092	59.8	70	25	5	1940-1945	16577	98.3	1.7	—
1950	3975	45.9	4689	54.1	8664	48.2	76	20	4	1946-1950	9031	93.2	6.8	—
1955	7728	57.4	5745	42.6	13473	48.3	76	18	6	1951-1955	13754	90.5	9.5	—
1960	12872	57.9	9342	42.1	22214	58.8	75	15	10	1956-1960	20674	88.8	11.2	—

1965	17356	58.6	12247	41.4	29603	53.9	79	12	9	1961-1965[1]	32849	89.1	10.9[2]	—
1966	19008	59.2	13082	40.8	32091	52.2	80	11	9	1966	8773	86.1	13.9	—
1967	20699	59.6	14003	40.4	34702	52.9	81	10	9	1967	8956	86.8	13.2	—
										1968	11646	84.1	15.9	—
										1969	11753	85.2	14.8	—
										1970	10168	89.5	10.5	—

SOURCE: M. C. Urquhart and K. A. H. Buckley (eds.), *Historical Statistics of Canada* (Toronto: Macmillan, 1965), pp. 169, 279, and Dominion Bureau of Statistics, *Canada Year Book*, 1962, p. 1116, for years up to 1960. Foreign investment figures thereafter from Dominion Bureau of Statistics, *Canadian Balance of International Payments*, and bond sales figures from Bank of Canada, *Statistical Summary*.

[1]Figures from 1961 onward are based on different compilations than those prior to 1961 and are therefore not strictly comparable.
[2]From 1961 to 1970 includes a few sales in Continental Europe.

> who were early to establish in Canada became widely known and built up extensive businesses. Among these were such companies as Canadian Allis Chalmers Company (later absorbed by Canadian General Electric Company), Westinghouse Company, International Harvester Company, the Canadian Fairbanks-Morse and others. In many cases advantage was taken of low-cost electrical energy provided by the power developments at Niagara Falls and in the province of Quebec, with the result that many American branches are located in the area served by these sources. The opening up of the extensive and valuable mining areas in Cobalt in 1908 and in other northern Ontario districts a few years later was responsible for the bringing to Canada of additional large amounts of American capital.[68]

U.S. investment amounted to 14% of non-resident investment in 1900 and by 1926 it amounted to 53%. What may have happened is this: the emerging importance of the incorporated Canadian industrial company around the turn of the century, a development that facilitated non-resident ownership of industry, came just at the time when the international structure of interest rates made the U.S. the most attractive source of capital for Canada. However, the relatively higher interest rates in Canada reflected also relatively higher marginal productivity of capital and so relatively attractive profit opportunities, and this was the basis for a persistent inflow of capital. Then, for reasons that are not all clear, Canadian investors greatly increased their share of total bond investments and foreign investors began to shift into equity investments, as suggested by the increase in non-resident investment accounted for by direct investment. A possible explanation is that the emergence of efficient bond-buying financial intermediaries in Canada came about as quickly as it did in the United States, so that Canada did not suffer a comparative disadvantage in supplying funds to the bond market; but Canada may have had a comparative disadvantage in supplying equity capital, in part because of the close association between the provision of such capital and the provision of managerial and other technology.

Whatever the reason, after the turn of the century Canadian investors came to dominate the Canadian bond market and U.S. investors concentrated increasingly on equity investment.

We turn now to a more detailed examination of the development of the capital market after the turn of the century.

---

68. G.H. Wood, "The Making of Canadian Financial History," *Monetary Times Annual*, June 7, 1927, pp. 122-3.

THE STOCK MARKETS

Earlier we referred to the "call" system of trading stocks that existed for many years on the Toronto and Montreal exchanges. The present "open" system of trading was adopted around the turn of the century, and it reflected the increasing volume of shares traded and numbers of shares listed. The two decades before the First World War saw rapid development of the stock exchanges, just as it saw rapid development of so many other aspects of the Canadian capital market. It was a period in which industrial stocks emerged prominently on the exchanges and this reflected the development of the incorporated form of industrial enterprise which we have already noted. The Montreal Stock Exchange in 1901 traded about 7,000 shares a day and had a membership of 45. By 1914 its membership was 75, daily turnover was about 10,000 shares and it listed 182 stocks. Membership was increased to 85 in 1920, but was reduced to 80 in 1927, where it has remained. By the turn of the century the highest price paid for a seat had been just over $12,000. This increased to over $20,000 in 1902 and 1903. In 1920 it reached $36,000 and in 1929 the peak price paid was $225,000. In the 1960s the price was around $40,000.

The Toronto Stock Exchange listed about 80 issues in 1900, and 200 in 1914. In 1906 its quotations began to be cabled to London and reported regularly in the London papers, and in 1909 in co-operation with the North Western Telegraph Company of Canada it introduced a ticker quotation service. A new building on Bay Street was occupied in 1913, where the exchange remained until it moved into its present building on Bay Street in 1937 and combined trading in industrial and mining stocks on the one floor. The period 1918-1924 saw an increase in listings as a result of activity in the mining industry. There was little disruption to its trading during the financial collapse of 1929 and the depression of the 1930s or even in 1933 when the United States exchanges were closed. In 1930 the exchange prohibited limited liability companies and incorporated partnerships from becoming members, because it was thought that in case of bankruptcy they would hinder trading. This decision was reversed in 1954, when corporations were permitted to become members, a year after the New York Stock Exchange introduced the change. Since then, as Table 14:5 shows, corporation memberships based on private companies have come to predominate with 84 out of a total of 96 memberships taking that form in 1970.

It was in 1934 that the Standard Stock and Mining Exchange with 51 members and the 62-member Toronto Stock Exchange merged to

Table 14:5 Toronto Stock Exchange Membership, Listings, Price of Seats 1947-1970

	MEMBERSHIP								LISTINGS			SEATS SOLD		
	NUMBER	TYPE OF ORGANIZATION			LOCATION OF HEAD OFFICE				IND.	MINES & OILS	TOTAL	PRICE		NO.
		PROP. SHIP	PARTNER-SHIP	CORP.	ONT.	QUE.	OTHER CAN.	U.S.A.				HIGH (IN 000's)	LOW	
1947	93	18	75	0	82	5	1	5				50	35	3
1948									493	357	850	35	27½	4
1949									503	364	867	38	35	6
1950									513	402	915	40	35	4
1951									517	440	957	51	40	7
1952	98	10	88	0	80	10	2	6	536	479	1015	90	51	8
1953									532	503	1035	75	50	4
1954									529	518	1047	60	55	3
1955									534	536	1070	100	75	7
1956									569	554	1123	130	105	5
1957	99	8	50	41	81	9	1	8	597	546	1143	120	120	1
1958									608	522	1130	100	75	4
1959	101	6	44	51					614	517	1131	140	110	5
1960	99	4	43	52					617	501	1118	90	90	1
1961	98	4	43	51	74	13	2	9	620	497	1117	80	75	2
1962	99	4	40	55	74	14	2	9	642	479	1121	101	90	4
1963	99	4	40	55	74	14	2	9	641	457	1098	71	60	2
1964	95	3	38	54	71	13	2	9	657	452	1109	75	70	5
1965	97	3	27	67	71	15	2	9	673	435	1108	105	90	3
1966	95	2	25	68	69	15	2	9	684	414	1098	105	90	2
1967	94	2	21	71	69	13	3	9	702	377	1079	92	65	7
1968	94	2	18	74	70	13	2	9	742	364	1106	98	98	1
1969	99	3	16	80	72	16	2	9	794	361	1155	125	98	14[1]
1970	96	1	11	84	69	16	2	9	817	360	1177	132	115	4

SOURCE: The Toronto Stock Exchange.

[1]Issue of thirteen treasury seats increased number of seats.

form the new Toronto Stock Exchange with 113 seats. There had grown up a Toronto Curb Market for securities not listed on the Toronto Stock Exchange, some of which were also listed on the Standard Stock and Mining Exchange, so the merger helped simplify the arrangement. But there seems to have been another reason for the merger. It has been pointed out that ". . . a great part of the impetus came from the office of the Attorney-General of Ontario. The Toronto Stock Exchange had come through the early thirties fairly well: not one member had become insolvent—a fact the Exchange attributed in part to its audit system inaugurated in 1929. The Standard Stock and Mining Exchange had not fared so well. Five individuals, representing the holders of 26 out of 51 memberships, had been arrested in the investigations following the market crash of 1929."[69]

In 1934 a new high-speed ticker system was introduced, followed in 1952 by a dial quotation service which enabled its members to obtain bid and ask prices; and in 1963 a Ferranti FP-6000 computer was installed which greatly speeded the market information made available to newspapers, extended the range of information available through the Dial Quotation System (including every fifteen minutes the latest levels of a large number of indexes), and operated the exchange's ticker service. A rather significant development occurred in 1956 when the exchange appointed its first permanent president, Arthur J. Trebilcock, Q.C., for it in a sense signalled the gradual evolution of the exchange from a sort of private brokers' club to a public institution. Until then the president had always been a temporary appointee and a prominent broker. In 1960 Lieutenant-General Howard D. Graham, Q.C., became president, followed in 1967 by the former chairman of the Ontario Securities Commission, Mr. John R. Kimber, Q.C. This move toward appointing an "outside" president was followed by the appointment of some "outside" members to the ten-member Board of Governors that governs the operation of the exchange. The trend is also clearly towards much closer public regulation of activities surrounding stock trading and underwriting, an area which we cannot examine here.

Other stock exchanges were formed after the turn of the century. There were informal and sporadic operations of a mining exchange in Montreal, but in 1926 the Montreal Curb Market was formed and it essentially took over the unlisted business of the Montreal Stock Exchange. From 1953 it has been known as the Canadian Stock Exchange.

---

69. See J. Peter Williamson, *Securities Regulation in Canada* (Toronto: University of Toronto Press, 1960), pp. 267-8.

The Vancouver Stock Exchange was formed in 1907, and the Winnipeg Stock Exchange in 1903, although it did not open for business until 1909. The Calgary Stock Exchange was incorporated in 1913, was closed from 1916 to 1926, but then reopened as a result of the revival of interest in oil shares. An Edmonton Stock Exchange was formed in 1953 but floor trading apparently did not develop and the other exchanges ceased recognizing it in 1957. The exchange closed in 1958.

In spite of the multiplication in the number of exchanges, the dominant trend until about 1955 was toward increased trading in Toronto at the expense of Montreal. After 1955, the Vancouver Exchange increased in relative size, accounting for about 8% of total trading in Canada (the 1969 ratio of 13% is misleading), while the Montreal Exchange, apart from a temporary resurgence in the late 1950s, continued until 1970 to decline in terms of the relative size of its trading activity. Table 14:6 shows these trends. So whereas in the period prior to 1900 the Montreal Stock Exchange clearly predominated, in the period after that the Toronto Exchange gradually acquired the reputation of having the broadest and deepest market in Canada. By 1948 even the volume of trading in industrial stocks on the Toronto Exchange exceeded that on the Montreal Exchange.

Table 14:6 Value of Stock Exchange Trading in Canada 1939-1971 (selected years)

	TORONTO	MONTREAL	VANCOUVER	CALGARY	WINNIPEG	TOTAL VALUE
	%	%	%	%	%	$MNS.
1939	56.3	41.5	1.7	.3	.2	520.6
1946	60.7	38.1	1.0	—	.1	1,233.5
1950	55.6	40.8	2.3	1.2	.1	1,623.6
1955	68.6	29.4	1.6	.4	.1	3,939.6
1960	63.1	34.6	2.1	.1	.1	1,940.2
1965	67.1	26.3	6.3	.2	.1	4,766.3
1966	67.9	23.8	7.5	.8	.1	4,236.8
1967	68.2	25.3	5.9	.6	—	5,193.3
1968	69.4	21.4	8.8	.4	—	7,229.0
1969	66.8	18.9	13.3	.9	.1	8,623.0
1970	68.5	22.6	8.5	.3	—	5,331.1
1971[1]	68.2	23.3	8.2	.2	—	1,787.0

SOURCE: The Toronto Stock Exchange. 1939 data directly from the individual exchanges.

[1]First quarter.

It is also interesting to examine the changing relative sizes of the Canadian stock exchanges and those of the United States, as is done in Table 14:7. In 1945 the Toronto and Montreal Exchanges accounted for 5.2% of the value of shares traded on exchanges in North America. This increased to 6.4% by 1950, then to 9.2% by 1955, but decline then set in. In 1960 the figure was only 4.0% and in 1967 it was down to 2.9%. The Toronto Stock Exchange was for a long period the third largest in North America in terms of value of shares traded, but by 1967 it had slipped to fifth place. After that it recovered slightly in relative size. It would appear that just when the Toronto Stock Exchange had firmly established itself as the major exchange in Canada, it began to lose business (in a relative sense) to the exchanges in the United States. It may be that this was because more Canadian issues became listed on the U.S. exchanges, possibly because more Canadians became interested in holding U.S. stocks,

Table 14:7 North American Stock Exchanges, Values of Shares Traded 1945-1970 (selected years)

EXCHANGES[1]	1945	1950	1955	1960	1967	1968	1969	1970
	%	%	%	%	%	%	%	%
New York	78.5	80.7	78.2	80.4	74.9	71.0	70.1	75.5
American	10.1	6.2	6.3	9.0	14.0	17.4	16.8	10.6
Midwest	1.7	2.1	2.2	2.6	3.0	3.0	3.2	3.5
Pacific Coast	1.7	1.9	1.7	1.9	2.7	2.6	3.0	3.7
Toronto	3.6	3.7	6.4	2.6	2.1	2.4	3.1	2.7
Philadelphia-Baltimore-Washington	.7	.8	.8	1.0	1.1	1.1	1.4	1.9
Montreal and Canadian	1.6	2.7	2.8	1.4	.8	.8	.9	.9
Boston	1.1	1.0	.7	.6	.6	1.0	.6	.6
Detroit	.3	.4	.4	.3	.4	.3	.1	.1
Vancouver	.1	.2	.1	.1	.2	.3	.6	.3
Other	.6	.3	.4	.1	.2	.1	.2	.1
	100	100	100	100	100	100	100	100
Value (millions of dollars)	17,144	24,465	41,972	47,247	167,389	204,347	185,013	136,824

SOURCE: Toronto Stock Exchange.

[1]Data made comparable over the period by summing values of shares traded for groups of exchanges that later merged to form the list shown.

particularly those of industries not present in Canada, and perhaps because of the increased foreign ownership of Canadian industry which reduced the supply of available equities. The tendency for Canadian brokerage firms to become members of the Midwest Stock Exchange, and even of the New York Stock Exchange, in the 1960s is not surprising in the light of these developments. It is possible that there will be further continental centralization of stock trading activity, with Canadian exchanges losing further ground to U.S. exchanges.

At the same time it may be noted that the New York Stock Exchange has also declined in relative size. The other regional U.S. exchanges have become more important, just as has the Vancouver Exchange. If this means that basic forces are discouraging complete centralization of activity in one exchange and in fact are facilitating the growth of regional exchanges, then the future of the Canadian stock exchanges may be quite satisfactory—in that they are regional exchanges in an essentially North American market.

The Canadian stock exchanges are incorporated under provincial law, and are self-governing, but have become increasingly subject to government regulation and in time may become essentially public institutions. This trend is indicated by the change in the type of individuals who have been presidents of the Toronto Stock Exchange. All nine presidents from 1861 to 1881 were born abroad (England, Scotland, and Ireland mainly) and all were prominent Toronto brokers. The first Canadian-born president, Robert Beatty, was appointed in 1882, and others soon followed, but all continued to be prominent brokers and were temporary appointees. Then, as noted earlier, in 1956 the exchange began to appoint permanent, non-industry presidents.

The Toronto Stock Exchange is governed by a Board of Governors, the Montreal Stock Exchange by a Governing Committee, the Canadian Stock Exchange by a Board of Management, the Vancouver Stock Exchange by a committee composed of representatives of all members, the Winnipeg Stock Exchange by a Governing Committee and the Calgary Stock Exchange by a Management Committee. As noted above, all the exchanges are provincially incorporated and are self-governing through their by-laws, rules and regulations, all of which have in recent years become increasingly detailed. At the same time, provincial securities legislation administered by such regulatory agencies as the Ontario Securities Commission have also become increasingly important, a technically detailed process that cannot be described here.

INVESTMENT DEALERS AND THE BOND MARKET

Before the First World War: We noted earlier the acceleration in the volume of bond financing after the mid 1890s and also that by 1905 the three investment dealers that even today are the largest in the bond business had already appeared. The decade or so prior to the First World War in fact saw the formation of a large number of Canadian bond houses and also saw active participation of United States bond houses in Canadian business. Both the substantial participation of investment houses in bond underwriting in that period and the range of prices being tendered are illustrated by the following reported tenders:

July 1st 1908 4½% serial Halifax Bonds $166,000 issue

		Price tendered
W.C. Brent & Co.		88.55
Dominion Securities Corporation Limited		91.77
Aemilius Jarvis & Co.		90.30
J.A. Mackay & Co.		91.00
Royal Bank of Canada		91.56
Wood, Gundy & Co.		89.66
J.C. MacIntosh & Co. and F.B. McCurdy & Co. jointly	$36,000	92.51
	30,000	92.89
	50,000	93.14
	50,000	93.39
	5,000	93.29

SOURCE: *Financial Post*, June 20, 1908, p. 1.

July 1909 4½% Owen Sound Bonds $155,000 issue

	Price tendered
Ontario Securities Co.	$156,377
Hanson Bros., Montreal	156,323
Wood, Gundy & Co.	155,612
W. C. Brent & Co.	155,529
G.A. Stimson & Co.	155,026
W.A. Mackenzie & Co.	153,294
British American Security Co.	152,675
R.C. Matthews & Co.	152,560

R. O'Hara & Co.	151,900
Aemilius Jarvis & Co.	151,016.50
Dominion Securities Corporation Ltd.	150,851

SOURCE: *Financial Post*, June 26, 1909, p. 8.

July 1916 5% 10-year Province of Nova Scotia $1,000,000 issue

	Price tendered
Wood, Gundy & Co.	100.2833
Kean, Taylor & Co. and Bank of Nova Scotia	100.027
Aemilius Jarvis & Co.	99.953
A.E. Ames Syndicate	99.8381
Canada Bond Co. & A.B. Leach & Co.	99.747
G.A. Stimson & Co.	99.53
Coffin & Burr	99.42
Royal Securities Corporation	99.377
R.C. Matthews & Co.	99.291
Brent, Noxon & Co.	99.277
Wm. A. Read & Co. and Dominion Securities Corporation	99.052
Macneill & Young	99.04
C.H. Meredith & Co. Ltd.	99.03
Merchants Bank	98.78
Field Richards & Co.	97.60
Harris, Forbes & Co. (received too late, 99.53)	

SOURCE: Files of A.E. Ames & Co.

The breadth that the underwriting business had achieved by 1911 is also indicated by Table 14:8, which summarizes the tenders for municipal issues in that year. It shows that there were on the average about five tenders for even small municipal issues, and about seven for all issues of over $10,000. The largest number of tenders received for any issue was fifteen and the smallest was two. In that year also, as many as eighteen bond dealers were advertising their facilities in one issue of the *Financial Post*. The syndicate system for underwriting even municipal issues was emerging.

This proliferation in the number of bond dealers in the decade ending in 1910 reflected, as we have already seen, a great acceleration in the volume of bond financing. While bonds were traded on the stock exchanges, the exchanges did not really lend themselves to initial distribution of municipal issues, that is to bond underwriting,

Table 14:8 Tenders for Municipal Bond Issues in 1911

Size of issues	No. of issues	Average no. of tenders	Range of no. of tenders Low	High
$ 0- 9,999	42	5	2	11
10,000- 24,999	33	7	2	15
25,000- 49,999	19	7	3	15
50,000- 99,999	14	7	4	10
100,000-249,999	14	7	2	13
250,000 and over	10	7	4	11
	132	6	2	15

SOURCE: Based on data in *Monetary Times Annual Review*, Jan. 6, 1912, pp. 70-2.

and to dealing in the large number of relatively small and diverse bond issues. Bond underwriting activity developed quite separately from the exchanges, direct dealings between bond dealers and bond investors became increasingly important, and so the "over-the-counter" market in bonds began to replace trading in bonds on the stock exchanges. Bond trading through the exchanges reached its peak in the 1920s, after which it quickly became insignificant. Also because of the great importance of the bond underwriting business, relative to the business of trading in outstanding bonds, much of the bond business involved bond dealers acting as principals—quite contrary to the stock business. Dealers early on began to hold portfolios of bonds, of both new and outstanding issues, whereas much of the business of stockbrokers did not involve them as principals. It is true, of course, that most bond houses had separate subsidiary organizations acting as stockbrokers.

Investment Dealers' Association: This development of a district bond underwriting and trading business had reached a point by about 1910 where the need for a bond dealers' organization, with its own by-laws and regulations, and serving as a pressure group for the trade, began to be recognized. Out of this need arose what today is the Investment Dealers' Association of Canada. It is the instrument through which self-regulation is exercised in the bond business, just as the stock exchanges are in the stock brokerage business.

The beginning of this development was December 11, 1911, when a meeting of Toronto bond dealers was held at the National Club, with G. H. Wood of Wood, Gundy & Company in the chair.[70] There was no unanimous feeling that an association should be formed, in part because some felt the public might regard the association as a combine. But the general idea was accepted and Wood was asked to explore the matter further. As a consequence of this, it was decided that rather than form a separate association the Bond Dealers' Association should be a section of the Toronto Board of Trade. Mr. H. R. O'Hara was appointed its first chairman, but it was not until 1913 that a constitution and by-laws were finally drafted and adopted. Besides O'Hara the first officials were J. H. Gundy, vice-chairman, W. C. Brent, treasurer, and C. H. Burgess, secretary. Also on the executive were W. L. McKinnon, J. A. Fraser and W. A. Mackenzie. When Mr. H. R. O'Hara lost his life through the sinking of the *Empress of Ireland* in June 1914, his place as chairman was taken by J. H. Gundy.

Problems for the industry arising from the impact of the First World War soon made the association quite active, particularly in ensuring that there would be no interference in the payment of bonds and coupons. Municipalities were circularized pointing out the need, for purposes of maintaining financial stability, of meeting bonded obligations when they were due. However, the association was disappointed when the Minister of Finance in 1915 offered his First War Loan without any consultation with its members, the feeling in Ottawa presumably being that the banks with their many branches would be adequate.

Montreal dealers had always decided against forming an association themselves. Then in early 1916 Quebec municipalities applied to the Quebec legislature for legislation that would, in effect, have changed the contracts between municipalities and holders of municipal bonds. The Montreal bond dealers made representations to the Premier against this course of action, and were well received. The incident illustrated the usefulness of an association.

Steps were soon taken to form one that would be national in scope. The Bond Dealers' Association of Canada came into being on June 16, 1916. At its first meeting the following were elected: E. R. Wood, Hon. president; C. Meredith and A. Jarvis, Hon. vice presidents; Wm. Hanson, president; A. E. Ames and J. M. Mackie, vice presidents; W. C. Pitfield, treasurer; C. H. Burgess, secretary. Others on the executive were J. H. Gundy, W. C. Brent, G. A. Morrow, G. W. Guthrie, A. H. B. Mackenzie and J. Nesbitt. All the large Toronto and Montreal dealers were represented. There were thirty-three founding

---

70. Details from a private memorandum written by C. H. Burgess of C. H. Burgess & Co. in 1919. He participated in the early meetings referred to here.

member companies. In 1925 the name of the association became The Investment Bankers' Association of Canada but in 1934, when the association was denied the right to use the term "bankers," it became "The Investment Dealers' Association of Canada."

The initial role of the Association was essentially to further the interests of its members. Gradually it also began to emphasize standards of conduct in the industry, financial standing and business conduct of its members, collection of statistical data, and also the provision of educational and training programs for young employees of its members.[71] However, its interest in basic research into the operation of the capital market has been insignificant.

The First World War: First World War financing was important for the development of the bond market and also for the position of the Bond Dealers' Association. The Second War Loan came along and again the association was not consulted in advance, although some of its voluntary suggestions were accepted. But when the results were in, it was found that more than three-quarters of all applications received had been turned in by members of the association. Therefore, when the third issue, the one of March 1917, was being planned, the government consulted frequently with the association. The Fourth War Loan was important for the development of the industry because of the great increase in the number of subscribers that were attracted to the issue. In the weeks preceding the issue the Minister of Finance, Sir Thomas White, asked A.E. Ames, President of the Bond Dealers' Association of Canada, to consider ways of selling yet another large issue. The bond market had deteriorated badly, and funds were urgently needed to finance the war and to purchase supplies being sent to Great Britain. Something special in bond selling seemed to be necessary. As a consequence of this, the Bond Dealers' Association suggested a plan for floating the loan that would involve a country-wide organization. Previous issues had been sold by usual underwriting methods, with dealers, brokers, banks and other financial institutions competing for subscriptions. This plan involved the pooling of all resources of dealers, of many brokers, insurance agents and other financial institutions, and the establishment of a huge selling organization with Dominion, provincial and local committees. The plan was accepted, the $150 million issue attracted $419 million subscriptions, no part of the issue was subscribed to directly by the banks, and instead of there being 25,000 to 41,000 subscribers as had been the case in the first three loans, the

---

71. See D. G. Fullerton, *op. cit.*, pp. 81-4.

number was 820,000. This was the first issue that really brought bonds into the hands of a very large number of Canadians. The Fifth War Loan of 1918 for $300 million attracted $690 million subscriptions and 1,080,000 subscribers; and the Sixth War Loan of 1919, for the same amount, had subscriptions of $678 million and 830,000 subscribers.[72] We have already noted that it was in this period that Canadians became major buyers of bond issues.

One final market development of First World War financing may be noted – the attempt at stabilizing the market. The first domestic war loan, dated December 1, 1915, was issued at 97½ (actually 96¼ after additional interest and discount for advance payment), and was listed on the stock exchanges and opened trading at 98. That was quite satisfactory from a marketing point of view. The Second War Loan, dated October 1, 1916, was priced net at about 97. Both issues for a while traded at around 98½. [73] But in early 1917, in consequence of Allied reverses in France, the market slumped and yet more funds were required to finance the war. The war loan dated March 1, 1917, was priced at 96 (after discount, 94.07) and was made payable also in U.S. dollars to attract U.S. funds. In spite of being over-subscribed, the bonds declined in price when first traded in mid April, and at the end of the year stood at 91¾. These conditions prompted the formation of the national selling organization already discussed, but they also illustrated the need for stability in bond trading activity if financial stability in general was to be protected. So the government appointed a market committee composed of bond dealers, with authority to fix prices. It began operations on January 22, 1918, the selling price for the new issue was set at 98⅞ and dealers agreed to buy bonds at 97⅞. The next war loan, in the fall of 1918, also came under the control of the committee. By the end of 1918 the market had so improved as to make committee support no longer necessary, and its operations ceased on December 21st of that year. In the one year it operated, about $70 million of bonds had passed through its hands, and trading at fixed prices had been agreed to by two hundred and forty dealers in bonds, including the exchanges.

But in the summer of 1919, with the "unpegging" of sterling and a consequent heavy inflow of securities sold in past years in the United Kingdom, bond prices declined. So when the war loan of late 1919 was issued, it and the two previous issues were placed under control of another marketing committee, beginning on January 22,

72. For details see Fullerton, *op. cit.* p. 40 and references there cited.

73. See "The Market Record of Canadian War Loan Issues," *Monetary Times Annual Review*, vol. 66, 1921, pp. 116-20.

1920. Control prices had soon to be reduced, and to help ease the pressure on the bond market the government solicited the assistance of dealers and exchanges in placing a voluntary embargo on the inflow of bonds from abroad. Selling pressure continued, control prices were reduced five times between January and August, and finally on November 29 the experiment had to be abandoned and free market forces again prevailed. Almost immediately prices improved.

In retrospect it would seem that the First World War had several important effects on the Canadian capital market. It hastened the shift of foreign financing from the United Kingdom to the United States; it greatly hastened the development of individual bond buying in Canada, increasing very significantly the number of individuals interested in the market; and it provided a volume of homogeneous and large-sized issues — the war loan issues — that permitted the development of a much more active *trading* market than had existed previously. Just as conditions prior to the war had already enabled the development of a broad and sophisticated bond and stock underwriting business engaging a substantial number of investment houses, so, as a consequence of the war, conditions suddenly permitted the emergence of the last important stage in the development of such a business — an active trading market. It may be noted parenthetically that in the Second World War, when government financing again substantially increased the supply of issues ideally suited for active trading (i.e., large and well distributed), the pioneering stabilization role of the marketing committee of the First World War was assumed by the Bank of Canada, and the National War Finance Committee assumed responsibilities that the dealer-sponsored national selling organization had assumed in the 1914-18 period. Apart from firmly establishing the Bank of Canada as a major force in the capital market, no other unique developments of permanent importance to the bond market seem to have arisen from Second World War financing. Of course it greatly increased the volume of securities of a kind that facilitated active security trading, as did First World War financing.

Trends after the First World War: The growth in the number of firms engaged in the bond business is in a general way indicated by the membership of the Investment Dealers' Association. Table 14:9 shows this membership from the year of the establishment of the Association. The thirty-three founding-year members grew to 105 by 1920. This acceleration was in part a consequence of the success of the Association's membership with respect to the 1917 war loan.

Table 14:9 Investment Dealers' Association of Canada, Number of Members 1916-1971

1916	33	1927	111	1938	122	1949	182	1960	198
1917	50	1928	126	1939	123	1950	196	1961	194
1918	72	1929	136	1940	114	1951	199	1962	187
1919	94	1930	134	1941	n.a.	1952	203	1963	189
1920	105	1931	124	1942	102	1953	205	1964	183
1921	103	1932	108	1943	102	1954	206	1965	181
1922	109	1933	101	1944	101	1955	208	1966	179
1923	100	1934	107	1945	102	1956	206	1967	169
1924	105	1935	113	1946	119	1957	204	1968	163
1925	108	1936	132	1947	137	1958	204	1969	158
1926	111	1937	128	1948	161	1959	199	1970	145
								1971	136

SOURCE: Figures for the years 1916-50 compiled by the author from Investment Dealers' Association material, while those for 1951 to 1969 were prepared for the author by the association. Membership count could not consistently be taken on the same day of the year, although from 1951 to 1970 it was always at the beginning of the year.

Members were drawn from all provinces and in this way it quickly became a nation-wide bond dealers' association. The membership fluctuated between 100 and 111 from 1920 to 1927, which is probably a reasonable indication of the size of the active bond dealer fraternity at that time; in the late 1920s, with the stock market boom, it rose to 136 and then by 1933 was down again to 101, and a similar increase occurred in the late 1930s only to be reduced again to as low as 101, as a consequence of the war. In effect the stable membership from 1920 to 1944 was just over one hundred. In the period after the Second World War it rose markedly, reaching almost 200 by 1951 and an all-time high of 208 in 1955. But after that the number declined persistently, largely through mergers, and by 1971 it was down to 136, which was below the 1948 figure. This occurred in a period of general prosperity, so the trend in the industry is toward fewer and larger dealers. It must be noted, however, that not all dealers in bonds are members of the Investment Dealers' Association. A study completed in early 1970 found that the combined membership total of the I.D.A., the Canadian Stock Exchange, the Montreal Stock Exchange, the Toronto Stock Exchange and the Vancouver Stock Exchange was 463, and that if overlapping memberships were eliminated there were 182 separate members of those organizations—indicating also the great extent to which the industry combines stock brokerage and bond business in individual houses. In addition to those 182 investment organizations, the study found that there were approximately 100 more securities firms licensed to carry on business in Canada.

However, in spite of the large number of bond dealers, there seems from the very beginning to have been a heavy concentration of underwriting business in a relatively few houses. Of a total of 233 securities issues compiled for the year 1927 and valued at $435 million, it would seem that about 60% were underwritten by, or had as their syndicate heads, only five investment dealers and one bank: A.E. Ames and Co., Dominion Securities Corporation Ltd., Wood, Gundy & Co., Royal Securities Corporation, Nesbitt, Thompson and Co. and the Bank of Montreal.[74] The five dealers alone accounted for 47% of the total. The Royal Commission on Banking and Finance reported that in 1962 eight out of 124 reporting firms accounted for 47% of total capital and 45% of total net income of that group of dealers. Another study completed in 1970 found that out of 114 investment dealers surveyed, 14 of them accounted for 50% of the offices of that group, 56% of the employees, 48% of the salesmen, and 40% of the shareholders.[75]

Possibly the major development of the 1920s was the emergence of Wood, Gundy & Co. as the dominant underwriter of securities issues, including particularly industrial securities. A.E. Ames and Co. seems to have been quite cautious in its underwriting activity in the 1920s, perhaps because of its unfortunate experience in 1903, and indeed it is commonly stated and believed that that house was the only major investment dealer not in a state of technical insolvency in the 1930s. Paradoxically, it would seem that while the aggressive underwriting activity of Wood, Gundy & Co. of the 1920s created a serious financial crisis for the company in the 1930s (one apparently overcome only through the patience of its banker), it also laid the foundation for its emerging as the dominant underwriting firm in the period following the near disastrous years of the Great Depression.

After the Second World War the major developments in the fixed-interest securities market were the increase and then the levelling off and decline in the number of dealers, the growth in the volume of underwriting, the shift in the ownership of bonds, and the emergence of a short-term money market.

We have already noted that since 1955 there has been a trend

---

74. Compiled from statistics in *Monetary Times Annual Review*, January 1928, vol. 80.

75. See *Report of the Committee to Study the Requirements and Sources of Capital and the Implications of Non-Resident Capital for the Canadian Securities Industry*, Investment Dealers' Association of Canada, Canadian Stock Exchange, Montreal Stock Exchange, Toronto Stock Exchange, Vancouver Stock Exchange, 1970.

Table 14:10 Gross New Canadian Securities Issues 1936-1970 (Annual average in millions of current dollars and percentage distribution)

PERIOD	GOVERNMENT OF CANADA		PROVINCIAL		CORPORATE BONDS		SUBTOTAL	
	$	%	$	%	$	%	$	%
1936-1940	366	—	148	—	160	—	674	—
1941-1945	2653	—	102	—	94	—	2849	—
1946-1950	1149	—	360	—	457	—	1966	—
1951-1955	1642	—	301	—	583	—	2526	—
1953-1957	2186	49.8	532	12.1	830	18.9	3548	80.8
1956-1960	3777	59.0	759	11.9	900	14.1	5436	85.0
1961-1965	3313	47.0	1379	19.6	1253	17.8	5945	84.4
1966-1970	5050	46.6	2722	25.1	1723	15.9	9495	87.6
1964	3383	44.9	1503	19.9	1379	18.3	6265	83.1
1965	2874	38.3	1469	19.6	1944	26.0	6287	83.9
1966	4159	44.1	2186	23.2	1696	18.0	8041	85.2
1967	3694	39.1	2847	30.1	1560	16.5	8101	85.7
1968	6597	53.9	2806	22.9	1614	13.2	11017	90.0
1969	6440	50.4	2947	23.1	1683	13.2	11070	86.7
1970	4359	42.3	2825	27.4	2064	20.0	9248	89.7
					Average Annual Growth Rates[1]			
1938-1968		9.1		10.2		8.2		9.2
1948-1968		7.7		10.6		6.9		8.2
1955-1968		6.4		13.4		5.9		7.9

SOURCE: Bank of Canada, *Statistical Summary.*

[1] Absolute figures used for 1938, 1948, 1955 and 1968 are five-year average figures centred on those years.

toward fewer dealers, as indicated by the decline in the membership of the Investment Dealers' Association. The development occurred at a time when the volume of new securities issues was steadily increasing. Table 14:10 shows the volume and growth rate of gross new Canadian securities issues. From 1938 to 1968 the volume of Government of Canada, provincial and corporate bond financing (in current dollars) grew at an annual rate of 9.2%, and over the period 1948 to 1968 it was 8.2%. This almost exactly equals the growth in G.N.P., for in the 1938-68 period it grew by 9.2% per annum and from 1948 to 1968 by 8.0%. In the 1955-67 period, a period for which more

MUNICIPALS		OTHER NON-CORP. BONDS		CORPORATE STOCKS CAN.		TOTAL CANADA		ABROAD
$	%	$	%	$	%	$	%	%
—	—	—	—	—	—			—
—	—	—	—	—	—			—
—	—	—	—	—	—			—
—	—	—	—	—	—			—
346	7.9	30	.7	466	10.6	4390	91.8	8.2
480	7.5	25	.4	457	7.1	6399	91.8	8.2
579	8.2	46	.6	477	6.8	7047	89.1	10.9
627	5.8	102	.9	614	5.7	10838	86.2	13.8
705	9.3	30	.4	541	7.2	7541	88.3	11.7
539	7.2	83	1.1	587	7.8	7496	87.8	12.2
682	7.2	52	.6	657	7.0	9432	86.1	13.9
774	8.2	81	.9	496	5.2	9452	86.8	13.2
530	4.4	99	.8	591	4.8	12237	84.1	15.9
552	4.3	31	1.0	1008	7.9	12761	85.2	14.8
595	5.8	145	1.4	318	3.1	10306	89.5	10.5
	n.a.		n.a.		n.a.		n.a.	
	n.a.		n.a.		n.a.		n.a.	
	4.7		9.9		2.1		7.2	

comprehensive data are available, gross new issues of all bonds (including municipal bonds) and common and preferred stocks increased by 7.2% per annum and G.N.P. by 7.4%. It may be noted that new corporate bond and stock issues grew at an annual rate of 5.9% and 2.1% from 1955 to 1968 compared with 6.4% for Government of Canada bonds, 13.4% for provincial bonds and 4.7% for municipal bonds. The much slower rate of growth of corporate stock issues than that of such macroeconomic aggregates as G.N.P., personal disposable income and personal savings itself suggests that the supply of Canadian equities is less than the demand for them, at prices that make them competitive with United States equities. This was also the conclusion reached by a major study commissioned by the Toronto Stock Exchange.[76]

We noted earlier that by the 1930s more than 80% of the bond financing was in Canadian dollars. By the mid 1950s, as Table 14:10 shows, this had increased to over 90%. But during the 1960s, a period of rapidly rising interest rates in Canada, bond financing in foreign markets again increased so that the proportion of new bond sales that were denominated in foreign currencies stood between 10% and 15%. Included in this trend were sales of bonds by Canadian provinces in Switzerland and Germany, as well as in the United States. Sales abroad of Canadian bond issues, as we have already seen, have had a long history and developments of the 1960s in this respect are not unique, or even unusual.

CURRENT CHARACTERISTICS OF INVESTMENT FIRMS

The preceding discussion has shown that the fraternity of investment dealers has developed over a long period of years. We can now pause to summarize its major current characteristics.

It must first of all be recognized that the large investment firms all engage heavily in the bond, stock and money markets, and that they account for a significant portion of that activity. For that reason it is not very accurate to think of the markets as being composed of "bond houses," "stockbrokers," and "money market dealers," and the term "investment firms" or "securities firms" is more appropriate. At the same time, as we shall see, there are firms that specialize in the various areas.

Stock brokerage function: Canadian securities firms may be regarded as fulfilling a number of different functions even though in practice those functions often are not performed separately.[77] First, they act as stockbrokers, buying and selling common and preferred stocks for clients on a commission basis, mostly through the facilities of the organized exchanges. Table 14:13 (on page 521) shows that this activity generates more than half of the income of the industry, indeed amounting in 1969 (which was an exceptional year) to about 76% of total income.

From 1946 to 1969 the volume of trading, as indicated by the value

---

76. See G. R. Conway, *The Supply of and Demand for Canadian Equities*, Toronto Stock Exchange, 1970.

77. *Report of the Committee to Study the Requirements and Sources of Capital, op. cit.*

of shares traded on all the stock exchanges, increased between 8% and 9% per annum, the same as G.N.P. (see Table 14:6).

Trading or secondary distribution: Dealers trade among each other in fixed-interest securities—bonds, debentures, notes and bills—and with clients, thereby facilitating changes in ownership of such securities through maintaining a secondary market in them. The market is referred to as an "over-the-counter" market but in fact it is an "over-the-telephone" market. This trading function requires dealers to hold an inventory of securities, that is, to buy and sell for their own account, and so, contrary to much of their stock business activity, they are principals in such activities. This activity, as well as their underwriting activity described below, means that to a limited extent they are financial intermediaries, for they borrow funds to hold other financial claims and often earn some interest income on the "carry" of their inventory.

About 10% of their gross income is in interest and dividend form (see Table 14:13). Additional income may be earned from this function through capital appreciation of inventory in a rising market, or through short-sales of securities in a falling market, although of course the "opportunity" for experiencing losses is also there since dealers must maintain some inventory in a falling market if they wish to continue to serve the function of making markets.

Primary distribution: A third function of the investment firms is to place new securities issues, that is, to engage in primary distribution of securities. This can take a number of different forms. If a bond or debenture issue is involved the issuer—provincial or municipal government or corporation—and dealer may negotiate on the nature and terms of the securities issue to be offered, with the dealer taking it on an agency or an underwriting basis. If the latter, then the dealer in effect guarantees the price to the issuer, and distributes it, taking any loss should it be necessary to reduce the price of the issue to make it sell. If a stock issue is involved it normally takes the form of an issue of rights to existing shareholders to take up additional shares, and the dealer may underwrite it (i.e., guarantee the amount of the issue price) or agree to take up shares not purchased by shareholders, at a price to be negotiated. In some cases a stock or bond issue is placed privately, in which case the dealer acts not as an underwriter but as an agent and negotiates the direct sale to one or a small number of buyers, usually large financial institutions. Provinces and municipalities sometimes call for public tenders, in which case the dealer may submit a tender and, if successful, become the underwriter of the issue. Finally, some stock exchanges, including the Toronto Stock Exchange, permit new issues of junior oil and mining companies (and in the case of one exchange, industrial companies) to be distributed by their members through the exchange itself – although much controversy has surrounded this use of exchange facilities.

As implied above, the method of placing new securities issues varies somewhat with the type of securities involved. In the case of Government of Canada bonds, the procedures are especially different. Terms (i.e., date of issue, maturity, coupon, price, size, delivery date, etc.) are decided by the government. The Department of Finance takes the leading role, but it has available to it the advice, experience and market knowledge of its debt manager and fiscal agent – the Bank of Canada. Typically the Minister of Finance, whenever he wishes to sell a bond issue, will issue a press release to that effect on a Thursday or Friday. Over the weekend the Bank of Canada will send a telegram giving the details of the issue to all the "primary distributors," which include the chartered banks, Quebec savings banks and over two hundred investment dealers and brokers. The telegram will indicate size of the issue, its coupon rate, price, yield, date of issue and delivery, dealer's commission, amount taken up by the Bank of Canada, amount offered firm to the particular distributor (which he may accept or reject in whole or in part) and amount of total issue still open for subscription. Dealers are requested not to sell the bonds below issue price until they receive a telegram informing them that the "price restrictions" have been lifted – usually at about the time of the delivery of the bonds. Normally dealers can sell bonds to any buyers they wish, that is, there are no "exempt institutions" whose orders are reserved for particular dealers. As soon as the primary distributors know their allotment of firm bonds they begin to place them through telephone communication with investors.

The Bank of Canada and government bond accounts act as underwriters for part of the issue. The Bank, through its securities traders in Toronto and Montreal, usually accumulates part of the maturing issue, directly or indirectly selling bonds out of its portfolio in exchange for it. It can therefore take up part of the new issue in payment for the maturing issue it holds, and in succeeding months it can sell the new issue in the market in exchange for other short-term bonds. The Bank and government accounts can also buy a new issue that is not selling well.

The only important exceptions to this general approach to selling Government of Canada securities relate to the government's sale of treasury bills, which are sold through a weekly auction, and the yearly issue of Canada Savings Bonds, dated November 1st, which are non-marketable securities always redeemable at par and sold for cash or through a payroll deduction plan with the help of an annual sales campaign.

The size, structure, maturity, and distribution of Government of Canada direct and guaranteed securities is shown on Table 14:11, from which the following trends are apparent. First, from 1946 to 1970 combined holdings of the Bank of Canada, chartered banks and Government of Canada accounts increased from 36% to 46% and the holdings of the general public category declined from 64% to 57%. Within the latter category the most pronounced change was the shift by individuals into Canada Savings Bonds out of marketable securities: at the end of 1946 the (basically) non-financial institutions category of "all other" resident holders accounted for about 28% of total government securities and Canada Savings Bonds were 7% of the total, whereas in 1969 the ratios were 11% and 29% respectively. Life insurance companies reduced their holdings from 10% of the total to 2% over that period and non-resident holders from 6% to 4%.

There has been a distinct shortening in the maturity of Government of Canada debt. Not only have Canada Savings Bonds – which are essentially demand securities – grown greatly in relative importance, but even excluding Canada Savings Bonds and perpetual bonds, the average term to maturity has been substantially reduced – from 9 years and 11 months in 1946 to 5 years and 4 months in 1970. The government in 1958 undertook a massive conversion of its debt into longer-term form.[78] Table 14:11 shows that by 1969 most of the debt had become "unconverted," as shown by the persistent shortening in the average maturity of the debt.

The underwriting role of the investment dealer comes to the fore in the marketing of new issues of municipal, provincial and corporation securities. The term "underwriter" has various meanings, but in North American securities markets it essentially refers to a dealer who purchases an issue outright from a borrower and resells it to investors; he is thus a principal and not just an agent in the transaction.[79] This means that if an issue can be sold only through reducing its issue price, the loss falls on the underwriter, not the borrower.

In the case of an issue of corporation securities, federal and provincial securities legislation requires that there must be filed with the authorities a prospectus outlining the details of the issue and that it must be made available to investors.[80] There is also a "Deed of Trust

78. For details see Fullerton, *op. cit.*, chap. 15 and Appendix C.
79. For a full discussion see Fullerton, *op. cit.*, chap. 9 and references there cited.
80. See below, p. 531.

Table 14:11 Government of Canada Direct and Guaranteed Securities: Structure, Maturity and Distribution 1938-1970 (selected years as of Dec. 31)

Structure	1938	1946	1950	1956	1960	1965	1968	1969	1970
	%	%	%	%	%	%	%	%	%
I *Direct debt*									
Treasury bills	6.2	2.6	9.4	10.3	11.2	10.4	12.0	12.1	14.1
Other unmatured market issues	93.7	80.8	79.0	67.6	59.0	53.7	54.3	53.2	51.2
Matured and outstanding	.1	.2	.3	.2	.1	.1	.1	.1	.1
Subtotal	100.0	83.5	88.7	78.1	70.3	64.2	66.4	65.4	65.4
Canada Savings Bonds	—	7.1	7.7	16.7	20.2	28.4	27.0	28.0	28.7
Other non-market issues	—	6.3	—	—	—	.8	1.8	2.3	1.9
Total	100.0	97.0	96.4	94.8	90.6	93.4	95.2	95.6	95.9
II *Guaranteed debt*		3.0	3.6	5.2	9.4	6.6	4.8	4.4	4.1
III *Total debt* $Mns.	4336	17313	15892	15234	17747	20681	23627	23902	25746
Average maturity[1] — total debt	10:7	9:11	8:1	6:4	9:5	7:9	6:4	5:10	5:4
(Years: months) — held by general public	—	n.a.	n.a.	7:11	11:6	10:4	8:10	7:10	7:10
Distribution									
	%	%	%	%	%	%	%	%	%
I *Bank of Canada*	4.2	11.0	12.4	15.9	15.5	16.8	16.7	17.2	16.7
II *Chartered Banks of Canada*	17.7	19.6	19.7	16.6	17.2	18.0	23.6	21.3	25.6
III *Government of Canada Accounts*	3.7	5.3	5.3	10.0	4.9	2.7	4.2	4.3	3.9
Subtotal	25.6	35.9	37.4	42.4	37.6	37.5	44.4	42.8	46.2

IV *General public*									
Provincial and municipal gov'ts		2.6	3.2	3.7	3.5	2.8	2.2	2.3	2.1
Life insurance companies		10.2	7.7	3.9	3.9	2.5	1.8	1.9	1.9
Other insurance companies		.9	1.4	2.3	2.7	2.7	2.7	2.9	2.4
Quebec savings banks		.4	.6	.3	.2	.1	.2	.1	.1
Trust companies }		1.1	1.2	.8	1.5	1.9	2.2	2.5	2.1
Mortgage loan companies }				.3	.4	.6	.5	.6	.5
Trusted pension funds }		28.5	25.6	2.1	2.7	1.6	1.3	1.4	1.3
All other resident market securities [2] }				16.8	15.7	11.3	11.5	11.1	9.8
Non-financial corporation		6.0	5.8	4.9	4.7	4.5	.9	.9	.4
Other financial institutions		1.1	.9	1.8	2.2	1.0	1.1	1.5	1.6
Canada Savings Bonds[3]		7.1	7.6	16.7	20.2	28.4	26.9	28.0	28.7
Subtotal	41.9	58.0	54.0	53.7	57.9	57.3	51.5	53.1	50.9
Non-resident	32.5	6.2	8.6	3.8	4.5	5.2	4.1	4.1	2.9
V Total $Mns.	4336	17313	15892	15234	17747	20681	23627	23902	25746

SOURCE: Bank of Canada, *Statistical Summary*.

[1] Excludes Canada Savings Bonds and Perpetual.
[2] Includes residual error.
[3] Held mainly by individuals.

and Mortgage," or "Trust Deed," that outlines conditions protecting the position of investors and prescribes procedures in the event of developments such as defaults in the payment of principal and interest; a trustee for the investors, usually a trust company, is appointed to ensure that the conditions of the deed are adhered to. The legal contract between the borrower and the underwriter, including all details of the financial arrangements between them and of the terms of the issue, takes the form of an "underwriting agreement" or "purchase agreement." However, one underwriter normally is not able to sell quickly the whole of an issue and usually does not wish to assume all of the underwriting risk involved. Therefore he will form syndicates of dealers, covered by syndicate agreements, under which underwriting risks and rewards are shared. Two groups of dealers are involved. First, there is the "banking group" covered by a "banking group agreement." It is the inner group that shares all risks and rewards of the underwriting, and participates in establishing terms of the issue. Then there is the less formal and very large "selling group," the members of which are permitted to subscribe for some of the issue. Their allotments may be small if the banking group finds that the issue is selling well. Price of the securities to the underwriter will be lower than to the banking group, to compensate him for his efforts; price to the banking group will be lower than to the selling group; and price to the selling group will be lower than to the investor. The spread between price to the underwriter and price to the investor varies from issue to issue, with $2 for a $100 corporate bond being quite common. As in the case of federal government securities, there are "price restrictions" when the issue is being distributed (although if it is moving badly accusations of deviations from them by members of the selling group are common), and there frequently is an "exempt list" of investors who are canvassed only by certain members of the banking group on behalf of the whole group. This basic approach to underwriting began to emerge in Canada just after the turn of the century, virtually as soon as it did in the United States.

Provincial bonds are frequently sold through negotiation with one or several dealers who are the "permanent" fiscal agents of the particular province. The fiscal agent will proceed with the underwriting much in the way described above, although there are no prospectus and trust deed requirements. Occasionally provincial issues are sold to syndicates by competitive tender, or are placed privately, or even distributed directly by the province. Many municipalities sell their issues to dealers or dealer syndicates, through public tender, while some also use the "fiscal agency" approach. The cost of funds varies substantially as between the various municipalities and provinces, depending on the market's view of the credit rating of the individual borrower, and the cardinal sin of default seems to affect such credit standing for many years.

The distribution of provincial, municipal and corporate bond holdings (see Table 14:12) has for the most part not changed dramatically since 1955. The most important changes were increased relative holdings of these bonds by pension funds and non-residents and reduced relative holdings of bonds by provincial governments, chartered banks and life insurance companies. The residual category of "all other resident" holders, which includes many individuals, accounted for 22% of the holdings of these bonds in 1968, non-resident buyers held 32% of them, life insurance companies 13%, trusteed pension plans 12%, provincial governments 7% and the chartered banks 4%.

Since the volume of gross new issues seems to have grown at about 8-9% per annum (see Table 14:10), that is also probably the average annual growth rate of bond trading and underwriting in Canada. The trading and underwriting function of the dealers seems to generate about 25% of their gross income (see Table 14:13), and largely accounts for the large size of their assets and their capital and loan requirements. Table 14:14 presents the most detailed investment dealers' balance sheet data available, but unfortunately it is not available for earlier years. Total assets amounted to $1,245 million, including a securities inventory of $755 million which was heavily weighted with short-term money market securities, an area of activity that we discuss later. But as can be seen, all manner of securities are represented in the inventories of the dealers. Those assets were financed largely with day-to-day and call loans ($707 million) but repurchase agreements, which we explain below, financed another $81 million.[81] The high level of accounts receivable and payable reflects the trading and underwriting activity of dealers. Table 14:15 provides additional detail on funds borrowed by investment firms, and covers the period 1963-9. Those data also suggest that funds borrowed by investment firms amount to about $800 million. They show, furthermore, that firms obtained half or more of their funds from

---

81. In addition to these D.B.S. data, the *Report of the Financial Industry Committee* includes balance sheet data for several years for 114 Canadian-owned firms and for one year for 167 Canadian-owned firms (p. 156). Total assets shown there amounted to $1,836 million based on balance sheets ending between April 1, 1968 and March 31, 1969, which is much larger than the D.B.S. balance sheet figure shown on Table 14:14, although dates differ. However, the figures of inventories of securities and borrowed funds are much the same as the D.B.S. figures, with the discrepancy explained largely by higher receivables and payables, and a larger capital and surplus.

Table 14:12 Distribution of Provincial, Municipal and Corporate Bond Issues 1955-1968 (selected years)

	PROVINCIAL DIRECT AND GUARANTEED BONDS			MUNICIPAL DIRECT AND GUARANTEED BONDS			CORPORATE AND OTHER BONDS			TOTAL		
	1955	1965	1968	1955	1965	1968	1955	1965	1968	1955	1965	1968
	%	%	%	%	%	%	%	%	%	%	%	%
Resident												
Bank of Canada	—	—	—	—	—	—	.2	1.9	2.2	.1	.7	.8
Chartered banks	7.9	2.8	2.1	9.9	6.3	5.7	10.6	4.9	5.2	9.4	4.3	3.9
Provincial governments	22.0	14.4	11.9	6.2	4.1	4.1	1.0	2.1	2.3	10.0	7.8	7.1
Municipal governments	.7	1.0	.9	5.2	7.4	8.8	—	.4	.2	1.3	2.0	2.1
Life insurance companies	8.7	8.8	6.4	17.0	13.4	11.0	31.8	22.3	20.8	20.1	14.8	12.4
Other insurance companies	3.5	3.2	3.2	3.4	2.8	3.2	1.6	2.2	2.7	2.7	2.8	3.0
Quebec savings banks	2.0	.6	.4	2.6	.5	.6	.4	.3	.4	1.4	.4	.4
Trust and mortgage loan cos.	2.4	2.0	1.9	2.4	2.5	2.0	1.9	2.7	2.6	2.2	2.4	2.2
Trusteed pension plan	31.0	16.9	14.4	32.8	12.0	11.1	18.6	9.4	9.3	26.1	13.1	12.0
All other resident (residual)		25.6	31.2		26.8	28.6		18.2	14.9		23.0	24.7
Total	78.2	75.3	72.3	79.6	75.8	75.1	66.1	64.4	60.6	73.4	71.3	68.5
Non-resident	21.8	24.7	27.7	20.4	24.2	24.9	33.9	35.6	39.4	26.6	28.7	31.5
Total $Mns.	4074	11946	17621	2203	5398	6366	4554	10709	13657	10831	28053	37658

SOURCE: Bank of Canada, *Statistical Summary*, Annual Supplements.

Table 14:13 Income and Expenses of 114 Canadian-Owned Investment Firms

	1965		1966		1967		1968		1969	
	$MNS.	%	$MNS.	%	$MNS.	%	$MNS.	%	$MNS.	%
Income										
Brokerage commission	83.7	59.5	92.4	62.3	85.6	60.4	120.9	63.6	214.3	75.6
Profits on trading and underwriting	43.0	30.6	41.1	27.7	39.9	28.1	47.2	24.8	72.0	22.5
Other (mainly interest and dividends)	14.0	9.9	15.0	10.1	16.3	11.5	22.1	11.6	33.1	10.4
Total	140.6		148.3		141.8		190.1		319.3	
Expenses										
Remuneration to employees (excluding shareholders and partners)	46.5	33.1	53.1	35.8	54.3	38.3	66.8	35.1	104.5	32.7
Other	46.1	32.8	53.1	35.8	57.6	40.6	72.6	38.2	104.4	32.7
Total	92.6	65.9	106.1	71.5	111.8	78.9	139.5	73.4	208.9	65.4
Income before shareholders' and partners' remuneration and income tax	48.0	34.1	42.2	28.5	29.9	21.1	50.6	26.6	110.5	34.6

SOURCE: *Report of the Committee to Study the Requirements and Sources of Capital and the Implications of Non-Resident Capital for the Canadian Securities Industry*, May 1970.

non-chartered bank sources. In 1969, for example, of $805 million of borrowed funds, $376 million came from non-bank sources. Also at least two-thirds of that $805 million was covered with short-term money market securities.

Table 14:14 shows that shareholders' equity in 1969 amounted to 9% of liabilities, or $112 million; another survey of 167 Canadian-owned firms placed it at 9.9% or $183 million.[82] The self-regulatory

82. See *Report of the Financial Industry Committee*, p. 155.

Table 14:14 Assets and Liabilities of Investment Dealers December 31, 1969, 1970

	$MNS. 1969	%	$MNS. 1970	%
Assets				
Cash	17.2	1.4	26.6	1.5
Canadian securities – total	745.2	59.9	1130.9	64.1
Bank term deposits	43.0	3.5	56.9	3.2
Finance company paper	128.0	10.3	162.4	9.2
Commercial paper	226.4	18.2	369.7	21.0
Canada treasury bills	98.1	7.9	182.9	10.4
Canada bonds less than three years	95.8	7.7	72.3	4.1
Canada bonds over three years	10.9	.8	60.5	3.4
Provincial	67.5	5.4	142.7	8.1
Municipal	15.0	1.2	13.2	.7
Corporation and institution bonds	40.8	3.3	57.0	3.2
Preferred and common shares	16.8	1.3	12.1	.7
Other investments	2.8	.2	1.2	.1
Foreign securities – total	9.4	.7	2.1	.1
Accounts receivable	426.0	34.2	563.4	31.9
Other assets	47.2	3.8	40.8	2.3
Total	1245.0	100	1763.8	100
Liabilities				
Loans – total	840.5	67.5	1226.4	69.5
Day-to-day loans	204.4	16.4	361.1	20.5
Overdrafts and call loans	502.6	40.4	696.5	39.5
Repurchase agreements	81.3	6.5	103.6	5.9
From associated companies	19.8	1.6	22.0	1.2
Other	32.4	2.6	43.2	2.4
Accounts payable	292.8	23.5	415.5	23.6
Share capital – total	111.7	9.0		
Preferred	25.2	2.0	28.9	1.6
Common	11.7	.9	14.6	.8
Retained earnings	67.3	5.4	72.6	4.1
Reserves	7.5	.6	6.7	.4
Total	1245.0	100	1763.8	100

SOURCE: D.B.S. *Financial Institutions Financial Statistics*, Queen's Printer, Ottawa, quarterly.

authorities imposed capital requirements on their members, but in the aggregate shareholders' equity is little different for investment firms than for other financial institutions. Under industry regulations

Table 14:15 Funds Borrowed by Investment Dealers 1963-1970

(PERCENTAGE DISTRIBUTION AND MILLIONS OF DOLLARS)

		1963	1964	1965	1966	1967	1968	1969	1970
Borrowed from chartered banks[1]									
Day-to-day loans	$mns.	150	188	200	218	278	249	203	268
	%	28.8	29.5	27.2	33.1	33.5	28.8	25.3	26.6
Call and short loans	$mns.	56	64	94	102	192	278	226	273
	%	10.7	10.0	12.8	15.5	23.1	32.1	27.9	27.1
Total	$mns.	206	252	294	320	470	527	429	541
	%	39.5	39.5	39.9	48.6	56.6	60.9	53.2	53.7
Non-banks borrowing secured by: Government of Canada securities[2]									
90 days to maturity or less	%	26.3	19.9	13.0	12.3	6.6	5.8	8.6	7.6
91 days to three years	%	10.7	8.0	6.4	5.0	4.0	2.2	2.5	1.6
Over three years	%	3.8	3.6	4.3	3.3	2.3	1.5	2.1	1.8
Total	$mns.	213	201	175	136	107	82	106	111
	%	40.9	31.5	23.7	20.6	12.9	9.5	13.2	11.0
Non-banks borrowing secured by: Other securities[3]									
One year maturity or less	%	11.9	21.2	28.7	24.7	26.5	27.7	31.2	33.0
Over one year	%	7.7	7.8	7.7	6.1	4.0	1.8	2.5	2.3
Total	$mns.	102	185	268	203	253	256	270	356
	%	19.6	29.0	36.4	30.8	30.5	29.6	33.6	35.3
Total	$mns.	521	637	736	659	830	866	805	1008
	%	100	100	100	100	100	100	100	100

SOURCE: Computed from data made available to us by the Investment Dealers' Association of Canada and from Bank of Canada *Statistical Summary*. Non-bank borrowing data includes all members of the I.D.A. and bank borrowing includes all loans made to investment dealers and brokers.

[1]Average of Wednesday figures.
[2]Average of month-end figures.
[3]Excludes stocks.

only those actively engaged in firms may be partners or shareholders, so that control rests with full-time officers and employees. Sources of equity capital also are restricted to them, which has raised the question of the adequacy of capital in the industry. An industry committee has recommended relaxation of restrictions relating to the use of outside capital, but it has recommended that a strong majority of voting capital always remain with the investors directly associated with the firm.[83] Public ownership and control of investment firms, in other words, was regarded as being undesirable. The New York Stock Exchange has endorsed the principle of public ownership of member firms with safeguards, and the matter of ownership and control of Canadian investment firms will undoubtedly continue to be a controversial issue in the years ahead.

Advisory and portfolio management services: Investment firms, including brokers and dealers, manage the investment portfolios of clients. They provide those clients with on-going advice relating to investment opportunities and portfolio management, and some manage mutual funds. Advice to corporations relates to issuing securities, company acquisitions, and mergers and economic conditions, while provincial and municipal borrowers also are serviced with information relevant to the issue and redemption of securities.

Number of firms and foreign ownership: In early 1970 there were 145 investment dealers who were members of the Investment Dealers' Association of Canada, while the Toronto Stock Exchange had 99 members, the Montreal Stock Exchange had 77, the Canadian Stock Exchange had 88, and the Vancouver Stock Exchange had 51 – a total of 463. However, because of duplication, that total represented only 182 separate firms. In addition, there were about 100 other firms licensed to do a securities business in Canada who were not members of the I.D.A. or exchanges. However, as already noted, a relatively few firms account for a significant proportion of the securities business. Of the 182 aforementioned member firms, 15 were non-resident controlled in early 1970, including 13 U.S. firms. Also, 9 of them were members of the Toronto Stock Exchange (out of a total membership of 99), 11 were I.D.A. members, 11 were members of the Canadian Stock Exchange, 8 of the Montreal Exchange and 3 of the Vancouver Exchange. Data for their income statements dated between April 1968 and March 31, 1969, show that they earned $10 million commissions on Canadian securities transactions with Canadian residents and $17.2 million on U.S. securities transactions with Canadian residents – with the total of $27 million being equal to about 11% of total brokerage commissions earned by 167 Canadian-owned firms surveyed. In addition to the 15 non-resident member firms, there were in early 1970 about 10 non-resident licensed securities firms that were not members of the Investment Dealers' Association or stock exchanges.

83. For a full discussion, see *ibid.*

The takeover of the old and historically interesting Canadian firm of Royal Securities Corporation Ltd. by the U.S. firm of Merrill Lynch, Pierce, Fenner & Smith Inc. in 1969 drew attention to the matter of foreign ownership in the industry. It is unlikely that further foreign takeovers of importance would be permitted. A committee of the industry concluded in 1970 that

> on the basis both of the cost-benefit analysis and of the "key sector" concept, we have concluded that any further non-resident control over Canadian securities firms that are members of the self-regulatory organizations to which we report should be prohibited. Neither the cost-benefit analysis nor the key sector concept leads to the conclusion that a prohibition of non-resident control should extend to Canadian firms already controlled by non-residents.... After the publication of this report, and subject to the exceptions proposed below, foreign securities firms should not be permitted to acquire memberships in the self-regulatory organizations to which we report.[84]

The Canadian firms, of course, could gain financially by regulations limiting entry of foreign firms, although some existing owners may suffer through being denied the possibility of selling their businesses to U.S. firms. The probabilty is that the rules of the self-regulatory bodies—the I.D.A. and the stock exchanges—will maintain foreign participation in the Canadian securities business at its present level, which is possibly around 10% of the total as far as stock trading is concerned and much less if underwriting activity is included. Obviously it will be important to ensure that adequate competition is maintained in the industry, particularly since some aspects of it are already heavily concentrated in a relatively few Canadian houses. Relaxation of the rules limiting public Canadian capital could serve to increase competition in the industry.

Differences between firms: In early 1970, of 114 firms surveyed, there were 14 firms with capital of over $3 million, 21 with capital of $1 million to $3 million, and 79 with capital of less than $1 million. The 14 accounted for 50% of the officers of the firms surveyed, 56% of the employees, and 48% of the salesmen. They also had 30 of the 37 offices outside of Canada, and 243 of the 511 offices in Canada.[85] In recent years 13 Canadian firms have become members of the Midwest Stock Exchange in the United States, one of the New York Exchange (and others are planning to become members), and about 10 are members or associate members of the Philadelphia-Baltimore-

---

84. *Ibid.*, pp. 138-9.
85. *Ibid.*, pp. 26, 153.

Washington Stock Exchange or the Boston Stock Exchange or both.[86] This undoubtedly resulted from the increased interest of Canadians in U.S. equities, which in turn probably reflected in part the scarcity of Canadian equities.

The large "integrated houses" engage in a full range of activity: originating, underwriting and distributing new securities issues of all kinds, including bonds and stocks; managing banking and selling groups formed for placing new issues; trading in securities, including stocks, bonds and short-term money market securities and placing new issues of the latter. They frequently maintain separate departments for underwriting, sales, trading, managing investors' securities portfolios, statistics, industry and economic research, accounting and delivering securities. The dealers referred to as "distributing houses" do not initiate new underwritings but frequently participate in placing new issues initiated by other houses, and engage in a broad range of the other securities activities. "Specialty houses" are more restricted in their activity. They may, for example, engage only in trading in bonds for speculative gain, or in trading in unlisted shares, or in placing municipal issues.[87]

Some important stockbrokers have no affiliated investment dealer firm at all, engage in no underwriting of issues and are generally inactive in the bond and money markets, apart from servicing accounts of clients, of which they may have a large number. It is sometimes argued by them that they thereby avoid the conflict of interest that could arise between servicing the portfolios of investor clients and distributing a new issue of a borrowing client – a potential conflict that may arise in the large, integrated investment firms. It is certainly true that specialization among investment firms is one way of avoiding such conflicts.

THE SHORT-TERM MONEY MARKET

Historical development: Special note must be taken of the development of one segment of the market for fixed-interest securities, namely the short-term money market, or as it is frequently referred to, "the money market." By money market we refer to the issue and distribution of and trade in highly liquid short-term financial claims. The market as such is therefore composed of (a) the issuers of money market securities, (b) the money market securities themselves, (c) the

---

86. *Ibid.*, p. 125.

87. See Investment Dealers' Association of Canada, *Brief to the Royal Commission on Banking and Finance*, 1962, Appendix A, Part 1, Exhibit "A," and as described in Fullerton, *op. cit.*, p. 85.

distributors of and traders in money market securities and (d) the buyers of such securities. Development of the market really involves developments in each of these aspects of the market.

Before examining the nature of that development, it is useful to consider why a money market is a desirable segment of a capital market. During the 1930s it was commonly thought that a money market, or "bill" market, was essential for the effective operation of a central bank,[88] and it is undoubtedly true that a central bank can manage the cash base of the banking system more efficiently if such a market exists. This is so not merely because it enables the central bank more easily to adjust the cash reserves of the banking system as a whole, but also because it enables individual banks to manage their cash reserves more efficiently and thereby maintain a more predictable cash reserve ratio. Furthermore, it enhances the central bank's knowledge of the state of current credit conditions. But if these were the only advantages to be gained, it is questionable whether development of a short-term money market would be worth the effort, particularly since other means exist for making cash reserve adjustments. More important is the improvement such a market makes possible in the portfolio composition of investors and in the capital structures of borrowers, including increased economic efficiency through greater competition in short-term lending and borrowing. Having in mind the balance between risk and income that various investors seek, and the varying time periods over which borrowers require funds, it is intuitively seen that a spectrum of financial claims that includes various short-term financial claims is likely to improve the positions of both borrowers and investors. Also, the short-term money market gives borrowers a source of short-term funds that is an alternative to bank loan accommodation, thereby increasing competition in an area of the capital market that in past years was highly institutionalized with rather limited interest rate flexibility. To commercial and industrial corporations the issue of commercial paper is a substitute for taking a short-term bank loan, as is the issue of finance company paper by sales finance companies. This in turn increases the flexibility of interest rates on bank loans. Similarly, the issue of short-term financial claims by financial institutions increases the flexibility of interest rates on ordinary deposits.

In Canada the short-term money market may be regarded as having begun on March 1, 1934, when Government of Canada treasury bills began to be sold by public tender. Until 1937 they were sold

88. Cf. E. P. Neufeld, *Bank of Canada Operations and Policy* (Toronto: University of Toronto Press, 1958), p. 48.

rather infrequently; then until June 30, 1953, they were sold every fortnight, while thereafter there has been an auction every week. Tenders are received at the Bank of Canada from the banks, investment dealers and Bank of Canada on Thursday before 12:00 noon and results are made known to tenderers by about 2 p.m.

Prior to the introduction of such treasury bills and the formation of the Bank of Canada in 1934, the chartered banks held their liquid assets in New York in the form of call loans and bankers' acceptances. The call loans they made to investment dealers and stockbrokers in Canada were not really very liquid. Until certain steps were taken to further develop the market in 1953, there was in fact not much of a market. From 1946 to 1952 the amount of treasury bills outstanding remained constant at $450 million, transactions were largely confined to the Bank of Canada and chartered banks, and dealers did not even carry an inventory of treasury bills.

In the early 1950s developments appeared that proved to be of long-term importance for the formation of the money market in general. It was in 1951 that the sales finance companies, including the largest Canadian sales finance company, Industrial Acceptance Corporation, began seriously to offer short-term finance company paper to investors; they did so apparently because of the curtailment of their bank lines of credit and the realization that over-reliance on the banks might make their position permanently vulnerable. In 1953 and 1954 the Bank of Canada took the initiative in developing a more active treasury bill market. On January 30, 1953, weekly instead of fortnightly treasury bill auctions began to be held, thereby improving the range of treasury bill maturities available to investors. In the same year the Bank of Canada encouraged the more active dealers in government securities to hold more treasury bills in inventory by giving emergency lines of credit to each of them against the security of such bills. This was extended in 1954 to include all Government of Canada securities three years to maturity or less and in 1962 bankers' acceptances as well, the latter now limited to 15% of a dealer's line of credit with the Bank. Accommodation takes the form of purchase and resale agreements under which the Bank of Canada agrees to buy limited amounts of such securities from a money market dealer and at the same time resells them to the dealer at a predetermined price for settlement one or several days hence – the difference between buying and selling prices constituting the cost of the accommodation to the dealer. The cost is basically equal to the last average treasury bill tender rate plus 1/4 of 1%. To further encourage dealer trading in treasury bills the Bank of Canada in 1954 began to widen the spread at which it would trade in them and it began to route payment for treasury bills through the clearing house instead of giving the banks instantaneous cash for them. At the same time the chartered banks began to extend day-to-day loans to money market dealers against money market securities, a form of loan that can be called or repaid up to 12 o'clock noon any day for settlement that day. Since both dealers and banks have lines of credit with the Bank of Canada, repayment and calling of such loans is an entirely impersonal matter. The banks also reduced their "over-certification" charge from 1/100% per diem to 1/250% in 1954, and in 1957 abolished it entirely for transfers of securities arising from a dealer's shifting day-to-day loan accommodation from one bank to another and from utilizing Bank of Canada lender-of-last-resort accommodation.[89]

Commercial paper began to appear in volume in 1958 and Canadian bankers' acceptances were introduced in 1962, while provinces and municipalities also became active borrowers in the market in the later 1960s. The province of Ontario introduced a weekly treasury bill auction in 1971.

Present structure of the money market: There are fifteen dealers in the money market, in the sense of dealers having lines of credit with the Bank of Canada, although probably much of the money market business is done by about five of them. The principal money market instruments are shown in Table 14:14. Data for some, particularly provincial and municipal treasury bills and promissory notes, are not available. While federal government treasury bills and short-term bonds constitute the largest volume of money market securities, the growth in the volume of finance company and commercial paper, and chartered bank deposits including "swapped" deposits, and trust and loan company deposits in the 1960s, was substantial. It may be noted that the banks in fact issue a variety of instruments: bearer deposit notes of up to one year to maturity with a minimum denomination of $100,000; a variety of deposit receipts, term notes and certificates of deposit for amounts as low as $5,000; U.S. dollar deposits; U.S. dollar deposits covered with a forward exchange contract, or "swapped" deposits; Eurodollar negotiable certificates of deposit, issued by U.K. branches of Canadian banks; and bankers' acceptances – a commercial draft drawn by a borrower and accepted or guaranteed by a chartered bank – with maturity up to 90 days and denominations of $100,000 and up in even multiples. Some provinces

---

89. A dealer requires a certified cheque to pay for securities before he himself receives payment for those securities later in the day, and the "over-certification" charge is the price of that accommodation.

issue treasury bills and promissory notes and some of their authorities and crown corporations issue notes as well, all usually in $100,000 denominations. The larger municipalities have also used the money market as a source of short-term funds, by issuing term and demand notes in denominations of $100,000 or more. Trust companies issue a variety of deposit receipts, short-term guaranteed trust certificates, and guaranteed investment certificates, as do mortgage loan companies, although the term "debenture" rather than guaranteed certificate is used to describe some of them. Sales finance or acceptance companies issue secured and unsecured promissory notes, some guaranteed by parent companies. The number of large Canadian corporations issuing prime commercial paper increased greatly in the 1960s and is now well over a hundred, including grain, distilling, textile, retail and oil companies; the paper has a minimum denomination of $100,000, and almost any term to maturity up to one year.

The money market dealers are active in distributing the money market instruments both as agents and as principals. They finance their inventories with chartered bank day-to-day loans (the cost of which is very sensitive to changing credit conditions), and with collateral or secured call loans from banks and from a wide range of other financial and non-financial corporations and also governments. This non-bank accommodation sometimes takes the form of a purchase and resale agreement.[90] For the lender, the purchase and resale agreement constitutes a convenient way of investing short-term funds for any desired period, and it is a virtually riskless investment since the lender holds collateral, usually money market securities. The investment dealers, by buying short-term securities from borrowers and financing them with funds obtained from bank and non-bank borrowers, often through purchase and resale agreements, have in fact moved a distance away from being merely distributors of securities toward becoming short-term lending financial intermediaries. Table 14:14 above shows that at the end of 1969 at least $591 million of the dealers' inventory of Canadian securities of $745 million was composed of short-term money market securities, including $128 million of finance company paper, $226 million of commercial paper and $194 million Government of Canada treasury bills and bonds under three years to maturity.

An exceedingly wide range of companies, institutions and governments have become buyers of money market securities. Since the

---

90. For numerous details about instruments available see Wood, Gundy Securities Ltd., *The Canadian Money Market*, Toronto, 1969.

banks are required to maintain a secondary reserve ratio—defined as including Government of Canada treasury bills, day-to-day loans and excess bank cash—they to some extent constitute a captive market for treasury bills. Of the total Government of Canada treasury bills outstanding over the last several years, about 16% were held by the Bank of Canada, 74% by the chartered banks, and 1% by Government of Canada accounts, with only 9% accounted for by all other financial and non-financial institutions and individuals. The trust companies have become important buyers of finance company and commercial paper, thereby engaging in short-term lending even though the legislation under which they operate prohibits them from making many large unsecured loans; they also make significant investments in the various types of chartered bank short-term instruments. The other financial and non-financial institutions also invest in non-government money market instruments, although to a much lesser extent than the trust companies.

There is no doubt that the Canadian short-term money market attained a remarkably high degree of sophistication and grew substantially in volume in the latter half of the 1960s, assisted in no small measure by the high rates of interest and general scarcity of funds that featured much of that period. The principal benefit to the nation from that development almost certainly was the increased competition in short-term lending and borrowing that it introduced into the Canadian capital market.

SECURITIES REGULATION AND INDUSTRY REGULATION

Regulation of the securities business essentially involves regulation of the placement of new issues by issuers and their agents, and regulation of trading in outstanding securities issues. The approach to regulation over the years has been a two-pronged one: "disclosure" provisions and "control of conduct" provisions. Both approaches have been applied to the new issues aspect of the business and also to trading in outstanding issues. Furthermore, they have been applied by the official authorities of the federal government and the ten provinces through legislation and through administrative actions of securities commissions, and by the industry itself through the by-laws of the stock exchanges, the Investment Dealers' Association of Canada and the Broker-Dealers' Association of Ontario. Over the years the trend has been away from "self-regulation," and toward governmental regulation, although the quality of self-regulation has improved.

Securities regulation by its very nature is a very complex subject, and we cannot review it here in detail.[91] However, a few important developments may be noted. First, until Manitoba passed its "Sale of Shares Act" in 1912, securities legislation in Canada had been confined largely to disclosure provisions relating to new issues, as found in the Companies acts of the federal government and the provinces. Secondly, the Manitoba act marked the beginning of "blue sky" legislation in Canada, in its strict sense of control over some of the activities of issuers of securities. Thirdly, in 1926 Manitoba again broke new ground by introducing provisions that formed the basis for later fraud prevention acts, that is, for legislative control not just over issues of securities but over traders in securities as well. These were the milestones that laid the basis for a comprehensive approach to official regulation of the securities business, even though the evolution and effective implementation of such an approach took many years. Indeed, the process was not nearly complete even in the late 1960s, as evidenced both by the abuses in new securities issues and stock trading that were revealed and by the serious attempts at that time on the part of the provinces to improve their regulation of the business.

We may now examine the history of security regulation in slightly more detail.

The spiritual forefather of modern Canadian securities legislation was the British Joint Stock Companies Act of 1844. Its approach was the one of disclosure, although for some years not very much was required to be disclosed and there was for a time even some retrogression from the original disclosure requirements. The 1844 act related essentially to disclosure of information surrounding the formation of a new company. This was extended in the Companies Act of 1867 to the raising of new capital by an existing corporation. In 1855 the government was empowered to inspect a company on the application of 20% of the shareholders. The Directors' Liability Act of 1890 imposed liabilities on directors and promoters for loss arising from untrue statements in prospectuses. The detailed prospectus provisions date from the Companies Act of 1900 which specified contents of prospectuses for promoters' as well as company issues—in fact, for virtually all issues offered to the public. Then by an act of 1907 the distinction between private and public companies was

91. For a thorough study of this matter, one on which we have depended heavily, see J. Peter Williamson, *op. cit.* See also J. W. Baillie, "The Protection of the Investor in Ontario," *Canadian Public Administration*, June 1965, pp. 172-268, and September 1965, pp. 325-432, and also Ontario, *Report of the Attorney General's Committee on Securities Legislation in Ontario*, March 1965.

introduced, the former being exempt from disclosure provisions, but the latter now being required to file a "statement in lieu of prospectuses" with respect to security issues not offered to the public. These English statutes greatly influenced Canadian security legislation. Professor Williamson has succinctly summarized the emergence of this legislation to 1912 and I quote him:

> The first general incorporation statute for the Dominion was the Canada Joint Stock Companies Letters Patent Act, 1869. Eight years later, the Canada Joint Stock Companies Act, 1877, introduced the requirement that a company's prospectus disclose corporate contracts, copying section 38 from the English Act of 1867. And in 1902 the English inspection provisions were copied.
>
> Nova Scotia introduced incorporation by letters patent in 1883, copying much of the Dominion Act of 1877. New Brunswick followed in 1885 and Prince Edward Island in 1888. All three included the prospectus provision from the English Act of 1867.
>
> The Northwest Territories copied its Companies Ordinance of 1888 from the Dominion Act of 1877, and then in 1901 adopted the complete prospectus provisions of the English Act of 1900, together with the Directors Liability Act and the inspection provisions. (In 1937 the Ordinance was repealed.) The Yukon Territory inherited the Ordinance of 1888 when it was formed in 1898.
>
> Other provinces soon adopted the same provisions. Nova Scotia added an inspection provision and the Directors Liability Act in 1900. Quebec adopted the inspection provision in 1907, and New Brunswick followed in 1916. Manitoba in 1905 adopted the inspection provisions from the Dominion Act of 1902, and in 1912 added an authorization for inspections where necessary "in the interest of justice," as well as when demanded by the holders of one-fifth of the voting capital.
>
> British Columbia in 1897 adopted the prospectus and inspection provisions of the English Act of 1890, and in 1914 the first Yukon Companies Ordinance was copied from the British Columbia Act. In 1899 Newfoundland (at that time still a British colony) copied most of the English Act of 1867, including the prospectus provision.
>
> Ontario did not introduce any securities regulation until 1891, but in that year it became the first Canadian jurisdiction to adopt the English Directors Liability Act. Six years later Ontario companies were required to furnish financial statements to stockholders, and the English inspection provisions were adopted.
>
> The Ontario Companies Act, 1907, drew on the English Act of 1900 for the content of a prospectus (the minimum subscription and inspection provisions were copied, too), but the Ontario Act went much further in its scope than did the English. The definition of "prospectus" was original. To the English coverage of "notices," etc., "offering securities for subscription or purchase," were added notices "published or issued for the purpose of being used to promote or aid in the subscription or purchase of such shares, debentures or securities."

Instead of taking the provision for statements in lieu of prospectus from the English Act of 1907, with its exception for private companies, the Ontario Act required all companies with more than ten security holders to file a prospectus and took a significant step in making a verbally solicited subscription voidable unless a copy of the prospectus had been delivered to the subscriber.

Then in 1912 Ontario did take the "private company" concept from the English Act of 1907, and adopted the "statement in lieu" provision as well.

The Ontario Act of 1912 is significant as the first act to cover underwritten offerings, as opposed to direct offerings by an issuer. The issuer was "deemed" to offer securities to the public for subscription, where any underwriter offered them. This of course put the burden of compliance with the Act on the issuer, rather than the underwriter.

It is apparent that up to 1912 security regulation was confined essentially to the new issue disclosure provisions of the Companies acts. The next stage was the emergence of "blue sky" legislation, which we will refer to later. Regulation of the activities of brokers and brokerage activity in this early period remained essentially in the hands of the self-governing stock exchanges. There was as yet no bond dealers' association and no machinery at all for regulating the activities of brokers, or securities salesmen, not members of the exchanges. It is true that a reading of the Toronto Stock Exchange Minutes reveals a gradual expansion of the exchange's by-laws and regulations, and since bonds were traded on the exchange, some of these regulations extended to the bond business. But conditions for becoming or remaining a member of the exchange seem to have been very rudimentary. An example of this, and one that is interesting in itself, for it relates to the emergence of one of Canada's largest brokerage houses and investment dealers, is contained in the Minutes of a Toronto Stock Exchange meeting of January 30, 1890:

> The application of Mr. Ames was further considered when in construction of the Rule placed upon it by the Chairman, it was decided that Mr. Ames was not yet eligible to become a Candidate, not having been in business as a Broker three months prior to his application.

What kinds of abuses existed in the absence of detailed regulations governing the securities business probably cannot be accurately documented and we cannot attempt to do so here. The following contemporary comment (i.e. of 1882) at least gives an impression of the nature of the problem:

> Gambling in its various forms is illegal. And yet what goes on every day at our Stock Exchanges? There men meet together, in person or by proxy, and stake large sums upon the contingency of stocks rising or falling in price. The *bulls* and the *bears* are organized bodies of men who play with loaded dice. They know or pretend to know something about a particular stock which the public does not know. Their knowledge or pretended knowledge is whispered about to catch the Grizzle Greenhorns; the *bulls* and *bears*, by concerted action, selling to one another, and resorting to a hundred kindred arts, can send the price of stocks up or down. They put their loaded dice against the unloaded dice of the public: the game is not fair; it is even more unfair, and therefore more disreputable, than most other forms of gambling. . . . If gambling in other forms, even where there is no "bank" with the odds in its favour, where the chances are equal and where skills make the difference, is put down by the strong arm of the law, is it not worse than an anomaly that a form of gambling in which the chances are not equal, in which there are loaded dice on one side, should be fostered by respectable institutions?[92]

It may simply be noted that multi-varied efforts by the exchanges and by provincial securities authorities to "unload" the dice were to extend over many decades, right up to the present, including recent attempts to control the activities of "insiders."

Soon after the turn of the century important new steps in regulation were taken. As noted earlier, it was really in 1912 that direct control over issuers of securities, as distinct from control through disclosure, was introduced into Canada by the Province of Manitoba. This took the form of "blue sky" legislation, a term that referred to the actions of promoters with schemes that "had no more basis than so many feet of blue sky," and one that was pioneered by the State of Kansas in 1911. The Supreme Court of the United States upheld the constitutionality of such legislation in 1917 and by 1933 all states of the United States except Nevada had "blue sky" laws.[93] State regulation took essentially three approaches or forms: anti-fraud legislation; registration of brokers and dealers; and registration of securities. Canada was much influenced by developments in the United States.

The "blue sky" legislation introduced into Canada by Manitoba in 1912 was largely a copy of the Kansas legislation. Saskatchewan followed in 1915 by copying the Manitoba legislation and Alberta did so in 1916, while New Brunswick copied the Alberta act in 1923.

---

92. *Monetary Times*, Oct. 27, 1882, p. 459.
93. See "Securities Legislation," *Encyclopaedia Britannica*, 1962, vol. 20, pp. 264A-264B.

Quebec introduced what was essentially a "disclosure" act in 1924. In general, important steps had been taken by the end of the 1920s to impose some official supervision onto issuers of securities and this through requiring certificates to be obtained before issuing securities (there were many exemptions), requiring issuers and sellers of such securities to be licensed and giving authorities the power to investigate issuers.

No similar progress, however, seems to have been made in regulating trading in outstanding securities. Again, in reading the minutes of the Toronto Stock Exchange, one sees evidence of an attempt to impose even more detailed regulation on members, but much trading escaped that exchange, for it was done on the loosely regulated Standard Stock and Mining Exchange. It was once more Manitoba that pioneered a new control approach in Canada, for in 1926 it introduced measures that were later to form the basis for much provincial fraud prevention legislation in Canada. The main aspect of the new legislation was the requirement that everyone who made or attempted to make a contract for the sale of securities in Manitoba had to obtain a licence from the Municipal and Public Utility Board; and any company issuing securities had to be approved by the Board. The latter provision caused the act to be declared *ultra vires* the constitution, for it required companies with a Dominion charter to obtain a certificate from the provincial authorities. Partly for this reason attention shifts to the 1928 "Security Frauds Prevention Act" of Ontario. But this Ontario act was an historically significant statute also because it was the first general act of its kind in Canada, combining anti-fraud provisions with provisions for the regulation of brokers and salesmen. Actions constituting fraud were listed in the act. Disclosure requirements relating to new issues were placed in the Companies Information Act. In 1929 six provinces met to compose uniform securities legislation, the result being a uniform Security Fraud Prevention Act of 1930, based largely on the 1928 Ontario act, and adopted by all provinces except New Brunswick. But unfortunately this unique instance of uniformity in Canadian securities legislation did not last long, as individual provinces, including Ontario, went their separate ways during the 1930s. Nevertheless, the principle that brokers and salesmen had to be registered, and so could lose their licence to work in the business, had firmly been adopted, as had the view that fraud had specifically to be legislated against in the securities business. While the principle that new securities issues had also to be regulated waned temporarily as a result of the constitutional difficulty referred to earlier, it had been effectively restored directly or indirectly by about 1945. It might also be noted parenthetically that the impact on other provincial legislation of the 1928 Ontario act showed unequivocally for the first time that in matters of securities regulation Ontario could, if it wished, play an influential role in Canada.

While the provinces were then developing their control legislation relating to the sale of new and outstanding securities issues, the Companies Act of the federal government continued to be amended and continued to emphasize the disclosure approach to corporate financial activity of federally incorporated companies, particularly through requirements relating to the content of prospectuses of new issues. The important Dominion act of 1917 was taken largely from the British act of 1908, and it included provisions relating to the filing, content and definition of a prospectus and of the use of a statement in lieu of prospectus; it employed the concept of the private company; and, significantly, it called for the disclosure of certain financial statements. A number of the provinces introduced similar provisions into the provincial companies acts over the years. The Dominion act of 1934 required that an issue of applications for shares had to be accompanied by a prospectus, and that except for existing holders of the securities involved, an applicant had to have a prospectus twenty-four hours before his application was accepted, and it banned house-to-house solicitation. But the act still did not apply to underwriters selling an issue on a firm commitment basis in contrast to an agency basis, and it curiously excluded the "in lieu of prospectus statement" requirements. All this was investigated by the Royal Commission on Price Spreads which, in its 1935 report, recommended a much stiffer Dominion Companies Act, one that would be a model for all the provinces.[94] As a consequence, the 1935 Dominion act extended the prospectus provisions to underwriters, prohibited the issue of shares with exclusive management rights, improved prospectus and annual report disclosure requirements, provided for disclosure of directors' transactions in a company's securities when requested by a shareholder, and prohibited speculation in such securities by directors.

Developments in the post–Second World War period began with the important Ontario Securities Act of 1945, which has been called Canada's first modern securities act.[95] It came in the wake of concern by the Ontario Royal Commission on Mining with fraudulent activity in the sale of new speculative issues. It included most of the

---

94. See Canada, *Report of the Royal Commission on Price Spreads*, Ottawa, 1937, pp. 38-45.
95. Williamson, *op. cit.*, p. 30.

control provisions for regulating the securities business in Ontario and built on the 1928 act and subsequent amendments, all of which were repealed. It should, however, be noted that the Ontario Securities Commission first appeared by name in legislation of 1933, prior to which a board existed to administer the act, and in 1937 the Commission was formally established.[96] Basically the act required greater disclosure concerning the details of new issues, but the Ontario Securities Commission was for the first time given power to close the Toronto Stock Exchange.

In 1947 the Ontario Broker-Dealers Act legally recognized the Broker-Dealers' Association in a further attempt to impose ethical standards on the highly speculative area of the stock business. By invoking a measure of self-government and internal regulation it was thought that many abuses not strictly in contravention of the Securities Act might be removed.

All the other provinces also developed distinct securities administrators under various names (i.e., commissions, superintendents, boards, administrators, registrars); virtually all moved toward a comprehensive securities act of the Ontario kind; and all retained the provincial companies acts, while in addition there was an Ontario Corporations Information Act and a Quebec Companies Information Act.[97] The federal government had only the Dominion Companies Act, and there was no federal securities commission, although matters such as fraud, wash sales, bucket shop operations and sales of shares held for customers are covered by the Criminal Code of Canada as well as by provincial securities acts and the by-laws of the stock exchanges.

Therefore, developments in securities regulation in the postwar period involved about two dozen statutes and eleven jursidictions, as well as the self-regulatory activities of the stock exchanges, Broker-Dealers' Association and the Investment Dealers' Association. This fantastically complex institutional framework for regulating the securities business was made even more confusing by the absence of material success in achieving uniformity in legislation through co-operation.

While we are not able to trace here the details of postwar regulatory changes, several general points may be noted. The first one is that it would seem that securities regulation gradually began to concern itself not just with disclosure and the prevention of fraud, but

---

96. For these and many other details referred to only briefly here see Baillie, *op. cit.*, and Williamson, *op. cit.*
97. See Williamson, *op. cit.*, p. 425.

also with attempting to raise in a detailed way the ethics of operations in the securities business quite apart from preventing fraudulent activities. The second point is that in this endeavour progress was apparently very slow. Some of the abuses that came to light illustrate this. Reporting in 1964, the Royal Commission on Banking and Finance discussed the abuses involved in primary distribution (i.e., distribution of new issues) through the Toronto Stock Exchange; the inadequate staffing of regulatory bodies; the inefficiency of having ten securities acts in Canada; the still inadequate disclosure requirements, including disclosure of insider trading; the undesirable aspects of takeover bids; the need for closer regulation of the issue of short-term securities which were exempt from regulation in many provinces; the failure to regulate closely the activities of securities salesmen as distinct from registering them; the exemption from registration of salesmen selling only certain exempt (mainly government) securities; the need for continued vigilance over high-pressured selling; the need for stricter listing and delisting rules of the stock exchanges; and the inadequate policing of manipulative trading activity. When it is remembered that these difficulties were noted in 1964, almost eighty years after the critical comments of the *Monetary Times* referred to earlier, and after much legislation had emerged, it is apparent that completely satisfactory regulation of the securities business is difficult to attain. The Province of Ontario has also examined securities legislation in detail through a committee that was headed by Mr. J. R. Kimber.[98] The resulting report covered particularly the area of insider trading, takeover bids, disclosure in financial statements, form, content and distribution of prospectuses, proxies and proxy solicitation, primary distribution through the Toronto Stock Exchange, the Ontario Securities Commission, and constitutional problems in securities regulation. The insolvency of the Atlantic Acceptance Corporation Limited, the financial difficulties of the British Mortgage and Trust Company, and the actions of the officers of Windfall Oils and Mines Limited (as revealed by a Royal Commission investigation) during the copper-zinc-silver discovery in 1964 of the Texas Gulf Sulphur Co. gave a new tone of urgency to the matter of securities regulation in Ontario. Both a tighter Ontario Securities Act, including stricter insider trading rules, and much tighter Toronto Stock Exchange regulations have resulted from all these intensive investigations of the industry. Nor is it without significance that Mr. J. R. Kimber, who headed the

98. See Province of Ontario, *Report of the Attorney General's Committee on Securities Legislation in Ontario*, March 1965.

Ontario government's securities legislation committee, became president of the Toronto Stock Exchange.

The really important issue for the future will be whether all this encouraging activity at the provincial level will produce satisfactory results or whether, in the end, it will be necessary to have a federal securities commission and appropriate federal securities legislation.

Particular note may be taken of the problems and inefficiencies involved in the present system of provincial securities commissions, quite apart from the duplication of administrative resources and the higher costs encountered by capital market participants in having to satisfy the requirements of a number of jurisdictions. First, some provinces do not have the resources to staff an effective securities commission. Secondly, interregional and international activity cannot be effectively controlled by a provincial jurisdiction. Thirdly, the abuses arising from a weak provincial securities commission and from inadequate regulation of interregional and international financial activity affects the whole of the Canadian capital market, for it affects investor confidence in general, both in Canada and abroad. Fourthly, conflicts and differences in regulations between provinces may lead to economically inefficient distribution of funds.

The international aspects of securities regulation are likely to become increasingly important, as international flows of private and public capital grow in size. It is inevitable that governments of countries affected by such flows will seek to co-operate in imposing desired regulation. Because Canada depends heavily on foreign capital for its development and because its own financial institutions are heavily and increasingly involved in international financial activity (e.g., Canadian investment dealers becoming members of the Midwest and New York Stock Exchanges), it is in her vital interest to encourage and influence such developments. Intelligent, informed and effective participation by Canada in the future development and control of the international capital market, including the international activities of Canadian institutions (matters that are likely to be exceedingly important), require that Canada speak with one strong voice in such matters and that the Government of Canada have available the expertise of a securities commission.

In general, it has become very apparent in recent years that financial activity relating to the issue of new securities and to trading in securities is almost entirely interprovincial and international in character. In other words, our capital market is in fact one *national* or even one *international* market in financial services, not a federation of regional or provincial markets. Efficiency lies in facilitating the free flow of such services. This in turn requires a system of regulation of securities activity that is designed with a national perspective. The same perspective is required to ensure that all Canadians will have equal protection from abuses in financial transactions. Its implication for the control of the securities business is basically that there should be comprehensive federal securities legislation and a national securities commission to administer it. Regional administration of capital market activity has become an anachronism in our world of massive movements of capital across provincial and international borders.

15

Interest Rates

Government Influences on the Rate of Interest

For a free capital market to function efficiently interest rates must be flexible. Inflexibility may arise from the influence of government through the rates that it commands its own financial intermediaries to charge and to pay, and through the statutory limitations that it may impose on rates charged and offered by private borrowers and lenders. Inflexibility may also result from market imperfections in the form of monopolistic tendencies arising from the relative size of financial institutions in relation to the market as a whole or, if funds do not flow easily from one region to another or between different credit markets in the same region, in relation to the size of markets in specific regions of the country or to the size of the particular credit market involved. Collusion, of course, is just as possible in a market for money as in any other market.

A distinction might be made between "institutional" interest rates, that is, the borrowing and lending rates of institutions, and "market" interest rates or the yields on marketable securities, the former being usually much less flexible than the latter, although eventually influenced by them. Governments have been concerned much more with institutional than with market rates of interest. Governments in Canada have concerned themselves with interest rates over the whole of the history of the capital market and it is to this influence that we first direct our attention. This will be followed by a discussion of the trends and patterns of interest rates in Canada over the last century.

Usury laws, that is, statutory limitations on rates that private lenders may charge, represent the oldest form of government influence on interest rates. In March 1777, the old Province of Quebec passed "An Ordinance for Ascertaining Damages on Protested Bills of Exchange, and fixing the rate of Interest in the Province of Quebec."[1] Section five of that ordinance was the one which introduced usury laws into Canada, and it reads as follows:

> And be it further enacted by the authority aforesaid, That it shall not be lawful upon any contract to take, directly or indirectly, for loan of any monies, wares, merchandize, or other commodities whatsoever, above the value of six pounds for the advance or forbearance of one hundred pounds for a year; and so after that rate for a greater or less sum or value, or for a longer or shorter time; and the said rate of interest shall be allowed and recovered in all cases where it is the agreement of the parties that interest shall be paid; and all bonds, contracts and assurances whatsoever, whereupon or whereby a greater interest shall be reserved and taken, shall be utterly void; and every person who shall either directly or indirectly take, accept and receive, a higher rate of interest, shall forfeit and lose for every such offence, treble of the value of the monies, wares, merchandize and other things lent or bargained for....

An 1811 act of Upper Canada included similar provisions,[2] as did the bank charters that began to appear in 1821.[3]

The first modification in the usury laws as such did not come until 1853, but even before that the emerging building societies operated under legislation that first modified substantially the limitations on interest rates that they could charge. It is not difficult to find contemporary criticism of the usury laws and many unsuccessful attempts were made to introduce modifying legislation. The criticism usually included the argument that the system, through widespread evasion, was not working; and also that it offended the forces of free demand and supply. Two commentaries may be quoted to give an impression of how some of the critics at the time regarded the laws and what they considered to be some of the consequences of imposing limits on interest rates.

First, in a letter addressed to the President of the Board of Trade, Toronto, in 1847 on "The Usury Laws with an Appendix," these comments appear:

> I can see no just cause or reason, why a man should be compelled by law to refuse 10 per cent for the loan or use of his *money*, any

1. 17 Geo. III, 1777, cap. 3.
2. 51 Geo. III, cap. 9.
3. For thorough discussion of the interest laws relating to the banks see Royal Bank of Canada, "History of the Statutory Ceiling on Bank Lending Rates in Canada," *Economic Trends and Topics*, June 1966.

> more than a man shall refuse to take ten dollars a ton for his *hay* when purchasers are ready and willing to give that price! If horses are starving and want food, they must be fed at whatever cost, and the law has laid no restrictions on the price of food, therefore it can be had and the horse can be fed and kept alive. But if a Merchant be "hard up," as it is termed and desirous of getting over a period of difficulty, and is willing to pay 10 per cent. for a loan for a short time,—and further, if he be so fortunate as to find a friend in whose sleek smiling face he can so far trace the lines of kindness as to encourage him to "pop the question," and asks, imploringly, "Can I have the favor of a temporary loan for two or three months?" he is met by the answer, "my money is in bank stock, which you know pays me 8 per cent?" The answer of the merchant is, "I will willingly give 10 per cent. if I can be accommodated, and ample security also." The rejoinder is, "No, the law allows the banks to *pay* 8 per cent. to their stockholders, but it does not allow me to *take* more than 6 per cent. from you....

While many did not take the usury laws seriously, the laws did tend to distort the way business was done. Besides being ignored by many, they were circumvented by many more. The most common way, perhaps, of circumventing them was to sell securities, including mortgages and notes, at a discount so that in effect the usurious element of interest—that in excess of 6%—was collected in advance. One most astute observer, whose identity is not known, made these observations on usury in a letter to a Toronto editor in October 1857:

> Values are of two denominations, *real* values, and *market* values. The real value of an article, is the cost of its production *at the moment of value*: the market value of this article is the cost of its production, *plus* such enhancement, or *minus* such depreciation, as may result from the current inequalities of supply and demand.... [Value] itself, whether real or market, is ... variable.
>
> These I hold to be the laws governing money, so far as money may be held an article for sale. And these laws, be it observed growing as they do, [arise] out of our social system as *necessary consequences* even though politicians be found to deal with them, as arbitrary or conventional.... The Law, it is true, says, that the interest of a hundred pounds for a year, shall not exceed six pounds; whereas the actual *practice* of every day, proves that the interest of money, like all other articles of trade, varies according to the social law of supply and demand, from six per cent. to even twenty per cent. If you limit the interest on a debenture to six per cent. in law, do you not see every day the sale of that debenture at a discount of 5, 10, 15, 20 per cent., setting aside that limit in fact? If I lend £80 for five years on a bond for £100, though the coupons attached to that bond, call for an annual interest in accordance with law, of six per cent. per annum, do I not receive in fact—in defiance of law—an interest per annum of over 12 per cent. On private notes, and on private mortgages, does not every one know, that the rate of interest

> brought by money, is in every case regulated by mutual conditions, in utter indifference to all attempts at Parliamentary restraint. . . .[4]

It was through this technique of circumventing the usury laws that the first Canadian life insurance company, the Canada Life Assurance Company, began its operations in 1847. For the first twelve years of its existence it did not make mortgages, but rather bought them at a discount from other holders; and in that period its many purchases of debentures were all at a substantial discount. In November 1848, for example, it bought two £50 Gore district debentures with 5 and 7 years to maturity at £40 and £36 respectively, thereby increasing the yield from 6% to over 11%; and in May 1849 it bought City of Hamilton debentures, also at a discount of about 20%. In June 1859, however, the Canada Life began to buy mortgages at par since the modification of the usury laws based on judicial interpretation of them favourable to life insurance companies[5] enabled it to stipulate a higher rate on the contract and within a short period it was itself making most of the mortgages it wished to invest in rather than buying them from other holders.

Our letter writer of 1857 also argued that the usury laws discriminated against the banks because they were less free than the private capitalist to evade them, and that this encouraged the activities of unscrupulous money brokers. It was also argued at the time that the usury laws militated against the inflow of foreign capital—capital which was sorely needed for the development of the country. While the laws could be evaded this was less easy for the banks than for private money lenders, and so for foreign capitalists who might wish to use the banks as intermediaries—the only reliable financial institutions available to them at the time. And there may have been a tendency for foreign investors to compare the legal rate of interest in Canada with the much higher market rates of interest in other countries.

It also appears that the usury laws tended to encourage the banks to concentrate on their foreign exchange and foreign bill business, to the detriment of the banks' domestic customers. If a bank discounted an international trade bill it made a return not only on the loan but also on the purchase and sale of foreign exchange. A contemporary observer put it this way:

> the Banks have other means of making money besides discounting paper, that is, selling exchange. . . . [The] bank which has the largest

4. See *Canadian Merchants' Magazine and Commercial Review*, Toronto, October 1857, vol. 2, no. 1, p. 33.
5. See below, p. 228.

> number of exchange customers generally makes the most money. We have an instance of this in the Bank of Montreal, the most prosperous institution in the Province; its customers have been almost exclusively importing houses. The importers are generally men of good credit here and at home, the nature of the business requiring a fair amount of capital and credit. In purchasing exchange they generally do so with paper, so that when the Bank sells an importer £1000 in exchange on London it makes say 1½% on the exchange, and 1½% on the 90 day paper, making 3 per cent. on the transaction, so that on all exchange transactions they make double the amount made in the ordinary mode of discounting. Now as the banks have always been limited by law to 6 per cent., and as money has generally been worth more than that rate, the banks to pay dividends that would be satisfactory to the stockholders, and offer inducements for further investments have made it their particular business and interest to build up importing houses.... Now if the laws of Usury were such that the Bank could always when there was competition for their funds between importer and manufacturer, charge the manufacturer an equivalent equal to what he makes by his exchange customer, then both would be equally served....[6]

Widespread evasion of the usury laws and the difficulty of enforcing them, together with the distortions which they created, appear to have provided convincing evidence that they should be relaxed. The first legal relaxation came with the establishment of building societies. In 1845 the Montreal Building Society was incorporated under an act[7] which was almost identical in its preamble and principal provisions to the "Act for the Regulation of Benefit Building Societies" passed by the United Kingdom Parliament in July 1836.[8] It was from the latter that the former act inherited the provision permitting the Montreal Building Society to receive a bonus on any shares for the privilege of receiving it in advance of being realized without being subject to the usury laws. This important legal modification of the usury laws was also incorporated in the "Upper Canada Building Society Act"[9] passed in 1846, which provided a strong impetus to the formation of such societies in Upper Canada. Similar legislation was passed by New Brunswick in 1847[10] and Nova Scotia in 1849.[11] Even as early as 1844 the Port Sarnia Syndicate was formed along lines of the English terminable building societies, putting out money collected to the highest bidder, and by 1850 a number of such socie-

6. "The New Usury Law," *Canadian Merchants' Magazine and Commercial Review*, September 1859, vol. 3, no. 5, pp. 353-6.
7. 8 Vic. cap. 94—March 29, 1845.
8. See also above, p. 186.
9. 9 Vic., cap. 20.
10. 10 Vic., cap. 83.
11. 12 Vic., cap. 42.

ties had been formed.[12] The next important legal modification of the usury laws came in 1850 when a private bill sponsored by John A. Macdonald amended the original terms of the statute incorporating the Trust and Loan Company, permitting that company to charge up to 8% interest.

An act of 1853[13] of the united Province of Canada abolished the penalties for usury and stipulated that contracts would be void only in respect of rates of interest in excess of 6%; but it also exempted the banks, insurance companies and other borrowing and lending institutions (excluding building societies) from those amendments, thereby perpetuating the usury laws, penalties and all, as far as they were concerned. However, an act of 1858[14] ended the voidance provision entirely, with the 6% applying only to contracts where no rate was stipulated, and provided that "It shall be lawful for any person or persons, other than those excepted in this Act to stipulate for, allow and exact, on any contract or agreement whatsoever, any rate of interest or discount which may be agreed upon," a clause that is almost the same as the one in the current Interest Rate Act. Again, financial institutions were excepted from these provisions, but the banks were permitted by the act to take interest up to 7% instead of the former 6%. By an act of 1856[15] chartered banks in the Province of Canada were permitted to charge ½% on 90-day paper in cases where paper was discounted at a different place from where it was payable, in addition to the 6% interest.

In 1866, under the Provincial Note Act,[16] the banks in the Province of Canada were relieved of the penalties continued by the act of 1858, and in 1867[17] this relief as well as the 7% ceiling provisions were extended to all banks in the newly formed Dominion. While the exemption of building societies from usury laws came through the Building Societies Act of 1846, the exemption of the life insurance companies from them came by judicial interpretation of the act of 1858. In the case of *Edinburgh Assurance Company* v. *Graham*[18] the restrictions continued by section 6 of the act of 1858 were held to apply only to companies formed for the purpose of lending money, and life companies were judged not to be such companies; and the company's requirement that borrowers should insure up to twice the

---

12. See above, p. 189.
13. 16 Vic., cap. 80.
14. 22 Vic., cap. 85.
15. 19 Vic., cap. 48.
16. 29-30 Vic., cap. 10.
17. 31 Vic., cap. 11.
18. 19 U.C.Q.B. 581.

value of the loan was in any case held not to be a violation of the usury laws.

So it can be seen that by Confederation there were no legal limitations in Central Canada on the rates charged on loans by individuals and by the three most important financial intermediaries of the day – banks, building societies and life insurance companies – although banks could not use the law to collect rates in excess of 7%. By various routes the usury laws had virtually disappeared in that part of British North America.

However, it was not long before a new twist was given to the argument that interest rates should be controlled by law. The earlier supporters of the usury laws seem to have seen the money lenders as exacting ruinous rates from an aware but helpless borrower in dire need of funds; but the new supporters came to emphasize the danger of lenders taking advantage of borrowers who were ignorant in matters of interest rates. Whereas the former led naturally to a policy of control, the latter could include a policy of disclosure as well as control. Legislation since Confederation has from time to time invoked both, but the problem has never been settled.

Legislation affecting interest rates after Confederation can be viewed as being related to chartered bank lending, mortgages, personal loans and merchandise credit. Power to legislate in these areas was divided between the federal government and the provinces by the terms of the British North America Act. The federal government was given power to legislate with respect to banks and banking, savings banks, bills of exchange and promissory notes, interest, bankruptcy and insolvency and the criminal law; all these powers might lead the federal government to legislate with respect to the granting of credit, and it could also influence that area through its power to incorporate companies granting credit.[19] The provincial governments could also incorporate credit granting institutions (except banks) and they were given power to legislate with respect to property and civil rights and matters of a merely local or private nature. These powers have induced the provinces to legislate in the area of consumer credit financing specific merchandise, since personal property and conditional sales agreements fall in the provincial domain. In so doing they have at times moved perilously close to legislating in the area of "interest," a federal matter.

---

19. For a discussion of these issues see Jacob S. Ziegel, "The Legal Regulation of Consumer Credit," in Jacob S. Ziegel and R. E. Olley, eds., *Consumer Credit in Canada*, proceedings of a Conference on Consumer Credit, Saskatoon, May 2-3, 1966, University of Saskatchewan, 1966, pp. 70-88, and *Report of the Special Joint Committee of the Senate and House of Commons on Consumer Credit and Cost of Living* (Ottawa: Queen's Printer, February 1967).

Let us now examine post-Confederation developments in the regulation of interest rates, beginning with the unification of interest rate legislation.

Many minute statutory changes affecting interest rates have appeared since interest rates were declared by the British North America Act to be a federal matter, but only the significant changes will here be outlined. Interest rate legislation that existed in the various British North American colonies at the time of Confederation was perpetuated by the federal government until 1886. Up to that date laws were passed that pertained to the individual provinces: Ontario and Quebec in 1873,[20] permitting religious, charitable and educational institutions there to charge up to 8%; Nova Scotia in 1873,[21] denoting 6% to apply to contracts where no rate was stipulated, limiting rates on loans made by persons on real estate and chattel mortgages to 7% and on personal loans to 10% with chartered banks specifically excluded from the provision; New Brunswick in 1875,[22] permitting any rates to be charged, excluding banks or incorporated companies which continued to be subject to the usury laws of the province; British Columbia in 1886,[23] stipulating 6% where no rate is indicated and limiting rates on sums awarded by judgment to not more than 12%. In 1886[24] all these acts, as well as the Prince Edward Island acts of 1868, were consolidated into one, and the separate provisions for the several provinces which were included were finally repealed in 1890.[25] However, since the B.N.A. Act gave provinces jurisdiction over property and civil rights, they have legislated in the field of conditional sales agreements and mortgages, and in their disclosure and "unconscionable" debt provisions they have in effect legislated in the field of interest rates. Constitutionally the issue of jurisdiction over interest rates does not seem to be settled, in that the definition of what constitutes interest is not clear and the separation of legislation on *interest rates*, which is a federal matter, from that on the *collection* of interest, which is a provincial matter, is very difficult.

Bank lending rates were relatively free from control until 1934. In 1871 the 7% interest rate ceiling and exemption from usury penalties were incorporated into the Bank Act,[26] while reference to the exemption was dropped in 1906 following repeal of all usury penalties in an

20. 36 Vic., cap. 70.
21. 36 Vic., cap. 71.
22. 38 Vic., cap. 18.
23. 49 Vic., cap. 44.
24. 49 Vic., cap. 127.
25. 53 Vic., cap. 34.
26. 34 Vic., cap. 5.

act of 1890.[27] The Privy Council ruled in 1913 that a bank could not legally demand a rate in excess of 7% and if it tried to do so it could only collect 5% – the latter being the legal rate payable in cases where no rate was stipulated in the contract; but the Privy Council also ruled that anyone voluntarily paying in excess of 7% could not recover the excess. So by the simple expedient of deducting interest in advance the banks could continue to charge any rate they wished, although they could not employ legal processes to recover interest in excess of 7%. In 1933 the Royal Commission on Banking and Currency reported that in its view the banks could not legally charge more than 7% under any circumstances and recommended that the ceiling be removed. Instead in 1934 the Bank Act was amended to reintroduce penalties for charging in excess of 7%, the first such penalties since 1866, and in 1944 the ceiling was reduced to 6%. Finally the Bank Act of 1967 raised the ceiling to 7¼% and provided that the ceiling would permanently be removed as soon as short-term government bond yields fell below 5% for one quarter of a year – with the result that the ceiling was entirely removed at the end of 1967. The banks, however, were required to disclose borrowing costs in per cent per annum terms to the borrower.

The first major national interest rate legislation after Confederation was the Orton Act of 1880[28] which pertained to interest on money secured by real estate mortgages. Its most important effect was virtually to abolish long-term sinking fund mortgages of individuals for it permitted borrowing individuals to pay off a mortgage after five years' interest had been paid, upon payment of a bonus equal to three months' interest. The act also stipulated that no interest on mortgages loaned could be recovered unless the amount of the principal and the rate of interest were clearly indicated; additional charges or fines raising interest beyond the stated rate were not permitted; and excess payments of interest or fines were made recoverable. There is little doubt that the impetus for this legislation came from abuses involving high interest rates exacted from unsuspecting borrowers.

The Orton Act provisions relating to mortgage loans noted above are still in force in the Interest Rate Act.[29] An amendment to the federal Loan Companies Act of 1934[30] permitted the Governor-in-Council on the recommendation of the Minister of Finance to cancel the charter of any federally incorporated loan company, including small companies, and to cancel any federal privileges of any provincial loan

27. 53 Vic., cap. 34.
28. 43 Vic., cap. 42.
29. R.S.C. 1952, cap. 156.
30. 24-25 Geo. V, cap. 56.

company which charged more than 2½% per month on the monthly balance owing by any borrower. These provisions, however, proved unworkable and were repealed in 1948.[31]

There are only two other important pieces of legislation affecting mortgage interest rates charged by private lenders. The first is that pertaining to residential mortgages made under the National Housing Act, which placed rigid limits on rates that could be charged; but since 1967 these rates have been tied to but 2¼% above long-term Government of Canada bond yields, adjusted quarterly. The second relates to loans partially guaranteed by the federal government and made by the chartered banks and other lending institutions, on which an interest ceiling was imposed until 1968, after which quarterly adjustments were provided for. The latter include loans under the Farm Improvement Loans Act, the Producer Interim Financing Act of 1951 and 1956, the Prairie Grain Loans Act of 1960, the Fisheries Improvement Loans Act of 1955, the Small Business Loans Act of 1961, the Home Improvement Loans since 1955 under the National Housing Act, the Veterans Business and Professional Loans Act since 1957. What these developments suggest is that government-inspired rigidities in institutional interest rates have diminished substantially in importance since 1967.

The disclosure aspects of the Orton Act, now part of the Interest Rate Act, seem to have had some effect in that they have provided a guide for the way contracts are written by reputable firms—which now includes most companies that make first mortgage loans. However, just as the usury loans used to be evaded by the practice of discounting securities, so the disclosure laws relating to mortgages can be evaded by the use of bonuses, discounts, and brokerage charges—a practice which seems to be most prevalent in the field of second mortgages.

Legislation relating specifically to personal loans was first introduced by the federal government in 1906 with the enactment of "An Act Respecting Money Lenders",[32] an act which was modelled fairly closely on the United Kingdom's Money Lenders Act of 1900 and was but a pale copy of a bill introduced by Senator Dandurand in 1899 entitled "An Act Respecting Usury." It limited the rate of interest to 12% per annum on loans smaller than $500 (pawnbrokers were excluded) and provided for penalties if the act was contravened. However, the act did not define the term "interest" and no department or agency of government was established to administer it, which

31. 11-12 Geo. VI, cap. 57.
32. 6 Edw. VII, cap. 32.

were the principal reasons why it was never effective. The 12% rate was exclusive of discounts, fines, and charges and such additional charges in excess of 12% were covered in the act only in the sense that a debtor could seek relief from them. Inevitably the principal effect of the bill was not to place a limit on rates on small loans, nor to enlighten small borrowers as to the rates of interest they were in practice paying, but only to provide some relief to small borrowers from over-burdensome debt arising from excessive interest charges, should they seek it. The low interest ceiling, considering the cost of and risk inherent in making small personal loans, probably invited abuse.

The deficiencies of the act were clearly indicated by the preamble of the 1939 Small Loans Act:

> Whereas it has become the common practice for money-lenders to make charges against borrowers claimed as discount, deduction from an advance, commission, brokerage, chattel mortgage and recording fee, fines and penalties, or for inquiries, defaults and renewals, which, in truth and substance are, in whole or in part, compensation for the use of money loaned or for the acceptance of the risk of loss or are so mixed with such compensation as to be indistinguishable therefrom and are, in some cases, charges primarily payable by the lender but required by the lender to be paid by the borrower; and whereas the result of these practices is to add to the cost of the loan without increasing the nominal rate of interest charged so that the provision of the law relating to interest and usury have been rendered ineffective....[33]

This act is important because it regulates the total cost of funds borrowed, not just the portion that might somehow be defined as constituting "interest", and because a department of the federal government—the Department of Insurance—was given responsibility for administering it. In this way the major deficiencies of the 1906 act were avoided and the latter act was repealed in 1956. The new act required that all money lenders (excluding chartered banks and registered pawnbrokers) making loans of $500 or less and charging more than 12% per annum had to be licensed under the act. Those adhering to the provisions of the act and licensed under it were given the privilege of charging up to 2% per month for a loan of more than 15 months. The act was amended in 1956[34] to include loans of $1,500 or less, with 2% per month on unpaid balances up to $300, 1% on unpaid balances from $300 to $1,000, and ½% on unpaid balances in excess of $1,000. Also, on loans of $500 or less made for a

---

33. 3 Geo. VI, cap. 23.
34. 4-5 Eliz. II., cap. 46.

period greater than 20 months or in excess of $500 for a period greater than 30 months, the cost of the loan could not exceed 1% per month on the unpaid balance.

This legislation therefore emphasizes absolute limits on rates of interest and does not rest merely on disclosure of rates, as does the imperfect legislation relating to mortgages on real estate. Indeed the disclosure approach alone was never seriously undertaken. The legislation does not apply to loans in excess of $1,500, the view being that such borrowers do not need to be artificially protected, nor does it apply to that very important field, the financing of merchandise purchases of individuals.

The provinces have also passed legislation relating to interest rates, even though the British North America Act gave jurisdiction over interest rates to the federal authority. They have passed Unconscionable Transactions Relief Acts, under which the courts can set aside loan agreements that appear to them to be unjustifiably harsh – including the matter of the rate of interest charged. Also under provincial legislation relating to credit unions and caisses populaires, these institutions can charge 1% per month on the unpaid balance, including all charges and penalties. The only exception is British Columbia, where credit unions can charge the same rates as loan companies operating under the Small Loans Act, and can charge up to 1¼% per month on loans not covered by the act, that is, those over $1,500 in amount.

Instalment credit for financing merchandise purchases was introduced by the finance companies just after the First World War and rose to prominence after the Second World War.[35] As we noted earlier, such retail sales finance credit usually involves personal property and conditional sale agreements, and legislation relating to it has been almost entirely provincial. Uniformity in provincial legislation has not yet been achieved. Legislation in existence imposes no limits on interest rates charged, except that in Quebec in the case of conditional sales of some durable goods valued up to $800, the creditor has no recourse against the security if he charges more than ¾% per month. Interest and other charges in *absolute* dollar amounts have for the most part been disclosed for a number of years but in the last several years most provinces have introduced legislation requiring all credit grantors to disclose the simple interest rate being charged.

In summary, usury laws have been re-introduced in several areas since Confederation but the disclosure approach to controlling interest rates is now emerging strongly. Beginning unsuccessfully in 1906 in the case of small loans, usury laws were successfully applied to

---

35. See above, p. 325.

such loans through the Small Loans Act of 1939 and credit union legislation. They differed from the original usury laws in that by increasing the minimum rates, they gave market forces much greater latitude for accommodating varying credit risks. From 1934 to 1967 they were also partially applied to the banks, but were then abolished, their place taken by disclosure provisions. The other form of usury law that existed for a period was the maximum limit on rates that private lenders could charge on mortgages guaranteed by the federal government and on other government guaranteed loans. The influence of government lending institutions such as the Farm Credit Corporation and the Industrial Development Bank can also tend to have the effect of placing limits on interest rates.

The improvement of the securities market and of the procedures for public borrowing have virtually solved the problem of disclosure as far as bonds and debentures are concerned. The spirit of the Orton Act seems also to have produced fairly complete disclosure of rates on real estate first mortgages—although, since full and honest disclosure there rests to a degree on the ethics of the industry rather than on legislation, cases of lapses in disclosure come to light from time to time. The weakness of the disclosure legislation is more apparent in the second mortgage market where the ethics of the industry do not appear to be as strong and reliable as in the case of first mortgage lenders. Disclosure in the case of small personal loans (but not large personal loans) has for long been relatively complete since most non-bank cash lenders must operate under the Small Loans Act, while the effective rate on chartered bank loans must now also be shown, as must the rate on most other personal credit because of recent provincial legislation. The only important problem areas from the point of view of disclosure seem to be second mortgages, and credit granted by merchants. It will be interesting to see whether in succeeding years legislation will drift again toward usury laws or will attempt seriously to follow the alternative route of carefully designed disclosure legislation. Present indications are that it will be the latter.

Interest Rates in Canada

Information relating to trends in interest rates in Canada prior to 1900 is difficult to compile. This is only partly because of the deficiencies of documentary material, the other reason being the absence of an active trading market in bonds in Canada over much of that period. Stocks were, of course, traded actively but because the large Canadian bond issues, particularly those of the Dominion, were for the most part sold in the United Kingdom, local trading in such securities was restricted. The smaller issues, those of the cities, counties, townships, and other municipal institutions which were sold in Canada, came in such small amounts as to make trading in them almost impossible. Newspaper references to the prices of such securities usually did not even indicate the terms of the issues referred to or the name of the issuing municipality. We must content ourselves therefore with obtaining a general impression of annual interest rate trends, rather than a detailed impression, and we must do this by examining series that undoubtedly do not meet standards of quality that exist in present-day series. We emphasize that it is the longer-term trends in which we are primarily interested, and that most of the series examined cannot be confidently viewed as showing accurately year-to-year changes in interest rates.

Long swings in interest rates: One of the most interesting aspects of the trends in Canadian interest rates, indeed in the interest rates of the western world in general, is the long swings or cycles evident in them. Chart 15:1 shows four series of bond yields: (a) Dominion government sterling bond yields in London 1867 to 1914; (b) Canadian bond yields in Canada composed as follows: from 1869 to 1897, Toronto bonds, from 1897 to 1920, Ontario bonds, from 1921 to 1971, Dominion bonds; (c) United Kingdom Consols; and (d) from 1867 to 1935 United States five best railway bonds and from 1936 to 1970 Moody's AAA corporate bonds. Consols reached a peak in yield in 1866 as did Canadian issues quoted in the London market, and it appears that the yields on better-quality issues in Canada also rose to a high level in that year. It is true of course that Canadian rates reached crisis levels in the late 1850s when the speculative boom collapsed. But, ignoring the interest rate highs established in the 1850s under exceedingly primitive market conditions, it would appear that with Confederation came the beginning of a long decline in Canadian interest rates on bonds that did not end until 1897, the same year as the low in yields on United Kingdom and Canadian securities in London, but several years before the low in yields in the United States. In Canada the years 1896 to 1897 saw bonds of the provinces of Ontario, Quebec and Nova Scotia, for example, yielding from 3⅛ to 3¼%; those of the large cities such as Toronto, Montreal, and London were yielding 3¼ to 3⅜%; those of the larger towns and

Chart 15:1—Trends in Long-Term Interest Rates in Canada, United Kingdom and United States 1867-1970

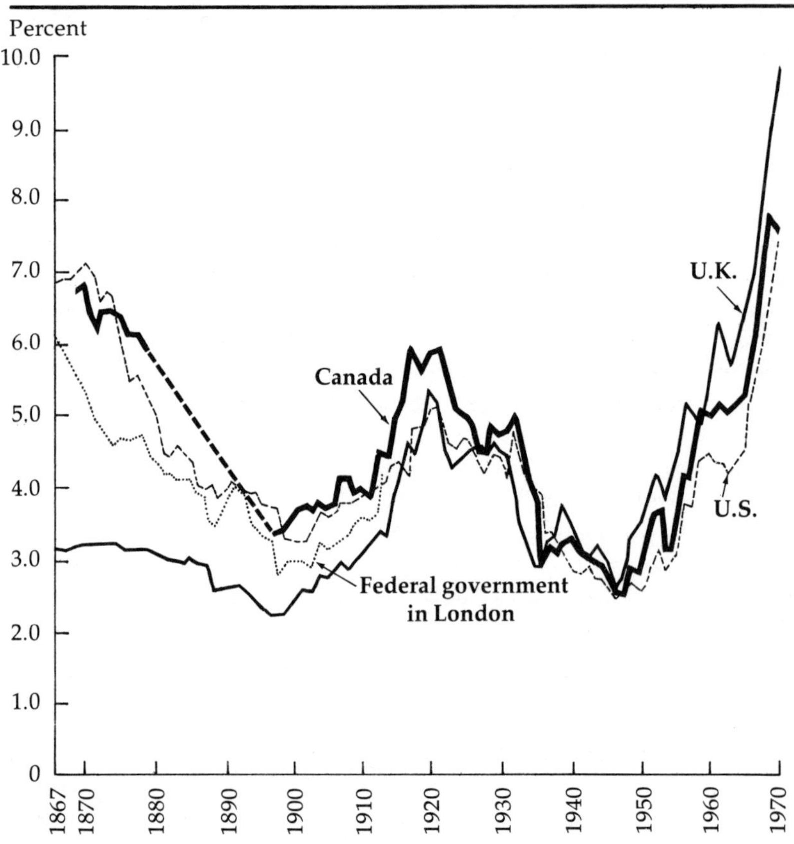

SOURCES:

1. From 1869 to 1880, 6% 20-year Toronto bond as quoted in the *Monetary Times*. No quotations are available from 1880 to 1897. From 1897 to 1900, estimated by the author from press reports. From 1900 to 1920, Province of Ontario bond yields as compiled by Wood, Gundy and Co. From 1921 to 1970, Government of Canada bond yields as compiled by the author from the *Financial Post* and from Bank of Canada, *Statistical Summary*. 1921-1925, 5½% 1934 Victory bond; 1926-1932, 4½% 1944 bond; 1933-1935, 4½% 1949 Conversion bond; 1936-1957, 15-year theoretical bond yield; 1958-1966, 3¼% 1979 bond; 1967-1970, 4½ 1983 bond issue. Average of end-of-quarter figures.
2. From 1867 to 1870, 5% 1885 Inscribed Stock; from 1871 to 1896, 5% 1903 bond; from 1897 to 1913, 3% 1938 bond. All data compiled from the *Economist*. Average of end-of-quarter figures.
3. Consols at various coupon rates. Data from 1867 to 1873 compiled by the author from the *Economist*, that from 1874 to 1970 from the United Kingdom, *Statistical Abstract*. Average of end-of-quarter figures.
4. From 1867 to 1935, January averages of five best railroad bonds, from F. R. Macaulay, *The Movement of Interest Rates, Bond Yields and Stock Prices*, National Bureau of Economic Research, New York, 1938. From 1936 to 1970, Moody's AAA corporate bonds, yearly average of monthly values.

townships yielded 3½ to 3⅝% and village bonds, 3¾% to 4%.[36] Then as the economic recovery began to emerge and later as war finance made its impact, interest rates rose substantially and a peak in bond yields was again established in 1920 and 1921, followed by a decline which reached its low in 1946. The period of increase in Canadian long-term bond yields after 1946 reached its peak in late 1969 and early 1970.

It is obvious from Chart 15:1 that the long swings in interest rates in Canada were generally similar to such swings in the United Kingdom and the United States.[37] At the same time, however, declines in Canadian and United States yields greatly exceeded those of the United Kingdom prior to 1897.

Table 15:1 shows that from 1867 to 1897 Canadian and U.S. bond yields declined by about the same amount, approximately 50%, while United Kingdom yields fell by only 30%. It was in the period 1897-1920 that the present pattern of bond yields was to a considerable degree established. With U.K. bond yields rising by about 140%, Canadian by about 90% and United States yields by only 40%, the three yields in absolute terms moved closer together; and after 1946 U.K. yields moved distinctly above Canadian and U.S. yields for a prolonged period – the first time this had ever happened.

It is also interesting to note from Table 15:1 that the percentage decline in Canadian yields over the thirty-year period 1867-1897 was almost identical to the percentage decline in the twenty-six year period 1920-1946; however the percentage increase in yield over the twenty-three-year period 1897-1920 was smaller than the increase over the twenty-four-year period 1946-1970. Yields of 1970 were in fact higher than any that had existed for over a century.

In a sense the most truly "Canadian" long-term interest rates prior to 1900 were the rates on mortgages in that they reflected local investment conditions more accurately than did the other securities with their less certain supply and less active Canadian participation. A general impression of the trend in mortgage rates can be obtained from Chart 15:2 which joins several series to cover the period 1852-1970, that is, one which includes the crisis rates of the 1850s. Beginning with a peak in about 1856 when land speculation drove mortgage rates to unrealistic levels – 16% was not uncommon – mortgage rates declined sharply until the early 1880s and then more gradually until about the turn of the century. Then they rose until

---

36. *Monetary Times*, Jan. 5, 1917, p. 112.

37. The decline in rates on German bonds and French Perpetual Rentes up to about 1897 was also very similar to the three declines shown in Chart 15:1 but their pattern differs after the First World War. See Oskar Morgenstern, *International Financial Transactions and Business Cycles*, National Bureau of Economic Research (Princeton: Princeton University Press, 1959), Charts 55, 56.

Table 15:1 Changes in Long-Term Bond Yields in Canada, United Kingdom and United States 1867-1970

	1867	1897	% Change	1897	1920	% Change	1920	1946	% Change	1946	1970	% Change
Canadian bonds												
Government of Canada (in London)	6.15	2.80	−55	–	–	–	–	–	–	–	–	–
Government of Canada (in Canada)	–	–	–	–	–	–	6.09	2.60	−57	2.60	7.50	188
Province of Ontario (in Canada)	–	–	–	3.25	5.95	83	5.95	2.75	−54	275	8.73	217
City of Toronto (in Canada)	7.10	3.40	−52	3.40	6.54	92	6.54					
City of Montreal borrowing costs[1]	7.00	3.50	−50	3.50								
United States bonds												
Railroad bonds – five best	6.83	3.64	−48	3.64	5.10	40						
Corporation AAA (Moody's)							6.12	2.53	−59	2.53	8.04	218
Government							5.32	2.19	−59	2.19	6.58	200
United Kingdom												
Consols	3.22	2.26	−30	2.26	5.41	139	5.41	2.60	−52	2.60	9.27	256

SOURCE: See notes to Chart 15:1.

[1]1868 to 1899.

Chart 15:2 — Interest Rates on Mortgages in Canada 1852-1970

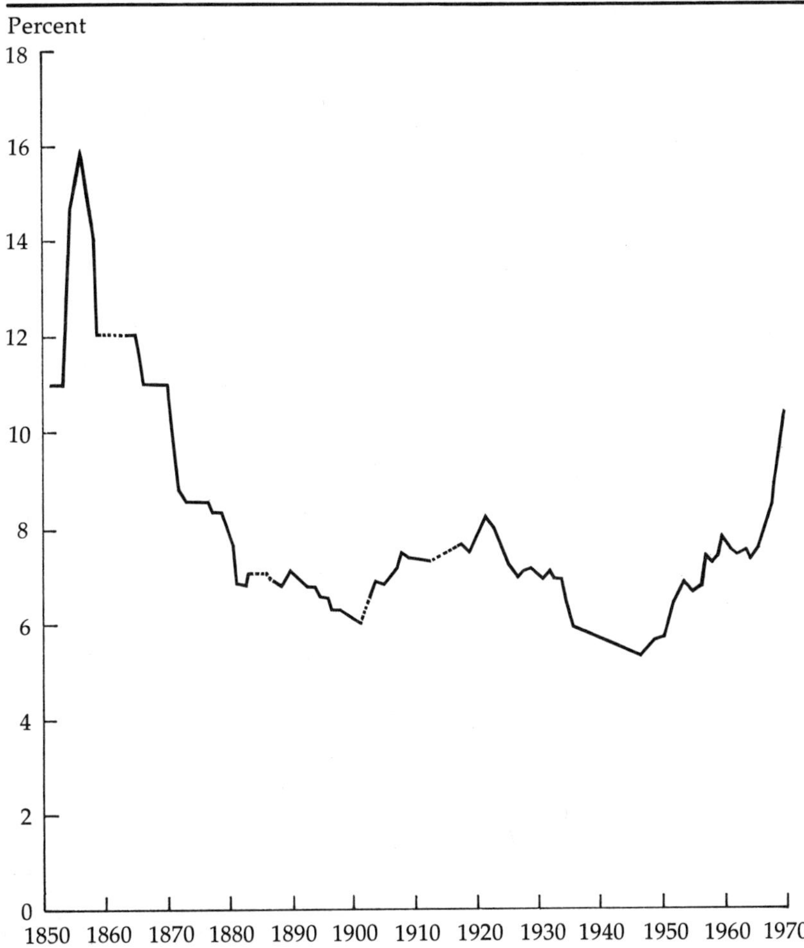

SOURCE: The yields shown here, particularly those of earlier years, can only be regarded as giving a very general indication of conventional mortgage rates. Data sources were: 1852-9, Minutes of the Board of Directors of the Canada Life Assurance Company; 1860-2 by interpolation; 1863-4 as reported in W. A. Douglas, "Ontario Loan and Savings Companies," *Canadian Economics*, Dawson Brothers, 1885, p. 266; 1885-6, interpolation; 1887-1912, estimated rate on mortgages and other securities current during the year of the Canada Permanent Mortgage Corporation as reported in Canada, Department of Finance, *Report of the Loan Companies and Building Societies*. Annual, 1887-1912, Queen's Printer, Ottawa; 1913-16, interpolation; 1917-61, rates on new and renewed mortgages during the year of the Canada Permanent Mortgage Corporation as shown in Dominion Mortgage and Investment Association Brief submitted to the Royal Commission on Banking and Finance, June, 1962, Appendix 9, and the same series for 1962-9 were kindly made available to me by the Canada Permanent Mortgage Corporation.

1922, that is for about 26 years, declined for the next 14 years, began to increase in 1946, and reached a peak in 1969 and 1970.

What information there is relating to yields on municipal debentures suggests a pattern not too different from that of the rate on mortgages. In the 1850s the debentures of Ontario towns and townships seem to have changed hands at rates yielding from about 9% to 11%. In the 1860s the range appears more like 7% to 8%; in the 1870s about 6¼% to 7½%; in the 1880s 5% to 6%; in the 1890s 3½% to 5%. The low point seems to have been reached in 1897.

The pattern of interest rates prior to 1914: Table 15:2 gives some impression of the pattern of certain Canadian interest rates prior to 1914. First of all it may be noted that over the five-year period ending in 1880 there was a 35 basis point (or 8%) spread between a Canada bond and a Quebec bond in London, and a 370 basis point (or 80%) spread between Canadian mortgage rates and the Canada bond in London, which was very similar to the spreads that existed from 1909 to 1912. But it is also true that these spreads varied substantially within the period. The Quebec bond generally moved within 35 to 80 basis points of the Canada bond, and mortgages generally moved from 300 to 370 basis points of Canada bonds. The Ontario bond yields from 1901 to 1913 were on average identical with those of Quebec, suggesting a roughly equal credit rating of the two provinces at that time.

The period 1867 to 1897 was one in which the difference in yields on Canadian securities in London and on the same securities in Canada disappeared. In the 1870s the yields on long-term Toronto bonds were approximately ½% to ¾% higher in Toronto than in London[38] but when the low in yields was reached in 1897 the difference had disappeared and on balance yields on Canadian bonds in Canada seem at times to have gone below yields on Canadian bonds in London. A series of yields on long-term Ontario bonds in Canada from 1900 to 1913 shows them to be very similar to the yields on Quebec Province long-term bonds over that period in the London market.[39]

This relative change in Canadian security yields in London and in Canada is also seen in the declining gap between the rate that a mortgage loan company paid on debentures sold in the United Kingdom and the rate earned on mortgages made in Canada. Table 7:5 (p.

---

38. See bond price quotations in the *Monetary Times*, 1869-1880, and the issues of the *Economist* for that period.
39. See Table 15:2.

212) provides this information for one company. It shows that whereas in the 1870s the difference between interest paid on sterling debentures and received on Ontario mortgages was 2.75% to 3.00%, in 1904 it was 1.50% and in 1920 1.25%. From 1873 to 1902 the yield gap between those two series declined by 125 basis points; while Table 15:2 shows that over that same period the yield gap between U.K. consols and Government of Canada sterling bonds declined by 116 basis points, that is, by a very similar amount. Also by 1902 the rate on sterling debentures sold by four mortgage loan companies was 3.92%, whereas the rate on their debentures sold in Canada was only 3.73%.[40] It would seem that the forces that made the United Kingdom an unattractive source of funds were far advanced by the turn of the century—essentially revealing themselves in a much more rapid decline in North American interest rates than U.K. interest rates—and that the First World War had the effect of confirming the permanence of these trends and helping to create interest rate levels that induced an outflow of capital, often through bond and debenture redemptions and repurchases from the United Kingdom.

Canadian and United States bond yields, 1900-1970: While directly comparable bond yields are not available, Chart 15:3 gives some impression of trends in and spreads between Canadian and United States federal government and corporate bond yields. The average yields of those series and the spread between them are shown in Table 15:3. The single most interesting point that emerges from that table is that Canadian corporate bonds since about the 1930s and federal government bonds since about the 1940s have on the average yielded around 25% more than similar U.S. bonds. So on the average capital in Canada seems to cost one-quarter more than in the United States.

Structure of bond yields and mortgage rates in Canada, 1948-1970: Table 15:4 shows average annual bond yields from 1948 to 1970, conventional residential mortgage rates from 1961 to 1970, and also the amount, in percentage terms, by which provincial, municipal and corporate bond yields and mortgage rates exceeded the yields on Government of Canada bonds. The first point to note is that from 1958 to about 1966 the gap between Government of Canada bond yields and the yield on the other bonds shown narrowed substantially—almost certainly because of the federal government's massive increase in long-term debt following its 1958 conversion loans.

40. See source to Table 7:5.

Table 15:2 Canadian Bond and Mortgage Yields and Yield of U.K. Consols 1870-1913 (Average of end-of-quarter figures)

	CANADA[1] BOND		QUEBEC[2] BOND		ONTARIO[3] BOND IN CANADA		CANADIAN MORTGAGES[4]		U.K. CON-SOLS[5]
	YIELD %	SPREAD ABOVE U.K. CONSOLS	YIELD %	SPREAD ABOVE CANADA BOND	YIELD %	SPREAD ABOVE CANADA BOND	YIELD %	SPREAD ABOVE CANADA BOND	
1870	5.95	190	—				11.00	585	3.25
1	4.95	170	—				9.50	455	3.25
2	4.85	160	—				8.75	390	3.25
3	4.70	145	—				8.50	380	3.25
4	4.60	135	—				8.50	390	3.25
5	4.60	139	—				8.50	390	3.21
6	4.65	148	5.10	45			8.50	385	3.17
7	4.65	151	5.00	35			8.50	385	3.14
8	4.70	155	5.00	30			8.25	355	3.15
9	4.45	137	4.75	30			8.25	380	3.08
1880	4.35	129	4.60	25			7.75	340	3.06
Average (1876-1880)	(4.55)	(143)	(4.90)	(35)			(8.25)	(370)	(3.12)
1881	4.20	119	4.45	25			6.75	255	3.01
2	4.20	122	4.45	25			6.75	255	2.98
3	4.15	117	4.55	40			7.00	285	2.98
4	4.15	117	4.55	40			7.00	285	2.98
5	4.10	108	4.45	35			(7.00)	290	3.02
6	3.90	92	4.25	35			(7.00)	310	2.98
7	3.95	99	4.15	20			6.86	291	2.96
8	3.60	98	4.10	50			6.82	322	2.62
9	3.50	86	4.00	50			6.80	330	2.64
1890	3.80	113	4.20	40			7.02	322	2.67
Average	(3.95)	(107)	(4.30)	(35)			(6.90)	(295)	(2.88)

1891	4.00	132	4.75	75			7.13	313	2.68
2	3.90	125	4.55	65			6.80	290	2.65
3	3.60	101	4.45	85			6.69	309	2.59
4	3.45	94	4.20	75			6.72	327	2.51
5	3.25	86	4.20	95			6.50	325	2.39
6	3.15	87	4.25	110			6.52	337	2.28
7	2.80	54	3.55	75			6.26	346	2.26
8	2.90	62	3.55	65			6.23	333	2.28
9	3.00	62	3.65	65			6.11	311	2.38
1900	3.00	47	3.70	70			6.05	305	2.53
Average	(3.30)	(84)	(4.10)	(80)			(6.50)	(320)	(2.46)
1901	3.00	33	3.70	70	3.65	65	6.00	300	2.67
2	2.95	29	3.65	70	3.75	80	(6.00)	305	2.66
3	3.05	27	3.70	65	3.80	75	6.45	340	2.78
4	3.20	36	3.75	55	3.75	55	6.92	372	2.84
5	3.10	33	3.80	70	3.80	70	6.82	372	2.77
6	3.15	30	3.80	65	3.60	45	6.99	384	2.85
7	3.25	26	3.95	70	3.65	40	7.18	393	2.99
8	3.30	40	3.95	65	4.10	80	7.48	418	2.90
9	3.50	51	3.90	40	4.10	60	7.36	386	2.99
1910	3.55	45	3.90	35	3.85	30	(7.34)	379	3.10
Average	(3.20)	(35)	(3.80)	(60)	(3.80)	(60)	(6.85)	(365)	(2.85)
1911	3.55	38	3.95	40	3.95	40	7.32	377	3.17
2	3.65	35	3.95	30	3.90	25	7.33	368	3.30
3	4.10	68	4.30	20	4.15	5	n.a.		3.42
Average	(3.75)	(45)	(4.05)	(30)	(4.00)	(25)	n.a.		(3.30)

SOURCE: Canada and Quebec bond yields computed from data in the *Economist*. Ontario yields from data published by Wood, Gundy & Co. Average of end-of-quarter figures. Canadian yields rounded off to 5 basis points.

1 From 1870-96, Canada 5% 1903 sterling bond; 1897-1913, Canada 3% sterling 1938 bond.
2 From 1876-94, Quebec 5% 1906 sterling bond; 1895-6, Quebec 4½% 1919 sterling bond; 1897-1913, Quebec 4% 1928 sterling bond.
3 From 1900-13, Ontario long-term bond yield in Canada, as computed by Wood, Gundy & Co.
4 See source of Table 15:2. These rates are rough approximations of levels of mortgage rates.
5 See note 3 of Chart 15:1.

Chart 15:3 — Canadian and United States Government and Corporate Bond Yields 1914-1970

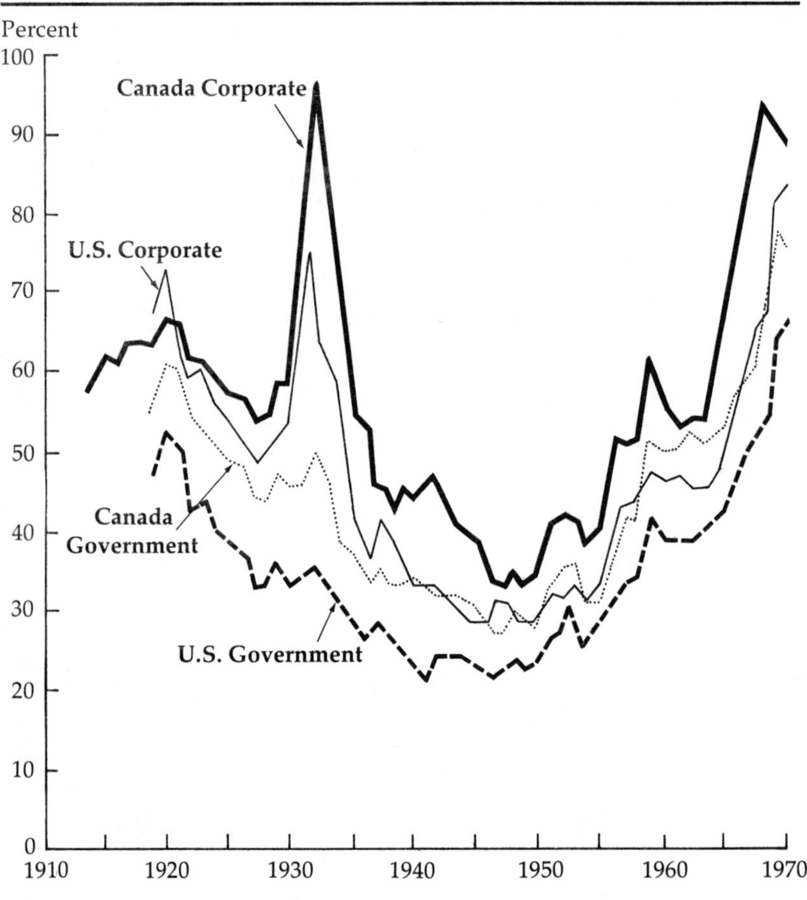

SOURCE: See Table 15:3.

Ignoring the years of the conversion loan distortion, provincial bond yields were about 13% higher than federal bond yields. Up to about 1958 the municipal bond yield shown stood about 25% above Canada bond yields, which by 1967-1970 had declined to about 18%. Corporate bond yields, from 1948 to 1957, were about 23% higher than federal government bond yields, and from 1967 to 1970 were about 17% higher. It would seem therefore that relative to federal government bond yields, municipal and corporate yields have drifted

Table 15:3 Canadian and United States Government and Corporate Bond Yields 1919-1970

	FEDERAL GOVERNMENT BOND				CORPORATE BOND			
	CANADA[1]	U.S.[2]	SPREAD BASIS POINTS	%	CANADA[3]	U.S.[4]	SPREAD BASIS POINTS	%
1914					5.70			
5					6.15			
6					6.04			
7					6.37			
8					6.37			
9	5.50	4.76			6.31	6.66		
1920	6.09	5.37			6.67	7.34		
Average	(5.80)	(5.07)	(73)	14	(6.49)	(7.00)	−51	−7
1921	6.00	5.03			6.52	6.36		
2	5.45	4.29			6.17	5.89		
3	5.20	4.36			6.13	6.08		
4	5.00	4.04			5.95	5.61		
5	4.95	3.85			5.74	5.40		
6	4.80	3.66			5.67	5.10		
7	4.50	3.30			5.41	4.83		
8	4.45	3.34			5.50	5.01		
9	4.85	3.62			5.85	5.17		
1930	4.62	3.25			5.85	5.38		
Average	(4.98)	(3.87)	(111)	29	(5.88)	(5.48)	(40)	(7)
1931	4.70	3.40			7.73	7.43		
2	5.00	3.61			9.60	6.31		
3	4.55	3.34			7.96	5.93		
4	3.90	3.10			5.50	4.79		
5	3.70	2.80			5.29	4.19		
6	3.35	2.67			4.61	3.67		
7	3.50	2.76			4.53	4.16		
8	3.34	2.61			4.23	3.95		
9	3.33	2.42			4.59	3.69		
1940	3.39	2.23			4.39	3.36		
Average	(3.88)	(2.89)	(99)	34	(5.84)	(4.75)	(109)	23
1941	3.23	2.05			4.54	3.35		
2	3.18	2.46			4.68	3.32		
3	3.17	2.49			4.38	3.14		
4	3.09	2.48			4.05	2.98		
5	3.06	2.36			3.96	2.80		
6	2.75	2.19			3.31	2.83		
7	2.73	2.27			3.28	3.12		
8	3.02	2.44			3.50	3.09		

Table 15:3 (continued)

9	2.92	2.29			3.30	2.86		
1950	2.79	2.34			3.40	2.88		
Average	(2.99)	(2.34)	(65)	28	(3.84)	(3.04)	(80)	(26)
1951	3.31	2.60			4.09	3.23		
2	3.60	2.70			4.20	3.19		
3	3.68	3.08			4.17	3.39		
4	3.11	2.55			3.82	3.13		
5	3.11	2.86			4.07	3.33		
6	3.66	3.12			5.10	3.89		
7	4.15	3.45			5.04	4.31		
8	4.10	3.50			5.18	4.38		
9	5.06	4.14			6.09	4.87		
1960	4.98	3.94			5.53	4.66		
Average	(3.88)	(3.19)	(69)	22	(4.73)	(3.84)	(89)	(23)
1961	5.06	3.94			5.31	4.71		
2	5.21	3.93			5.35	4.52		
3	5.06	4.03			5.45	4.55		
4	5.17	4.15			5.48	4.58		
5	5.26	4.24			6.03	4.84		
6	5.73	4.68			6.77	5.69		
7	6.09	4.91			7.52	6.51		
8	6.94	5.34			8.11	6.80		
9	7.82	6.31			9.32	8.13		
1970	7.50	6.50			8.87	8.35		
Average	(5.98)	(4.80)	(118)	(25)	(6.82)	(5.87)	(95)	(16)

[1] Average of end-of-quarter figures 1919 and 1920 estimated by the author from press reports. 1921-5 5½% 1934 Victory bond; 1926-32 4½% 1944 bond; 1933-7 4½% 1949-59 bond; 1938-40 3% perpetual bond; 1941-57 15-year theoretical bond yield as computed by Bank of Canada; 1958-67 3¼% 1979 bond; 1968-70 4½% 1983 bond.

[2] Average of figures of last month in the quarter and the monthly figure used was a daily average figure for that month. From 1919 to 1941 bonds were partially tax exempt. Data for them came from Board of Governors of the Federal Reserve System, *Banking and Monetary Statistics*, 1943, pp. 468-71. From 1942 to 1970 average of last month in the quarter with the monthly figure being a Wednesday average figure. Data from Board of Governors of the Federal Reserve System, *Federal Reserve Bulletin*. From 1919 to 1925 bonds were 8 years to maturity or more; from 1926 to 1941, 12 years or more; from 1942 to 1953, 15 years or more; from 1954 to 1970, 10 years or more.

[3] Year-end figures 1914-54 data from series published by Wood, Gundy & Co. 1955-70, McLeod, Young, Weir and Co. Ltd. figures for industrial and utility yields.

[4] December figure for Moody's total corporate bond yield.

downward while provincial yields have remained about the same. In the decade ended 1970 conventional residential mortgage rates were about 34% higher than federal government bond yields.

Structure of Canadian provincial bond yields, 1921-1970: The provincial bond yields shown in Table 15:4 are an average of yields on bonds issued by the various provinces. It may be interesting to note the changing structure of yields among the provinces. Table 15:5 shows yields on bonds of individual provinces as well as the individual provincial bond yields as a proportion of the average bond yield of all the provinces. It is apparent that important changes in relative credit standing, as implied by bond yields, have occurred. From 1936 to 1945 Alberta defaulted on the principal of its maturing issues and paid interest at only one-half the coupon rate. Its credit rating naturally suffered as Table 15:5 shows, but fortunately it did not have to borrow for many years; and when its bonds again appeared, its rating was better relative to the other provinces than it had been prior to the default, with its bond yield being actually below the provincial average yield in 1968-1970. Saskatchewan's credit rating also suffered in the 1930s but it recovered completely by 1951, and since then has improved steadily and in 1969 was among the best of the provinces. The yields of British Columbia, Manitoba, and Nova Scotia bonds have usually been close to the provincial average, while that of Ontario has usually been below the average and New Brunswick and Newfoundland – in the post–Second World War period – above the average. Earlier we saw that just after the turn of the century the credit rating of Quebec was about the same as and sometimes better than that of Ontario – that is, about the best among the provinces. Table 15:5 suggests that this continued to be the case until 1962. After that its bond yields rose steadily relative to those of Ontario and to that of the provincial average yield. In 1968, 1969 and 1970 its bonds yielded clearly more than any other province except Newfoundland.

Using the average bond yields for the years 1968, 1969 and 1970 as a criterion, the implied relative credit standing of the provinces in declining order was as follows: Ontario, Saskatchewan, Alberta, Nova Scotia, Manitoba, New Brunswick, British Columbia, Prince Edward Island, Newfoundland, Quebec. This, of course, is only a rough approximation of credit standing, and as the data in Table 15:5 show, there are year-to-year changes in relative yields. The spread in basis points between the highest and lowest bond yield of the provinces in 1970 was 92, or 5½%; in the 1921-1930 period when interest rates were much lower (see Table 15:5) it was 32 basis points,

Table 15:4 Structure of Canadian Bond Yields 1948-1971

	GOVERNMENT OF CANADA[1]	PROVINCIAL[2]		MUNICIPAL[2]		CORPORATE[2]		PRIME CONVENTIONAL[3] MORTGAGES	
	YIELD	YIELD	PERCENT ABOVE CANADA YIELD	YIELD	PERCENT ABOVE CANADA YIELD	YIELD	PERCENT ABOVE CANADA YIELD	YIELD	PERCENT ABOVE CANADA YIELD
1948	2.93	3.15	7	3.47	18	3.49	19		
1949	2.83	3.14	11	3.55	25	3.47	22		
1950	2.77	3.12	13	3.46	25	3.43	24		
Average	(2.84)	(3.14)	(11)	(3.49)	(23)	(3.46)	(22)		
1951	3.22	3.73	16	4.18	30	3.93	22		
1952	3.56	4.12	16	4.64	30	4.26	20		
1953	3.67	4.14	13	4.65	26	4.43	20		
1954	3.14	3.49	11	3.92	25	4.00	27		
1955	3.11	3.42	10	3.74	20	3.87	25		
1956	3.64	4.26	17	4.69	29	4.49	23		
1957	4.20	4.98	19	5.49	31	5.29	26		
1958	4.15	4.75	14	5.16	24	4.95	19		
1959	5.08	5.64	11	5.99	18	5.57	10		
1960	5.18	5.65	9	6.00	16	5.69	10		
Average	(3.90)	(4.42)	(13)	(4.84)	(24)	(4.65)	(19)		
1961	5.05	5.49	9	5.71	13	5.45	8	7.00	39
1962	5.11	5.50	8	5.71	12	5.43	6	6.97	37
1963	5.09	5.43	6	5.59	10	5.42	6	6.97	37
1964	5.18	5.53	7	5.67	9	5.51	6	6.97	35
1965	5.21	5.59	7	5.75	10	5.67	9	7.02	35

1966	5.69	6.29	11	6.46	14	6.44	13	7.66	35
1967	5.94	6.70	13	6.95	17	7.01	18	8.07	36
1968	6.75	7.60	12	7.80	16	7.85	16	9.07	34
1969	7.58	8.40	11	8.84	17	8.69	17	9.84	30
1970	7.91	9.04	14	9.44	19	9.22	17	10.44	32
1971 1st. Q.	6.76	7.81	15	8.12	20	8.29	23	9.65	43
Average	(5.95)	(6.56)	(10)	(6.79)	(14)	(6.67)	(12)	(8.00)	(34)

SOURCE: Bank of Canada, McLeod, Young, Weir and Co. Ltd., Central Mortgage and Housing Corporation.

[1] 1948-9, theoretical 15-year bond yield. Thereafter basically an average of bonds ten years to maturity and over. Monthly average using last-Wednesday-of-month figures.

[2] Average of near month-end figures of ten provincial, ten municipal, and twenty corporate bonds.

[3] Average of rates charged by institutional lenders on residential mortgages.

Table 15:5 Structure of Provincial Bond Yields 1921-1970

	B.C. yield	% of Av.	Alta. yield	% of Av.	Sask. yield	% of Av.	Man. yield	% of Av.	Ont. yield	% of Av.
1921-1930	5.13	104	5.10	103	4.99	101	4.99	101	4.90	99
1931-1940	4.55	98	6.64	143	5.69	122	4.93	106	3.78	81
1941-1950	2.98	89	4.48	134	4.08	120	3.22	96	2.63	79
1951-1960										
1961-1969										
1948	3.10	98	—	—	3.87	122	3.13	99	3.08	97
1949	3.13	100	—	—	3.60	115	3.16	101	3.06	97
1950	3.11	99	—	—	3.50	111	3.07	98	3.02	96
1951	3.67	98	—	—	3.76	101	3.65	98	3.56	95
1952	4.06	99	—	—	4.13	100	4.10	99	4.00	97
1953	4.08	99	—	—	4.21	102	4.13	100	3.92	95
1954	3.38	97	—	—	3.61	103	3.51	101	3.39	97
1955	3.23	94	—	—	3.59	105	3.47	101	3.29	96
1956	4.11	96	—	—	4.38	103	4.21	99	4.16	98
1957	4.84	97	—	—	5.07	102	4.98	100	4.91	99
1958	4.38	92	—	—	4.92	104	4.83	102	4.72	99
1959	5.50	98	—	—	5.67	101	5.65	100	5.54	98
1960	5.36	95	—	—	5.67	100	5.67	100	5.68	101
1961	5.24	95	—	—	5.51	100	5.54	101	5.51	100
1962	5.34	97	—	—	5.54	101	5.56	101	5.42	99
1963	5.54	102	—	—	5.41	100	5.33	98	5.34	98
1964	5.58	101	—	—	5.49	99	5.51	100	5.42	98
1965	5.56	99	—	—	5.57	100	5.55	99	5.48	98
1966	6.28	100	—	—	6.24	99	6.20	99	6.06	96
1967	6.77	101	—	—	6.57	98	6.61	99	6.39	95
1968	7.59	100	7.42	98	7.42	98	7.47	98	7.20	95
1969	8.51	101	8.26	98	8.17	97	8.34	99	8.23	97
1970	9.02	100	8.89	98	8.75	97	9.00	100	8.73	97

SOURCE: Data for average yields for the periods 1921-30, 1931-40, and 1941-50 computed from year-end bond prices shown in Government of Canada, Department of Insurance, *Lists of Securities.* These data can only be regarded as rough approximations. Data for individual years 1948-70 from unpublished material kindly made available to us by McLeod, Young, Weir and Co. Ltd. are averages of near month-end figures.

and the gap in percentage terms was again 7%. This spread as well as the changing pattern of provincial bond yields shows that not all provinces are equal in the bond market and each must pay some attention to the effect of the fiscal activity on its credit worthiness.

Que. yield	% of Av.	N.B. yield	% of Av.	P.E.I. yield	% of Av.	N.S. yield	% of Av.	Nfld. yield	% of Av.	Average yield
4.81	97	4.86	98	4.87	98	4.96	100	–	–	4.95
3.88	83	4.26	92	4.09	88	4.11	88	–	–	4.66
3.31	97	3.55	100	2.93	86	2.93	88	–	–	3.35
2.98	94	3.38	107	3.10	98	3.15	100	–	–	3.16
2.74	87	3.55	113	3.20	102	3.17	101	–	–	3.14
2.96	94	3.60	115	3.09	98	3.11	99	–	–	3.14
3.52	94	4.39	118	3.90	105	3.76	101	–	–	3.73
3.92	95	4.67	114	4.29	104	4.10	99	–	–	4.12
3.84	93	4.48	108	4.19	101	4.12	99	–	–	4.14
3.39	97	3.79	109	3.57	102	3.51	101	–	–	3.49
3.36	98	3.76	110	3.41	100	3.46	101	–	–	3.42
4.10	96	4.46	105	4.28	101	4.26	100	–	–	4.26
4.84	97	5.18	104	5.17	104	5.07	101	–	–	4.98
4.56	96	4.83	102	5.00	105	4.92	104	–	–	4.75
5.52	98	5.88	104	5.82	103	5.71	101	–	–	5.64
5.59	99	5.67	100	5.83	103	5.71	101	–	–	5.65
5.42	99	5.54	101	5.65	103	5.53	101	–	–	5.49
5.50	100	5.55	101	5.65	103	5.52	100	–	–	5.50
5.46	101	5.44	100	5.54	102	5.40	99	–	–	5.43
5.61	101	5.58	101	5.67	103	5.38	97	–	–	5.53
5.70	102	5.70	102	5.75	103	5.38	96	–	–	5.59
6.48	103	6.37	101	6.49	103	6.18	98	–	–	6.29
6.94	104	6.82	102	6.94	104	6.61	99	–	–	6.70
7.92	104	7.77	102	7.85	103	7.50	99	8.08	106	7.60
8.82	105	8.29	99	8.50	101	8.23	98	8.75	104	8.40
9.65	107	8.99	99	9.09	101	8.89	98	9.43	104	9.04

16
Concluding Observations

The details of the growth and development of the various types of Canadian financial institutions have now been recounted, as has the chronology of their appearance over the last century and a half, and also the growth of financial intermediary assets over the last century. What remains to be done is to view the whole of that development and record certain over-all impressions and generalizations about the evolution and current character of the Canadian financial system.

The first generalization that can safely be made is that there has seldom been a period when there have not been important evolutionary developments in the Canadian financial system. The period before Confederation, the period after Confederation to the turn of the century, the period from then until the end of the Second World War, and the post–Second World War—each of these periods witnessed the exceedingly rapid growth of *some* type of financial intermediaries, each saw the emergence of some *new* types of financial intermediaries, and each saw refinement of the brokerage-oriented financial institutions. Financial institutions have appeared in Canada remarkably soon after they emerged in the United States and United Kingdom. About the only institutions that might at all be regarded as uniquely Canadian are the trust companies and, perhaps in some respects, the caisses populaires.

The rate of growth of total financial intermediary assets in per capita constant dollar terms was not the same over the whole of that period, but there were extended periods prior to the turn of the century when that growth was as rapid as, or more rapid than, after the Second World War.

There has been a substantial diffusion of Canadian financial intermediary assets among the different types of financial intermediaries since Confederation. In 1870 the two largest, the chartered banks and mortgage loan companies, accounted for 82% of the total; after 1904 the two largest were the chartered banks and life insurance companies, and their assets accounted for 72% of total Canadian financial intermediary assets in 1910 and 1926, 61% in 1950 and 43% in 1968.

It is also apparent that there is nothing sacrosanct about the position of importance of particular types of financial intermediaries. This is seen especially in the relative decline in size of the chartered banks, Quebec Savings Banks, Post Office Savings Bank, mortgage loan companies, life insurance companies and, recently, the sales finance companies. The failure or inability of financial intermediaries to adjust to changing "tastes" of investors, or changing requirements of borrowers, or changing competitive environment, or even simply their *delay* in adjusting to them, it seems, is soon reflected in their rates of growth. There is no reason at all to believe that the future will be different in this respect than the past. It is on the whole indirect evidence of a healthy, competitive environment.

There has been a trend toward reduced dominance by individual companies in some important sectors of the financial system. The Bank of Montreal lost its position of pre-eminence as several of the other banks grew to match it in size; the Canada Life Assurance Company declined substantially in relative size over many years, as did the Sun Life after its unusual growth up to the end of the 1920s; among mutual funds the largest of them, the Investors Group, has over the past decade declined in relative size; and while the largest of the trust companies, Royal Trust, has been increasing in relative size, so have several of the other larger trust companies.

While there has been a decrease in the dominance of the largest companies, there has been increased concentration among the several largest companies in some sectors of the financial system. The five largest chartered banks accounted for 44% of total assets in 1880, 64% in 1910, 83% in 1940 and 93% in 1969; the four largest trust companies (company and guaranteed funds) accounted for 43% of total assets in 1926, 42% in 1955 and 54% in 1968. On the other hand among Canadian federally registered life insurance companies the five largest had 84% of total assets in 1900, 71% in 1945 and 64% in 1968; while the eight largest mutual fund management companies were directly responsible for the management of 95% of mutual fund assets in 1957, 85% in 1963 and 79% in 1969. The degree of concentration of assets that still exists in the larger companies of all these sectors makes it necessary for government to develop an explicit and economically rational merger policy. For example, mergers between the larger companies may be very undesirable in some sectors, but not in others, and mergers between companies of different sectors might also be highly desirable in some cases while not in others. The danger is that the absence of such a policy will lead to over-concentration of financial business in some sectors, and will impede desirable evolutionary developments.

In most sectors the number of financial intermediaries in operation has increased or remained relatively constant, but the number of chartered banks decreased from a peak of 51 in 1875 to 11 in 1925 and in 1971 there were only 9. There were 24 federally registered life insurance companies in operation in 1869, in 1905 there were 40, in 1945 there were 46, and in 1969 the number in operation was 127; while the number of federally registered fire and casualty insurance companies increased from 27 in 1875 to 264 in 1969. We have compiled 60 trust companies as being in operation in 1947, 52 in 1958, 65 in 1966 and 61 in 1969. There were 65 federally registered small loan companies and money lenders in operation in 1940, 56 in 1950, 83 in 1965 and 69 in 1968. The total number of sales finance companies is not known but in addition to the 10 that account for about 90% of the industry, there were 18 others that were members of the Federated Council of Sales Finance Companies in 1969 and apparently there were well over 100 other small, local instalment finance companies. There were 8 mutual funds in 1946, 15 in 1950, 65 in 1960 and 134 in 1969. The number of members of the Investment Dealers' Association was 105 in 1920, 134 in 1930, 114 in 1940, 196 in 1950, 198 in 1960 and 145 in 1969, and there were well over 100 other securities dealers and brokers in operation in 1969. Almost all the provinces as well as the federal government have established loan schemes for farmers and for encouraging industrial development, as well as for a variety of other purposes.

The number of retail financial outlets or branches in Canada cannot be meaningfully measured because of the widespread granting of credit through retail stores. However the total number of chartered bank branches, branches of registered small loan companies and trust companies, and the number of credit union locals totalled 8,738 in 1954, 10,901 in 1960 and 13,515 in 1969. This amounted to about 1,750 people per branch in 1954, and about 1,550 in 1969.

All the foregoing developments would seem to suggest indirectly that there has been considerable competitive ferment among Canadian financial intermediaries, both between companies within particular sectors of the financial system and between sectors themselves.

The latter point justifies elaboration. As different types of financial intermediaries first emerged there seem to have been sharp functional lines of demarcation between them, and this was partly because of the bias of the legislators. Just by way of example, the banks could issue bank notes but not debentures and could make unsecured loans and buy securities but could not make mortgage loans, and they could not sell insurance; the mortgage loan companies could issue debentures but not bank notes and could make mortgage loans and buy securities, but could not make unsecured loans; the trust companies at first could not make unsecured loans or take deposits or issue debentures or generally engage in "the business of banking," but they could take funds in trust and make secured and real estate mortgage loans; the life insurance companies could not enter the savings deposit business or make unsecured loans, but could make mortgage loans and buy securities. A number of other examples of such division of activities could be cited. However, as time went on, the barriers dividing the activities of financial institutions began to break down. The thin edge of the wedge first appeared in the 1850s when the permanent building societies began to take deposits and this not because they were specifically permitted to do so but because they were not specifically prohibited from doing so. The trust companies, after several decades of operation, in effect received legislative approval for engaging in deposit business, and their guaranteed investment certificates were in practice the same as debentures. Credit unions and caisses populaires were also permitted to engage in the deposit business. In this way inter-bank competition for deposits was augmented by competition from other types of intermediaries, and after the Second World War this began to include the chequing deposit business. As a result of changes in the 1967 Bank Act the chartered banks were permitted to issue debentures, which further reduced the differences between the banks and their closest competitors as far as the accumulation of funds was concerned.

This process also emerged on the lending side. Trust companies and life insurance companies from the beginning of their existence were active in mortgage lending, as were the caisses populaires, competing with the mortgage loan companies, and they competed for new securities issues as did the chartered banks. New institutions also emerged to compete with the banks in the area of short-term lending. The credit unions and caisses populaires began to make personal cash loans, as did the reputable consumer loan companies that first appeared in the 1920s, and the sales finance companies began to offer instalment credit after 1916, while the life insurance companies made policy loans. After the Second World War the principal changes were the growth to new prominence of some of the aforementioned competitors; the entry of the chartered banks into mortgage lending and consumer credit business; and entry of the trust companies into short-term lending through their purchase of commercial and finance company paper (which had become close substitutes for bank loans) and into unsecured short-term lending through a broadening of their powers under the basket clause. It was in this way that "lending" competition between types of institutions emerged over the years.

Since there is now exceedingly little difference between chartered banks and their competitors in their legal powers and actual practices relating to the accumulation of funds and the lending of those funds, there is no longer a very meaningful functional definition of a chartered bank. Also, since some of those competitors are provincially incorporated, it must be the case that the provinces are exercising jurisdiction over types of activity identical to that carried on by the chartered banks, and therefore over "banking," contrary to the intentions of the British North America Act. Jurisdictional lines separating the federal and provincial areas of authority in the regulation of non-bank financial intermediaries have always been indistinct and the evolution of the financial system has increased the problem. Unquestionably an area of high priority in future should be the rationalization of federal and provincial jurisdiction with respect to the supervision and control of financial intermediaries and the supervision and control of the securities business – that is, the issue of and trading in securities.

There has emerged substantial competition between intermediaries for funds seeking equity investments. The brokers and investment dealers of course have managed such accounts for many decades. At the turn of the century the closed-end funds began to emerge and in the 1930s the mutual funds. After the Second World War the trust companies and some banks also began to offer mutual funds. The life insurance companies began to offer segregated pension fund plans with funds invested in equities, and the trust companies began to establish equity-based pooled investment funds for small estates and registered retirement pension funds for individuals and groups. So today the individual Canadian equity investor has a remarkably wide range of choices not only within the mutual funds industry, but also outside that industry.

This increased similarity between types of financial intermediaries, both in the accumulation and the distribution of funds, is a most desirable development from the viewpoint of maintaining and improving further the efficiency of the capital market. It is also the basic reason why recent federal legislation limiting inter-financial-intermediary ownership and interlocking directorships is desirable. Competitive policy must be aimed at preserving and encouraging competition both between companies in particular sectors of the financial system and between sectors themselves. It is not at all inconceivable that such policy, through legislative changes, should in future facilitate some of the existing financial intermediaries to transform themselves into banks if their healthy development seems to call for it. For example, the possibility that the caisses populaires locals in Quebec might in time, assisted by the equity interest the Desjardins movement has in La Banque Provinciale du Canada, evolve into an efficient branch system, is quite intriguing and certainly should not be legally impeded. Also the possibility that a large instalment finance company together with its multiple-branch small loan company subsidiary might be able to improve its long-term prospects by broadening out and evolving into a national chartered bank, should not be discouraged – particularly since the sales finance companies as such may have entered a period of relative decline in size. Similarly so for the larger trust companies.

An important part of the development of the financial system has been the increased relative importance of both federal and provincial government financial intermediaries, amounting in 1968 to 23% of total Canadian financial intermediaries' assets. Since normal competitive criteria are not relevant for appraising their efficiency and since the market place has little interest in appraising them, techniques and procedures should be developed that will make it possible to determine in an ongoing way whether those intermediaries are in fact achieving the objectives they were designed to achieve and whether they are doing so in an economically efficient way. They have become too important to be ignored.

Foreign ownership in the financial system is not likely to emerge as an important issue in future. The banks are overwhelmingly owned by Canadians and legislation not only prevents their shifting into non-resident hands but also limits the growth of the one chartered bank that is not Canadian-owned. In 1968, 43 of the 122 federally registered life insurance companies in Canada accounted for 69% of life insurance in force of such companies and all, except 7 of the smaller ones, were Canadian-owned. Further foreign ownership is limited both by the predominance of mutualization in the industry and by ownership control legislation, and the proportion of total life business done by foreign-owned companies in Canada declined on balance after the Second World War, as it had done ever since the first Canadian companies appeared. Almost all the trust and mortgage loan companies are essentially Canadian-owned and federal legislation limits foreign ownership of the federal companies. By their very nature the mutual funds (although not the management companies), credit unions and caisses populaires, and pension funds are essentially Canadian-owned. In general, over 85% of private financial intermediary assets seem to be accounted for by Canadian-owned companies, and since all government intermediaries are Canadian-owned, over 90% of total financial intermediary assets are Canadian-owned.

Among financial intermediaries the only sector that is dominated by foreign companies is the fire and casualty insurance business where in 1968, 81% of premiums written were written by non-resident owned or controlled companies. In the sales finance industry the Canadian-owned companies seem to account for approximately 60% of the business, but the large foreign-owned companies have been increasing their share of industry assets and may well continue to do so. There is little chance that any of the large Canadian-owned sales finance companies will pass into foreign hands since the federal government has already prevented one such transfer, and federal control legislation that would explicitly require government approval for the transfer of ownership of such companies is on the way.

Nor is it likely that foreign ownership of securities dealers and brokers is likely to increase much. The industry itself, through its control of membership in the stock exchanges and Investment Dealers' Association, seems to favour limiting it, and at present the Canadian institutions among them seem to account for 90% or more of the securities business in Canada. Of course there is the possibility, as there is also in the case of the life insurance and sales finance industry, that the existing foreign-owned companies through superior management could increase their share of the business. If this were to happen then the foreign ownership issue could arise in a very troublesome form. Should one protect Canadian companies that have been shown, through their loss of market share, to be less efficient than foreign-owned companies? Should special procedures be taken to examine regularly the relative competitive strength of Canadian companies, and should remedial action be taken if they seem not to be maintaining their market position, or their efficiency in the case of sectors, such as the banking sector, where no meaningful foreign competition is permitted to exist? This could be the nature of the foreign ownership debate in future as far as the financial system is concerned.

There has been a significant extension of lender-of-last-resort facilities in the financial system. Historically these had been available only to the chartered banks, since 1935 through the facilities of the Bank of Canada. After the Second World War, Central Mortgage and Housing Corporation was given authority to make such loans to approved National Housing Act lenders on the security of government-guaranteed N.H.A. mortgages. Through the Canada, Ontario, and Quebec deposit insurance corporations, lender-of-last-resort facilities have been extended to those institutions whose deposit and certain other liabilities are partially covered with deposit insurance – including the trust companies and mortgage loan companies. The Investment Companies Act will extend this privilege to the companies, mainly instalment finance companies, covered by that act. Therefore the risk of well-managed and credit-worthy financial intermediaries facing bankruptcy through a "money panic" has been minimized, while the threat of runs on deposit institutions has been reduced through the introduction of deposit insurance.

By international comparison it seems that Canada has, over the last century and a half, developed a remarkably sophisticated and comprehensive financial system, and one that is quite flexible in its ability to change. It seems to adopt without much delay financial innovations that develop elsewhere, and there is considerable indirect evidence of the existence of strong competitive forces. There are even now financial institutions that will have to adapt quickly or face an inevitable decline in their future growth experience. Challenges to management abound in many companies and sectors.

Such challenges also exist for government. The operation of government financial intermediaries should be continuously appraised against objective criteria. Rationalization of federal-provincial jurisdiction, supervision, and control over private financial institutions is necessary not only for improving further the effectiveness of the control function, but also for minimizing the administrative costs of such control, including the cost to financial institutions in complying with control regulations. Government controllers should concern themselves more with economic efficiency criteria when designing and implementing control legislation than they have done in the past, if only because of the importance of encouraging and perpetuating both inter-company and inter-sector competition in the capital market. They must also develop a rational merger policy, as far as financial institutions are concerned. The need to ensure the perpetuation of effective domestic competition is especially important now that the impact of competition from abroad will be somewhat subdued through the limitation of foreign ownership in Canada's financial system.

Statistical Appendix

One important purpose of our study has been to trace the growth of Canadian financial intermediaries in general and to determine the changing relative size of particular types of financial intermediaries. This necessitated making an estimate of financial intermediary assets. In order to see clearly the unfolding pattern of financial intermediation, annual rather than less frequent estimates of such assets seemed to be necessary. Deficiencies of the data also suggested that undue reliance should not be placed on the estimates for a particular year, especially in earlier years, a problem that is largely avoided if annual estimates are used. So we made the decision to make such estimates, and these estimates for the years 1870 to 1970 are included in this appendix. However, not all figures for 1969 and 1970 were available prior to publication, and some data for 1867, 1868, and 1869 are included. Appendix Table A summarizes the data by showing the assets of broad groupings of financial intermediaries, and their relative size, in current dollars, and for selected years in constant dollars and as a proportion of Gross National Product. The basic groups are:

1 All Canadian financial intermediary assets
2 Private financial intermediary assets
3 Chartered bank Canadian assets
4 Private non-bank financial intermediary assets
5 Public financial intermediary assets
6 Federal government financial intermediary assets
7 Federal government monetary financial intermediary assets, i.e. including Dominion note issue up to 1934 and Bank of Canada assets thereafter
8 Provincial financial intermediary assets

In other words, these groupings show private and public financial intermediary assets, with the former classified into bank and non-bank sub-groups and the latter into federal and provincial sub-groups. Appendix Table B shows the assets on an annual basis in current dollars of the individual types of financial intermediaries as well as the percentage distribution of total financial intermediary assets among those types. It is Table B that shows the changing relative size of particular financial intermediary assets.

Before we discuss the sources and quality of the estimates, a word about their degree of comprehensiveness may be useful. It is our impression that the assets recorded here would account for more than 95% of the assets of organized financial intermediaries over virtually the whole of the period. Not included, because of absence of data for earlier years, are the assets of provincially incorporated life insurance companies, provincially incorporated fire and casualty insurance companies and fraternal benefit societies other than those incorporated by Ontario (see discussion below for details), and investment dealers and stockbrokers. We estimate that in 1968 these probably amounted to about 2% of total financial intermediary assets, and they seem not to have ever been important. Also unavailable are the figures for the assets of the local private bankers which were numerous in Ontario before the turn of the century. Nor is the book credit of merchants included.

The concept of assets we attempted to employ was calendar year-end assets in current dollars at market prices arising from business in Canada. Assets arising from foreign operations were excluded wherever possible, although these are examined when discussing the institutions themselves. Needless to say many compromises had to be made with the concept referred to above. Not all assets were reported at year end, so figures nearest to the year end were frequently used. Some assets were reported at book value, rather than market value, and some at amortized values, and this had to be accepted. In the case of certain government pension and savings schemes, "total liabilities" figures had to be used. The concept of "assets arising out of business done in Canada" is not entirely satisfactory, nor even unambiguous, since an intermediary may borrow in one country and lend in another. Sometimes the data available showed "Canadian assets," sometimes "assets held in Canada," and in a few minor cases no distinction at all had been made between Canadian and foreign business. Fortunately a reasonably satisfactory adjustment was possible in the two cases that mattered – the chartered banks and the life insurance companies. Because of all the aforementioned difficulties, year-to-year comparisons of assets should generally not be made; however, the trends they reveal over a longer period seem to us quite reliable.

Figures of Gross National Product at Market Prices and G.N.P. Implicit Price Index for 1870 to 1920 are from O. J. Firestone, *Canadian Economic Development, 1867-1953* (London: Bowes & Bowes Limited, 1958), and for the years thereafter from Dominion Bureau of Statistics, *National Income and Expenditure Accounts* (Ottawa, Queen's Printer).

We may now examine the sources and nature of the estimates pertaining to the assets of the various types of financial intermediaries shown in Appendix Table B.

PRIVATE FINANCIAL INTERMEDIARIES

Chartered banks: Up to 1929 data came from C. A. Curtis, "Statistics of Banking," *Statistical Contributions to Canadian Economic History*, vol. I (Toronto: The Macmillan Company of Canada Limited, 1931). After that from "Monthly Return of the Chartered Banks," *Canada Gazette* (Ottawa, Queen's Printer), and Bank of Canada, *Statistical Summary*. Bank of Canada estimates of the chartered banks' Canadian assets were used over the period for which they were available. Prior to that the Curtis estimates of total assets were used, from which were subtracted all foreign assets that could specifically be identified.

Quebec Savings Banks: Total assets figures were used as reported in *Canada Gazette* (Ottawa, Queen's Printer), and Bank of Canada, *Statistical Summary*.

Life insurance companies: Statistics relate to federally registered Canadian companies and all foreign companies and came from *Report of the Superintendent of Insurance for Canada* (Ottawa, Queen's Printer), and Bank of Canada, *Statistical Summary*. Bank of Canada estimates of assets in Canada were accepted for the period for which they were available, prior to which time we adjusted total reported assets to exclude assets abroad. Prior to 1900 this adjustment was not possible for Canadian companies, but it was also a period when their foreign business was relatively small.

Fraternal benefit societies: Included in this series are all the assets of federally registered Canadian societies and assets in Canada of foreign societies for the whole of the period. From 1900 onward the series also includes assets in Ontario of Ontario-registered fraternal (or friendly) societies. From 1900 to 1918 assets of Quebec-registered provident mutual benefit associations are included; many of these seem then to have transferred to federal registry, for the series declined to insignificance, and since a complete series of their assets was not available in any case, they were omitted after 1918.

Assets in Canada of foreign societies for 1902-1919 were estimated by interpolation but were relatively small. Assets for Ontario societies for 1902-4, 1908, 1921-2, were estimated by interpolation. Assets of Quebec provident mutual benefit associations for 1900-1909 were estimated by applying to them the growth rate of federally registered societies. Estimates of assets of federally registered companies for 1888 and 1889 were arrived at by extrapolation. To total reported assets of federally registered societies for 1890-1896 have been added an estimate of the assets of the Independent Order of Foresters which had been excluded from those figures until 1896.

Data from *Report of the Superintendent of Insurance for Canada* (Ottawa, Queen's Printer); *Report of the Superintendent of Insurance and Registrar of Friendly Societies of Ontario* (Toronto, Queen's Printer); and Province of Quebec, *Sessional Papers* (Quebec, Queen's Printer).

Fire and casualty insurance companies: For 1967 and 1968 data from D.B.S., *Financial Institutions—Financial Statistics* (Ottawa, Queen's Printer), which figures coincide almost exactly with overlapping year figures of a preceding series used. Prior to 1967, data include total assets of federally registered Canadian fire and casualty insurance companies, and assets in Canada of Ontario joint-stock fire and casualty insurance companies, of Ontario purely mutual companies and up to 1933 of a category referred to as Ontario cash mutual companies. Data from Canada, Department of Insurance, *Report of the Superintendent of Insurance for Canada* (Ottawa, Queen's Printer), and Ontario, *Report of the Superintendent of Insurance and Registrar of Friendly Societies for Ontario* (Toronto, Queen's Printer).

Building societies and mortgage loan companies: The compilation of this series was one of the most difficult and important in this study. Basic references were Canada, Department of Finance, *Report of the Affairs of Loan Companies and Building Societies* (later data compiled and published by the Department of Insurance) (Ottawa, Queen's Printer); Ontario, *Report of the Registrar of Loan and Trust Corporations* (Toronto, Queen's Printer); and *Monetary Times*. Figures of assets of over one hundred individual companies were transferred to a work sheet and where official data—especially in earlier years—omitted particular companies from time to time, these gaps were filled either with data reported in the press or by interpolation. After the First World War until 1959, data used were essentially those in Canada, Department of Insurance, *Report of the Superintendent of Insurance, Loan and Trust Companies* (Ottawa, Queen's Printer). From 1960 to 1968 data used were those in D.B.S., *Business Financial Statistics*, and

Financial Institutions–Financial Statistics (Ottawa, Queen's Printer), which series matched closely the one used in preceding years. Assets of all "investment contract" companies are included from 1960 onward, and of Investors Syndicate which accounted for most of the assets of that group of companies, over the whole of the period since its formation in 1940.

Trust companies: Data prior to 1961 compiled from individual company balance sheets (in earlier years); Canada, Department of Finance, *Report of the Affairs of Loan Companies and Building Societies* (Ottawa, Queen's Printer); Canada, Department of Insurance, *Report of the Superintendent of Insurance, Loan and Trust Companies* (Ontario, Queen's Printer); *Report of the Registrar of Loan and Trust Companies* (Toronto, Queen's Printer). From 1961 onward data from D.B.S., *Business Financial Statistics and Financial Institutions—Financial Statistics* (Ottawa, Queen's Printer), which series, as figures for overlapping series show, is almost identical with that used for years before 1961.

Consumer loan and sales finance companies: Total asset data for 1960-1968 from D.B.S., *Business Financial Statistics* and *Financial Institutions–Financial Statistics* (Ottawa, Queen's Printer). Consumer loan company assets were then estimated by adding together assets of small loan companies and money-lenders as shown in *Report of the Superintendent of Insurance for Canada, Small Loan Companies and Money-Lenders* (Ottawa, Queen's Printer), as well as an estimate of the assets of consumer loan companies not covered by that report, that is, of those making "large" loans and so not covered by the *Small Loans Act.* The latter involved taking the figure for outstandings for consumer loan companies as reported in Bank of Canada, *Statistical Summary,* subtracting from it the outstandings of small loan companies and money-lenders as shown in the Superintendent's *Report* and regarding the result as the assets of such consumer loan companies. The estimate of sales finance company assets is arrived at by subtracting the figure for consumer loan company assets from that of total assets of sales finance and consumer loan companies. From 1948 to 1959 the total asset figure came from Bank of Canada, *Statistical Summary, Annual Supplements,* with breakdown estimated as above. For the years 1940-1947 figures for consumer loan companies from the Superintendent's *Report,* which in those years seems to have included most of the companies. Estimates for assets of sales finance companies for 1926-1938 came from D.B.S., *Working Document on Selected Corporation Financial Statistics 1926-1946,* August 1958 under the classification "Personal and Business Credit"; the series may not be a satisfactory one but none better was available, and its general trend seems to reflect the experience of the large individual companies of that period for which some data are available.

Mutual Funds: Data for 1963 onward from D.B.S., *Business Financial Statistics* and *Financial Institutions—Financial Statistics* (Ottawa, Queen's Printer), quarterly. Prior to that, data were compiled from statistics in the *Financial Post, Survey of Industrials* and *Survey of Investment Funds,* Toronto, annual, and from company data directly in earlier years. Data are based on market values and assets of funds investing only in other funds are excluded.

Non-resident funds: Compiled from the *Financial Post, Survey of Industrials* and *Survey of Investment Funds,* Toronto, annual.

Closed-end funds: Data for 1957 onward from *Financial Post* sources as above, except that holding companies as shown below are excluded, as is UNAS which we place under "development" companies. Prior to 1957 data compiled from *Financial Post* and company sources.

Holding companies: Compiled from company and *Financial Post* data. Includes assets of Argus Corporation, Power Corporation of Canada, and Canadian Power and Paper Securities Ltd. and predecessor company.

Credit unions and caisses populaires—locals: Data for 1967 onward from D.B.S., *Financial Institutions—Financial Statistics,* and prior to that from Canada, Department of Agriculture, *Credit Unions in Canada,* annual, and D.B.S., *Canada Year Book* (Ottawa, Queen's Printer), annual. Assets for some earlier years had to be estimated by interpolation.

Credit unions and caisses populaires—centrals: Data for 1950-1953 from Gilles Mercure, *Credit Unions and Caisses Populaires,* Working paper prepared for the Royal Commission on Banking and Finance (Ottawa, Queen's Printer), 1962. That for 1954-1966 from Canada, Department of Agriculture, *Credit Unions in Canada* (Ottawa, Queen's Printer), and for 1967 onward from D.B.S., *Financial Institutions—Financial Statistics* (Ottawa, Queen's Printer).

Trusteed Pension Funds: For the years 1957 onward data from D.B.S., *Trusteed Pension Plans* (Ottawa, Queen's Printer), annual. For 1950-1957 data estimated by using procedures outlined in *Report of* *the Royal Commission on Banking and Finance* (Ottawa, Queen's Printer, 1964), p. 257. Estimates for the period 1939-1949 were more difficult to make and the results must be treated with great caution. We found that from 1957 to 1966 the growth rate of trusteed pension plans was very similar to that of the federal and provincial government annuity, insurance and superannuation funds, and also that if this correlation was used to estimate the 1950 figure for trusteed pension funds, the estimated figure was very close to the one arrived at by using the procedure of the Royal Commission on Banking and Finance referred to above. We therefore simply assumed that the correlation held also prior to 1950 and used the series for the government funds to estimate the size of trusteed pension funds. However, it did not seem justifiable to use this procedure for years prior to 1939 and so we arbitrarily began to include trusteed pension funds in our tabulation in that year.

Development and other financing companies: Development companies included are Roynat Ltd.; Canadian Enterprize Development Corporation; Charterhouse Group Canada Ltd.; and UNAS Securities Ltd.

The only "other" financing firm included is Export Finance Corporation of Canada Ltd., whose assets in millions of dollars for the years 1961 to 1968 (using end of April of succeeding year figures) were: $68, $96, $139, $221, $180, $91, $25 and $10.

All data came from company annual reports.

PUBLIC FINANCIAL INTERMEDIARIES

The reader is referred to Ervin J. Doak, *Government Financial Intermediation in Canada* (unpublished Ph.D. thesis, University of Toronto, 1970), for a very useful statistical compilation of government financial intermediary operations.

Dominion Notes: Data from C. A. Curtis, "Statistics of Banking," *Statistical Contributions to Canadian Economic History* (Toronto: The Macmillan Company of Canada Limited, 1931), vol. I, Bank of Canada, *Statistical Summary*, and *Canada Gazette* (Ottawa, Queen's Printer).

Bank of Canada: Data from Bank of Canada, *Statistical Summary.*

Post Office and Federal Government Savings Banks: Canada, *Public Accounts* and D.B.S., *Canada Year Book* (Ottawa, Queen's Printer), annual. Figure used is total deposits.

Federal Government Annuity, Insurance and Pension Account: Canada, *Public Accounts* (Ottawa, Queen's Printer), annual. Figure used is "total liabilities."

Industrial Development Bank: Industrial Development Bank, *Annual Reports*, Ottawa.

Farm Credit Corporation: Farm Credit Corporation and its predecessor Farm Improvements Loan Board, *Annual Reports*, Ottawa.

Veterans' Land Act loans: Canada, *Public Accounts* (Ottawa, Queen's Printer).

Central Mortgage and Housing Corporation: C.M.H.C., *Annual Reports*, Ottawa. Prior to 1946 data relate to National Housing Act loans made by the Government of Canada.

Export Credits Insurance Corporation: E.C.I.C., *Annual Reports*, Ottawa, now called the Export Development Corporation.

Canada Deposit Insurance Corporation: Canada, *Public Accounts* (Ottawa, Queen's Printer).

Canada Pension Plan: Canada, *Public Accounts* (Ottawa, Queen's Printer).

Caisse de dépôt et placement du Québec: *Annual Reports*, Quebec.

Provincial savings institutions: Includes Province of Alberta Savings Office and Treasury Branches, Manitoba Provincial Savings Office, Province of Ontario Savings Office and Newfoundland Savings Office. Data from Bank of Canada, *Statistical Summary*, and from *Public Accounts* of the provinces. Figures used are deposit liabilities of the institutions.

Provincial annuity, insurance and pension accounts: *Public Accounts* of the provinces. Figure used is "total liabilities."

Provincial agricultural loan programs: *Public Accounts* of the provinces. Figure used is "loans outstanding." We have included loan schemes that were not purely transitory in nature and that were not related to a particular project or emergency relief operation. For example we have excluded loans to the Canadian Pacific and other railway companies, relief loans, loans to support hard-pressed wheat pool organizations in the 1930s, and a number of schemes that always remained insignificant in size.

Provincial industrial loan programs: *Public Accounts* of the provinces, and annual reports in some cases. See chapter 13 for more details of the types of programs and institutions included.

Provincial miscellaneous loan programs: The only ones included in this category up to 1968 were housing loans and student loans. Data from *Public Accounts* of the provinces.

Appendix Table A
Canadian Financial Intermediaries
Canadian Assets 1870-1970
Summary

CURRENT DOLLAR DATA

1. All Financial Intermediaries
2. Private Financial Intermediaries
3. Chartered Banks
4. Private Non-Bank Financial Intermediaries
5. Public Financial Intermediaries
6. Federal Government Financial Intermediaries
7. Federal Government Monetary Financial Intermediaries
8. Provincial Government Financial Intermediaries

CONSTANT DOLLAR DATA (1935-39=100)

1. All Financial Intermediaries
2. Private Financial Intermediaries
3. Chartered Banks
4. Private Non-Bank Financial Intermediaries
5. Public Financial Intermediaries
6. Federal Government Financial Intermediaries
7. Federal Government Monetary Financial Intermediaries
8. Provincial Government Financial Intermediaries
9. G.N.P. Implicit Price Index

ASSETS AS A PROPORTION OF GROSS NATIONAL PRODUCT CURRENT DOLLAR DATA

1. All Financial Intermediaries
2. Private Financial Intermediaries
3. Chartered Banks
4. Private Non-Bank Financial Intermediaries
5. Public Financial Intermediaries
6. Federal Government Financial Intermediaries
7. Federal Government Monetary Financial Intermediaries
8. Provincial Government Financial Intermediaries
9. G.N.P. at Market Prices (millions of dollars)

Appendix Table A (continued)
Canadian Financial Intermediaries
Canadian Assets 1870-1970
Summary

CURRENT DOLLAR DATA

							1869		1870	
	$ MNS.	%	$ MNS.	%	$ MNS.	%	$ MNS.	%	$ MNS.	%
1. All							126.7	100.0	141.9	100.0
2. Private							117.5	92.7	129.9	91.5
3. Ch. Bks.							95.2	75.1	103.1	72.6
4. Pr. N.B.							22.3	17.6	26.8	18.9
5. Public							9.2	7.3	12.0	8.4
6. Federal							9.2	7.3	12.0	8.4
7. Fed. Mon.							5.8	4.6	7.4	5.2
8. Prov.	–		–		–		–		–	

CONSTANT DOLLAR DATA (1935-39=100)

					1870
1. All					236.1
2. Private					216.1
3. Ch. Bks.					171.5
4. Pr. N.B.					44.6
5. Public					20.0
6. Federal					20.0
7. Fed Mon.					12.3
8. Prov.					–
9. Prices					60.1

ASSETS AS A PROPORTION OF GROSS NATIONAL PRODUCT CURRENT DOLLAR DATA

	%	%	%	%	%
1. All					30.9
2. Private					28.3
3. Ch. Bks.					22.5
4. Pr. N.B.					5.8
5. Public					2.6
6. Federal					2.6
7. Fed. Mon.					1.6
8. Prov.					–
9. G.N.P.					459

Canadian Financial Intermediaries
Canadian Assets 1870-1970
Summary

	1871		1872		1873		1874		1875	
CURRENT DOLLAR DATA										
	$ MNS.	%	$ MNS.	%	$ MNS.	%	$ MNS.	%	$ MNS.	%
1. All	171.0	100.0	203.4	100.0	227.5	100.0	261.3	100.0	249.3	100.0
2. Private	154.7	90.5	185.6	91.2	208.2	91.5	242.1	92.6	231.0	92.6
3. Ch. Bks.	121.6	71.1	146.8	72.2	163.0	71.6	190.6	72.9	173.5	69.6
4. Pr. N. B.	33.1	19.4	38.8	19.1	45.2	19.9	51.5	19.7	57.5	23.1
5. Public	16.3	9.5	17.8	8.8	19.3	8.5	19.2	7.3	18.3	7.3
6. Federal	16.3	9.5	17.8	8.8	19.3	8.5	19.2	7.3	18.3	7.3
7. Fed. Mon.	11.0	6.4	11.6	5.7	12.1	5.3	12.1	4.6	11.3	4.5
8. Prov.	–		–		–		–		–	
CONSTANT DOLLAR DATA										
1. All										
2. Private										
3. Ch. Bks.										
4. Pr. N.B.										
5. Public										
6. Federal										
7. Fed. Mon.										
8. Prov.										
9. Prices										
ASSETS AS A PROPORTION OF GROSS NATIONAL PRODUCT CURRENT DOLLAR DATA										
	%		%		%		%		%	
1. All										
2. Private										
3. Ch. Bks.										
4. Pr. N.B.										
5. Public										
6. Federal										
7. Fed. Mon.										
8. Prov.										
9. G.N.P.										

Canadian Financial Intermediaries
Canadian Assets 1870-1970
Summary

	1876		1877		1878		1879		1880	
CURRENT DOLLAR DATA										
	$MNS.	%	$MNS.	%	$MNS.	%	$MNS.	%	$MNS.	%
1. All	259.4	100.0	264.8	100.0	271.2	100.0	266.2	100.0	289.9	100.0
2. Private	240.9	92.9	244.7	92.4	251.9	92.9	242.9	91.2	259.9	89.6
3. Ch. Bks.	173.7	67.0	168.4	63.6	171.0	63.0	153.7	57.7	160.7	55.4
4. Pr. N.B.	67.2	25.9	76.3	28.8	80.9	29.8	89.2	33.5	99.2	34.2
5. Public	18.5	7.1	20.1	7.6	19.3	7.1	23.3	8.8	30.0	10.3
6. Federal	18.5	7.1	20.1	7.6	19.3	7.1	23.3	8.8	30.0	10.3
7. Fed. Mon.	11.1	4.3	11.6	4.4	10.1	3.7	12.3	4.6	14.2	4.9
8. Prov.	–		–		–		–		–	
CONSTANT DOLLAR DATA										
1. All									489.7	
2. Private									439.0	
3. Ch. Bks.									271.4	
4. Pr. N.B.									167.6	
5. Public									50.7	
6. Federal									50.7	
7. Fed. Mon.									24.0	
8. Prov.									–	
9. Prices									59.2	
ASSETS AS A PROPORTION OF GROSS NATIONAL PRODUCT CURRENT DOLLAR DATA										
	%		%		%		%		%	
1. All									49.9	
2. Private									44.7	
3. Ch. Bks.									27.6	
4. Pr. N.B.									17.1	
5. Public									5.2	
6. Federal									5.2	
7. Fed. Mon.									2.4	
8. Prov.									–	
9. G.N.P.									581	

Canadian Financial Intermediaries
Canadian Assets 1870-1970
Summary

	1881		1882		1883		1884		1885	
CURRENT DOLLAR DATA										
	$ MNS.	%	$ MNS.	%	$ MNS.	%	$ MNS.	%	$ MNS.	%
1. All	331.6	100.0	373.9	100.0	371.3	100.0	373.6	100.0	400.9	100.0
2. Private	294.8	88.9	331.6	88.7	325.3	87.6	324.2	86.8	345.9	86.3
3. Ch. Bks.	188.0	56.7	217.7	58.2	205.9	55.4	198.3	53.1	207.9	51.8
4. Pr. N.B.	106.8	32.2	113.9	30.5	119.4	32.2	125.9	33.7	138.0	34.4
5. Public	36.8	11.1	42.3	11.3	46.0	12.4	49.4	13.2	55.0	13.7
6. Federal	36.8	11.1	42.3	11.3	46.0	12.4	49.4	13.2	55.0	13.7
7. Fed. Mon.	15.0	4.5	16.1	4.3	16.8	4.5	16.4	4.4	17.8	4.4
8. Prov.	—		—		—		—		—	
CONSTANT DOLLAR DATA										
1. All										
2. Private										
3. Ch. Bks.										
4. Pr. N.B.										
5. Public										
6. Federal										
7. Fed. Mon.										
8. Prov.										
9. Prices										
ASSETS AS A PROPORTION OF GROSS NATIONAL PRODUCT CURRENT DOLLAR DATA										
	%		%		%		%		%	
1. All										
2. Private										
3. Ch. Bks.										
4. Pr. N.B.										
5. Public										
6. Federal										
7. Fed. Mon.										
8. Prov.										
9. G.N.P.										

Canadian Financial Intermediaries
Canadian Assets 1870-1970
Summary

	1886		1887		1888		1889		1890	
CURRENT DOLLAR DATA										
	$ MNS.	%	$ MNS.	%	$ MNS.	%	$ MNS.	%	$ MNS.	%
1. All	410.1	100.0	431.9	100.0	460.9	100.0	476.6	100.0	498.6	100.0
2. Private	354.0	86.3	374.8	86.8	401.3	87.1	419.6	88.0	443.6	89.0
3. Ch. Bks.	204.9	50.0	216.2	50.0	232.6	50.5	237.5	49.8	246.9	49.5
4. Pr. N.B.	149.1	36.4	158.6	36.7	168.7	36.6	182.1	38.2	196.7	39.4
5. Public	56.1	13.7	57.1	13.2	59.6	12.9	57.0	12.0	55.0	11.0
6. Federal	56.1	13.7	57.1	13.2	59.6	12.9	57.0	12.0	55.0	11.0
7. Fed. Mon.	15.3	3.7	15.7	3.6	16.6	3.6	15.1	3.2	15.6	3.1
8. Prov.	–		–		–		–		–	

CONSTANT DOLLAR DATA	1886	1887	1888	1889	1890
1. All					848.0
2 Private					754.4
3 Ch. Bks.					419.9
4. Pr. N.B.					334.5
5. Public					93.5
6. Federal					93.5
7. Fed. Mon.					26.5
8. Prov.					–
9. Prices					58.8

ASSETS AS A PROPORTION OF GROSS NATIONAL PRODUCT
CURRENT DOLLAR DATA

	1886	1887	1888	1889	1890
	%	%	%	%	%
1. All					62.1
2. Private					55.2
3. Ch. Bks.					30.7
4. Pr. N.B.					24.5
5. Public					6.8
6. Federal					6.8
7. Fed. Mon.					1.9
8. Prov.					–
9. G.N.P.					803

Canadian Financial Intermediaries
Canadian Assets 1870-1970
Summary

	1891		1892		1893		1894		1895	
CURRENT DOLLAR DATA										
	$ MNS.	%	$ MNS.	%	$ MNS.	%	$ MNS.	%	$ MNS.	%
1. All	519.9	100.0	567.4	100.0	579.1	100.0	593.8	100.0	616.5	100.0
2. Private	464.2	89.3	506.7	89.3	516.2	89.1	528.2	89.0	547.3	88.8
3. Ch. Bks.	256.0	49.2	283.0	49.9	282.4	48.8	285.5	48.1	296.1	48.0
4. Pr. N.B.	208.2	40.0	223.7	39.4	233.8	40.4	242.7	40.9	251.2	40.7
5. Public	55.7	10.7	60.7	10.7	62.9	10.9	65.6	11.0	69.2	11.2
6. Federal	55.7	10.7	60.7	10.7	62.9	10.9	65.6	11.0	69.2	11.2
7. Fed. Mon.	16.2	3.2	18.8	3.3	19.8	3.4	21.2	3.6	22.4	3.6
8. Prov.	—		—		—		—		—	
CONSTANT DOLLAR DATA										
1. All										
2. Private										
3. Ch. Bks.										
4. Pr. N.B.										
5 Public										
6. Federal										
7. Fed. Mon.										
8. Prov.										
9. Prices										
ASSETS AS A PROPORTION OF GROSS NATIONAL PRODUCT CURRENT DOLLAR DATA										
	%		%		%		%		%	
1. All										
2. Private										
3. Ch. Bks.										
4. Pr. N.B.										
5. Public										
6. Federal										
7. Fed. Mon.										
8. Prov.										
9. G.N.P.										

Canadian Financial Intermediaries
Canadian Assets 1870 - 1970
Summary

	1896		1897		1898		1899		1900	
CURRENT DOLLAR DATA										
	$ MNS.	%	$ MNS.	%	$ MNS.	%	$ MNS.	%	$ MNS.	%
1. All	635.7	100.0	669.3	100.0	716.0	100.0	774.8	100.0	831.8	100.0
2. Private	565.0	88.9	594.6	88.8	641.0	89.5	695.2	89.7	747.2	89.8
3. Ch. Bks.	303.1	47.7	321.0	48.0	355.1	49.6	397.3	51.3	437.3	52.6
4. Pr. N. B.	261.9	41.2	273.6	40.9	285.9	39.9	297.9	38.4	309.9	37.2
5. Public	70.7	11.1	74.7	11.2	75.0	10.5	79.6	10.3	84.6	10.2
6. Federal	70.7	11.1	74.7	11.2	75.0	10.5	79.6	10.3	84.6	10.2
7. Fed. Mon.	21.7	3.4	24.6	3.7	24.6	3.4	26.4	3.4	28.4	3.4
8. Prov.	–		–		–		–		–	
CONSTANT DOLLAR DATA										
1. All									1477.4	
2. Private									1327.1	
3. Ch. Bks.									776.7	
4. Pr. N. B.									550.4	
5. Public									150.3	
6. Federal									150.3	
7. Fed. Mon.									50.4	
8. Prov.									–	
9. Prices									56.3	
ASSETS AS A PROPORTION OF GROSS NATIONAL PRODUCT CURRENT DOLLAR DATA										
	%		%		%		%		%	
1. All									78.7	
2. Private									70.7	
3. Ch. Bks.									41.4	
4. Pr. N. B.									29.3	
5. Public									8.0	
6. Federal									8.0	
7. Fed. Mon.									2.7	
8. Prov.									–	
9. G.N.P.									1057	

Canadian Financial Intermediaries
Canadian Assets 1870 - 1970
Summary

	1901		1902		1903		1904		1905	
CURRENT DOLLAR DATA										
	$ MNS.	%	$ MNS.	%	$ MNS.	%	$ MNS.	%	$ MNS.	%
1. All	880.6	100.0	958.8	100.0	1049.2	100.0	1125.8	100.0	1219.1	100.0
2. Private	791.7	89.9	863.4	90.0	945.7	90.1	1015.5	90.2	1107.6	90.8
3. Ch. Bks.	466.3	53.0	524.9	54.7	587.5	56.0	633.9	56.3	700.9	57.5
4. Pr. N.B.	325.4	37.0	338.5	35.3	358.2	34.1	381.6	33.9	406.7	33.4
5. Public	88.9	10.1	95.4	9.9	103.5	9.9	110.3	9.8	111.5	9.1
6. Federal	88.9	10.1	95.4	9.9	103.5	9.9	110.3	9.8	111.5	9.1
7. Fed. Mon.	30.3	3.4	34.4	3.6	41.1	3.9	47.8	4.2	49.0	4.0
8. Prov.	—		—		—		—		—	
CONSTANT DOLLAR DATA										
1. All										
2. Private										
3. Ch. Bks.										
4. Pr. N.B.										
5. Public										
6. Federal										
7. Fed. Mon.										
8. Prov.										
9. Prices										
ASSETS AS A PROPORTION OF GROSS NATIONAL PRODUCT CURRENT DOLLAR DATA										
	%		%		%		%		%	
1. All										
2. Private										
3. Ch. Bks.										
4. Pr. N. B.										
5. Public										
6. Federal										
7. Fed. Mon.										
8. Prov.										
9. G.N.P.										

Canadian Financial Intermediaries
Canadian Assets 1870 - 1970
Summary

	1906		1907		1908		1909		1910	
CURRENT DOLLAR DATA										
	$ MNS.	%	$ MNS.	%	$ MNS.	%	$ MNS.	%	$ MNS.	%
1. All	1383.7	100.0	1407.0	100.0	1446.8	100.0	1618.6	100.0	1780.1	100.0
2. Private	1263.9	91.3	1281.0	91.0	1306.4	90.3	1471.5	90.9	1628.9	91.5
3. Ch. Bks.	835.4	60.4	832.5	59.2	823.3	56.9	947.8	58.6	1060.4	59.6
4. Pr. N. B.	428.5	31.0	448.5	31.9	483.1	33.4	523.7	32.4	568.5	31.9
5. Public	119.8	8.6	126.0	9.0	140.4	9.7	147.1	9.1	151.2	8.5
6. Federal	119.8	8.6	126.0	9.0	140.4	9.7	147.1	9.1	151.2	8.5
7. Fed. Mon.	56.5	4.1	62.6	4.4	79.4	5.5	87.0	5.4	90.7	5.1
8. Prov.	–	–	–		–		–		–	
CONSTANT DOLLAR DATA										
1. All									2568.7	
2. Private									2350.5	
3. Ch. Bks.									1530.2	
4. Pr. N.B.									820.3	
5. Public									218.2	
6. Federal									218.2	
7. Fed. Mon.									130.9	
8. Prov.									–	
9. Prices									69.3	
ASSETS AS A PROPORTION OF GROSS NATIONAL PRODUCT CURRENT DOLLAR DATA										
	%		%		%		%		%	
1. All									79.6	
2. Private									72.9	
3. Ch. Bks.									47.4	
4. Pr. N. B.									25.4	
5. Public									6.8	
6. Federal									6.8	
7. Fed. Mon.									4.0	
8. Prov.									–	
9. G. N. P.									2235	

Canadian Financial Intermediaries
Canadian Assets 1870 - 1970
Summary

	1911		1912		1913		1914		1915	
CURRENT DOLLAR DATA										
	$ MNS.	%	$ MNS.	%	$ MNS.	%	$ MNS.	%	$ MNS.	%
1. All	2024.8	100.0	2227.3	100.0	2303	100.0	2415	100.0	2529	100.0
2. Private	1848.0	91.3	2050.2	92.0	2111	91.7	2193	90.8	2289	90.5
3. Ch. Bks.	1213.6	59.9	1345.5	60.4	1323	57.4	1358	56.2	1415	56.0
4. Pr. N. B.	634.4	31.3	704.7	31.6	788	34.2	835	34.6	874	34.6
5. Public	176.8	8.7	177.1	8.0	192	8.3	222	9.2	240	9.5
6. Federal	176.8	8.7	177.1	8.0	192	8.3	222	9.2	240	9.5
7. Fed. Mon.	115.2	5.7	115.8	5.2	131	5.7	162	6.7	179	7.1
8. Prov.	–		–		–		–		–	
CONSTANT DOLLAR DATA										
1. All										
2. Private										
3. Ch. Bks.										
4. Pr. N. B.										
5. Public										
6. Federal										
7. Fed. Mon.										
8. Prov.										
9. Prices										
ASSETS AS A PROPORTION OF GROSS NATIONAL PRODUCT CURRENT DOLLAR DATA										
	%		%		%		%		%	
1. All			92.3							
2. Private			84.9							
3. Ch. Bks.			55.7							
4. Pr. N. B.			29.2							
5. Public			7.3							
6. Federal			7.3							
7. Fed. Mon.			4.8							
8. Prov.			–							
9. G. N. P.			2414							

Canadian Financial Intermediaries
Canadian Assets 1870-1970
Summary

	1916		1917		1918		1919		1920	
CURRENT DOLLAR DATA										
	$MNS.	%	$MNS.	%	$MNS.	%	$MNS.	%	$MNS.	%
1. All	2777	100.0	3286	100.0	3748	100.0	4028	100.0	4172	100.0
2. Private	2532	91.2	2949	89.7	3350	89.4	3593	89.2	3710	88.9
3. Ch. Bks.	1631	58.7	1985	60.4	2346	62.6	2529	62.8	2535	60.8
4. Pr. N. B.	901	32.4	964	29.3	1004	26.8	1064	26.4	1175	28.2
5. Public	245	8.8	337	10.2	398	10.6	435	10.8	462	11.1
6. Federal	245	8.8	337	10.2	392	10.4	415	10.3	434	10.4
7. Fed. Mon.	181	6.5	273	8.3	327	8.7	319	7.9	312	7.5
8. Prov.	–		–		6	.2	20	.4	28	.6
CONSTANT DOLLAR DATA										
1. All									2893	
2. Private									2573	
3. Ch. Bks.									1758	
4. Pr. N. B.									815	
5. Public									320	
6. Federal									301	
7. Fed. Mon.									216	
8. Prov.									19	
9. Prices									144.2	
ASSETS AS A PROPORTION OF GROSS NATIONAL PRODUCT CURRENT DOLLAR DATA										
	%		%		%		%		%	
1. All									75.4	
2. Private									67.1	
3. Ch. Bks.									45.8	
4. Pr. N. B.									21.2	
5. Public									8.4	
6. Federal									7.8	
7. Fed. Mon.									5.6	
8. Prov.									.5	
9. G. N. P.									5529	

Canadian Financial Intermediaries
Canadian Assets 1870-1970
Summary

	1921		1922		1923		1924		1925	
CURRENT DOLLAR DATA										
	$MNS.	%	$MNS.	%	$MNS.	%	$MNS.	%	$MNS.	%
1. All	3996	100.0	3945	100.0	4111	100.0	4324	100.0	4345	100.0
2. Private	3548	88.8	3499	88.7	3642	88.6	3819	88.3	3871	89.1
3. Ch. Bks.	2337	58.5	2189	55.5	2247	54.6	2314	53.5	2275	52.4
4. Pr. N. B.	1211	30.3	1310	33.2	1395	33.9	1505	34.8	1596	36.7
5. Public	448	11.2	446	11.3	469	11.4	505	11.7	474	10.9
6. Federal	411	10.3	393	10.0	396	9.6	414	9.6	384	8.8
7. Fed. Mon.	281	7.0	257	6.5	249	6.0	262	6.0	227	5.2
8. Prov.	37	.9	53	1.2	73	1.7	91	2.1	90	2.2

CONSTANT DOLLAR DATA

1. All
2. Private
3. Ch. Bks.
4. Pr. N.B.
5. Public
6. Federal
7. Fed. Mon.
8. Prov.
9. Prices

ASSETS AS A PROPORTION OF GROSS NATIONAL PRODUCT
CURRENT DOLLAR DATA

	%	%	%	%	%
1. All					
2. Private					
3. Ch. Bks.					
4. Pr. N. B.					
5. Public					
6. Federal					
7. Fed. Mon.					
8. Prov.					
9. G. N. P.					

Canadian Financial Intermediaries
Canadian Assets 1870-1970
Summary

CURRENT DOLLAR DATA

	1926		1927		1928		1929		1930	
	$MNS.	%	$MNS.	%	$MNS.	%	$MNS.	%	$MNS.	%
1. All	4544	100.0	5025	100.0	5497	100.0	5843	100.0	5744	100.0
2. Private	4080	898	4551	90.6	5021	91.3	5365	91.8	5282	92.0
3. Ch. Bks.	2267	49.9	2544	50.6	2781	50.6	2873	49.2	2635	45.9
4. Pr. N. B.	1813	39.9	2007	39.9	2240	40.7	2492	42.6	2647	46.1
5. Public	464	10.2	474	9.4	476	8.6	478	8.2	462	8.0
6. Federal	369	8.1	373	7.4	369	6.7	363	6.2	340	5.9
7. Fed. Mon.	210	4.6	221	4.4	222	4.0	204	3.5	175	3.0
8. Prov.	95	2.1	101	2.0	107	2.0	115	1.9	122	2.1

CONSTANT DOLLAR DATA

	1926	1927	1928	1929	1930
1. All	3904	4370	4801	5041	5097
2. Private	3505	3957	4385	4629	4687
3. Ch. Bks.	1948	2212	2429	2479	2338
4. Pr. N. B.	1558	1745	1956	2150	2349
5. Public	399	412	416	412	410
6. Federal	317	324	322	313	302
7. Fed. Mon.	180	192	194	176	155
8. Prov.	82	88	93	99	108
9. Prices	116.4	115.0	114.5	115.9	112.7

ASSETS AS A PROPORTION OF GROSS NATIONAL PRODUCT
CURRENT DOLLAR DATA

	1926	1927	1928	1929	1930
	%	%	%	%	%
1. All	88.3	90.4	90.8	95.2	100.4
2. Private	79.3	81.8	83.0	87.4	92.3
3. Ch. Bks.	44.0	45.7	46.0	46.8	46.1
4. Pr. N. B.	35.2	36.1	37.0	40.6	46.3
5. Public	9.0	8.5	7.9	7.8	8.1
6. Federal	7.2	6.7	6.1	5.9	5.9
7. Fed. Mon.	4.1	4.0	3.7	3.3	3.0
8. Prov.	1.8	1.8	1.8	1.9	2.1
9. G. N. P.	5146	5561	6050	6139	5720

Canadian Financial Intermediaries
Canadian Assets 1870-1970
Summary

	1931		1932		1933		1934		1935	
CURRENT DOLLAR DATA										
	% MNS.	%	$ MNS.	%	$ MNS.	%	$ MNS.	%	$ MNS.	%
1. All	5764	100.0	5631	100.0	5685	100.0	5919	100.0	6280	100.0
2. Private	5295	91.9	5128	91.1	5174	91.0	5351	90.4	5574	88.8
3. Ch. Bks.	2582	44.8	2463	43.7	2476	43.6	2515	42.5	2676	42.6
4. Pr. N. B.	2713	47.1	2665	47.3	2698	47.4	2836	47.9	2898	46.1
5. Public	469	8.1	503	8.9	511	9.0	568	9.6	706	11.2
6. Federal	344	6.0	372	6.6	371	6.5	421	7.1	543	8.6
7. Fed. Mon.	174	3.0	191	3.4	183	3.2	217	3.7	308	4.9
8. Prov.	125	2.2	131	2.3	140	2.4	147	2.6	163	2.5
CONSTANT DOLLAR DATA										
1. All	5438		5860		6035		6191		6535	
2. Private	4995		5336		5492		5597		5800	
3. Ch. Bks.	2436		2563		2628		2631		2784	
4. Pr. N. B.	2559		2773		2864		2966		3016	
5. Public	442		523		542		594		735	
6. Federal	324		387		394		440		565	
7. Fed. Mon.	164		199		194		227		320	
8. Prov.	118		136		149		154		170	
9. Prices	106.0		96.1		94.2		95.6		96.1	
ASSETS AS A PROPORTION OF GROSS NATIONAL PRODUCT CURRENT DOLLAR DATA										
	%		%		%		%		%	
1. All	122.8		147.6		162.8		149.1		146.0	
2. Private	112.8		134.4		148.2		134.8		129.6	
3. Ch. Bks.	55.0		64.6		70.9		63.4		62.2	
4. Pr. N. B.	57.8		69.9		77.3		71.4		67.4	
5. Public	10.0		13.2		14.6		14.3		16.4	
6. Federal	7.3		9.8		10.6		10.6		12.6	
7. Fed. Mon.	3.7		5.0		5.2		5.5		7.2	
8. Prov.	2.7		3.4		4.0		3.7		3.8	
9. G. N. P.	4693		3814		3492		3969		4301	

Canadian Financial Intermediaries
Canadian Assets 1870-1970
Summary

	1936		1937		1938		1939		1940	
CURRENT DOLLAR DATA										
	$MNS.	%	$MNS.	%	$MNS.	%	$MNS.	%	$MNS.	%
1. All	6636	100.0	6867	100.0	7054	100.0	7808	100.0	8066	100.0
2. Private	5846	88.1	6015	87.6	6155	87.2	6769	86.7	6900	85.5
3. Ch. Bks.	2803	42.2	2864	41.7	2948	41.8	3315	42.4	3303	40.9
4. Pr. N.B.	3043	45.8	3151	45.9	3207	45.5	3454	44.2	3597	44.6
5. Public	790	11.9	852	12.4	899	12.7	1039	13.3	1166	14.4
6. Federal	627	9.4	691	10.1	731	10.4	878	11.2	1001	12.4
7. Fed. Mon.	357	5.4	390	5.7	405	5.7	527	6.7	627	7.8
8. Prov.	163	2.4	161	2.3	168	2.4	161	2.2	165	2.1
CONSTANT DOLLAR DATA										
1. All	6696		6746		6943		7738		7645	
2. Private	5899		5909		6058		6709		6540	
3. Ch. Bks.	2828		2813		2902		3285		3131	
4. Pr. N. B.	3071		3095		3156		3423		3409	
5. Public	797		837		885		1030		1105	
6. Federal	633		679		719		870		949	
7. Fed. Mon.	360		383		399		522		594	
8. Prov.	164		158		165		160		156	
9. Prices	99.1		101.8		101.6		100.9		105.5	
ASSETS AS A PROPORTION OF GROSS NATIONAL PRODUCT CURRENT DOLLAR DATA										
	%		%		%		%		%	
1. All	143.2		131.0		133.8		138.9		120.2	
2. Private	126.2		114.8		116.7		120.4		102.8	
3. Ch. Bks.	60.5		54.6		55.9		59.0		49.2	
4. Pr. N.B.	65.7		60.1		60.8		61.4		53.6	
5. Public	17.0		16.2		17.0		18.5		17.4	
6. Federal	13.5		13.2		13.9		15.6		14.9	
7. Fed. Mon.	7.7		7.4		7.7		9.4		9.3	
8. Prov.	3.5		3.1		3.2		2.9		2.4	
9. G. N. P.	4634		5241		5272		5621		6713	

Canadian Financial Intermediaries
Canadian Assets 1870-1970
Summary

	1941		1942		1943		1944		1945	
CURRENT DOLLAR DATA										
	$MNS.	%	$MNS.	%	$MNS.	%	$MNS.	%	$MNS.	%
1. All	8893	100.0	9796	100.0	10987	100.0	12494	100.0	14139	100.0
2. Private	7447	83.7	8051	82.2	9043	82.3	10122	81.0	11324	80.1
3. Ch. Bks.	3670	41.3	4164	42.5	4910	44.7	5706	45.7	6517	46.1
4. Pr. N. B.	3777	42.5	3887	39.7	4133	37.6	4416	35.3	4807	34.0
5. Public	1446	16.2	1745	17.8	1944	17.7	2372	19.0	2815	19.9
6. Federal	1283	14.4	1580	16.1	1779	16.2	2202	17.6	2642	18.7
7. Fed. Mon.	843	9.5	1048	10.7	1308	11.9	1687	13.5	2032	14.4
8. Prov.	163	1.8	165	1.7	165	1.5	170	1.3	173	1.2

	1941	1942	1943	1944	1945
CONSTANT DOLLAR DATA					
1. All	7814	8239	8925	9838	10876
2. Private	6544	6771	7346	7970	8711
3. Ch. Bks.	3225	3502	3989	4493	5013
4. Pr. N. B.	3319	3269	3357	3477	3698
5. Public	1271	1468	1579	1868	2165
6. Federal	1127	1329	1445	1734	2032
7. Fed. Mon.	741	881	1062	1328	1563
8. Prov.	143	139	134	134	133
9. Prices	113.8	118.9	123.1	127.0	130.0

	1941	1942	1943	1944	1945
ASSETS AS A PROPORTION OF GROSS NATIONAL PRODUCT CURRENT DOLLAR DATA					
	%	%	%	%	%
1. All	107.4	95.4	99.4	105.4	119.2
2. Private	89.9	78.4	81.8	85.4	95.4
3. Ch. Bks.	44.3	40.6	44.4	48.2	54.9
4. Pr. N. B.	45.6	37.9	37.4	37.3	40.5
5. Public	17.4	17.0	17.6	20.0	23.7
6. Federal	15.5	15.4	16.1	18.6	22.3
7. Fed. Mon.	10.2	10.2	11.8	14.2	17.1
8. Prov.	2.0	1.6	1.5	1.4	1.4
9. G. N. P.	8282	10265	11053	11848	11863

Canadian Financial Intermediaries
Canadian Assets 1870-1970
Summary

	1946		1947		1948		1949		1950	
CURRENT DOLLAR DATA										
	$MNS.	%	$MNS.	%	$MNS.	%	$MNS.	%	$MNS.	%
1. All	15065	100.0	15863	100.0	17394	100.0	18444	100.0	20589	100.0
2. Private	12179	80.8	12831	80.9	13927	80.1	14649	79.4	16297	79.2
3. Ch. Bks.	6924	46.0	7067	44.6	7705	44.3	7853	42.6	8636	41.9
4. Pr. N. B.	5255	34.9	5764	36.3	6222	35.8	6796	36.8	7661	37.2
5. Public	2886	19.2	3032	19.1	3467	19.9	3795	20.6	4292	20.8
6. Federal	2688	17.8	2827	17.8	3219	18.5	3528	19.1	4020	19.5
7. Fed. Mon.	1949	12.9	1926	12.1	2059	11.8	2126	11.5	2350	11.4
8. Prov.	198	1.4	205	1.3	248	1.4	267	1.5	272	1.3
CONSTANT DOLLAR DATA										
1. All	11251		10887		10638		10837		11826	
2. Private	9096		8806		8518		8607		9361	
3. Ch. Bks.	5171		4850		4712		4614		4960	
4. Pr. N. B.	3924		3956		3806		3993		4400	
5. Public	2155		2081		2120		2230		2465	
6. Federal	2007		1940		1969		2073		2309	
7. Fed. Mon.	1456		1322		1259		1249		1350	
8. Prov.	148		141		152		157		156	
9. Prices	133.9		145.7		163.5		170.2		174.1	
ASSETS AS A PROPORTION OF GROSS NATIONAL PRODUCT CURRENT DOLLAR DATA										
	%		%		%		%		%	
1. All	126.7		120.4		115.0		113.2		114.7	
2. Private	102.5		97.4		92.1		89.9		90.8	
3. Ch. Bks.	58.2		53.7		50.9		48.2		48.1	
4. Pr. N. B.	44.2		43.8		41.1		41.7		42.7	
5. Public	24.3		23.0		22.9		23.3		23.9	
6. Federal	22.6		21.5		21.3		21.6		22.4	
7. Fed. Mon.	16.4		14.6		13.6		13.0		13.1	
8. Prov.	1.7		1.6		1.6		1.6		1.5	
9. G. N. P.	11885		13169		15127		16300		17955	

Canadian Financial Intermediaries
Canadian Assets 1870-1970
Summary

	1951		1952		1953		1954		1955	
CURRENT DOLLAR DATA										
	$MNS.	%	$MNS.	%	$MNS.	%	$MNS.	%	$MNS.	%
1. All	21839	100.0	23487	100.0	25324	100.0	27499	100.0	30539	100.0
2. Private	16943	77.6	18428	78.5	19882	78.5	21773	79.2	24531	80.3
3. Ch. Bks.	8589	39.3	9148	38.9	9592	37.9	10291	37.4	11575	37.9
4. Pr. N. B.	8354	38.3	9280	39.5	10290	40.6	11482	41.8	12956	42.4
5. Public	4896	22.4	5059	21.5	5442	21.5	5726	20.8	6008	19.7
6. Federal	4612	21.1	4743	20.2	5104	20.2	5347	19.4	5591	18.3
7. Fed. Mon.	2444	11.2	2381	10.1	2437	9.6	2401	8.7	2620	8.6
8. Prov.	284	1.3	316	1.3	338	1.3	379	1.4	417	1.4
CONSTANT DOLLAR DATA										
1. All	11234		11581		12487		13349		14725	
2. Private	8716		9087		9804		10569		11828	
3. Ch. Bks	4418		4511		4730		4995		5581	
4. Pr. N. B.	4297		4576		5074		5574		6247	
5. Public	2518		2494		2683		2780		2897	
6. Federal	2372		2339		2517		2596		2696	
7. Fed. Mon.	1257		1174		1202		1165		1263	
8. Prov.	146		156		167		184		201	
9. Prices	194.4		202.8		202.8		206.0		207.4	
ASSETS AS A PROPORTION OF GROSS NATIONAL PRODUCT CURRENT DOLLAR DATA										
	%		%		%		%		%	
1. All	103.7		97.7		100.0		109.0		109.5	
2. Private	80.5		76.6		78.5		86.3		87.9	
3. Ch. Bks.	40.8		38.0		37.9		40.8		41.5	
4. Pr. N. B.	39.7		38.6		40.6		45.5		46.4	
5. Public	23.2		21.0		21.5		22.7		21.5	
6. Federal	21.9		19.7		20.2		21.2		20.0	
7. Fed. Mon.	11.6		9.9		9.6		9.5		9.4	
8. Prov.	1.3		1.3		1.3		1.5		1.5	
9. G. N. P.	21060		24042		25327		25233		27895	

Canadian Financial Intermediaries
Canadian Assets 1870-1970
Summary

	1956		1957		1958		1959		1960	
CURRENT DOLLAR DATA										
	$MNS.	%	$MNS.	%	$MNS.	%	$MNS.	%	$MNS.	%
1. All	32777	100.0	34876	100.0	39112	100.0	41384	100.0	44948	100.0
2. Private	26350	80.4	27924	80.1	30876	78.9	32471	78.5	35189	78.3
3. Ch. Bks	11942	36.4	12274	35.2	13676	35.0	13442	32.5	14192	31.6
4. Pr. N. B.	14408	44.0	15650	44.9	17200	44.0	19029	46.0	20997	46.7
5. Public	6427	196	6952	19.9	8236	21.0	8913	21.5	9759	21.7
6. Federal	5973	18.2	6452	18.5	7712	19.7	8335	20.1	9124	20.3
7. Fed Mon.	2548	7.8	2659	7.6	2944	7.5	2968	7.2	3044	6.8
8. Prov.	454	1.4	500	1.4	524	1.3	578	1.4	635	1.4
CONSTANT DOLLAR DATA										
1. All	15281		15932		17626		18247		19577	
2. Private	12284		12756		13914		14317		15326	
3. Ch. Bks.	5567		5607		6163		5927		6181	
4. Pr. N. B.	6717		7149		7751		8390		9145	
5. Public	2996		3176		3712		3930		4250	
6. Federal	2785		2947		3475		3675		3974	
7. Fed. Mon.	1188		1215		1327		1309		1326	
8. Prov.	212		228		236		255		276	
9. Prices	214.5		218.9		221.9		226.8		229.6	
ASSETS AS A PROPORTION OF GROSS NATIONAL PRODUCT CURRENT DOLLAR DATA										
	%		%		%		%		%	
1. All	104.5		106.0		114.7		114.2		119.0	
2. Private	84.0		84.8		90.6		89.6		93.2	
3. Ch. Bks.	38.1		37.3		40.1		37.1		37.6	
4. Pr. N. B.	45.9		47.6		50.4		52.5		55.6	
5. Public	20.5		21.1		24.2		24.6		25.8	
6. Federal	19.0		19.6		22.6		23.0		24.2	
7. Fed. Mon.	8.1		8.1		8.6		8.2		8.0	
8. Prov.	1.4		1.5		1.5		1.6		1.7	
9. G. N. P.	31374		32907		34094		36226		37775	

Canadian Financial Intermediaries
Canadian Assets 1870-1970
Summary

	1961		1962		1963		1964		1965	
CURRENT DOLLAR DATA										
	$ MNS.	%	$ MNS.	%	$ MNS.	%	$ MNS.	%	$ MNS.	%
1. All	49711	100.0	53541	100.0	59029	100.0	64954	100.0	73412	100.0
2. Private	38904	78.3	42069	78.6	46570	78.9	51202	78.8	57972	79.0
3. Ch. Bks.	15644	31.5	16397	30.6	17858	30.2	18694	28.8	21196	28.9
4. Pr. N. B.	23260	46.8	25672	47.9	28712	48.6	32508	50.0	36776	50.1
5. Public	10807	21.7	11472	21.4	12459	21.1	13752	21.2	15440	21.0
6. Federal	10099	20.3	10722	20.0	11618	19.7	12791	19.7	14351	19.6
7. Fed. Mon.	3243	6.5	3231	6.0	3445	5.8	3642	5.6	3956	5.4
8. Prov.	708	1.4	750	1.3	841	1.3	961	1.4	1089	1.5
CONSTANT DOLLAR DATA										
1. All	21529		22861		24740		26588		29028	
2. Private	16849		17963		19518		20959		22923	
3. Ch. Bks.	6775		7001		7484		7652		8381	
4. Pr. N. B.	10074		10962		12034		13306		14542	
5. Public	4680		4898		5222		5629		6105	
6. Federal	4374		4578		4869		5236		5674	
7. Fed. Mon.	1404		1380		1444		1491		1564	
8. Prov.	307		320		352		393		431	
9. Prices	230.9		234.2		238.6		244.3		252.9	
ASSETS AS A PROPORTION OF GROSS NATIONAL PRODUCT CURRENT DOLLAR DATA										
	%		%		%		%		%	
1. All	127.2		126.4		129.8		130.5		133.7	
2. Private	99.5		99.3		102.4		102.8		105.6	
3. Ch. Bks.	40.0		38.7		39.3		37.6		38.6	
4. Pr. N. B.	59.5		60.6		63.2		65.3		67.0	
5. Public	27.6		27.1		27.4		27.6		28.1	
6. Federal	25.8		25.3		25.6		25.7		26.1	
7. Fed. Mon.	8.3		7.6		7.6		7.3		7.2	
8. Prov.	1.8		1.8		1.8		1.9		2.0	
9. G. N. P.	39080		42353		45465		49783		54897	

Canadian Financial Intermediaries
Canadian Assets 1870-1970
Summary

	1966		1967		1968		1969		1970	
CURRENT DOLLAR DATA										
	$MNS.	%	$MNS.	%	$MNS.	%	$MNS.	%	$MNS.	%
1. All	80366	100.0	89373	100.0	100310	100.0				
2. Private	62206	77.4	68466	76.6	76791	76.6				
3. Ch. Bks.	22507	28.0	25199	28.2	28939	28.9	31000		33616	
4. Pr. N. B.	39699	49.4	43267	48.4	47852	47.7				
5. Public	18160	22.6	20907	23.4	23519	23.4				
6. Federal	16020	19.9	17766	19.9	19282	19.2				
7. Fed. Mon.	4207	5.2	4412	4.9	4636	4.6				
8. Prov.	2140	2.7	3141	3.5	4237	4.2				

	1966	1967	1968	1969	1970
CONSTANT DOLLAR DATA					
1. All	30394	32689	35445		
2. Private	23526	25042	27135		
3. Ch. Bks.	8512	9217	10226	10462	10900
4. Pr. N. B.	15014	15825	16909		
5. Public	6868	7647	8310		
6. Federal	6059	6498	6813		
7. Fed. Mon.	1591	1614	1638		
8. Prov.	809	1149	1497		
9. Prices	264.4	273.4	283.0	296.3	308.4
ASSETS AS A PROPORTION OF GROSS NATIONAL PRODUCT CURRENT DOLLAR DATA					
	%	%	%	%	%
1. All	130.8	136.0	140.5		
2. Private	101.3	104.2	107.6		
3. Ch. Bks.	36.6	38.3	40.6	39.5	39.8
4. Pr. N. B.	64.6	65.9	67.0		
5. Public	29.6	31.8	32.9		
6. Federal	26.1	27.0	27.0		
7. Fed. Mon.	6.8	6.7	6.5		
8. Prov.	3.5	4.8	5.9		
9. G. N. P.	61421	65722	71388	78560	84468

Appendix Table B
Canadian Financial Intermediaries
Canadian Assets 1870-1970
(millions of dollars and per cent of total)

Private

1. Chartered Banks
2. Quebec Savings Banks
3. Life Insurance Companies
4. Fraternal Benefit Societies
5. Fire and Casualty Insurance Companies
6. Building Societies and Mortgage Loan Companies
7. Trust Companies
8. Consumer credit companies
   (a) Consumer loan companies
   (b) Sales Finance Companies
9. Investment Companies
   (a) Canadian Mutual Funds
   (b) Non-Resident Owned Mutual Funds
   (c) Closed-End Funds
   (d) Holding Companies
10. Caisses Populaires and Credit Unions – Locals
11. Caisses Populaires and Credit Unions – Centrals
12. Trusteed Pension Funds
13. Development and other companies

Public

14. Dominion Notes
15. Bank of Canada
16. Government and Post Office Savings Banks
17. Federal Annuity, Insurance and Pension Account
18. Industrial Development Bank
19. Farm Credit Corporation
20. Veterans Land Act
21. Central Mortgage and Housing Corporation
22. Export Credits Insurance Corporation
23. Canada Deposit Insurance Corporation
24. Canada Pension Plan
25. Caisse de dépôt et placement du Québec
26. Provincial Savings Institutions
27. Provincial Superannuation and Pension Accounts
28. Provincial Agricultural and Fisheries Loans
29. Provincial Industrial Development Loans
30. Provincial Miscellaneous Loan Plans

Appendix Table B (continued)
Canadian Financial Intermediaries
Canadian Assets 1870-1970

	1867		1868		1869		1870	
	$MNS.	%	$MNS.	%	$MNS.	%	$MNS.	%
Private								
1. Ch. Bks.					95.2	75.1	103.1	72.6
2. Q.S.B.					3.9	3.1	5.2	3.7
3. Life Ins.					2.6	2.0	3.4	2.4
4. Frat. Soc.								
5. Fire & Cas.					4.2	3.3	4.5	3.2
6. Mtge. Loan					11.6	9.2	13.7	9.6
7. Trust								
8. Cons. Loan								
(a) Con. L.								
(b) Fin.								
9. Inv. Cos.								
(a) Mut.								
(b) Non-Res.								
(c) Closed								
(d) Holding								
10. CP&CU-lcs.								
11. CP&CU-cens.								
12. Pension								
13. Dev. & other								
Public								
14. Dom. Notes	4.3	71.7	4.3	63.2	5.8	4.6	7.4	5.2
15. B. of C.								
16. P.O.	1.7	28.3	2.5	36.8	3.4	2.7	4.6	3.2
17. Fed. Ann.								
18. I.D.B.								
19. F.C.C.								
20. V.L.A.								
21. C.M.H.C.								
22. E.C.I.C.								
23. C.D.I.C.								
24. C.P.P.								
25. C. de dépôt								
26. Pr. Sav.								
27. Pr. Ann.								
28. Pr. Ag. Lo.								
29. Pr. Ind. Lo.								
30. Pr. Misc.								

Canadian Financial Intermediaries
Canadian Assets 1870-1970

	1871		1872		1873		1874		1875	
	$MNS.	%	$MNS.	%	$MNS.	%	$MNS.	%	$MNS.	%
Private										
1. Ch. Bks.	121.6	71.1	146.8	72.2	163.0	71.6	190.6	72.9	173.5	69.6
2. Q.S.B.	7.1	4.2	7.8	3.8	8.5	3.7	8.4	3.2	8.3	3.3
3. Life Ins.	3.7	2.2	4.3	2.1	5.4	2.4	6.0	2.3	6.9	2.8
4. Frat. Soc.										
5. Fire & Cas.	5.5	3.2	6.1	3.0	7.0	3.1	8.2	3.1	8.4	3.4
6. Mtge. Loan	16.8	9.8	20.6	10.1	24.3	10.7	29.0	11.1	33.9	13.6
7. Trust										
8. Cons. Loan										
(a) Con. L.										
(b) Fin.										
9. Inv. Cos.										
(a) Mut.										
(b) Non-Res.										
(c) Closed										
(d) Holding										
10. CP&CU-lcs.										
11. CP&CU-cens.										
12. Pension										
13. Dev. & other										
Public										
14. Dom. Notes	11.0	6.4	11.6	5.7	12.1	5.3	12.1	4.6	11.3	4.5
15. B. of C.										
16. P.O.	5.3	3.1	6.2	3.0	7.2	3.2	7.1	2.7	7.0	2.8
17. Fed. Ann.										
18. I.D.B.										
19. F.C.C.										
20. V.L.A.										
21. C.M.H.C.										
22. E.C.I.C.										
23. C.D.I.C.										
24. C.P.P.										
25. C. de dépôt										
26. Pr. Sav.										
27. Pr. Ann.										
28. Pr. Ag. Lo.										
29. Pr. Ind. Lo.										
30. Pr. Misc.										

Canadian Financial Intermediaries
Canadian Assets 1870-1970

	1876		1877		1878		1879		1880	
	$ MNS.	%	$ MNS.	%	$ MNS.	%	$ MNS.	%	$ MNS.	%
Private										
1. Ch. Bks.	173.7	67.0	168.4	63.6	171.0	63.0	153.7	57.7	160.7	55.4
2. Q.S.B.	8.5	3.3	7.1	2.7	6.9	2.5	7.3	2.7	8.9	3.1
3. Life Ins.	7.4	2.8	8.1	3.0	8.5	3.1	9.6	3.6	9.8	3.4
4. Frat. Soc.										
5. Fire & Cas.	9.2	3.5	9.5	3.6	9.1	3.4	9.5	3.6	9.1	3.1
6. Mtge. Loan	42.1	16.2	51.6	19.5	56.4	20.8	62.8	23.6	71.4	24.6
7. Trust										
8. Cons. Loan										
(a) Con. L.										
(b) Fin.										
9. Inv. Cos.										
(a) Mut.										
(b) Non-Res.										
(c) Closed										
(d) Holding										
10. CP&CU-1cs.										
11. CP&CU-cens.										
12. Pension										
13. Dev. & other										
Public										
14. Dom. Notes	11.1	4.3	11.6	4.4	10.1	3.7	12.3	4.6	14.2	4.9
15. B. of C.										
16. P.O.	7.4	2.8	8.5	3.2	9.2	3.4	11.0	4.1	15.8	5.4
17. Fed. Ann.										
18. I.D.B.										
19. F.C.C.										
20. V.L.A.										
21. C.M.H.C.										
22. E.C.I.C.										
23. C.D.I.C.										
24. C.P.P.										
25. C. de dépôt										
26. Pr. Sav.										
27. Pr. Ann.										
28. Pr. Ag. Lo.										
29. Pr. Ind. Lo.										
30. Pr. Misc.										

Canadian Financial Intermediaries
Canadian Assets 1870-1970

	1881		1882		1883		1884		1885	
	$ MNS.	%	$ MNS.	%	$ MNS.	%	$ MNS.	%	$ MNS.	%
Private										
1. Ch. Bks.	188.0	56.7	217.7	58.2	205.9	55.4	198.3	53.1	207.9	51.8
2. Q.S.B.	10.3	3.1	10.6	2.8	10.6	2.8	10.6	2.8	10.7	2.7
3. Life Ins.	12.0	3.6	13.6	3.6	15.4	4.1	17.9	4.8	20.5	5.1
4. Frat. Soc.										
5. Fire & Cas.	8.8	2.6	8.8	2.4	9.3	2.5	10.0	2.7	10.2	2.5
6. Mtge. Loan	75.7	22.8	80.9	21.6	84.1	22.6	87.4	23.4	96.6	24.1
7. Trust										
8. Cons. Loan										
(a) Con. L.										
(b) Fin.										
9. Inv. Cos.										
(a) Mut.										
(b) Non-Res.										
(c) Closed										
(d) Holding										
10. CP&CU-lcs.										
11. CP&CU-cens.										
12. Pension										
13. Dev. & other										
Public										
14. Dom. Notes	15.0	4.5	16.1	4.3	16.8	4.5	16.4	4.4	17.8	4.4
15. B. of C.										
16. P.O.	21.8	6.6	26.2	7.0	29.2	7.9	33.0	8.8	37.2	9.3
17. Fed. Ann.										
18. I.D.B.										
19. F.C.C.										
20. V.L.A.										
21. C.M.H.C.										
22 E.C.I.C.										
23. C.D.I.C.										
24 C.P.P.										
25. C. de dépôt										
26 Pr. Sav.										
27. Pr. Ann.										
28. Pr. Ag. Lo.										
29. Pr. Ind. Lo.										
30. Pr. Misc.										

Canadian Financial Intermediaries
Canadian Assets 1870-1970

	1886		1887		1888		1889		1890	
	$MNS.	%	$MNS.	%	$MNS.	%	$MNS.	%	$MNS.	%
Private										
1. Ch. Bks.	204.9	50.0	216.2	50.0	232.6	50.5	237.5	49.8	246.9	49.5
2. Q.S.B.	11.3	2.8	12.0	2.8	12.3	2.7	12.7	2.7	12.8	2.6
3. Life Ins.	22.8	5.6	27.1	6.3	31.4	6.8	36.9	7.7	43.1	8.6
4. Frat. Soc.	—		—		1.0	0.2	1.2	0.2	1.4	0.3
5. Fire & Cas.	10.9	2.6	12.0	2.8	13.4	2.9	15.1	3.2	17.4	3.5
6. Mtge. Loan	104.1	25.4	107.5	24.9	110.6	24.0	116.2	24.4	122.0	24.5
7. Trust										
8. Cons. Loan										
(a) Con. L.										
(b) Fin.										
9. Inv. Cos.										
(a) Mut.										
(b) Non-Res.										
(c) Closed										
(d) Holding										
10. CP&CU-lcs.										
11. CP&CU-cens.										
12. Pension										
13. Dev. & other										
Public										
14. Dom. Notes	15.3	3.7	15.7	3.6	16.6	3.6	15.1	3.2	15.6	3.1
15. B. of C.										
16. P.O.	40.8	9.9	41.4	9.6	43.0	9.3	41.9	8.8	39.4	7.9
17. Fed. Ann.										
18. I.D.B.										
19. F.C.C.										
20. V.L.A.										
21. C.M.H.C.										
22. E.C.I.C.										
23. C.D.I.C.										
24. C.P.P.										
25. C. de dépôt										
26. Pr. Sav.										
27. Pr. Ann.										
28. Pr. Ag. Lo.										
29. Pr. Ind. Lo.										
30. Pr. Misc.										

Canadian Financial Intermediaries
Canadian Assets 1870-1970

	1891		1892		1893		1894		1895	
	$MNS.	%	$MNS.	%	$MNS.	%	$MNS.	%	$MNS.	%
Private										
1. Ch. Bks.	256.0	49.2	283.0	49.9	282.4	48.8	285.5	48.1	296.1	48.0
2. Q.S.B.	13.9	2.7	14.8	2.6	14.9	2.6	15.2	2.6	16.4	2.7
3. Life Ins.	48.2	9.3	55.7	9.8	61.6	10.6	68.1	11.5	73.2	11.9
4. Frat. Soc.	1.7	0.3	2.0	0.4	2.4	0.4	2.9	0.5	3.5	0.6
5. Fire & Cas.	18.0	3.5	19.1	3.4	20.0	3.4	20.2	3.4	20.8	3.4
6. Mtge. Loan	126.4	24.3	132.1	23.3	134.9	23.3	136.3	23.0	137.3	22.3
7. Trust										
8. Cons. Loan										
(a) Con. L.										
(b) Fin.										
9. Inv. Cos.										
(a) Mut.										
(b) Non-Res.										
(c) Closed										
(d) Holding										
10. CP&CU-lcs.										
CP&CU-cens.										
12. Pension										
13. Dev. & other										
Public										
14. Dom. Notes	16.2	3.2	18.8	3.3	19.8	3.4	21.2	3.6	22.4	3.6
15. B. of C.										
16. P.O.	39.5	7.6	41.9	7.4	43.1	7.4	44.4	7.5	46.8	7.6
17. Fed. Ann.										
18. I.D.B.										
19. F.C.C.										
20. V.L.A.										
21. C.M.H.C.										
22. E.C.I.C.										
23. C.D.I.C.										
24. C.P.P.										
25. C. de dépôt										
26. Pr. Sav.										
27. Pr. Ann.										
28. Pr. Ag. Lo.										
29. Pr. Ind. Lo.										
30. Pr. Misc.										

Canadian Financial Intermediaries
Canadian Assets 1870-1970

	1896		1897		1898		1899		1900	
	$ MNS.	%	$MNS.	%	$ MNS.	%	$ MNS.	%	$ MNS.	%
Private										
1. Ch. Bks.	303.1	47.7	321.0	48.0	355.1	49.6	397.3	51.3	437.3	52.6
2. Q.S.B.	16.8	2.6	17.1	2.6	17.8	2.5	19.1	2.5	20.8	2.5
3. Life Ins.	81.1	12.8	88.4	13.2	95.4	13.3	104.0	13.4	108.7	13.1
4. Frat. Soc.	4.2	0.7	5.0	0.7	6.1	0.8	7.2	0.9	8.5	1.0
5. Fire & Cas.	21.7	3.4	22.9	3.4	23.8	3.3	25.7	3.3	27.6	3.3
6. Mtge. Loan	138.1	21.7	136.0	20.3	137.1	19.1	135.1	17.4	134.7	16.2
7. Trust	–		4.2	0.6	5.7	0.8	6.8	0.9	9.6	1.2
8. Cons. Loan										
(a) Con. L.										
(b) Fin.										
9. Inv. Cos.										
(a) Mut.										
(b) Non-Res.										
(c) Closed										
(d) Holding										
10. CP&CU-lcs.										
11. CP&CU-cens.										
12. Pension										
13. Dev. & other										
Public										
14. Dom. Notes	21.7	3.4	24.6	3.7	24.6	3.4	26.4	3.4	28.4	3.4
15. B. of C.										
16. P.O.	49.0	7.7	50.1	7.5	50.3	7.0	53.1	6.8	56.1	6.7
17. Fed. Ann.					.1	...	.1	...	.1	...
18. I.D.B.										
19. F.C.C.										
20. V.L.A.										
21. C.M.H.C.										
22. E.C.I.C.										
23. C.D.I.C.										
24. C.P.P.										
25. C. de dépôt										
26. Pr. Sav.										
27. Pr. Ann.										
28. Pr. Ag. Lo.										
29. Pr.Ind.Lo.										
30. Pr. Misc.										

Canadian Financial Intermediaries
Canadian Assets 1870-1970

	1901		1902		1903		1904		1905	
	$ MNS.	%	$ MNS.	%	$ MNS.	%	$ MNS.	%	$ MNS.	%
Private										
1. Ch. Bks.	466.3	53.0	524.9	54.7	587.5	56.0	633.9	56.3	700.9	57.5
2. Q.S.B.	22.2	2.5	23.4	2.4	25.1	2.4	26.7	2.4	29.1	2.4
3. Life Ins.	115.2	13.1	123.0	12.8	130.7	12.4	142.4	12.6	151.9	12.5
4. Frat. Soc.	9.8	1.1	11.4	1.2	13.4	1.3	15.4	1.4	18.0	1.5
5. Fire & Cas.	29.2	3.3	31.3	3.3	33.8	3.2	35.4	3.1	37.9	3.1
6. Mtge. Loan	138.2	15.7	137.4	14.3	140.1	13.4	144.4	12.8	149.4	12.2
7. Trust	10.8	1.2	12.0	1.2	15.1	1.4	17.3	1.5	20.4	1.7
8. Cons. Loan										
(a) Con L.										
(b) Fin.										
9. Inv. Cos.										
(a) Mut.										
(b) Non-Res.										
(c) Closed										
(d) Holding										
10. CP & CU-lcs.										
11. CP & CU-cens.										
12. Pension										
13. Dev. & other										
Public										
14. Dom. Notes	30.3	3.4	34.4	3.6	41.1	3.9	47.8	4.2	49.0	4.0
15. B. of C.										
16. P.O.	58.4	6.6	60.8	6.3	62.1	5.9	62.0	5.5	61.9	5.1
17. Fed. Ann.	.2	...	.2	...	.3	...	.5	...	.6	...
18. I.D.B.										
19. F.C.C.										
20. V.L.A.										
21. C.M.H.C.										
22. E.C.I.C.										
23. C.D.I.C.										
24. C.P.P.										
25. C. de dépôt										
26. Pr. Sav.										
27. Pr. Ann.										
28. Pr. Ag. Lo.										
29. Pr. Ind. Lo.										
30. Pr. Misc.										

Canadian Financial Intermediaries
Canadian Assets 1870-1970

	1906		1907		1908		1909		1910	
	$MNS.	%	$MNS.	%	$MNS	%	$MNS	%	$MNS	%
Private										
1. Ch. Bks.	835.4	60.4	832.5	59.2	823.3	56.9	947.8	58.6	1060.4	59.6
2. Q.S.B.	30.8	2.2	31.4	2.2	32.4	2.2	34.4	2.1	37.1	2.1
3. Life Ins.	158.8	11.5	165.5	11.8	182.8	12.6	196.8	12.2	212.3	11.9
4. Frat. Soc.	20.4	1.5	22.4	1.6	25.0	1.7	28.8	1.8	32.4	1.8
5. Fire & Cas.	41.8	3.0	46.3	3.3	49.8	3.4	53.7	3.3	58.9	3.3
6. Mtge. Loan	151.9	11.0	155.2	11.0	164.0	11.3	177.9	11.0	193.4	10.9
7. Trust	24.8	1.8	27.7	2.0	29.1	2.0	32.1	2.0	34.4	1.9
8. Cons. Loan										
(a) Con. L.										
(b) Fin.										
9. Inv. Cos.										
(a) Mut.										
(b) Non-Res.										
(c) Closed										
(d) Holding										
10. CP&CU-lcs.										
11. CP&CU-cens.										
12. Pension										
13. Dev. & other										
Public										
14. Dom. Notes	56.5	4.1	62.6	4.4	79.4	5.5	87.0	5.4	90.7	5.1
15. B. of C.										
16. P.O.	62.6	4.5	62.6	4.4	59.9	4.1	58.3	3.6	58.0	3.2
17. Fed. Ann.	.7	...	.8	...	1.1	.1	1.8	.1	2.5	.1
18. I.D.B.										
19. F.C.C.										
20. V.L.A.										
21. C.M.H.C.										
22. E.C.I.C.										
23. C.D.I.C.										
24. C.P.P.										
25. C. de dépôt										
26. Pr. Sav.										
27. Pr. Ann.										
28. Pr. Ag. Lo.										
29. Pr Ind. Lo.										
30. Pr. Misc.										

Canadian Financial Intermediaries
Canadian Assets 1870-1970

	1911		1912		1913		1914		1915	
	$MNS.	%	$MNS.	%	$MNS.	%	$MNS.	%	$MNS.	%
Private										
1. Ch. Bks.	1213.6	59.9	1345.5	60.4	1323	57.4	1358	56.2	1415	56.0
2. Q.S.B.	42.2	2.1	45.5	2.0	44	1.9	42	1.7	44	1.7
3. Life Ins.	235.6	11.6	263.5	11.8	326	14.1	350	14.5	364	14.4
4. Frat. Soc.	36.5	1.8	40.1	1.8	43	1.9	46	1.9	68	2.7
5. Fire & Cas.	65.6	3.2	74.4	3.3	71	3.1	80	3.3	73	2.9
6. Mtge. Loan	209.7	10.4	228.1	10.2	243	10.6	255	10.6	260	10.3
7. Trust	44.8	2.2	53.1	2.4	61	2.6	62	2.6	63	2.5
8. Cons. Loan										
(a) Con. L.										
(b) Fin.										
9. Inv. Cos.										
(a) Mut.										
(b) Non-Res.										
(c) Closed										
(d) Holding										
10. CP&CU-lcs.	–		–		–		–		2	.1
11. CP&CU-cens.	–		–		–		–			
12. Pension										
13. Dev. & other										
Public										
14. Dom.Notes	115.2	5.7	115.8	5.2	131	5.7	162	6.7	179	7.1
15. B. of C.										
16. P.O.	58.3	2.9	57.0	2.6	56	2.4	54	2.2	54	2.1
17. Fed. Ann.	3.3	.2	4.3	.2	5	.2	6	.2	7	.3
18. I.D.B.										
19. F.C.C.										
20. V.L.A.										
21. C.M.H.C.										
22. E.C.I.C.										
23. C.D.I.C.										
24. C.P.P.										
25. C. de dépôt										
26. Pr. Sav.										
27. Pr. Ann.										
28. Pr. Ag. Lo.										
29. Pr. Ind. Lo.										
30. Pr. Misc.										

Canadian Financial Intermediaries
Canadian Assets 1870-1970

	1916		1917		1918		1919		1920	
	$MNS.	%	$MNS.	%	$MNS.	%	$MNS.	%	$MNS.	%
Private										
1. Ch. Bks.	1631	58.7	1985	60.4	2346	62.6	2529	62.8	2535	60.8
2. Q.S.B.	48	1.7	49	1.5	53	1.4	58	1.4	63	1.5
3. Life Ins.	383	13.8	411	12.5	445	11.9	487	12.1	541	13.0
4. Frat. Soc.	70	2.5	77	2.3	78	2.1	80	2.0	82	2.0
5. Fire & Cas.	77	2.8	94	2.9	107	2.8	109	2.7	141	3.4
6. Mtge. Loan	258	9.3	261	7.9	254	6.8	259	6.4	277	6.6
7. Trust	63	2.3	69	2.1	64	1.7	67	1.7	67	1.6
8. Cons. Loan										
(a) Con. L.										
(b) Fin.										
9. Inv. Cos.										
(a) Mut.										
(b) Non-Res.										
(c) Closed										
(d) Holding										
10. CP&CU-lcs.	2	.1	3	.1	3	.1	4	.1	4	.1
11. CP&CU-cens.										
12. Pension										
13. Dev. & other										
Public										
14. Dom. Notes	181	6.5	273	8.3	327	8.7	319	7.9	312	7.5
15. B. of C.										
16 P.O.	56	2.0	54	1.6	53	1.4	42	1.0	39	0.9
17. Fed. Ann.	8	.3	10	.3	11	.3	12	.3	14	.3
18. I.D.B.										
19. F.C.C.										
20. V.L.A.	—		—		1	...	42	1.0	69	1.6
21. C.M.H.C.										
22. E.C.I.C.										
23. C.D.I.C.										
24. C.P.P.										
25. C. de dépôt										
26. Pr. Sav.	—		—		—		1	...	2	...
27. Pr. Ann.										
28. Pr. Ag. Lo.	—		—		6	.2	9	.2	13	.3
29. Pr. Ind. Lo.	—		—		—		—		—	
30. Pr. Misc.	—		—		—		10	.2	13	.3

Canadian Financial Intermediaries
Canadian Assets 1870-1970

	1921		1922		1923		1924		1925	
	$MNS.	%	$MNS.	%	$MNS.	%	$MNS.	%	$MNS.	%
Private										
1. Ch. Bks.	2337	58.5	2189	55.5	2247	54.6	2314	53.5	2275	52.4
2. Q.S.B.	64	1.6	64	1.6	68	1.6	71	1.6	73	1.7
3. Life Ins.	599	15.0	664	16.8	727	17.7	818	18.9	887	20.4
4. Frat. Soc.	83	2.1	83	2.1	84	2.0	89	2.0	92	2.1
5. Fire & Cas.	130	3.2	135	3.4	141	3.4	149	3.4	155	3.6
6. Mtge. Loan	263	6.6	275	7.0	274	6.7	273	6.3	277	6.4
7. Trust	67	1.7	83	2.1	94	2.3	98	2.3	104	2.4
8. Cons. Loan										
(a) Con. L.										
(b) Fin.										
9. Inv. Cos.										
(a) Mut.										
(b) Non-Res.										
(c) Closed										
(d) Holding										
10. CP&CU-lcs.	5	.1	6	.2	7	.2	7	.2	8	.2
11. CP&CU-cens.										
12. Pension										
13. Dev. & other										
Public										
14. Dom. Notes	281	7.0	257	6.5	249	6.0	262	6.0	227	5.2
15. B. of C.	–		–		–		–		–	
16. P.O.	35	.8	32	.8	34	.8	34	.8	33	.8
17. Fed. Ann.	17	.4	21	.5	26	.6	30	.7	36	.8
18. I.D.B.										
19. F.C.C.										
20. V.L.A.	78	2.0	83	2.1	87	2.1	88	2.0	88	2.0
21. C.M.H.C.										
22. E.C.I.C.										
23. C.D.I.C.										
24. C.P.P.										
25. C. de dépôt										
26. Pr. Sav.	4	.1	13	.3	24	.6	27	.6	29	.7
27. Pr. Ann.	–		1	...	2	...	3	.1	3	.1
28. Pr. Ag. Lo.	16	.4	21	.5	26	.6	36	.8	34	.8
29. Pr. Ind. Lo.										
30. Pr. Misc.	17	.4	18	.4	21	.5	25	.6	24	.6

Canadian Financial Intermediaries
Canadian Assets 1870-1970

	1926		1927		1928		1929		1930	
	$MNS.	%	$MNS.	%	$MNS.	%	$MNS.	%	$MNS.	%
Private										
1. Ch. Bks.	2267	49.9	2544	50.6	2781	50.6	2873	49.2	2635	45.9
2. Q.S.B.	76	1.7	79	1.6	80	1.4	78	1.3	78	1.4
3. Life Ins.	984	21.6	1098	21.8	1233	22.4	1340	22.9	1491	26.0
4. Frat. Soc.	94	2.1	96	1.9	101	1.8	100	1.7	103	1.8
5. Fire & Cas.	162	3.6	176	3.5	193	3.5	207	3.5	217	3.8
6. Mtge. Loan	289	6.4	295	5.9	296	5.4	287	4.9	291	5.0
7. Trust	117	2.6	135	2.7	154	2.8	224	3.8	250	4.4
8. Cons. Loan	24	.5	30	.6	40	.7	56	1.0	40	.7
(a) Con. L.	—		—		—		1	...	1	—
(b) Fin.	24	.5	30	.6	40	.7	55	.9	39	.7
9. Inv. Cos.	59	1.3	89	1.8	133	2.4	189	3.2	165	2.9
(a) Mut.										
(b) Non-Res.										
(c) Closed	50	1.1	75	1.5	100	1.8	135	2.3	109	1.9
(d) Holding	9	.2	15	.3	33	.6	54	.9	56	1.0
10. CP&CU-lcs.	8	.2	9	.2	10	.2	11	.2	12	.2
11. CP&CU-cens.										
12. Pension										
13. Dev. & other										
Public										
14. Dom. Notes	210	4.6	221	4.4	222	4.0	204	3.5	175	3.0
15. B. of C.										
16. P.O.	32	.7	31	.6	28	.5	26	.4	25	.4
17. Fed. Ann.	43	.9	52	1.0	61	1.1	70	1.2	80	1.4
18. I.D.B.										
19. F.C.C.	—		—		—		3	.1	6	.1
20. V.L.A.	84	1.8	69	1.4	58	1.0	60	1.0	54	.9
21. C.M.H.C.										
22. E.C.I.C.										
23. C.D.I.C.										
24. C.P.P.										
25. C. de dépôt										
26. Pr. Sav.	31	.7	34	.7	37	.7	38	.6	39	.7
27. Pr. Ann.	4	.1	4	.1	5	.1	6	.1	5	.1
28. Pr. Ag. Lo.	36	.8	40	.8	43	.8	50	.8	58	1.0
29. Pr. Ind. Lo.	—		—		—		—		—	
30. Pr. Misc.	24	.5	23	.4	22	.4	21	.4	20	.4

Canadian Financial Intermediaries
Canadian Assets 1870-1970

	1931		1932		1933		1934		1935	
	$MNS.	%	$MNS.	%	$MNS.	%	$MNS.	%	$MNS.	%
Private										
1. Ch. Bks.	2582	44.8	2463	43.7	2476	43.6	2515	42.5	2676	42.6
2. Q.S.B.	80	1.4	77	1.4	76	1.3	75	1.3	77	1.2
3. Life Ins.	1599	27.7	1611	28.6	1678	29.5	1789	30.2	1839	29.3
4. Frat. Soc.	117	2.0	120	2.1	121	2.1	124	2.1	123	2.0
5. Fire & Cas.	213	3.7	208	3.7	203	3.6	210	3.5	218	3.5
6. Mtge. Loan	300	5.2	294	5.2	286	5.0	284	4.8	276	4.4
7. Trust	233	4.0	225	4.0	225	4.0	228	3.8	229	3.6
8. Cons. Loan	33	.6	22	.4	22	.4	29	.5	36	.6
(a) Con. L.	1	...	1	...	2	...	3	...	3	...
(b) Fin.	32	.6	21	.4	20	.4	26	.4	33	.5
9. Inv. Cos.	125	2.2	94	1.7	72	1.3	81	1.4	83	1.3
(a) Mut.	–		–		1	...	3	...	4	.1
(b) Non-Res.										
(c) Closed	72	1.2	47	.8	43	.8	50	.8	53	.8
(d) Holding	53	.9	47	.8	28	.5	28	.5	26	.4
10. CP&CU-lcs.	13	.2	14	.2	15	.3	16	.3	17	.3
11. CP&CU-cens.										
12. Pension										
13. Dev. & other										
Public										
14. Dom. Notes	174	3.0	191	3.4	183	3.2	217	3.7	–	
15. B. of C.	–		–		–		–		308	4.9
16. P.O.	24	.4	24	.4	23	.4	23	.4	22	.4
17. Fed. Ann.	90	1.6	99	1.8	110	1.9	126	2.1	151	2.4
18. I.D.B.										
19. F.C.C.	8	.1	10	.2	10	.2	10	.2	18	.3
20. V.L.A.	48	.8	48	.8	45	.8	45	.8	44	.7
21. C.M.H.C.										
22. E.C.I.C.										
23. C.D.I.C.										
24. C.P.P.										
25. C. de dépôt										
26. Pr. Sav.	33	.6	31	.6	30	.5	33	.6	41	.6
27. Pr. Ann.	7	.1	8	.1	10	.2	11	.2	19	.3
28. Pr. Ag. Lo.	67	1.2	75	1.3	83	1.4	87	1.5	87	1.4
29. Pr. Ind. Lo.										
30. Pr. Misc.	18	.3	17	.3	17	.3	16	.3	16	.2

Canadian Financial Intermediaries
Canadian Assets 1870-1970

	1936		1937		1938		1939		1940	
	$MNS.	%	$MNS.	%	$MNS.	%	$MNS.	%	$MNS.	%
Private										
1. Ch. Bks.	2803	42.2	2864	41.7	2948	41.8	3315	42.4	3303	40.9
2. Q.S.B.	81	1.2	84	1.2	90	1.3	93	1.2	86	1.1
3. Life Ins.	1945	29.3	2029	29.5	2079	29.5	2112	27.0	2221	27.5
4. Frat. Soc.	125	1.9	129	1.9	131	1.8	133	1.7	136	1.7
5. Fire & Cas.	219	3.3	217	3.2	226	3.2	232	3.0	244	3.0
6. Mtge. Loan	263	4.0	258	3.8	257	3.6	256	3.3	252	3.1
7. Trust	238	3.6	241	3.5	234	3.3	232	3.0	222	2.8
8. Cons. Loan	48	.7	69	1.0	72	1.0	66	.8	89	1.1
(a) Con. L.	4	.1	5	.1	5	.1	6	.1	17	.2
(b) Fin.	44	.7	64	.9	67	.9	60	.8	72	.9
9. Inv. Cos.	105	1.6	104	1.5	96	1.4	91	1.2	89	1.1
(a) Mut.	7	.1	8	.1	11	.1	12	.2	9	.1
(b) Non-Res.										
(c) Closed	67	1.0	63	.9	57	.8	54	.7	58	.7
(d) Holding	31	.5	33	.5	28	.4	25	.3	22	.3
10. CP&CU-lcs.	(19)	.3	(20)	.3	(22)	.3	(23)	.3	25	.3
11. CP&CU-cens.										
12. Pension	–		–		–		216	2.8	233	2.9
13. Dev. & other										
Public										
14. Dom. Notes	–		–		–		–		–	
25. B. of C.	357	5.4	390	5.7	405	5.7	527	6.7	627	7.8
16. P.O.	22	.3	23	.3	23	.3	23	.3	22	.3
17. Fed. Ann.	177	2.7	201	2.9	221	3.1	243	3.1	264	3.3
18. I.D.B.										
19. F.C.C.	28	.4	32	.5	35	.5	37	.5	38	.5
20. V.L.A.	42	.6	42	.6	41	.6	38	.5	36	.4
21. C.M.H.C.	1		3		6	.1	10	.1	14	.2
22. E.C.I.C.										
23. C.D.I.C.										
24. C.P.P.										
25. C. de dépôt										
26. Pr. Sav.	46	.7	47	.7	47	.7	44	.6	45	.6
27. Pr. Ann.	20	.3	23	.3	25	.4	12	.2	13	.2
28. Pr. Ag. Lo.	86	1.3	84	1.2	90	1.3	100	1.3	103	1.3
29. Pr. Ind. Lo.										
30. Pr. Misc.	11	.1	7	.1	6	.1	5	.1	4	...

Canadian Financial Intermediaries
Canadian Assets 1870-1970

	1941		1942		1943		1944		1945	
	$MNS.	%	$MNS.	%	$MNS.	%	$MNS.	%	$MNS.	%
Private										
1. Ch. Bks.	3670	41.3	4164	42.5	4910	44.7	5706	45.7	6517	46.1
2. Q.S.B.	87	1.0	90	.9	105	1.0	126	1.0	143	1.0
3. Life Ins.	2318	26.1	2421	24.7	2572	23.4	2717	21.7	2882	20.4
4. Frat. Soc.	140	1.6	144	1.5	152	1.4	158	1.3	164	1.2
5. Fire & Cas.	259	2.9	269	2.7	280	2.5	293	2.3	320	2.3
6. Mtge. Loan	247	2.8	242	2.5	246	2.2	253	2.0	261	1.8
7. Trust	226	2.5	226	2.3	234	2.1	255	2.0	279	2.0
8. Cons. Loan	99	1.1	64	.6	58	.5	60	.5	69	.5
(a) Con. L.	19	.2	19	.2	22	.2	25	.2	30	.2
(b) Fin.	80	.9	45	.4	36	.3	35	.3	39	.3
9. Inv. Cos.	83	.9	85	.9	99	.9	109	.9	147	1.0
(a) Mut.	9	.1	10	.1	11	.1	13	.1	16	.1
(b) Non-Res.										
(c) Closed	54	.6	55	.6	64	.6	72	.6	84	.6
(d) Holding	20	.2	20	.2	24	.2	24	.2	47	.3
10. CP&CU-lcs.	31	.3	44	.4	69	.6	93	.7	146	1.0
11. CP&CU-cens.										
12. Pension	287	3.2	302	3.1	318	2.9	352	2.8	396	2.8
13. Dev. & other										
Public										
14. Dom. Notes	—		—		—		—		—	
15. B. of C.	843	9.5	1048	10.7	1308	11.9	1687	13.5	2032	14.4
16. P.O.	22	.2	24	.2	28	.2	34	.3	36	.2
17. Fed. Ann.	331	3.7	425	4.3	367	3.3	407	3.2	458	3.2
18. I.D.B.	—		—		—		—		10	.1
19. F.C.C.	37	.4	35	.4	30	.3	25	.2	23	.2
20. V.L.A.	34	.4	32	.3	30	.3	34	.3	53	.4
21. C.M.H.C.	16	.2	16	.2	16	.1	15	.1	25	.2
22. E.C.I.C.	—		—		—		—		5	...
23. C.D.I.C.										
24. C.P.P.										
25. C. de dépot										
26. Pr. Sav.	42	.5	46	.5	54	.5	67	.5	73	.5
27. Pr. Ann.	13	.1	16	.2	17	.2	19	.2	20	.1
28. Pr. Ag. Lo.	105	1.2	100	1.0	91	.8	82	.6	78	.6
29. Pr. Ind. Lo.										
30. Pr. Misc.	3	—	3	—	3	—	2		2	...

Canadian Financial Intermediaries Canadian Assets 1870-1970

	1946		1947		1948		1949		1950	
	$MNS.	%	$MNS.	%	$MNS.	%	$MNS.	%	$MNS.	%
Private										
1. Ch. Bks.	6924	46.0	7067	44.6	7705	44.3	7853	42.6	8636	41.9
2. Q.S.B.	159	1.0	173	1.1	185	1.1	198	1.1	204	1.0
3. Life Ins.	3066	20.4	3260	20.6	3472	20.0	3758	20.4	3998	19.4
4. Frat. Soc.	170	1.1	178	1.1	167	1.0	173	.9	187	.9
5. Fire & Cas.	352	2.3	396	2.5	443	2.5	497	2.7	551	2.7
6. Mtge. Loan	288	1.9	313	2.0	328	1.9	353	1.9	387	1.9
7. Trust	305	2.0	333	2.1	367	2.1	394	2.1	441	2.1
8. Cons. Loan	124	.8	227	1.4	232	1.3	308	1.7	468	2.3
(a) Con L.	43	.3	61	.4	72	.4	83	.4	103	.5
(b) Fin.	81	.5	166	1.0	160	.9	225	1.2	365	1.8
9. Inv. Cos.	148	1.0	135	.8	144	.8	165	.9	204	1.0
(a) Mut.	16	.1	17	.1	20	.1	36	.2	59	.3
(b) Non-Res.										
(c) Closed	80	.5	76	.5	76	.4	81	.4	89	.4
(d) Holding	52	.3	42	.3	48	.3	48	.3	56	.3
10. CP&CU-lcs.	188	1.2	221	1.4	254	1.5	282	1.5	312	1.5
11. CP&CU-cens.									34	.2
12. Pension	455	3.0	528	3.3	630	3.6	708	3.8	875	4.2
13. Dev. & other										
Public										
14. Dom. Notes	–		–		–		–		–	
15. B. of C.	1949	12.9	1926	12.1	2059	11.8	2126	11.5	2350	11.4
16. P.O.	36	.2	36	.2	38	.2	39	.2	37	.2
17. Fed. Ann.	527	3.5	611	3.8	718	4.1	811	4.4	979	4.8
18. I.D.B.	16	.1	28	.2	29	.2	30	.2	31	.2
19. F.C.C.	22	.1	22	.1	23	.1	25	.1	27	.1
20. V.L.A.	108	.7	145	.9	167	1.0	175	.9	189	.9
21. C.M.H.C.	25	.2	48	.3	174	1.0	271	1.5	395	1.9
22. E.C.I.C.	5	...	11	.1	11	.1	11	...	12	...
23. C.D.I.C.										
24. C.P.P.										
25. C. de dépôt										
26. Pr. Sav.	89	.6	94	.6	119	.7	124	.7	122	.6
27. Pr. Ann.	24	.2	27	.2	36	.2	36	.2	39	.2
28. Pr. Ag. Lo.	83	.6	83	.5	85	.5	88	.5	93	.4
29. Pr. Ind. Lo.	–		–		2	...	3	...	3	...
30. Pr. Misc.	2	...	1	...	6	...	16	.1	15	.1

Canadian Financial Intermediaries
Canadian Assets 1870-1970

	1951		1952		1953		1954		1955	
	$MNS.	%	$MNS.	%	$MNS.	%	$MNS.	%	$MNS.	%
Private										
1. Ch. Bks.	8589	39.3	9148	38.9	9592	37.9	10291	37.4	11575	37.9
2. Q.S.B.	205	.9	218	.9	226	.9	243	.9	265	.9
3. Life Ins.	4236	19.4	4522	19.2	4858	19.2	5226	19.0	5599	18.3
4. Frat. Soc.	194	.9	202	.9	212	.8	224	.8	234	.8
5. Fire & Cas.	604	2.8	673	2.9	765	3.0	851	3.1	920	3.0
6. Mtge. Loan	400	1.8	422	1.8	457	1.8	522	1.9	582	1.9
7. Trust	455	2.1	477	2.0	490	1.9	637	2.3	717	2.3
8. Cons. Loan	565	2.6	813	3.5	1025	4.0	998	3.6	1244	4.1
(a) Con. L.	119	.5	156	.7	161	.6	222	.8	289	.9
(b) Fin.	446	2.0	657	2.8	864	3.4	776	2.8	955	3.1
9. Inv. Cos.	266	1.2	297	1.3	333	1.3	572	2.1	829	2.7
(a) Mut.	90	.4	110	.5	146	.6	202	.7	278	.9
(b) Non-Res.	–		–		–	–	121	.4	223	.7
(c) Closed	104	.5	114	.5	112	.4	146	.5	177	.6
(d) Holding	72	.3	73	.3	75	.3	103	.4	151	.5
10. CP&CU-lcs.	359	1.6	424	1.8	489	1.9	552	2.0	653	2.1
11. CP&CU-cens.	45	.2	52	.2	54	.2	65	.2	77	.2
12. Pension	1025	4.7	1180	5.0	1378	5.4	1589	5.8	1832	6.0
13. Dev. & other	–		–		3	...	3	...	4	...
Public										
14. Dom. Notes	–		–		–		–		–	
15. B. of C.	2444	11.2	2381	10.1	2437	9.6	2401	8.7	2620	8.6
16. P.O.	38	.2	39	.2	38	.2	37	.1	36	.1
17. Fed. Ann.	1416	6.5	1567	6.7	1773	7.0	1977	7.2	2186	7.2
18. I.D.B.	30	.1	34	.1	40	.2	43	.2	46	.2
19. F.C.C.	29	.1	32	.1	36	.1	41	.1	46	.2
20. V.L.A.	198	.9	163	.7	162	.6	162	.6	161	.5
21. C.M.H.C.	445	2.0	515	2.2	607	2.4	672	2.4	481	1.6
22. E.C.I.C.	12	...	12	...	11	...	14	...	15	...
23. C.D.I.C.										
24. C.P.P.										
25. C. de dépôt										
26. Pr. Sav.	120	.5	129	.5	129	.5	143	.5	152	.5
27. Pr. Ann.	46	.2	56	.2	65	.2	69	.2	81	.3
28. Pr. Ag. Lo.	98	.4	104	.4	116	.4	134	.5	150	.5
29. Pr. Ind. Lo.	6	...	13	...	14	...	19	.1	21	.1
30. Pr. Misc.	14	.1	14	...	14	...	14	...	13	...

Canadian Financial Intermediaries Canadian Assets 1870-1970

	1956		1957		1958		1959		1960	
	$MNS.	%	$MNS.	%	$MNS.	%	$MNS.	%	$MNS.	%
Private										
1 Ch. Bks.	11942	36.4	12274	35.2	13676	35.0	13442	32.5	14192	31.6
2. Q.S.B.	273	.8	286	.8	303	.8	298	.7	311	.7
3. Life Ins.	6010	18.3	6511	18.7	6933	17.7	7474	18.1	8007	17.8
4. Frat. Soc.	244	.7	250	.7	267	.7	286	.7	311	.7
5. Fire & Cas.	948	2.9	1057	3.0	1161	3.0	1242	3.0	1388	3.1
6. Mtge. Loan	624	1.9	666	1.9	736	1.9	815	2.0	945	2.1
7. Trust	745	2.3	786	2.3	970	2.5	1079	2.6	1306	2.9
8. Cons. Loan	1612	4.9	1684	4.8	1675	4.3	1981	4.8	2322	5.2
(a) Con. L.	369	1.1	372	1.1	413	1.0	496	1.2	563	1.2
(b) Fin.	1243	3.8	1312	3.8	1262	3.2	1485	3.6	1759	3.9
9. Inv. Cos.	991	3.0	989	2.8	1221	3.1	1352	3.3	1331	3.0
(a) Mut.	347	1.0	354	1.0	429	1.1	557	1.3	609	1.4
(b) Non-Res.	302	.9	306	.9	399	1.0	390	.9	333	.7
(c) Closed	195	.6	167	.5	201	.5	215	.5	207	.5
(d) Holding	147	.4	162	.5	192	.5	190	.4	182	.4
10. CP&CU-lcs.	761	2.3	852	2.4	1009	2.6	1158	2.8	1314	2.9
11. CP&CU-cens.	86	.3	104	.3	128	.3	138	.3	172	.4
12. Pension	2110	6.4	2460	7.0	2791	7.1	3200	7.7	3583	8.0
13. Dev. & other	4	...	5	...	5	...	6	...	7	...
Public										
14. Dom. Notes	—		—		—		—		—	
15. B. of C.	2548	7.8	2659	7.6	2944	7.5	2968	7.2	3044	6.8
16. P.O.	35	.1	34	.1	34	.1	29	.1	29	.1
17. Fed. Ann.	2427	7.4	2713	7.8	3302	8.4	3565	8.6	3955	8.8
18. I.D.B.	53	.2	74	.2	90	.2	99	.2	107	.2
19 F.C.C.	55	.2	70	.2	93	.2	122	.3	164	.4
20. V.L.A.	157	.5	154	.4	151	.4	152	.4	166	.4
21. C.M.H.C.	682	2.1	732	2.1	1082	2.8	1382	3.3	1642	3.6
22. E.C.I.C.	16	...	16	...	17	...	18	...	17	...
23. C.D.I.C.										
24. C.P.P.										
25. C. de dépôt										
26. Pr. Sav.	157	.5	161	.5	167	.4	160	.4	167	.4
27. Pr. Ann.	93	.3	107	.3	117	.3	153	.4	175	.4
28. Pr. Ag. Lo.	165	.5	186	.5	189	.5	211	.5	229	.5
29. Pr. Ind. Lo.	26	.1	29	.1	31	.1	33	.1	42	.1
30. Pr. Misc.	13	...	17	...	20	...	21	...	22	...

Canadian Financial Intermediaries
Canadian Assets 1870-1970

	1961		1962		1963		1964		1965	
	$ MNS.	%	$ MNS.	%	$ MNS.	%	$ MNS.	%	$ MNS.	%
Private										
1. Ch. Bks.	15644	31.5	16397	30.6	17858	30.2	18694	28.8	21196	28.9
2. Q.S.B.	336	.7	357	.7	373	.6	403	.6	430	.6
3. Life Ins.	8574	17.2	9205	17.2	9943	16.8	10638	16.4	11424	15.6
4. Frat. Soc.	324	.6	348	.6	377	.6	406	.6	439	.6
5. Fire & Cas.	1487	3.0	1549	2.9	1621	2.7	1760	2.7	1949	2.6
6. Mtge. Loan	1110	2.2	1300	2.4	1544	2.6	1936	3.0	2426	3.3
7. Trust	1590	3.2	1894	3.5	2321	3.9	2860	4.4	3439	4.7
8. Cons Loan	2340	4.7	2726	5.1	3191	5.4	3686	5.7	4228	5.8
(a) Con L.	608	1.2	729	1.4	829	1.4	923	1.4	1082	1.5
(b) Fin.	1732	3.5	1997	3.7	2362	4.0	2763	4.2	3146	4.3
9. Inv. Cos.	1684	3.4	1724	3.2	1858	3.1	2266	3.5	2742	3.7
(a) Mut.	841	1.7	945	1.8	1115	1.9	1507	2.3	1949	2.6
(b) Non-Res.	341	.7	255	.5	134	.2	66	.1	63	.1
(c) Closed	264	.5	257	.5	307	.5	310	.5	343	.5
(d) Holding	238	.5	267	.5	302	.5	383	.6	387	.5
10. CP&CU-lcs.	1506	3.0	1674	3.1	1920	3.2	2212	3.4	2542	3.5
11. CP&CU-cens.	199	.4	238	.4	267	.4	303	.5	357	.5
12. Pension	4036	8.1	4530	8.5	5127	8.7	5766	8.9	6541	8.9
13. Dev. & other	74	.1	127	.2	170	.3	272	.4	259	.4
Public										
14. Dom. Notes	–		–		–		–		–	
15. B. of C.	3243	6.5	3231	6.0	3445	5.8	3642	5.6	3956	5.4
16. P.O.	27	...	26	...	24	...	23	...	22	...
17. Fed. Ann.	4246	8.5	4747	8.9	5131	8.7	5684	8.8	6392	8.7
18. I.D.B.	125	.2	167	.3	205	.3	229	.4	262	.4
19. F.C.C.	219	.4	279	.5	352	.6	458	.7	608	.8
20. V.L.A.	177	.4	196	.4	217	.4	236	.4	256	.3
21. C.M.H.C.	2002	4.0	1999	3.7	2070	3.5	2281	3.5	2574	3.5
22. E.C.I.C.	60	.1	77	.1	174	.3	238	.4	281	.4
23. C.D.I.C.										
24. C.P.P.										
25. C. de dépôt										
26. Pr. Sav.	181	.4	167	.3	186	.3	203	.3	215	.3
27. Pr. Ann.	200	.4	228	.4	262	.4	295	.4	335	.4
28. Pr. Ag. Lo.	253	.5	276	.5	302	.5	333	.5	358	.5
29. Pr. Ind. Lo.	50	.1	53	.1	62	.1	83	.1	129	.2
30. Pr. Misc.	24	...	26	...	29	...	47	.1	52	.1

Canadian Financial Intermediaries
Canadian Assets 1870-1970

	1966		1967		1968		1969		1970	
	$MNS.	%	$MNS.	%	$MNS.	%	$MNS.	%	$MNS.	%
Private										
1. Ch. Bks.	22507	28.0	25199	28.2	28939	28.9	31000		33616	
2. Q.S.B.	461	.6	506	.6	571	.6	542		568	
3. Life Ins.	12127	15.1	12912	14.4	13667	13.6	14334		n.a.	
4. Frat. Soc.	453	.6	488	.5	506	.5	503		n.a.	
5. Fire & Cas.	2163	2.7	2304	2.6	2516	2.5	2758		3088	
6. Mtge. Loan	2570	3.2	2772	3.1	2978	3.0	3292		3778	
7. Trust	3923	4.9	4353	4.9	4980	5.0	5771		6564	
8. Cons. Loan	4374	5.4	4501	5.0	4927	4.9	5652		5502	
(a) Con. L.	1198	1.5	1338	1.5	1556	1.6	1702		n.a.	
(b) Fin.	3176	4.0	3163	3.5	3371	3.4	3950		n.a.	
9. Inv. Cos.	2839	3.5	3374	3.8	4312	4.3	4108		3615	
(a) Mut.	2090	2.6	2645	3.0	3372	3.4	3192		2806	
(b) Non-Res.	49	.1	51	.1	51	.1	50		40	
(c) Closed	349	.4	373	.4	455	.5	472		426	
(d) Holding	351	.4	305	.3	434	.4	394		343	
10. CP&CU-lcs.	2926	3.6	3382	3.8	3758	3.7	4103		4570	
11. CP&CU-cens.	407	.5	459	.5	520	.5	562		658	
12. Pension	7250	9.0	8068	9.0	8972	8.9	10003		11059	
13. Dev. & other	206	.2	148	.2	145	.1	149		n.a.	
Public										
14. Dom. Notes	—		—		—		—		—	
15. B. of C.	4207	5.2	4412	4.9	4636	4.6	4888		5405	
16. P.O.	21	...	19	...	—	—	—		—	
17. Fed. Ann.	7235	9.0	7700	8.6	8409	8.4	9240		9922	
18. I.D.B.	305	.4	341	.4	379	.4	423		498	
19. F.C.C.	777	1.0	955	1.1	1085	1.1	1161		1213	
20. V.L.A.	311	.4	383	.4	423	.4	472		493	
21. C.M.H.C.	2879	3.6	3567	4.0	3961	3.9	4428		4981	
22. E.C.I.C.	285	.4	357	.4	357	.4	293		348	
23. C.D.I.C.	—	—	32	...	32	...	31		11	
24. C.P.P.	681	.8	1353	1.5	2108	2.1	2932		3844	
25. C. de dépôt	183	.2	419	.5	684	.7	990		1326	
26. Pr. Sav.	233	.3	260	.3	294	.3			n.a.	
27. Pr. Ann.	374	.5	373	.4	406	.4			n.a.	
28. Pr. Ag. Lo.	415	.5	431	.5	460	.5			n.a.	
29. Pr. Ind. Lo.	204	.3	259	.3	242	.2			n.a.	
30. Pr. Misc.	50	.1	46	.1	43	...			n.a.	

Index